AF593381

American Art at the Flint Institute of Arts

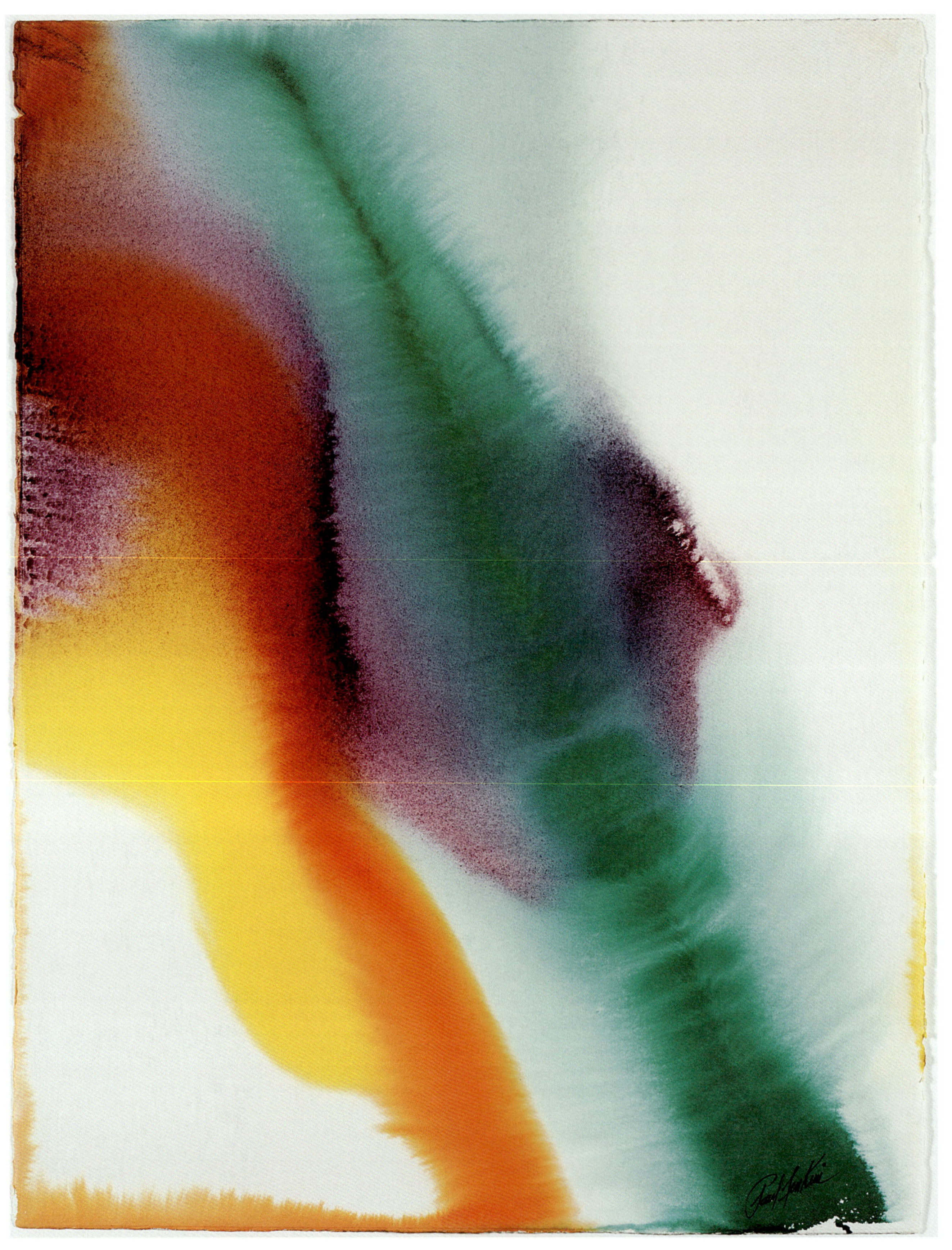

American Art at the Flint Institute of Arts

INTRODUCTORY ESSAY BY WILLIAM H. GERDTS

CONTRIBUTIONS BY
Kelly Baum
Monique M. Desormeau
Melissa Miller Farr
John B. Henry III
Melina Kervandjian
Valerie Ann Leeds
Akella Reason
R. Sarah Richardson
Sue Scott
Kristie Everett Zamora

FLINT INSTITUTE OF ARTS
in association with HUDSON HILLS PRESS | NEW YORK AND MANCHESTER

FIRST EDITION

Published in the United States by:

HUDSON HILLS PRESS LLC
74-2 Union Street
Manchester, Vermont 05254

Distributed in the United States, its territories and possessions, and Canada by National Book Network, Inc. Distributed in the United Kingdom, Eire, and Europe by Windsor Books International.

Founding Publisher: Paul Anbinder
Executive Directors: Randall Perkins and Leslie van Breen

Editor: Fronia Simpson
Designer: Christopher Kuntze
Proofreader: Kathleen Achor
Manuscript editor, indexer: Judith Hanson
Color separations by Pre Tech Color, Wilder, Vermont
Printed and bound by CS Graphics Pte., Ltd., Singapore

FRONTISPIECE
Paul Jenkins, American born 1923
Phenomena Tang Jade, 1978
Watercolor on paper, 29⅞ × 22⅜ in.
Signed lower right: *Paul Jenkins*
Gift of Mr. Irving Sniderman (1998.18)

LIBRARY OF CONGRESS CATALOGUING-IN-PUBLICATION DATA

American art at the Flint Institute of Arts / William H. Gerdts . . .
[et al].– 1st ed.
p. cm.
1-55595-219-4 hardcover (alk. paper)
1-55595-220-8 softcover (alk. paper)
1. Art, American–Catalogues. 2. Art–Michigan–Flint–Catalogues. 3. Flint Institute of Arts–Catalogues. I. Gerdts, William H., 1949– II. Flint Institute of Arts.
N6505.A6258 2003
709'.73'07477437—dc21 2003014854

Contents

Donors to the Collection

Mrs. Harlan A. Way
Mrs. Cecil Boksenbom
Mary Mallery Davis
Messrs. Samuel N. Tomkin and Sidney Freeman
Mr. and Mrs. Jerome O. Eddy
Mr. and Mrs. Keith Davis
Mrs. Aimee Mott Butler
Mark and Charlotte Lippincott
Mr. and Mrs. B. Morris Pelavin
Mr. and Mrs. Carroll McGregor Boutell
Enos A. and Sarah DeWaters
Mr. Irving Sniderman
Mr. and Mrs. Jay C. Thompson
Edgar William and Bernice Chrysler Garbisch
Mr. and Mrs. Donald E. Johnson
Mr. and Mrs. William L. Richards
Mrs. Arthur Jerome Eddy
Dr. and Mrs. Victor J. Cervenak
Mr. and Mrs. David Martin
Mrs. R. S. Bishop
Mrs. Arthur M. Davison
Mrs. Ralph Harmon Booth
F. Karel Wiest
Mr. Stanley Gillen
Anthony E. and Richard D. van Benschoten
Mr. and Mrs. John Lord Booth
Mr. and Mrs. Charles Stewart Mott
Michael Gorman
Bernard J. and Arlene D. Harris
Michael A. and Natalie Pelavin
Mr. and Mrs. Harold L. Frank
Ellen and Richard U. Levine
James W. Sibley
Estate of Mrs. Ernest C. Schnuck
Mr. J. Curtis Willson
Jerald Webster
Mr. and Mrs. Kaye Goodwin Frank
Mr. and Mrs. Martin Ryerson
Mr. Patrick Martin
Mr. Max Greenfield
Gertrude and Leonard Kasle
Mrs. Bernard Stroh
Dr. Julius Stone
Russell J. Cameron
The Bishop Trust
Michael Rosenfeld Gallery
Hudson's
Dr. Stuart Hodge Memorial
The Dennis Oppenheim Foundation
Harvey J. Mallery Charitable Trust
Founders Society
S. L. Hudson Gallery
Hirschl and Alder Galleries
Flint Public Trust
The Whiting Foundation
Loeb Charitable Trust
Richard Florsheim Art Fund
Dedalus Foundation
Viola E. Bray Charitable Trust
J. L. Hudson Company Acquisitions Challenge Grant
Friends of Modern Art
Samuel and Alma Catsman Foundation
National Endowment for the Arts

Foreword

On the occasion of the Flint Institute of Arts' seventy-fifth anniversary, we are pleased to present this volume of highlights from its holdings of American art. Long out of date the last catalogue featuring works from the Institute's permanent collection, published in 1978, was a selection of 100 works by both European and American masters. The need for a new collection catalogue is clearly apparent. The more than 120 American paintings and sculptures presented here were chosen not only for their inherent quality but also to display the breadth and depth of the Institute's American works in these media. The American collection also comprises, in addition to painting and sculpture, decorative and applied arts, prints, textiles, mixed media, and ethnographic material, a range too vast to include in this publication. The print collection alone numbers more than 2,500 images, most of which are American, and is deserving of at least one volume of its own.

The impetus behind this publication was Ellen Holtzman of the Henry Luce Foundation, who contacted the Flint Institute of Arts in 1998 to inquire about the collection. After learning of the Institute's outstanding American works, she suggested we produce a catalogue, which would not only serve as an important reference in the field but also make the American collection available to a wider audience. The Foundation provided lead funding for the project, which stimulated additional support from local foundations and individuals.

What becomes evident on reviewing the collection is the exceptional quality and depth this small museum has attained as a result of the vision, leadership, and generosity of the community it exists to serve. The American collection is particularly rich, with significant works that span the years from the newly founded republic to contemporary pieces that attest to the diversity of the country more than two centuries later. An overview of many of the Institute's American holdings and their significance to art history is provided by William H. Gerdts, Professor Emeritus at the City University of New York.

Flint, Michigan, even in its early days, when it was known for making carriages, has been considered among the most cultured of the small communities in the Midwest. About 1910 it entered a period of radical change that led to the tremendous growth and expansion of the automobile industry. Figures like William (Billy) C. Durant, J. Dallas Dort, Walter P. Chrysler, and Charles W. Nash established what would become General Motors. Of these captains of industry, some chose to lead from Flint and, in the process, contributed to the long and distinguished history of the Flint Institute of Arts. Many of the city's great leaders had the vision and the courage, through good times and bad, to sustain the service, creativity, and commitment to excellence that have become the hallmarks of the Institute. Today, the collection is their most enduring legacy, one that reveals the tastes, intellect, and interests of a community that had such an impressive and lasting influence on American industry and design.

The Flint Institute of Arts was established in 1928 primarily as an art school. On 5 April of that year, it ran a half-page advertisement in the *Flint Journal* announcing "classes designed to help the amateur find pleasant and adequate means of expression in drawing and painting as well as laying a good foundation for beginners with professional aspirations." Today, it still functions as a teaching institution dedicated to art education. Its large school and active education department reflect the interests of many in the community who support the continuance of this vital activity.

Over the years, as public demand for expanded offerings increased, the Institute relocated to more appropriate and accommodating facilities. At the same time, a tradition was established of presenting loan exhibitions of the highest-quality art from collectors, dealers, and museums. As a result of an impressive array of shows, the Institute encountered a chronic need for more gallery space. From the modest space it occupied in 1928 in the Brownson-Fisher Building on East Third Street, the Institute moved to two other addresses downtown before moving to its present location. Progressively bigger, each space provided more and larger studio classrooms and galleries.

In 1929, the Institute's first purchase of art—Tunis Ponsen's *The Old Pier*—was selected as the viewers' choice from an exhibition and was purchased with funds collected in a donation box beneath the painting. By 1930 the Institute had incorporated, its stated purpose "to stimulate the love of beauty and to cultivate public taste." That same year the board of trustees approved an accessions committee and accepted the first gifts into the collection, which included twenty lithographs by the American artist Boris Lovet-Lorski. Prophetically, the *Flint Journal* wrote: "The first gift may someday be productive of great results. If we look into the future, would we see in Flint

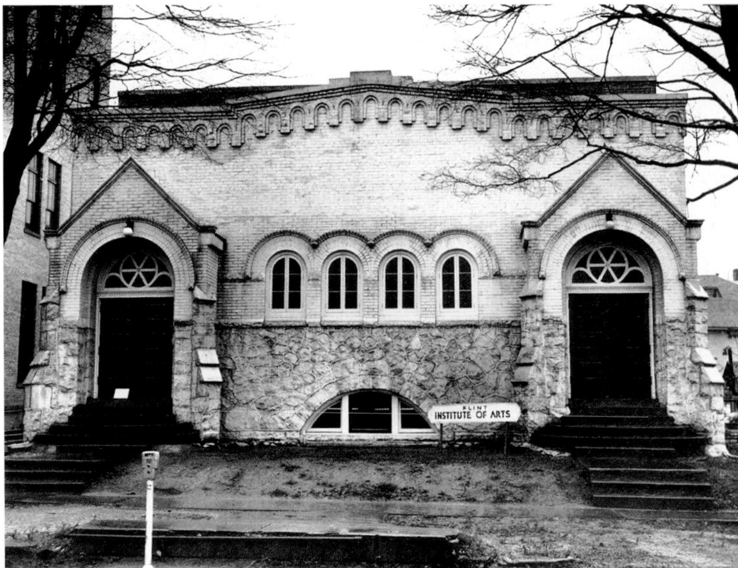

215 W. First Street, Flint Institute of Arts site 1941–1958

a beautiful building where students could pass in and out of classes and where collections of fine paintings, sculpture, and art objects would be on display?" In 1931 the Institute received its first major donation of paintings, from the Flint native and Chicago resident Arthur Jerome Eddy. Eddy had an international reputation as an author and collector of avant-garde art, and his gift included outstanding works by the American painters Leon Kroll, Leonard Ochtman, Henry Oliver Walker, and Frederick Carl Frieseke.

The Institute had only just opened and was already well on its way to building a collection of importance and depth. In these early years, many Flint collectors, among them Mr. and Mrs. John Lord Booth, Mary Mallery Davis, Enos A. and Sarah De Waters, Mr. and Mrs. Donald E. Johnson, Mr. and Mrs. Charles Stewart Mott, Mr. and Mrs. William L. Richards, and George C. Willson, donated works. The years of the Great Depression slowed the rate of acquisitions somewhat, but during the 1940s and 1950s the Institute acquired important American paintings by John Francis Murphy, Robert William Vonnoh, William Wendt, Roy Lichtenstein, Carl Milles, and Zoltan Sepeshy.

A new chapter in the history of the Flint Institute of Arts commenced in 1958, when it moved for the last time, into the newly built De Waters Art Center, located in the heart of Flint's Cultural Center. The 85,000-square-foot building was the first facility the Institute occupied that was specifically designed as a museum and art school. In 1959 the Institute hired Dr. Stuart Hodge, who served as director for twenty-one years and made many of the most impressive acquisition decisions. That same year, plans were announced to expand the galleries to house recent gifts of French and Italian Renaissance art. Also included in the expansion plans was an "interim" gallery for permanent collections, reflecting a heightened awareness of adding to the Institute's holdings that continues today. By 1961 two wings were added, collection policies were formed, funds for acquisitions were established, and the process of refining the collection had begun. Four years later an exhibition of the entire permanent collection, then totaling about one hundred works, took place. The show signaled the beginning of a new era of intensified collecting. For the remainder of the decade, the Institute received donations of and purchased significant works by American artists including Richard Anuszkiewicz, Mary Bauermeister, Harry Bertoia, Ralph Albert Blakelock, Alexander Calder, Mary Cassatt, Bruce Crane, Jasper Cropsey, Adolph Gottlieb, George Rickey, and Andrew Wyeth. Among the many donors were Mrs. Aimee Mott Butler, Mrs. Jay C. Thompson from the estate of Mrs. George Crapo Willson, and Mrs. R. H. Bishop. An acquisitions endowment was established in 1968, and the collection policies were revised by the trustees to emphasize nineteenth- and twentieth-century European and American art. Also that year, Edgar and Bernice Chrysler Garbisch gave the first of several gifts of American naïve paintings. By 1970 the collection had grown more than tenfold.

During the following two decades several important donations took the collection in many directions—sixty-five African sculptures from Justice and Mrs. G. Mennen Williams; Native American artifacts from Richard Pohrt; Asian objects from Miss

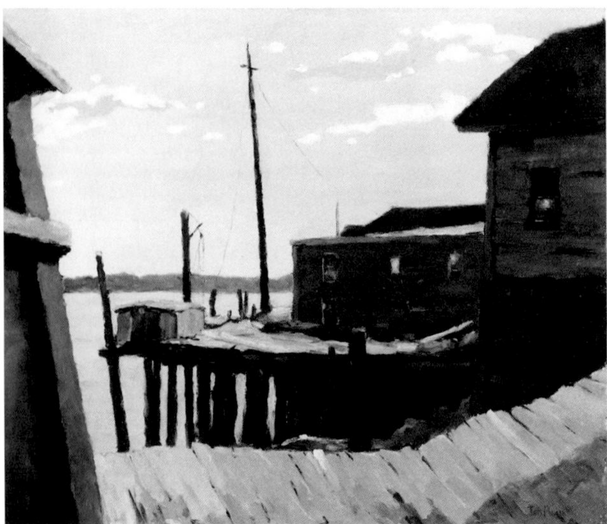
Tunis Ponsen, *The Old Pier,* cat. no. 60

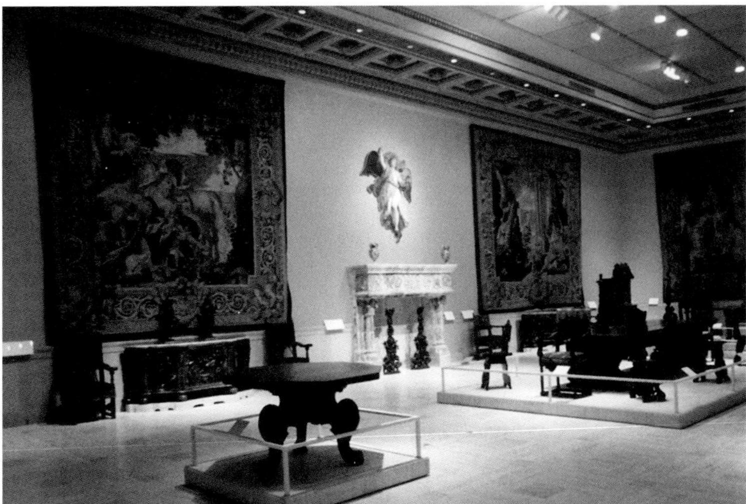

Flint Institute of Arts' Viola E. Bray Renaissance Gallery

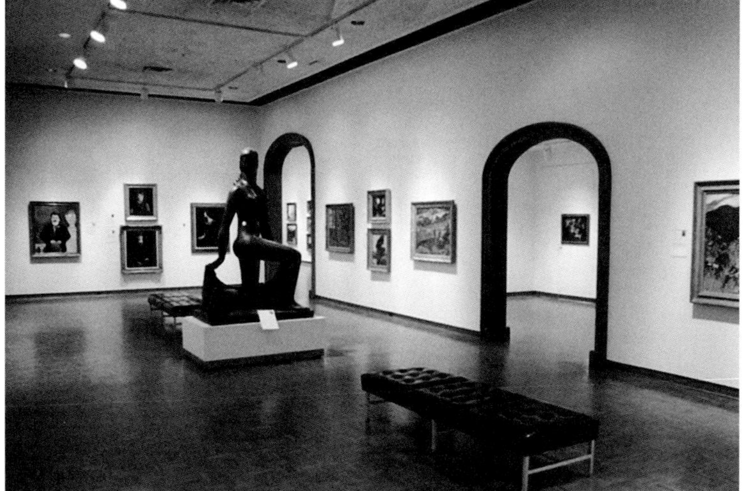

Flint Institute of Arts' Willson Galleries

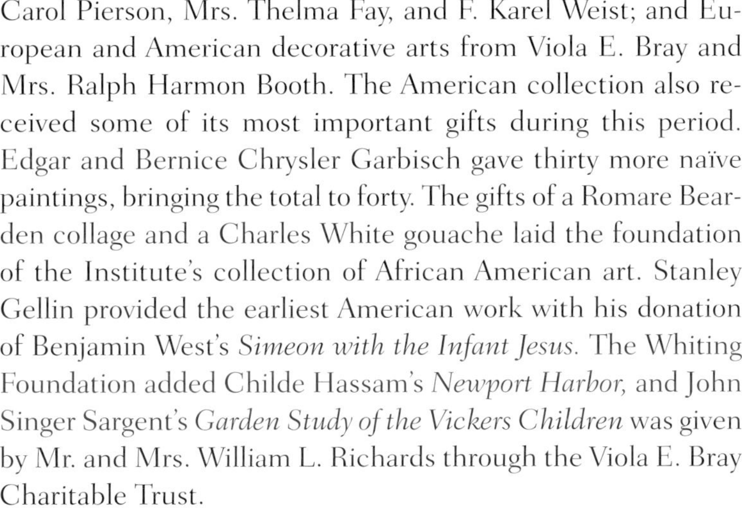

Carol Pierson, Mrs. Thelma Fay, and F. Karel Weist; and European and American decorative arts from Viola E. Bray and Mrs. Ralph Harmon Booth. The American collection also received some of its most important gifts during this period. Edgar and Bernice Chrysler Garbisch gave thirty more naïve paintings, bringing the total to forty. The gifts of a Romare Bearden collage and a Charles White gouache laid the foundation of the Institute's collection of African American art. Stanley Gellin provided the earliest American work with his donation of Benjamin West's *Simeon with the Infant Jesus.* The Whiting Foundation added Childe Hassam's *Newport Harbor,* and John Singer Sargent's *Garden Study of the Vickers Children* was given by Mr. and Mrs. William L. Richards through the Viola E. Bray Charitable Trust.

Beginning in the 1990s and continuing to the present, the museum accelerated its collecting. Increased support from its auxiliary support groups—the Founders Society and the Friends of Modern Art—and an anonymous gift of $1,000,000 to the endowment fund enabled the Institute to expand its holdings significantly. Important American purchases by the Founders Society added works by Arthur B. Davies, James Daugherty, William A. Harper, and Charles Hawthorne. The Friends of Modern Art contributed contemporary paintings and sculpture by David Barr, Robert Goodnough, Duayne Hatchett, Tony King, Seymour Lipton, Robert Natkin, Thomas Pfannerstill, Victor Rodriguez, and Beatrice Wood, among others. The museum also continues to add contemporary art with endowment-fund purchases of works by Melvin Edwards, Robert Gniewek, Robert Motherwell, and Dennis Oppenheim.

At the turn of the millennium, the Flint Institute of Arts was in the process of reevaluating its American collection in preparation for this book. With the assistance of the Collections Committee and the diligence of the staff and two adjunct curators, Dr. Valerie Ann Leeds and Sue Scott, several works were deaccessioned to obtain the funds needed to purchase "missing links" in its holdings, especially modernist and Regionalist paintings and sculptures. This enabled the Institute to obtain works by Thomas Hart Benton, Emil Bisttram, Konrad Cramer, Frederick Carl Frieseke, George L.K. Morris, Theodore Roszak, Max Weber, and Larry Rivers. The curators also took the opportunity to add significant works by the African American artists Chakaia Booker, Hughie Lee-Smith, and Whitfield Lovell.

The process of building a collection is never complete—there will always be missing links, discoveries of overlooked and underestimated artists, and, of course, new creations by contemporary artists. Nevertheless, a museum's collection is a product of the vision and intellect of the community leaders who contributed to the process. In the case of the Flint Institute of Arts, the collection reflects the spirit of a community of intelligent, informed, and generous people striving to encourage, enlighten, and inspire their neighbors and guests.

John B. Henry III
DIRECTOR

CONTRIBUTORS

KB	Kelly Baum
MMD	Monique M. Desormeau
MMF	Melissa Miller Farr
JBH	John B. Henry III
MK	Melina Kervandjian
VAL	Valerie Ann Leeds
AR	Akella Reason
RSR	R. Sarah Richardson
SS	Sue Scott
KEZ	Kristie Everett Zamora

Acknowledgments

This publication of the highlights from the Flint Institute of Arts' American collection is the result of the generosity and hard work of a great many people. In acknowledging the contributions of those whose efforts made this book possible, I wish to begin by thanking all who generously contributed works of art or funding for the acquisition of works of art featured in this book. Donors have been identified in the curatorial information accompanying each catalogue entry and in the section titled Donors to the Collection on page 6.

Additional research was conducted and insightful narratives were written about the works in the collection by several noteworthy scholars. I am most grateful to William H. Gerdts, Professor Emeritus of the Graduate Center, City University of New York, for his eloquent introduction to the collection. I also wish to thank Melina Kervandjian, independent scholar, Houston; Kelly Baum, curator, Blanton Museum, University of Texas, Austin; and R. Sarah Richardson, doctoral candidate, City University of New York, for their scholarly research and clear and concise narratives.

The Institute was fortunate to have Dr. Valerie Ann Leeds, independent scholar, and Sue Scott, Adjunct Curator of Contemporary Art, Orlando Museum of Art, serve as adjunct curators of American art during the preparation and production of this book. Their efforts not only contribute knowledge to the field but also serve to bring each work to life for the reader. Each brought valuable knowledge and experience to the process of selecting, ordering, and writing the entries included in this volume. Both traveled frequently to Flint to meet with the Institute's Collections Committee and staff. Sue, whose specialty is American postwar art, wrote forty of the narratives. In addition to writing forty-five narratives, Valerie accepted the additional responsibility of project manager, organizing schedules and managing the detailed preparation of the manuscript and illustrations before their delivery to Hudson Hills Press. Valerie also coordinated research assignments and copyediting for the publication. She was assisted by Flint Institute of Arts staff members Kristie Everett Zamora, Coordinator of Exhibitions; Monique M. Desormeau, Curator of Education; and Melissa Miller Farr, Registrar, all of whom contributed to the writing of this publication. Melissa, in turn, was instrumental in scheduling conservation for selected works and arranging the photography for the book. Melissa, along with Flint Institute of Arts research interns Mike Martin and Duncan Cardillo, assisted with file retrieval and in-house research. I wish to thank Duncan Cardillo also for researching and securing rights to reproduce works in the collection.

I am most grateful to the following artists, representatives, representative organizations, and institutions that gave permission or assisted the Flint Institute of Arts in obtaining the right to reproduce the images that are featured in the catalogue: George Adams, George Adams Gallery; Lucienne Allen; Richard Anuszkiewicz; Cristin O'Keefe Aptowicz, Artists Rights Society; Mary Bauermeister; Lillian Brenwasser, Kennedy Galleries; Edward R. Brohel, Plattsburgh State Art Museum; Staffan Carlén, Millesgården; Jean Collier, Bayly Art Museum; Aileen B. Cramer; Charles M. Daugherty; Maxwell Davidson IV, Maxwell Davidson Gallery; Molly Eppard, Hollis Taggart Galleries; Melvin Edwards; Marie Evans, Alexandre Gallery; Robert Fishko, Forum Gallery; Helen Frankenthaler; T. Kinney Frelinghuysen, George L.K. and Suzy Frelinghuysen Morris Foundation; Ann M. Garfinkle, Estate of Morris Louis; John Gittins; Robert Gniewek; Robert Goodnough; Edmund and Susan Gordon, The Frances Barrett White Trust; Sara Greenberger; Grace Hartigan; Karen S. Kadlecsik, Marlborough Gallery; Gerome Kamrowski; Katherine Kaplan, Kraushaar Gallery; Lisa Koonce, Babcock Galleries; Suzanne Kreps, O. K. Harris Gallery; Shelley Lee, Estate of Roy Lichtenstein; Robert Lococo, Lococo Gallery Inc.; Nancy Lucscombe, Dedalus Foundation; Andrea Mihalovic, VAGA; Marjorie Minkin; Richard N. Murray; Peter T. Nesbett, The Jacob and Gwendolyn Lawrence Foundation; Robert Natkin; Suzanne Obuck, Salander-O'Reilly Galleries; Claes Oldenburg; Dennis Oppenheim; Sandra Paci, D. C. Moore Gallery; David Buchanan Parrish; Philip Pearlstein; Beverly Pepper; Jim Peters; Plattsburgh State Art Museum, Rockwell Kent Gallery and Collection; Karen Polack, Sperone Westwater, Anne S. Porter; Franklin Riehlman, Franklin Riehlman Gallery; Marie Rose; Roy Saper, Saper Galleries; Michael Sepeshy; Penelope Schmidt, Estate of Michael Graves; John Solum, The Daugherty Archives; Sique Spence, Nancy Hoffman Gallery; Clara Diament Sujo, CDS Gallery; Richard Wattenmaker, Archives of American Art; Jerald Webster; Andrew Wyeth, Mary Landa, The Wyeth Collection; Virginia Zabriskie, Trong Nguyen, Zabriskie Gallery; Jonathan Zorach, Zorach Collection LLC.

This project benefited greatly from the advice and technical skill it received from specialists in the field. Judith Hanson edited the preliminary draft before sending it to Hudson Hills Press. In addition to her virtuosity as an editor, I am grateful to Judith for her patience and restraint when deadlines were missed. I would like to thank Paul Anbinder, Founding Publisher of Hudson Hills Press, for his guidance during the preparation of this publication; Randall Perkins and Leslie van Breen, Executive Directors of Hudson Hills Press, for their direction and patience; Fronia W. Simpson, editor, for her refinements to the text; and Christopher Kuntze, designer, for the imaginative presentation of this volume. I would like to thank Kenneth Katz, who examined the condition of the collection and conserved works in need of attention, and Robert Hensleigh, Assistant Director of Photography at the Detroit Institute of Arts, who photographed objects in the collection in preparation for this publication. I would also like to thank staff members Regina Schreck, Assistant Curator; Bryan Christie, Facilities Manager/Preparator; and Henry Lovelady and Don Howell, Preparators, who handled objects with expert care and patience as the collection was examined, transported, photographed, stored, or reinstalled during the lengthy process of preparing this book.

This publication would not have been possible without the financial support of several generous donors, and I would like to acknowledge each one of them. The Henry Luce Foundation must be thanked above all. Its grant served as a lead gift and inspired others to contribute. I would like to thank the Dietrich Foundation, the Charles Stewart Mott Foundation, and the Viola E. Bray Trust for their generous contributions toward the scholarly research needed to complete the project. I would also like to thank Mr. and Mrs. Herbert Booth, the Founders Society of the Flint Institute of Arts, and the Friends of Modern Art for contributing to the production costs of the publication.

Finally, special thanks must be given to Ellen Holtzman of the Henry Luce Foundation, who was the initial inspiration for this project. Ellen had heard about the museum's outstanding collection of American art and contacted me in 1998 to recommend cataloguing the collection for the benefit of scholars and the enjoyment of the public at large. Ellen, thank you for taking the initiative and for the guidance you gave to make this publication possible.

JBH

Flint Institute of Arts | The American Painting and Sculpture Collection

WILLIAM H. GERDTS

The most celebrated art museum collections in this country as well as in Europe are those that aspire to display art both from around the world and over the course of history, such as those enshrined in the National Gallery of Art in Washington, D.C., and the Metropolitan Museum of Art in New York City. Institutions in smaller cities, some younger communities, or those less financially well endowed, have made a virtue of their limitations by concentrating on a particular area of or period in the history of art while still aspiring to comprehensiveness within their chosen mandate. Some institutions are concerned only with modern or contemporary art, whereas others have taken as their criterion a national, regional, or local focus. For instance, the museums in Montclair and Newark, both in New Jersey, have been successful and gained prominence for their specialization in American art, though both also have other collections and specialties.

The Montclair and Newark museums were founded at the beginning of the twentieth century. The Flint Institute of Arts is a younger museum, and its establishment the year before the start of the Great Depression did not augur well for its success. Yet the Institute has amassed an extraordinary group of American paintings over the past seventy-five years, one that enables the visitor to survey generally, if not specifically, the history of this country's pictorial achievement and to enjoy a number of individual masterworks worthy of any collection, private or institutional, in the United States.

The Flint Institute of Arts' American Collection begins with Philadelphia's Benjamin West, the most celebrated American-born artist of the period, who is represented by a lovely, moving biblical scene, *Simeon with the Infant Jesus,* painted when West had succeeded to the presidency of the Royal Academy in London, where he had settled in 1763. In its tender and emotional restraint and coloristic and compositional simplicity, the work evokes the tenets of the then-dominant Neoclassical style while representing "historical" art, considered the highest form of artistic expression, both for the technical challenges it presented the artist and the inspirational impact it had on the viewer.

Such historical works found relatively little patronage back in West's native land until fairly well into the nineteenth century. In the early decades of that century, portraiture remained the primary form of artistic expression, with Gilbert Stuart—trained in London and active successively in New York, Philadelphia, Washington, and finally Boston—its most celebrated master. From his last years dates the fine likeness *Portrait of Samuel Jackson Gardner,* a typical three-quarter bust portrait, the sitter erect and sure of countenance, with soft, pearly flesh tones that many of Stuart's contemporaries strove to emulate. The collection at Flint is rich in portraits by more naïve, usually self-taught painters of the period, sometimes termed "folk" or "primitive" artists. Some of these artists, such as the maker of the marvelous group portrait *The Fowler Children,* remain unidentified, though research through both family records and stylistic comparisons is ongoing. Others, such as Sheldon Peck of Vermont, later one of the earliest artists in Illinois, who painted the pair of portraits *Mr. Murry* and *Mrs. Murry,* have been carefully studied and identified by scholars. Beyond Peck's flat, linear manner, one can see in *Mr. Murry* the provincial emulation of Stuart's very sophisticated treatment of Samuel Jackson Gardner—in pose, expression, and even in the swag of "grand manner" drapery behind the figure.

William Matthew Prior, who painted *Baby in Pink and White or Little Janey in Pink and White Dress,* is another well-identified "primitive," although in his case one who advertised

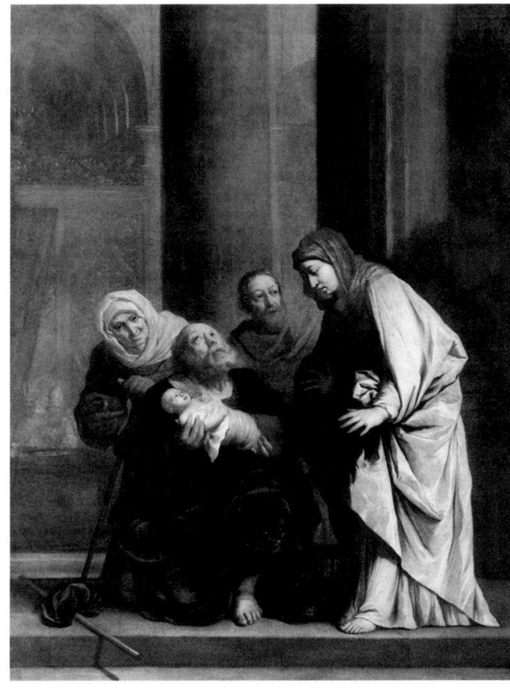

Benjamin West, *Simeon with the Infant Jesus,* cat. no. 1

a sliding scale of fees based on degree of finish, distinguishing between the more linear likenesses, as here, and more costly "three-dimensional" portraits. Many of the so-called primitives essayed more ambitious canvases as well. Erastus Salisbury Field, who worked in the Connecticut River Valley in Massachusetts, was a marvelous portraitist, but he also painted biblical and exotic scenic works such as *The Taj Mahal,* surely based on a published print. Still another well-known, somewhat naïve painter was Thomas Chambers, esteemed for his dramatic landscape and marine paintings, here represented by *Old Sleepy Hollow Church,* a spooky, moonlit image where the ruined church and ominous graveyard project the eerie spirit of Washington Irving's tale "The Legend of Sleepy Hollow."

By the beginning of the nineteenth century, painters began seriously to investigate themes other than portraiture, especially when institutions arose that offered them, through annual exhibitions, access to an art-loving and, with luck, art-collecting public. Robert Street was a prolific portrait painter in Philadelphia in the first half of the nineteenth century, though not an especially elegant one. Today probably his best-known painting is *The Basket of Apples,* painted in 1818 and one of the few still lifes of the period executed by a professional artist in this country. The still-life tradition in the United States had been established in Philadelphia just a few years earlier by Raphaelle Peale, and Street's simple, symmetrical composition and clear rendering of forms were almost surely inspired by Peale. By the middle of the century, the austerity of such work was overtaken by a sense of abundance, both literal and visual, most recognized today in the paintings of the German-born émigré Severin Roesen, the painter of *Still Life with Fruit.* Here, in a celebration of American bountifulness and the good life, dozens of pieces of fruit, an abundance of leaves and trailing tendrils, and even a bird's nest compete for the viewer's attention. An alternative still-life mode was introduced into American painting about 1860, one that can be seen in *Still Life: Overturned Cup of Raspberries* by Carducius Plantagenet Ream, the first celebrated still-life specialist in Chicago. Here, the fruits of nature are returned to a natural setting, rather than set out formally on a tabletop. By the end of the century, however, the tabletop still life received new impetus toward even greater mimesis and even illusionistic deception in the work of William Michael Harnett. Harnett's 1884 *Still Life,* painted in Munich during his six years abroad, reflects his emulation of the seventeenth-century Dutch models on view in the Bavarian capital's art museum.

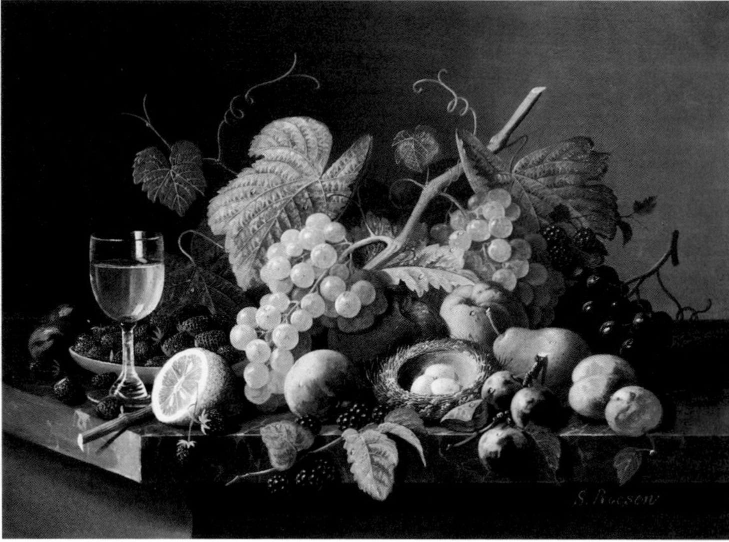

Severin Roesen, *Still Life with Fruit,* cat. no. 17

It was with landscape painting, however, that America was most identified for much of the nineteenth century—American history was its *natural* history. Once the wilderness was tamed, Americans, increasingly citified, sought pictorial and emotional relief in scenes of nature, and thus was born the well-known Hudson River School. One of the country's first masters of pure landscape was Thomas Doughty, the painter of *Landscape with Two Figures,* who turned to this theme in the second decade of the century. Increasingly, however, scenic artists came to identify and depict settled landscapes. One such painter was George Henry Durrie, a specialist in the winter landscape, such as *Winter Scene.* The Flint Institute's most complete expression of the realist aesthetic and celebratory nature of the Hudson River School is Jasper Cropsey's *Hudson River View, Summer,* where an exciting, glowing sunset of almost godly light prevails over a placid scene in the foreground, while the river seems to extend toward the infinity with which the vast American continent was identified. A subset of paintings by artists of the midcentury focused instead on a tranquil meditation on nature, pictures often small in scale but emphasizing horizontal breadth rather than depth. Among those who specialized in this approach to landscape, which has come to be known as Luminism, was Martin Johnson Heade, whose *Sunrise on the Marshes,* painted near Newburyport, Massachusetts, is probably the most celebrated landscape in the Institute's collection.

The post–Civil War period saw dramatic changes in American landscape painting. For one, a more painterly mode replaced the smooth surfaces sought by earlier artists and their patrons. For another, many artists began to concentrate not on vast panoramas but on more intimate fragments of nature, where the drama of nature's mood was drawn from seasonal identity, cloud patterns, and weather conditions. This, as in Alexander Helwig Wyant's *Early Autumn,* Ralph Blakelock's *A Mountain Road near Gorham, N.H.,* and Hugh Bolton Jones's *Landscape,* represented a retreat from national glorification to a concentration on the artists' personal, often poetic, responses to the landscape and reflected American fascination with and emulation of the work of the French Barbizon painters. Such pictures, as these, might be unpopulated; alternatively, the emphasis might be on rural scenery, with farm buildings and animals, as in Thomas Moran's *A Pastoral Landscape,* Bruce Crane's *Long Island Farm, Springtime,* and J. Francis Murphy's *Landscape.* Murphy became extraordinarily successful after the turn of the twentieth century, recognized as a leader of the Tonalists, in whose work an often near-barren piece of land would be infused with a poetic luminosity in which only a single color tone dominated.

Increasingly, however, as American painters more frequently sought training abroad, principally in Paris and Munich, they chose to emphasize the figure as often as the landscape. Figure painting was hardly new to American art. But the earlier, more sentimental and anecdotal approach, which continued in the works of the immensely popular John George Brown, such as *How d'ye?*—notable for its concentration on an African American subject—was replaced by either more ambitious, academic subjects, such as Henry Oliver Walker's modernized biblical theme in *Hagar and Ishmael,* or by the more straightforward renderings of subjects of modern life. The latter was the province of the French Impressionists and was taken up by their American followers, most notably Mary Cassatt, whose involvement with modern-life subjects led to her distinction as the only American to exhibit with Claude Monet, Auguste Renoir, and their colleagues. Cassatt's colorful, monumental image of her sister, *Lydia at a Tapestry Frame,* is one of the glories of the Flint collection. Equally outstanding is the *Garden Study of the Vickers Children* by John Singer Sargent, another of the great American expatriates of the later nineteenth century. This work, equally a portrait and a decorative figure arrangement, was created just at the time the artist decisively changed his base of operation from Paris to London. In its informality, vigorous brushwork, and flat patterning, it reflects the impact of Edouard Manet and the Impressionists.

At first, however, when Americans became aware of Impressionism in the 1880s, many were repelled by the mundane, sometimes ugly and pessimistic, subjects of the French Impressionist figure painters. Thus American artists, both abroad and at home, instead often applied Impressionist strategies of bright color, broken brushwork, and flickering light to landscape themes. This can be seen in the *French Landscape* by William Harper, one of the leading African American painters of the period, much of whose short creative life was spent abroad. These traits are also abundantly displayed in *Newport Waterfront,* a characteristic painting by Childe Hassam, the most celebrated and successful of the American Impressionists, whose pictures celebrate America's colonial traditions in what was considered the most acceptable advanced aesthetic of the time. Other painters, such as Leonard Ochtman, working near the Connecticut artists' colony of Old Lyme, chose in paintings such as *Along the Mianus River* a quieter, less scintillating mode, mixing the brighter colorism of Impressionism with the softer, more gentle tendencies of Tonalism.

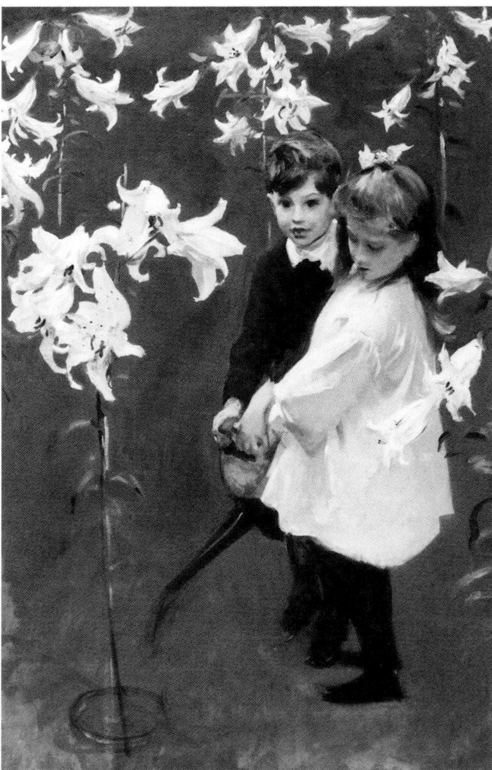

John Singer Sargent, *Garden Study of the Vickers Children,* cat. no. 37

By the beginning of the twentieth century, American artists began to explore the more decorative, less illusionistic strategies of Post-Impressionism, seen here in Maurice Prendergast's *Bathers.* Prendergast was a member of The Eight, the group of New York artists who ushered in a vigorous new urban realism in their exhibition at the Macbeth Gallery in New York in February 1908. Robert Henri's *Catharine* is one of his series of pictures called *My People*—unidealized and unadorned, directly painted images of representative types. The Eight also included

Arthur B. Davies, a painter of visionary figurative works such as *Four Figures.* Urban realism of the period is seen most impressively in the Flint Institute's collection in *Terminal Yards* by Henri's associate Leon Kroll, a work shown in the historic Armory Show held in New York in 1913, which for the first time ushered in European modernism on a large scale.

The Flint Institute of Arts' collection offers examples of the increasing awareness of regional art developments in the twentieth century. Thus, Tunis Ponsen, whose *The Old Pier* is very likely a scene along the shore of Lake Michigan, was a Michigan and Chicago painter of urban realism, while William Wendt was a Chicago painter who became a major figure in the Laguna Beach artists' colony in Southern California, where *Rocks and Sea* was likely painted. Charles Burchfield, working in Buffalo, New York, was one of the country's greatest watercolor specialists, in his later years painting romantic fantasies of nature, such as *Nighthawks at Twilight* and *Northwoods in Spring.* Precisionism, a movement beginning in the 1920s that often emphasized the clean-cut mechanical forms of industry, had a leading representative in Milwaukee, Wisconsin, in Edmund Lewandowski, seen here in his *Dynamo.* Emil Bisttram, one of the most radical modernists in the artists' colony of Taos, New Mexico, created such abstractions from nature in his *Sea Pattern.*

In the late 1940s abstraction became the dominant artistic mode and New York the art capital not only of the United States but of the world. Abstract Expressionism was the predominant art form for the next several decades, with artists' gestural expressions mirroring on canvas their personal dynamics and emotional passions. Many smaller institutions in the United States—and not a few larger ones—shied away from including works by the leading Abstract Expressionists in their collection, reflecting the lack of comprehension and even dismay on the part of their constituency. Flint did not, and thus, by both gift and purchase, the Institute has a splendid, if small, group of such paintings, including one from Robert Motherwell's *Elegy* series, *Elegy to the Spanish Republic #173,* Willem de Kooning's *Woman,* Hans Hofmann's *Untitled,* and Adolph Gottlieb's *Conflict,* which contrasts motionless and solid shapes with active, disintegrating ones. And if Jackson Pollock, the most innovative painter of this group, is not represented in the collection, *Happy Lady,* a superb example by his artist-wife, Lee Krasner, emulates Pollock's gestural, all-encompassing methodology yet expresses her own, more subtle, and restrained sensibility.

The Flint Institute of Arts has also kept up with many of the subsequent movements in American art, both abstract and figurative. In the aftermath of the vigorous paint application of Abstract Expressionism, a number of painters such as Helen Frankenthaler, here with *Minotaur,* and Paul Jenkins, in *Phenomena Forking Paths,* developed an alternative methodology of staining their canvases with thin, overlapping layers of color, substituting almost transparent planes of color for the thick, often three-dimensional paint surfaces of the Abstract Expressionists. Similar, but with more solid areas of color, were Color Field painters such as Morris Louis, creating paintings that abjure even more traditional spatial illusionism, as seen here in *I-31.* Equally abstract, though offering an antithetical approach to color and space, is Josef Albers's series of pictures, represented here by *Study for Homage to the Square: With a Veil,* where the interaction of overlapping squares of different colors communicated optical recession or progression. This was but a short step to Op Art—severely geometric compositions such as Richard Anuszkiewicz's *Inflexional I,* a painting that visually plays tricks on the viewer's perceptions, imparting spatial and coloristic oscillation.

Realist art was relegated to a back seat during the middle years of the twentieth century, though such masters as Andrew Wyeth, drawing on his Pennsylvania and Maine environments in such works as *The Sweep,* maintained a dedication to reality that continues to earn him popular acclaim. The reaction to abstraction, however, occurred even at the height of the movement in the very painterly realist figural work of Fairfield Porter, such as his *Jimmy in Black Rocker.* Pop Art, which developed in the 1960s, took popular, mundane visual objects and elements of daily life, from store goods to billboards, and elevated them, often through enlargement, to the level of "high art," as

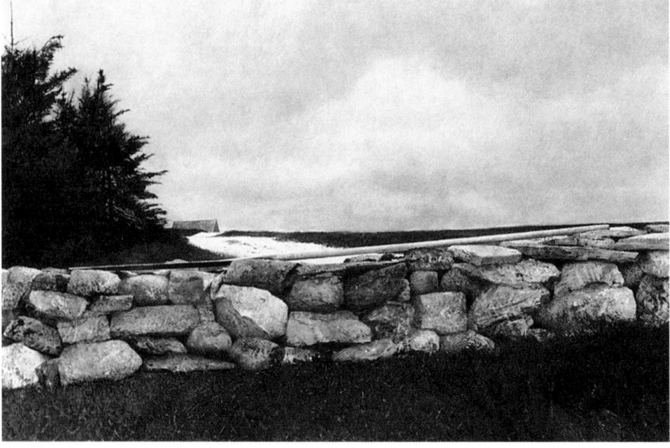

Andrew Wyeth, *The Sweep,* cat. no. 74

seen in *Golden Cake,* a work by the San Francisco painter Wayne Thiebaud.

Even later decades of the century, however, witnessed the development of new approaches to realism in such traditional genres as landscapes, as seen in Neil Welliver's cool, pure images of Maine, here exemplified by *Cedar Water Brook.* Stone Roberts is one of a new breed of realists intent on visually enumerating the details of contemporary life in the juxtaposition of figures with their environment, as in *Portrait of a Marriage.* One of the most celebrated figurative painters working today is Philip Pearlstein, who has concentrated on studio close-ups of cropped nudes. Pearlstein's *Entrance to Lincoln Tunnel, Daytime,* which links him to the Photorealists, is a departure from his figurative work, though its spatial disjuncture—the viewer moves from the foreground window immediately both far out and far down to the scene below—is consistent with his spatial manipulation in his more usual figural paintings. More traditional is the work of Richard Maury, as in his *Interior with Stefania,* which suggests an updating of the celebrated work of the great seventeenth-century Dutch painter Jan Vermeer.

Perhaps it is the genre of still-life painting that has particularly enjoyed a revival under the rubric of contemporary realism during the last two decades. In the academic work of Deborah Diechler, modern tableware in *The Chocolate Thief* replaces the tankards and beakers of the Dutch old masters. Jack Beal has often expanded this genre to include a wider perimeter, placing his arrangements within a portion of an interior with accompanying figures. This establishes the still life as a significant element within an environment of domestic contentment, although, as in *Sondra with Gladioli,* the flowers maintain their primacy within the compositional scheme.

A special feature of the collection at Flint is its small but important collection of works by African American artists. These include the aforementioned landscape by William Harper, working in France, and modern examples by some of the leading black artists of the last century, such as the stylized figurative picture *South African Gold Miners* by Jacob Lawrence, probably the most celebrated African American painter of the century, and Charles White's more naturalistic *Wanted Poster Series #17.* White, one of the finest draftsmen among twentieth-century American artists, often focused, as here, on both the suffering and nobility of his people. Romare Bearden also chose similar themes as well as even more universal ones in his *Prevalence of Ritual: Reverend John's Sermon No. 1,* interpreting them in bright colors and bold, jagged, and fragmented patterns in the medium of collage.

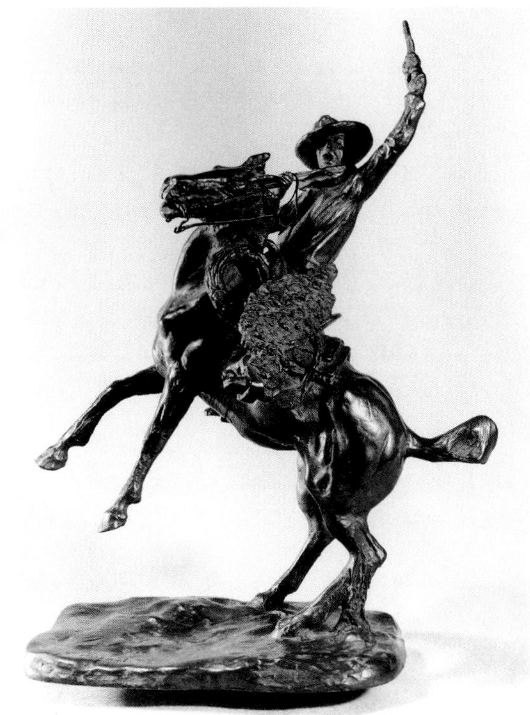

Charles Russell, American 1865–1926
Smoking Up, modeled 1903; bronze, 13½ × 10⅝ in.
Signed on bottom: *C. M. Russell* (1969.31)

One of the major lacunae of the collection of the Flint Institute of Arts is examples of the American marmoreans—those sculptors in marble who, for two generations in the second and third quarters of the nineteenth century, developed their careers abroad. Almost all of them based their careers in Florence or Rome, working in emulation of the ancient Greek and Roman sculptors. Recognized as Neoclassicists, they constituted the first school of American sculptors. By the end of the nineteenth century, marble had given way to bronze as the preferred medium of American sculptors, with many artists turning to more indigenous subject matter. These include those artists who chose to represent action themes drawn from the American West, most notably the painter-sculptors Frederic Remington and Charles Russell, the latter represented by *Smoking Up.* Other sculptors, such as Anna Hyatt Huntington, specialized in the depiction of wild animals, such as *Yawning Panther.* Huntington not only represents the American contingent of *animaliers* who had begun to come to the fore in France in the mid–nineteenth century but also the prominence that women achieved in sculpture, comparatively earlier than in painting.

Early modernism often took the form of stylization in American sculpture, notably in the Art Deco bronze heads of Boris Lovet-Lorski—here in *Sieglinde,* drawn from Richard Wagner's operatic *Ring* cycle—and in William Zorach's monumental *Spirit of the Dance.* Abstract Expressionism had its sculptural contingent in such vigorous works as Seymour Lipton's *Wind Drift,* where open space becomes an important element vis-à-vis the solid and jagged forms of mottled metal. But modern sculpture was able to go beyond painting, adding movement as a significant element in the formal repertoire of art. This achievement has been associated especially with Alexander Calder and mobiles such as *Red Fish Tail* that he developed from the late 1940s on. Flat pieces of painted sheet metal hanging from extended rods move with wind patterns, changing their relationship with one another and creating a variety of arrangements. Similarly, and at about the same time, George Rickey developed spiky, stainless-steel abstract kinetic sculptures such as *Column I.* More recent artistic developments in American painting are mirrored in the sculpture of the last three or four decades. This includes Claes Oldenburg's Pop sculptures, based on mundane objects such as foodstuffs, household objects, and cosmetics, or an icon of popular culture such as Mickey Mouse, simplified and cubistic, in his *Geometric Mouse, Scale C.* Contemporary figurative realism has found its ultimate sculptural expression in the figures of everyday Americana by Duane Hanson, such as his *College Student*—wearing "real" clothes, holding his "real" book, and as startlingly lifelike as the viewer him- or herself.

The painting and sculpture collection of the Flint Institute of Arts encompasses a remarkably complete spectrum of American achievement. Within that survey there are a number of truly world-class examples—paintings such as those by Heade, Cassatt, and Sargent, as well as many modern examples—that would enhance the collections of any major institution in this country, great or small, an achievement in which Flint should take great pride.

Catalogue

Benjamin West AMERICAN 1738–1820

1 | *Simeon with the Infant Jesus*, c. 1796

Oil on canvas, 48 × 35⅝ in.

Unsigned

Gift of Mr. Stanley Gillen (1972.1)

Benjamin West was the first American artist to gain international acclaim and to influence developments in European painting. He was born in Springfield, Pennsylvania, about ten miles west of Philadelphia, the youngest of ten children. His father, a Quaker, had emigrated from England to the state of Pennsylvania in 1715 or 1716. Edward Penington, a distant cousin, taught West to paint and invited the nine-year-old to Philadelphia. It was there that he met the English artist William Williams (1727–1791), who lent him art books. By the age of fifteen West was considered a prodigy—he even sold a few of his paintings for a pound or two, then a considerable sum. He also apparently received some art training from John Valentine Haidt, a goldsmith who immigrated to America in 1754. West became a protégé of Reverend William Smith, a classical scholar and Anglican minister who had come to America from Scotland in 1754 at the invitation of Benjamin Franklin. Smith served as a mentor to West and promoted the young artist's career in his publication, *The American Magazine and Monthly Chronicle for the British Colonies.* Between 1757 and 1760, West worked as a portrait painter in order to finance a trip to Europe to study art. In 1760 the Allens and the Shippens, two leading Philadelphia families, provided him with free passage to Italy and advanced him £300 for copies of Old Master paintings he was to paint for them during his trip.

West was also the first professional American artist to train in Italy. As part of his studies, he made copies of classical and religious subjects that reflected the influence of this exposure to Renaissance art and the then-fashionable Rococo and Neoclassical styles. In 1763, presumably on his way back to America, he stopped in London, where he remained for many years on the advice of his patrons. He was influential in bringing the new Neoclassical approach to contemporary English painters, one that they had hitherto largely ignored. He showed two such works, completed in Rome, at the Society of Arts exhibition in London in 1766. William Allen, his patron, wrote to Benjamin Chew in Philadelphia that "He is really a wonder of a man and has so far outstripped all the painters of his time [in getting] into high esteem at once. . . . If he keeps his health he will make money very fast."[1] In 1768, West was one of a group of artists who seceded from the Society of Artists to form a new organization, the Royal Academy of Arts. He continued to exhibit there every year but one from 1769 until 1819 and, after the death of Joshua Reynolds, became the Academy's second president. In December 1805, West resigned the post due to factional disputes, but returned to office a year later and remained until his death.

In England, West's work was first recognized by the Anglican clergy, who commissioned him to paint classical and biblical subjects. Archbishop Drummond introduced him to King George III, who became West's friend and patron. Like the Anglican bishops, the king was interested in reintroducing art in the Church, which had been largely absent since the Reformation due to its association with Catholicism. Between 1768 and 1800, West received numerous commissions from the English king, including work for a proposed private chapel at Windsor on the History of Revealed Religion. Although West completed most of the paintings for the chapel, the project itself was never completed. In 1772, West was appointed Historical Painter to the King and in 1791 became Surveyor of the King's Pictures. From 1780 to 1810, he received a stipend of £1,000 per year from the Crown. From 1780 on, West focused on religious subject matter, primarily related to the Windsor project, although he also worked for William Beckford, the English collector and writer, and completed various church and public commissions.

Simeon with the Infant Jesus shows the Presentation of the Infant Jesus to the Lord in the Temple. Mary and Joseph are at the right of the scene. On the floor next to Mary, a caged pair of turtledoves can be seen in the shadows. As was customary, the birds had been brought to the Temple as a sacrifice. The elderly Saint Simeon, who had been promised he would live long enough to see Jesus, holds the Child in his arms as he gazes upward toward the Lord. Behind him is Saint Anna the Prophetess, who referred to the Child as the Redeemer.

The painting was exhibited at the Royal Academy in 1796 and then joined the collection of George III. When the collection was dismantled, the work became the property of Sibton Vicarage. When the vicarage was sold, the painting was purchased by a Mr. Hart, who subsequently sold it to Mr. Stanley Gillen, the man who donated it to the Flint Institute of Arts. According to a letter from the donor, the picture is in its original frame.

While West is well known as a painter, he had a more direct and powerful effect on American art as a teacher and mentor. He opened his London studio to other American artists, including Gilbert Stuart, Charles Willson Peale, Ralph Earl, and John Trumbull, who studied there during their European travels and received West's guidance and encouragement. MMD

1. D. A. Kimball and M. Quinn, "William Allen–Benjamin Chew Correspondence, 1763–1764," *Pennsylvania Magazine of History and Biography* (1966), p. xc.

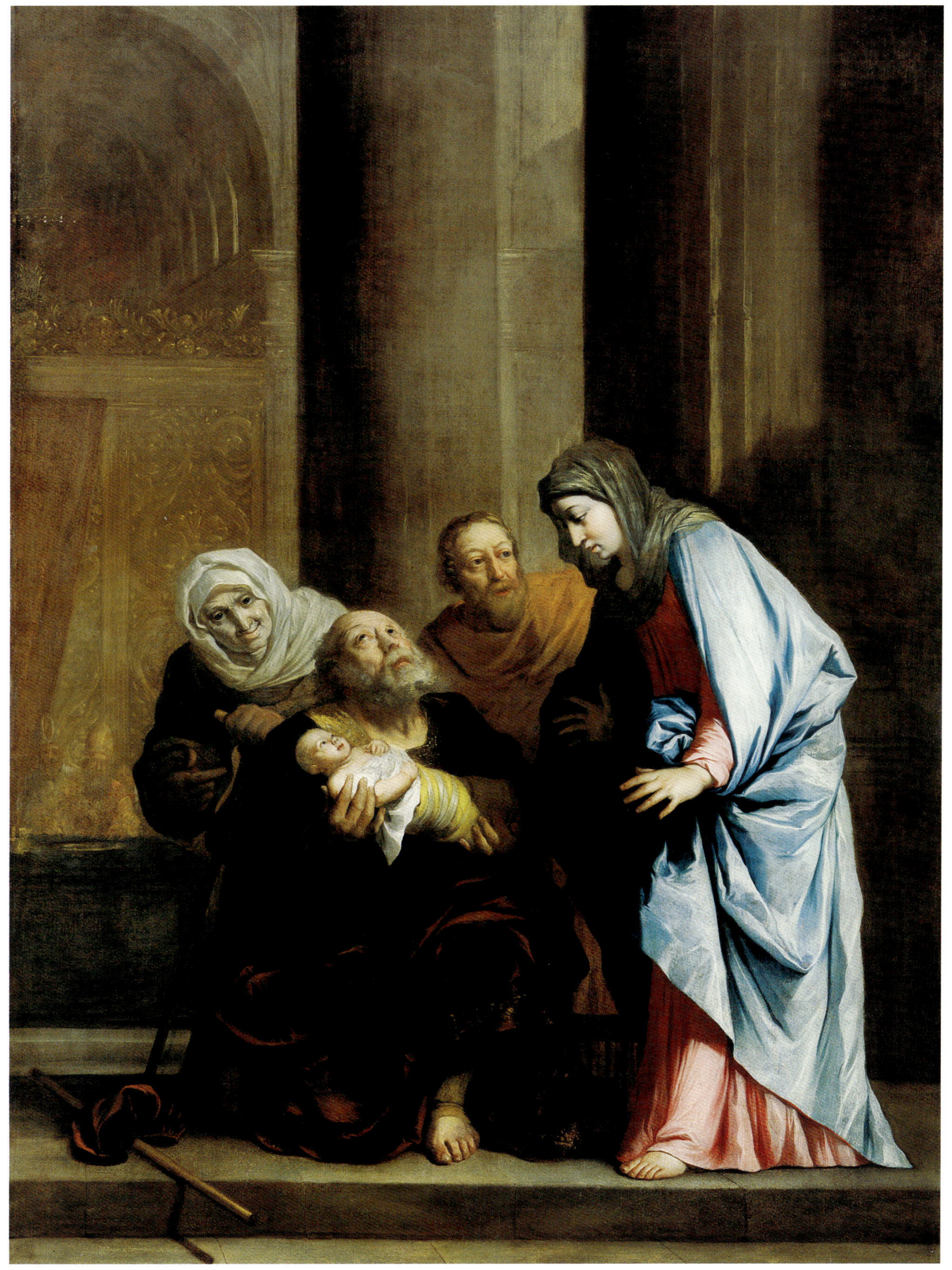

Robert Street AMERICAN 1796–1865

2 | *The Basket of Apples,* 1818

Oil on board, 10 × 14 in.

Signed and dated lower right: *Street 1818*

Gift of the Viola E. Bray Charitable Trust via Mr. and Mrs. William L. Richards (1964.4)

A native of Germantown, Pennsylvania, the versatile Robert Street painted still lifes, history and religious paintings, and landscapes in addition to the portraits for which he is best known. In nearby Philadelphia, Street found a thriving art and cultural center thanks in large part to the efforts of Charles Willson Peale and his talented and prolific family. In addition to his famous natural history museum, Peale founded the short-lived Columbianum in 1795, which provided young artists with training and encouraged art patronage. Even more important for the Philadelphia art community and for Street in particular was Peale's participation in the establishment of the Pennsylvania Academy of the Fine Arts, an institution that held annual exhibitions and served as an educational facility complete with imported classical casts. Beginning in 1815 Street exhibited extensively at the Pennsylvania Academy.

An avid art collector who greatly admired the old masters, Street assembled a group of works attributed to such artists as Peter Paul Rubens, Anthony van Dyck, and Annibale Carracci.[1] In 1840 Street exhibited his own paintings alongside the older works, composed primarily of works that are now assumed to have been fakes, the product of the large-scale duping of nineteenth-century American collectors by dealers of the "old masters." Held in the Artists' Fund Hall in Philadelphia, the show served in part to declare some of Street's influences and to borrow on the artistic authority of these well-known European painters to validate the work of the American artist.

The Basket of Apples, Street's only located still life, is a meticulously painted and highly detailed image that employs the illusionistic, trompe-l'oeil style contemporaneously practiced by members of the Peale family, most notably Raphaelle and James. Here Street depicts a grouping of apples, carefully arranged within an elegant, silver wire–worked basket. Despite the fact that the composition is extraordinarily balanced and nearly symmetrical (a nod to the Neoclassical style that was still influential in Philadelphia), Street is also committed to focusing on the banal to achieve a measure of realism. He chooses, for example, to paint local and commonplace, rather than exotic, fruit, and he reveals each flaw. In this vein, he deliberately contrasts the brown spots of the blemished apples with the cool perfection of the silver basket.

By focusing on the apple, the most frequently painted fruit in nineteenth-century American art and one long connected to American national identity, Street also paints a still life that suggests its "American-ness."[2] The first fruit tree domesticated in this country and a leading agricultural product, particularly in the Northeast, the apple attained its popularity because of its versatility, hardiness, and prevalence, achieved in part by itinerant seed distributors, among them the legendary Johnny Appleseed, the alter ego of John Chapman (1774–1845). The apple also captured the attention of numerous nineteenth-century writers, such as Ralph Waldo Emerson (1803–1882), who recommended it as the "national" or "American" fruit. The preacher and writer Henry Ward Beecher (1813–1889) declared that the apple was both American and democratic: "The apple is . . . the true democratic fruit . . . It is so easy of propagation . . . It is neither dainty nor dyspeptic . . . a genuine democrat. It can be poor, while it loves to be rich. . . . The apple tree is the common people's tree. . . ."[3] MK

1. Perhaps inspired by Charles Willson Peale, who named his children after old master artists, Street's own appreciation of these painters influenced the naming of his sons—including Rubens, Del Sarto, Correggio, and Claude Lorraine Street—all of whom became (unsuccessful) artists.

2. On the history and significance of the apple in American art and culture, see Bruce Weber, *The Apple of America: The Apple in Nineteenth-Century American Art,* exh. cat. (New York: Berry-Hill Galleries, 1993).

3. Quoted in ibid., p. 10.

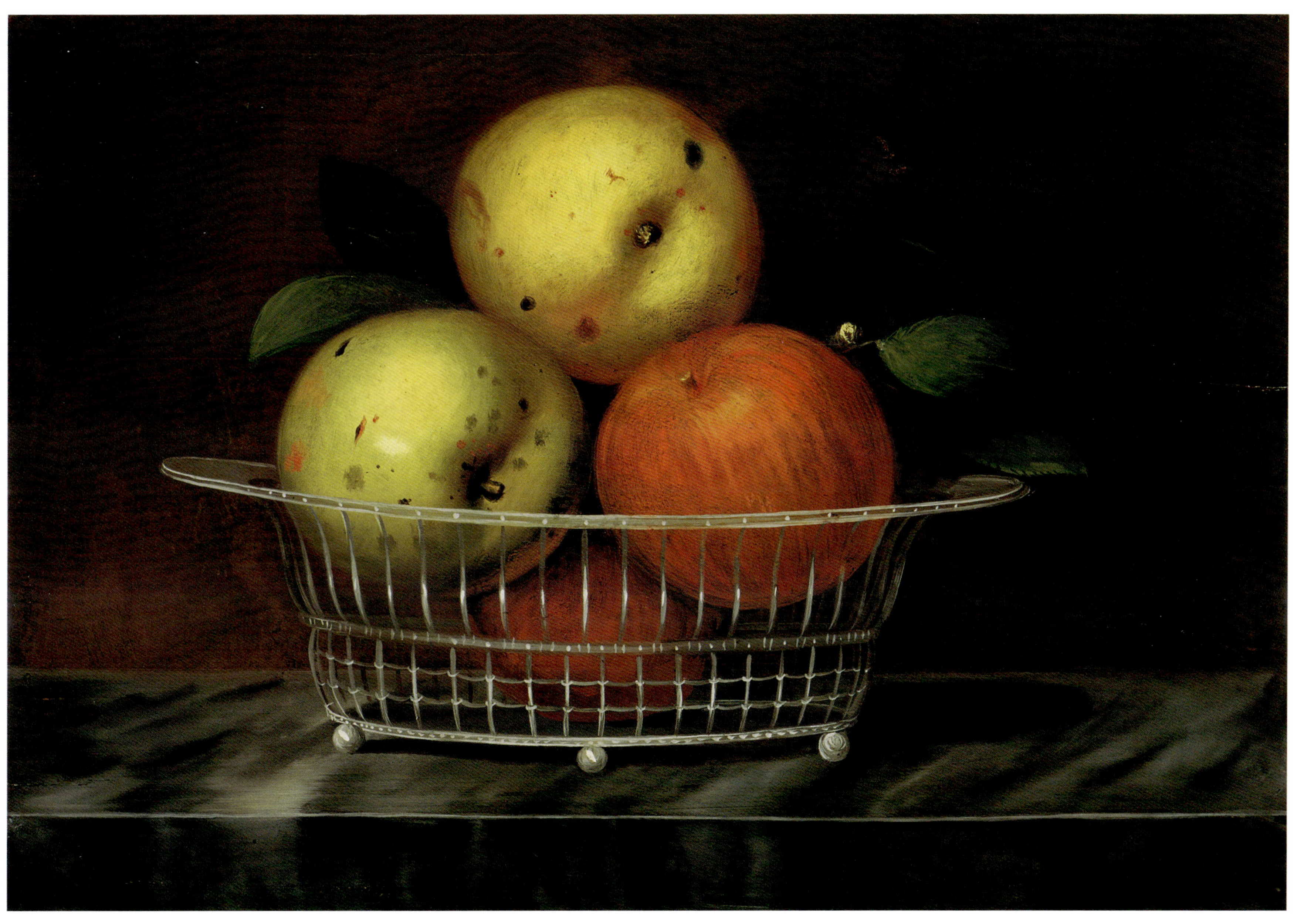

Attributed to Joshua Johnson AMERICAN, ACTIVE 1796–1824

3 | *Portrait of an African American Man,* c. 1820

Oil on panel, 19 × 13¾ in.

Unsigned

Gift of Edgar William and Bernice Chrysler Garbisch (1981.7)

Joshua Johnson, perhaps the most successful and well-known of the early African American artists, achieved acclaim as a skilled portraitist during the Federal period. His birthplace is unknown, though he was rumored to be from the West Indies and was possibly a former slave. A self-taught painter, he was primarily active in Baltimore, where he appears in city directories beginning in 1797. He garnered numerous commissions from prominent Southern families, especially in and around Baltimore, and was able to earn a living making portraits. Although his works are mainly multifigure, he also executed a number of single-figure compositions in the manner of *Portrait of an African American Man*.

A sizable body of work has been attributed to Johnson's hand, yet he is known to have signed only one work, and none is dated. His painting style is characterized by precisely rendered, geometricized features, a thinly applied paint surface, careful attention to clothing and visual details, and sensitive portrayals of character. His subjects are Caucasian, with the exception of the Flint portrait and two other examples. The second work depicting an African American was also acquired by the Garbisches (subsequently given to the National Gallery of Art, Washington, D.C.). It is a close version of the Flint painting except for the placement of the sitter, who faces the opposite direction; they may have originally been conceived of as a pair. The third portrait of an African American is also of an unidentified male (Bowdoin College Museum of Art, Brunswick, Maine).

The Flint portrait is notable not only for the rarity of the subject but also for its elaborate background. Johnson generally painted plain dark backgrounds, but in this work a red swag or curtain is drawn back at the right to reveal a ship in the distance. The vessel has been identified as the *New Philadelphia*—a passenger steamer that traversed the Hudson River from New York to Albany; it was the first ship to have African Americans serve as waiters on board. Since painted portraits often include clues to a sitter's profession, it is possible that this individual was affiliated with the steamer in some way. The Flint portrait, while typical of the artist's work in its stiff pose, is a skillful and perceptive portrayal of the sitter's expression. Johnson's ability to capture a subject's likeness in oil places him in the highest ranks of naïve portrait painters. VAL/AR

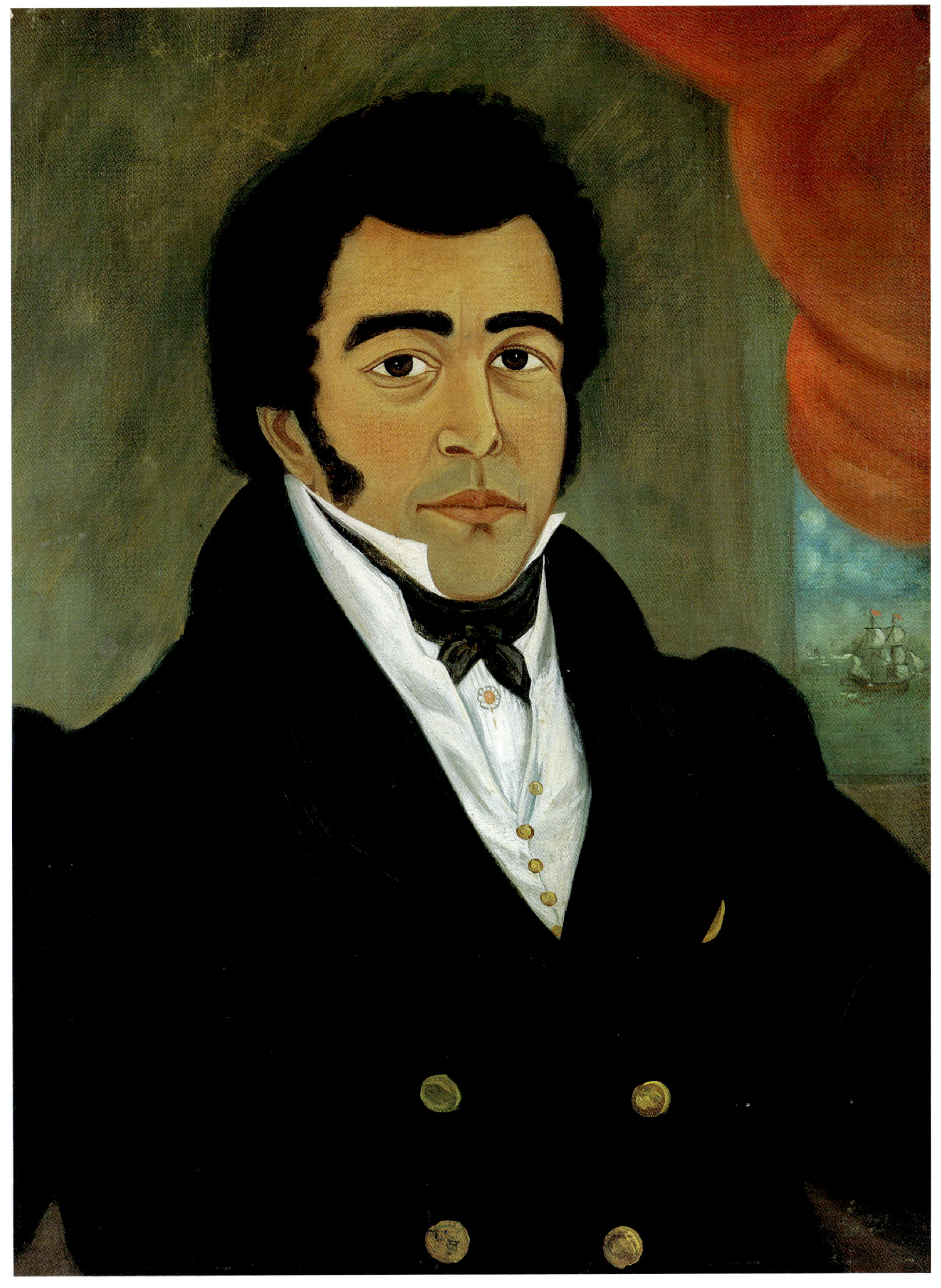

Almira Wheaton AMERICAN 1804–1881

4 | *Lady in Straw Hat*, c. 1824/25

Watercolor on paper, 13⅞ × 9⅞ in.

Inscribed in two hands on verso: *This was a lesson in watercolor made about 1824 or 1825 by Almira Wheaton mother of Levi Saben*

Gift of Edgar William and Bernice Chrysler Garbisch (1981.9)

In the nineteenth century, women of the upper classes were encouraged to cultivate their artistic skills, especially in watercolor, which was considered an important reflection of a feminine culture and refinement. Ladies were generally given art lessons to develop their technique, and this work by Almira Wheaton, as indicated by the inscription on the verso, is likely the product of such study. The artist's bold technique in a difficult and unforgiving medium reveals her confidence and precision in interpretation. The sitter was also a member of the upper class, as seen in her highly decorative bodice and hat. The draftsmanship is competent and, although it lacks modeling and depth, the artist has clearly conveyed the physical attributes of the subject as well as captured her spirit.

Little is known of Wheaton except that she lived most of her life in Winchester, New Hampshire, and married Mowry Saben in 1836, with whom she had eight children. Of these offspring, only one, the Levi mentioned in the inscription, survived beyond childhood. Wheaton is one of many unrecognized naïve American artists of the nineteenth century who reflected the country's growing interest in culture and the arts. VAL/AR

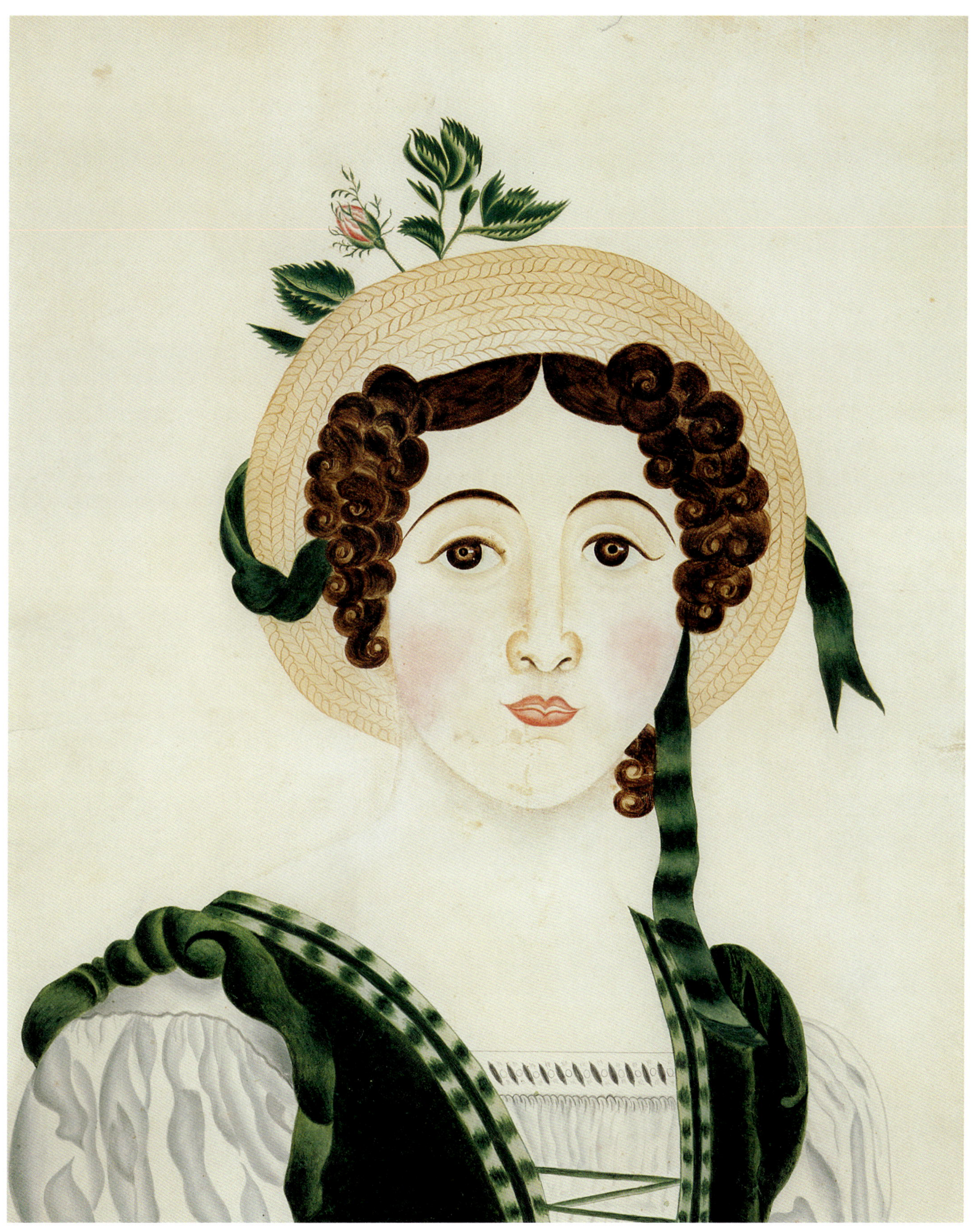

Sheldon Peck AMERICAN 1797–1868

5 | *Mr. Murry,* c. 1820–25

Oil on panel, 27¼ × 21⅞ in.

Unsigned

Gift of Edgar William and Bernice Chrysler Garbisch (1968.24)

6 | *Mrs. Murry,* c. 1820–25

Oil on panel, 27¾ × 22⅝ in.

Unsigned

Gift of Edgar William and Bernice Chrysler Garbisch (1968.25)

Sheldon Peck, born in Cornwall, Vermont, was most likely a self-taught artist who specialized in portraiture. Although there is no record of his having received formal training, he may have consulted art instruction books, widely available at the time, to acquire basic technical skills.

It is difficult to assign a specific body of work to Peck, as he did not sign his paintings. Based on works attributed to him on stylistic evidence, his career falls into three discrete phases. The first commenced about 1820, when he undertook works depicting his immediate family. These compositions, three-quarter-length portraits on wood panels, are executed in a somber palette with minimal decorative detail and flattened perspective, and the subjects often display a dour expression.

The second phase of his career began in 1828, when he moved to Onondaga County in upstate New York. He continued painting three-quarter-length poses but started to employ a brighter palette and more elaborate detail and settings. This change can be seen especially in decorative costume details such as Mrs. Murry's colorful scarf and the lace collars and in the gold-bordered drapery swags, furniture, books, and fruit, all of which provide background context. It is to this mature period in his artistic development that the Flint portraits belong. The direct gaze, stern expression, and lack of spatial depth seen in the portraits of Mr. and Mrs. Murry typify Peck's portraiture.

In 1836 Peck was implicated in a local social scandal that resulted in his relocating to Illinois. After a brief residence in Chicago, he and his family moved to Lombard, Illinois, where he remained for the rest of his life. There he initiated the third period of his career, painting larger, more complex, multifigure compositions in heightened color, some of which are full-length. Despite his development as an artist, Peck appears to have opted to paint in a provincial, naïve style, one that was apparently appreciated by his local clientele, rather than adopting a more sophisticated approach. VAL/AR

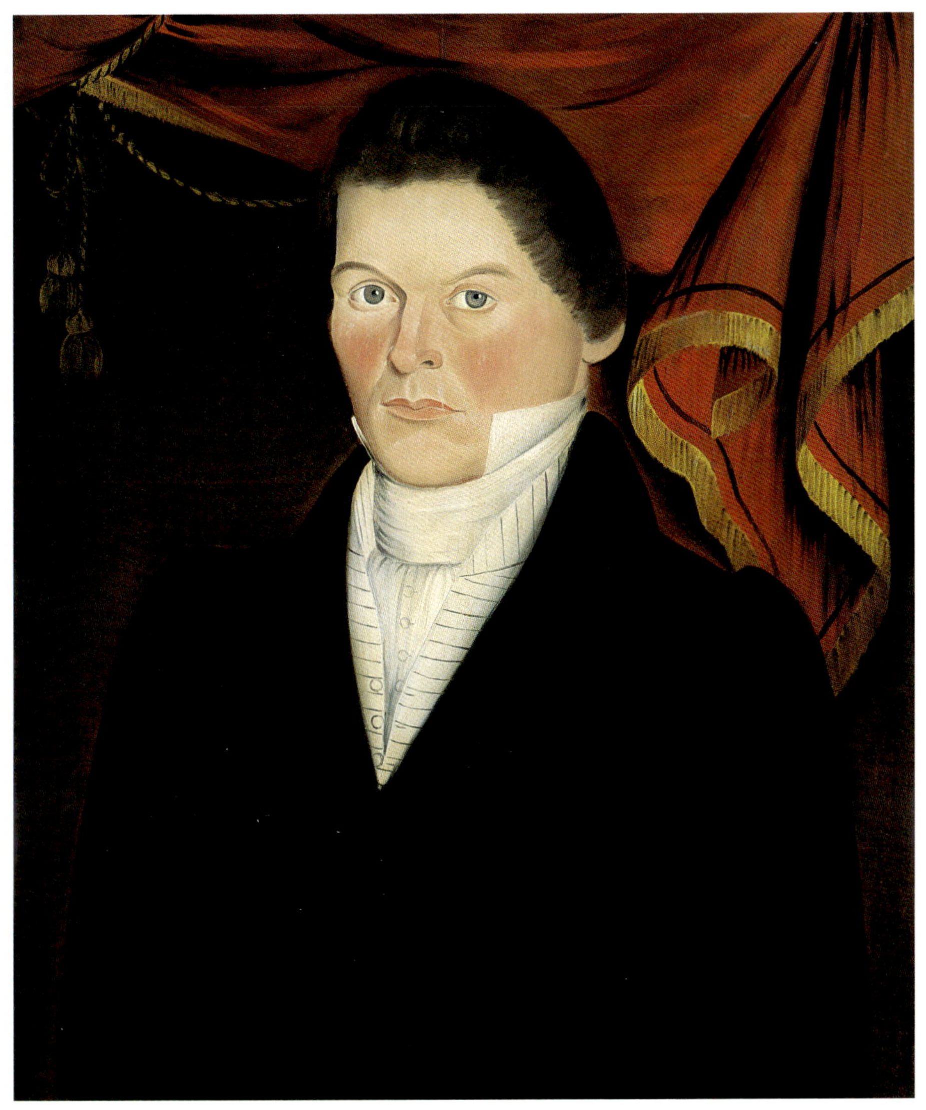

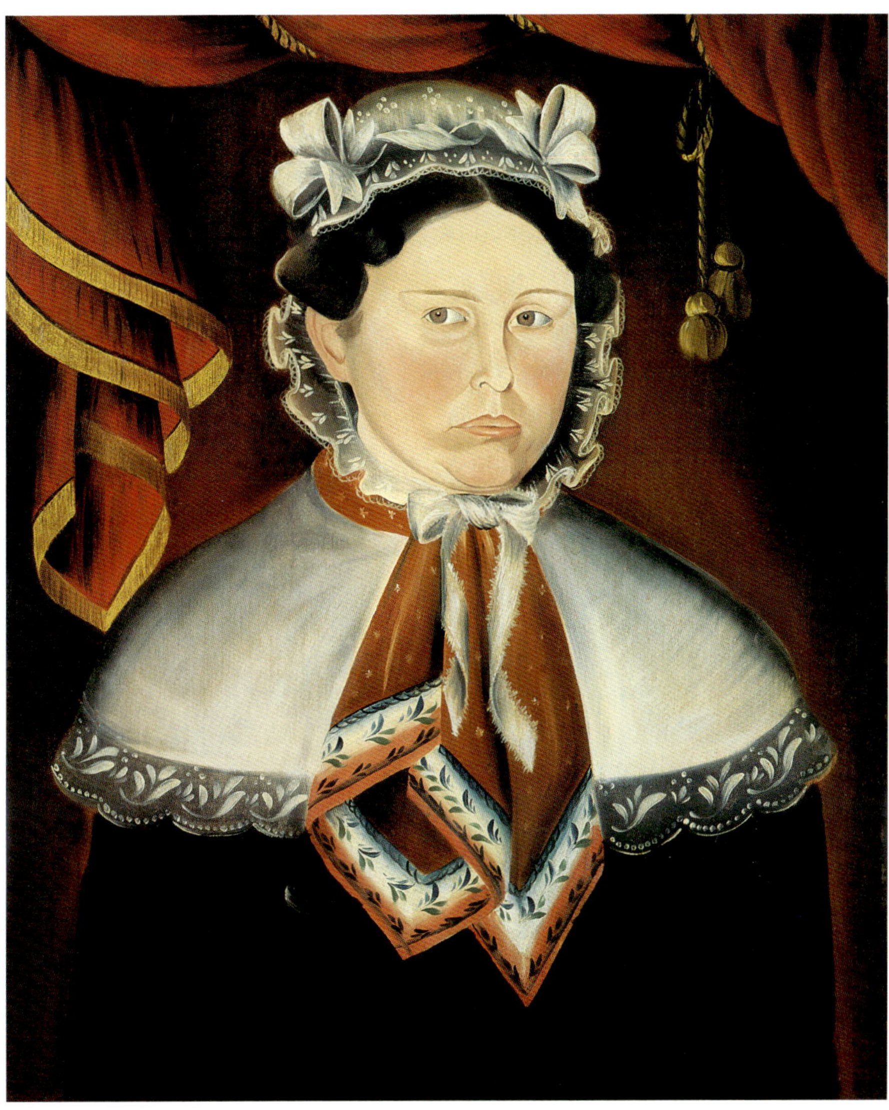

Gilbert Stuart AMERICAN 1755–1828

7 | *Portrait of Samuel Jackson Gardner,* 1825

Oil on canvas, 27¼ × 22¼ in.

Unsigned

Gift of Mrs. Arthur M. Davison (1961.1)

During his lifetime, Gilbert Stuart achieved professional recognition as a painter of prominent figures in noble, political, and social circles. The son of a Newport, Rhode Island, tobacco dealer, Stuart began making portraits in his early teens. After training with the Scottish artist Cosmo Alexander and traveling with him to Edinburgh, Stuart returned to Newport. By 1775 intimations of war made finding commissions difficult, and Stuart moved to London. There he worked as an assistant in the studio of the American expatriate artist Benjamin West, for whom he finished portraits and painted backgrounds. Stuart soon established his own business as a portraitist—his clients were attracted to his fluid brushstrokes, soft outlines, and coloristic canvases, features he drew from the styles of his English contemporaries Thomas Gainsborough and George Romney. In 1787, the same year that he exhibited for the first time at the Royal Academy of Arts, Stuart moved to Dublin, where he continued to receive important commissions. After five years of success in Ireland, and a total of eighteen years abroad, Stuart returned to the United States in 1792.

Stuart's best-known work was created shortly thereafter, when he was hired to paint George Washington. From the three portraits done from life—now known, respectively, as the "Vaughan" portrait (1795; National Gallery of Art, Washington, D.C.), the unfinished "Athenæum" portrait (1796; Boston Athenæum, on deposit at the Museum of Fine Arts, Boston), and the "Landsdowne" portrait (1796; National Portrait Gallery, Washington, D.C.)—Stuart made 111 copies. These images sold very well to a public keenly interested in its new national leader. By the early 1800s Stuart's sitters included the most wealthy and prominent citizens of the new nation and, despite a sometimes difficult demeanor and a tendency to finish paintings long past the dates clients expected them, his reputation as a portraitist was firmly established. The notable Americans of his time who sat for him included Thomas Jefferson, Abigail Adams, Paul Revere, and John Jacob Astor.

Samuel Jackson Gardner (1788–1864) was a prominent citizen of Boston, where Stuart had moved permanently in 1805. After studying law at Harvard, from where he graduated in 1807, Gardner worked as a lawyer in Roxbury, Massachusetts, and held political office. In 1850 he became the editor of the *Newark (New Jersey) Daily Advertiser,* a position he held through the Civil War. Stuart's image of Jackson is typical of his mature style: the face is both idealized and well-defined, while Gardner's clothes and the background are rendered in broader, sketchier brushstrokes. This distinction between detailed faces and more generalized backgrounds grew particularly pronounced in Stuart's later career. Stuart often placed the sitter slightly off center, which is unusual.[1]

During his later years in Boston, many artists sought Stuart's advice and, after his death in 1828, artists including Samuel F. B. Morse, John Vanderlyn, and John Trumbull composed a resolution naming Stuart the Father of American Portraiture. RSR

1. Richard McLanathan, *Gilbert Stuart* (New York: Harry N. Abrams, 1986), p. 141.

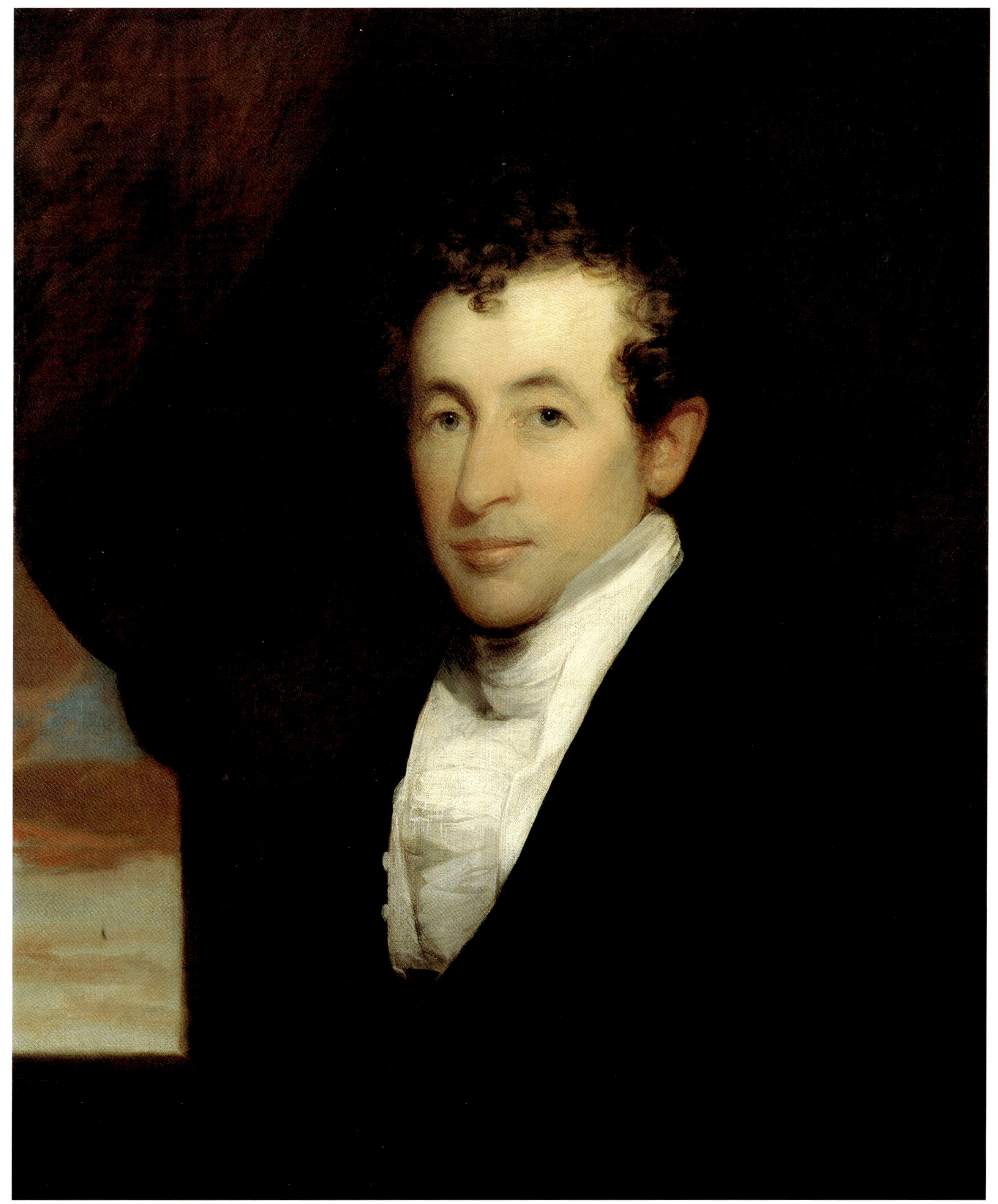

Joseph H. Davis AMERICAN, ACTIVE 1832–38

8 | *Isaac T. Demeritt,* 1835

Watercolor, pen and ink, and pencil on paper, 12 × 9 in.

Inscribed on recto: *[Isaac T. Demeritt. Painted at the Age of 24. 1835]*

Gift of Edgar William and Bernice Chrysler Garbisch (1972.75)

Davis, who often signed his works, "Joseph H. Davis, Left-Hand Painter," is an enigmatic figure who left behind a significant body of work. Little is known of his life, though his naïve painting technique is identifiable in a relatively small number of portraits executed in watercolor. Beyond his singular style, he also had a distinctive penchant for including ornately lettered inscriptions beneath his paintings, which included both single- and multifigured standing or seated portraits. Documentation of his subjects indicates that he worked in New Hampshire and Maine. Although his works tend to follow a set formula, they offer sociological insight into the life and status of the subjects.

Davis's watercolor portraits are characterized by careful draftsmanship and a delicate touch. Other defining traits include strongly outlined figures, often in dark colors, set against a pale background, and an interest in decorative details, most often seen in colorful, ornately patterned carpets that border the lower portion of the compositions. He pictures his sitters in profile with a flattened perspective, both in his single portraits, like *Isaac T. Demeritt,* and in his complex multifigure works. Although nothing definite is known about the model beyond his name and age written beneath the likeness, he may have resided in Ossipee, New Hampshire. Davis also painted a John F. Demeritt in the following year, and it is probable that Isaac was related to John, as artists of the time frequently painted several members of the same family. VAL/AR

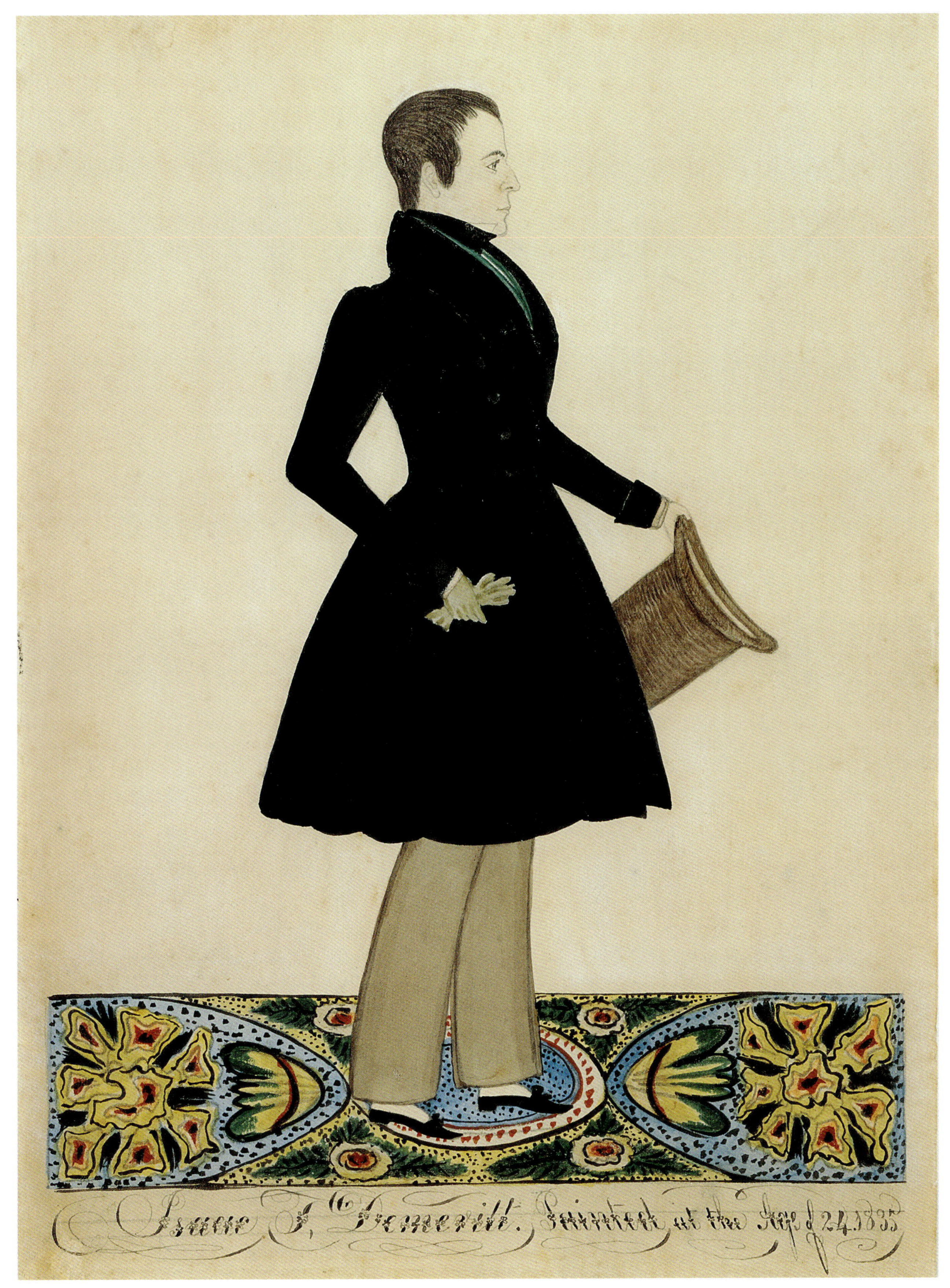
Isaac J. Demeritt. Painted at the Age of 24. 1835

Noah North AMERICAN 1809–1880

9 | *Major J. R. Jackman,* c. 1835–36

Oil on panel, 28⅛ × 23¾ in.

Inscribed on verso: *Major Jackman, husband of Gracie*

Gift of Edgar William and Bernice Chrysler Garbisch (1968.21)

10 | *Gracie Beardsley Jefferson Jackman and Her Daughter,* c. 1835–36

Oil on panel, 28½ × 23⅝ in.

Inscribed and dated on verso: *Gracie Beardsley Jefferson, wife of J. R. Jackman 1835–6*

Gift of Edgar William and Bernice Chrysler Garbisch (1968.22)

Noah North, born in Alexander, New York, was a largely self-taught portrait painter who worked in New York, Ohio, Connecticut, and possibly Kentucky. He may have studied art with Van Rensselaer Hawkins for several years, though likely on an informal basis. By 1833 North had established himself as a portraitist in upstate New York, producing a number of naïve depictions of area residents. *Major J. R. Jackman* and *Gracie Beardsley Jefferson Jackman and Her Daughter* are among these early works. After 1834 North extended his geographic scope, painting in Orleans County and the Rochester, New York, area. North moved to the Cleveland, Ohio, area in 1836, and it is believed that he may also have worked in Cincinnati as well as Kentucky, but no works can be specifically linked to these places. By 1841 North returned to upstate New York, where he settled, married, and started a family. In 1844 North was listed in the census as a painter, and in the same year he placed advertisements in newspapers promoting his skills as a "Carriage, Sign, House, and Ornamental Painter." The range of his production, not unusual for an American artist of the time, was most likely necessary for him to earn a living. He also developed an interest in politics, joining the local Whig party and winning the election for assessor in 1845 and 1846.

In the 1850s North moved to Darien, Connecticut, close to the New York border, where he served as a justice of the peace. He subsequently moved to Attica, New York, where he worked at various endeavors to support himself. Although he continued to paint portraits, no works executed after the 1840s have been ascribed to him. It is possible that the reduction in his artistic output was due to the increasing popularity of the daguerreotype and the resulting decline in the painted portrait during that decade. As a result, the later years of North's life were financially difficult.

North achieved a degree of technical skill in capturing likenesses despite his lack of academic training, as seen in these two works. Employing a naïve style, such as sharp modeling of the facial features and a flattened perspective, North was still able to realize a high degree of detail and realism in the characterizations of the models. He employed a varied palette, using brighter tones in the features and clothing of the sitters that contrast with the darker backgrounds. To provide context for his subjects, North frequently included the top of a high-backed Hitchcock-type of stenciled chair in his portrait compositions, a detail that can be seen in the portrait of Gracie Beardsley Jackman and her daughter. In the portrait of Major Jackman, the artist employs another frequently used device, that of resting the sitter's arm on the top rail of a chair that has a lower back.

Major Jackman (1793–1877) was born in Vermont and settled in Alexander, New York, in 1816. Of modest origins, Jackman became a lawyer and county judge. His wife, Gracie Beardsley Jackman (1803–1864), was probably born in Hungersfield, New York. The couple married when the bride was thirteen, and they had at least seven children. The child depicted in this portrait could be one of the two daughters born to them in the 1830s. The drooping rose in the child's hand may serve as a symbol of mourning, implying that the child had died by the time the work was painted. The patronage of the Jackmans, prominent residents of Alexander, was surely important to North's burgeoning career as a portrait painter. VAL/AR

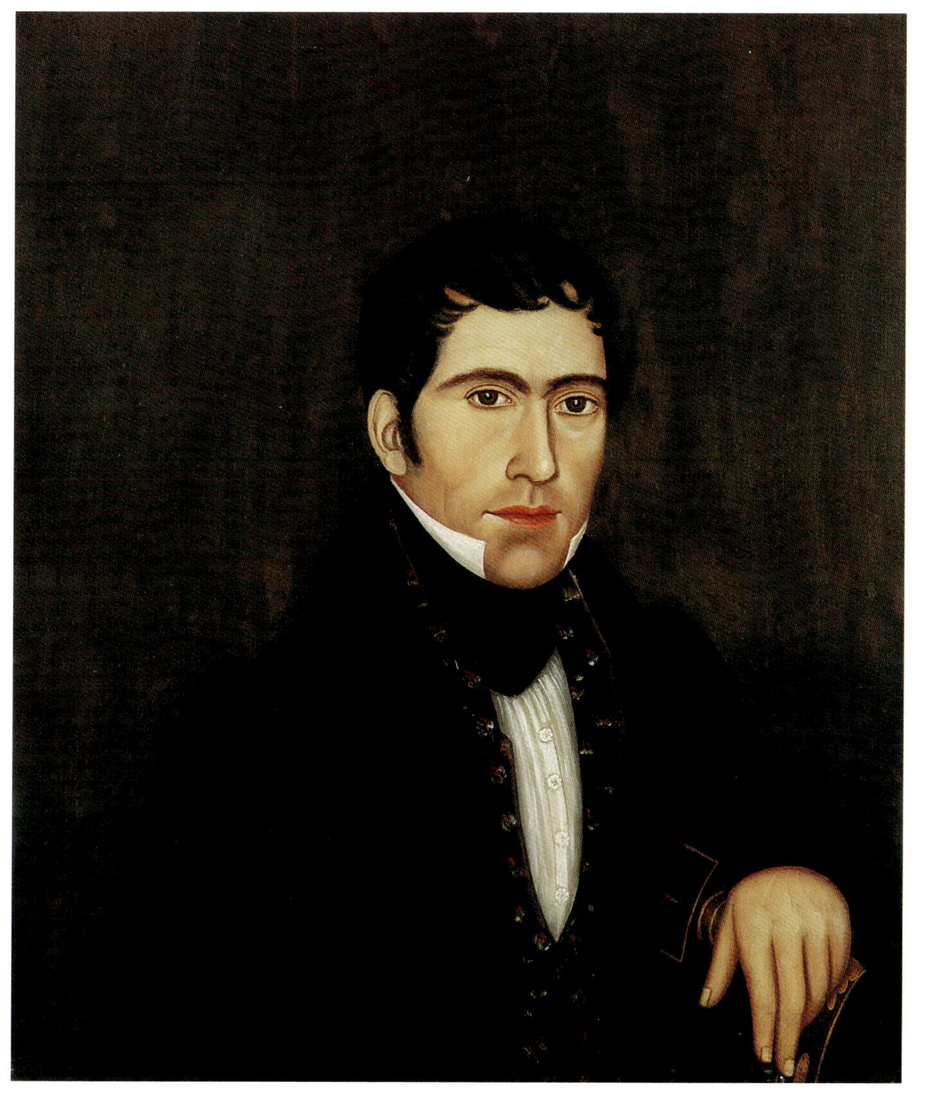

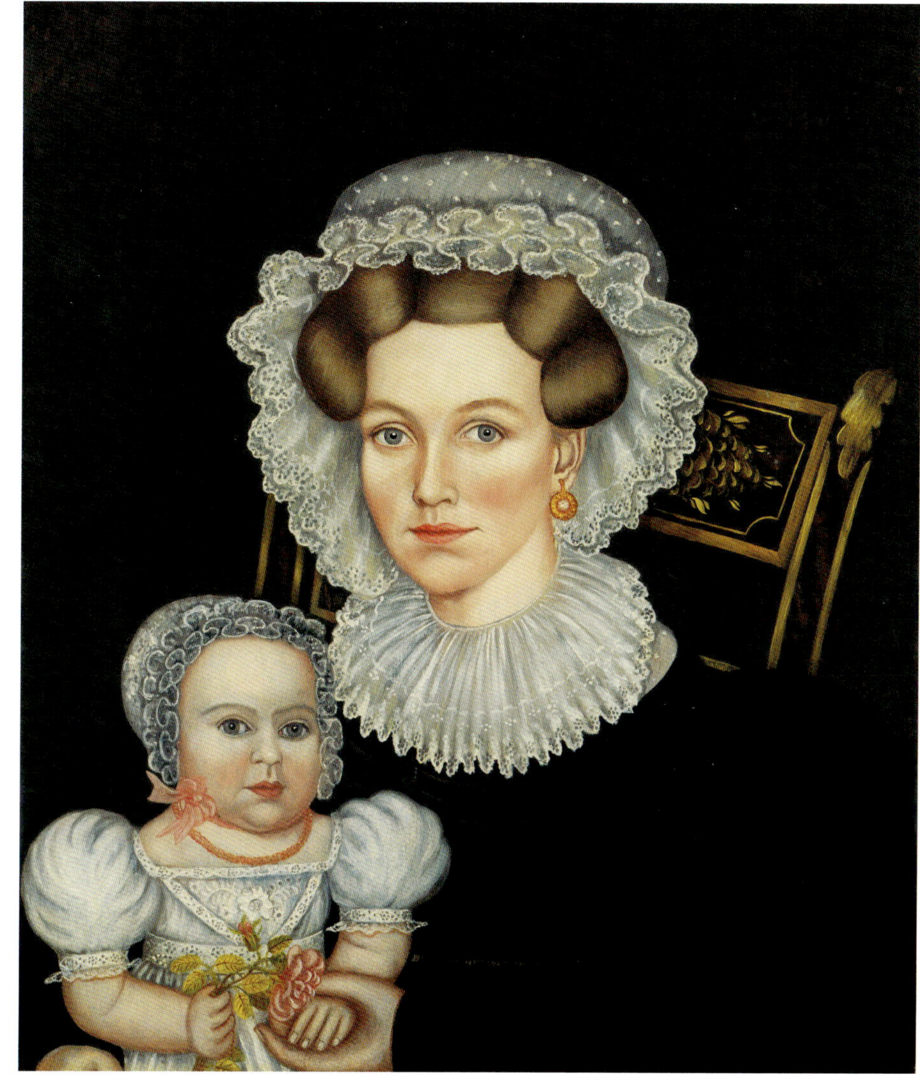

Attributed to Thomas Coke Ruckle AMERICAN, BORN IRELAND C. 1775–1873

11 | *Humming Bird, Red Bird, Baltimore Bird, Robbin, Flicker, Blue Bird,* 1842

Oil on panel, 12 × 10 in.

Dedicated, titled, dated, and signed on verso: *To Martha Jane / Humming Bird, Red Bird, Baltimore Bird, Robbin, Flicker, Blue Bird / Spring 1842* T. R.

Gift of Edgar William and Bernice Chrysler Garbisch (1981.3)

This painting, attributed to Thomas Coke Ruckle, depicts six birds, each, with the exception of the hummingbird, perched on a branch of a flowering tree. Ruckle, born of German parents in Ireland, immigrated to America in 1798. Although he is not known to have had any formal training, he established himself as a painter and glazier in Baltimore, where he is listed in city directories from 1799 to 1850. Ruckle concentrated on portraits and landscapes, and although this painting of birds is rather unusual for the artist, it is not unique; there is a similar version in the collection of the Baltimore Museum of Art. Despite his intuitive skill, clearly evident in this painting, Ruckle retains a naïve style that lacks an overall sense of perspective and realistic spatial relationships—the birds, organized rhythmically on the evenly spaced branches, are depicted in flat profile and do not overlap. Nevertheless, their physical attributes are precisely rendered, more like a natural history illustration than a spontaneous scene from life. While this accurate depiction of birds reveals the artist's powers of observation and his ability to record the physical world, the lively palette, decorative quality, and immense charm of the painting captivate the viewer. VAL/AR

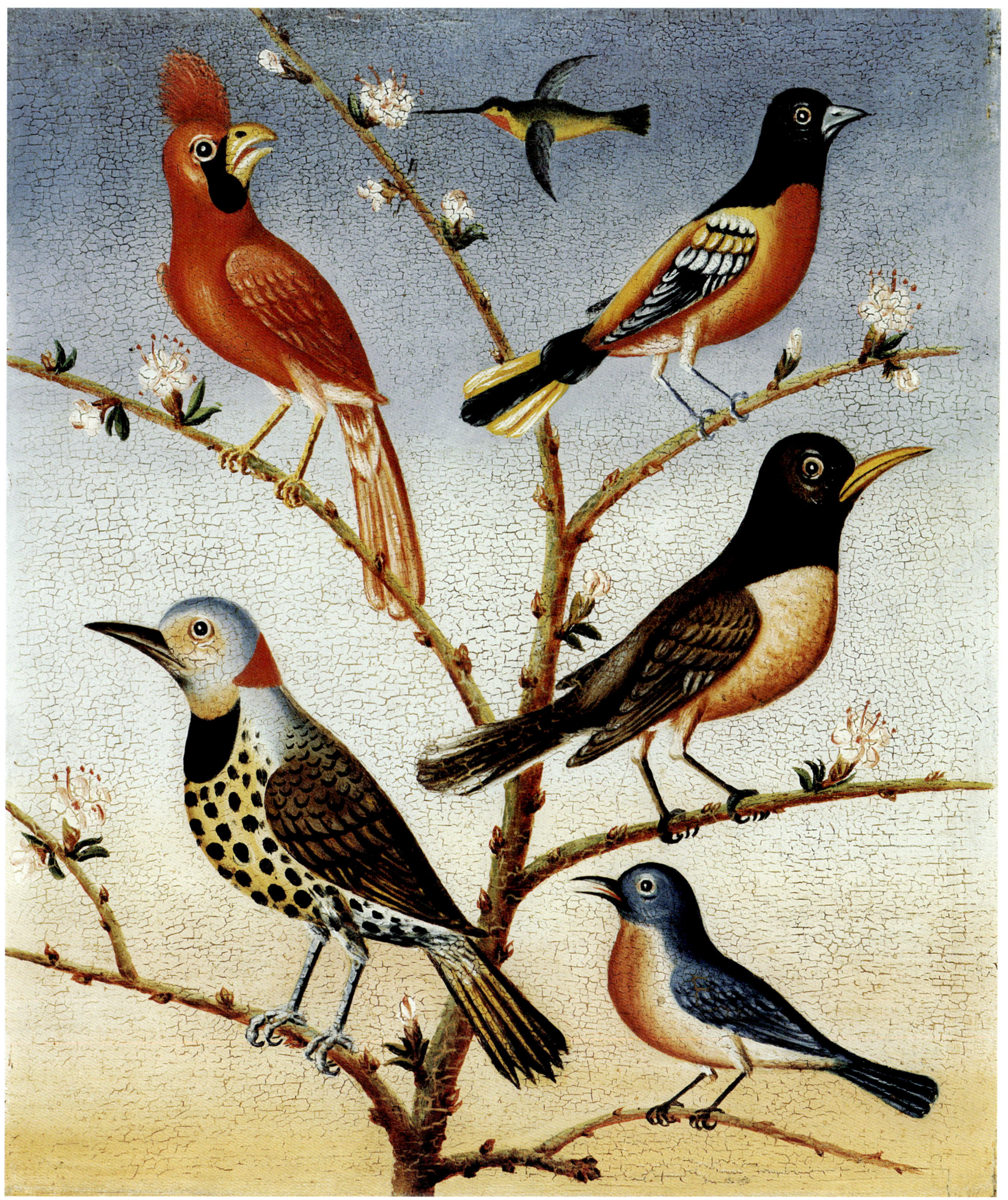

Attributed to William Matthew Prior AMERICAN 1806–1873

12 | *Baby in Pink and White or Little Janey in Pink and White Dress,* c. 1840

Oil on canvas, 24¼ x 20¼ in.

Unsigned

Gift of Edgar William and Bernice Chrysler Garbisch (1968.19)

William Matthew Prior, born in Bath, Maine, is one of the earliest known itinerant portraitists in America. A painter by the time he was seventeen, he also advertised his skill as a specialist in "ornamental" painting. He had a highly commercial approach—newspaper advertisements state that he would vary the degree of detail, modeling, and finish in a likeness in proportion to the amount the client was willing to pay. He traveled throughout New England and the mid-Atlantic states, venturing as far south as Baltimore in pursuit of work. He eventually settled in 1841 in Boston, where he married into a family of painters that included his brother-in-law, the portrait painter Sturtevant J. Hamblin, and George Hatwell. Prior and Hamblin worked in a similar and distinctive style, and authorship of unsigned works executed in this style is often attributed to what is known as the Prior-Hamblin School. Prior achieved recognition for his portraits, but the varied artistic approaches he took and the different degrees of finish resulting from a sliding-fee structure make it difficult to date them.

Although he lacked professional training, Prior became highly skilled in capturing likenesses, and it is for this accomplishment that he is best known. He often painted children, and the faces of his many youthful subjects and his most simple (that is, low-fee) interpretations have elegantly refined features that are imbued with an inherent sophistication. His work is characterized by outlines, sharp tonal contrasts, a distinctive palette, and graceful, fluid brushstrokes, all of which can be seen in *Baby in Pink and White.* The work, while unsigned, is typical of Prior's known works in style and compositional arrangement.

As is often seen in naïve portraits of the period, an element of symbolic significance has been introduced into the composition—the child has been depicted with one shoe removed. While its exact meaning is not known, it often implied mourning in the artistic vocabulary of the time. VAL/AR

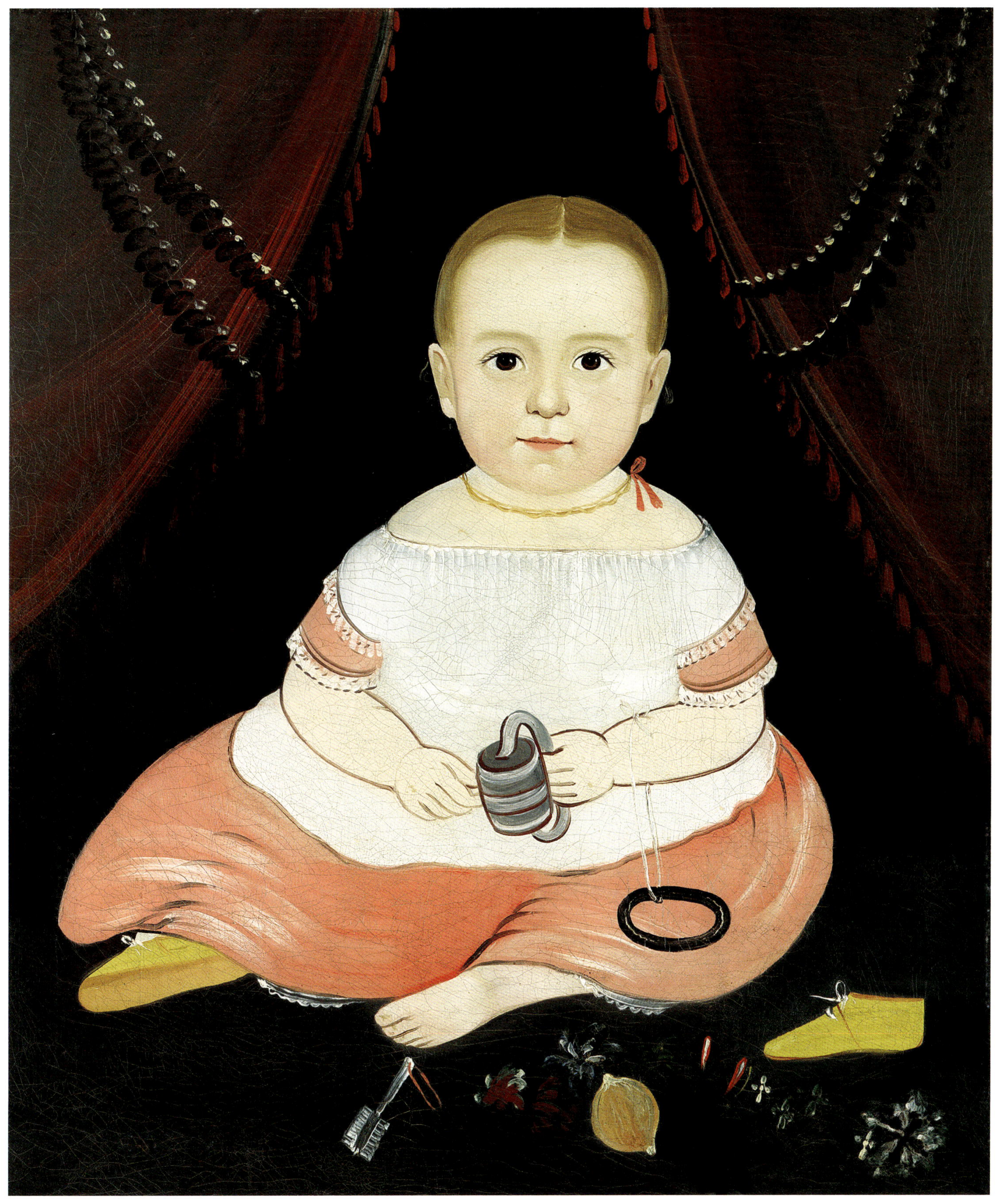

Thomas Chambers AMERICAN, BORN ENGLAND C. 1808–1866 OR LATER

13 | *Village in the Foothills,* c. 1850

Oil on canvas, 22½ × 30⅜ in.

Unsigned

Gift of Edgar William and Bernice Chrysler Garbisch (1972.73)

14 | *Old Sleepy Hollow Church,* c. 1850

Oil on canvas, 18¾ × 24⅜ in.

Unsigned

Gift of Edgar William and Bernice Chrysler Garbisch (1968.18)

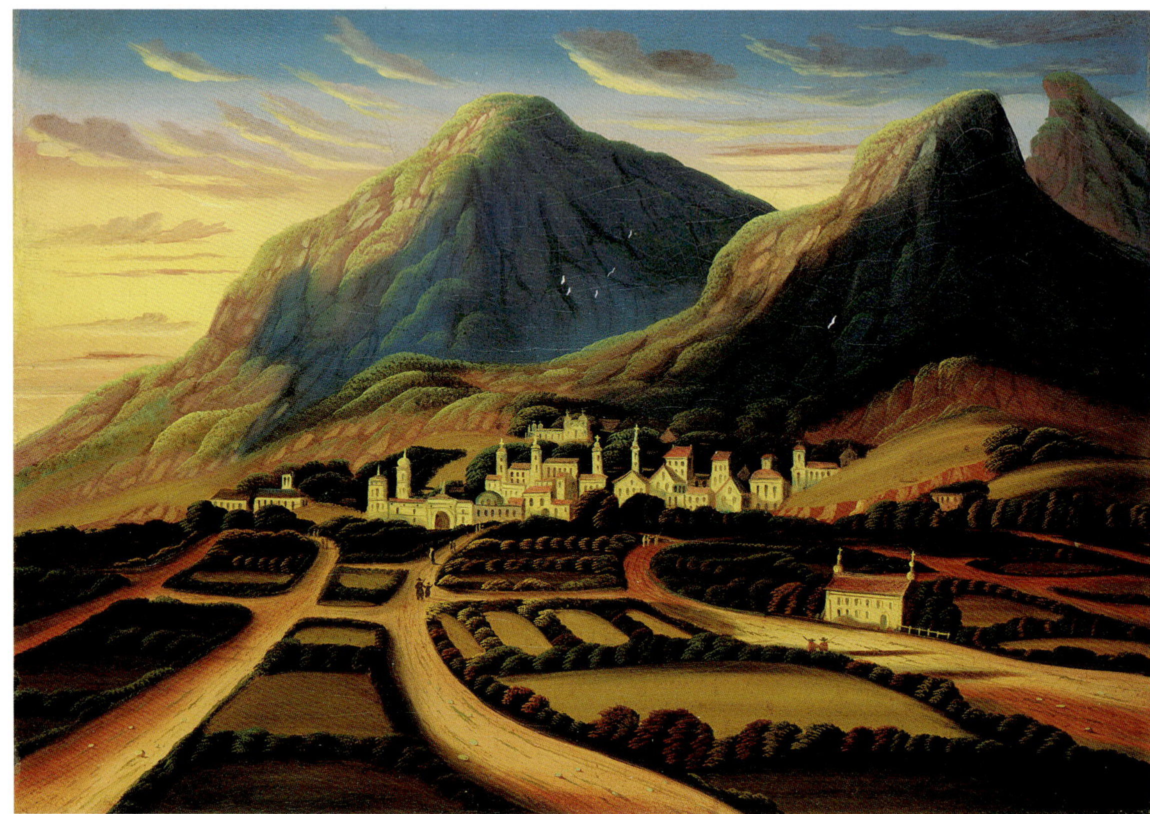

Thomas Chambers was born in England and immigrated to the United States in 1832. He was active as an artist from 1834, when he first appears in the New York City directory as a painter of landscapes. He later advertised himself as a portrait painter, although no works by him in this genre have been uncovered. He resided in New York City from 1834 until 1840; in Boston from 1843 to 1851; in Albany from 1852 to 1857; and again in New York City from 1858 to 1859 and 1861 to 1866. His whereabouts and activities after 1866 are unknown.

Chambers was drawn to landscape themes and was especially taken with the Hudson River Valley area, although his oeuvre includes other locations as well as river, harbor, and marine scenes. In addition, like many itinerant artists of the time, he also regularly executed works whose compositions are appropriated from the work of other artists or from prints. His landscapes are typically moody and romanticized, as is the case with *Old Sleepy Hollow Church,* an eerie, moonlit scene of a roofless, abandoned stone church and old cemetery. The subject of the painting almost certainly originates in literature—Washington Irving's "Legend of Sleepy Hollow" (1819)—rather than in the still-extant church in upstate New York, which would explain the rather Gothic presentation. Though more subdued in tone, Chambers's *Village in the Foothills* also represents nature in an imaginative and highly stylized manner. The source of this work has not been identified. It is possible that it is a composite of several views or that it derives purely from the artist's imagination. More likely, however, it originates in a print, as the setting, with mountains rising sharply from the plain, seems more European than American.

Chambers's distinctive technique can be inherently dramatic, a style accentuated by his use of dark outlines and an especially opulent palette. He renders perspective in a convincing manner but employs somewhat naïve draftsmanship. Chambers signed relatively few works, but his individual approach has enabled scholars to assign a significant body of work to his hand. VAL/AR

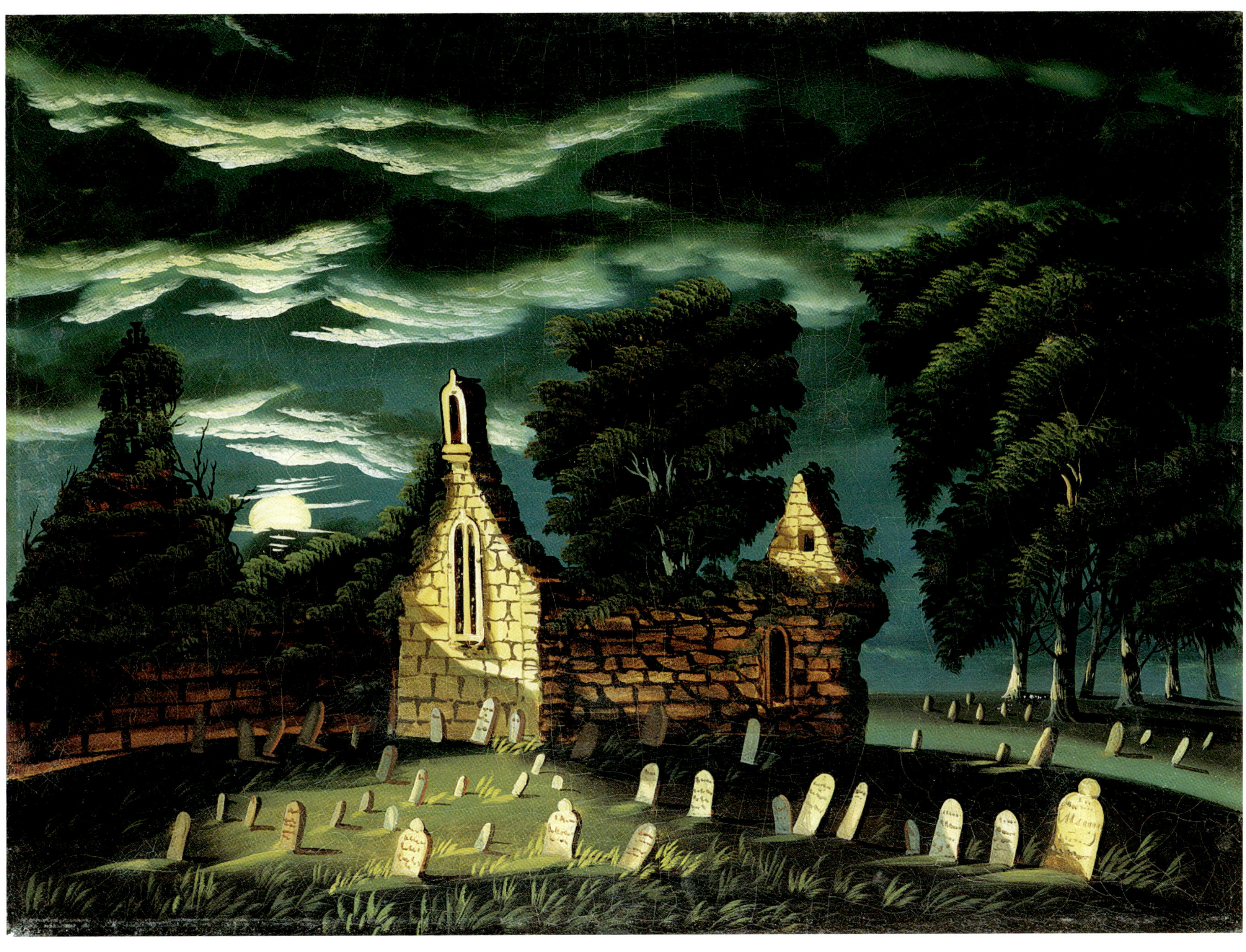

Erastus Salisbury Field AMERICAN 1805–1900

15 | *The Taj Mahal,* c. 1850

Oil on canvas, 24¼ × 34⅛ in.

Unsigned

Gift of Edgar William and Bernice Chrysler Garbisch (1968.20)

Erastus Salisbury Field, a naïve painter of historical, biblical, and landscape subjects, was initially recognized for his portraits. Born in rural Massachusetts, Field showed an early interest in painting. In 1824 he went to New York City to study art with the artist-inventor Samuel F. B. Morse. He remained there for three months, until Morse's wife, who had become gravely ill, died, an event that terminated his tutelage. With only this training, he returned to Massachusetts and began to paint portraits, traveling throughout New England in his quest for work. He began to employ the new medium of photography soon after its invention in 1839, the use of which helped him to improve his technique. In the ensuing years, he refined his approach, achieving his own style and garnering renown, especially in the Connecticut River Valley, for his skill as a portraitist.

In the early 1840s Field again went to New York, where he remained until 1848, when he returned to Massachusetts. After that time, he undertook landscape and historical subjects in addition to portraiture. He drew on literary sources, books, and popular prints of the time for his subject matter and also seems to have used his imagination, as he began to depict exotic locales with a visionary quality, almost like a stage set.

The Taj Mahal, located in Agra, India, was a subject that seems to have especially intrigued Field, as he painted it on at least three occasions. Shah Jahan built the well-known monument in 1630–48 as a memorial to his deceased wife, and it has been suggested that Field painted these works after 1859 in response to the death of his own wife. Given that Field is not known to have visited India, the subject was most likely familiar to him through books and prints. There are two other known depictions of the Taj Mahal painted by Field, one in the collection of the National Gallery of Art, Washington, D.C. (originally, like the Flint version, in the Garbisch Collection), the other in the collection of the Museum of Fine Arts, Springfield, Massachusetts. The latter example closely resembles the Flint Institute of Arts' version in its attention to visual details, deep-hued palette, and overall conception. VAL/AR

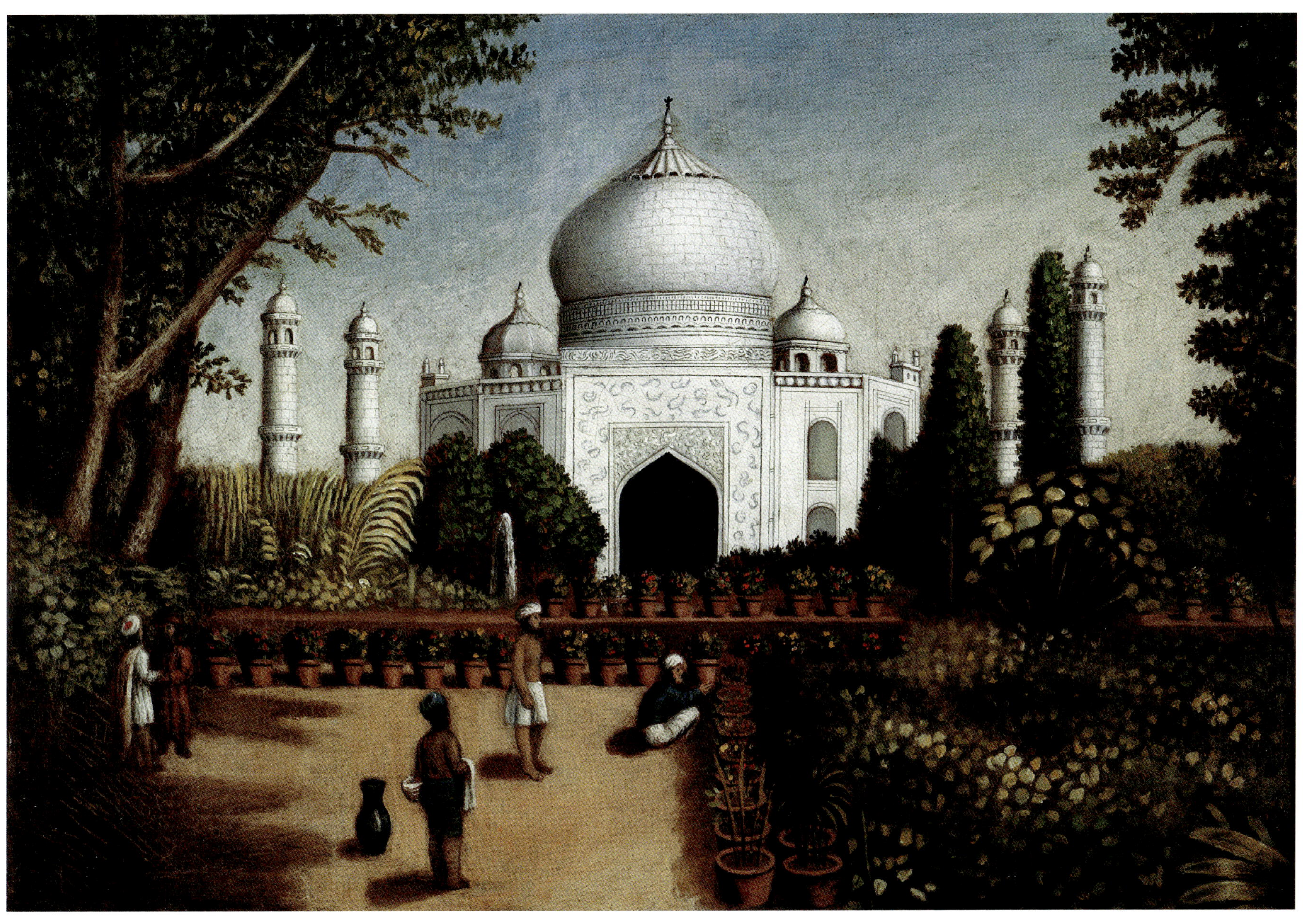

Unknown artist AMERICAN, 19TH CENTURY

16 | *The Fowler Children,* c. 1854

Oil on canvas, 49 × 61¼ in.

Unsigned

Gift of the Estate of Mrs. Ernest C. Schnuck (1976.1)

John Nash Fowler (1812–1879), a wealthy shipowner and lumberman originally from Clayton, New York, commissioned this portrait of his youngest children in 1854. Delia, age sixteen, is at the left. Seated next to her, in the middle, is her fourteen-year-old brother, Milo, while Gertrude, age nine, kneels on the ground to the right. The three, dressed in their best clothes, occupy most of the composition, giving the impression that they are practically in the viewer's space. A wood lattice behind Delia and Milo creates a barrier that separates the two children from a vast panoramic landscape that is revealed in minute detail behind Gertrude.

The painting's lush surface treatment and precise detail show the hand of a talented and observant artist. The incongruity in scale between the figures and the landscape in the background, however, marks this as the work of a self-taught itinerant painter. Family records refer to the painter only as "he" and state that he was from Philadelphia. It is also known that the artist lived with the Fowler family for three months while working on the portrait. This unnamed painter was paid $300 for his services, a considerable sum for the time, attesting that his skill was well appreciated. Unfortunately, his identity remains unknown, as the work is unsigned and his name is not noted in any extant papers.

John Fowler was one of the owners of Fowler & Esselstyn, a shipping firm that operated one of the largest fleets on the Great Lakes in the mid–nineteenth century. Originally based along the St. Lawrence River in Clayton, New York, the firm relocated to Detroit in 1856. According to a history of Jefferson County, New York, written by L. H. Everts in 1878, Fowler's shipping business continued to be as successful in Detroit as it had been in Clayton. In fact, to secure trading rights with Canada—which were only granted to vessels built on British soil—Fowler & Esselstyn established a shipyard at the foot of Wolf (or Grand) Island in the St. Lawrence River, Canada.

The portrait of the Fowler children was brought to Detroit when the family relocated in 1856 and was displayed in their home at 500 Woodward Avenue. On Fowler's death in 1879, Delia brought the painting to Flint, where she had settled with her husband. For many years, the work hung in the family residence at 414 East Court Street. In 1976 Delia's granddaughter, Adelaide Schnuck, donated the painting to the Flint Institute of Arts. MMD

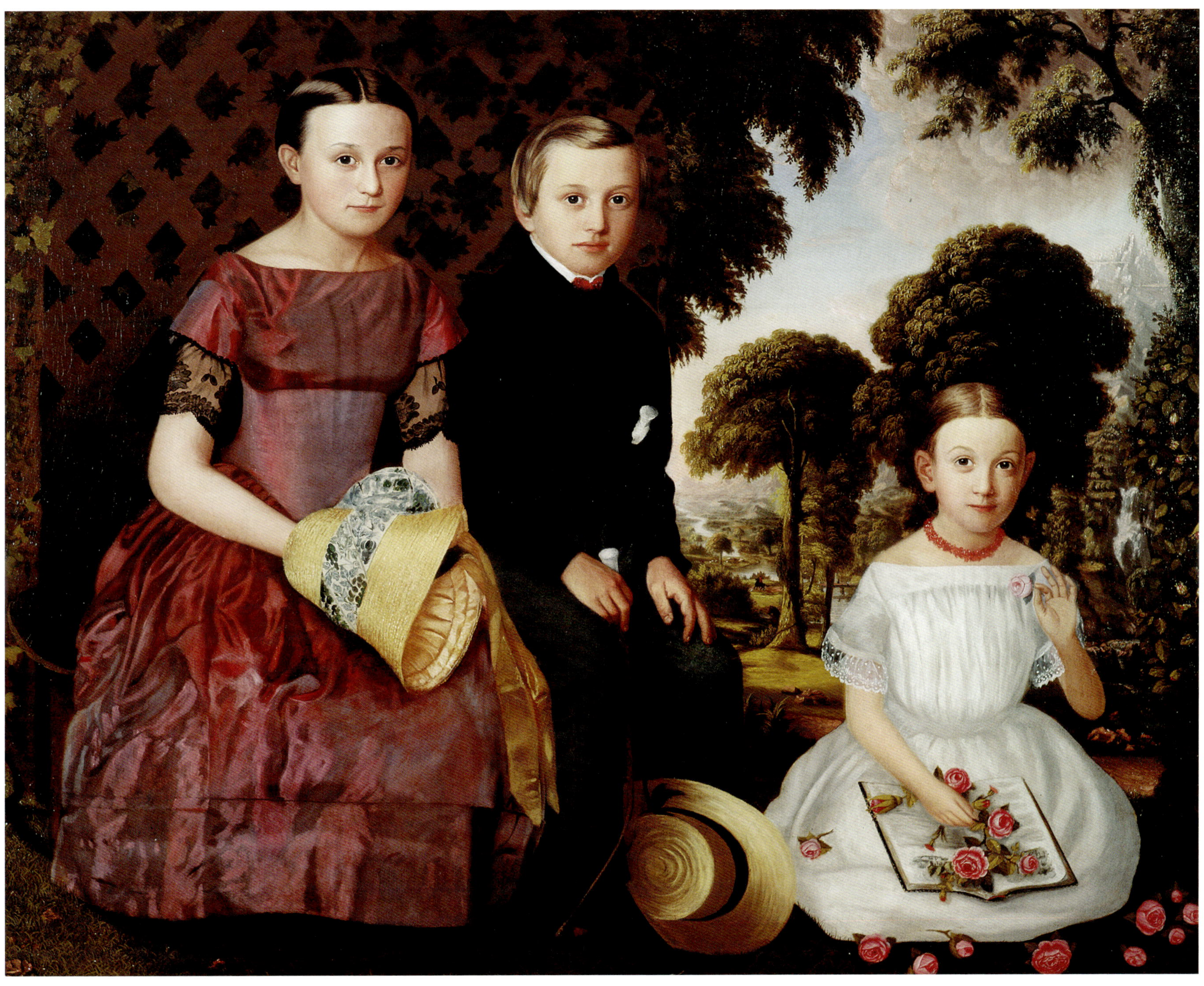

Severin Roesen AMERICAN, BORN GERMANY C. 1815–1872

17 | *Still Life with Fruit,* c. 1855

Oil on canvas on panel, 17¾ × 24¼ in.

Signed lower right: *S. Roesen*

Gift of Mr. and Mrs. John Lord Booth, by exchange (1994.2)

Severin Roesen was a prolific painter who produced tabletop still lifes, predominantly of fruit and flower subjects. Greatly influenced by the Dutch still-life tradition, Roesen's paintings present nature's bounty in displays of fruit and or flowers offered up on a table, as in *Still Life with Fruit.* These images, executed in a meticulously rendered realist style in both horizontal and vertical formats, are composed of a stock set of objects artfully arranged and repeated in various configurations. Elaborate floral arrangements, sliced lemons, glasses of wine, stems of grapes and berries, pomegranates, and bird's nests are among the hallmarks of Roesen's compositions. The representation of objects such as glassware and bird's nests and such surfaces as wood and marble tabletops are the common means for a still-life artist to convey artistry and technical virtuosity, and Roesen was no exception. It is probable that much of his work was done on commission, for he did close variants of a number of paintings.

Despite his prodigious output, few facts about Roesen's life are known. It is believed that he was born in Germany, possibly in Cologne, about 1815. He moved to America in 1848, settling in New York, where he remained for ten years. He began exhibiting at the American Art-Union in New York the year he arrived and continued to show there until it closed, in 1852. His association with the American Art-Union, which exhibited his work and distributed prints after his paintings, surely enhanced his reputation and following.

Still Life with Fruit has been ascribed to about 1855 and thus is an early, but mature, work, executed while Roesen was living in New York. The manner of painting is distinguished by a detailed execution that includes droplets of condensation on the fruit and embellishment of the blackberries hanging over the edge of the tabletop, both of which create a sense of depth in the composition. His skill at precise rendering is thought to be due to early training as an enamel painter. Despite the small scale and fine detail of many of Roesen's still lifes, they have a feeling of monumentality, especially the horizontal compositions, as evidenced by *Still Life with Fruit.* This work, typical of many of his arrangements, has a strong diagonal axis created by the grape stems, while the vine tendrils counter the static quality of the composition.

In 1859, a few years after the creation of this *Still Life with Fruit,* Roesen appears in Harrisburg, Pennsylvania. It is believed that he then moved to Williamsport, Pennsylvania, in 1861, where he remained until 1872. Unfortunately, nothing more is known of Roesen after this time. VAL

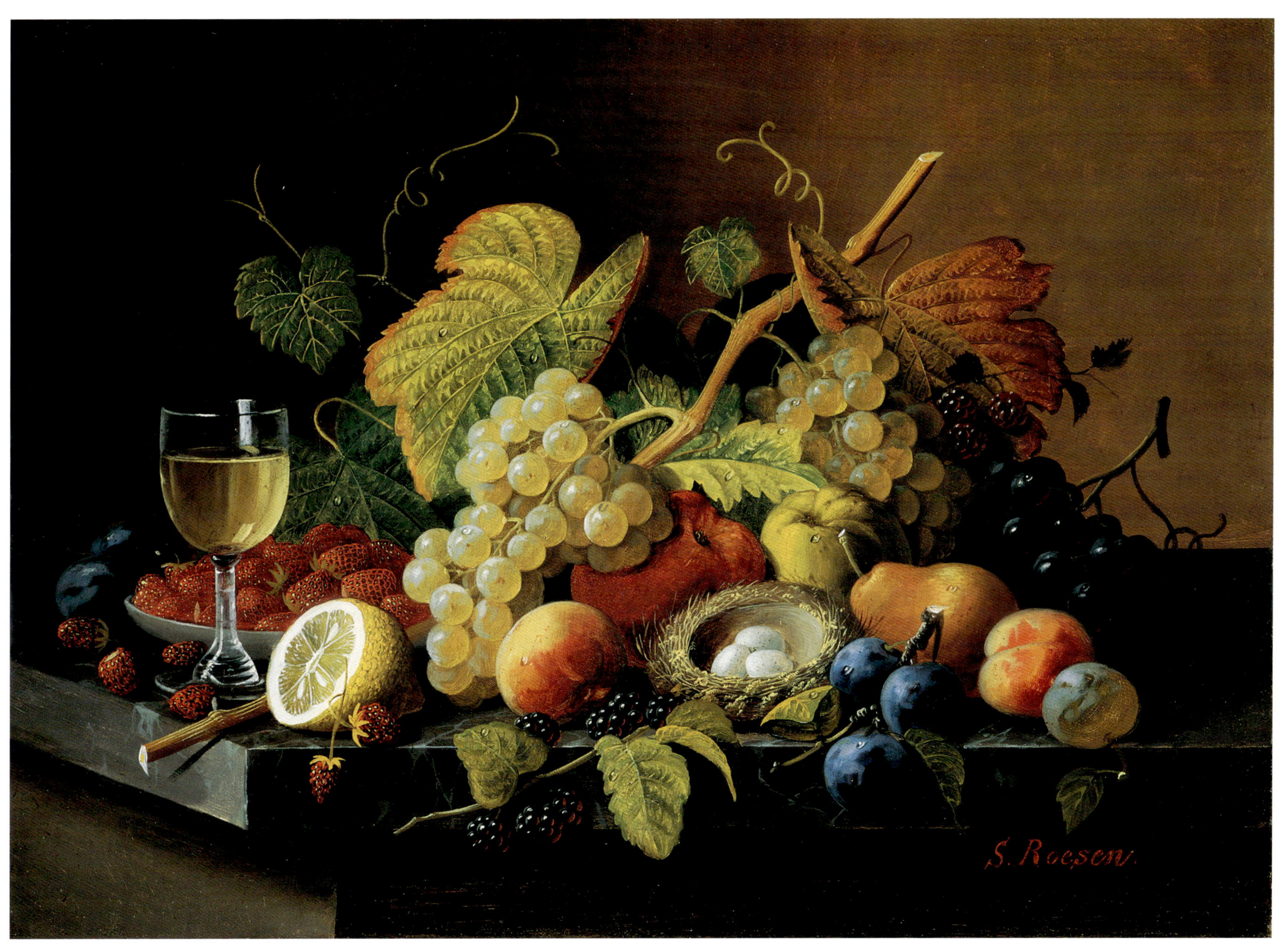
S. Roesen.

Thomas Doughty AMERICAN 1793–1856

18 | *Landscape with Two Figures,* 1855

Oil on board, 8¼ × 10¼ in.

Signed and dated on verso: *T. Doughty 1855*

Gift of Dr. and Mrs. Victor J. Cervenak (1997.88)

Thomas Doughty, a forerunner to the Hudson River School, was the first American painter to dedicate himself to landscape subjects. Born in Philadelphia, he was largely self-taught. He initially worked in the leather trade and, although he first exhibited at the Pennsylvania Academy of the Fine Arts in 1816, he did not become a full-time artist until 1820. He continued to show frequently at the Pennsylvania Academy, where he became an Academician in 1824, and also exhibited at the Boston Athenæum when he lived in that city from 1828 to 1830. He spent the following two years in Philadelphia before making his way back to Boston, where he stayed until 1837, when he left for a visit to England. He settled in New York on his return in 1838, making visits to New Orleans in 1844, London in 1845, and Paris in 1846. Ill from 1848 to 1850, he produced little work after that time, and died in poverty several years later.

Throughout the 1830s and 1840s Doughty frequently traveled throughout the Northeast, often producing landscapes such as *Landscape with Two Figures.* The locations, however, tend to be generalized and rarely can be identified. These picturesque scenes, executed in a naturalistic style, gained a successful following through exhibitions, and his work remained popular until his later years. The paintings —most often pastoral views with a body of water and an occasional diminutive figure or two set within the landscape with trees framing the composition—are generally marked by a sense of quietude and a genuine feeling for nature. *Landscape with Two Figures* is such a work, which shows two small, vaguely defined figures, possibly two women, enjoying the bucolic setting. He frequently depicted woodland and autumn scenes, although his palette is usually characterized not by the golds and reds typical of the fall season for which he became known, but by his mastery of the "silvery tone," as Henry T. Tuckerman observed.[1] Although Doughty was not as influential as his successor Thomas Cole, the founder of the Hudson River School, he had a role in laying the foundation of the landscape tradition on which the school rests. As Thomas Hofland observed in 1839 in *The Knickerbocker:* "The American School of landscape is decidedly and peculiarly original; fresh, bold, brilliant, and grand . . . we may mention Doughty, of Boston, as eminently combining these qualities . . . He must undoubtedly be considered the master and founder of a new school—no small honor in this imitative age."[2] *Landscape with Two Figures,* with its calm mood, diffused atmospheric light, and romanticized view of nature, typifies the artist's intimate, sylvan landscapes. VAL

1. Henry T. Tuckerman, *Lives of the Artists* (1867; reprint, New York: James F. Carr, 1966), p. 507.

2. Thomas R. Hofland, "The Fine Arts in the United States," *The Knickerbocker* 14 (July 1839), p. 50.

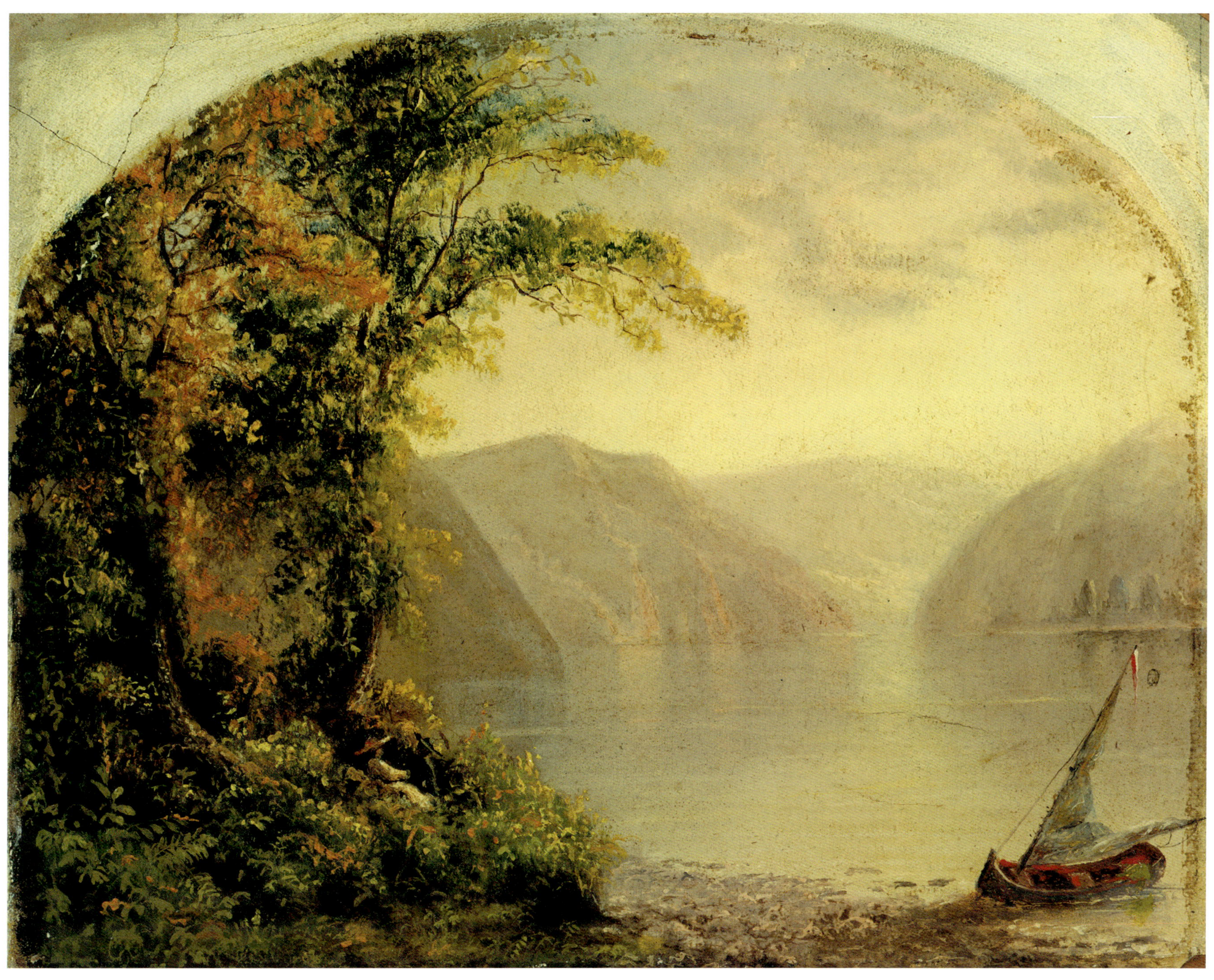

M. O'Neil AMERICAN 19TH CENTURY

19 | *Civil War Encampment,* c. 1863

Oil on canvas, 25 × 37¼ in.

Signed lower left: *M O'Neil*

Gift of Edgar William and Bernice Chrysler Garbisch (1968.26)

Beyond the name of the artist as shown in the signature, nothing is known about the painter of this Civil War scene. Rather than depicting a heroic scene of the war, such as an active military engagement, the composition pictures a Union Army encampment. The static subject, with its open vista and high horizon line, in combination with the diminutive scale of the figures, has similarities with typical topographical studies from the late eighteenth and early nineteenth centuries. O'Neil has used a tight and deliberate technical approach, executing the work in a meticulous style with attention to minute detail.

On careful examination it is evident that some of the soldiers sport red trousers, the uniform adopted in America in emulation of the Algerian Zoave troops who fought for France in the Crimean War. The 11th Infantry of New York is perhaps the best-known Zoave-inspired regiment, although there were others who also saw active service in the Civil War. In addition to several from New York, other regiments came from Pennsylvania, Illinois, and Missouri. The artist may have been a participant in the war and was recording a personal experience on the spot, or he may have been documenting the scene from memory. It is also possible that he was simply using his imagination, a conjecture supported by the evenly rhythmic repetition of the stylized mountain formation. VAL/AR

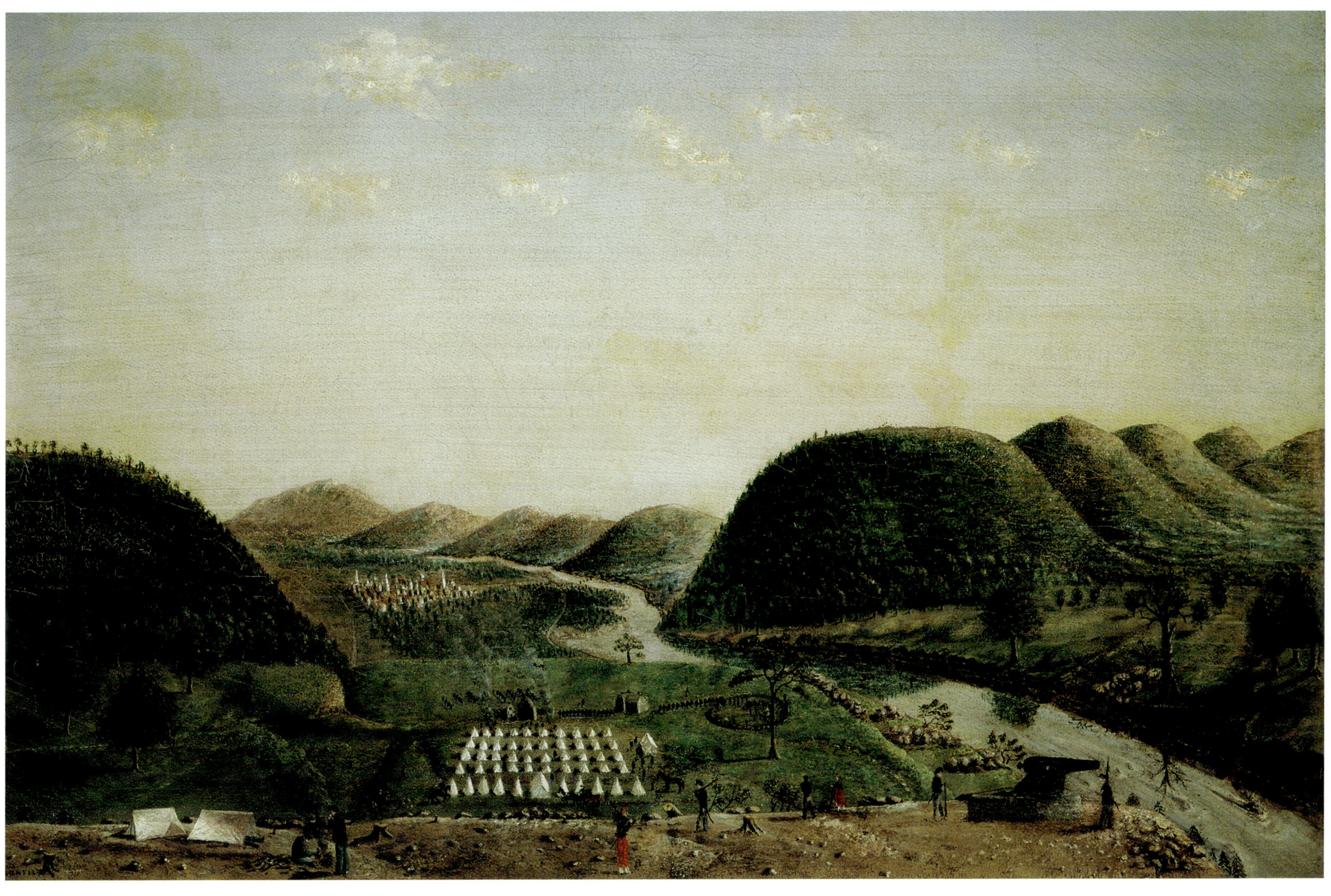

George Henry Durrie AMERICAN 1820–1863

20 | *Winter Scene,* 1857

Oil on board, 26¼ × 36 in.

Signed and dated lower left: *G.H.D. 1857*

Gift of Hirschl & Adler Galleries, Inc., New York City (1979.203)

George Henry Durrie, although primarily recognized as a painter of winter scenes, experimented with a variety of genres early in his career. Born in New Haven, Connecticut, where he spent much of his life, he studied with the portraitist Nathaniel Jocelyn, as did his brother John, who also became an artist. Between 1840 and 1842 Durrie mainly painted portraits, working in New Jersey and Connecticut; he then returned to Connecticut. He first showed his work at the National Academy of Design in 1843, and two years later he submitted his first snow scenes to the Academy's annual exhibition.

By the mid-1840s Durrie's work began to concentrate on outdoor genre scenes depicting everyday rural life. After a considerable absence from exhibiting at the Academy, he submitted two winter scenes in 1857, the year he painted *Winter Scene.* His fame became more widespread in the 1860s, when Currier & Ives distributed prints after his images, which gained him a wider audience and further renown.

Durrie received little professional training beyond his studies with Jocelyn. Despite this, he developed a manner of painting that, while naïve in style, is at once sophisticated in its attention to detail and composition and meticulous in its realism. He seems to have developed this style independent of outside influences, since he worked largely on his own, outside major art centers. His overall production can tend toward the formulaic, as he often returned to similar subject matter and employed a stock set of motifs, such as a horse and sleigh.

Winter Scene is an especially lively composition, with several different groups of figures engaged in activities such as playing and chopping wood throughout the expansive horizontality of the composition. The scene is typical of Durrie's outdoor genre scenes and offers an interesting record of farm life in mid-nineteenth-century America. Durrie is able to capture a sense of intimacy and charm exceptional in a landscape. In contrast to the production of his contemporaries of the Hudson River School, who celebrated grand vistas of an unsullied American landscape, his work revels in the simple, everyday pleasures of country life. VAL

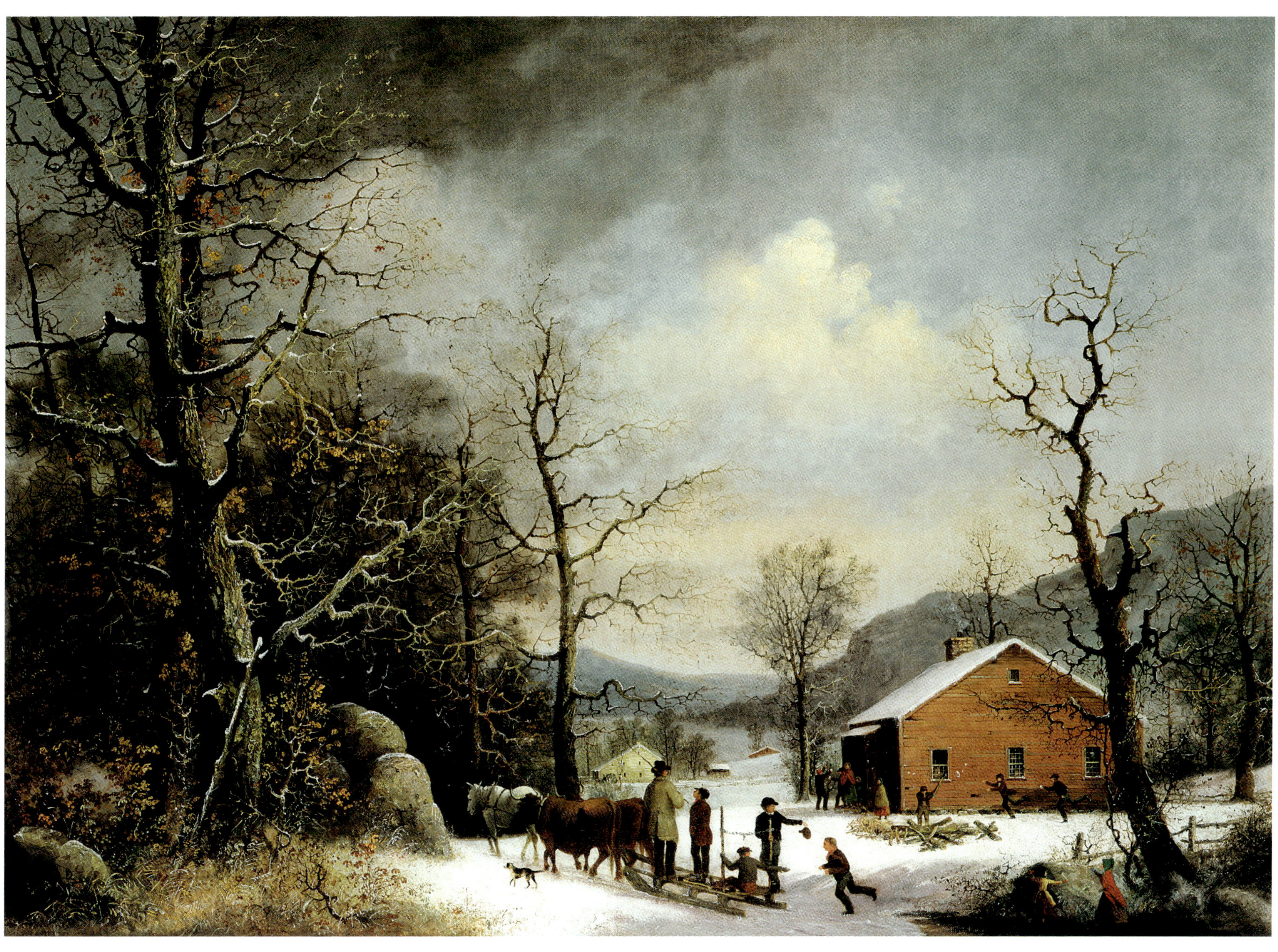

Jasper Francis Cropsey AMERICAN 1823–1900

21 | *Hudson River View, Summer,* 1872

Oil on canvas, 33⅜ × 53¼ in.

Signed and dated lower left: *J F Cropsey 1872*

Gift of Mr. and Mrs. Jay C. Thompson (1963.9)

Jasper Francis Cropsey was born in Rossville, Staten Island. He showed an early predisposition toward architectural drafting and drawing, skills in which he excelled. He became an apprentice to the architect Joseph Trench, who encouraged him in his artistic aspirations. Cropsey received some private instruction in art and took several classes at the National Academy of Design; these brief endeavors constitute his professional training.

In 1843 Cropsey opened his own architectural firm and began exhibiting at the National Academy of Design's annual exhibitions. Concentrating on landscape painting, he found particular inspiration in Greenwood Lake, New Jersey. He became an Associate of the Academy in 1844 and was accorded full Academician status in 1851. Cropsey left for Italy in 1847 with his new bride, remaining there for two years. On his return, he settled in New York City and focused on painting pastoral scenery of New Jersey, Pennsylvania, New Hampshire, Maine, and the Hudson River Valley. Cropsey traveled to Europe again in 1856, this time to London, where he stayed for seven years. Despite his extended residence abroad, he continued to paint American scenes.

In the mid-1850s Cropsey began to gain recognition for his autumnal scenes. Close in spirit to Thomas Cole, leader of the Hudson River School, Cropsey belonged to a second generation of artists working in the style. *Hudson River View, Summer* aptly displays Cropsey's technique of dramatizing bucolic scenes with a dynamic compositional structure, vibrant brushwork, and a luminous and diffused golden light with warm tonalities. His frequent use of classical compositional formulas, reintroduced by Cole—foreground, middle ground, and background, framed by a prominent edifice to the side, often including a tree—is evident in *Hudson River View, Summer.* The painting has small visual details woven into the expansive panoramic view of the Hudson River: in the foreground, a boating party has landed on the lower shore, cows grace the upper right embankment, and farther in the distance are two houses overlooking the river. Cropsey expertly uses these compositional devices to direct attention throughout the work, a technique he often employed in his works of the 1860s and 1870s. These visual diversions were nearly always small in scale so as not to detract from the natural setting, which was his principal subject. Humans, when they appear in Cropsey's paintings, are subordinate to nature, and, typical of American art at this time, the Emersonian philosophy of Transcendentalism was an important influence.

The most singular aspect of *Hudson River View, Summer* is the sky, sublime in its array of color and light effects that denote an approaching summer sunset. This majestic landscape is exceptional in scale and numbers among the artist's more monumental compositions.[1] Cropsey continued to work in the tradition of the Hudson River School until his death, long after the popularity of the style, which had fallen out of favor in the 1880s, had waned. VAL

1. For the most thorough catalogue to date of Cropsey's major works, see William S. Talbot, *Jasper F. Cropsey* (New York: Garland Publishing, 1977). It is surprising, considering the large scale, technical mastery, and artistic significance of the work, that it has remained overlooked and seems not to have been shown in any major exhibition. It is possible that the work originally had a different title, one that is currently unknown.

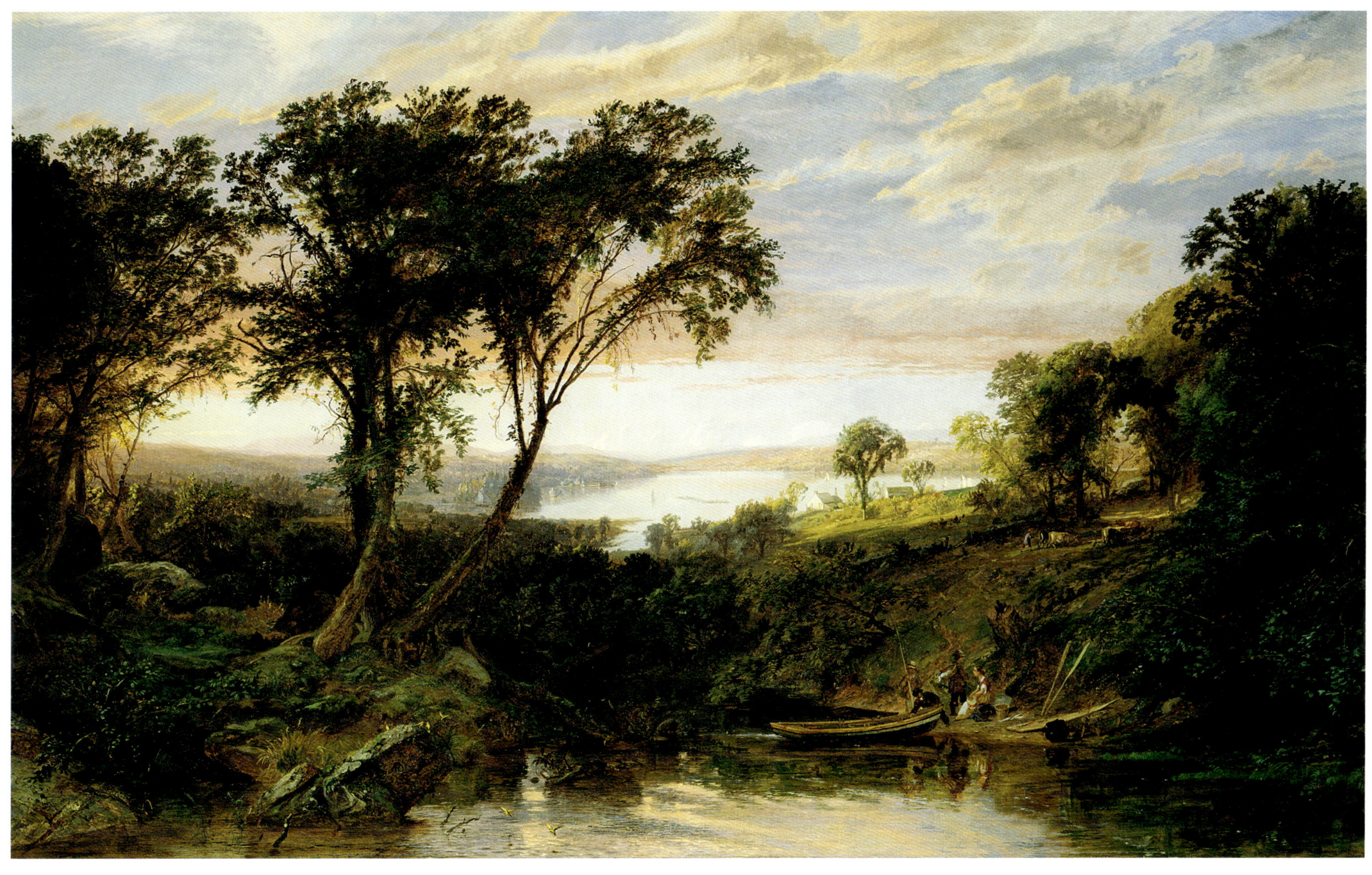

Martin Johnson Heade AMERICAN 1819–1904

22 | *Sunrise on the Marshes,* 1863

Oil on canvas, 26¼ × 50⅜ in.

Signed and dated lower right: *M J Heade 63*

Gift of Mr. and Mrs. William L. Richards through the Bray Charitable Trust (1963.5)

Despite a peripatetic nature, Martin Johnson Heade exhibited great consistency in his choice of subjects. He concentrated on painting flower still lifes; landscapes, a group of which were inspired by travel to the tropics; close-ups of flora and fauna in situ; and marsh scenes depicting areas in the Northeast and Florida.

Heade was born in Lumberville, Pennsylvania. He took lessons in art from the well-known naïve painter Edward Hicks but did not receive extensive formal training. In 1840 he visited Europe, spending two years in Rome. He returned to America in 1842, settling first in New York before moving to Philadelphia in 1847. He left again for Europe the following year, visiting Rome and France, and then went back to United States, where he lived in several cities for short periods before returning to New York in 1859. There he became a tenant of the Tenth Street Studio Building, where he met several of the foremost landscape painters of the time. This exposure appears to have inspired his predisposition toward landscape painting and contributed to finding his artistic voice.

Never settling in any one place for very long, Heade was in Boston from 1861 to 1863, where he furthered his pursuit of landscape subjects. Between 1860 and the 1880s, Heade concentrated on New England coastal and marsh views, a subject with which he is most identified and one to which he returned for more than forty-five years.[1] *Sunrise on the Marshes* dates from 1863, four years after he first initiated this type of landscape, and the sophistication of the work shows how rapidly he refined the paradigm. The expansive voids of space, exaggerated horizontality, and warm glow of light seen in *Sunrise on the Marshes* are characteristic of his marsh compositions. Despite the use of wide panoramic views, Heade instills a sense of intimacy and quietude in these luminous landscapes through the atmosphere and other artistic devices. It becomes apparent that the works are a vehicle for the artist's exploration of subtly nuanced light effects. The minimal scenes often include just the most basic elements—water, land, and sky—with only an occasional visual interruption of cows, figures, boats, trees, and, most often, haystacks. *Sunrise on the Marshes* is notable for its prominent placement of the figures, which are larger in scale than those usually seen in Heade's landscapes.

An extended visit in 1863 to Brazil, where he went to execute illustrations of hummingbirds, proved to be an important inspiration. He made two more trips to South America, one in 1866 and another in 1870, both of which provided a rich source of new tropical themes, including landscapes and regional flora and fauna, especially orchids and hummingbirds.

Heade married in 1883 and moved to St. Augustine, Florida, which had a burgeoning artists' colony. There he continued painting landscapes and flower still lifes for his remaining years. He exhibited at the annual exhibitions of many of the major art organizations, though he had no particular affiliations and achieved only modest success in his day. VAL

1. For more on Heade's life and art, see Theodore E. Stebbins Jr. et al., *Martin Johnson Heade* (New Haven: Yale University Press, 1999); and Theodore E. Stebbins Jr., *The Life and Work of Martin Johnson Heade: A Critical Analysis and Catalogue Raisonné* (New Haven: Yale University Press, 2000).

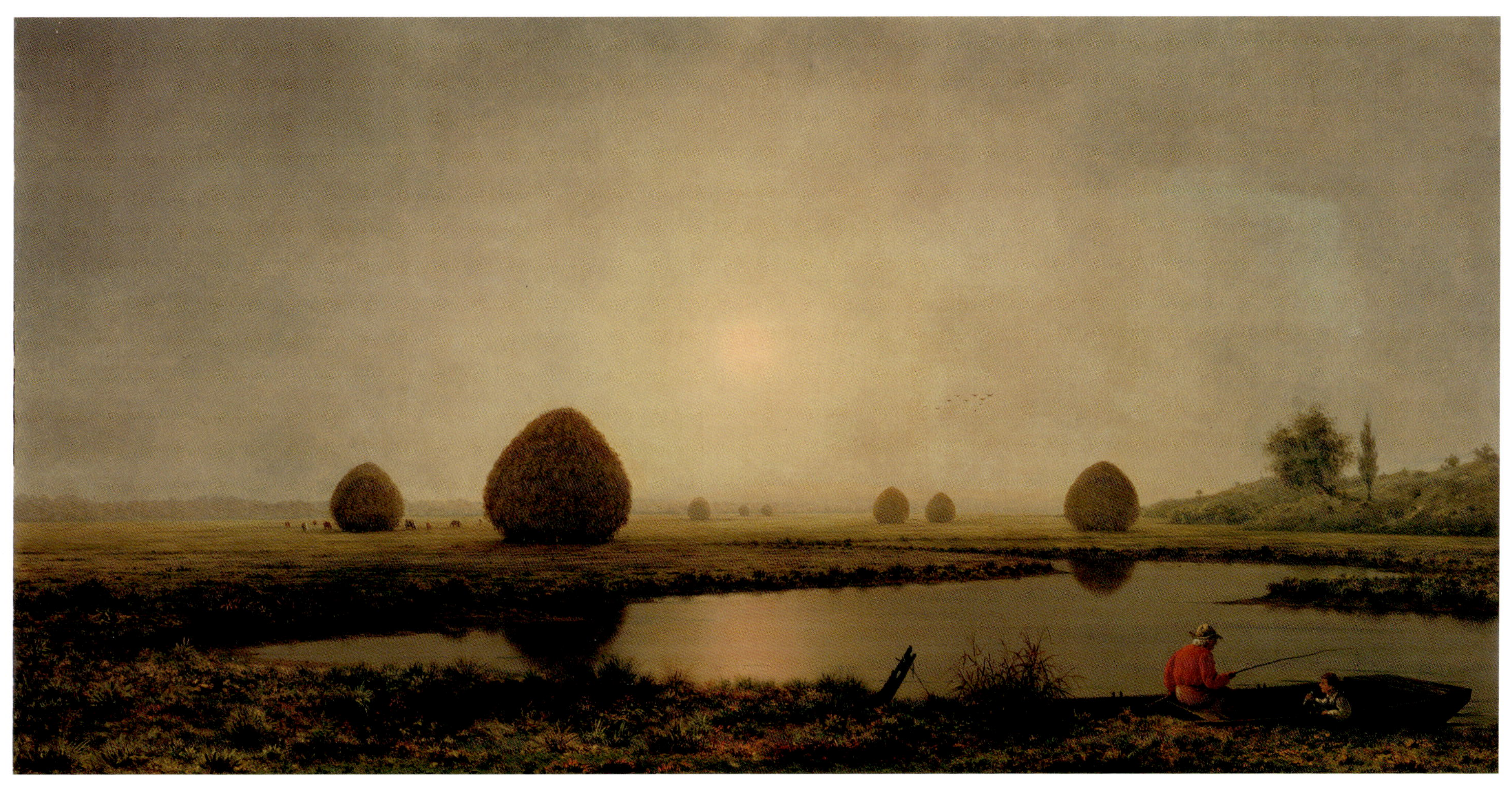

John George Brown AMERICAN, BORN ENGLAND 1831–1913

23 | *How d'ye?* c. 1875–80

Oil on canvas, 23½ × 17 in.

Signed lower right: *J.G. Brown N.A.*; stamped on verso: *The J.G. Brown Sale*

Gift of Enos A. and Sarah De Waters, by exchange (1993.34)

Although few outside the art world know his name today, John George Brown was one of the most popular and successful genre painters in the post–Civil War era. He was a shrewd businessman who took care to build his career by joining organizations, exhibiting his work in cities throughout the United States, copyrighting his paintings, and reproducing his work as prints to reach a wider audience. He had a keen sense of what the public wanted and the ability to adjust to changes in public taste. He is best known for his paintings of poor street urchins. These children, common in the bustling cities of late-nineteenth-century America, were pictured in a somewhat less than realistic way by Brown—they do wear patched and ragged clothes but are otherwise clean, well-fed, and healthy. This type of portrayal appealed to the viewer's sympathy yet avoided much of the anguish many Americans felt in the years after the war when faced with the reality of a large class of urban poor, especially abandoned children forced to live in the streets.

Born in England and originally trained as a glass cutter, Brown came to the United States in 1853 and settled in Brooklyn, New York. He took a job at the Brooklyn Flint Glass Company but continued his study of art, which he had begun while working as an apprentice glassworker in Newcastle upon Tyne. His academic training and exposure to contemporary English painting influenced his earliest works, as did the sentimental nature of Victorian genre painting.

In September 1855 Brown married Mary Owen, the daughter of his employer. It is believed that Brown's father-in-law encouraged and supported his interest in art. William Owen died in 1856 during a yellow-fever epidemic. The following year, the glass company failed, along with many other businesses in the great financial panic of 1857. Needing to support his family, Brown turned to portrait painting, especially pictures of children. He enrolled in classes at the National Academy of Design and, in 1858, began his impressive record of exhibitions by submitting two paintings to the Academy's annual show. About this time, he came to the attention of Samuel P. Avery, a prominent art dealer. Most contemporary accounts credit Avery with helping launch Brown's career as a genre painter, as he was one of the first, in 1858 or 1859, to purchase one of Brown's paintings in this style. By 1860 Brown's scenes of children were popular with the public, and the artist had taken a painting studio in the Tenth Street Studio Building, where most of the prominent artists of his day established themselves. By 1869 he was elected president of the National Academy.

How d'ye? (pronounced "howdy") is the epitome of Brown's depictions of rural America. Like many paintings from the years following the Civil War, the work symbolized America's lost innocence as well as her hopes for the future. The subject of the composition is a recently emancipated African American youth. It is an unusual work for the time in that the boy is the focus of the painting rather than a minor figure, and in that he is portrayed in a factual and realistic manner, without condescension. There is, however, no larger sense of social commentary. The brushwork and the dappled sunlight that filters through the trees—an effect Brown increasingly utilized in his country scenes—create a charming scene of an innocent, perhaps mischievous, boy enjoying a carefree moment.

The theme of the work refers to a well-established vocabulary that can be traced back to William Sidney Mount's country boys of the 1840s. It was further developed by Eastman Johnson in the early 1860s and subsequently refined by Winslow Homer in the 1870s. As typified by Johnson's *The Barefoot Boy* (reproduced as a chromolithograph by Prang in 1867), the depiction of the country boy has the following essential features: bare feet; rolled-up pants often supported by suspenders; a loose-fitting long-sleeved white shirt and rumpled hat, usually of straw; and a fresh face with a happy expression. As in his later urban scenes, Brown includes details, such as the boy's ragged clothes, to suggest the poverty experienced by many farm families after the war.

Brown's city scenes first appeared in the early 1870s, perhaps influenced by a change in patronage. Economic, social, and artistic factors later in the decade led Brown to redirect the focus of his work to the poor street urchins of the city. By the end of the decade, Brown was thoroughly associated with this city-urchin theme, especially the bootblack, the subject for which he is best known. MMD

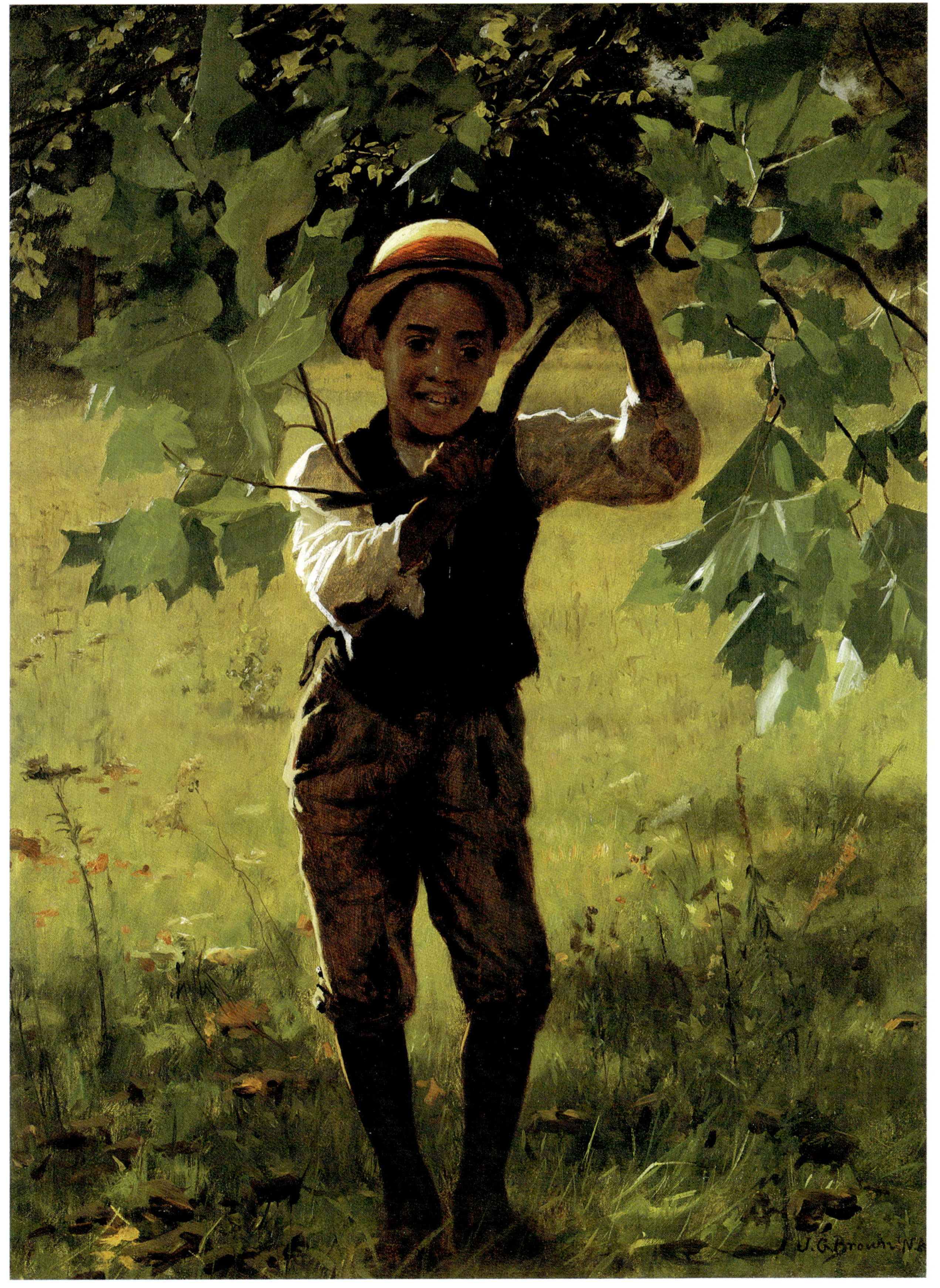

Carducius Plantagenet Ream AMERICAN 1837–1917

24 | *Still Life: Overturned Cup of Raspberries,* n.d.

Oil on canvas, 9¼ × 12½ in.

Signed lower right: *C. P. Ream*

Gift of F. Karel Wiest in memory of Julie Garrett (1982.415)

A practitioner of the flourishing still-life genre in mid-nineteenth-century America, Carducius Plantagenet Ream, a successful and well-known artist in his day, earned the sobriquet "the King of Fruit Painters."[1] His brother Morston Constantine Ream was also a still-life painter. Carducius was born in Lancaster, Ohio, and was for the most part self-taught, although he did study abroad for a period. Primarily recognized as a still-life painter, he also executed marine scenes, landscapes, portraits, and some animal subjects. He worked in New York City from 1876 to 1878 and then settled in Chicago. In addition to American venues, he exhibited at London's Royal Academy of Arts and the Paris Salon. Specializing in delicate compositions of scrupulously rendered fruit, Ream often elected to show it tumbling from a container, as seen in the porcelain cup depicted in *Still Life: Overturned Cup of Raspberries.* A master at verisimilitude, he skillfully painted objects of many diverse materials and textures, including glass and metal, porcelain dishes, and reed baskets, all interspersed within or containing the fruit subjects. In *Still Life: Overturned Cup of Raspberries,* he expertly captures the smooth, shiny surface of the porcelain cup, which contrasts with the natural matte texture of the fruit. Ream sometimes elected to paint the fruit in a natural setting, as he did in this still life, which he executes with a minute attention to detail in the manner advocated by the nineteenth-century British artist and critic John Ruskin. VAL

1. For more on Carducius Ream, see Giselle D'Unger, "Carducius Plantagenet Ream," *Chicago Fine Arts Journal* 16 (October 1905), pp. 428–31. The artist's first name has appeared with various spellings, most commonly Caducis or Carducius.

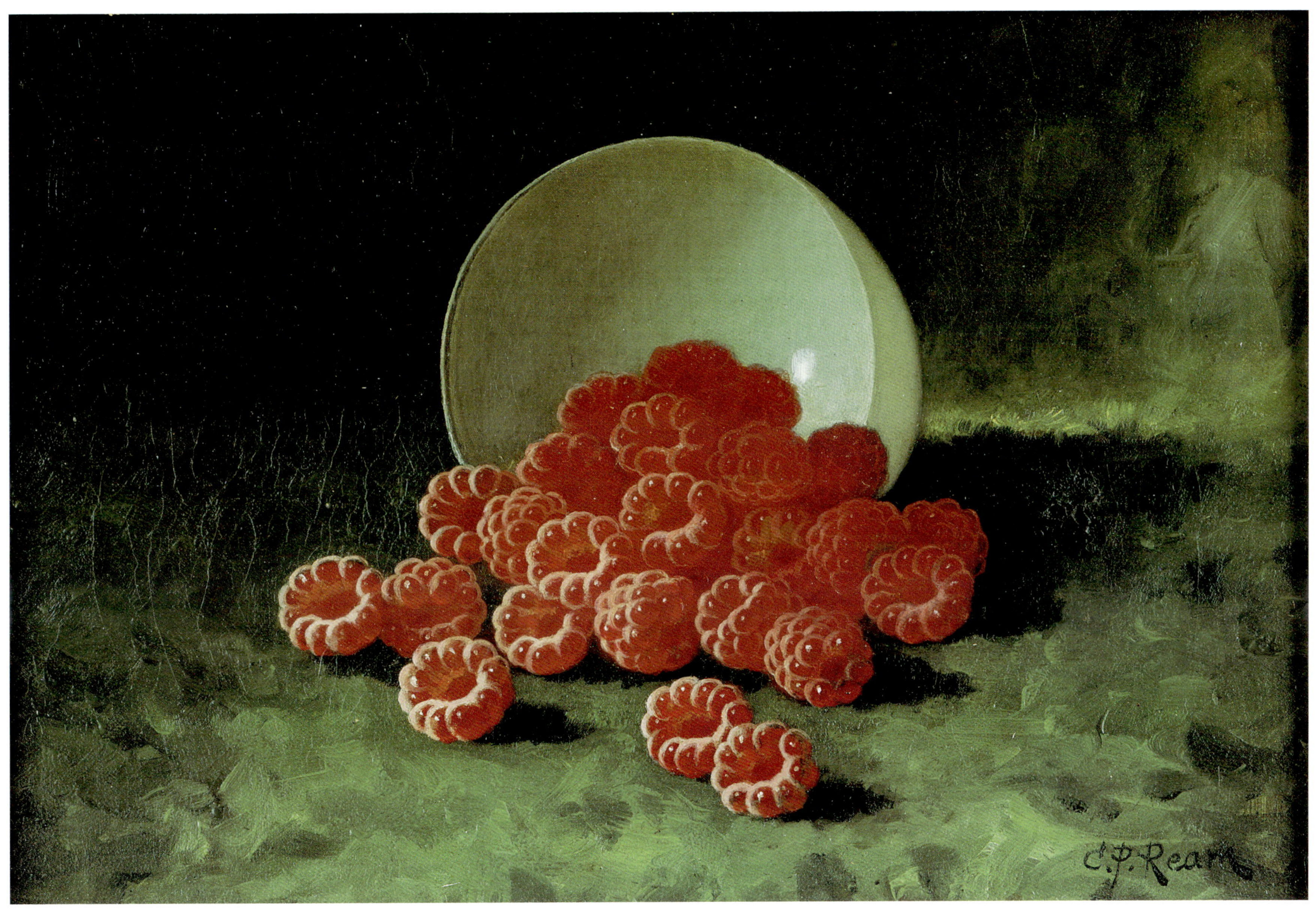

William Michael Harnett AMERICAN, BORN IRELAND 1848–1892

25 | *Still Life (Copper tankard, box, apples, wine bottles, ginger pot, cigar box, and peeled orange),* 1884

Oil on panel, 9⅜ × 12⅝ in.

Signed and dated lower right: *Harnett München 1884.*

Gift of Mr. and Mrs. William L. Richards through the Viola E. Bray Charitable Trust (1963.8)

William Harnett, born in Ireland, immigrated with his family to Philadelphia when he was still an infant. From the artisan class, he originally trained to be an engraver of silverware. He continued to work in that profession while studying art at the Pennsylvania Academy of the Fine Arts and later at the Cooper Union and the National Academy of Design in New York. In about 1875 he gave up silver engraving and its steady income for oil painting, supporting himself by making small, precisely detailed still lifes. His career, which lasted only eighteen years, can be divided into three distinct six-year periods: 1874 to 1880, spent mostly in Philadelphia; 1880 to 1886, spent in Munich and Paris; and 1886 until his death in 1892, spent entirely in New York City. He began painting small tabletop still lifes early in his career, continuing with this subject during his years in Europe. Originally focusing on humble, everyday objects—mugs, pipes, books, currency, and writing materials—he began to include rarer and more expensive objects such as tankards, medieval books, and Turkish rugs during his European period. Although his style changed little after his return to the United States, his late work includes many paintings depicting a single object set against a green wood door.

Still Life (Copper tankard, box, apples, wine bottles, ginger pot, cigar box, and peeled orange), painted in Munich in 1884, is one of approximately thirty works by Harnett that include fruit, a subject in which he specialized while in Philadelphia and New York from 1875 to 1877 and again from 1881 to 1884 while in Germany. Harnett's observation of nature is almost scientific in its detail. No element is emphasized over another—fruit is scattered throughout the picture, leading the viewer's gaze throughout the composition.

Like much of the work of this period, the painting is small in scale. Precisely painted, the elements composing the still life are carefully placed and balanced. Some are positioned close to the viewer, whereas others serve as intermediaries between the viewer and the objects placed farther in the background. They occupy a shallow space close to the picture plane and are arranged so that they move backward and upward from the table's edge. Countering this receding movement is the diagonally placed cigar box with the Chinese ginger jar on top of it, the opposing diagonal of the champagne bottle, and the knife in the immediate foreground. The horizontal plane of the table and the vertical Curaçao bottle and copper tankard add stability to the composition. These foreground objects are brought into even sharper focus by their placement against what appears to be a shadowed corner of a room, the angle of which meets the back corner of the top of the table. This compositional device, common in seventeenth-century Dutch still-life painting, did not appear in Harnett's work before his European sojourn.

Harnett's experience as an engraver helped him achieve the remarkable precision and superb draftsmanship that make his pictures so convincingly lifelike. Although popular with the public, his paintings, like those of other trompe-l'oeil artists of the time, were generally dismissed by the art world as mere foolery. Languishing in obscurity in the years after his death, his work was not rediscovered until 1939, when an enormously successful exhibition at the Downtown Gallery in New York reintroduced it to the general public. MMD

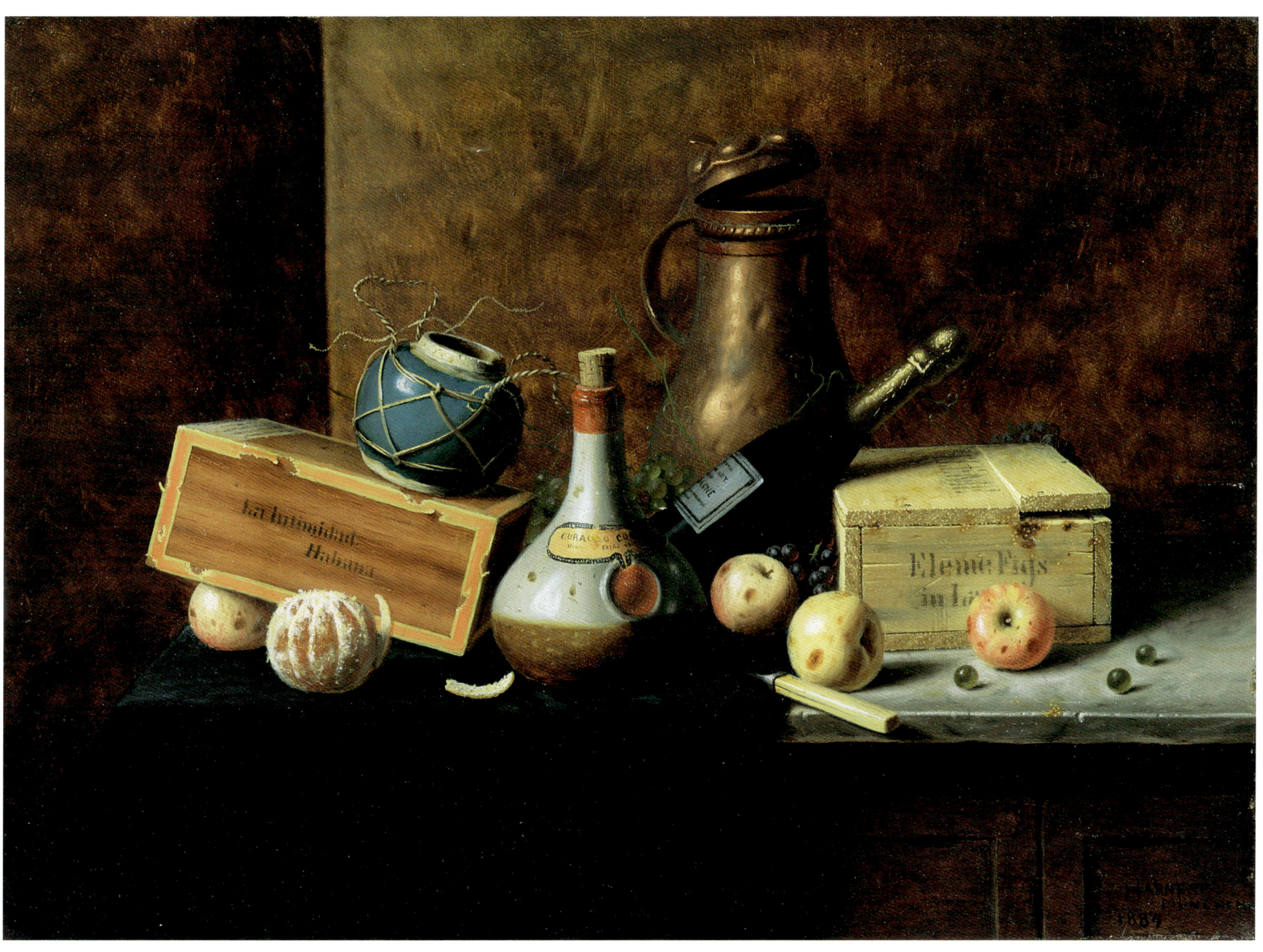
La Intimidad
Habana
Eleme Figs

Ralph Albert Blakelock AMERICAN 1847–1919

26 | *A Mountain Road near Gorham, N.H.*, c. 1879–85

Oil on canvas, 16⅜ × 24½ in.

Signed lower right: *R A Blakelock*; inscribed on verso on stretcher: *R A Blakelock A Mountain Road near . . . Gorham, N.H. White Mt.*

Gift of Mrs. Jay C. Thompson from the estate of Mrs. George Crapo Willson (1969.30)

The story of Ralph Blakelock's life is an especially tragic and compelling one, yet it is the singular quality of his work that truly distinguishes him. Born into a financially comfortable family, Blakelock attended what later became City College in New York City from 1864 to 1866, but left to pursue painting. Largely self-taught, he began exhibiting at the National Academy of Design in 1867. He traveled to the West in 1869 and 1872, visiting Wyoming, Utah, California, and Mexico as well as Panama and the West Indies.

Blakelock was an experimental artist who employed unorthodox techniques, often using thickly layered paint in a distinct palette of somber earth tones which he combined with glazes, sometimes applying a pumice stone and incorporating tobacco juice in an effort to achieve romanticized visual effects. His work did not evolve along a linear course but varied in method and style from one composition to another.

Blakelock had nine children and a wife to support, which he attempted to do by selling his art. He experienced much hardship and was frequently in dire financial straits, a situation made worse by the fact that his work, perceived as unconventional, was not commercially successful. Unlike the more popular landscapists, he was not interested in accurately recording the natural world, instead preferring to use nature as a vehicle for self-expression. It was an approach that resulted in haunting and evocative images. Subjects to which the artist most often returned were Indian encampments and moonlit landscapes with dark trees silhoutted against moody, atmospheric skies. Although he is known for painting pure landscapes and is especially identified with moonlit scenes, small-scale figures and shanties were occasionally included in his compositions.

By 1891 Blakelock's mental condition began to deteriorate, and in 1899 he was committed to a local mental hospital. He was transferred to the State Hospital for the Insane in Middletown, New York, two years later, and he remained there until 1916. After a brief release into the guardianship of a Mrs. Van Rensselaer Adams, he returned to a private institution in 1918 and died the following year while in the care of Mrs. Adams in Elizabeth, New York.

Blakelock's *A Mountain Road near Gorham, N.H.* is exceptional in several respects. Although the palette is somber and dark, it is brighter than his typical landscape compositions. More refined and detailed in conception and technique than many of his paintings, the lean-to and small figure in the middle right distance and the lacy foliage of the tree are especially well rendered. It is also notable that, as the title indicates, the painting appears to depict an actual place, which is unusual in Blakelock's oeuvre—more often, his landscape compositions were abstracted and generalized, veiled in a romanticized hazy atmosphere. Although it is not known when Blakelock visited New Hampshire, the use of a specific locale in the title makes it likely that he did visit the area. It would surely date before his first institutionalization, in 1899; based on style and the inscription on the stretcher, the work could be ascribed to his middle period, about 1879–85.[1] Stylistically, it relates to others of the period, including *The Vista* (c. 1879–85; The Minneapolis Institute of Arts) and *Woods at Sunset* (1879–85; Montclair Art Museum, Montclair, New Jersey).

A few years into his confinement at Middletown, Blakelock returned to painting. He achieved notoriety and popular attention in this late period, and his work began to command substantial prices. He was made an Associate of the National Academy in 1913 and an Academician in 1916, the year of his brief release in the care of Mrs. Adams. The elevation of Blakelock's artistic status, however, had a negative side effect: numerous copies and forgeries of the artist's work began to appear on the market. This problem has left a cloud over his reputation and has made it difficult to evaluate and determine the parameters of his oeuvre. His artistic legacy is, however, unquestioned—the product of a visionary artist, whose art evolved independently, Blakelock's work is unique and stands apart from that of his contemporaries. VAL

1. An inscription on the inner side of three stretcher bars is stamped, "The Pfleger Pat, Pat Feb 2nd 1886." The work stylistically relates to other works from the later 1880s. For the most thorough treatment of Blakelock's life and work, see Abraham A. Davidson, *Ralph Albert Blakelock* (State College, Pa.: Penn State University Press, 1996).

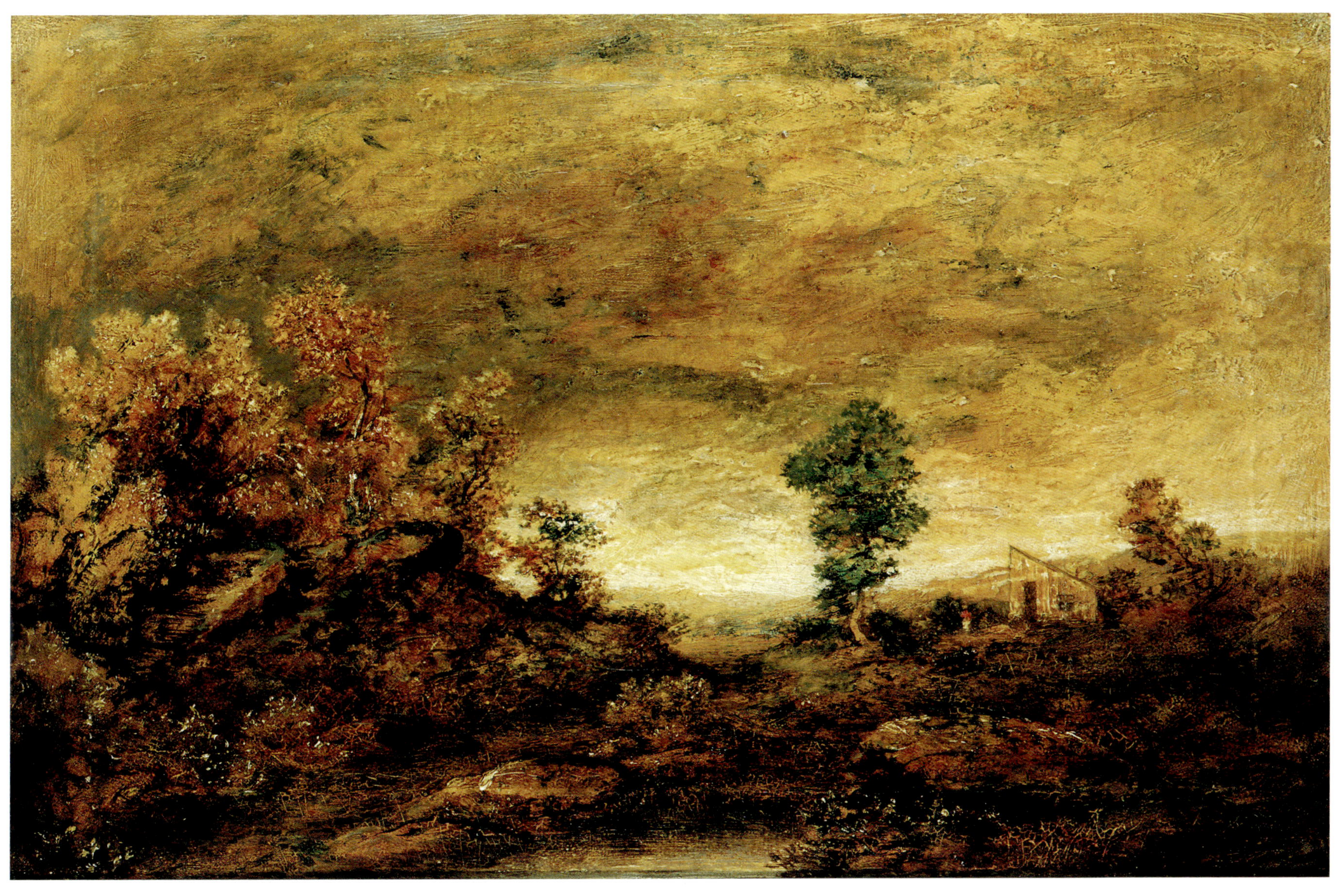

Thomas Moran AMERICAN, BORN ENGLAND 1837–1926

27 | *A Pastoral Landscape,* 1889

Oil on canvas, 43⅛ × 61⅛ in.

Signed and dated lower right: *T. Moran 1889*

Gift of Mr. and Mrs. Carroll McGregor Boutell in honor of Mr. and Mrs. Frank J. Boutell (1990.71)

Part of the romantic tradition in late-nineteenth-century landscape painting, Moran is most recognized for his idealized scenes celebrating the American West, though he depicted other areas, notably Florida and Long Island, New York. Born in Bolton, Lancashire, England, his family moved to the United States in 1844, settling in Philadelphia. In 1853 he apprenticed to a wood engraver, but by 1856 he had committed himself to painting, first exhibiting at the Pennsylvania Academy of the Fine Arts. He returned to England in 1861 and there studied the work of J. M.W. Turner, who proved to be an inspirational force in his development. On his return to America, Moran participated in several expeditions to the western territories and recorded views of the uncharted pristine wilderness. In 1871 he accompanied the Hayden Geological Survey to Yellowstone, and in 1873 he was part of the Powell Expedition that traversed the Grand Canyon. Moran settled in New York City in 1881 and lived there until he relocated in 1916 to Santa Barbara, where he spent the remainder of his years.

Moran visited Long Island several times for extended periods during the late 1870s and early 1880s. He and his wife, the artist Mary Nimmo, whom he had married in 1863, acquired property in East Hampton in 1883, and they completed work on a cottage and studio on the property the following year. This region became a source of subject matter for Moran's painting in the subsequent decades. Popularly associated with scenes of the West, Moran also painted many Long Island subjects and exhibited them with frequency, including at the National Academy of Design annual exhibitions in 1882, 1884, 1885, 1889, and 1890. A work he showed in 1889, *A Pastoral,* is possibly the Flint Institute's or a variant. In a review of the 1889 annual exhibition, a critic noted that "'A Pastoral' . . . possesses an undeniable scenic grandeur . . . Its only fault as a composition is that it is a little too perfect. . . ."[1]

Moran's artistic interpretations, while generally seen as realism, are actually more like romanticized naturalism, as he believed that an artist must be free to exercise license:

> I place no value on literal transcripts from nature. My general scope is not realistic; all my tendencies are toward idealization. Of course, all art must come through nature or naturalism, but I believe that a place as a place has no value in itself for the artist only so far as it furnishes the material from which to construct a picture.[2]

Moran's paintings were largely produced from on-site sketches and completed in his studio, where he would make adjustments to the composition, altering perspective, combining several views, adding or deleting details, and intensifying the palette to achieve specific effects. Although his works are highly finished, Moran's painting style is more expressive and romanticized than mere literal representation.

In *Pastoral Landscape* Moran has concentrated on the bucolic lushness of the low-lying Long Island marshland by giving a velvety quality to the paint surface. He added picturesque notes to the composition by placing a figure off to the right, with cows dotting the pasture and a house in the distance. This was a favorite type of scene for Moran, more intimate than his western views, and he produced a number of related compositions. Such works include *The Passing Shower* (c. 1880s; The Samuel B. and Marion W. Lawrence Collection), *Autumn* (c. 1893–97; The Philbrook Museum of Art, Tulsa, Oklahoma), *June, East Hampton* (1895; private collection), and *View of East Hampton* (1900; Hollis Taggart Galleries, New York). East Hampton was a place to which Moran returned from far-flung travels and which appeared to serve as an emotional anchor for him until late in his life. He maintained his residence and studio in East Hampton through 1922 and produced numerous scenes of the area until his final years. VAL

1. "The Academy Exhibition," *New York Evening Post,* 5 April 1889, p. 9.

2. Quoted in *Thomas Moran, 1837–1926,* exh. cat. (Riverside, Calif.: The Picture Gallery, University of California, 1963), p. 18, quoted from G. W. Sheldon, *American Painters,* 1879.

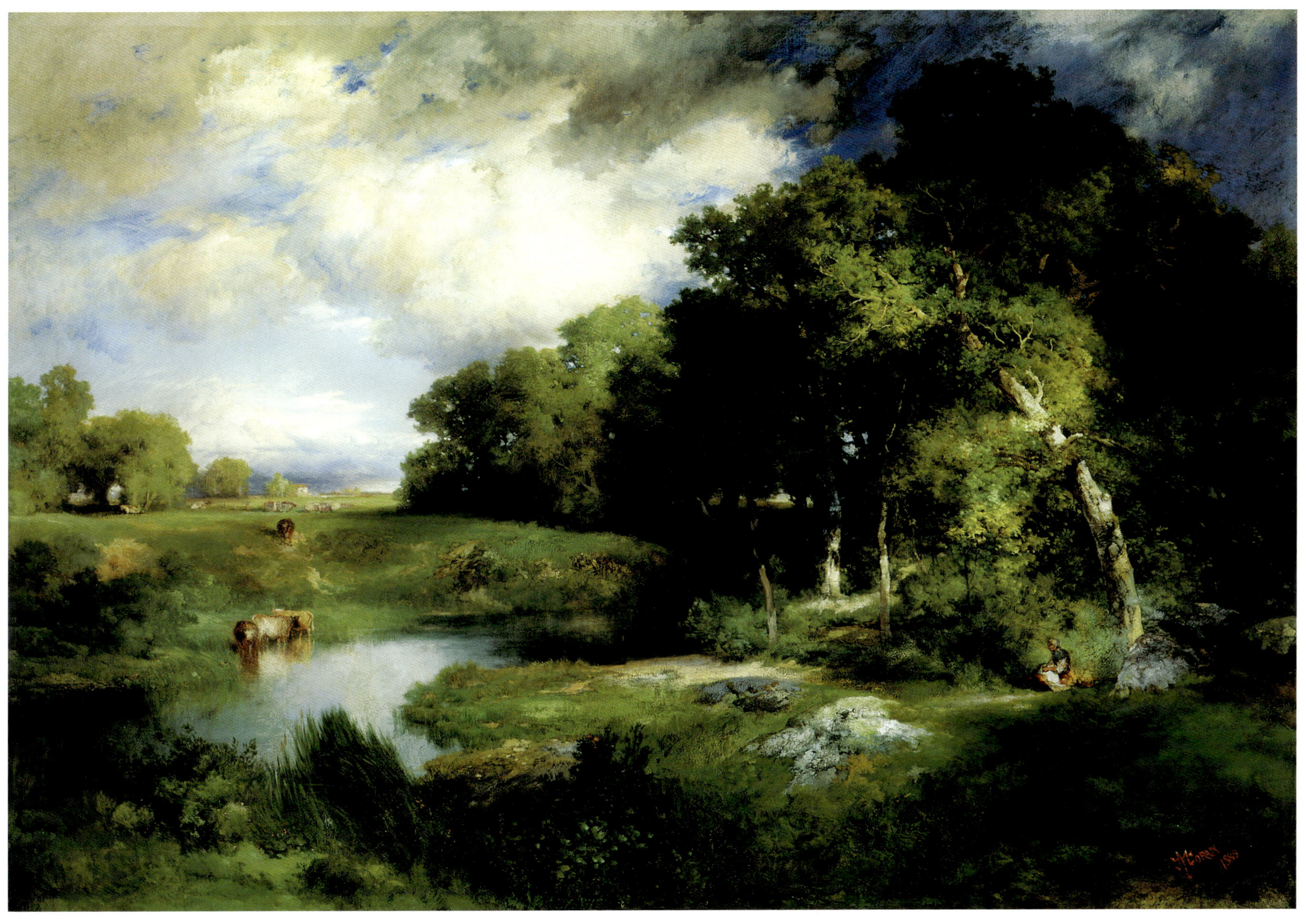

Hugh Bolton Jones AMERICAN 1848–1927

28 | *Landscape*, c. 1880s

Oil on canvas 14 × 20⅛ in.

Signed lower right: *H. Bolton Jones*

Gift of Mrs. Harlan A. Way in memory of Myrtle Peterson Baldwin (1962.2)

The work of Hugh Bolton Jones belongs to the burgeoning trend of plein-air painting in late-nineteenth-century America, and he became especially noted for depicting bucolic scenes of the northeastern countryside in the spring and summer. The critic Samuel Isham observed of his work: "all the minutiae of nature which characterized the old Hudson River School is there, but the execution is surer and more artistic, and the coloring in its truthfulness and delicacy and in the absence of the brown studio tones shows the influence of the French open-air school."[1]

Jones was born in Baltimore, where he began his studies at the Maryland Institute. He first showed his work at the National Academy of Design in 1874 and departed two years later for France, where he settled in the artists' colony at Pont-Aven and started producing landscape studies *en plein air.* He also spent some time traveling, visiting North Africa and Spain in 1877. During his five years abroad, he exhibited work at the Paris Universal Exposition, the Paris Salon, and the Royal Academy of Arts in London. He returned to America in 1881 and settled in New York, where he and his brother, the artist Francis Coates Jones, established a studio. The following year he was nominated as an Associate of the National Academy of Design, becoming a full Academician in 1883. In addition to these establishment credentials, he was also involved with the Society of Independent Artists.

Jones's career is characterized by three distinct phases: the early period, during which he resided in Baltimore; the time he spent abroad; and, finally, the years when he was based in New York.[2] He was an artist who did not submit to prevailing artistic vogues, retaining a traditional academic approach to landscape subjects. *Landscape* belongs to the last period of Jones's career, when he produced numerous poetic scenes in and around New England, especially South Egremont, Massachusetts, where he and his family spent many summers. The site for this particular work, however, remains undetermined.

Known for possessing a gentle and contented nature, Jones's personality can be seen in his art. During his mature years, he focused on pure landscape compositions in which he was clearly preoccupied with light and its changing visual effects. He favored cool, silvery colors, eschewing his earlier predilection for darker earth tones, and he often achieved a pristine clarity in the depiction of the atmosphere and reflections on water. He would frequently include a waterway disappearing into the distance and frame the composition with trees on a riverbank, both stylistic devices he employed in this work. In rendering the essential elements of a landscape—sky, atmosphere, reflections, foliage, and tree branches—Jones exhibits a delicacy in the handling of paint that creates a sense of quiet tranquility, one that celebrates the universality of nature. VAL

1. Samuel Isham, *The History of American Painting* (New York: The Macmillan Company, 1944), p. 444.

2. For the most thorough account of the life and career of Hugh Bolton Jones, see Joan Hanson Zeizel, "Hugh Bolton Jones, American Landscape Painter," master's thesis, George Washington University, Washington, D.C., 1972.

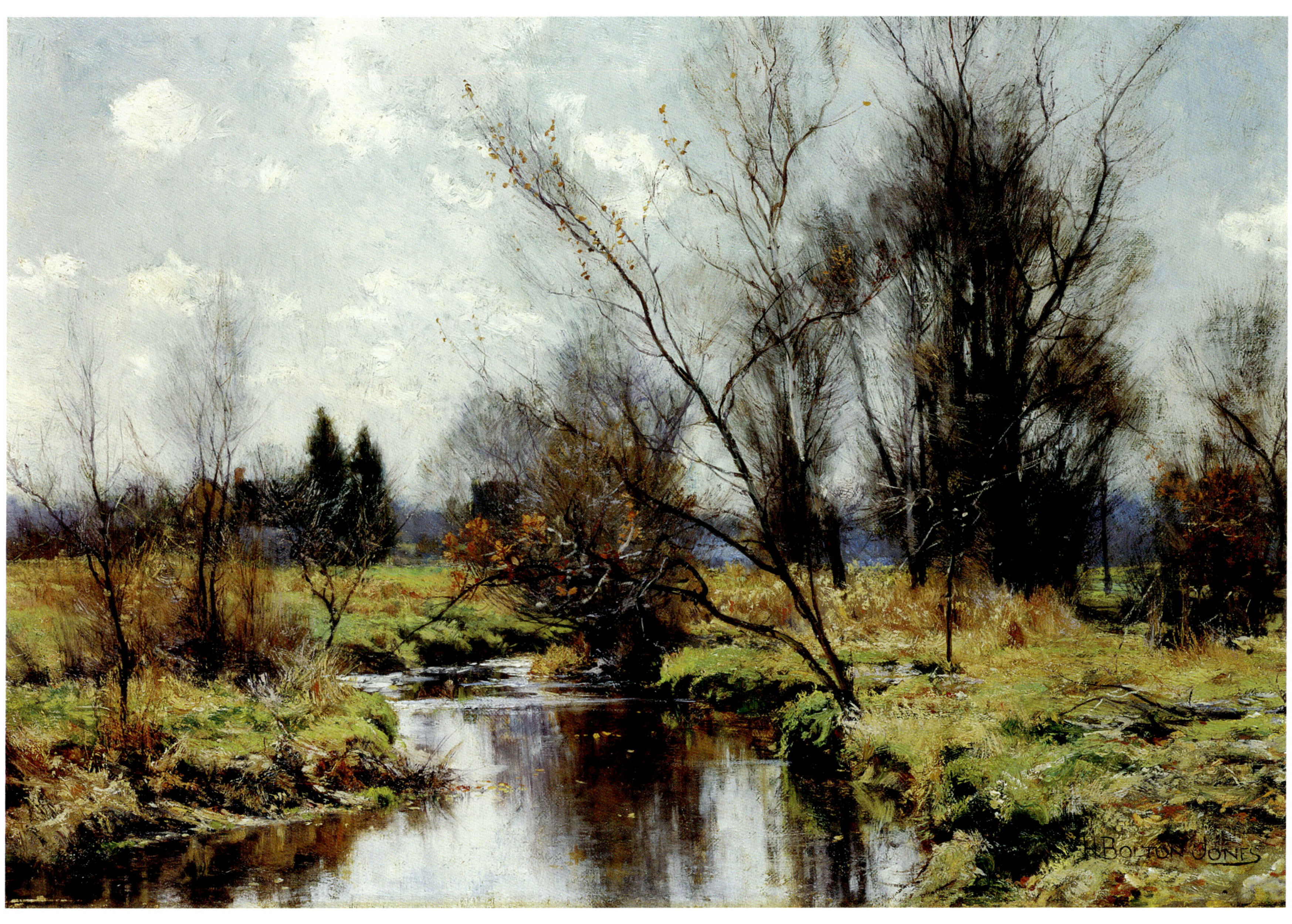
H BOLTON JONES

Bruce Crane AMERICAN 1857–1937

29 | *Long Island Farm, Springtime* (also known as *A Morning in Spring, Long Island*), 1881

Oil on canvas, 29⅜ × 53⅜ in.

Signed, inscribed, and dated lower left: *R. Bruce Crane N.Y. 1881*

Gift of Mr. and Mrs. William L. Richards through the Viola E. Bray Charitable Trust (1967.37)

Bruce Crane was born and raised in New York City, where he was exposed to the city's art museums and galleries through his father, an amateur painter. As a young man, Crane worked as a draftsman for a New Jersey architect but started painting in earnest when he began studying with the artist Alexander Helwig Wyant in about 1876 or 1877. Wyant's painterly approach to landscapes and his later work in a Tonalist style remained important influences throughout Crane's life. His formal training also included courses at the Art Students League from 1878 to 1882.

During the summers of 1880 and 1881 Crane lived on the eastern end of Long Island, where he became acquainted with the older, more established landscape painter Thomas Moran and his contemporaries, the artists Frederick Dellenbaugh and Charles Yardley Turner.[1] For his Long Island paintings, Crane chose as his subjects inland views of farms and windmills rather than scenes of the nearby seashore. Many of the Long Island works have anecdotal or narrative elements, such as the group of geese that appears in the center of the Flint Institute of Arts' painting. Geese—as well as the windmill and pile of stacked wood—are motifs that frequently appear in other paintings by Crane.[2]

In addition to scenes of Long Island, in the early years of his career Crane often depicted suburban and rural areas in other parts of New York State, New Jersey, and Connecticut. The work from this period, which includes *Long Island Farm, Springtime,* is characterized by subdued colors, tight brushwork, and attention to detail. After the early 1880s, however, Crane developed the style that defined the better-known part of his career. In 1882 he spent the summer in the French town of Grez-sur-Loing, where he and other American artists, including Kenyon Cox, Birge Harrison, and Alexander Harrison, grew interested in the French Barbizon painters. Crane was particularly drawn to the group's earth tones, painterly technique, and appreciation of unembellished nature. By the turn of the century, Crane had developed these elements into full-fledged Tonalism, and after about 1900 he painted contemplative, moody landscapes characterized by diffused light and hazy outlines that were far less literal than his early work.

In addition to his participation in the groups of artists gathered on Long Island and at Grez-sur-Loing, Crane was also very involved with the artists' colony at Old Lyme, Connecticut, and served as a member of the Lyme Art Association. In fact, Crane's activities included most of the major artists' organizations of the period, among them the Society of American Artists, the American Water Color Society, the National Arts Club, and the Salmagundi Club. In 1876 Crane began exhibiting regularly at the National Academy of Design, where he was elected a full member in 1901. RSR

1. Crane may have summered on Long Island in other years as well; see Charles Teaze Clark, "Bruce Crane, Tonalist Painter," *Antiques* 122, no. 5 (November 1982), p. 1060.

2. Ibid., p. 1066.

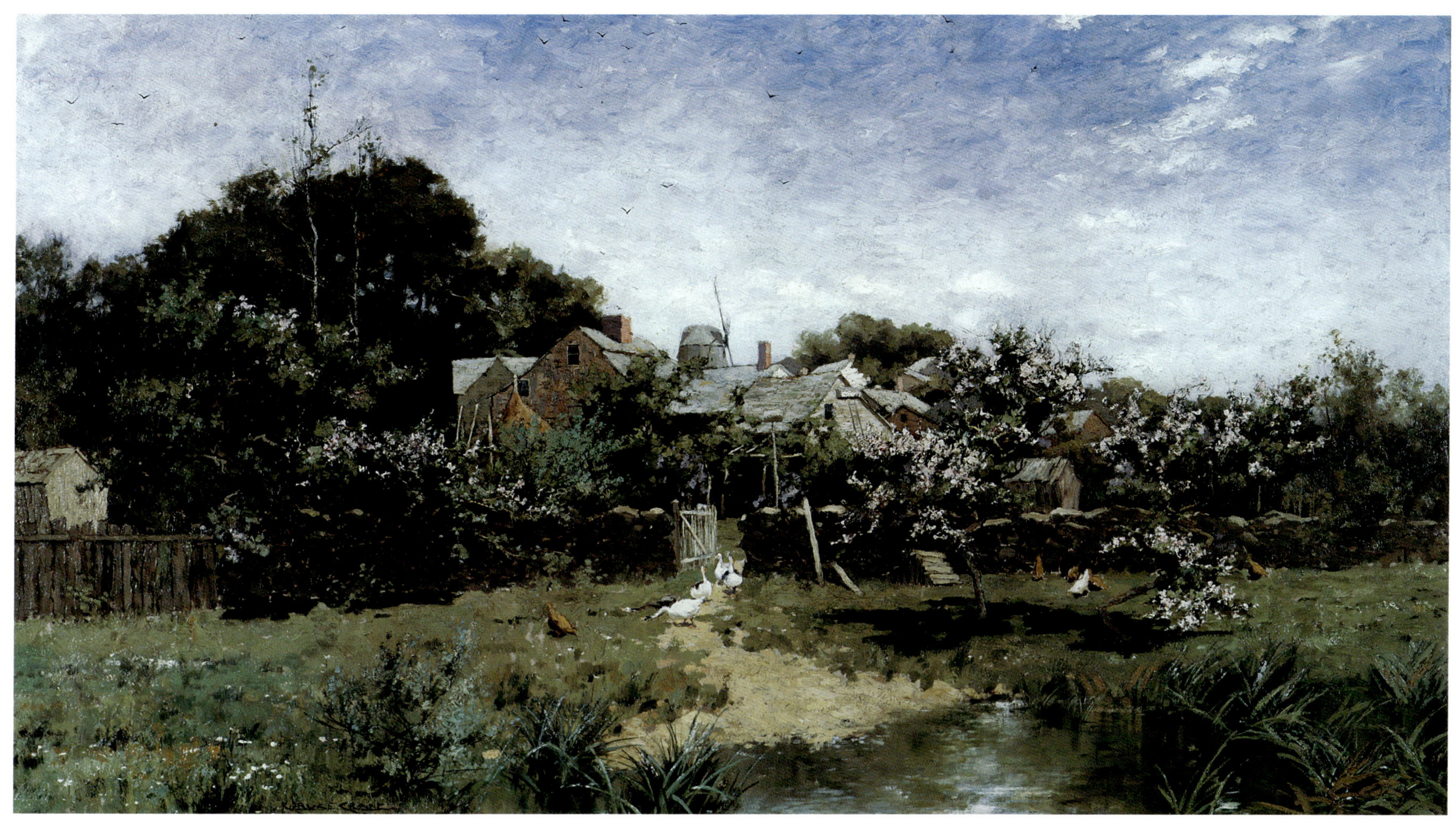

Alexander Helwig Wyant AMERICAN 1836–1892

30 | *Early Autumn*, c. 1875–90

Oil on canvas, 12 × 16¼ in.

Signed lower right: *A H Wyant*

Gift of the Flint Public Trust (1972.35)

The work of Alexander Helwig Wyant can be classified as Tonalist, a style of landscape painting that flourished in late-nineteenth-century America. Born and raised in Ohio, Wyant was inspired to pursue an artistic career after seeing some paintings by George Inness in 1857. He sought out the older artist, whose encouragement led Wyant to enroll in the National Academy of Design in New York. He remained there for a year, returning to Ohio for two years before moving back to New York to resume his studies at the Academy. He first exhibited in 1864 at the Academy's annual exhibition and left in 1865 for two years of study in Europe. The works he saw in London, especially those of J. M.W. Turner and John Constable, were of great importance in shaping his ideas about landscape painting. He settled in New York in 1867 and was made an Associate of the Academy in 1868 and an Academician the following year. He also became active in other art organizations, such as the American Water Color Society, the Society of the American Artists, and the Century Association.

In 1873 Wyant joined a government-sponsored expedition to the Southwest, where he suffered an incapacitating stroke that affected the use of his right hand. Undeterred, Wyant taught himself to paint with his left hand and continued his career as a landscape painter. After 1880 the artist began to frequent the Keene Valley area in the Adirondack Mountains of New York State, and in 1889 he moved to Arkville, New York, in the Catskills, where he became a neighbor of the Tonalist artist J. Francis Murphy.

Wyant's work underwent a visible transformation after his stroke. Previously employing a tight realist technique based on close observation in the manner of the Hudson River School, his later style became more painterly and expressive, with abundant layering and broad strokes of paint. This new, freer approach with richly impastoed surfaces invoked associations with the Barbizon School, notably the work of Narcisse Diaz de La Peña. Wyant, like the Barbizon painters, also began to depict small-scale, intimate views of the bucolic countryside that were more generalized in conception. He became known for capturing impressions of light at different times of the day, especially twilight, an interest he retained from his youth. He noted in 1866: "I saw an effect of evening over the little lake or pond . . . [which] grew upon me . . . by a sort of force which is almost comprehensible. . . . It was the moment when the sun has not yet set but when the conflict between the light and darkness is to me of all those conflicts the grandest."[1]

It is this momentary effect, so often seen in an autumnal sky, that Wyant recorded in *Early Autumn*. Wyant's late Tonalist style is evident in this work, in which he restricts the use of bright hues, relying on subtlety and the skilled blending of color. In his later years, the artist became interested in Johann Wilhelm von Goethe's *On the Theory of Colors*, and his comments in an interview at the time appear to reflect this influence: "Now the gray of a picture should be chock-full of primaries—of red, yellow, and blue, or of violet-gray and greenish-gray—if the result is to be delicious and satisfying."[2] Wyant applied this idea to the sky in *Early Autumn*, in which he realized the last satisfying glimpse of ethereal light on the horizon. VAL

1. Alexander Wyant to Thomas Turlay, 17 March 1866, Wyant Papers, Archives of American Art, Smithsonian Institution, microfilm roll 70-48, frames 672–73.

2. Quoted in "Alexander H. Wyant," *Harper's Weekly*, 23 October 1880, p. 677.

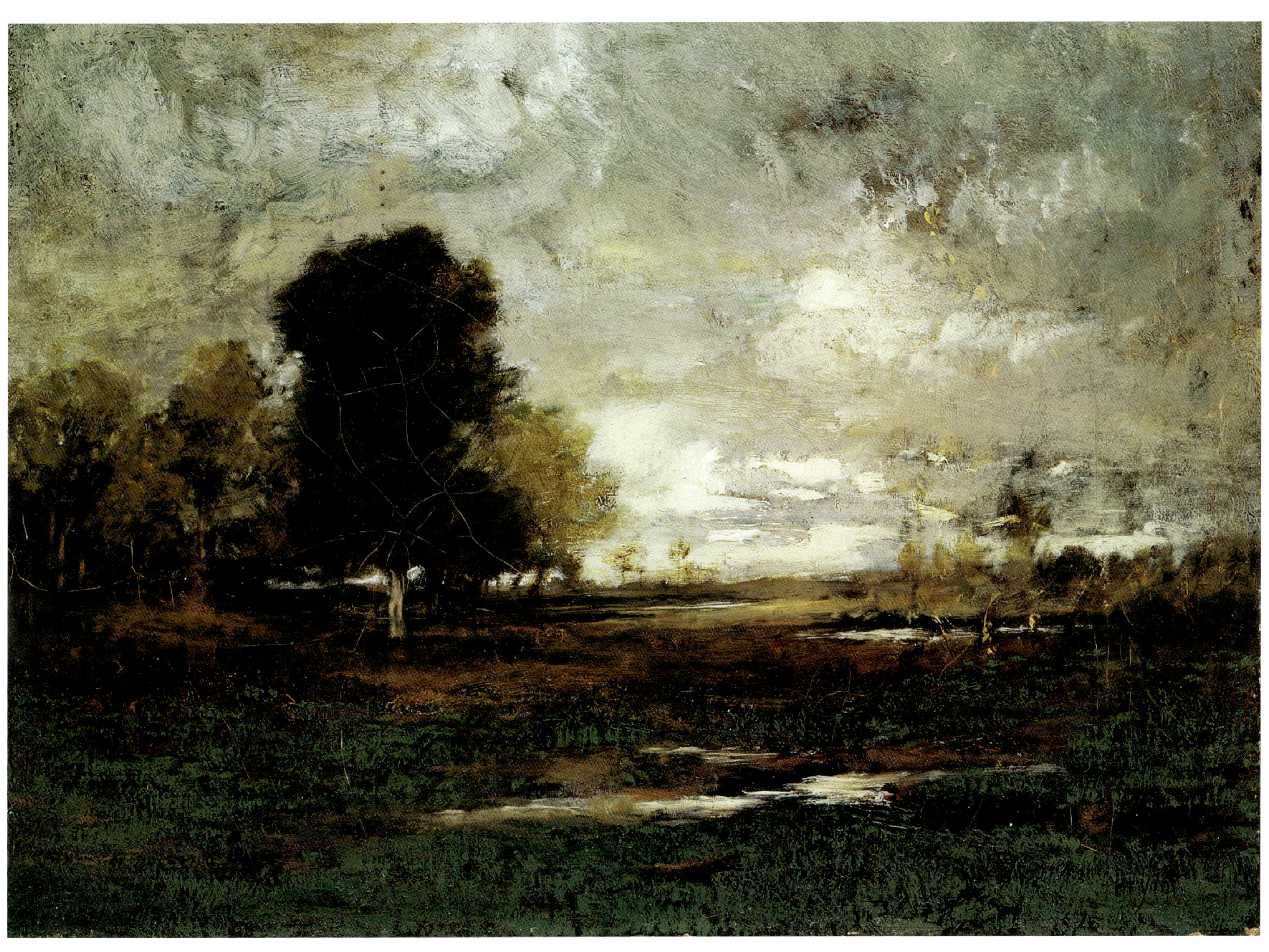

Leonard Ochtman AMERICAN, BORN THE NETHERLANDS 1854–1934

31 | *Along the Mianus River,* 1892

Oil on canvas, 24⅛ × 36 in.

Signed and dated lower left: *Leonard Ochtman 1892*

Gift of Mr. and Mrs. Jerome O. Eddy (1940.5)

Born in Zonnemain, Holland, Leonard Ochtman immigrated in 1866 with his family to America, where they settled in Albany, New York. For ten years, from age sixteen to twenty-six, he worked as a draftsman for a wood engraver in Albany. Although his only professional training in the fine arts was a single session at the Art Students League in 1879, he began exhibiting at the National Academy of Design in 1882. He continued to show there regularly throughout his career. He traveled to Europe in about 1885 and, on his return, took up residence in New York City, where he acquired a studio on Union Square. Soon after, his work attracted critical attention and he became a respected figure in the city's art community. He was made an Associate of the National Academy in 1898 and an Academician in 1904. Ochtman was accorded many prizes and honors throughout his career and became an influential teacher. He built a studio in Riverside, Connecticut, where he held classes from 1891 to 1896, after which he moved to Mianus, Connecticut, the area he had depicted in *Along the Mianus River* in 1892. About 1900 he moved to Cos Cob, Connecticut, where he remained until his death.

Ochtman concentrated on landscape subjects and became particularly identified with scenes of rural Connecticut. He was exposed to the work of the Barbizon painters and became associated with Dwight Tryon, who also admired that group of artists. Through these influences, Ochtman modified his own approach, becoming a Tonalist painter who concentrated on quiet, intimate landscape compositions that are executed in a subdued and limited palette. These artists, generally working in an impressionistic mode and *en plein air,* were interested in capturing the effects of light in nature. Charles Caffin noted in his contemporary survey of American painting that "Among the artists of this country who have taken the lead in studying nature in the light of open air, Ochtman has won a foremost position. He is keenly sensitive to the quiet moods of nature and to the manifestation of subtlest quality. Few canvases equal his in refinement of observation and delicate tonality."[1]

Along the Mianus River is executed with a measured restraint typical of Ochtman's sensitive and lyrical interpretation of the Connecticut countryside. The composition, a scene viewed from an elevated ridge that overlooks the river, is divided by horizontal bands of foreground and sky that emphasize the quiet, stable ambiance of the scene. Ochtman entered the painting in the 1892 Annual Exhibition at the National Academy of Design, where it was singled out in a review as a "dreamy autumn scene."[2] The work is also one of three Ochtman submitted to the 1893 World's Columbian Exposition in Chicago, where it won an award.

Other compositions of the Connecticut region include *Night on the Mianus River* (c. 1901; location unknown) and *On the Mianus River* (1896; Bruce Museum, Greenwich, Connecticut), which were shown at the National Academy of Design's 1897 annual exhibition. The latter work shows a different vista seen from a lower vantage point but it is executed in a similar way. Both the Flint Institute's painting and the Bruce's *On the Mianus River* exhibit hallmarks of Ochtman's style that include the brushy application of paint to the canvas; blended, low-keyed tones; and a horizontal composition. VAL

1. Charles Caffin, *The Story of American Painting* (New York: Frederick A. Stokes, 1907), p. 345.

2. "The Academy Show," *The Art and Amateur* 27 , no. 1 (1 June 1892), p. 5.

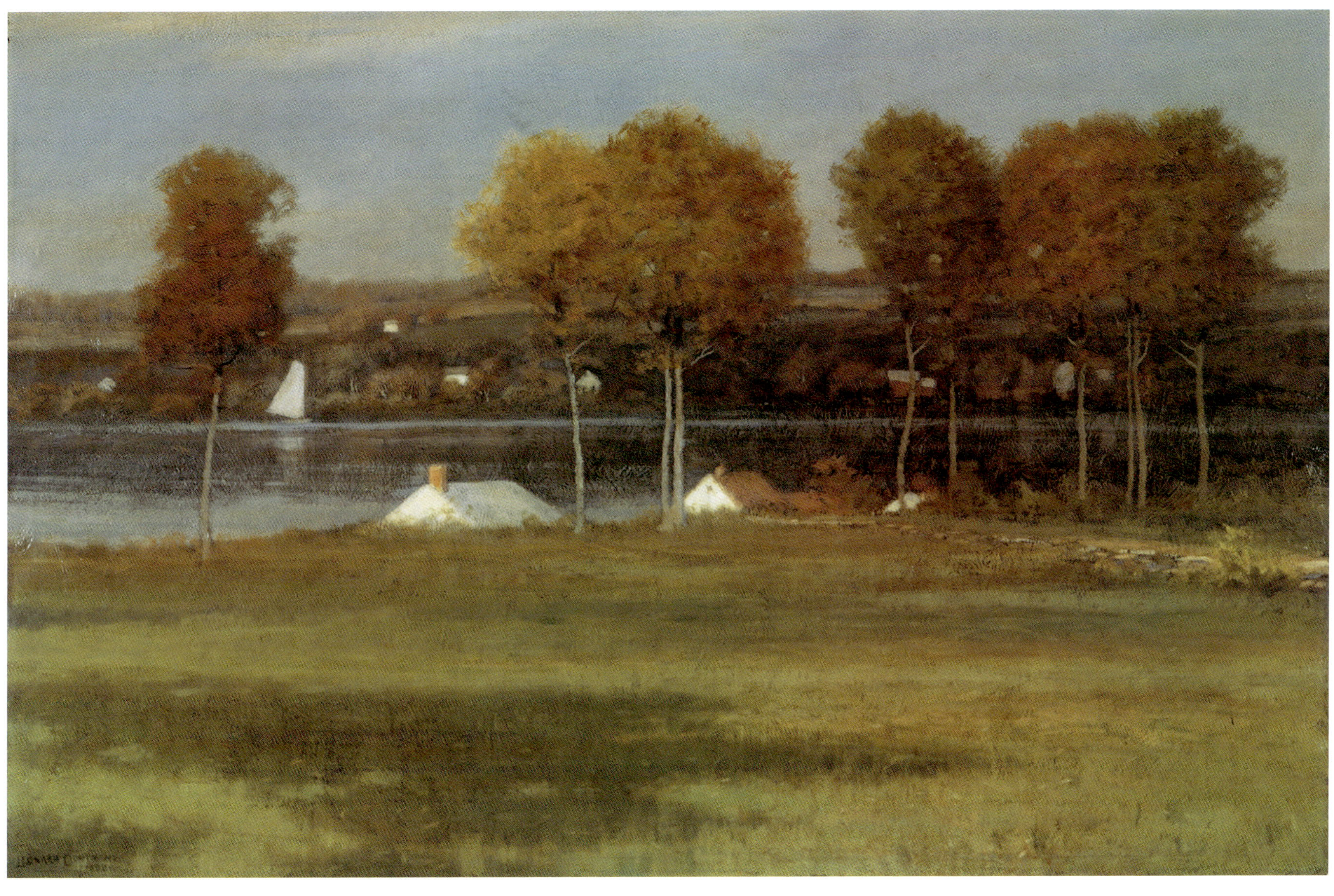

John Francis Murphy AMERICAN 1853–1921

32 | *Landscape,* 1898

Oil on canvas, 15⅞ × 22⅛ in.

Signed and dated lower left: *J. Francis Murphy 98*

Gift of Mr. and Mrs. Donald E. Johnson (1941.4)

Known as the American Corot, J. Francis Murphy was a painter of Tonalist landscapes, a style that flourished in the final decades of the nineteenth and into the early twentieth century. Murphy's reputation rested on these subdued works executed in subtly modulated tonalities, a type exemplified by *Landscape.*

Murphy had virtually no professional training as an artist. Born in Owego, New York, he worked as a sign painter in Chicago, where he briefly attended the School of the Art Institute. In 1875 he moved to New York City, where he depicted landscapes of the surrounding rural areas rather than urban views. He first exhibited at the National Academy of Design in 1876, won the Hallgarten Prize, and was nominated an Associate of the Academy in 1885. He was elected an Academician two years later. By the late 1880s Murphy had achieved success and recognition for his work. In 1887 he built a summer residence in Arkville, New York, in the Catskills, where he would spend extended periods of time, although he also maintained a Manhattan residence at the Chelsea Hotel. Alexander Helwig Wyant, a self-taught artist with whom he became acquainted in New York City, became a neighbor in Arkville when he moved there in 1889.

Murphy had been exposed to a variety of influences when he first arrived in New York, many of which informed his stylistic development, most notably the work of his friend Wyant and George Inness. Seeking a more expressive mode of interpretation and aspiring to capture an emotional response to nature in his work, he modified his earlier, more detailed, and literal realism, which was akin to that of the Hudson River School, and used an increasingly fluid, painterly approach. After the turn of the century, Murphy's brushwork became bolder and more defined, yet even these works are quiet and intimate. *Landscape,* typical of Murphy's muted tonal landscapes, conveys a sense of introspective spirituality. The spare composition, framed on two sides by trees, has a dusky sky and a dense, hazy atmosphere that contributes to an overall moody ambiance. The scene is likely derived from the landscape of Arkville, as it bears a strong resemblance to *The Old Barn* (1906; The Metropolitan Museum of Art, New York), a work executed eight years later. By this time in his career, however, Murphy was not interested in recording specific topography but rather sought the poetic inspiration seen in these two works. As Eliot Clark stated, "He reflects little of his actual environment except the light, the tone, and the effect of atmosphere, and uses his simple store of the objective world to reflect his subjective nature."[1]

In 1899 Murphy was invited to participate in the 1900 Universal Exposition in Paris, but he had no available works to submit. In November of that year, he contacted Mr. W. B. Lockwood, the owner of *Landscape,* stating in a letter to him that "In my opinion you possess one of my best pictures and it occurred to me that it would be a work that would well represent me at the Paris Exposition."[2] Lockwood agreed to lend the work, and thus it was one of two canvases that represented Murphy in the exposition, for which he won an honorable mention.[3] VAL

1. Eliot Clark, *J. Francis Murphy* (New York: privately printed by Frederic Fairchild Sherman, 1926), p. 37.

2. John Francis Murphy to W. B. Lockwood, 13 November 1899, Archives, Flint Institute of Arts.

3. The other work was *Under Grey Skies* (watercolor and pastel, 1893, lent by H. H. Harrison, Esq.; currently in the collection of the Indianapolis Museum of Art). For more on the 1900 Paris Universal Exposition, see *Paris 1900: The "American School" at the Universal Exposition,* ed. Diane P. Fischer, exh. cat. (New Brunswick, N.J.: Rutgers University Press in association with the Montclair Art Museum, 2000). This publication lists Murphy's painting *Landscape* as unlocated.

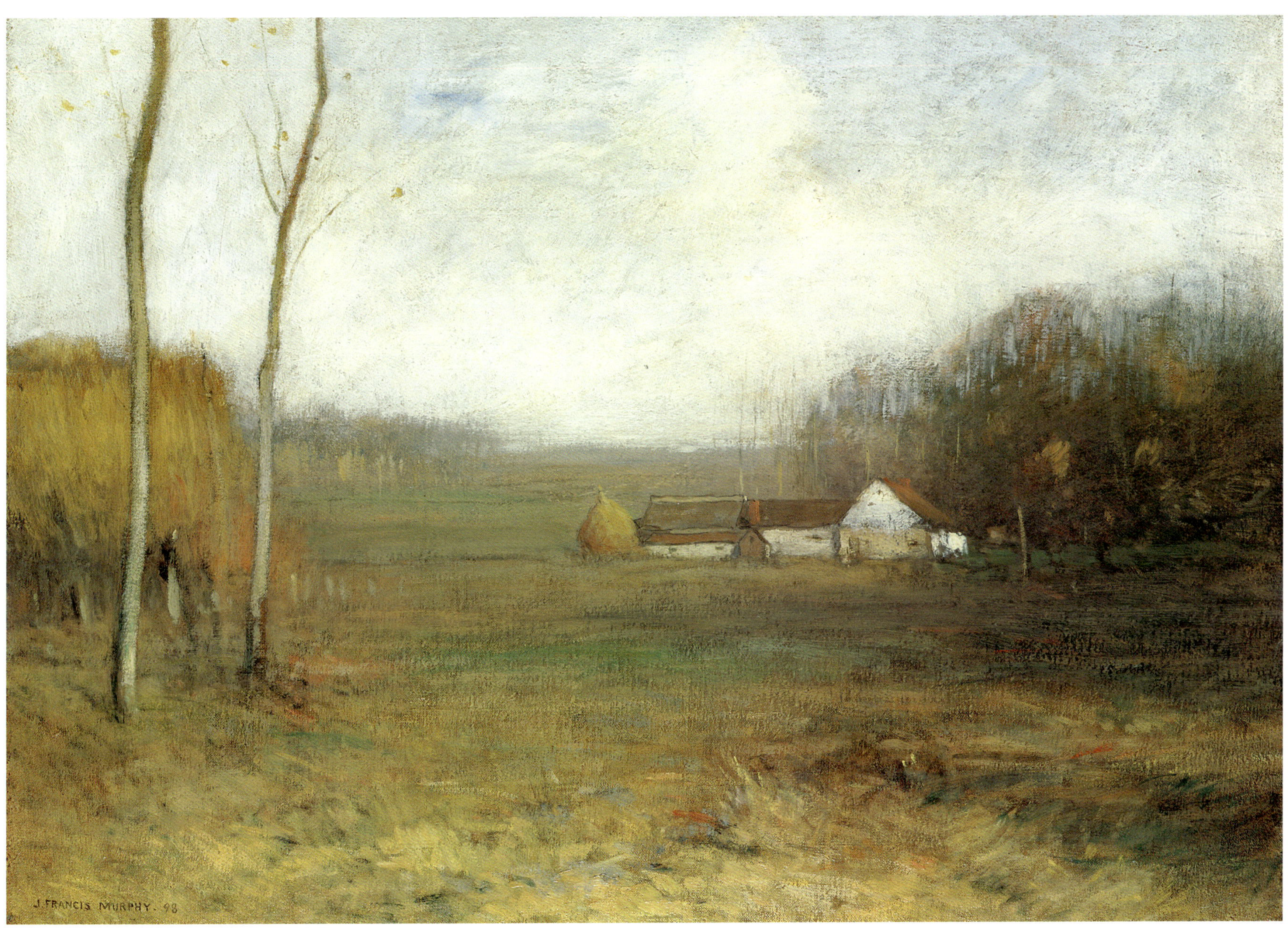
J. FRANCIS MURPHY. 98

Henry Oliver Walker AMERICAN 1843–1929

33 | *Hagar and Ishmael,* 1892

Oil on canvas, 24⅜ × 18⅞ in.

Signed and dated lower left: *H.O. Walker 1892*

Gift of Mrs. Arthur Jerome Eddy (1931.1)

The Boston-born Henry Oliver Walker spent the first part of his professional life pursuing commercial endeavors. It was not until the mature age of thirty-four, when he traveled to Paris to study with the academic painter Léon Bonnat—whose pupils included Thomas Eakins, Henri de Toulouse-Lautrec, Gustave Caillebotte, and Raoul Dufy—that Walker began to devote himself seriously to establishing an artistic career. On his return to America, Walker enjoyed considerable success as an easel and mural painter, receiving several commissions for public murals, including ones at the Library of Congress, the Massachusetts State House, and the Minnesota State Capitol Building.

Walker worked primarily in New York City and in his studio in Cornish, New Hampshire, where he was part of an artists' colony, established in 1885, that thrived for more than twenty years. Walker and the other members of the Cornish Colony, among them Augustus Saint-Gaudens, Thomas Wilmer Dewing, and George de Forest Brush, were influenced by classical antiquity and the Renaissance and also shared an interest in depicting traditional themes. *Hagar and Ishmael* reflects Walker's pursuit of traditional, in this case biblical, subject matter. In the painting, Walker depicts Abraham's illegitimate son, Ishmael, supported by the protective arm of his mother, Hagar. The two had been cast into the wilderness at the request of Abraham's wife, Sarah. In the melancholy, resigned figure of Hagar, Walker captures a mother's concern for her child and her trepidation about the future.

A critic who saw *Hagar and Ishmael,* first exhibited with the Society of American Artists in New York, wondered about the appropriateness of the biblical title: "Mr. Walker's picture not only suggests, but evidently is a simple family group, to which the title was affixed probably as an afterthought."[1] The hint of derision aside, this comment is a response to the simplicity of the image of a modestly attired mother and her son. The representation of biblical or historical figures as everyday people was a practice that had become increasingly popular around the middle of the nineteenth century, in part owing to the growing influence of the realist aesthetic. The pensive expressions, simple clothing, outdoor setting, and muddy earth tones of Walker's palette recall, for example, Jules Bastien-Lepage's *Joan of Arc* (1879; The Metropolitan Museum of Art, New York).

After Walker's death in 1929, Will H. Low recalled how the artist was able simultaneously to evoke the classical and remain firmly grounded in "reality": "Walker had, with his gifts of refinement and distinction that aided him in the idealization of his figures, a strong sense of reality."[2] MK

1. See "The Society of American Artists," *The Art Amateur* 27, no. 1 (June 1892), p. 3. Walker again exhibited *Hagar and Ishmael,* along with two other works, at the 1893 World's Columbian Exposition, a fair held in Chicago to celebrate the four-hundredth anniversary of Columbus's explorations in the New World.

2. Will H. Low, "Henry Oliver Walker: A Tribute by Will H. Low in Memory of Our Late Distinguished American Painter," *New York Herald-Tribune,* January 1929, curatorial files, Flint Institute of Arts.

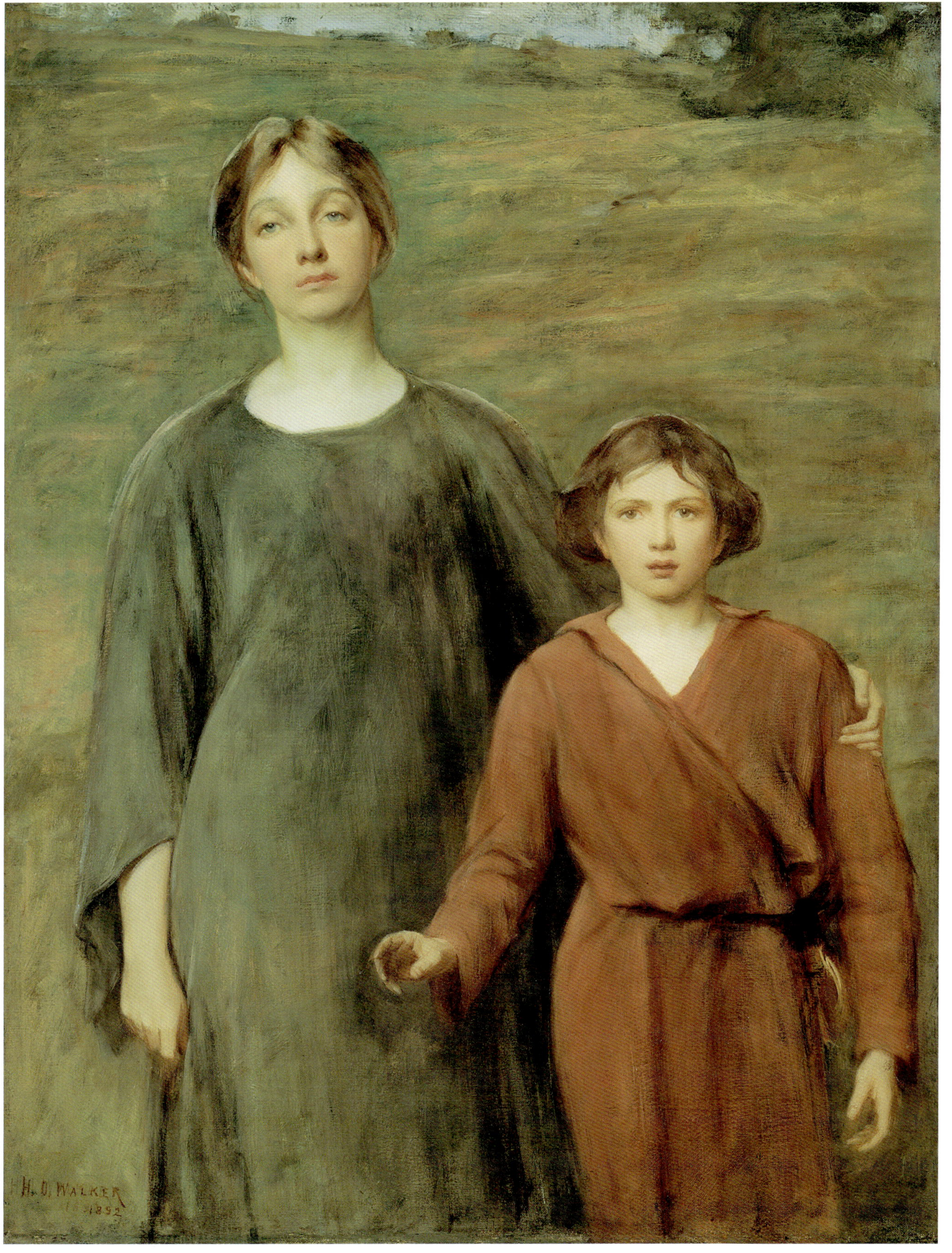
H. O. WALKER
1892

Anna Vaughn Hyatt Huntington AMERICAN 1876–1973

34 | *Yawning Panther,* 1911–22

Bronze mounted on black Belgian marble, 5 × 15½ × 4⅜ in.

Signed on genitals: *Hyatt*

Gift of the Founders Society (1984.14)

Anna Hyatt Huntington is best known for her expressive, anatomically accurate sculptures of animals. The daughter of a paleontologist, Huntington trained first in Boston and then at New York's Art Students League with Hermon MacNeil and Gutzon Borglum. She had her first solo exhibition early in her career, when she showed forty animal sculptures at the Boston Arts Club in 1901. In 1907 she left the United States to work in Paris and Italy. Huntington received numerous awards and sculpture commissions in the following decades, including an honorable mention in the 1910 Paris Salon, as well as awards from the National Academy of Design, the Pennsylvania Academy of the Fine Arts, and the National Sculpture Society. She also won a silver medal at the Panama-Pacific International Exposition in 1915, and in 1922 was made a Chevalier of the French Legion of Honor. Her public sculpture includes the equestrian monument *Joan of Arc* in New York City (1915) and *El Cid Compeador* in Seville (1927). With Huntington's critical acclaim came financial success: a 1912 article listed her among the twelve women in America earning $50,000 per year.[1]

Yawning Panther was completed between 1911 to 1922, after Huntington had already achieved critical recognition. Casts of the sculpture were sold by the Gorham Company Founders of Providence, Rhode Island, a firm with which Huntington had a long-standing arrangement for casting and marketing her work. In 1928 the foundry offered it in two sizes.[2] The sculpture is characteristic of Huntington's work. The energy expressed by the exposed fangs, the elegant line of the body—from the curved tail to the neck and front paws—and the highly realistic portrayal of the straining muscles are all elements frequently seen in her sculpture. Her animal images are typified by such dynamic action—she portrayed her dogs, horses, lions, monkeys, and tigers in poses of play, fighting, and repose. Scholars have connected Huntington's facility with anatomy to her lifelong proximity to animals—she spent her childhood summers on a farm, studied the creatures at the Bronx Zoo, and later in life trained horses and kept a menagerie at her estate.

After her marriage to the railway scion and collector Archer M. Huntington, Anna Hyatt Huntington pursued philanthropic art activities. Together they created Brookgreen Gardens, near Charleston, South Carolina, for which they collected and commissioned sculpture. The garden, which opened to the public in 1932, was the first and largest sculpture garden in the United States of its time. In 1939 the Huntingtons donated their Fifth Avenue mansion to the National Academy of Design, which remains the institution's home. RSR

1. Cited in Katherine Weems, "Anna Hyatt Huntington," *National Sculpture* 22, no. 4 (winter 1973–74), p. 10.

2. *Famous Small Bronzes: A Representative Exhibit Selected from the Works of Noted Contemporary Sculptors,* exh. cat. (New York: Bronze Division of the Gorham Company, 1928), p. 14.

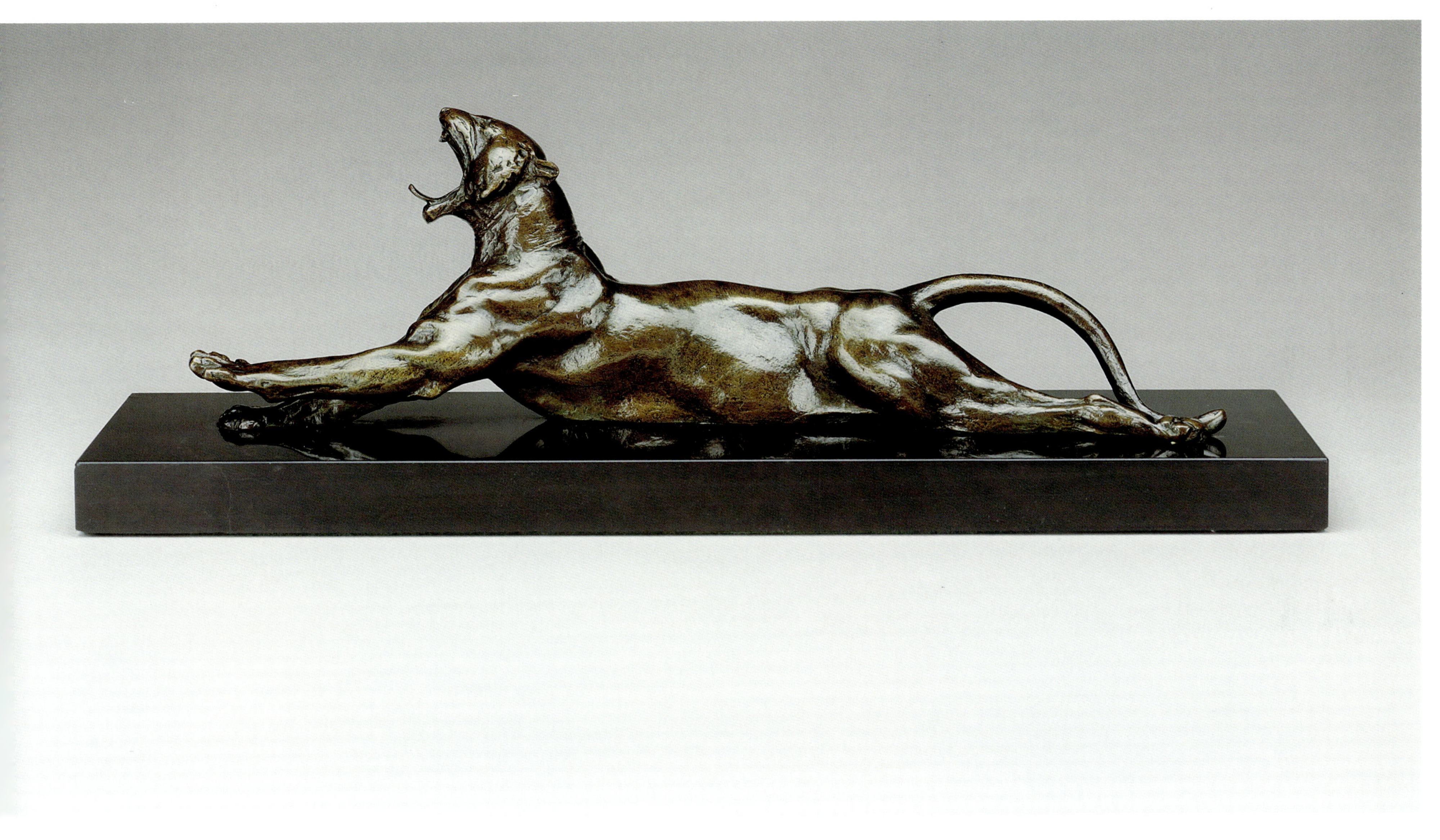

Robert William Vonnoh AMERICAN 1858–1933

35 | *Portrait of Jerome A. Eddy, Sr.*, 1894

Oil on canvas, 23⅛ × 18 in.

Signed, inscribed, and dated lower right: *Vonnoh, Chicago 94*

Gift of Jerome O. Eddy (1940.3)

Robert Vonnoh was one of the first Americans to adopt the Impressionist style of painting. Born in Hartford, Connecticut, he was raised in Boston, where he attended the Massachusetts Normal Art School. He left for Paris in 1880 to further his training and enrolled at the Académie Julian, where he studied for three years with the noted teachers Gustave Boulanger and Jules-Joseph Lefebvre. On his return to Boston, he began to teach and established himself as a portraitist.

Vonnoh returned to France briefly in 1886 and again in 1887, the latter time remaining in Paris for four years. During this period he participated in various European exhibitions, including the Paris Salon, where he won an honorable mention in 1889. Moving back to Boston for a short time in 1891, he went to Philadelphia later that year, where he taught at the Pennsylvania Academy of the Fine Arts through 1895. An influential teacher, he counted among his students such noted artists as Robert Henri, William Glackens, John Sloan, Edward Redfield, and Maxfield Parrish. He married the sculptor Bessie O. Potter in 1899, with whom he spent time at the artists' colonies of Old Lyme, Connecticut, and Grez-sur-Loing, France. Made an Associate of the National Academy of Design in 1900, he was elected an Academician in 1906. Due to failing eyesight, Vonnoh painted little from the mid-1920s until his death in Nice ten years later.

Though an early convert to Impressionism, probably by the mid-1880s, not all of Vonnoh's art falls into this category. His landscapes, painted *en plein air*, were freely executed with a brilliant Impressionist palette, but he also continued to paint portraits in a second style, a somber mode derived from nineteenth-century French academic portraiture, as seen in *Portrait of Jerome A. Eddy, Sr.* As Eliot Clark noted in an article devoted to the work of Vonnoh:

> Among landscape painters few have had the technical mastery or the constructive understanding to render the figure convincingly. . . . Robert Vonnoh has the rare ability not of combining the two but seeing each subject for itself. As a portrait painter he has not sacrificed likeness, and his brush has responded to his knowing understanding of character. . . . But Vonnoh is also conscious of the function of an official portrait, and his presentments of distinguished sitters have a formal elegance without sacrificing personality.[1]

Portrait of Jerome A. Eddy, Sr. reflects Vonnoh's immense skill in portraiture. The work pictures Jerome A. Eddy (1829–1905), father of Arthur Jerome Eddy, the Chicago lawyer and writer who was also a noted collector of avant-garde art and a major purchaser at the 1913 Armory Show. The elder Eddy was born in Stafford, New York, in 1829 and moved with his family to Flint, Michigan, when he was nine years old. A prominent citizen known for his geniality and refinement, he was involved in various business ventures in the city, including lumber, real estate, and the proprietorship of the *Genessee County Democrat*, a local newspaper.[2] This portrait was executed in Chicago in 1894, possibly during a visit to his son, and was donated to the Flint Institute of Arts by the sitter's grandson.

Vonnoh, as he often did in his portraits, has captured the stately demeanor and amiable disposition of the subject as well as imbued the characterization with a certain nobility. He has appropriated a painterly technique, especially evident in the visage, beard, and hands of the sitter. Strong contrasts of white have been used in a traditional manner to highlight the subject's features and expression. Remarkably, at the time Vonnoh produced this incisive portrait, he was also painting bright Impressionist scenes, most often landscapes with dappled sunlight and vividly colorful fields and flowers. VAL

1. Eliot Clark, "The Art of Robert Vonnoh," *Art in America* 16 (August 1928), p. 224. See also Harold Donaldson Eberlein, "Robert W. Vonnoh: Painter of Men," *Arts and Decoration* 2 (September 1912), pp. 381–83, 402, 404.

2. *Biographical History of Genessee County, Michigan* (Indianapolis: B. F. Bowen & Company, n.d.), pp. 267–68, curatorial files, Flint Institute of Arts.

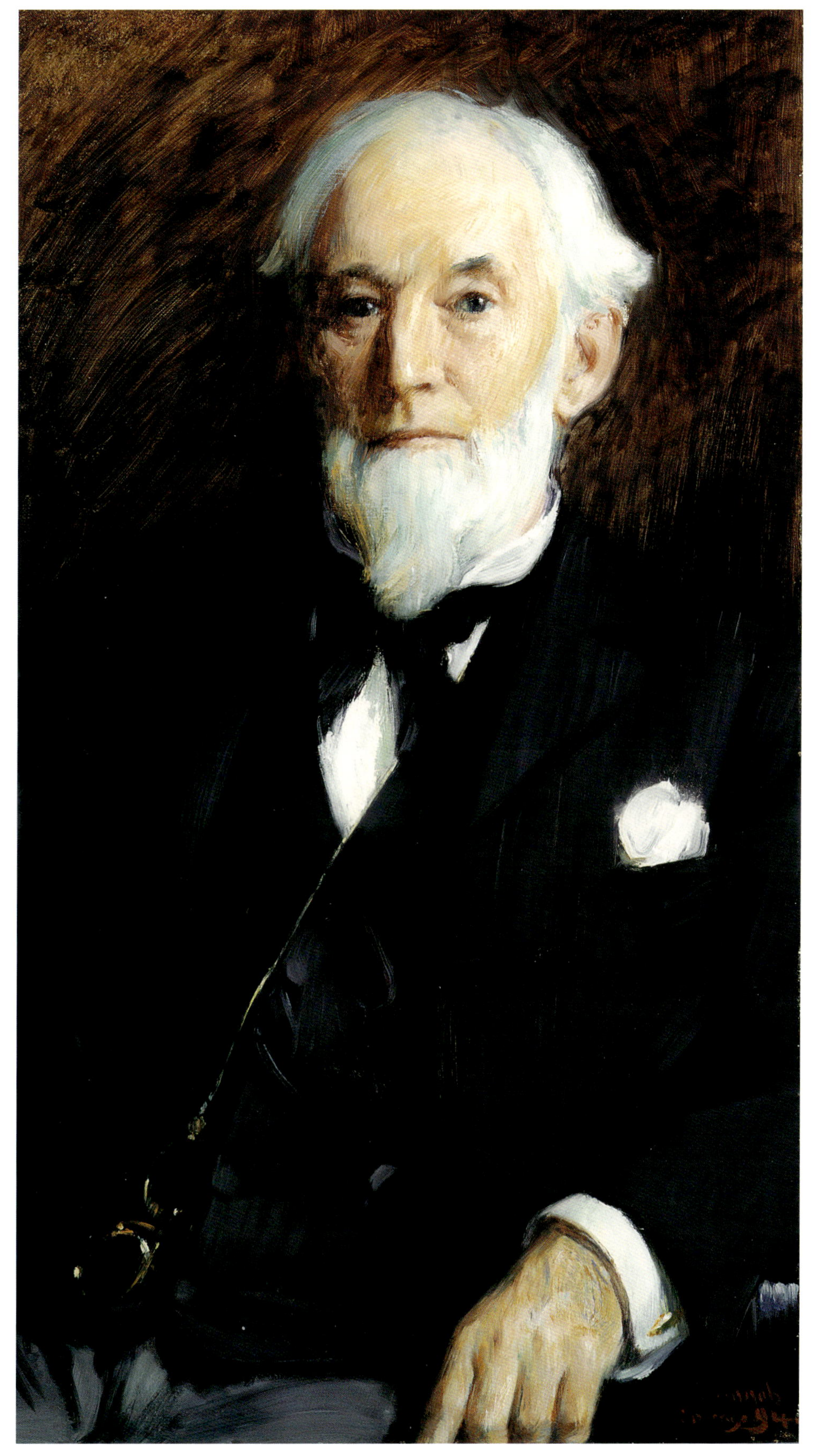

Mary Stevenson Cassatt AMERICAN 1844–1926

36 | *Lydia at a Tapestry Frame,* c. 1881

Oil on canvas, 25⅝ × 36⅜ in.

Signed lower right: *Mary Cassatt*

Gift of The Whiting Foundation (1967.32)

Mary Cassatt, born in the United States but an expatriate for most of her life, holds a unique position: she was the only American to be invited to exhibit with the French Impressionists. Born in Pennsylvania, she spent four years of her childhood—from 1851 to 1855—abroad. In 1860 Cassatt began her study of art at the Pennsylvania Academy of the Fine Arts, which she continued until 1862. She found the American system too constraining for a woman and so set out for Paris, arriving there in December 1865. She studied with the noted French painters Jean-Léon Gérôme and Thomas Couture until 1870, when she returned to the United States at the outbreak of the Franco-Prussian War.

Cassatt returned to Europe the following year and visited London, Paris, Parma, and Seville, where she studied works of the old masters. Her work was accepted at the Paris Salons of 1868, 1870, and 1872–76, but as her style became more decisively aligned with Impressionism she received increasingly harsh criticism, and in 1877 her submission to the Salon was rejected. Edgar Degas invited Cassatt to exhibit with the Impressionists, and she was one of only two known women (Berthe Morisot was the other) to show in the independent exhibitions. Later she recorded her response to Degas's overture: "At last I could work with complete independence, without considering the opinions of a jury. I had already recognized who were my true masters. I admired Manet, Courbet, and Degas. I hated conventional art. I began to live."[1] She participated in the Impressionist shows of 1879, 1880, 1881, and 1886, and her acquaintance with Degas developed into a close, lifelong friendship. Cassatt remained a resident of Paris and traveled to America infrequently, visiting in 1900, 1904, and, for the last time, in 1908–9. In 1909 she was elected an Associate of the National Academy of Design in New York, an honor she declined. By 1914 she was afflicted by failing eyesight, which prevented her from working in her remaining years.

By the late 1870s, she had fully embraced an Impressionist aesthetic. Although Degas and Manet were important influences in shaping her artistic style and outlook, Cassatt ultimately established her own subject matter and manner of painting. Unlike most women of the time, Cassatt was independent (she never married) and an active participant in a male-dominated profession. She was, however, especially drawn to female-oriented subject matter, especially that of the upper class, to which she herself belonged. Leisure pursuits such as boating, theater going, reading, needlework, and other social activities were favorite subjects, although she is best known for intimate portrayals of mothers and children. Cassatt often used members of her family as sitters and executed few portraits of men.

Her sister, Lydia, with whom she was close, served as model for a number of compositions. In addition to this celebrated painting in the Flint Institute of Arts' collection, other works include *The Garden* (1880; The Metropolitan Museum of Art, New York), *Lydia Seated in the Garden with a Dog in Her Lap* (c. 1880; private collection), *Lydia Seated on a Terrace Crocheting* (c. 1881–82; formerly collection of Charles and Joan Hermanowski), and *The Cup of Tea* (c. 1880; Museum of Fine Arts, Boston). Several of the works, including *Lydia at a Tapestry Frame,* attest to her sister's abilities at needlework, a skill that measured the refinement of upper-class women of the time. The Flint painting is notable in that it is the final portrait Cassatt painted of Lydia, who was ill with Bright's disease at the time the work was executed. Lydia died in November 1882, a short time after its completion.

Lydia at a Tapestry Frame is exceptional for Cassatt in its freedom of execution, evidenced by the loose brushwork and strokes of pigment applied to outline and accent certain details; this is readily apparent in the dark lines defining the tapestry frame. Typical of Cassatt's earlier technique, Lydia's face is carefully rendered in a more restrained and careful manner, as the artist captures her sister's frail condition, her peaked complexion, and subdued expression.

The high esteem in which Cassatt was held by the French Impressionists reflects her exceptional artistic abilities, and her work, with its concentration on the limited social sphere of the feminine world, had a singular place and significant impact on the future acceptance of women artists. VAL

1. Quoted in Adelyn Breeskin, *Mary Cassatt, 1844–1926,* exh. cat. (Washington, D.C.: National Gallery of Art, 1970), from Achille Segard, *Un Peintre des enfants et des mères,* 3d ed. (Paris, 1913), p. 2.

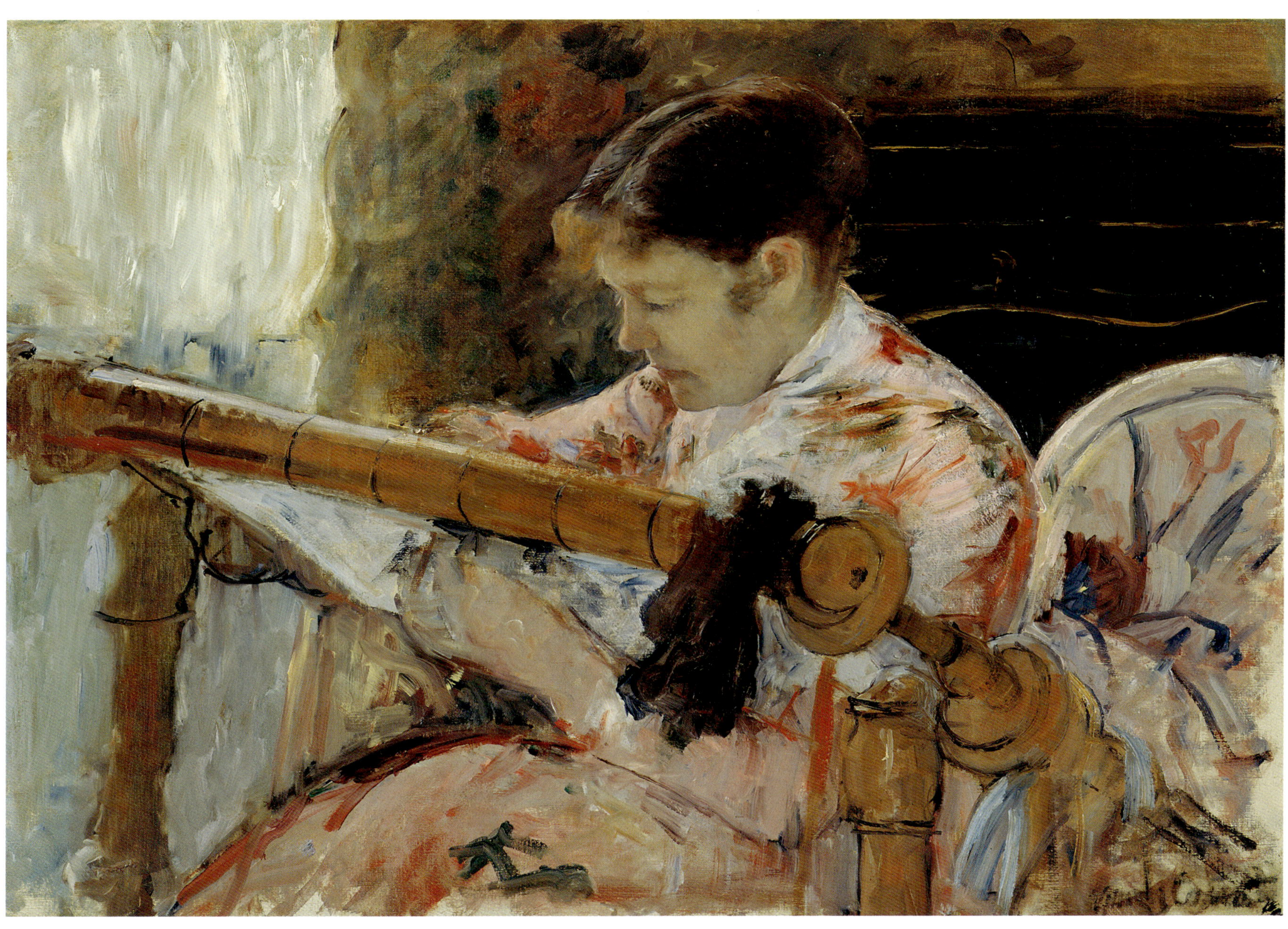

John Singer Sargent AMERICAN, BORN ITALY 1856–1925

37 | *Garden Study of the Vickers Children,* 1884

Oil on canvas, 54½ × 36 in.

Unsigned

Gift of the Viola E. Bray Charitable Trust via Mr. and Mrs. William L. Richards (1972.47)

Born in Florence, Italy, to American parents who had strong roots in the colonial Northeast, John Singer Sargent was a sophisticated and peripatetic expatriate who established his reputation with his flattering portraits of the American and European upper classes. Although he lived most of his life abroad, he retained his American citizenship and periodically worked in this country. He had an exceptional natural technical mastery and relied on keen powers of observation, yet his fluent style was born of exposure to cosmopolitan international influences and European training. He first studied art at the Accademia delle Belle Arti in Florence in 1873–74 and then worked in the atelier of the noted French portraitist Carolus-Duran for nearly five years, beginning in 1874. Additional instruction was received at the Ecole des Beaux-Arts in Paris in 1874, 1875, and 1877, as well as some classes with another French academic portraitist, Léon Bonnat. He also spent much time studying the old masters and the work of the eighteenth-century British masters of portraiture, Joshua Reynolds and Thomas Gainsborough.

The year 1884 saw the completion and first public exhibition of the artist's most well-known portrait, *Madame X,* a depiction of Madame Virginie Gautreau, the American wife of a prominent Parisian banker. When displayed at the Paris Salon, the work was widely condemned as scandalous, a reception that induced Sargent to exile himself to England.[1] Later that same year, Sargent painted *Garden Study of the Vickers Children,* an important transitional work in his career. He commenced painting *Garden Study* that summer, while visiting Mr. and Mrs. Albert Vickers at their home in Sussex, England. Although many of Sargent's portraits are in the grand manner, he also excelled at more informal portrayals. The composition, one of eleven portraits Sargent made of the Vickers family, depicts their children, Vincent and Dorothy, amid stalks of lilies as they water the flowers in a seemingly spontaneous outdoor scene. *Garden Study of the Vickers Children* is executed in a naturalistic manner, with broad, fluid brushstrokes and flat areas of unmodulated color. The lower portion of the composition is not fully resolved in its details, and the thinly transparent application of paint over the opaque ground color suggests dimensionality. This work would later serve as a prototype for *Carnation, Lily, Lily, Rose* (c. 1885–86; Tate Gallery, London), a masterwork done in an essentially Impressionist style.[2] *Carnation, Lily, Lily, Rose* was enthusiastically praised when displayed at the 1887 London Royal Academy exhibition, a response that helped rehabilitate Sargent's damaged reputation.

As Sargent regained popular acclaim, he reestablished his social position and was eventually embraced by British society. This acceptance ensured a stream of portrait commissions, which he worked at steadily, until he wearied of the genre. By 1907 Sargent declared to a friend, "I abhor and abjure them and hope never to do another, especially of the Upper Classes."[3] Some time would pass, however, before he was able to act on his resolve, but he began to concentrate on subjects that were more personally compelling and artistically more rewarding to him. In his later years he especially favored travel subjects and outdoor scenes done in watercolor and oil in a loose, spontaneous style. Sargent's last years were devoted to the completion of a series of American mural commissions for the Boston Public Library, the Museum of Fine Arts, Boston, and the Harvard University Library. VAL

1. For more on the events surrounding Sargent's move from Paris to London, see Albert Boime, "Sargent in Paris and London: A Portrait of the Artist as Dorian Gray," in *John Singer Sargent,* exh. cat. (New York: Whitney Museum of American Art, 1986), pp. 88–96.

2. *Carnation, Lily, Lily, Rose,* although based in a general way on some basic artistic ideas Sargent was exploring in *Garden Study of the Vickers Children,* is less about portraiture than the Flint painting and is a more complex and fully resolved composition. *Carnation, Lily, Lily, Rose* depicts different subjects and a different locale than the earlier work—it was painted in Broadway, in the Cotswolds, during the summers of 1885 and 1886, while Sargent was visiting his friend, the artist Frank Millet. The models for the work—Kate, the daughter of Millet, and also two daughters of the illustrator Frederick Barnard—are depicted in Millet's garden lighting Japanese paper lanterns.

3. John Singer Sargent to Ralph Curtis, quoted in Stanley Olsen, *John Singer Sargent: His Portraits* (London: Barrie and Jenkins, 1986), p. 228.

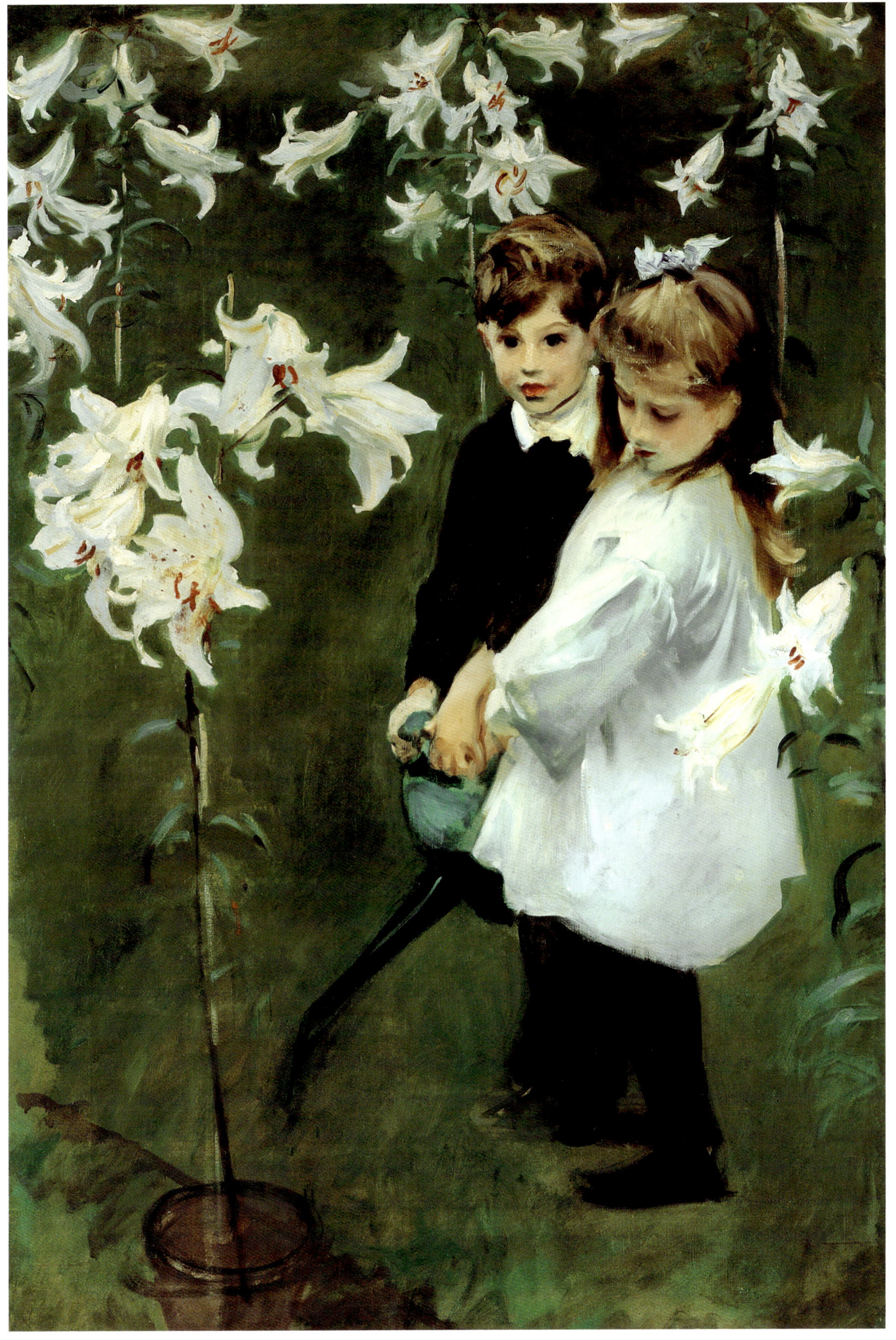

(Frederick) Childe Hassam AMERICAN 1859–1935

38 | *Newport Waterfront,* 1901

Oil on canvas, 26¼ × 24⅛ in.

Signed and dated lower right: *Childe Hassam 1901*

Gift of The Whiting Foundation through Mr. and Mrs. Donald E. Johnson (1972.31)

Childe Hassam, one of the foremost American Impressionists, was a versatile and prolific artist. He excelled in several media—oil, watercolor, pastel—and was also a skilled printmaker. Of his varied subject matter, he is especially noted for New England land- and seascapes as well as urban scenes of Boston and New York.

Hassam was born in Dorcester, Massachusetts, and was apprenticed to a wood engraver in Boston in 1879. He later established his own studio and worked as a professional illustrator. In 1881 he studied art at the Lowell Institute and had his first solo show, composed of watercolors, at a Boston gallery the next year. He briefly visited Europe for the first time in 1883 and returned in 1886 for an extended stay, enrolling at the Académie Julian in Paris. There he studied under Gustave Boulanger and Jules-Joseph Lefebvre and showed at the 1888 Paris Salon and the 1889 Paris Universal Exposition, where he won medals. Returning to America in 1889, he settled in New York City, bringing with him the influence of the French Impressionists, whose ideas he had begun to incorporate into his art. He traveled often, especially in the Northeast and to Europe. A frequent exhibitor at the National Academy of Design, Hassam was elected an Associate in 1902 and an Academician in 1906. He was also a key figure in The Ten, a group of artists who were largely associated with Impressionism, who showed together regularly from 1898 until they disbanded in 1919.

Newport Waterfront is one of a group of harbor scenes Hassam executed of Gloucester, Provincetown, and Newport. He appears to have commenced painting these views about 1890, when he first visited Gloucester, north of Boston, and he produced them over the ensuing years. In 1900 he went to Provincetown, at the tip of Cape Cod, and in September and October 1901 to Newport, Rhode Island. New England coastal towns held a particular allure for Hassam; as his biographer observed: "How he loved the whole New England coast. . . . To many an attentive eye, the familiar Hassam magic has altered and enhanced the Gloucester scene, the Provincetown scene, the Newport scene. Those places transcended their former selves, because the invisible had been made visible through the painter's art."[1]

Newport Waterfront pictures the quaint historic town from Goat Island, looking landward to the harbor. The blue sky is punctuated by the strong verticality of the boat masts and the white colonial-style church steeple. The work depicts nearly the same view as two other compositions, *Newport, October Sundown* (private collection) and *Catboats, Newport* (Pennsylvania Academy of the Fine Arts, Philadelphia), both painted in 1901. *Catboats, Newport,* which focuses on schooners in the harbor, was shown at the Pennsylvania Academy annual exhibition in 1902. *Newport, October Sundown* depicts dusk on a brisk, cloudless fall day, whereas the Flint and Pennsylvania Academy paintings are daytime scenes taken from a more distant vantage point. The steeple of Trinity Church and the same architectural landmarks and landscape are evident in the three compositions, and all are portrayed from a somewhat elevated perspective that allows the viewer to fully survey the scene.

The harbor paintings appear to have been executed spontaneously, in part due to the artist's Impressionist technique. Extant studies, however, reveal that these works were actually carefully conceived compositions.[2] Hassam's use of Impressionist daubs of light, vivid colors applied to the canvas to define form is particularly evident in *Newport Waterfront.* He remained loyal to the Impressionist aesthetic approach throughout his career, well past its vogue and into the twentieth century. VAL

1. Adeline Adams, *Childe Hassam* (New York: American Academy of Arts and Letters, 1938), p. 94.

2. Warren Adelson et al., *Childe Hassam: Impressionist* (New York: Abbeville Press, 1999), p. 210. It is noted in this publication that a group of related drawings is in the collection of the Carnegie Museum of Art, Pittsburgh.

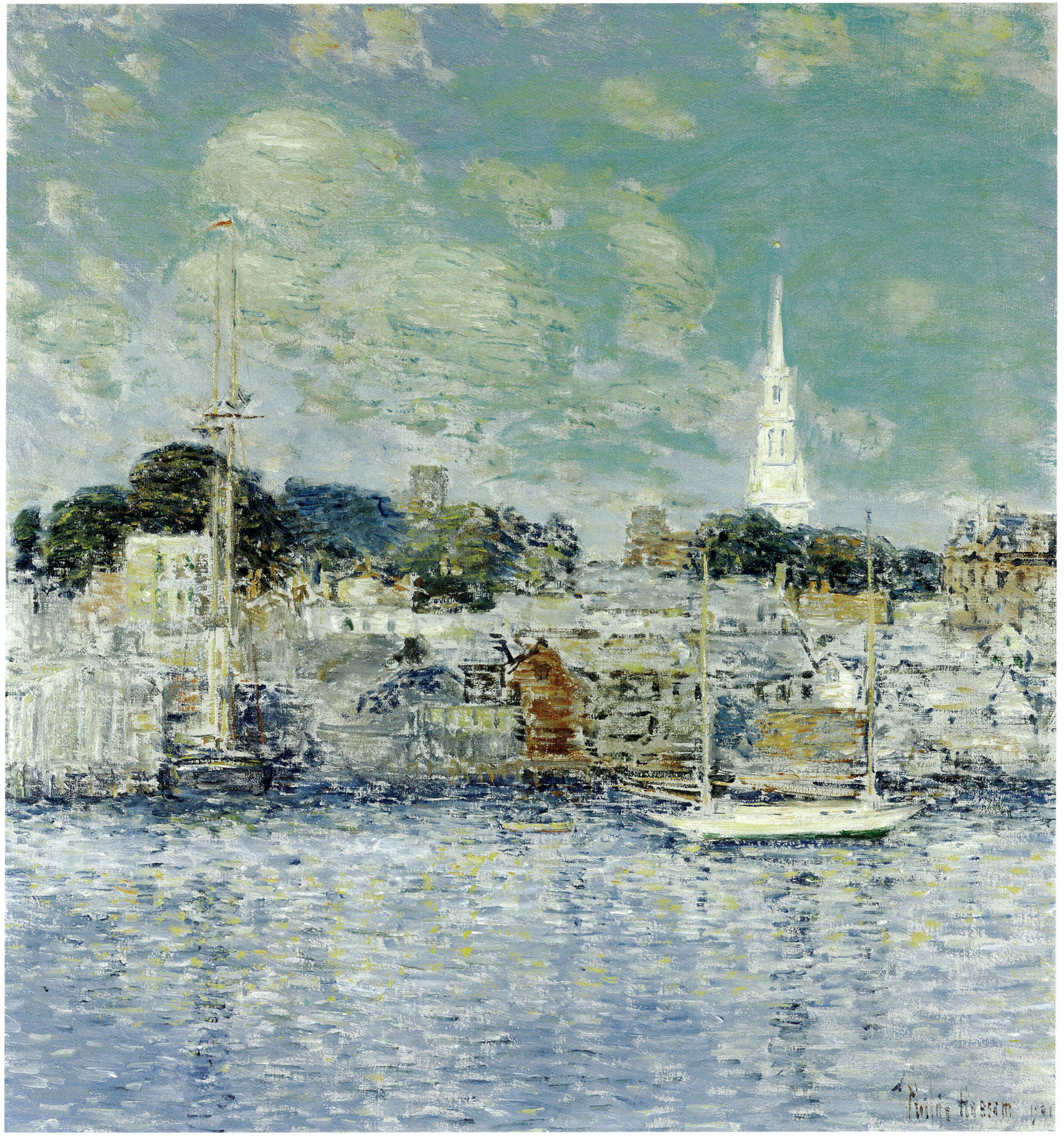

Frederick Carl Frieseke AMERICAN 1874–1939

39 | *Two Women on the Grass,* c. 1914 or earlier

Oil on board, 18 × 23⅜ in.

Signed lower left: *F C Frieseke*

Gift of David M. and Patrick Martin in memory of Virginia Davison Martin, by exchange, gift of Mr. Max Greenfield, by exchange, gift of Mr. and Mrs. Donald E. Johnson, by exchange, gift of Gertrude and Leonard Kasle, by exchange, gift of Mrs. Bernhard Stroh, by exchange, and gift of Dr. Julius Stone, by exchange (2002.1)

Born in Ossowa, Michigan, the Impressionist painter Frederick Frieseke was among the many turn-of-the-century Americans who sought and found his artistic voice in France. Frieseke first pursued his creative interests at the Art Institute of Chicago and the Art Students League in New York. He began his career as a cartoonist for such periodicals as *Puck, Truth,* and the *New York Times.* In 1897 Frieseke set sail for Europe and eventually settled in France, where he would spend most of his adult life and where he was encouraged by his teachers at the Académie Julian and at James McNeill Whistler's Académie Carmen, both in Paris, to devote himself to painting.

In Paris, Frieseke, like so many others who were drawn to this thriving artistic and cultural world capital, found a supportive and engaged art community and institutions as well as a significant American expatriate contingent. This American presence was important to Frieseke throughout his life and, in particular, during the summers when he joined fellow Americans at artists' colonies, first at Le Pouldu in Brittany (1901) and then in Giverny (1905–20). Beginning about 1886 with the arrival of the painters Theodore Robinson and Willard Metcalf, Giverny became an important gathering place for American artists, who were initially drawn to the site because of the presence there of Claude Monet. While the roster of artists at Giverny changed and expanded over the years, a general dedication to plein-air painting and Impressionist brushstrokes and palette remained relatively constant throughout Frieseke's long tenure at the colony.

Frieseke's *Two Women on the Grass* is representative of his Giverny output in its emphasis on representing light and color patterns and in its focus on figures, more specifically women, out-of-doors and integrated within a natural setting. Using a staccato application of paint, particularly in rendering the foliage that surrounds the figures, and a light palette of whites, pinks, lavenders, greens, yellows, and blues, Frieseke juxtaposes two women, one clothed and bejeweled and the other completely nude save for her bathing turban. Here, as he often does, Frieseke pursues the decorative, which in his oeuvre is interchangeable with the feminine, by identifying and exaggerating the patterns of the natural world in relation to the bodies, accessories, and clothing of women. In general, his paintings suggest little interest in depicting women as individuals with personalities, emotions, or thoughts. Instead, his female figures are primarily vehicles for studying color and light.

Frieseke repeatedly paints a feminine world characterized by quiet, stillness, isolation, and serenity. Whether his figures are rendered in private gardens or on riverbanks, they occupy a civilized arcadia that merges the contemplative and restful potential of nature with certain bourgeois material comforts, including parasols and jewelry that serve both aesthetic and utilitarian purposes. *Two Women on the Grass* exemplifies Frieseke's interest in this type of arcadia, with the women allegorically representing civilization and nature. Here, civilization appears in the guise of the clothed woman who treads with her parasol carefully through the oddly compressed space. She is contrasted with the personification of nature, the nude woman who turns her back on the viewer. MK

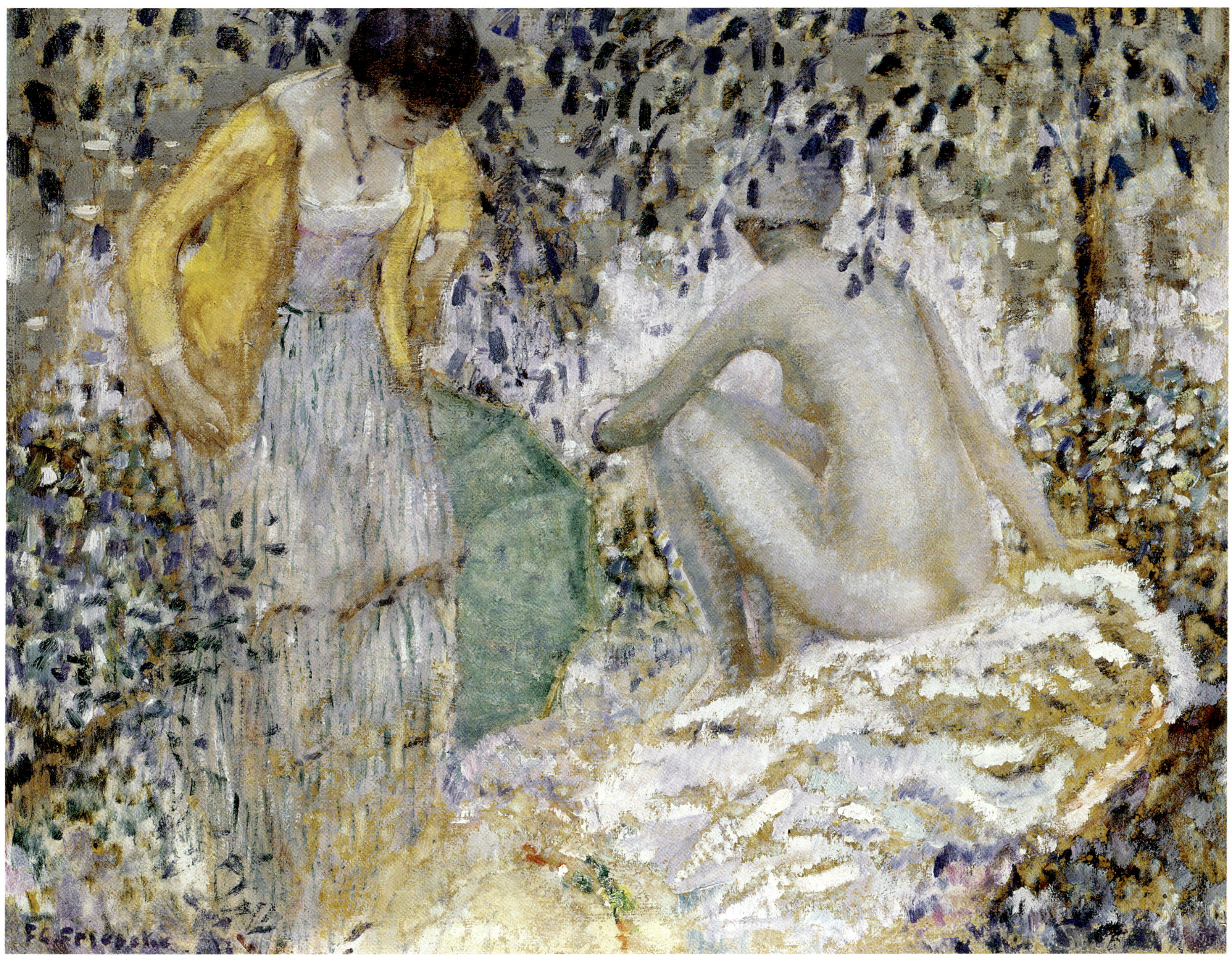

William A. Harper AMERICAN, BORN CANADA 1873–1910

40 | *French Landscape,* c. 1905–9

Oil on canvas, 13⅝ × 11⅛ in.

Signed lower right: *W. A. Harper*

Gift of the Founders Society (2000.65)

Although one the most important African American artists of the late nineteenth and early twentieth century, relatively little is known about William Harper. What documentation is available is both vague and contradictory, but it is known that he actively exhibited, won awards for his work, and traveled abroad, to France, England, and Mexico. It is also clear that he left behind an important and accomplished body of work. Moreover, the success he achieved in his lifetime, despite his working-class origins and the tremendous obstacles facing an African American not long after the Civil War, is a testament to his considerable talent as an artist.

Harper, born near Cayuga, Ontario, moved with his family to the United States in either 1881 or 1885. They settled on a farm in Illinois, where he spent the remainder of his youth. It was in this pastoral setting that he developed his love of nature and decided to become an artist.[1] After spending some time at a college in Jacksonville, Illinois, Harper began his art education at the Art Institute of Chicago in 1895, ultimately graduating with second honors in 1901. Moving to Houston in 1902, Harper taught drawing in the public schools until 1903, when he left for France. He would remain there until 1905, returning to America in 1907–8.[2] It was during one of these stays abroad that he met and became a pupil of Henry Ossawa Tanner (1859–1937),[3] who was the most-established African American artist of the nineteenth century. Harper studied with Tanner for a relatively short period of time, but the influence of the older artist can nevertheless be seen in Harper's oeuvre. The work of the Barbizon painters and the Impressionists also had a significant impact on Harper's painting, most notably the Impressionists' use of light and color. In addition, Harper was able to meet and work with the American artists William Wendt and Charles Francis Browne while in France.

At some point a date of about 1905 was assigned to *French Landscape.* While Harper's earlier style has a definite Barbizon influence, the more impressionistic qualities of his later work—quick brushstrokes, a sense of movement in the composition, and an Impressionist palette—dominate this painting. Therefore, a date of 1907–9, after his return to the United States, may be more accurate.

Harper's work was frequently exhibited. Forty-three paintings were shown at the Art Institute of Chicago over a period of eight years, from 1903 until his death in 1910. He was included in the Art Institute's Annual Exhibition of American Paintings and Sculpture and its Annual Exhibition of Works by Artists of Chicago and Vicinity. He also showed at the Chicago Municipal Art League in 1905 and 1908, winning awards at both exhibitions—from the Art League in 1905 and first prize from the Fortnightly Club in 1908—and exhibited at the Pennsylvania Academy of the Fine Arts in 1909. Such a full schedule is indicative of the acceptance he received and the remarkable position he held in the art world of his time.

Harper died at the tragically young age of thirty-seven, at the American Hospital in Mexico City. A memorial exhibition and sale of sixty of his paintings were held at the Art Institute of Chicago four months after his death. *French Landscape* may have been included in that exhibition, but it is impossible to confirm with the available extant documentation.[4] MMF

1. Barbara A. Hudson, *Walter O. Evans Collection of African American Art,* exh. cat. (Savannah, Ga.: Beach Institute, King-Tisbell Museum, 1991), p. 19.

2. Harper may have been awarded a fellowship to study in Europe; see *Henry O. Tanner, William A. Harper, William E. Scott: A Mentor and His Influence,* exh. cat. (Washington, D.C.: Evan-Tibbs Collection, 1985), p. 12.

3. The date of Harper and Tanner's meeting is uncertain; it is variously reported as 1903–5 and 1907–8.

4. At least thirteen descriptive titles could refer to the Flint's *French Landscape;* see *Exhibition of Paintings by William A. Harper,* exh. cat. (Chicago: The Art Institute of Chicago, 1910).

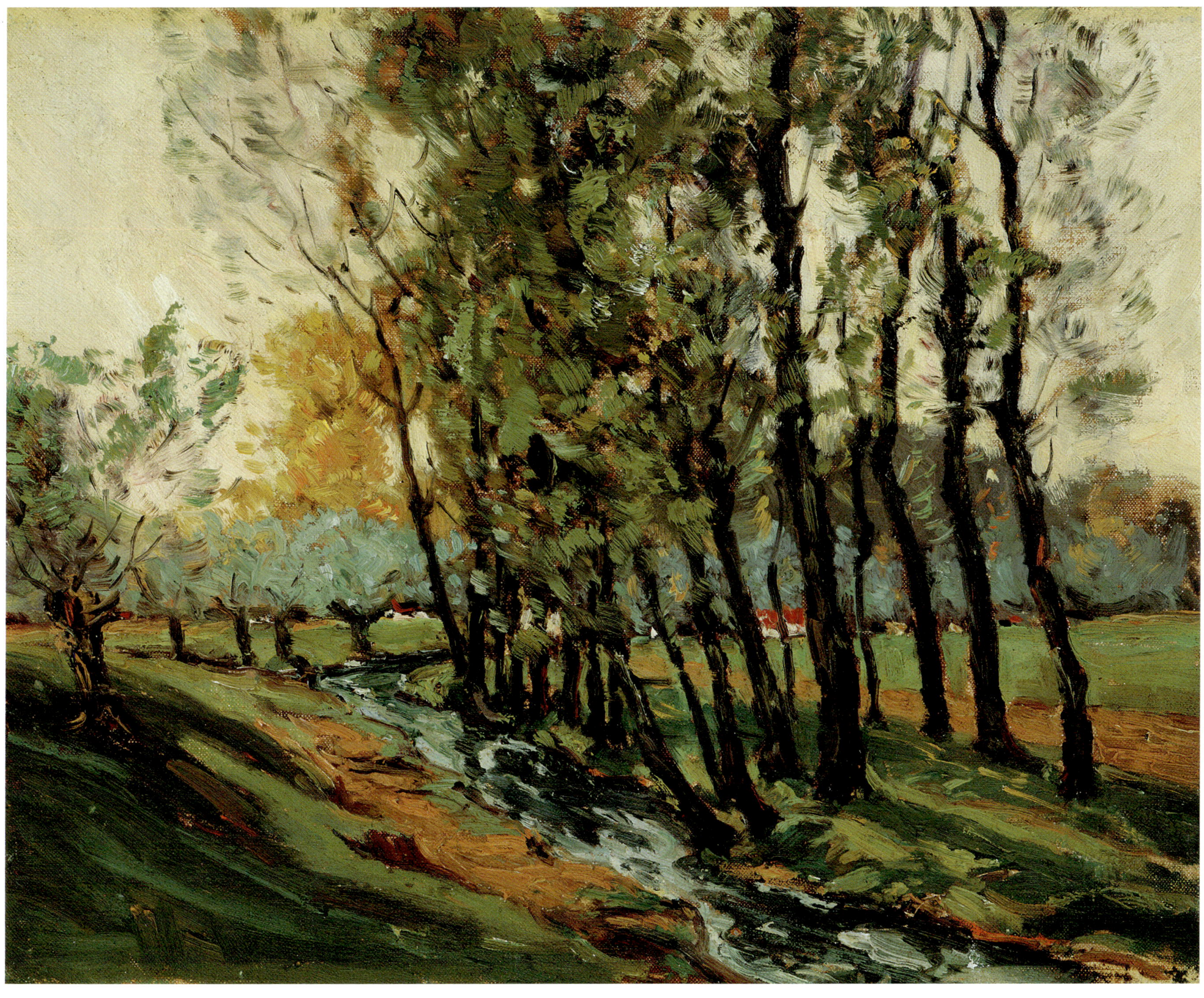

Richard Hayley Lever AMERICAN, BORN AUSTRALIA 1876–1958

41 | *Flowers,* n.d.

Oil on canvas, 14½ × 18¼ in.
Signed lower left: *Hayley Lever*
Gift of Mrs. Ralph Harman Booth (1939.5)

The Australian-born Hayley Lever was in many respects a citizen of the world, one who made important artistic associations in Europe and America while refusing to pigeonhole himself by identifying with a specific group or style. Lever moved from his birthplace of Adelaide, Australia, to London in 1893. About 1900 he settled at the artists' colony of St. Ives in Cornwall, where he focused on painting the seascapes and landscapes for which he is best known. In 1911 the American Impressionist Ernest Lawson, a member of The Eight and a frequent visitor to the colony at St. Ives, persuaded Lever to immigrate to the United States.

In America Lever became a successful painter and teacher who taught at the Art Students League and conducted summer classes in Gloucester, Massachusetts. An active participant in the New York art community, Lever exhibited at the Whitney Studio Club and the Macbeth Gallery and coorganized the New Society of Artists with Robert Henri, George Bellows, and John Sloan. Despite his friendship with artists connected to The Eight and the Ashcan School, Lever pursued a more independent path, continuing to make expressive, often boldly painted, impressionistic canvases.

Lever's exposure to the work of Vincent van Gogh significantly influenced the development of his style. His own paintings embraced an expressiveness similar to that of van Gogh's and he, too, appreciated and emulated the stylization, flatness, asymmetry, and decorativeness found in Japanese prints. In *Flowers,* Lever presents a vigorously painted vase of chrysanthemums, placed asymmetrically in the picture space. His appreciation for Japanese art may have influenced the subject matter of *Flowers* in a literal way, as the chrysanthemum has an important place in the history and culture of Japan. A popular and prevalent motif, chrysanthemums were featured on the Japanese imperial crest and on the official seals of prominent families.

In *Flowers,* Lever employs a muted palette of whites, lavenders, greens, and spots of pink and focuses on blooms that are neither perfect nor perfectly arranged. On the right side of the composition, for example, several flowers droop toward the simple table. This positioning and the flowers' imperfections allow him to inject a certain amount of character into the image and to accomplish the difficult feat of suggesting movement in a *still* life. The drooping flowers may also be an acknowledgment that the chrysanthemum is a flower that blooms in the fall, a season traditionally associated with the end of life. Moreover, Lever may be reiterating the flowers' allusion to death in his use of lavender tones, a color associated with mourning rituals from the Victorian period until World War I.
MK

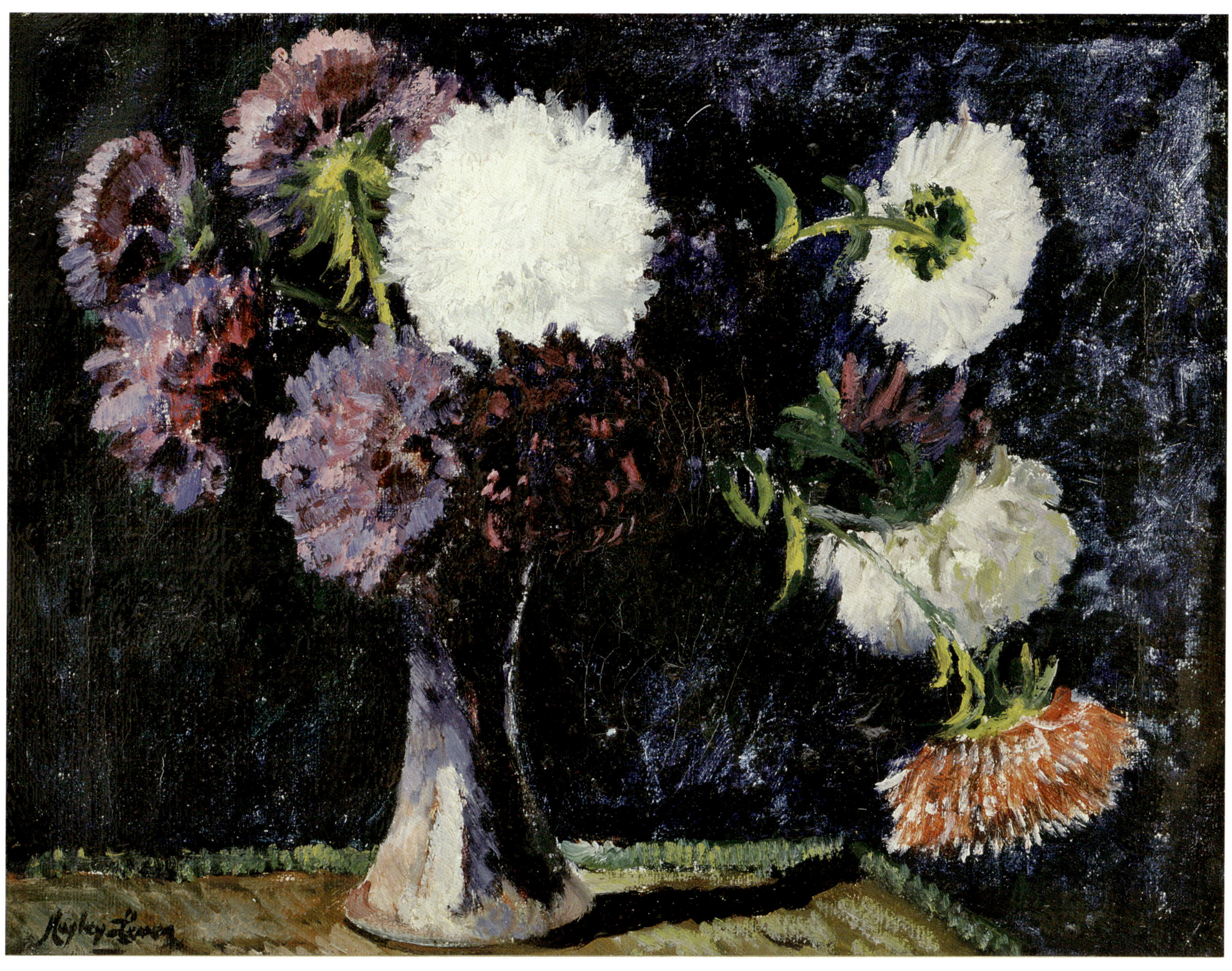

William Wendt AMERICAN, BORN GERMANY 1865–1946

42 | *Rocks and Sea,* c. 1930–40

Oil on canvas, 28 × 36 in.

Signed lower right: *WM Wendt*

Gift of Mr. and Mrs. Jerome O. Eddy (1940.2)

William Wendt, known as the dean of Southern California landscape painters, was born in Bentzen, Germany. His family came to the United States in 1880, when he was fifteen, and settled in Chicago. Though largely self-taught—his training consisted of two evening sessions at the School of the Art Institute of Chicago—he established himself as a successful artist quite early in his career. He won the Yerkes Prize at the Chicago Society of Artists in 1893, the first of many awards he garnered from a variety of arts organizations and at expositions during his long career.

Wendt first visited California, the state with which he is most identified, in 1894 and moved to Los Angeles twelve years later with his wife, the sculptor Julia Bracken. There he became one of the founding members of the California Art Club, an influential regional organization, serving as its president from 1911 to 1916 and again in 1918. He was also elected an Associate of the National Academy of Design in New York, where he was a consistent exhibitor. Wendt built a second studio in Laguna Beach in 1918, relocating there permanently about 1923.

In his work, Wendt focused on pure landscape subjects, which progressed from a Tonalist approach to an increasingly bold Impressionist style. His paintings are characterized by a pronounced contrast of light and shadow, vigorous brushwork, and strong colors, especially green, gold, and orange, which he most often employed to depict the hills of the California chaparral.

Though recognized for his compositions of the Southern California landscape, Wendt also excelled at marine subjects like *Rocks and Sea,* a theme he pictured with more frequency after his move to Laguna Beach. *Rocks and Sea,* by highlighting a portion of a panoramic view, captures both a sense of intimacy and a sense of monumentality. The date ascribed to this work is based on stylistic criteria, as his later work exhibits rougher and choppier brushwork with less modulated color transitions. Though in the end an Impressionist, Wendt was also a romantic who celebrated the power of nature in his scenes depicting the Far West, often imbuing them with religious and spiritual overtones. VAL

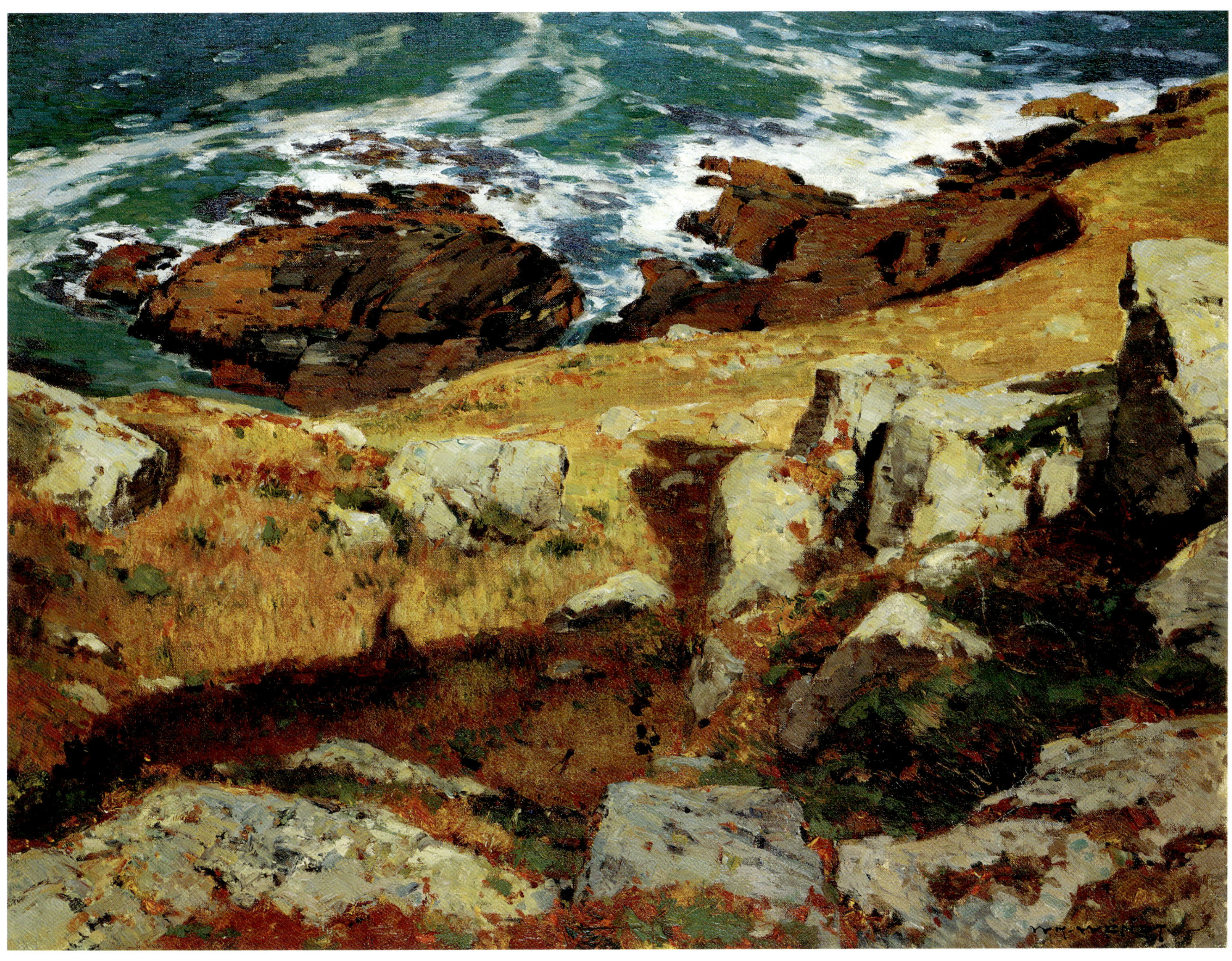

Charles Webster Hawthorne AMERICAN 1872–1930

43 | *Boy with Pitcher,* n.d.

Oil on canvas, 30 × 25 in.

Unsigned

Gift of the Founders Society (2002.10)

Charles Webster Hawthorne achieved a reputation as an extraordinary portrait and figure painter. His works often suggest a paradoxical appreciation for both the light effects of the Impressionists and the tonalities and bravura handling of such old masters as Frans Hals, whose paintings he studied and admired during a trip to the Netherlands in 1898. At the age of eighteen, Hawthorne moved from his home in Richmond, Maine, to New York City, where he began lessons at the Art Students League. To support himself, Hawthorne, the son of a sea captain, found work on the docks of New York, a profession he would eventually leave to devote himself more completely to his art. In 1896 he worked with the Impressionist painter William Merritt Chase at Chase's summer school in Shinnecock, Long Island. His friendship with the artist resulted in the pair's collaboration on the opening of Chase's New York School of Art. Hawthorne also became an important teacher, opening his own school, the Cape Cod School of Art, in Provincetown, Massachusetts, in 1899.

Hawthorne's *Boy with Pitcher* is a striking representation of a young working-class boy, who appears to be an apprentice in a ceramic workshop. The extremely fair, gap-toothed child, rendered with whites and buttery yellows, wears a white apron and holds a white ceramic vase, decorated with a delicate floral motif. Although the source of light is external to the painting, the boy effectively illuminates the composition as he emerges from the dark, murky background. Hawthorne's fascination with light and its appearance indoors is apparent in many of his canvases, and he is known to have been particularly interested in instructing his students about achieving light effects: "Make your canvases drip with sunlight. Exaggerate to give the impression inside that you feel outside."[1]

Boy with Pitcher revisits a theme particularly popular with such American artists as Chase and Frank Duveneck, whose tenures in Munich in the 1870s resulted in a number of pictures featuring young apprentices. Hawthorne's sensitive representation of the boy also recalls the many perceptive and insightful portraits of children painted by his slightly older contemporary, Robert Henri. Like Henri, Hawthorne succeeds in depicting a child without sentimentality and suggests, albeit in a vague way, something of the boy's interior life. Although the apron and the pitcher indicate that he is in the midst of work, his faraway gaze implies that he has become somewhat mentally distracted from his tasks, perhaps performing them automatically while his mind wanders. Despite the possibility that the child has been forced to work at a very young age, Hawthorne suggests that he does not suffer either physically or emotionally. Allowing the boy to maintain a youthful gentleness and naïveté, Hawthorne's painting does not reflect the concerns over child labor that were increasingly voiced at the turn of the century.[2] MK

1. Charles Webster Hawthorne, "Hawthorne on Painting," reprinted in Richard Mühlberger, *Charles Webster Hawthorne: Paintings and Watercolors* (Chesterfield, Mass., 1999), p. 93. Hawthorne's essay was first published in 1938.

2. The National Child Labor Committee was established in 1904, and the first Federal child labor bill was proposed in 1906.

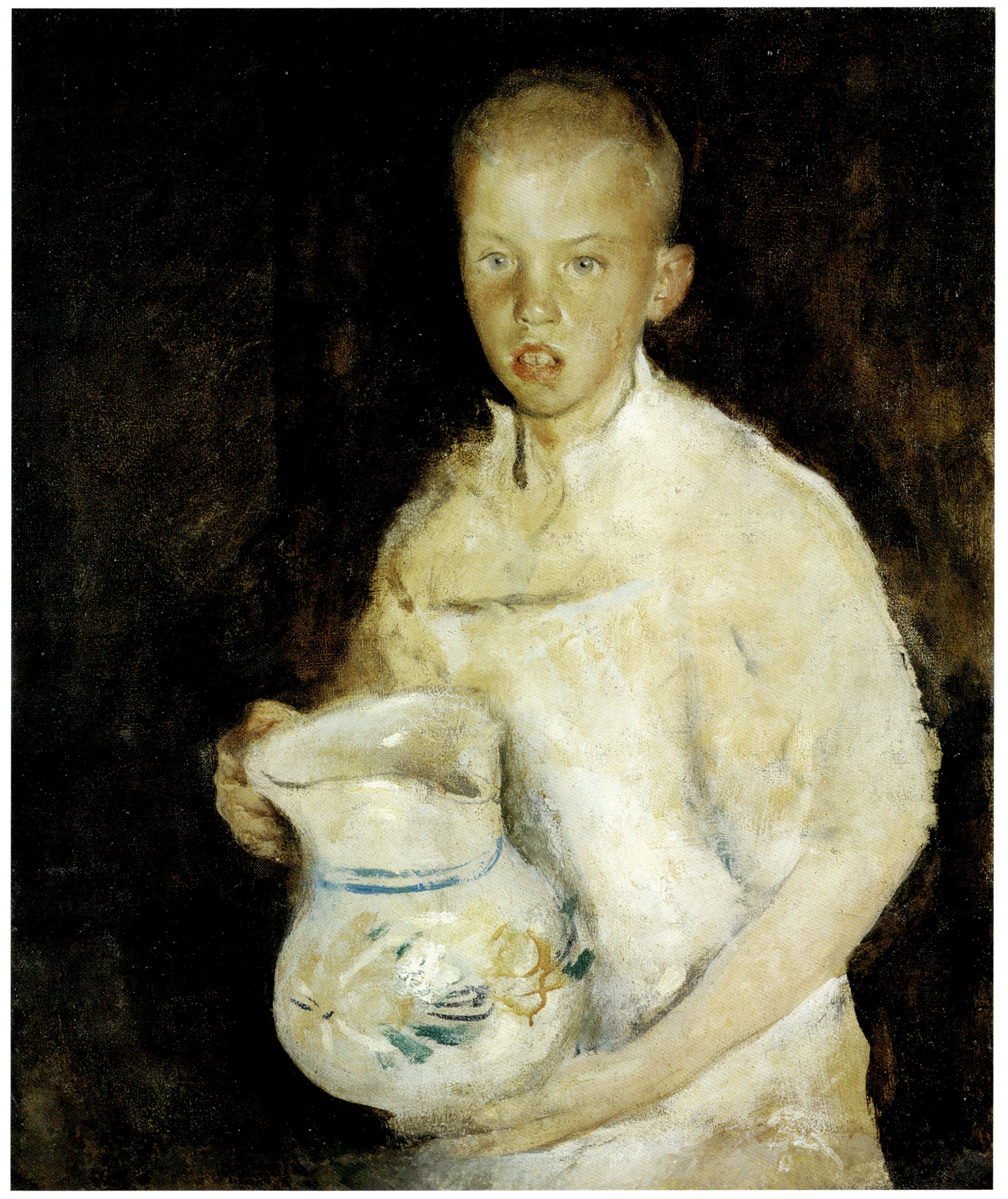

Robert Henri AMERICAN 1865–1929

44 | *Catharine,* 1924

Oil on canvas, 24½ × 20⅜ in.

Signed lower left: *ROBERT HENRI*; inscribed on verso: *Robert Henri "Catharine" 197M*

Gift of James W. Sibley in memory of Harriet Cumings Sibley (1984.7)

Robert Henri, the influential portrait painter, teacher, and exhibition organizer, is particularly noted for his depictions of Irish children, such as *Catharine,* which he painted in Ireland in 1924. Henri was born in Cincinnati and spent his formative years in Cozad, Nebraska. He entered the Pennsylvania Academy of the Fine Arts in 1886 and studied there intermittently with Thomas Anshutz, Robert Vonnoh, and Thomas Hovenden. He left for Europe in 1888 and enrolled in the Académie Julian in Paris. In 1891 he was admitted to the Ecole des Beaux-Arts but returned to America later that year to study again at the Pennsylvania Academy. He continued to travel to Europe, however, making repeated visits over the next few years. In 1900 he moved from Philadelphia to New York City. To earn money he taught at numerous institutions, including The New York School of Art and the Art Students League. He was extremely supportive of other artists and was active in organizing alternative exhibitions, including the famed exhibition of The Eight in 1908, the 1910 Exhibition of Independent Artists, and the MacDowell Club exhibitions.

Henri first visited Ireland in 1913, following the Armory Show. He recounted that it was a happy accident that led him to visit the remote island of Achill in County Mayo in northwestern Ireland—he simply picked it out on a map.[1] Though by nature a peripatetic traveler, Henri was probably also drawn to Ireland because his second wife, Marjorie, was of Irish descent, and his friend John Butler Yeats, father of the famous poet, often spoke of it. Dire financial straits and the outbreak of World War I prevented Henri from traveling abroad after his 1913 visit, but in 1923 his mother died and an inheritance from her gave him financial freedom. He left for Madrid that year and stayed for eight months before traveling back to Achill Island in 1924, where he remained from May to November. It was toward the end of this visit that Henri painted *Catharine.*

Henri's late career, which spans the period from 1924 until he ceased painting in 1928 due to failing health, was devoted to painting the children of the outlying fishing village of Dooagh on Achill Island. He had a continuing fascination with and respect for his youthful subjects, seeing in them an optimism, simplicity, and wisdom that he conveyed in his portrayals. He remarked that "If you paint children you must have no patronizing attitude toward them. Whoever approaches a child without humility, without wonderment and without infinite respect, misses . . . what is before him. . . ."[2] Henri's paintings of Irish children were the manifestation of his lifelong passion for representing the essential spirit of each individual he depicted. He noted a special vitality in the Irish children and expressed the "hope that some of this emotion will find its way into what I tell of Achill folk in my portraits."[3]

Catharine is an exceptional portrait, notable for its colorful palette, with its interplay of purple, reddish orange, and bright green accents, and for the way Henri captures the subject's innocence. The free and seemingly effortless technique seen in this likeness is typical of Henri's late Irish portraits. Works such as *Catharine* are deceptive in this respect, for they are actually carefully conceived compositions, the result of years of study and experimentation with various color and compositional theories and approaches. VAL

1. Mary L. Alexander, *Cincinnati Daily Times-Star,* 10 March 1926, clipping file, estate of Robert Henri, Le Clair Family Collection; Henri to Alice Klauber, 11 March 1914, Klauber Papers, Archives, San Diego Museum of Art.

2. Robert Henri, *The Art Spirit,* ed. Margery Ryerson (1923; reprint, New York: Harper & Row, 1984), pp. 237–38.

3. Violet Organ, "Robert Henri: His Life and Letters," n.d., p. 118, estate of Robert Henri, Le Clair Family Collection.

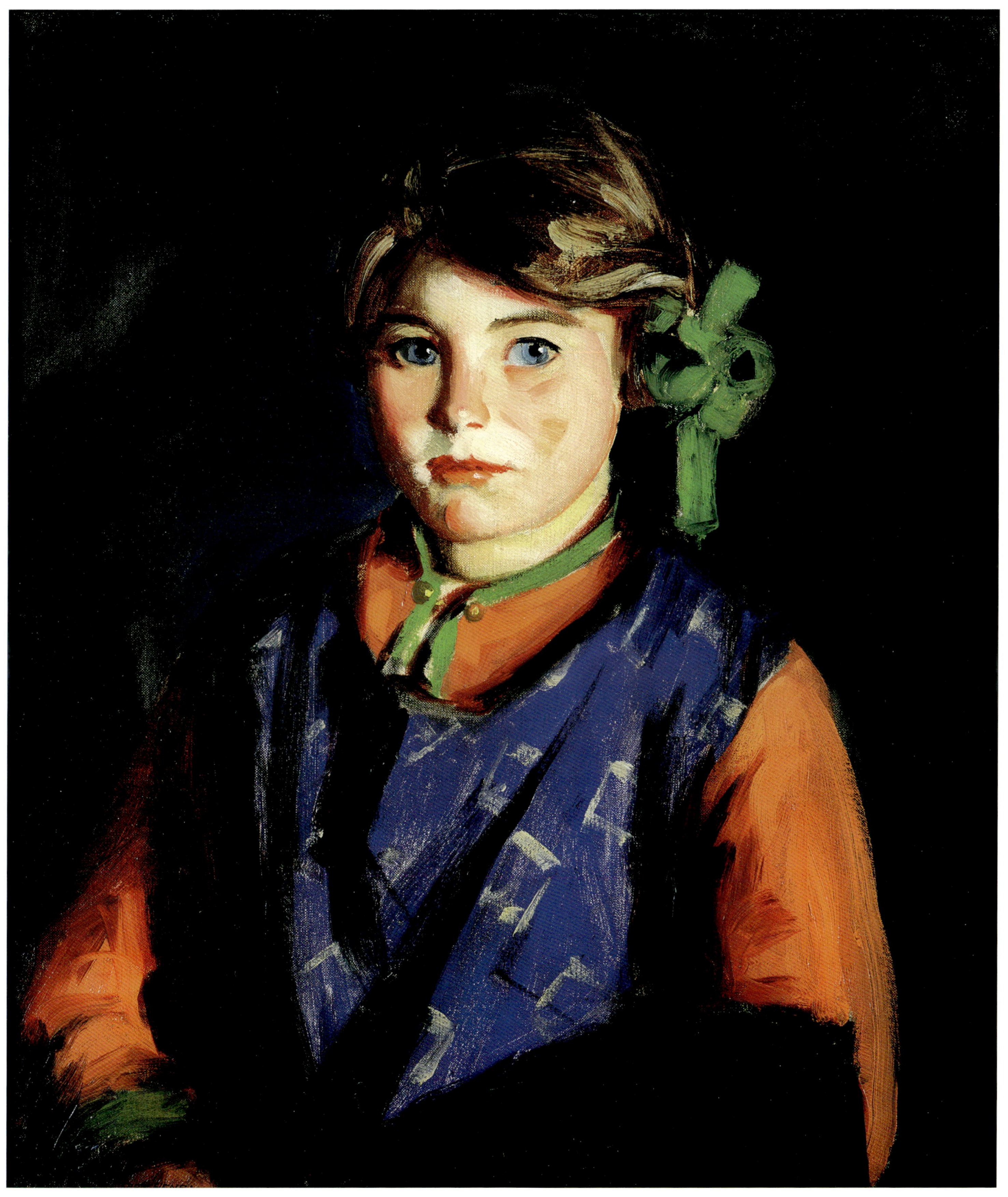

Arthur B. Davies AMERICAN 1862–1928

45 | *Four Figures,* 1911

Oil on canvas, 16 × 20 in.
Signed lower right: *Arthur B. Davies*
Gift of the Founders Society (1997.92)

46 | *Three Male Figures—A Study,* n.d.

Pastel on brown paper, 13¼ × 10¾ in.
Signed lower left: *Arthur B. Davies*
Gift of Mr. and Mrs. Ryerson (1939.9)

Born in Utica, New York, Arthur B. Davies was an imaginative and artistic child. When his family relocated to Chicago in 1879, he attended the Chicago Academy of Design. From 1880 to 1882 he worked in Mexico as an engineering draftsman. He returned to Chicago and studied briefly at the Art Institute before moving to New York in 1886. There he studied art, taking classes at the Art Students League and making his living as a magazine illustrator. He had his first solo show in 1896 at Macbeth Galleries in New York and embarked on a long-term relationship with that firm. Davies was working in a unique style that differed considerably from that of his contemporaries, and he attracted a following that included a number of important and wealthy patrons. He made several excursions abroad and became enamored of the new developments in contemporary art to which he was exposed during these visits.

Though he did not work in a realist style, Davies became allied with Robert Henri and his followers, who were rebelling against the conservative academic ideas of the National Academy of Design. Like several other artists in Henri's circle, Davies's nomination as an Associate of the Academy in 1907 was rejected. He did show at the National Academy in 1908 but afterward sought other exhibition venues. The Academy's rejection helped galvanize Davies's interest in independent causes, and he worked closely with Henri on the 1910 Exhibition of Independent Artists. Ideological differences between Henri and Davies, however, soon precipitated a rift between them. Davies continued to be aligned with independent artists and became one of the principals in the organization of the Armory Show, which introduced art of the European avant-garde to American audiences. He was also elected president of the Association of American Painters and Sculptors, the administrative body that orchestrated the Armory Show. In addition to painting and organizing exhibitions, Davies was a prolific graphic artist who produced a sizable body of drawings and prints, including pastels, aquatints, and lithographs. He had made prints early in his career and returned to the medium in 1916.

Though Davies was sympathetic to and interested in radical art, his own production was more visionary in conception, in the tradition of such independent artists as the English Pre-Raphaelites, the French Symbolists, Puvis de Chavanne, Gustave Moreau, and the American visionaries Albert Pinkham Ryder, Ralph Blakelock, and Elihu Vedder. He had no interest in producing a literal depiction of the world around him, and his work had little in common stylistically with the realism of Henri and the Ashcan School artists. Dreamlike idylls populated with sylphs and allegorical figures in friezelike arrangements, all cloaked in moody atmospheric effects, characterize the better part of Davies's production. *Four Figures* and *Three Male Figures—A Study* are typical examples of his stylized technique in oil and pastel, respectively, from the period before the Armory Show.

A contrived naïve approach with classicizing figures situated in arcadian surroundings became the hallmarks of Davies's style. As his friend Bryson Burroughs observed of Davies's work:

> These landscapes though founded on views of particular places, are entirely ideal and romantic in expression. He made over the landscapes before him, changing it into the landscape of his imagination where dryads might wander or unicorns graze. The latter was his reality . . . he eliminated . . . such details of form and of color as might frustrate his artistic impulse.[1]

After the Armory Show, his work underwent a dramatic transformation—inspired by Cubism, he began incorporating some of its ideas in his art, even experimenting with abstraction. However, he abandoned that manner of working by about 1920 and

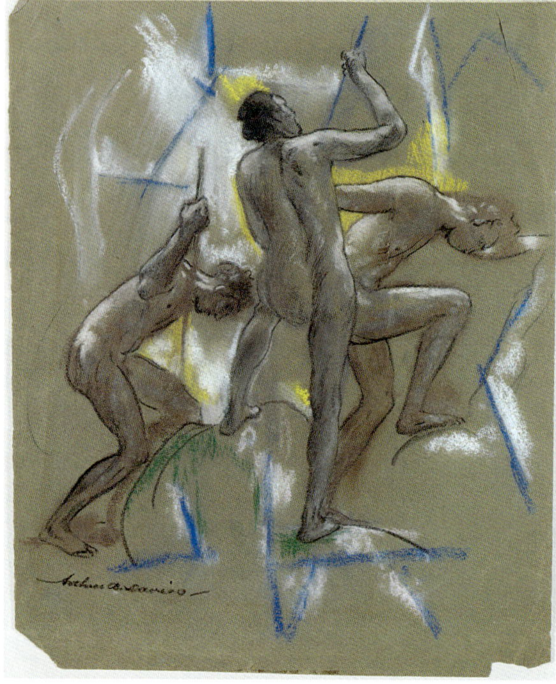

reverted to painting in the style of his earlier years. He also produced many poetic landscapes. Davies was an immensely influential artist in his time, though today his importance is underestimated, perhaps due to the difficulty of classifying his work.
VAL

1. Bryson Burroughs, introduction to *Catalogue of a Memorial Exhibition of the Works of Arthur B. Davies,* exh. cat. (New York: The Metropolitan Museum of Art, 1930), pp. xvii–xviii.

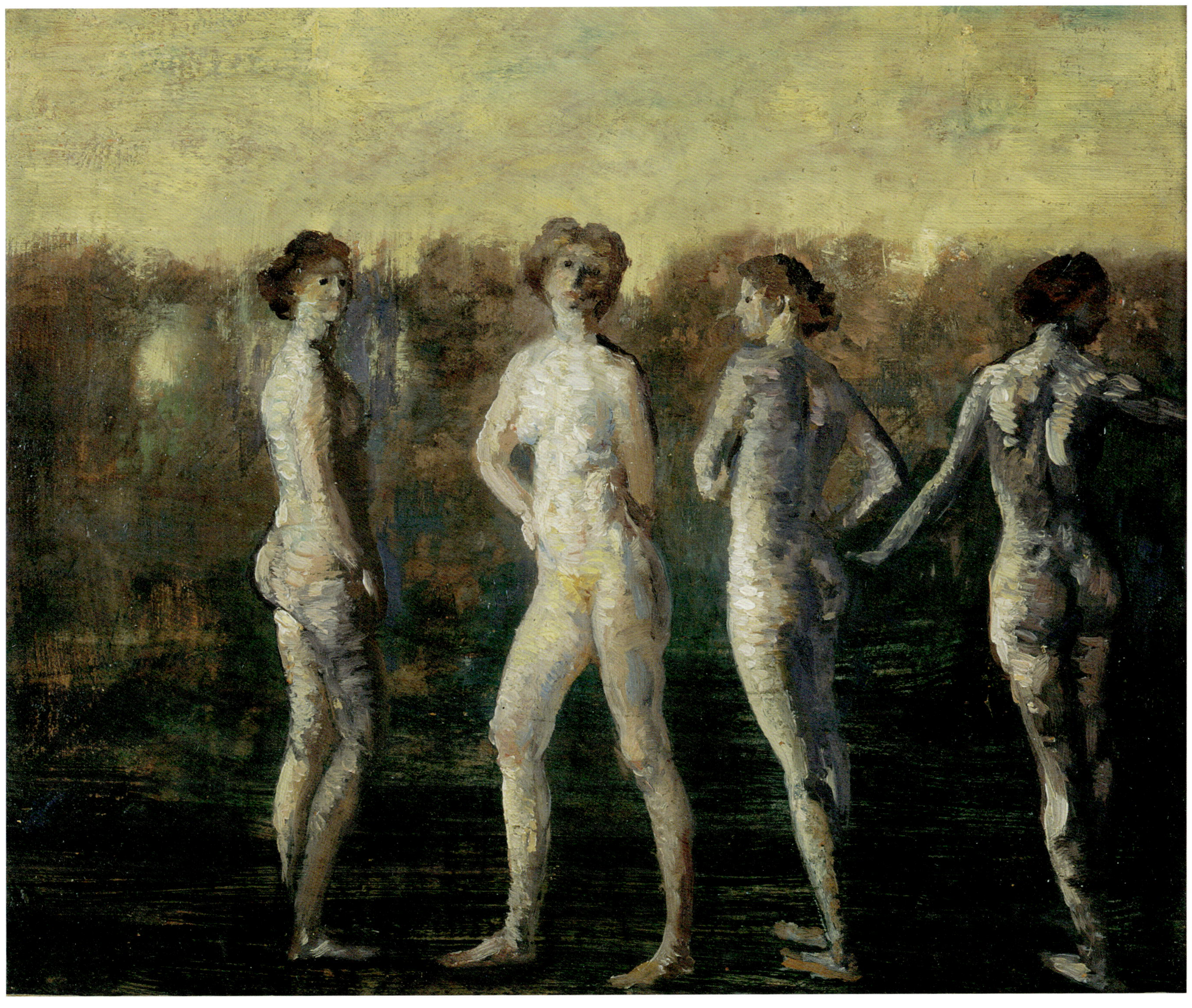

Leon Kroll AMERICAN 1884–1974

47 | *Terminal Yards,* 1913

Oil on canvas, 46½ × 52½ in.

Signed and dated lower right: *Kroll 1913*

Gift of Mrs. Arthur Jerome Eddy (1931.4)

Leon Kroll, known as a figurative painter and the dean of the American nude, made his initial mark on the art world with urban landscapes of the New York area, a type exemplified by *Terminal Yards.* Born in New York City, he studied at the Art Students League with the Impressionist John Henry Twachtman and also took classes at the National Academy of Design. He traveled to Paris in 1908 and attended the Académie Julian, studying with Jean-Paul Laurens; there he became influenced by the work of Paul Cézanne, whose modernist ideas he slowly assimilated into his own technique. Kroll returned to New York in 1910 and began focusing on Manhattan cityscapes, work that gained him critical attention. These paintings were original in conception. As Kroll himself observed, "Those New York pictures are really quite my own: I never saw anybody paint in exactly that way. You can't recognize anybody's influence in those New York pictures, at all."[1] *Terminal Yards* belongs to this series of urban scenes and is one of the artist's most important works.

The composition presents a panoramic view from Weehawken Heights in New Jersey looking across the railroad yards. Beyond is the Hudson River, with the New York skyline visible in the distance. In these cityscapes, Kroll tended to favor such bird's-eye vistas depicted from unusual vantage points. The sweeping curve of the railroad tracks lends a sense of dynamism to the composition, which is punctuated by the puffs of smoke from the train engines. Kroll painted *Terminal Yards* on location on a bitterly cold Christmas Day in a burst of creative inspiration.[2] He produced at least two other related major canvases and a small panel painting seen from different vantage points: *West Shore Terminal* (1913; location unknown), also a snow scene; *View of Manhattan from the Terminal Yards, Weehawken* (1913; Montgomery Museum, Alabama), a similar view, but without snow; and *Manhattan from Hoboken* (1915; Collection of Samuel B. and Marion W. Lawrence).

Terminal Yards was selected for inclusion in the important 1913 International Exhibition of Modern Art—more commonly known as the Armory Show—by Arthur B. Davies and Walt Kuhn, two of the principal organizers of the show. The painting was Kroll's only submission. The picture was singled out from the many other works on view by the former president, Theodore Roosevelt, who called it "one of the most striking in the show,"[3] and was purchased by the noted Chicago collector Arthur Jerome Eddy, who became an important patron of Kroll's work.

Kroll continued to paint and exhibit urban scenes until the later 1920s, but by then he had increasingly turned to more pastoral subjects. During his career, Kroll won many prizes and awards, painted murals, and was an influential teacher at the Art Students League and the National Academy of Design. Though he experimented with some modernist ideas, he remained firmly entrenched in the realist tradition throughout his life. VAL

1. Leon Kroll, *Leon Kroll: A Spoken Memoir,* ed. Nancy Hale and Fredson Bowers (Charlottesville: University Press of Virginia, 1983), p. 30.

2. Ibid., p. 33.

3. Theodore Roosevelt, "A Layman's Views of an Art Exhibition," *The Outlook,* 22 March 1913, as quoted in *1913 Armory Show 50th Anniversary Exhibition 1963,* exh. cat. (Utica, N.Y.: Munson-William-Proctor Institute, 1963), p. 162.

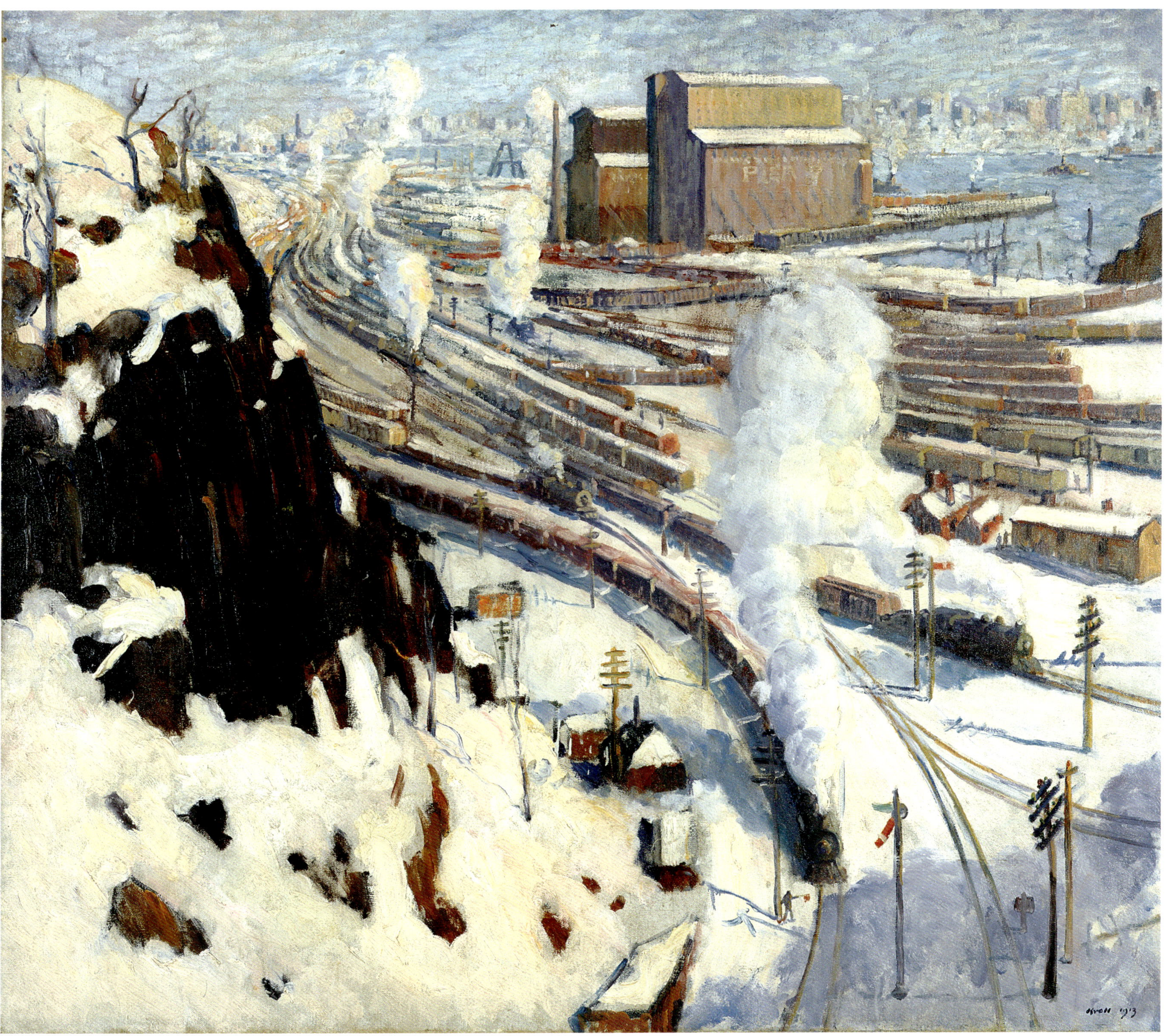

Maurice Brazil Prendergast AMERICAN, BORN CANADA 1859–1924

48 | *Bathers,* c. 1918–23

Oil on canvas, 17½ × 24⅛ in.
Signed lower left: *Prendergast*
Gift of Mr. and Mrs. William L. Richards, by exchange (1993.33)

In American art, Prendergast's work represents a bridge between a nineteenth-century aesthetic and a twentieth-century modernist approach. One of this country's most original artists, he absorbed influences from abroad while developing an approach uniquely his own. He is especially recognized for his picturesque idylls depicting the leisure class engaged in recreational activities—people promenading, wading, and swimming are among his most typical themes, most often set, like *Bathers,* in New England coastal locales. In this work, Prendergast has captured a sense of spontaneity and movement, where brilliance of color and expressive brushwork contribute to the overall vibrancy of the composition. Prendergast was particularly recognized for his proficiency in watercolor, a medium in which he often worked. Though *Bathers* is an oil, the artist has achieved the feeling of transparency often seen in watercolor by using flattened forms and areas of color that he has simply outlined and by leaving portions of the canvas bare.

Prendergast was born in St. Johns, Newfoundland, but his family moved to Boston when he was nine. He studied in Paris between 1891 and 1894 at the Académies Julian and Colarossi. He frequently traveled abroad, most often to France, where he painted and kept up with the most advanced ideas in contemporary art. In 1907 in France Prendergast saw an exhibition of the work of Paul Cézanne, which he declared was "perfectly marvelous. He left everything to the imagination, they were great for their simplicity and suggestive qualities."[1] Prendergast was among the earliest of American artists to understand the ideas of the European avant-garde, notably those espoused by Cézanne and the Fauves, which he assimilated into his work. The vivid nonnaturalistic colors, abstracted forms, and flattened space seen in *Bathers* typify the individualized approach he actively cultivated.

Prendergast's artistic independence allied him with antiacademic concerns. He exhibited with The Eight, insurgent artists who rebelled against the National Academy of Design, in the show held in 1908 at Macbeth Galleries in New York. He also participated in the 1910 Exhibition of Independent Artists and was appointed to both the Domestic and Foreign Selection Committees for the 1913 Armory Show. Ultimately, Prendergast defined his own artistic course, apart from current fashions, and he remained an independent and progressive painter well into the twentieth century. VAL

1. Maurice Prendergast to Mrs. Williams, October 1907, quoted in *Maurice Prendergast: Art of Impulse and Color,* exh. cat. (College Park, Md.: University of Maryland Art Gallery, 1976), p. 23.

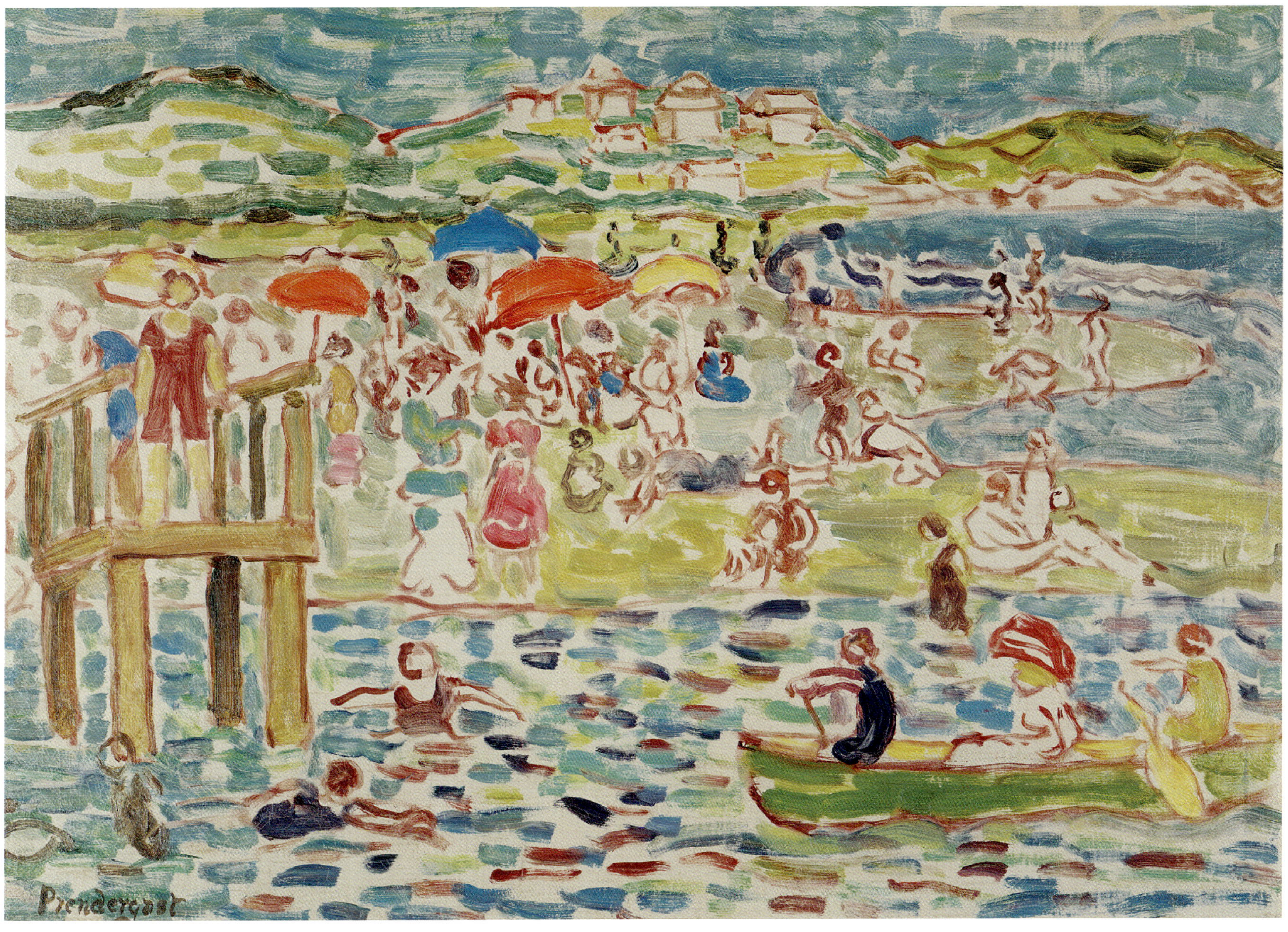
Prendergast

Konrad Cramer AMERICAN, BORN GERMANY 1888–1963

49 | *Abstraction,* c. 1913

Oil on board, 16¼ × 13¾ in.

Unsigned

Gift of Mr. and Mrs. Carroll McGregor Boutell in honor of Mr. and Mrs. Frank J. Boutell, by exchange (2002.7)

The German-born Konrad Cramer, among the earliest painters of purely abstract works, served as an important conduit of ideas between the avant-garde of his native country and artists of nascent American modernism. After studying in Karlsruhe, Germany, in 1910 Cramer went to Munich, where he met the American artist Florence Ballin, whom he married later that year. While in Munich, Cramer was exposed to vanguard art and ideas, which, particularly in Munich, emphasized new forms of expression with particular significance placed on form and color and on the evocation of spirituality. He was especially influenced by Wassily Kandinsky and Franz Marc, founders of the Blaue Reiter, and he avidly read Kandinsky's writings, including the seminal *Concerning the Spiritual in Art.* Of the European avant-garde artists, Cramer fell most profoundly under Kandinsky's spell, to the point of emulating his style and appropriating the title *Improvisation* for some of his works.[1]

In 1911 Cramer and his wife moved to the United States, where they settled in New York. There they met Mabel Dodge and attended her salons and also became acquainted with the impresario Alfred Stieglitz, through whom they encountered others who shared progressive ideas on art. The couple soon moved to Woodstock, a burgeoning artists' colony in upstate New York, where Cramer became an influential figure and exponent of modernist ideas. He inspired other artists, including Andrew Dasburg and Henry Lee McFee, to explore new directions in their work.

Cramer is believed to have commenced painting his own abstract compositions about 1910, well before the Armory Show, the international exhibition that introduced European modern art to an American audience. He, along with Manierre Dawson, Arthur Dove, Marsden Hartley, and Morgan Russell, was one of the first artists in America to pursue abstract painting. *Abstraction* was likely executed about 1913 and pays homage to Kandinsky's abstract compositions. While distinctly Cramer's own creation, *Abstraction* appears to have developed from ideas that originated with Kandinsky and Marc. Although Cramer depicted objects extracted from and distantly based in nature, he has taken the work into the abstract realm by the use of geometricized forms and a vivid palette that does not suggest the natural world.

Despite his early enthusiasm, Cramer did not pursue a long-term investigation of pure abstraction. By about 1917 he began to turn away from this mode of expression in favor of a Cubist-based vernacular that was an interpretation of discernible subject matter. For the remainder of his life, Cramer embraced traditional subject matter, favoring landscapes and still lifes, and later also became very involved with the medium of photography. VAL

1. For more on Konrad Cramer and his place in the art of his time, see *Concerning Expressionism: American Modernism and the German Avant-Garde,* exh. cat. (New York: Hollis Taggart Galleries, 1998), pp. 56–61; and Gail Levin and Marianne Lorenz, *Theme and Improvisation: Kandinsky and the American Avant-Garde, 1912–1950,* exh. cat. (Dayton: Dayton Art Institute, 1992), pp. 27–29, 68–69.

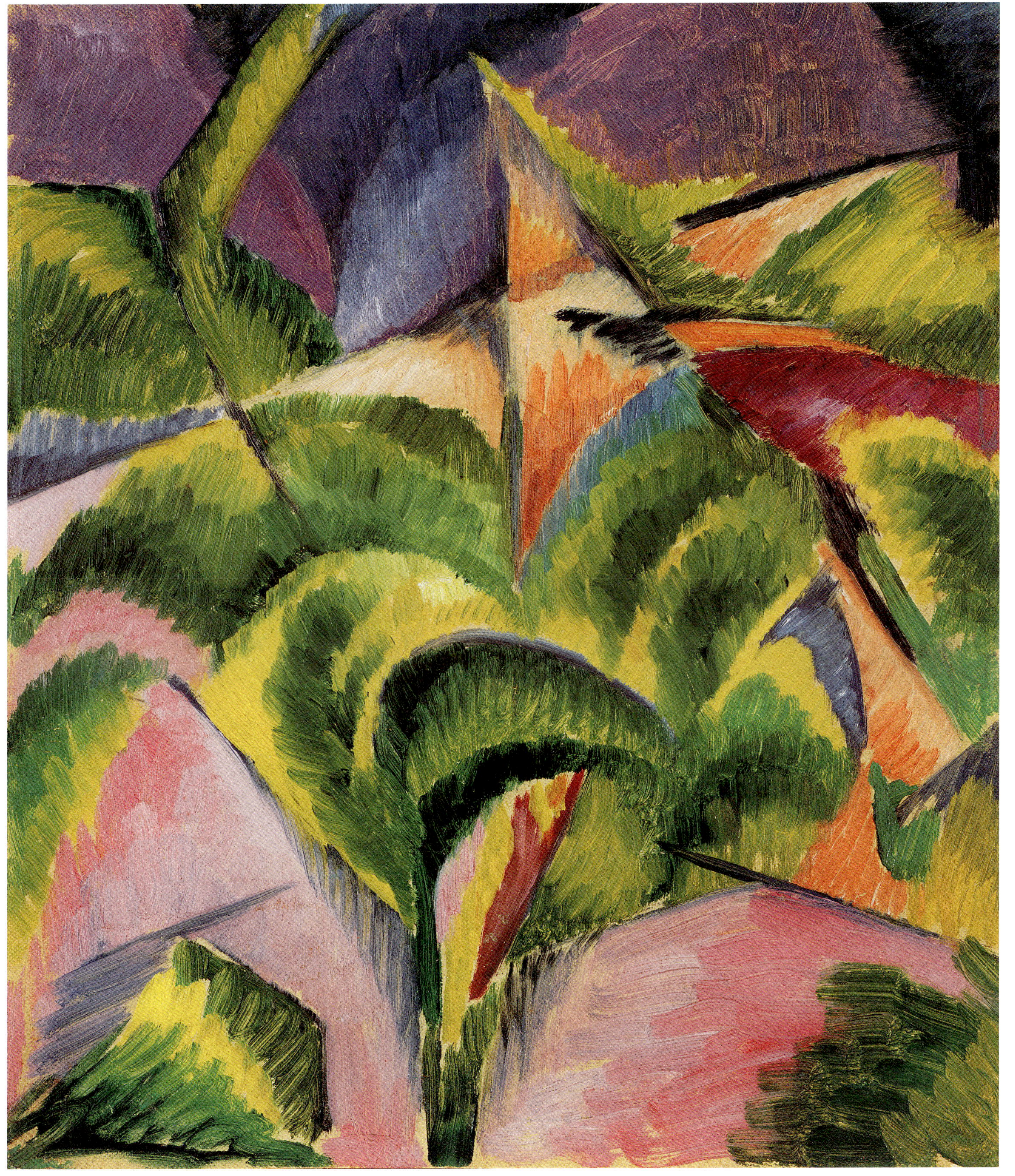

Max Weber AMERICAN, BORN RUSSIA 1881–1961

50 | *Untitled (Cubist Still Life)*, before 1920

Oil on canvas mounted on board, 36 × 30 in.

Signed lower left: *Max Weber*

Bequest of Mary Mallery Davis, by exchange (2002.5)

One of the first American artists to study abroad, assimilate the tenets of European modernism, and introduce them to artists back home, Max Weber was integral to the evolution of modern art in this country. Henri Matisse, from whom he received critiques in Paris, was influential, but the work of Paul Cézanne and Pablo Picasso proved to be even more profound forces in shaping Weber's artistic development.

Born in Bialystock, Russia, Weber immigrated in 1891 with his family to the United States, where they settled in Brooklyn. He studied art at Pratt Institute with the teacher and theorist Arthur Wesley Dow from 1898 to 1900, departing for Paris in 1905. There he trained at the Académie Julian and worked under Jean-Paul Laurens. He returned to New York in 1909, bringing with him the new artistic ideas he had gleaned from his exposure to progressive European art, which he had begun to integrate into his work and advocate to others. The year following his return, Alfred Stieglitz included Weber in an important group show at Gallery 291, which was devoted to avant-garde art. This important first step was followed by a solo show at 291 in 1911, which launched Weber's career. A teacher and writer as well as a prolific artist, Weber was an innovative painter who knew of and experimented with various styles and techniques. After his time in Europe, he worked in a Cubist mode and also investigated nonobjective compositions, though he later reintroduced subject matter by turning to Social Realism. He explored various media, from painting and drawing to collage, printmaking, and sculpture.

The compositional arrangement of *Untitled (Cubist Still Life)* employs reductive forms and flattened spatial planes, technical approaches that owe a debt to Cézanne, whose simplifying and geometricizing of shapes and mass were precursors to Cubism. Like Cézanne, Weber also attempted to move beyond basic formal concerns and instill deeper meaning into his work. He declared, "Sometimes I feel that even inanimate objects crave a hearing, and have a desire to participate in the motion of time and its indentations. . . . Things live in us and through us."[1]

Beyond the obvious visual parallels between *Untitled (Cubist Still Life)* and the still-life compositions of Cézanne, evident in the irregular angularity of the drapes, the exaggerated, uneven form of the fruit bowl, and the flattening of the perspective of the floor and tabletop, Weber found influential ideas in the work of Picasso, also a prodigious still-life painter. He met the innovative painter during a visit to France and was one of the first artists to comprehend and absorb Picasso's ideas about Cubism, experimenting with the style after his return to New York in 1909. He continued to investigate various permutations of it throughout the next decade, although he would also execute works that were not fully Cubist in approach, like this one. The painting does, however, make an obvious reference to Analytic Cubism in its monochromaticism, one of the style's key characteristics. It likely dates to sometime between 1910 and 1920 and clearly reflects the artist's understanding of the work of Cézanne and Picasso, although Weber has made an original artistic statement by synthesizing many of their ideals with his own interpretation. The monumentality of this composition makes it an unusual work for the artist, who generally employed a more diminutive scale for such subjects.

Although Weber's reputation did not ascend to the heights of the European artists he admired, he is recognized as an important American modernist who was an early proponent of new artistic developments and innovations. VAL

1. Max Weber, *Essays on Art* (1916; reprint, New York: Gerald Peters Gallery, 2000), pp. 14–15.

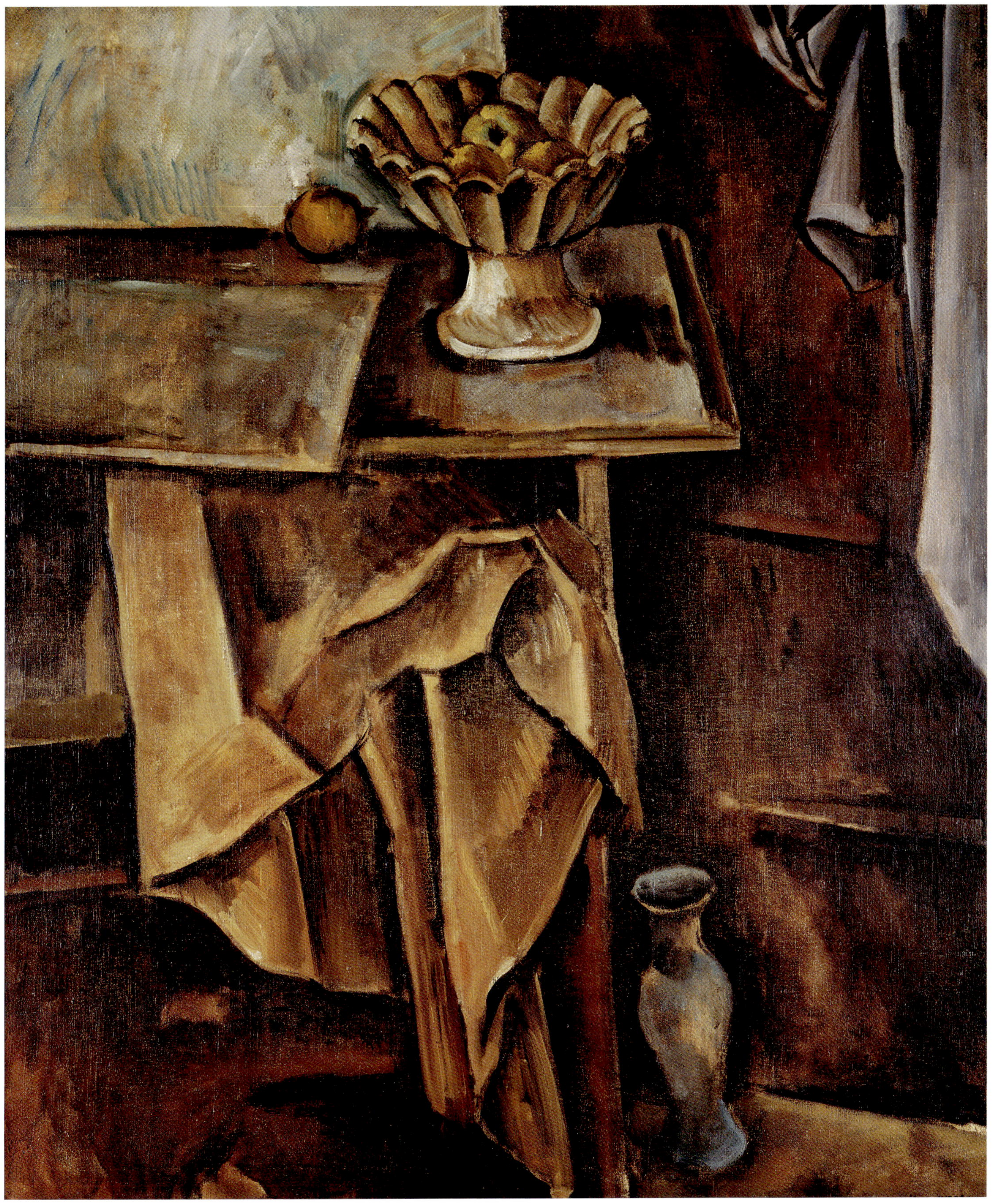

Carl Milles AMERICAN, BORN SWEDEN 1875–1955

51 | *Jonah and the Whale,* 1932

Bronze, 15⅜ × 11 x 8¾ in.

Signed on right side: *C. Milles*

Bequest of Michael Gorman (1959.5)

Known for his large-scale public sculptures and fountains, Carl Milles is also important for his role in the founding of the Cranbrook Academy of Art in Bloomfield Hills, Michigan. The Academy was the inspiration of George and Ellen Booth, who, after a visit to the American Academy in Rome, envisioned the creation of a similar art school at their estate, Cranbrook. The Booths invited the Finnish architect Eliel Saarinen, then teaching at the University of Michigan, to help develop the idea. Saarinen and the original faculty, which included Milles and other internationally renowned artists and designers such as Arthur N. Kirk, Zoltan Sepeshy, and Eliel's son, Eero, collaborated on the implementation of the Booths' vision.[1] The Cranbrook Academy of Art is an extraordinary campus, where the landscape, sculptures, and buildings function together as a seamless whole. Eliel Saarinen, who also designed the Academy's original buildings, called Cranbrook an "historical document." In 1931 Milles was hired as a professor of advanced sculpture; he continued in residence until 1951, teaching such students as Marshall Fredericks and Duane Hanson as well as executing more than seventy sculptures that are installed throughout the grounds.

Carl Milles, born Wilhelm Carl Emil Andersson in Stockholm, Sweden, left school in 1892 to apprentice as a carpenter and cabinetmaker. In 1897 he moved to Paris, where he took classes in anatomy at the Ecole des Beaux-Arts. He also studied with and worked as a studio assistant for the renowned sculptor Auguste Rodin. Milles left Paris in 1904, spending the next few years in Rome, Stockholm, and Austria. In 1908 he moved back to Sweden. Milles's training as a woodworker, along with his work with Rodin, is evident in the organic and expressionist qualities that inform his sculpture.

Jonah and the Whale was made as a study, or maquette, for a large-scale fountain that Milles was to create for the Cranbrook campus. Documents note, however, that the work was "originally done for Kingswood [an elementary school for girls], but the trustees rejected it."[2] There is no existing evidence indicating the reason for the trustees' displeasure with the sculpture; perhaps it was due to what could be seen as the irreverent nature of the piece.

Milles's Jonah, emerging from the mouth of a rather small whale, looks shocked and bewildered. The whale, awkwardly positioned in a dramatic U, with an upwardly thrust tail and jutting fins, precariously grasps the disproportionately large Jonah in its outstretched tongue, creating an unbalanced diagonal that lends a great deal of movement to the work. It also helps to make the composition somewhat comical, apparently an intentional effect. As Milles stated, "I made this fountain to be used in the courtyard in Kingswood. It was the first thing I started here at Cranbrook. When I started it I didn't know what to do, but wanted to make a joke for the children. I thought it would be right to have Jonah appearing with a surprised look on his face. I like it and would like to do another Jonah—more amusing."[3] He clearly succeeded in making Jonah more amusing than suffering; it is the most whimsical of his sculptures at Cranbrook. Several of his works have a light tone, but his only other truly humorous work is *The Animal Acrobats* (Collection of Millesgården, Sweden), a maquette for an unrealized fountain tentatively titled *Anything Is Possible in the New World,* intended for the city of Harrisburg, Pennsylvania. Other Milles fountains in the United States can be found in Chicago, Kansas City, New York, and St. Louis.

In 1951 Milles left his position at Cranbrook and moved to Rome, where he had a studio at the American Academy. He spent his summers at Millesgården in Sweden and died in Lidingö in 1955, shortly after he was awarded the Founder's Medal at Cranbrook. His home at Millesgården is now an open-air museum of his work. MMF

1. Cranbrook Academy of Art website, www.cranbrook.edu/archives/brief_hi.htm, accessed 15 February 2002.

2. Clipping, *Milles Sculpture at Cranbrook,* 1964(?), Archives, Cranbrook Foundation, Bloomfield Hills, Michigan, p. 2.

3. Ibid.

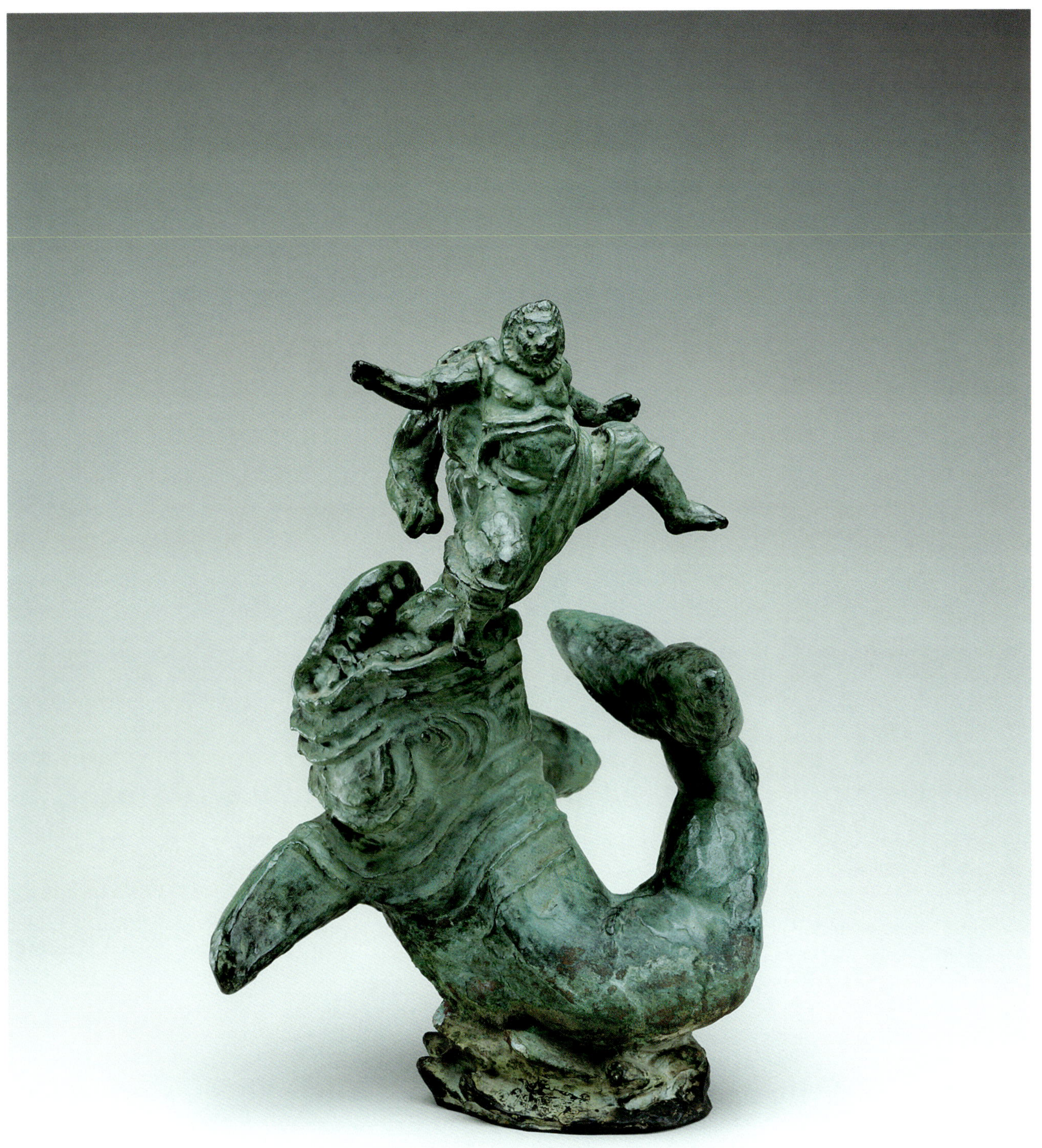

Zoltan Sepeshy AMERICAN, BORN HUNGARY 1898–1974

52 | *Patterns*, n.d.

Oil and tempera on wood, 33¼ × 45 in.

Signed lower right: *Z. Sepeshy*

Gift in memory of Michael A. Gorman (1959.2)

In his life and art, Zoltan Sepeshy spanned two centuries and two continents, during which time he witnessed significant changes in the perception and philosophy of contemporary art. From an era that saw Paul Cézanne and Pablo Picasso as wild innovators and living into an era that embodied such then-radical developments as abstraction, Minimalism, and Conceptual art, he forged a career as an artist and educator, exhibiting nationally and achieving recognition as one of the leading artists of Michigan.

Sepeshy, born in Kassa, Hungary, was the only child of landed gentry. He was given the benefit of private education and tutoring, which culminated in study at the Fine Arts Academy in Vienna and four and a half years at the Royal Academy of Fine Arts in Budapest, where he earned degrees in art and art education. He immigrated to the United States in 1921, stopping for a period of time in New York before relocating to Detroit, Michigan. The young artist could not know the importance of this move, chosen because an uncle resided in the vicinity. He lived in Michigan for the remainder of his life, where he flourished not only as a leading artist but as an influential and effective educator and administrator, serving in various capacities at the Cranbrook Academy of Art for thirty-six years.

Sepeshy's early years in the United States were a profound departure from the aristocratic life he had lived in Europe. He supported himself with odd jobs in order to paint and from 1922 to 1925 worked as an architectural draftsman for Albert Kahn. He traveled around the United States, studied with Walter Ufer in New Mexico, and in 1928–29 went to Europe. Sepeshy moved away from the romanticized interiors and landscapes he had learned to depict as a student and became increasingly interested in American Scene painting. "I painted with a vengeance," he observed of the time. "I paint not floral table set-ups, manicured scenery, maidens in salon outfits and happy little people, but railroad bridges, factories, miners, grimy city scenes, unemployed park habitués."[1]

By the mid-1920s Sepeshy had made a name for himself in Detroit: in 1925 he won the Art Founders Prize of the Detroit Institute of Arts (again in 1936) and in 1930 was awarded the J. L. Hudson Purchase Prize at the annual Michigan Artists Exhibition at the Detroit Institute of Arts. He had his first one-man exhibition in New York at the Newhouse Galleries in 1932. His style at the time was akin to that of the School of Paris, relating to Cézanne and the Cubists, and although *Patterns* is undated, the Cubist planes, tilted perspective, and Cézannesque palette indicate it may have been executed around this time. The painting shows his attempts to synthesize his European training with a more personal view. Sepeshy continued to exhibit in New York and nationally throughout the 1940s and was honored with such national awards as the IBM Award at the Golden Gate International Exposition in San Francisco (1940), the Award of the National Academy of Arts and Letters in New York (1946), and the Carnegie Institute First Prize in Pittsburgh (1947).

Initially, Sepeshy's development as an artist paralleled his life as a teacher and administrator as he achieved recognition in these arenas. In 1931 he was invited to teach at the Cranbrook Academy of Art. He later served as visiting artist and eventually chaired the painting department. In 1947 he was named director of Cranbrook Academy, and from 1959 to 1966 he served as its president. In the late 1940s Sepeshy's subject matter moved from American genre scenes to mostly religious themes,[2] a period in his career that coincided with a decline in the time he spent in the studio and a resulting drop in productivity. These changes in style, subject, and productivity may have been caused as much by the shift in critical thought in the art world—away from representation and toward abstraction—as much as to the increasing demands of teaching and administration. Nevertheless, Sepeshy's contribution to the arts in Michigan remains substantial, both as an artist and as an administrator. SS

1. James Houghton, *Zoltan Sepeshy Remembered*, exh. cat. (Muskegon, Mich.: Muskegon Museum of Art, 2002), p. 6.

2. Ibid., p. 12.

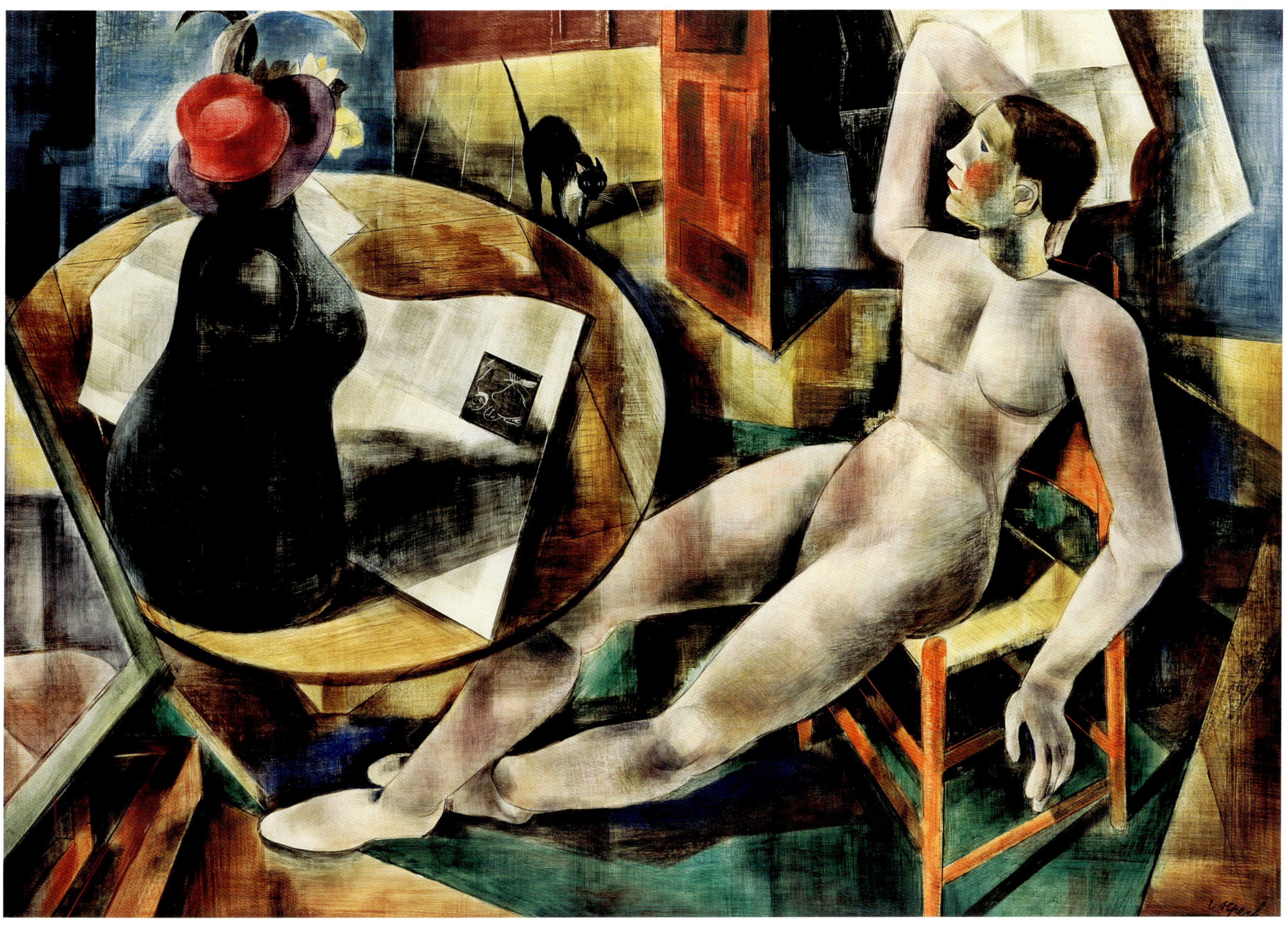

William Zorach AMERICAN, BORN LITHUANIA 1887–1966

53 | *Spirit of the Dance,* 1932

Bronze, 76 × 31 × 48 in.

Signed and dated, front left corner of base: *c 3 Zorach 1932*

Gift of Mr. and Mrs. Charles Stewart Mott (1965.10)

William Zorach, renowned as a sculptor, began his career as a painter. Born Zorach Samovich in Lithuania, he came to America with his family when he was three years old and grew up in Cleveland, Ohio. In 1908 he commenced two years of formal study at the National Academy of Design in New York. In 1910 he left for France, where he remained until 1911, spending most of his time in Paris. There he encountered Post-Impressionism, Fauvism, and Cubism, all of which influenced his own painting. In Paris he met Marguerite Thompson, also an artist, whom he married in 1912. He had participated in the 1911 Salon d'Automne in France and on his return to America exhibited in the 1913 Armory Show and the 1916 Forum Exhibition, allying himself with modernism and against the prevailing art establishment. He first took up sculpture in 1917 and by 1922 he had abandoned oil painting to concentrate on the new three-dimensional medium. He began teaching at the Art Students League in 1929, which he continued until his death, thereby directly influencing several generations of sculptors.

Zorach was one of the modern pioneers of direct carving, a method that advocated the use of natural materials and a return to the more direct involvement of the sculptor's hand in the fabrication of the sculpture. He especially favored stone but worked in a variety of materials. Though he was influenced by his friendship with the sculptor Gaston Lachaise, who was likewise inclined toward figurative subjects, particularly female nudes, Zorach's sculptures are more angular and severe. He was also inspired by works of the past, noting that his sculpture "owes most to the great period of primitive carving in the past, not to the moderns or to the classical Greeks, but to the Africans, the Persians, the Mesopotamians, the archaic Greeks, and, of course, to the Egyptians."[1]

Zorach had his first solo show, at the Kraushaar Gallery in New York, in 1924, which was followed by another at the Downtown Gallery in 1931. The Downtown Gallery was run by Edith Halpert, who was also acting as an adviser to the Rockefellers on the decoration of Radio City Music Hall at Rockefeller Center. She was involved in the decision to hire the young designer Donald Deskey to plan the interior space, and it was he who chose Zorach's *Spirit of the Dance* installed as the centerpiece of the theater's lower-level lounge. The sculpture, which depicts a nude woman dancer kneeling at the end of a performance, was considered to be controversial because of its unabashed nudity and was temporarily removed from view. The notoriety garnered much attention for the work and the artist, although the sculpture was eventually replaced.[2]

Spirit of the Dance is a signature work of the artist and one that defined his stature as a leading sculptor of his generation. The sculpture evolved from drawings Zorach submitted for the commission. Once Zorach saw where the sculpture was to be placed, he realized his initial three-foot-high conception would not be suitable and that the piece needed to be on a monumental scale, six and a half feet high, which would make the kneeling figure nine feet tall if standing. He made a plaster original and cast it in aluminum for Radio City. A second cast was made in bronze; the Flint Institute of Arts' cast, also in bronze, is the third version.[3] The work was also realized in a small-scale version, of which seven casts were executed.

With its classicized interpretation of rounded and stylized forms, *Spirit of the Dance* relates to other female figurative subjects Zorach produced in the 1930s. Whether in small or large scale, his work is generally characterized by a sense of intimacy and grandeur in equal measure, and these qualities are clearly in evidence in *Spirit of the Dance.* Zorach was striving to make his sculpture an expression of spirituality, noting that:

> There will always be sculptors who will make the pretty and obvious, but there will also be sculptors who are fired with a desire to express the deepest aspirations of humanity, who are absorbed with a vision of new and marvelous possibilities of expression who burn with emotion that only some exalted rhythm or some powerful distortions can express.[4]

Spirit of the Dance, in its monumentality and its vision of the new, is the embodiment of Zorach's artistic ideals. VAL

1. William Zorach, as quoted in *Artnews* (November 1959), curatorial files, Flint Institute of Arts.

2. William Zorach, *Art Is My Life: The Autobiography of William Zorach* (Cleveland: The World Publishing Company, 1967), p. 91.

3. Notes, curatorial files, Flint Institute of Arts.

4. William Zorach, *William Zorach* (New York: American Artists Group, 1945), p. 32.

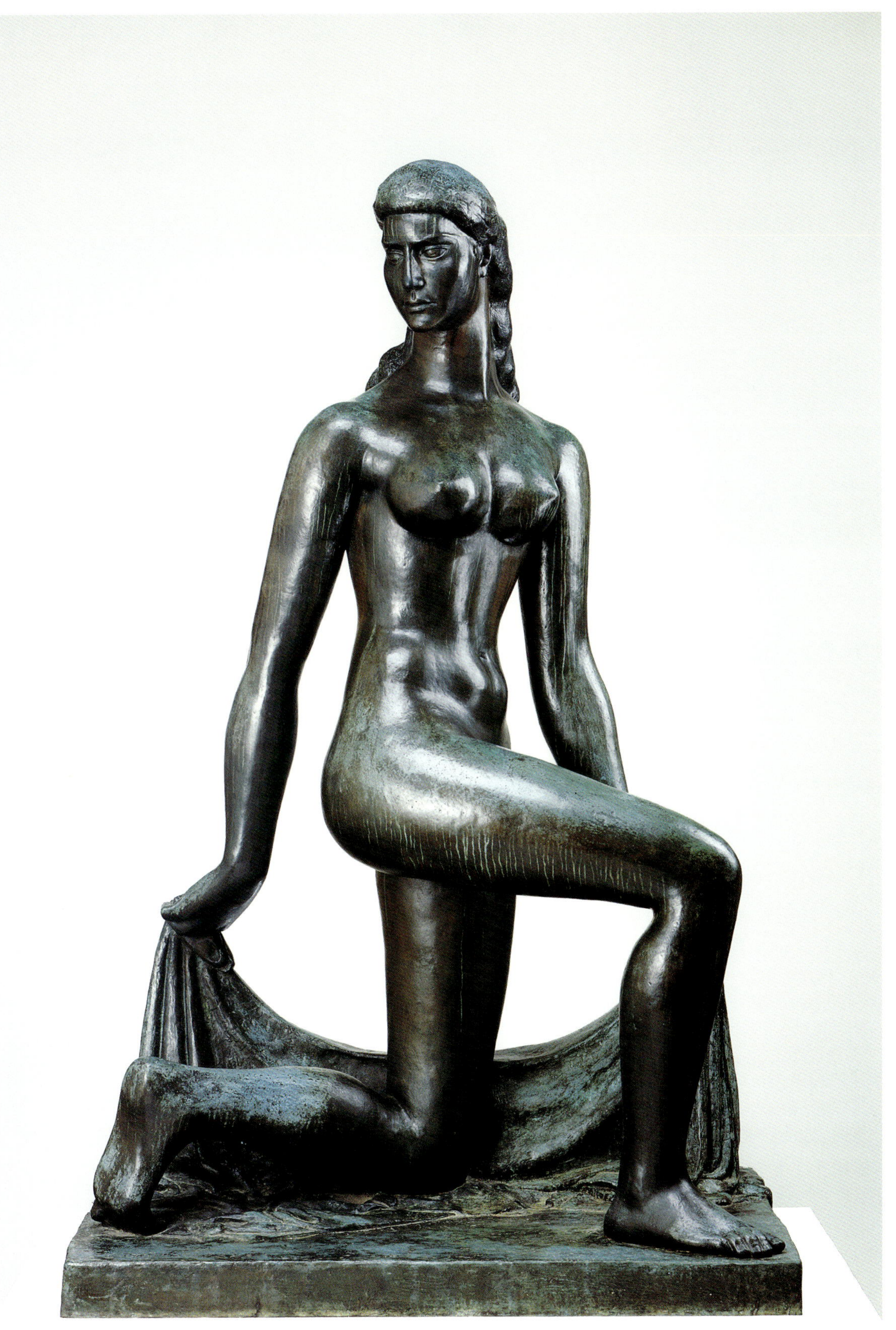

Charles Burchfield AMERICAN 1893–1967

54 | *Nighthawks at Twilight*, 1917/49

Watercolor on paper, 34⅜ × 48½ in.

Signed and dated lower right: *C E B 1917–49*

Gift of the Viola E. Bray Charitable Trust (1964.3)

55 | *Northwoods in Spring*, 1951–64

Watercolor on paper, 56 × 40 in.

Signed and dated lower left: *C E B 1951–64*

Bequest of Mary Mallery Davis (1990.31)

Charles Burchfield, a native of Ohio, was raised in the town of Salem and studied at the Cleveland Institute of Art from 1912 to 1916. Between 1911 and 1920 Burchfield worked intermittently at the Mullins Company, a metal fabricating plant, and painted in his spare time. He moved to Buffalo, New York, where he was employed as a designer for M. H. Birge and Sons, a wallpaper manufacturing concern. In 1925 he moved to Gardenville, a suburb of Buffalo, with his wife and growing family, which eventually included five children. Four years later he gave up his job to paint full-time.

Although Burchfield has come to be regarded as one of the realists known as the American Scene painters, or Regionalists, it was a label he rejected. His work, in fact, is more that of a romantic visionary and is remarkable for its imaginative landscapes, most frequently executed in watercolor.

Burchfield's career falls into three distinct phases. From 1916 through the 1920s he concentrated on what he called "childhood moods," which are nostalgic and enchanting expressions of landscapes inspired by Salem, Ohio. The works from this time are fantastical evocations of the natural world that summon various sentiments ranging from awe and wonder to mysterious foreboding and a sense of the macabre. His emotional response to nature resulted in haunting images based in reality but which relied primarily on his creative vision. Such feelings are aroused through the use of exaggerated natural forms and the visualization of sound. Burchfield noted:

> Most adults spurn the things of their childhood and consider the yearnings for such things in a grown man as a weakness. Perhaps it is, but it is still my belief that it is of such stuff that real art is made. As an artist grows older he has to fight disillusionment, and learn to establish the same relation to nature as an adult as he had when a child—it will not be like it, but the ratio of emotion will be the same.[1]

It is from this early period that the essential conception for *Nighthawks at Twilight* derives. Burchfield began work on the watercolor in 1917, which the artist later termed his "golden year," during which he executed more than two hundred images. This period was followed by a stylistic change around the time of his move to Gardenville. He began to paint the local urban landscape in a less fanciful style, one inclined toward realism. He achieved a national reputation with this body of work, and his association with Regionalism dates to this time, since he chose to depict bleak street scenes and views of industrial areas in New York State.

Burchfield's third phase commenced in the beginning of the 1940s with a break from realism and a revisiting of his earlier, more evocative approach. This return was characterized by an even more pronounced emphasis on expressing his response to the environment than the work of the late 1910s and the 1920s. The late works exhibit a particular mood of Gothic foreboding in their embellished and stylized execution, an effect he achieves by employing startling contrasts of dark and light, abundant black outlines, and boldly stylized draftsmanship. *Northwoods in Spring*, of 1951–64, is from this period, and it shares with the earlier *Nighthawks at Twilight* an ominous and sinister aura. As Burchfield later remarked of the earlier work: "'Nighthawks' needs no comment I guess, I love to see them frolicking in the vanguard of a storm—I think they must use the swirling eddies of wind. . . . How I envy them. . . . And I love the eeriness of the woods at nightfall."[2] He creates this vision by employing elongated and exaggerated forms, heavy use of black, and undulating lines and contours, a style that is similar to that which he used again in works of his late period.

In the 1940s Burchfield resumed work on a number of images he had begun in 1917, reworking and augmenting the compositions with additional sections of paper and repainting the images to suit his new ideas. As he explained: "Working on 1917 watercolors—with great pleasure and assurance. . . . And I

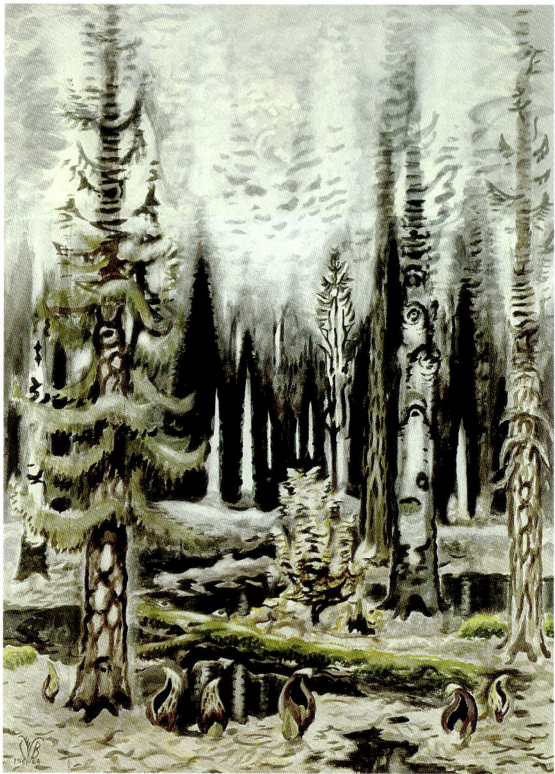

came to an important decision regarding the plans that I have had since 1944 for enlarging certain of these into more important compositions & ideas—and that was, to . . . correct and complete the ideas on their present scale."[3] Burchfield returned to work on *Nighthawks at Twilight*, conceived in 1917, completing it in 1949 in the more mannered and stylized approach found in late works like *Northwoods in Spring*.
VAL

1. Charles Burchfield, as quoted in *Charles Burchfield: Catalogue of Paintings in Public and Private Collections* (Utica, N.Y.: Munson-Williams-Proctor Institute, 1970), p. 7.

2. Burchfield to Lawrence Fleischman, 17 March 1956, Burchfield Papers, Archives of American Art, Smithsonian Institution, quoted in Ruth Osgood Trovato, *Extending the Golden Year: Charles Burchfield Centennial*, exh. cat. (Clinton, N.Y.: Emerson Gallery, Hamilton College, 1993), p. 57.

3. Burchfield, diary, 6–15 July 1954, in *Charles Burchfield's Journals: The Poetry of Place*, ed. J. Benjamin Townsend (Albany: State University of New York Press, 1993), p. 534.

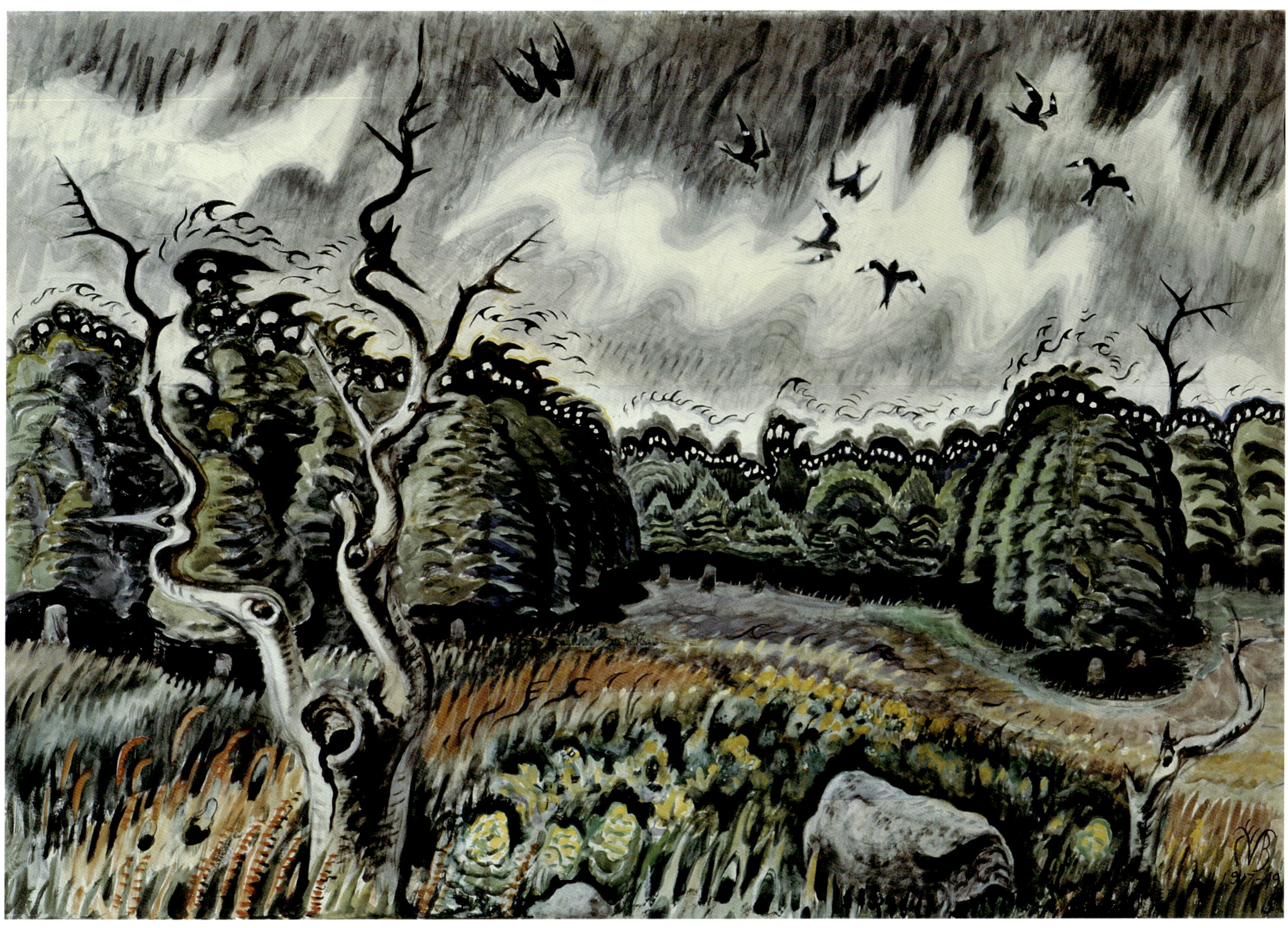

Thomas Hart Benton AMERICAN 1889–1975

56 | *Boomtown,* c. 1927

Oil on Masonite, 15½ × 11⅜ in.

Signed upper right: *Benton*

Bequest of Mary Mallery Davis, by exchange (2002.6)

Thomas Hart Benton, known as a purveyor of images of the Heartland, is an artist whose reputation is singularly identified with America. Like Grant Wood and John Steuart Curry, he was labeled a Regionalist, one of a group of artists whose work celebrates the distinct character of the Midwest. Benton, however, stated that he felt the term "suggested too narrow a range ... to be applicable. We went from place to place ... from region to region.... I was after a picture of America in its entirety.... A large part of my own work had been concerned with industrial and metropolitan factors."[1] *Boomtown,* a recent acquisition by the Flint Institute of Arts that represents rapid industrial expansion in a small Heartland town, is just such an image.

Born in Neosho, Missouri, Benton began his art studies at the Art Institute of Chicago in 1907, departing the following year for further training in Paris, where he attended the Académie Julian for three years. While there, he embraced abstraction and subscribed to the color-oriented ideas of Synchromism for a short time, befriending the expatriate American Stanton Macdonald-Wright, one of the movement's founders. Benton left Synchromism behind as his own style of realism coalesced; in the process, the work of Renaissance and Mannerist masters began to greatly inform his artistic approach. An advocate of documenting one's native surroundings, Benton generally rendered scenes of everyday American life, both urban and rural, an emphasis that became known as American Scene painting.[2]

Boomtown was painted as Benton was achieving artistic maturity and beginning his career as a Regionalist. In 1926 he started making trips through the South and Midwest, recording images of the American experience. This painting is one of a number of finished oil studies Benton made of Borger, in the Texas Panhandle, where he arrived in the autumn of 1927. The small, provincial community was undergoing massive growth as the result of the discovery of oil in the area. Benton's studies of the town were made in preparation for his first Regionalist masterwork of the same title (1928; Memorial Art Gallery, University of Rochester, New York), a painting that illustrates the results of the rapid growth, development, and speculation on a remote town. Like the romanticized "Wild West," the "Boomtown" represents a fall from an idyllic state that is part of American mythology.

In the Flint Institute's work, Benton's signature stylistic devices—allusion to narrative, exaggerated and sinuous lines, caricature, and rhythmic and repetitive use of form—are fully apparent. He has employed stark tonal contrasts that revolve around shades of blue and yellow. The low storefronts, automobile, telephone pole, and Stetson-wearing oilmen, as well as the vast land spreading out beyond the settlement, are archetypal imagery for Benton's vision of small-town life. In this study, Benton has realized in a visual shorthand the essence of what he later expanded in the Memorial Art Gallery painting—both offer a critical assessment of the effects of industrial and commercial expansion. While the specific image of Flint's *Boomtown* is not evident in the larger painting, the two works are clearly related and derive from the same source.

Flint's *Boomtown* also has a connection to another work by Benton, *The Changing West,* a scene from one of the artist's most important mural cycles, *America Today,* commissioned by the New School for Social Research in New York City.[3] In the center of *The Changing West,* a vignette of a small-town street shown at an angle similar to that in *Boomtown,* figures are depicted on the sidewalk in front of a storefront with gasoline pumps. This work, too, is drawn from the town of Borger. *Boomtown* is a Regionalist ode to small-town America and, as made explicit in the large version of *Boomtown* and *The Changing West,* it is also a story of the impact of growth and progress and the resulting loss of innocence.

In his maturity, Benton completed a number of important mural cycles and became a staunch critic of modernism. In addition to painting, he was an influential teacher, first at the Art Students League from 1927 to 1935 and then at the Kansas City Art Institute (1935–41), after which he returned to his home state of Missouri for the remainder of his life. VAL

1. Thomas Hart Benton, "American Regionalism: A Personal History of the Movement," *The University of Kansas Review* 18 (autumn 1951), p. 42.

2. For more on Benton's life and art, see Henry Adams, *Thomas Hart Benton: An American Original* (New York: Alfred A. Knopf, 1989).

3. For the most thorough assessment of the *America Today* murals, see Emily Braun and Thomas Branchick, *Thomas Hart Benton: The America Today Murals* (Williamstown, Mass.: Williams College Museum of Art, 1985).

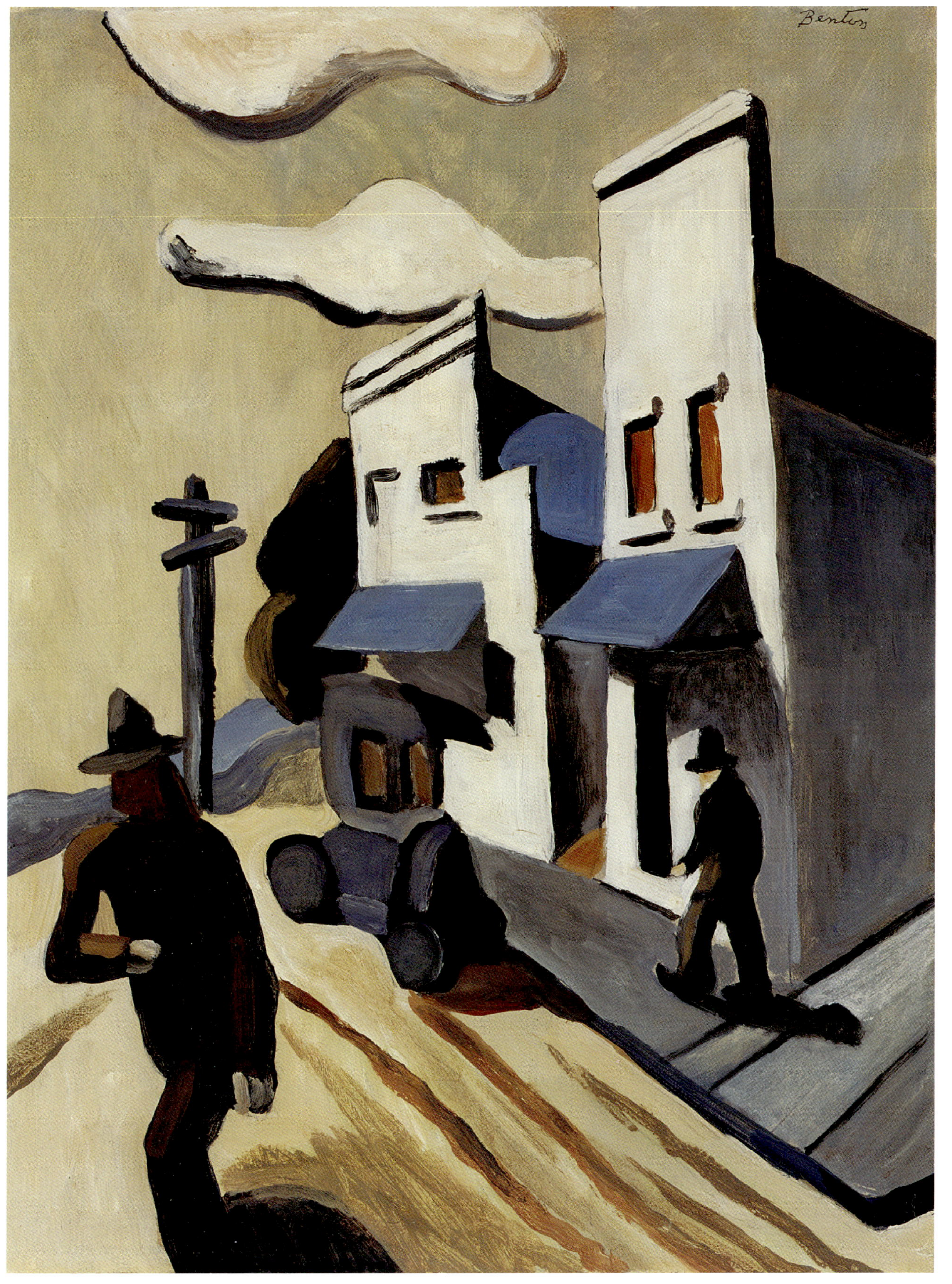
Benton

Boris Lovet-Lorski AMERICAN, BORN LITHUANIA 1894–1973

57 | *Sieglinde,* c. 1930s

Carved plaster with ebony-like finish,
10⅜ × 5½ × 2 in.

Unsigned

Bequest of Mary Mallory Davis (1990.53)

The work of Boris Lovet-Lorski, one of the foremost sculptors working in the Art Moderne style during the 1920s and 1930s, is largely overlooked today. Born in Lithuania, he studied at the Imperial Academy of Fine Arts in St. Petersburg. He left in 1916 as the Bolshevik Revolution commenced, going first to Western Europe and then to America, where he settled in Boston with his brother in 1920. Shortly after his arrival, he was given his first solo show in that city and was offered the position of head of the sculpture department at the Layton School of Art in Milwaukee. He accepted the post and remained there for two years, afterward moving to New York City, where he had another solo exhibition that helped him achieve some critical success. In 1926 he decided to go to Paris, where the acceptance of three sculptures at that year's Salon d'Automne contributed to his growing renown. Having established a thriving reputation, he received many portrait commissions and lived intermittently in Los Angeles from 1932 to 1934, where his work was much sought after by Hollywood society.

Lovet-Lorski had a supreme regard for the medium of sculpture, which he declared "seems to me like the work of God, for it is creation . . . something from nothing; first a lump of clay, then something that expresses life, beauty, thought and emotion."[1] His work embodies streamlined Art Moderne principles, evident especially in its refined sleekness and technical virtuosity. Extraneous details eliminated, his sculptures are elegant and idealized and suggest a strong classical influence. As the noted art critic Mary Fanton Roberts remarked, "The work of this man gives one a sense of great power and reserve strength. He does not seem to exhaust himself on any subject, but in every case you are given . . . beauty . . . a curious combination of old Greek simplicity and Russian intensity."[2] This effect is further enhanced by the artist's frequent choice of exquisite and rare materials—exotic marbles, slate, brass, onyx, jade, and ebony, most often hand-carved—and the highly refined and polished surfaces of the pieces.

Sieglinde is informed by archaic sources and influences, particularly non-Western, and its exaggerated features and proportions are typical of his artistic and subjective vision. Truth is subordinated to design and the result is a highly mannered conception. The masklike appearance of *Sieglinde,* as well as its flatness and exaggerated form, most likely have their genesis in African art, which was enjoying an international vogue with artists in the 1930s. Lovet-Lorski became recognized for his stylized interpretations of the female figure, usually heads and torsos, and of animals, especially the horse. In 1939, at the height of his reputation, he became handicapped by severe arthritis and was forced to give up carving but continued to do modeling for some years. VAL

1. Boris Lovet-Lorski, quoted in Martin Bush, *Boris Lovet-Lorski: The Language of Time,* exh. cat. (Syracuse, N.Y.: Syracuse University, 1967), p. 37, from *Milwaukee Journal,* 21 January 1923.

2. Mary Fanton Roberts, "Art Reviews: A Point of View," *Arts and Decoration* 28 (March 1928), p. 335.

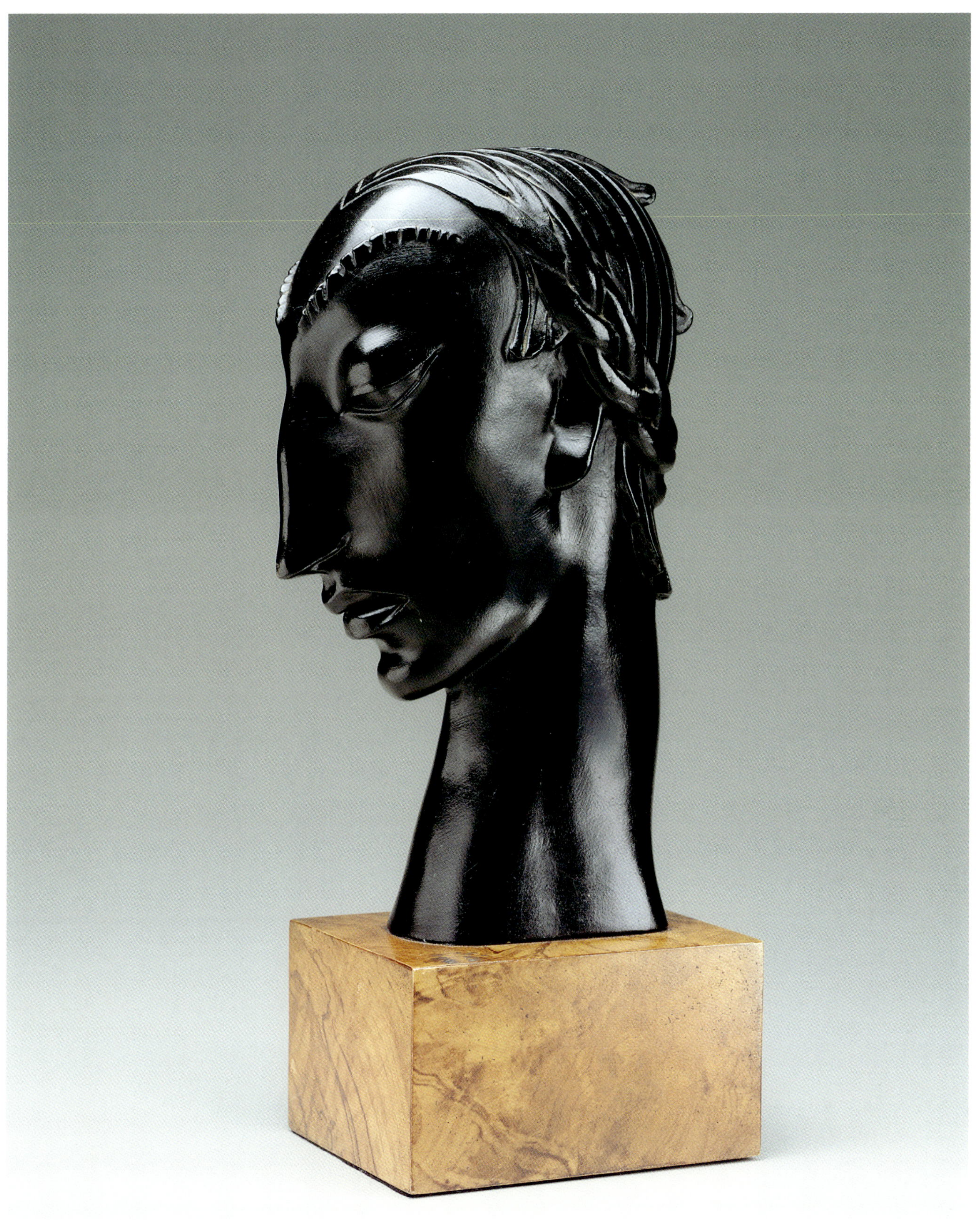

Sergei Y. Soudeikine AMERICAN, BORN RUSSIA 1886–1946

58 | *Sarah and Her Uncle*, c. 1940s

Oil on board, 21⅞ × 17¾ in.

Unsigned

Museum purchase (2000.67)

The Russian-born Sergei Soudeikine earned an international reputation as a painter and stage designer. After attending the Moscow Institute of Painting, Sculpture, and Architecture, he embarked on a multifaceted career that took him to Paris, where he exhibited with the Russian contingent at the 1906 Salon d'Automne, and then to New York, where he settled permanently in 1922. Responding to the avant-garde art movements of his time, Soudeikine began to work in a sometimes whimsical and fantastic Symbolist style, one he would later leave behind in favor of a kind of primitivism that partly responds to painters like Pablo Picasso.

In *Sarah and Her Uncle,* Soudeikine incorporates the strategies of simplification found in such works as Picasso's proto-Cubist *Portrait of Gertrude Stein* (1906; The Metropolitan Museum of Art, New York). Primarily rendered in dark tonalities, the modest and pensive African American figures are volumetrically constructed and their heads slightly enlarged and exaggerated. Almost sculptural and certainly monumental, their physical substantiveness suggests strength of character and perseverance.

It is significant that Soudeikine painted this double portrait of two well-dressed and extremely dignified African Americans just on the heels of the Harlem Renaissance of the 1920s and 1930s. During the Harlem Renaissance, the African American community, led by artists and intellectuals centered in Harlem, New York, enjoyed an extremely vital and productive period. Characterized by a flourishing of art, music, and literature, this renaissance was spearheaded by such culturally and intellectually important figures as W.E.B. Du Bois and Langston Hughes.

Sarah and Her Uncle must be seen in relation to the achievements of this period and to its emphasis on taking pride in oneself and in one's history and culture. Although the sitters' identities and the circumstances surrounding the work's conception are not known, it is likely that these figures understood that having a portrait painted could be an empowering affirmation of status within a community. In addition to emphasizing their dignified bearing, Soudeikine uses a number of objects to suggest that his subjects are accustomed to maintaining an immaculate appearance outside the portrait studio and that they are well educated and financially comfortable. Sarah's uncle, for example, holds a book, which implies both literacy and an intellectually curious mind, while his gold pocket watch reiterates his seriousness and indicates that he is an organized individual who must keep track of a number of obligations. It also denotes that he has the means to acquire what is likely a costly timepiece.

In addition to *Sarah and Her Uncle,* Soudeikine painted other works featuring African Americans, among them *Colored People Dancing,* which he exhibited at the Society of Independent Artists in 1924. Additionally, in his work as a stage designer, he made drawings for the first production of George Gershwin's opera *Porgy and Bess* (1935) in Charleston, South Carolina, which relates the difficulties of residents of Catfish Row, an African American community in Charleston.

Soudeikine's work for the stage eventually overshadowed his painting career, and he was frequently asked to collaborate with such international theater, opera, and ballet figures as Sergei Diaghilev and Konstantin Stanislavsky. After his immigration to the United States, he worked as a principal set designer for the Metropolitan Opera in New York City. MK

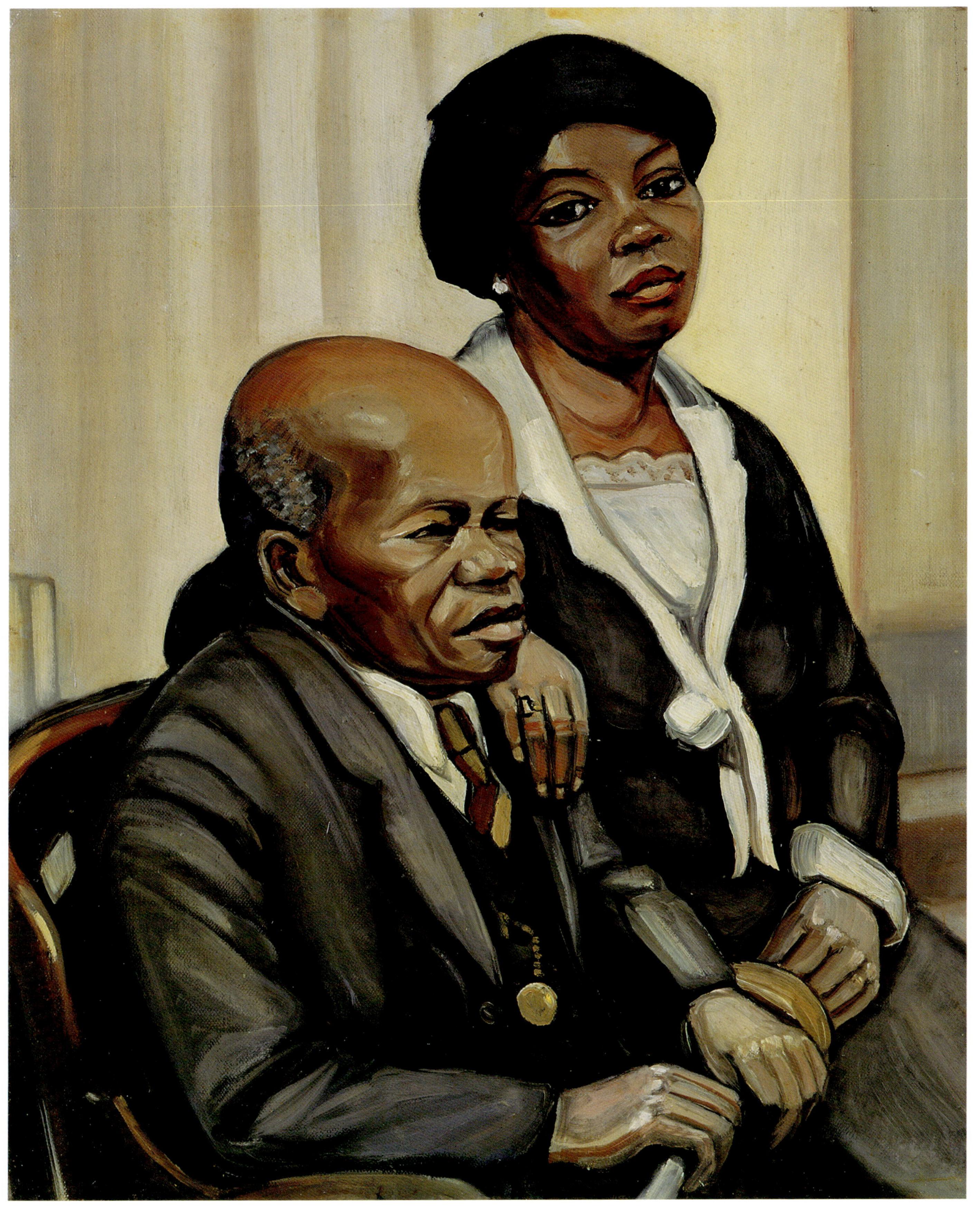

James Daugherty AMERICAN 1887–1974

59 | *Commuters Return*, c. 1930s

Oil on Masonite, 18¼ × 30⅛ in.

Signed lower left: *J. Daugherty*

Gift of the Founders Society (1998.21)

James Daugherty's long career encompassed work in avant-garde easel painting, numerous public murals, and illustrations for a wide variety of publications. Raised in Indiana, Ohio, and Washington, D.C., Daugherty enrolled at Washington's Corcoran School of Art in 1903 and in 1904 entered the Darby Summer School of Painting in Darby, Pennsylvania, run by Thomas Anshutz and Hugh Breckenridge. After finishing high school that fall, Daugherty enrolled at the Pennsylvania Academy of the Fine Arts, studying under William Merritt Chase; his classmates included Charles Sheeler and Morton Livingston Schamberg. Daugherty first began working in newspaper illustration after he moved to New York in 1907. Illustration remained very important to him throughout his career; he worked for numerous newspapers and magazines, including the *New Yorker,* and enjoyed recognition for his book illustrations over several decades.[1]

In New York, Daugherty had access to the most progressive European currents in art, and about 1913 he developed a style of painting that borrowed elements from Cubism and Futurism. By 1915 he was working in a Synchromist manner of abstracted, highly colored planes and volumes. He became involved with the Société Anonyme, established by Katherine Dreier and Marcel Duchamp to promote understanding and appreciation of modern art. Daugherty contributed to the organization's first exhibition in 1920 and also participated in the group's later shows.

In the early 1920s Daugherty adapted elements of his avant-garde style to develop a more representational art while continuing to use the bright palette, fragmented spatial construction, and distorted figures of his Synchromist work. The more than fourteen mural commissions he received in the 1920s and 1930s are among his best-known artworks. Most of the subjects of these murals are accessible themes typical of American Scene painting: everyday civic and political life, American farms and cities, workers, moviegoers, and children at school.

Commuters Return shares both style and subject with Daugherty's mural paintings of the 1930s. The bright colors are applied in broad areas that suggest the elements of the scene rather than provide specific details. He does not create an illusion of actual human flesh and musculature: the legs of the blond woman at the left, for instance, are formed with pronounced strokes of two colors of paint. The busy scene, with its many figures and vignettes, is calmer than some of Daugherty's vertiginous mural compositions, but it still recalls the energy the artist brought to larger projects. Its subject matter, however, links *Commuters Return* with Daugherty's other work, and with American Scene painting in general. Several of Daugherty's murals deal with aspects of working life, and a section of one created for the Fairfield Court public housing project in Stamford, Connecticut, was originally titled *Home from Work*.[2]

Many artists of the 1930s, and particularly those involved with public murals, were interested in the idea of art as a social and democratic tool. It was felt that, by making intelligible art available to a large audience—and by celebrating daily activities of ordinary Americans—art could help convey civic values and build a stronger nation. About his Fairfield Court murals, Daugherty said they "are supposed to be good fun. . . . I have tried to tell a story in understandable visual terms that can be easily associated with our experience of the immediate past."[3] In a similar way, *Commuters Return* takes pleasure in the quotidian. RSR

1. Daugherty also wrote books—he was both author and illustrator of *Andy and the Lion* (1938) and *Daniel Boone* (1939), for which he won a Caldecott Honor Medal and the John Newberry Medal, respectively. See Rebecca E. Lawton, "James Daugherty's Mural Drawings," *American Art Review* 10, no. 3 (June 1998), p. 191 n. 2.

2. The final title for the panel was *Homecoming*. Rebecca E. Lawton, *Heroic America: James Daugherty's Mural Drawings from the 1930s*, exh. cat. (Poughkeepsie, N.Y.: Frances Lehman Loeb Art Center, Vassar College, 1998), pp. 53–54.

3. "A Shy Artist Paints Bold Murals," *Life* 3, no. 17 (25 October 1937), p. 48.

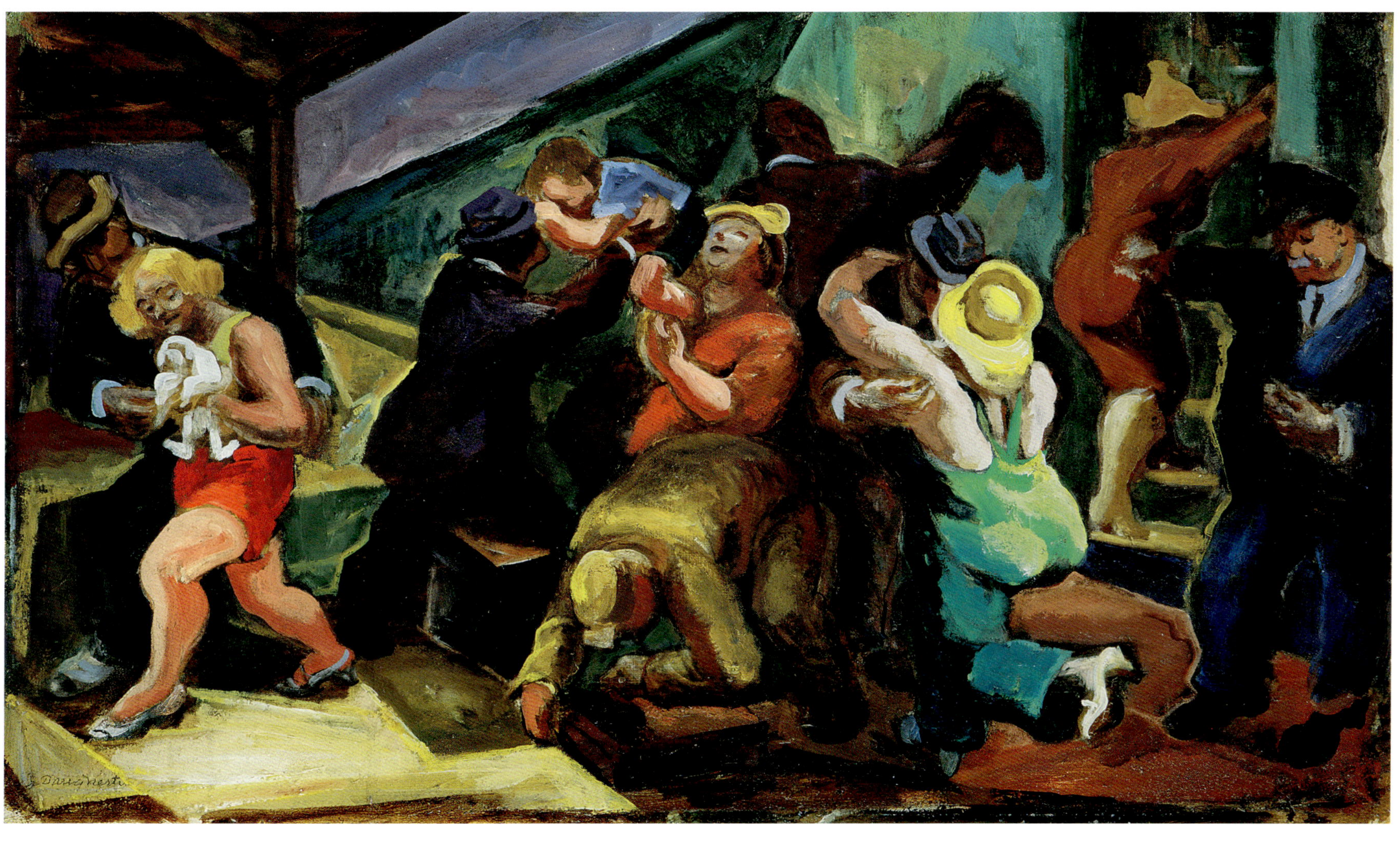

Tunis Ponsen AMERICAN, BORN THE NETHERLANDS 1891–1968

60 | *The Old Pier,* n.d.

Oil on canvas, 26¼ × 30¼ in.

Signed lower right: *Tunis Ponsen*

Flint Institute of Arts purchase by popular subscription (1929.1)

Tunis Ponsen emigrated in 1913 from the Netherlands to the United States. He settled in Muskegon, Michigan, and worked as a decorator, painting and hanging wallpaper. During this time, he developed a relationship with Lulu Miller, the director of the Hackley Art Gallery (now the Muskegon Museum of Art). Miller encouraged Ponsen's artistic ambitions, giving him solo exhibitions in 1922 and 1923. In 1924 he moved to Chicago, where he took classes at the Art Institute of Chicago, studying with, among others, George Oberteuffer, Karl Buehr, and Leon Kroll. Ponsen made his first trip to the East Coast in 1926, traveling to Provincetown, Massachusetts. There he made the acquaintance of Charles Hawthorne, with whom he briefly studied.[1] He would continue to vacation, and paint, in various locations along the Atlantic Coast, and it is likely that *The Old Pier* was executed on one of these trips.[2]

Ponsen's work exhibits qualities associated with both avant-garde styles as well as those of a more conservative nature. His paintings of the urban Chicago environment demonstrate the most modernist tendencies, whereas his landscapes tend to be comparatively traditional. As he said, "You know, I just paint the thing I see the way I feel it. I have no particular theories. I just try to paint well."[3] *The Old Pier* follows Ponsen's ability to work in whatever style, or combination of styles, he considered best suited to the subject. Although the color and tone of the painting are conservative, a more experimental edge is provided by the two cut-off buildings in the foreground—especially the red building at the left, which leans at a sharp angle—the general perspective, and the undulating deck.

Ponsen enjoyed a great deal of success during his lifetime, exhibiting widely in the Illinois and Michigan area. He won several awards and was respected as an established member of the Chicago art scene. He began teaching at the Chicago Academy of Fine Arts in 1945, a position he retained for twenty-two years, until just before his death. As with many artists with regional reputations, he was all but forgotten by historians and critics after his death. A discovery of more than one thousand of his works in the early 1990s brought his work back to public awareness.

The Old Pier, purchased by popular subscription, was the first work of art to enter the Flint Institute of Arts' permanent collection. It hung at the Institute for one year in the 1929 Michigan Artists Exhibition, where it was installed with a box for donations underneath. Ponsen's work is also represented in the collections of the Detroit Institute of Arts, the Art Institute of Chicago, the Toledo Museum of Art, and the Pennsylvania Academy of the Fine Arts.

As noted in a catalogue that accompanied a 1938 exhibition of his work:

> There is a kind of blunt Dutch honesty in a painting by Tunis Ponsen. . . . Ponsen's paintings "grow" on you. At first they may strike you as a trifle harsh, perhaps a bit too blunt. But go back to the creations again and you will appreciate that while Ponsen's method is conscientiously abrupt, it is not audacious. While it is very direct, it is far from crude. You begin to feel the downright integrity of the artist. These paintings are not color poems, mood symphonies or anything of the sort. This is prose, straightforward and deliberate . . . shorn of all superlatives, done by a man well trained in the grammar of art.[4] MMF

1. Susan S. Weininger, *The Lost Paintings of Tunis Ponsen (1891–1968),* exh. cat. (Muskegon: Muskegon Museum of Art, 1994), p. 23 n. 21.

2. Weininger suggests that Ponsen painted *The Old Pier* in the spring of 1929 in Boothbay Harbor, Maine; see ibid., p. 23.

3. Quoted in ibid., p. 19 n. 5.

4. Critical assessment of a 1938 exhibition at the Drake Hotel in Chicago; see *The (Hidden) Estate Paintings of Tunis Ponsen (1891–1968),* exh. pamphlet (Saper Galleries, East Lansing, Mich., 1997).

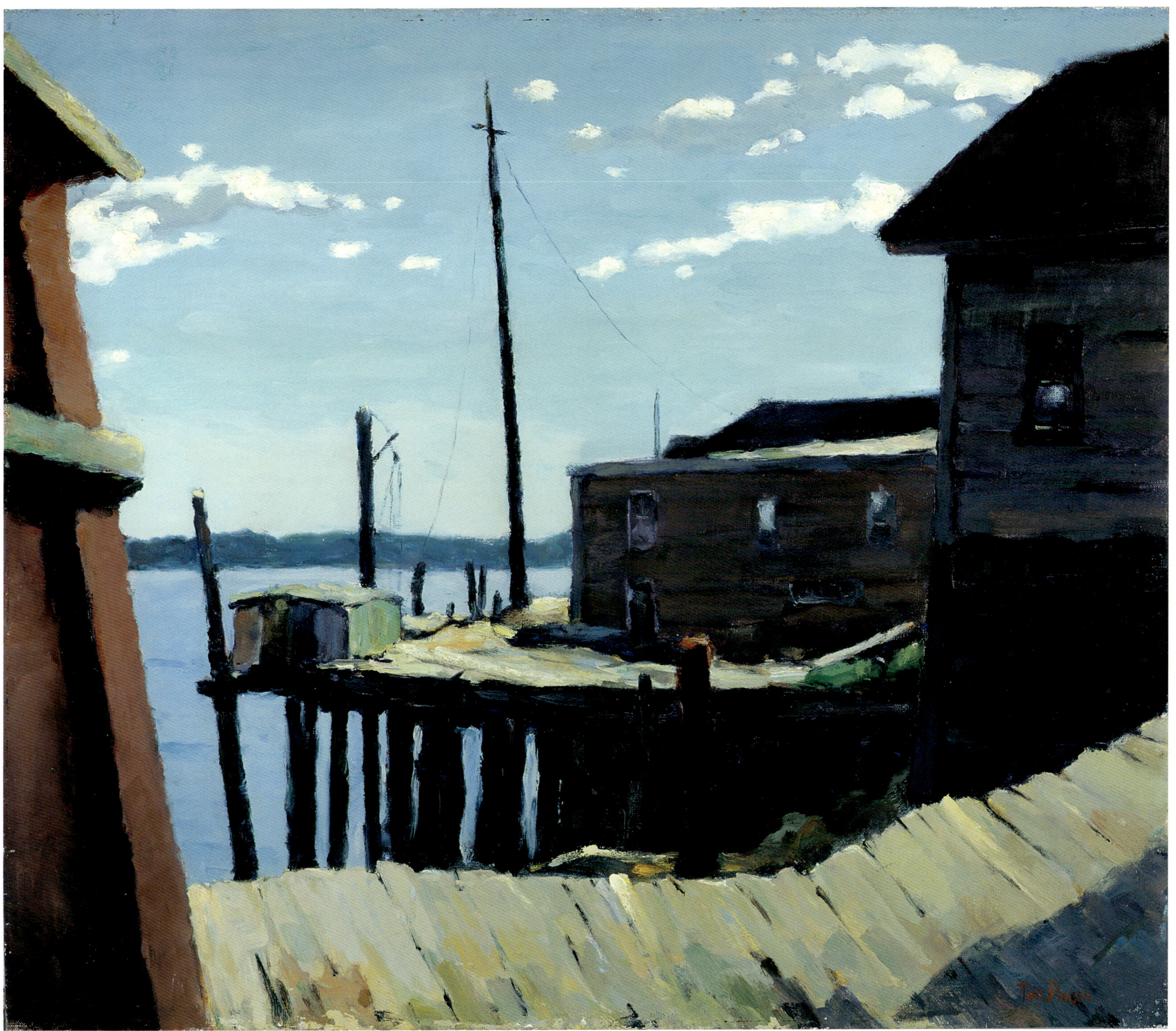

Gifford Beal AMERICAN 1879–1956

61 | *The Abandoned Quarry,* 1951

Oil on canvas, 35¾ × 58½ in.

Unsigned

Gift of Anthony E. and Richard D. van Benschoten in memory of their mother Elizabeth H. Beal (1999.12)

Gifford Beal was one of a group of independent realists who later became associated with Robert Henri's extended circle. He received traditional training from 1892 to 1901 with William Merritt Chase, including classes at both his New York School of Art and his summer school at Shinnecock, Long Island. Other teachers included Frank Vincent DuMond and Henry Ward Ranger at the Art Students League. From a family of substantial means, Beal attended Princeton University at the same time he pursued his studies in art. Receiving his degree in 1900, he began showing at the National Academy of Design the following year, which he continued to do regularly for the rest of his life. He was also a frequent exhibitor at the Pennsylvania Academy of the Fine Arts. Beal won many prizes and awards in his long career, receiving his first in 1903, just two years after he began to show his work. In 1908 he was nominated as an Associate of the National Academy of Design; he became a full Academician in 1914. He also continued his association with the Art Students League, serving as its president for several terms between 1916 and 1930. Beal traveled with some frequency, visiting Europe twice as well as making a number of trips to Caribbean locales, including Puerto Rico, the Bahamas, Bermuda, Cuba, and Haiti. The influences on his work, however, remained decidedly American. Starting in 1923, he spent many summers in the coastal fishing village of Rockport, Massachusetts, a place that proved to be an important inspiration. He produced a significant body of work depicting the region, including *The Abandoned Quarry,* executed in 1951.

Beal's oeuvre consists of several types of subjects. He made many circus scenes, as did his brother, Reynolds Beal. As a landscapist, Gifford painted numerous images of New York City and the surrounding region, particularly Central Park, and is also especially noted for his works depicting the Gloucester and Rockport areas in Massachusetts. His early style exhibits some similarities to that of other realists, such as Leon Kroll, Rockwell Kent, and John Sloan, though his work became more distinctive as he matured. In his later years, he embraced a more expressive and spirited use of color and line and his brushwork is blunter, with more vitality and freedom than seen earlier. In his final stylistic phase, he moved toward an abstracted and simplified approach that reflects acceptance of some of the basic precepts of modernist painting. All these tendencies can be seen in *The Abandoned Quarry,* painted a few years before his death.

The large scale of *The Abandoned Quarry* is indicative of its significance and Beal's intention to use it as an exhibition piece. The work was one of his final achievements, winning the Samuel Finley Breese Morse Gold Medal at the National Academy's annual exhibition in 1954. It was also shown at the Century Association the same year, was included in the 1955 and 1979 exhibitions of the artist's work held at Kraushaar Galleries in New York, and was featured in the American Academy of Arts and Letters memorial exhibition held in 1956 to honor his career.

Beal was a dedicated artist who remained independent in his artistic vision. He did not take up social commentary in his work, electing instead to focus on formal issues such as color and form, though he often painted subjects with activity or narrative elements. A critic observed that his work was "not mere reporting—rather, he infused a quality of personal vision into his paintings of Rockport quarry . . . and other recurrent themes."[1] Although somewhat traditional in his training and approach and fairly entrenched in the Academy system, Beal did take part in alternative independent exhibitions. At the same time he was showing at established venues, he was invited to participate in the 1913 Armory Show (though his works do not seem to have arrived) and exhibited at the MacDowell Club and with the New Society of Artists. VAL

1. "Memorial Tribute: Exhibition at the American Academy Pays Homage to Gifford Beal," *New York Times,* 16 December 1956, artist files, American Academy of Arts and Letter, New York.

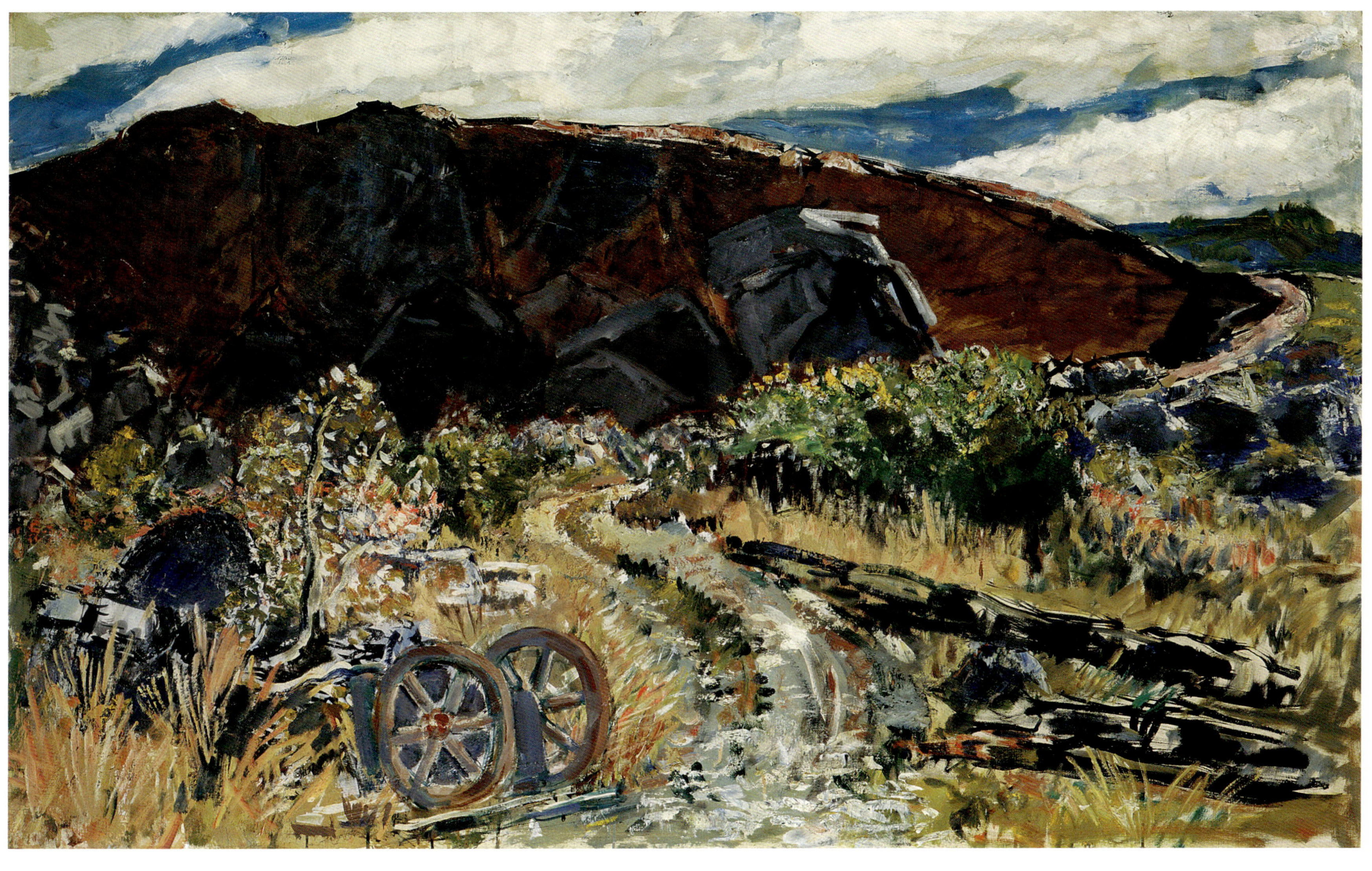

Rockwell Kent AMERICAN 1882–1971

62 | *Au Sable River, Winter,* c. 1961–62

Oil on canvas, 22¼ x 28 in.

Signed lower right: *Rockwell Kent*

Gift of Mr. and Mrs. Jerome O. Eddy, by exchange (1994.5)

Primarily a painter, Rockwell Kent was also an exceptional graphic artist as well as an adventurer, writer, lecturer, insurgent, and political activist. He was born in Tarrytown Heights, New York, and attended Horace Mann School and Columbia University School of Architecture. His training in art included study with William Merritt Chase from 1900 to 1903 and instruction from Kenneth Hayes Miller, Abbott Handerson Thayer, and Robert Henri. Henri in particular was a great influence, though Kent later broke away from his circle. Possessed of a rebellious and irascible disposition, Kent was frequently involved in anti-establishment political causes and antiacademic art organizations. He was an important figure in the planning of the 1910 Exhibition of Independent Artists and organized another independent show on his own the following year. He also published several books, one of them an autobiography, and was a prolific illustrator, both of his own writings and of others' works. Kent was a great traveler and visited a number of far-flung locations, including Alaska, Tierra del Fuego, Greenland, Puerto Rico, Brazil, and Newfoundland.

In 1927 Kent purchased a farm in Au Sable Forks, New York, near the Adirondacks, which he named Asgaard, Norse for "Farm of the Gods."[1] It became his emotional center as well as his home, the place to which he returned from his journeys. He tried to make it a self-supporting dairy farm, though unsuccessfully. He took on commercial projects to help finance the farm and his wandering lifestyle. Kent had a keen sense of place, and both his home and the places he visited stimulated and informed his artistic production. The region around the farm and the nearby Adirondacks served as an important source for his paintings, especially from the 1940s through the 1960s. *Au Sable River, Winter* belongs to this late period.

Kent's paintings are simplified, yet realistic representations of the natural world. After shedding the painterly approach instilled by his former teachers Chase and Henri, Kent developed his own brand of realism, one in which the details of a scene are eliminated, resulting in a stylized representation. This approach is even more exaggerated in his late scenes, which become increasingly static and austere. In smoothing out lines and forms in works such as *Au Sable River, Winter,* where precision and linearity become primary, his late painted work came to resemble his graphic compositions.

According to his notes, Kent painted *Au Sable River, Winter* in 1961 or 1962 on a cold, snowy day in what he described as "uncomfortable conditions," at a place one-half mile north of Au Sable Forks.[2] Kent has aptly conveyed the bleakness of the day and captured the beauty of the region that he found so inspiring. VAL

1. Caroline M. Welsh and Scott R. Ferris, *The View from Asgaard: Rockwell Kent's Adirondack Legacy,* exh. cat. (Blue Mountain Lake, N.Y.: The Adirondack Museum, 1999), p. 11.

2. Rockwell Kent, artist's notes, 8 January 1967, curatorial files, Flint Institute of Arts.

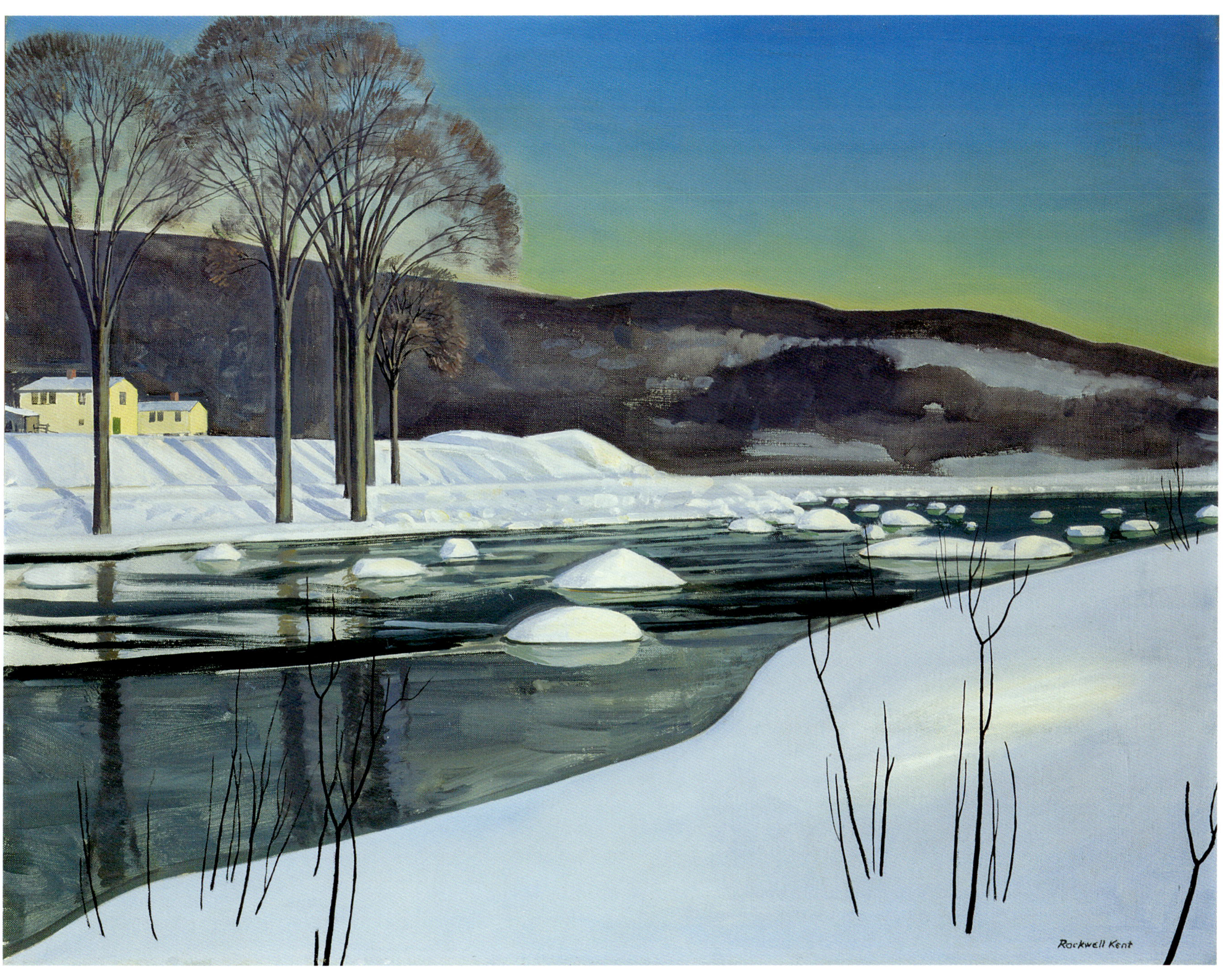
Rockwell Kent

Lucienne Bloch AMERICAN, BORN SWITZERLAND 1909–1999

63 | *The Barn,* 1940

Tempera on board, 8 × 9 in.

Signed, inscribed, and dated lower right corner: *Lucienne Bloch Flint 1940*

Gift of Mrs. R. S. Bishop (1948.1)

Born in Geneva, Switzerland, Lucienne Bloch was the third child of the composer Ernst Bloch and his wife, the musician Margarethe Augusta Schneider. Raised in privileged circumstances, Lucienne immigrated with her family in 1917 to the United States, where they settled in Cleveland. It was there that she had her first instruction in art, as a scholarship student at the Cleveland School of Art. Her formal training continued in Paris, where she studied sculpture with Antoine Bourdelle and painting with André Lhote. She also attended the Ecole des Beaux-Arts from 1925 to 1928 and traveled and worked throughout Europe, making wood-engraved bookplates as well as glass sculpture for the Royal Leerdam Factory in Holland. Her work attracted the attention of Frank Lloyd Wright, who invited her to teach sculpture at his school, Taliesin, in Spring Green, Wisconsin.

Bloch returned to the United States in August 1931, when she was given a solo exhibition of her glass sculptures in New York. It was during this time that she met the Mexican artists Frida Kahlo and Diego Rivera, who were in New York preparing for an exhibition of Rivera's work at the Museum of Modern Art. Inspired by Rivera and his painting, Bloch enthusiastically offered to grind his colors. She accompanied the couple to Michigan, where Rivera had been commissioned to paint large frescoes at the Detroit Institute of Arts. Bloch not only helped him there but also shared the couple's home for nearly six months. She followed Rivera back to New York, where she assisted him with his controversial Rockefeller Center mural, notorious for Rivera's inclusion of, and refusal to remove, a portrait of Lenin among the images. (The standoff eventually led to the work's being destroyed before its completion.) Bloch ground colors and transferred Rivera's sketches to the plastered walls in preparation for painting. Her most important role, however, may have been that of chief photographer. Her images document the painting as it progressed from the initial stages through the unfinished fresco's destruction; they constitute the sole visual record of the work.

As a muralist, Bloch created her own works under the auspices of the New York City Works Progress Administration/Federal Art Project. It was while working with Rivera that she fell in love with the artist's chief plasterer, Stephen Pope Dimitroff. Bloch and Dimitroff eventually married and collaborated as an artistic team, he handling the plaster and she the painting. Her most acclaimed works include *The Evolution of Music* at George Washington High School in upper Manhattan and *The Cycle of a Woman's Life* for the House of Detention for Women. In 1940 Bloch and Dimitroff left New York for the Midwest, where they settled in Flint, Michigan, Dimitroff's hometown. There they continued their artistic endeavors and also taught at the Flint Institute of Arts. *The Barn,* painted during Bloch's residence in Flint, includes a portrayal of their young son, Pencho, who is the model for the boy holding the cat in this depiction of a typical southeastern Michigan farm scene. KEZ

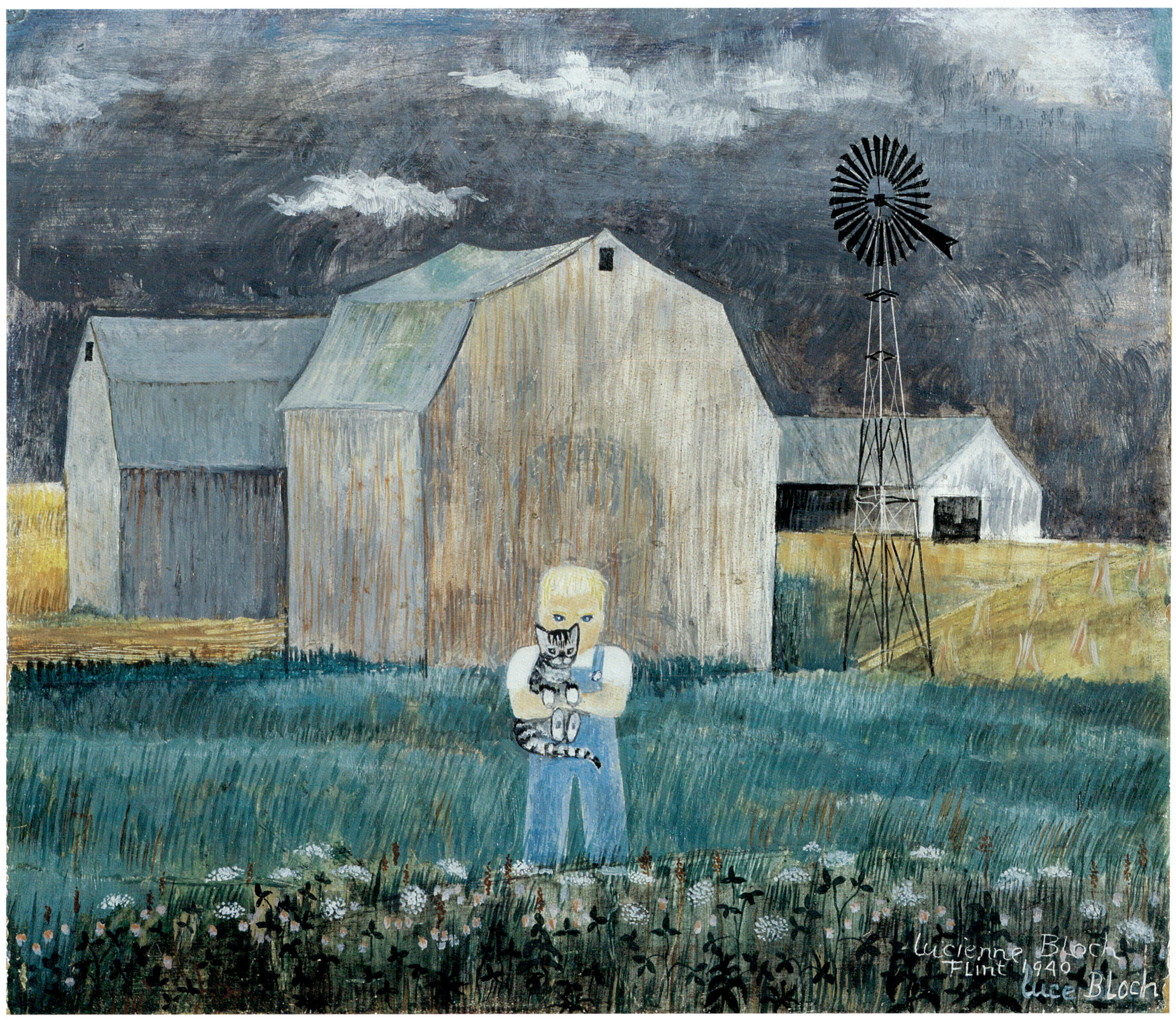
Lucienne Bloch
Flint 1940
Luce Bloch

Theodore Roszak AMERICAN, BORN POLAND 1907–1981

64 | *Musical Still Life,* 1932

Aluminum, 20¼ × 13 × 5½ in.

Unsigned

Bequest of Mary Mallery Davis, by exchange (2002.4)

Theodore Roszak and his family emigrated from Poland to Chicago when the artist was an infant. First trained in art at the Art Institute of Chicago, Roszak later moved to New York, where he studied at the National Academy of Design and also took courses with the painter George Luks. A fellowship in 1929 allowed Roszak to spend an extended period in Europe, where he was exposed to the latest developments in abstract art, including the machine aesthetic of the Bauhaus that would ultimately shape his career.

After his return to New York in 1931, Roszak received a fellowship from the Tiffany Foundation; the two-year period of foundation support, spent in Oyster Bay, Long Island, and Staten Island, was a fruitful time when Roszak refined some of his most important ideas. He began exploring three-dimensional art by modeling clay and working with plaster. Roszak also grew interested in the use of industrial materials and techniques and expanded his knowledge of the tools used to manipulate them.

Musical Still Life represents the fundamental developments of this period. The medium—aluminum—reflects his interest in industrial materials and in the principles of Constructivism, both of which he pursued further in later sculptural work. The pyramidal arrangement in the center of the relief consists of shapes that are not entirely recognizable but suggest musical instruments: the sound hole of a violin, the bow or a neck of an instrument, and the strings connecting two elements in the top of the composition. This iconography had personal significance (Roszak was an accomplished violinist) and also relates to other images from the same period, such as the plaster relief *Musical Elements as Architectural Forms* (1933; destroyed).[1] The triangular composition of abstracted shapes, sometimes set on a vertical background or support, is repeated in numerous drawings and other reliefs from 1931 to 1933. A painted plaster version of the Flint Institute of Arts' work, also titled *Musical Still Life* (1932; estate of Theodore Roszak), incorporates wood pieces and chair caning around the edge of the relief.[2] The iconography of the two works is almost identical, but the bright colors of the polychromed piece and the quality of its wood and caning lend it an almost handcrafted feel that is very different from the smooth, brushed-aluminum surface of the Flint Institute relief.

In keeping with Bauhaus ideals, Roszak explored clean-cut surfaces, reminiscent of industrial products, in his sculptural work for the next fifteen years. In the mid-1940s Roszak shifted to expressionistic welded sculptures, and in his later career he created large-scale drawings. Roszak's public projects included the bell tower for the Massachusetts Institute of Technology's chapel designed by Eero Saarinen (1955–56) and the eagle on the facade of the United States Embassy building in London (1960). RSR

1. Illustrated in Howard E. Wooden, *Theodore Roszak: The Early Works, 1929–1943*, exh. cat. (Wichita, Kans.: Wichita Art Museum, 1986), p. 38, fig. 28.

2. Illustrated in Douglas Dreishpoon, *Theodore Roszak: Constructivist Works, 1931–1937*, exh. cat. (New York: Hirschl & Adler Galleries, 1992), p. 21, cat. no. 2.

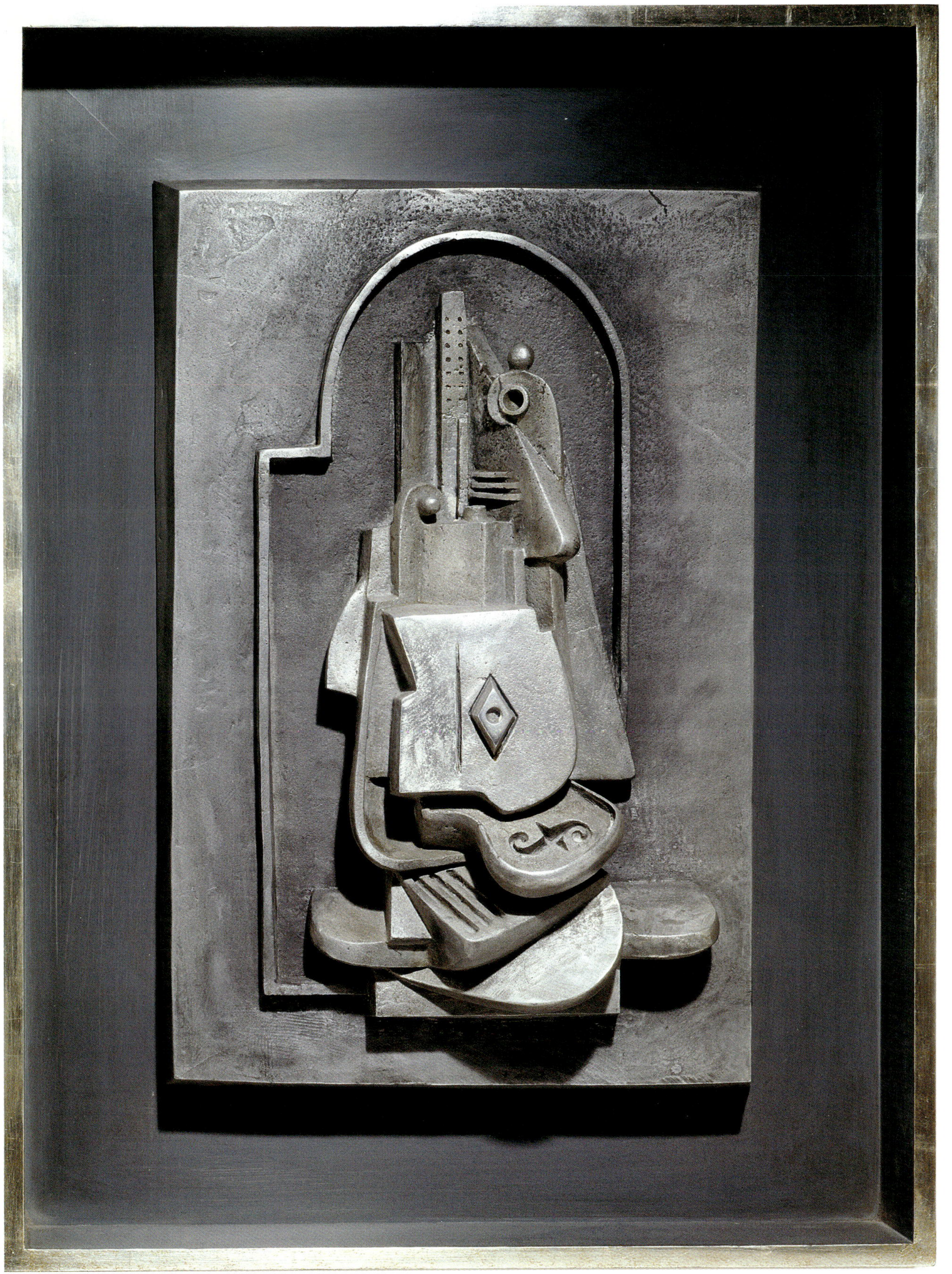

George L. K. Morris AMERICAN 1905–1975

65 | *Rotary Motion,* 1938

Oil on canvas, 30 × 26 in.

Signed lower right: *Morris;* dated lower left: *1938*

Gift of Mr. and Mrs. Martin Ryerson, by exchange (2002.2)

In addition to his accomplishments in avant-garde painting and sculpture, George L. K. Morris promoted and wrote extensively on modern art. Morris, who came from an affluent background and was known as one of the "Park Avenue Cubists," attended Yale University, where he edited the *Yale Literary Magazine*. After college, he studied in New York at the Art Students League and from 1929 to 1930 lived in Paris, where he took courses with Fernand Léger and Amédée Ozenfant at the Académie Moderne.

In Paris, Morris began developing his lifelong commitment to abstract art, and by the mid-1930s his work became almost entirely free of recognizable imagery.[1] Morris drew from several modern idioms, particularly Analytic Cubism and the biomorphism of such artists as Joan Miró and Jean Arp, combining hard-edged geometric imagery with curvilinear shapes to create clear and organized compositions. Interested in the optical contrasts of surface and depth, Morris customarily layered the elements of his paintings—such as the slender black shapes atop the white forms in *Rotary Motion*—and "floated" them on a shallow, often light-colored, background.[2]

Morris had extensive connections in the contemporary art world of New York, which allowed him to observe its nuances and also lent him particular influence in the writing and art organizing that were important parts of his career. Albert Eugene (A.E.) Gallatin, a distant cousin and family friend, developed an extensive collection of modern art and founded the Museum of Living Art at New York University, which he devoted to modernism. Gallatin named Morris a curator of the museum in 1933.[3] With Gallatin, Morris founded and wrote regularly for *Plastique,* a Paris-based journal concerned with the study of abstract art. Morris also collaborated in the creation of the *Partisan Review;* his column, "Art Chronicle," was continued in later years by other noted critics, including Robert Goldwater and Clement Greenberg. He also contributed to numerous other publications, including *Life* and *Artnews*.

In 1936 a group of avant-garde artists in New York organized the American Abstract Artists (AAA), which aimed to promote abstraction through exhibitions, lectures, films, and publications. Although the group's members worked in a variety of nonrepresentational styles, they were most closely associated with Synthetic Cubism. Early members included Morris, Balcomb Greene, Ilya Bolotowsky, Willem de Kooning, and Lee Krasner. Through his essays for the AAA's annual yearbook and his *Partisan Review* column, Morris came to be seen as the spokesman for the organization. He served as the group's president from 1949 to 1951 and remained active in the AAA, as well as other artists' groups, throughout his life. RSR

1. Notable exceptions are works completed during World War II, when Morris incorporated recognizable imagery into some pieces.

2. Melinda A. Lorenz, *George L. K. Morris: Artist and Critic* (Ann Arbor, Mich.: UMI Research Press, 1982), p. 54.

3. Debra Bricker Balken and Deborah Menaken Rothschild, *Suzy Frelinghuysen and George L. K. Morris, American Abstract Artists,* exh. cat. (Williamstown, Mass.: Williams College Museum of Art, 1992), p. 17.

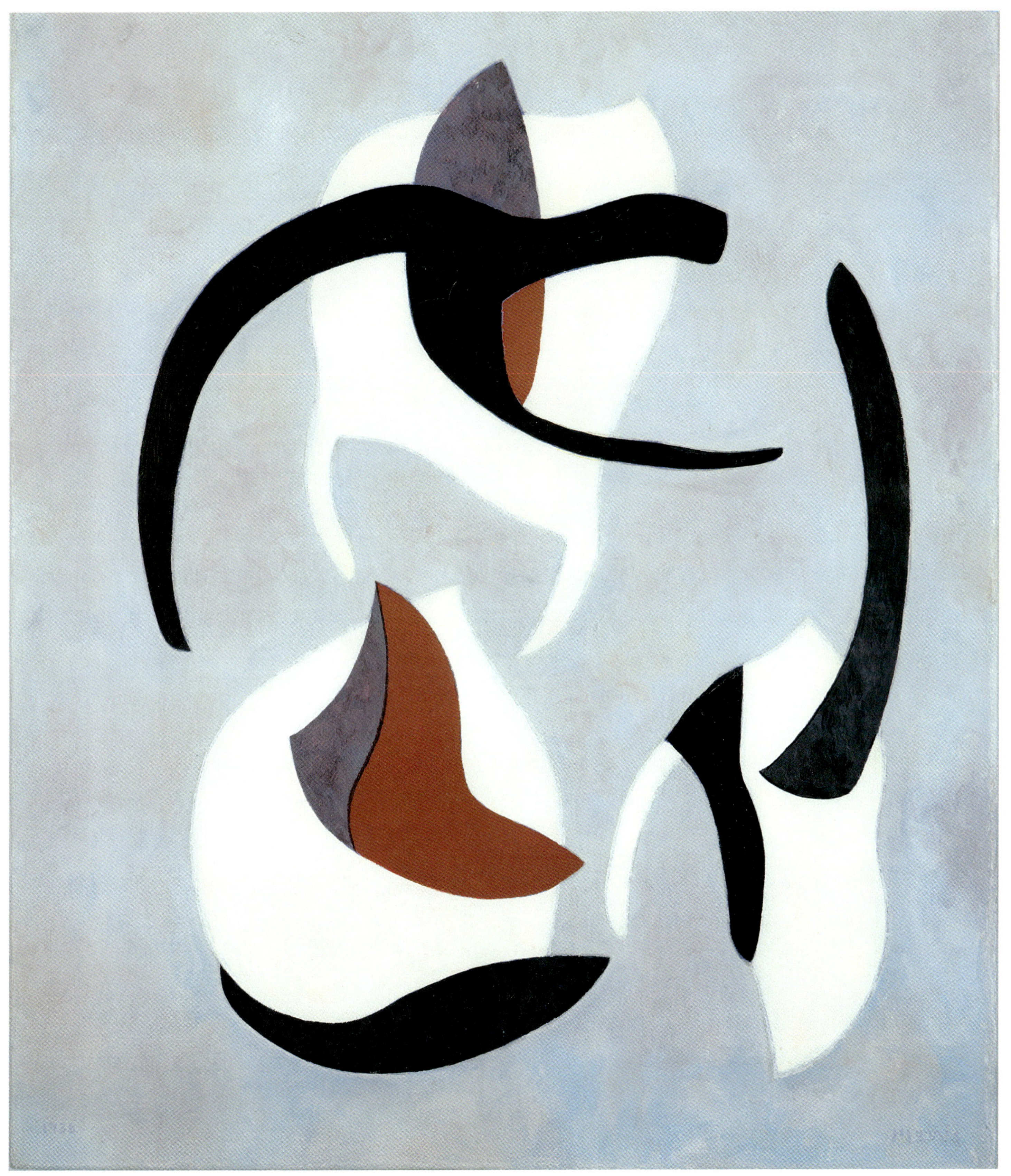

Emil Bisttram AMERICAN, BORN HUNGARY 1895–1976

66 | *Sea Pattern,* c. 1957–58

Oil on canvas, 24 × 27 in.
Signed lower right: *Bisttram*
Museum purchase (2000.68)

Emil Bisttram is recognized as an influential figure in the Taos, New Mexico, artists' colony as well as for his work as an abstract painter. He is especially noted for his role as one of the founders of the Transcendental Painting Group, a loose confederation of southwestern abstract artists who shared a similar artistic philosophy.

Bisttram was born in Hungary and immigrated with his family to America, where they settled in New York City's Lower East Side in 1907. Originally trained as a cabinetmaker, he was determined to pursue a career in art. To this end, he first attended night school for illustration and received instruction at a number of institutions, including the National Academy of Design, Cooper Union, Parsons School of Design, and the Art Students League, studying with Leon Kroll, Jay Hambidge, and Howard Giles, among others. Hambidge was an especially important figure in Bisttram's development, for he introduced him to Dynamic Symmetry, a compositional approach that was based on proportional relationships, a method to which Bisttram became committed. He served an apprenticeship for two years before setting out on his own, building a successful art agency along with teaching at the New York School of Fine and Applied Arts and Master Institute of the Roerich Museum in New York. In 1930 Bisttram received a Guggenheim Fellowship. He went to Mexico to study with Diego Rivera, an artist who subsequently exerted a profound stylistic influence on Bisttram, one that persisted for a number of years but eventually faded.

Bisttram's reputation is inextricably linked to New Mexico and the Taos artists' colony. He first visited New Mexico in 1930 but, like Stuart Davis and Edward Hopper, initially found its landscape inhibiting. Despite this, he settled in Taos full-time two years later. There he founded the Taos School of Art, which was afterward renamed the Bisttram School of Art. The school later relocated, first to Phoenix and then to Los Angeles, where Bisttram would spend part of each year. During the 1930s he also became involved in the New Deal art program and worked on a number of murals, including several in New Mexico. Instrumental in the development of Taos as an art center, he cofounded, with Raymond Jonson, the Transcendental Painting Group. Committed to producing and promoting nonobjective art as an expression of universal spirituality, these artists sought deeper meaning in abstraction, reacting against the formalism of many of its practitioners. Though active for only three years, the group was of major importance in the cultural development of New Mexico.

Bisttram was an experimental artist, and his work includes a variety of approaches, ranging from modernist to nonobjective. Late in his career, Bisttram returned to identifiable subject matter and a more painterly technique. In the second half of the 1940s he produced a series of compositions devoted to marine subjects, a theme that interested him through the 1950s. The Flint Institute's *Sea Pattern* is likely from the latter part of this period, as it exhibits the characteristically expressive brushwork and overlapping forms he used at that time. Although interpretative, the work refers to the natural world and reveals detectable forms, such as seagulls, an octopus, and other sea life, within the abstracted design. Bisttram's painting remained based on highly theoretical concepts into his late years—the composition of *Sea Pattern* was likely conceived according to the principles of Dynamic Symmetry, with the coloration based on the palettes of the noted theoretician Denman Ross.[1]
VAL

1. I would like to express my gratitude to Ruth Pasquine for generously sharing her knowledge of Emil Bisttram's life and work (conversation with the author, 18 April 2001). See also Pasquine, "The Politics of Redemption: Dynamic Symmetry, Theosophy, and Swedenborgianism in the Art of Emil Bisttram (1895–1976)," Ph.D. diss., City University of New York, 2000, for more on Bisttram and his theoretical approaches.

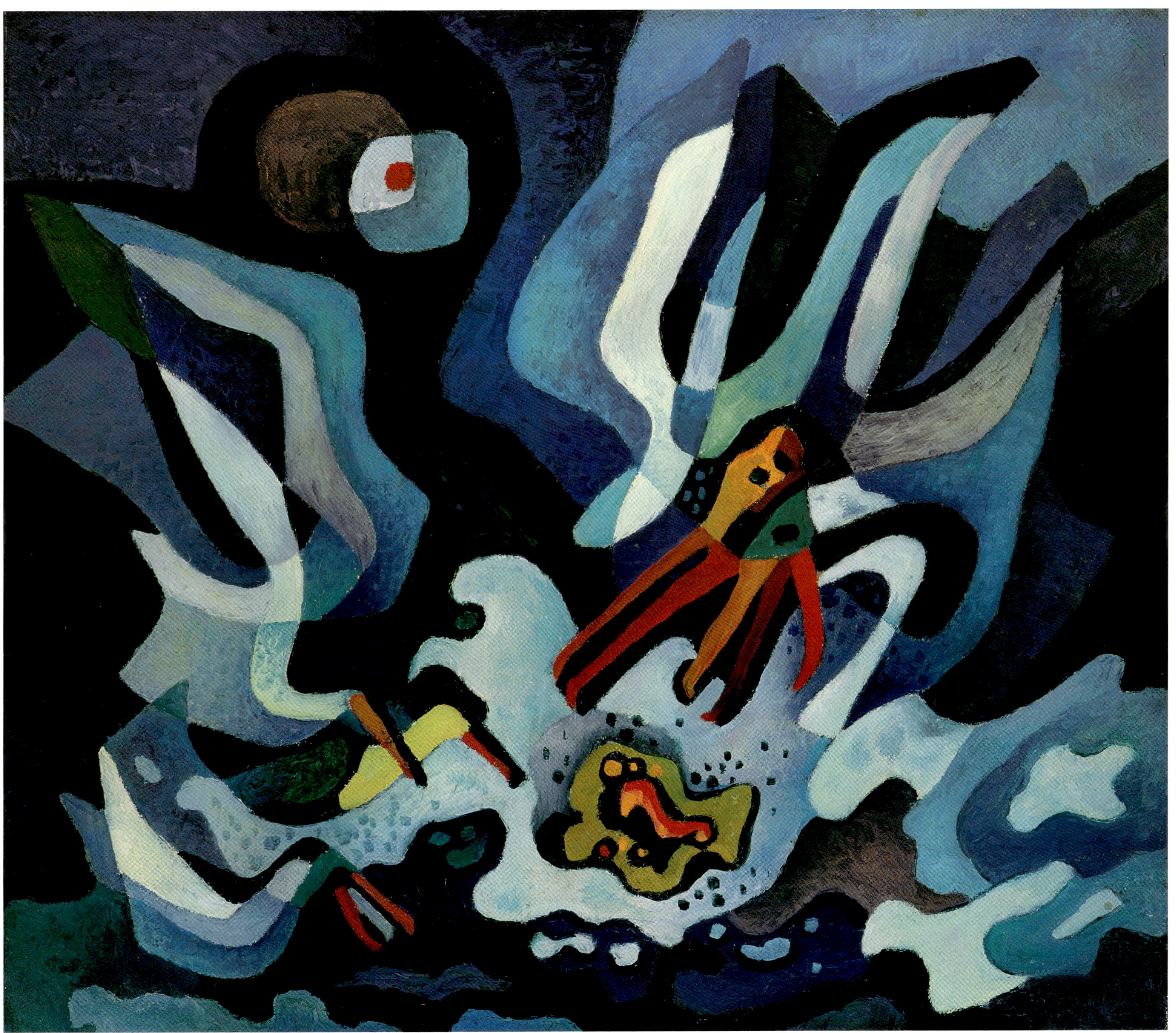

Gerome Kamrowski AMERICAN BORN 1914

67 | *Via Space Ward,* 1948

Oil on board, 29¼ × 22 in.

Signed lower left: *Kamrowski*

Gift of Mr. and Mrs. Kaye Goodwin Frank (1964.7)

André Breton, the founder of Surrealism, names Gerome Kamrowski—whom he had met in 1944—as the most authentic of the American Surrealists and lauded him for the quality, originality, and experimentalism of his work.[1] In a similar vein, Robert Motherwell, later known as an Abstract Expressionist, complimented Kamrowksi as being "the most Surrealist of us all."[2]

Kamrowski was born in Minnesota and began his study of art at the St. Paul School of Art. He left his home state in 1932 and went to New York City the following year, where he took classes at the Art Students League, after which he returned to the St. Paul School. He became affiliated with the mural program in the Works Progress Administration in Minnesota about 1935 and also began to work in a nonobjective manner around the same time. His exposure to Surrealist ideas, then much in fashion, came through not only his art studies but also publications. In 1937 he attended the short-lived New Bauhaus school in Chicago, where both Alexander Archipenko and László Moholy-Nagy were instructors. That same year Kamrowski was the recipient of a Guggenheim Fellowship and attended the Hans Hofmann School in Provincetown, Massachusetts. The year 1941 marked the beginning of Kamrowski's dedication to Surrealism. He was one of the first American artists to experiment with automatism, becoming more involved as his friendships with William Baziotes and Jackson Pollock developed, and he adopted many related techniques such as *frottage, fumage,* and the pouring of pigment.

The Chilean Surrealist Roberto Matta was a significant influence on Kamrowski's work, as was the French artist André Masson. Kamrowski used abstract, biomorphic imagery with occasional recognizable references, but in the end it is often metaphysical concepts and the inner cosmography of humankind that are depicted. This can be seen in *Via Space Ward,* which evokes a sense of the universe and alludes to phenomena of space and the cosmos. In the 1940s Kamrowski became drawn to more intense coloration and sometimes employed, as in this work, such vivid hues as bright pink, orange, purple, or blue.

Kamrowski remained a committed Surrealist and continued his association with the European Surrealists following their departure from New York after World War II. Although he had been a central figure in the development of American Surrealism, he did not achieve the degree of recognition indicated by the success of his early career. One reason may be that Kamrowski moved from New York City to Ann Arbor in 1946 and became an instructor at the University of Michigan, a post he held for many years. Although he continued to exhibit his work with other abstract artists at East Coast venues, he was no longer part of the avant-garde. VAL

1. Martica Sawin, "Gerome Kamrowski: The Most Surrealist of Us All," *Arts Magazine* 62 (December 1987), p. 74.

2. Quoted in ibid.

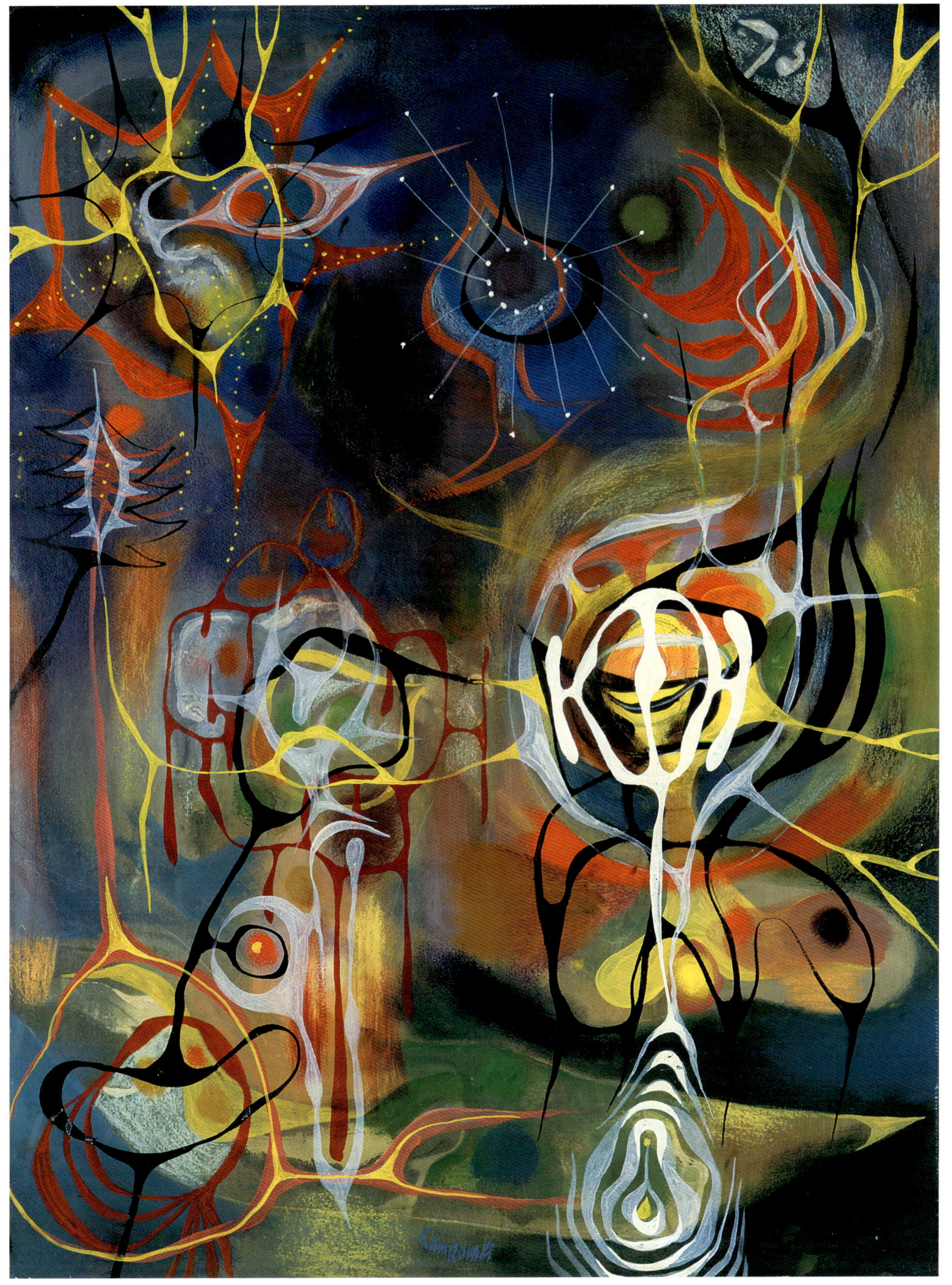

Edmund Lewandowski AMERICAN 1914–1998

68 | *Dynamo,* 1948

Oil on canvas, 36⅛ × 30⅞ in.
Signed and dated lower right: *Lewandowski 1948 (C)*
Gift of Mr. and Mrs. Harold L. Frank, by exchange (1993.38)

Edmund Lewandowski was born in Milwaukee, where he attended the Layton School of Art from 1931 to 1934. After graduation, he took a position as a teacher in the local public school system to support himself, although he continued to paint. In 1936 Edith Halpert, an important New York art dealer, invited him to join the Downtown Gallery. In the same year he became involved with painting murals for the Federal Art Project, and from 1939 to 1940 he executed murals at post offices in Minnesota, Illinois, and Wisconsin. In 1947 he took a position at the Layton School of Art, his alma mater, and from 1949 through 1954 he served on the faculty of Florida State University in Tallahassee. He then returned to Milwaukee to become director of the Layton School of Art, where he remained until 1972, when he was appointed chairman of the Art Department at Winthrop College in Rock Hill, South Carolina.

Lewandowski's affiliation with Precisionism commenced about the time he joined the Downtown Gallery. It was then that he became acquainted with the paintings of Charles Sheeler, with which his work is often compared. Sheeler's art had a great impact on Lewandowski's development. Sheeler also acted as a mentor to the young painter, recommending him for commercial commissions. The influence of the older artist is clear when one compares such works as Sheeler's *Incantation* (1946; The Brooklyn Museum) with Lewandowski's *Dynamo,* executed two years later. Lewandowski practiced the Precisionist mode throughout his career and extended the movement's influence to the Midwest. Like other artists working in the style, including Sheeler, Ralston Crawford, Charles Demuth, and Niles Spencer, Lewandowski was interested in technology, machinery, and industrial subject matter. He recalled that "from as far back as I can recall, the cityscapes, farms, and the depiction of industrial power and technological efficiency has had a great attraction for me. . . . Rather than present reality I try to treat these observations with personal honesty and distill these impressions to visual order."[1] He was also interested in vernacular themes, as can be seen in his depictions of barns set within pastoral Wisconsin landscapes.

Lewandowski attained artistic maturity and was at the pinnacle of his career by the 1940s and was noted for geometricizing objects in hard-edged quasi-abstractions of machinery and industrial forms, as evidenced by *Dynamo.* He noted that "our machines are as representative of our culture as temples and sculpture were of the Greeks. They are classically beautiful and represent physically the material progress the nation has made."[2] Lewandowski can be seen as a contemporary classicist for his cool rational interpretations of the artifacts of industry, which he asserts "have an esthetic impact on me such as the cathedrals might have had on artists of older times."[3] VAL

1. Quoted in Martha Severns, *Greenville County Museum of Art: The Southern Collection* (New York: Hudson Hills Press in association with the Greenville County Museum of Art, 1995), p. 194.

2. Quoted in "Noted Painter of Marine, Industrial Life at FSU," *Tallahassee Democrat,* October 1949, Archives, Flint Institute of Arts.

3. Quoted in "Lewandowski Discovers Formula for Success," *Milwaukee Sentinel,* 3 July 1954, Archives, Flint Institute of Arts.

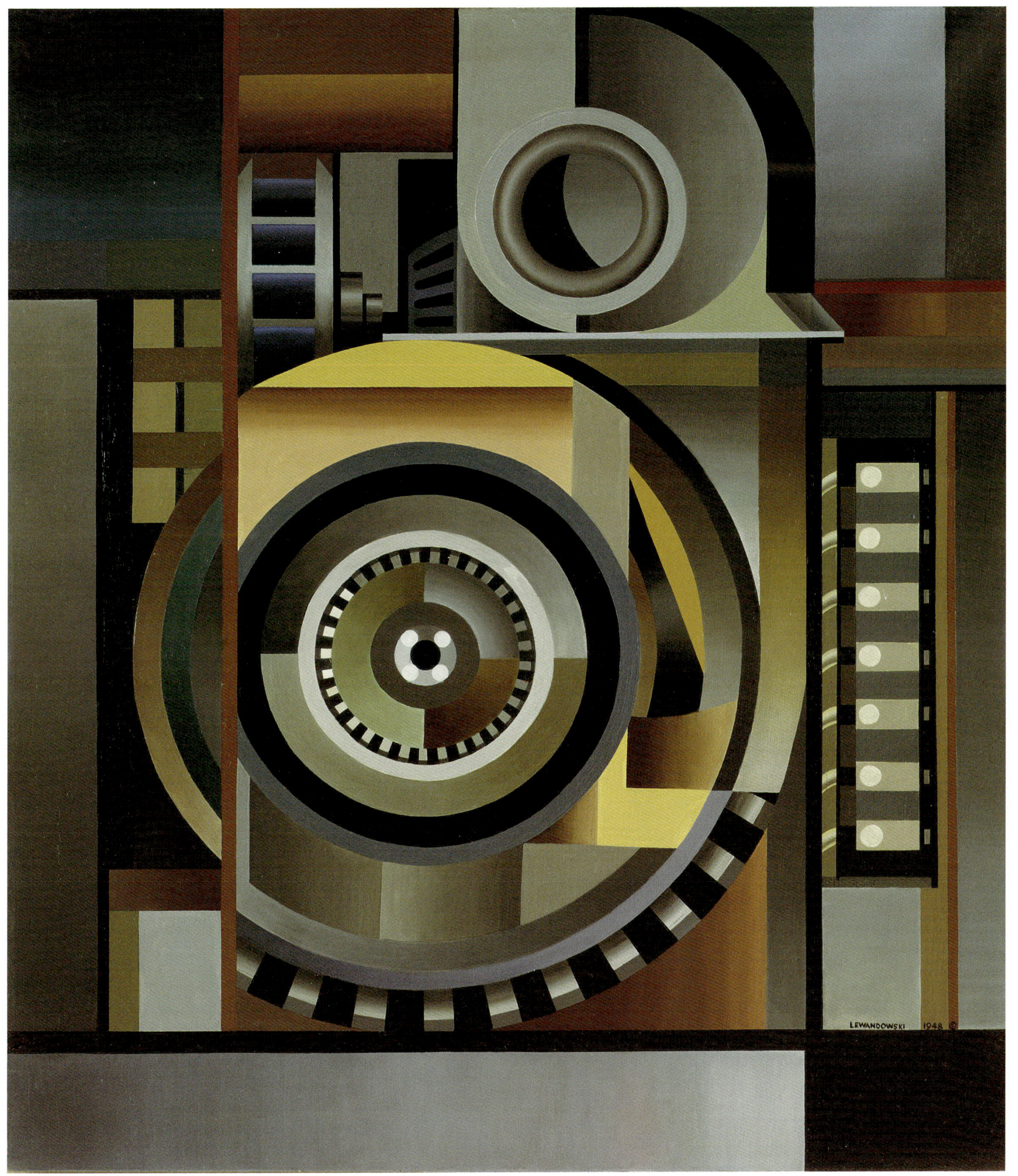
LEWANDOWSKI 1948 ©

Jacob Lawrence AMERICAN 1917–2000

69 | *South African Gold Miners,* 1946

Gouache on paper, 26½ × 27½ in.

Signed and dated lower left: *Jacob Lawrence '46*

Flint Institute of Arts purchase with a grant from the Harvey J. Mallery Charitable Trust (1991.23)

In 1937 Jacob Lawrence began to create visual stories based on African American history, the subjects of which have included civil rights, racism, the rights of the worker, and poverty in America. Flat shapes, sharp angles, slashing diagonals, and a tilted perspective characterize his style. Lawrence effectively uses these elements to express his strong feelings about the struggle of African Americans for equality. Although his work focuses on African American history and culture, it is universal in theme—the struggle of all people for freedom and justice.

Lawrence was born in Atlantic City, New Jersey, and was raised in Harlem during the Great Depression. Although he was unable to attend school for very long, other African American artists, including Charles Alston and Augusta Savage, recognized his talent and encouraged him. His first encounter with art was in an after-school program at the Utopia Children's Center, where his mother had enrolled him. He began painting at the Harlem Art Workshop, a program funded by the Works Progress Administration. In 1936 he enrolled at the American Artists School. Two years later, he was hired by the Works Progress Administration's Federal Art Project, where he worked in the easel division. By 1941, at twenty-four, he had received major recognition for an exhibition of his series of sixty paintings, *The Migration of the Negro*. The following year, the Museum of Modern Art in New York and the Phillips Collection in Washington, D.C., jointly purchased the series, each institution taking thirty paintings.

In 1946 *Fortune* magazine commissioned Lawrence to make illustrations for its October cover story, an article on mining in South Africa. The miners' strike of that year brought attention to the plight of South African migrant workers, who labored in unsafe conditions for low wages. Although government response to the strike was brutal, with hundreds of the 160,000 striking miners killed or injured, the event was seen as a turning point, the foundation for the politicization and unionization of the working class of South Africa. *South African Gold Miners* is one of two gouaches Lawrence created for the *Fortune* commission. The other, *African Gold Miners* (Hirshhorn Museum and Sculpture Garden, Smithsonian Institution, Washington, D.C.), was selected for the cover of the magazine.

In *South African Gold Miners,* five bare-chested black men dressed in white pants wield pickaxes and shovels against a brightly colored background of hills, mine shafts, and railroad tracks. The flat planes and bold colors of the background create an abstract pattern of shapes that suggests the steep perspective of the hills while functioning as a two-dimensional ground on which the figures stand. The interaction of negative and positive shapes heightens this effect. For instance, the yellow-ocher shovel blade in the center foreground is both a tool and an opening in the red ground, while the blue shovel blade, below the figure at the top center of the composition, is both tool and sky. Lawrence's way of working, from a preliminary drawing of the overall design to the final addition of elements and details as he painted, allowed his process to remain open and fluid as he progressed. Each time he added or changed a color in his composition, he transformed the balance and dynamics of the composition.

In this painting, as in all his work, Lawrence treats his subjects with the utmost respect and imbues them with a monumental dignity, one that honors labor and the preservation of self-worth in the harshest of social conditions. MMD

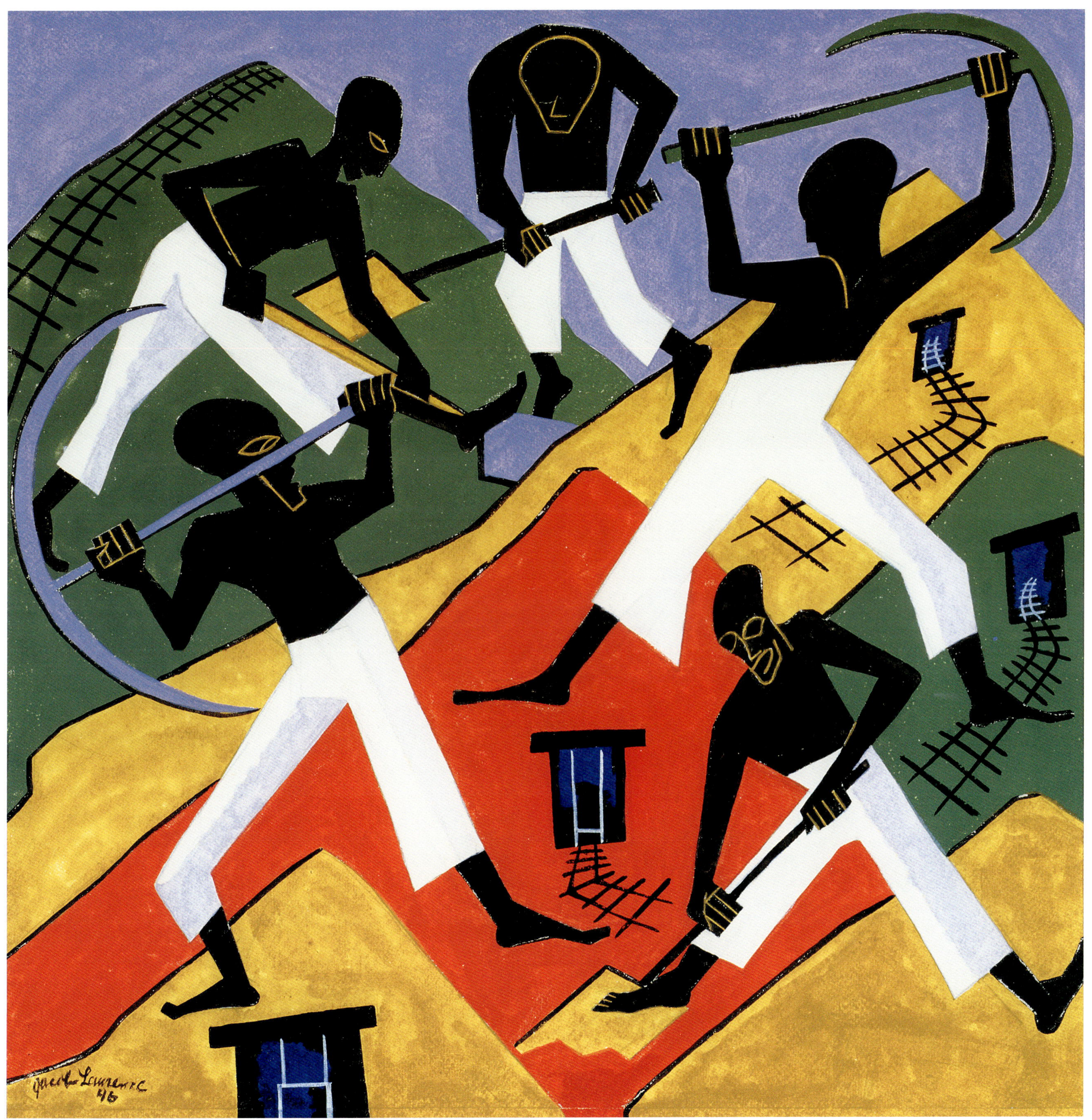

Milton Avery AMERICAN 1893–1965

70 | *Blue Sea,* 1945

Watercolor on paper, 22 × 30 in.

Signed and dated lower right: *Milton Avery 1945*

Bequest of Mary Mallery Davis (1990.30)

71 | *Bicycle Rider by the Loire,* 1954

Oil on canvas, 38 x 55 in.

Signed and dated lower left: *Milton Avery 1954*

Bequest of Mary Mallery Davis (1990.19)

The work of Milton Avery was out of step with the art trends of his day: he remained committed to depicting the world in a representational manner while some of his contemporaries achieved renown with a new style—gestural Abstract Expressionism—that rejected subject matter as outdated. Although his work was well regarded by other artists, especially the avant-garde abstract painters Mark Rothko, Adolph Gottlieb, and Barnett Newman, he met with little critical and commercial success during his lifetime.

Avery was born in upstate New York. Sometime about 1911 he briefly enrolled in a lettering class at the Connecticut League of Art Students in Hartford before transferring to life drawing. He remained a student there until 1918, then studied for two additional years at the Art Society of Hartford while doing factory and construction work to earn a living. In 1925 he moved to New York City to be with Sally Michel, an artist he had met the previous summer in Gloucester, Massachusetts; they married in 1926. His new wife took a job to enable him to paint full-time and, from then until 1938, Avery attended sketching classes several times a week at the Art Students League.

At fifty-nine Avery finally had his first solo exhibition, at the Phillips Memorial Art Gallery, in Washington, D.C., followed by two concurrent New York gallery exhibitions in 1945. Unfortunately, little of his work sold. In 1949 he had a severe heart attack that left him in poor health, although he remained productive until his final year.

Like many artists, Avery often sought inspiring summer locales, and he spent a number of seasons in the towns of Gloucester and Provincetown on the coast of Massachusetts. He also frequented Woodstock, New York; Peterborough, New Hampshire; and Vermont. Gloucester, an area to which he repeatedly returned, likely served as the inspiration for *Blue Sea,* since he spent the summer of 1945 there, the year the watercolor was executed. While Avery was equally accomplished at figurative subjects, still lifes, and portraits, it is landscapes, especially seascapes, that he favored throughout his career and for which he is especially renowned. *Blue Sea* relates to a number of major seascape compositions he painted during the 1940s and 1950s, a group that includes such works as *Green Sea* (1954; The Metropolitan Museum of Art, New York), *Sea Grasses and Blue Sea* (1958; The Museum of Modern Art, New York), and *Dunes and Sea II* (1960; Whitney Museum of American Art, New York).

The mid-1940s represents a turning point for Avery in other respects, beyond achieving recognition; he began to further simplify his artistic conceptions, eliminating nonessential detail. The noted critic Clement Greenberg remarked that:

> Nature is flattened and aerated in Avery's landscapes, but not deprived in the end of its substantiality—which is restored to it as it were by the substantiality and solidity of the picture itself as a work of art. The painting floats, but it also coheres and stays in place, as tight as a drum and as open as light. . . . Avery is able to convey the integrity of nature more vividly than the Cubists could . . . And whereas Cubism had to eventuate in abstraction, Avery has continued to develop and expand his art without abandoning the description of nature.[1]

Blue Sea illustrates these observations, which became even more pronounced in the artist's later years, as seen in *Bicycle Rider by the Loire.* Much like Henri Matisse, Avery reveled in the purely sensuous lines and contours of natural forms. During the late phase of his development, Avery, always a skilled colorist, became even more assertive in his selection and use of color, notable in the rich blue tones of *Blue Sea.* He also turned to exceptional combinations that produce resonant tonal harmonies, exemplified by the unusual juxtaposition of gold, maroon, and brown hues in *Bicycle Rider by the Loire.* Avery traveled to Europe for the first time in 1952. The trip included time in

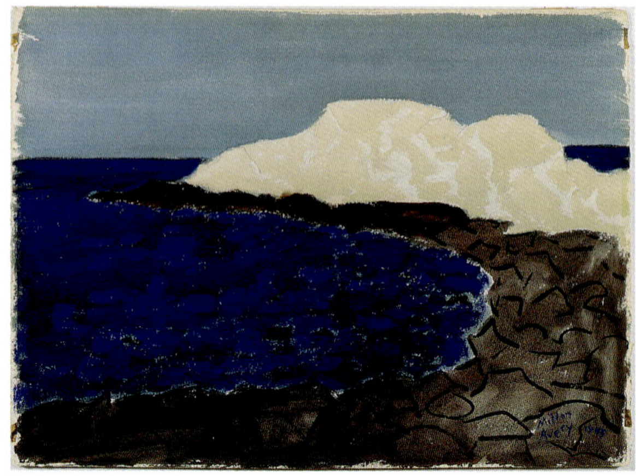

France, where he surely sketched the subject matter for *Bicycle Rider by the Loire.*

Both *Blue Sea* and *Bicycle Rider by the Loire* contain many of the distinguishing characteristics of Avery's style: a lyrical sense of line, economy of detail (his faces rarely have features), spare compositions, the elimination of nonessential visual references, flattened spatial dimensions, unnaturalistic proportions, and a tranquil mood. In contrast to his earlier work, these two paintings from Avery's late period make use of increasingly abstracted forms. Although it shares certain affinities with the work of Matisse (the application of color and fluidity of line, the rejection of explicit details), Marsden Hartley (a reductivist approach and similarities in subject matter), and John Marin (an expressive use of the watercolor medium and in the brushwork), Avery's art remains distinctly his own. A painter who interpreted the world around him in a representational style that ran counter to pure abstraction, Avery nonetheless pushed his art close to the border of nonobjectivity in his later years, a development evident in both of the Flint Institute's paintings. VAL

1. Clement Greenberg, "Milton Avery," *Arts Magazine* 32 (December 1957), p. 44.

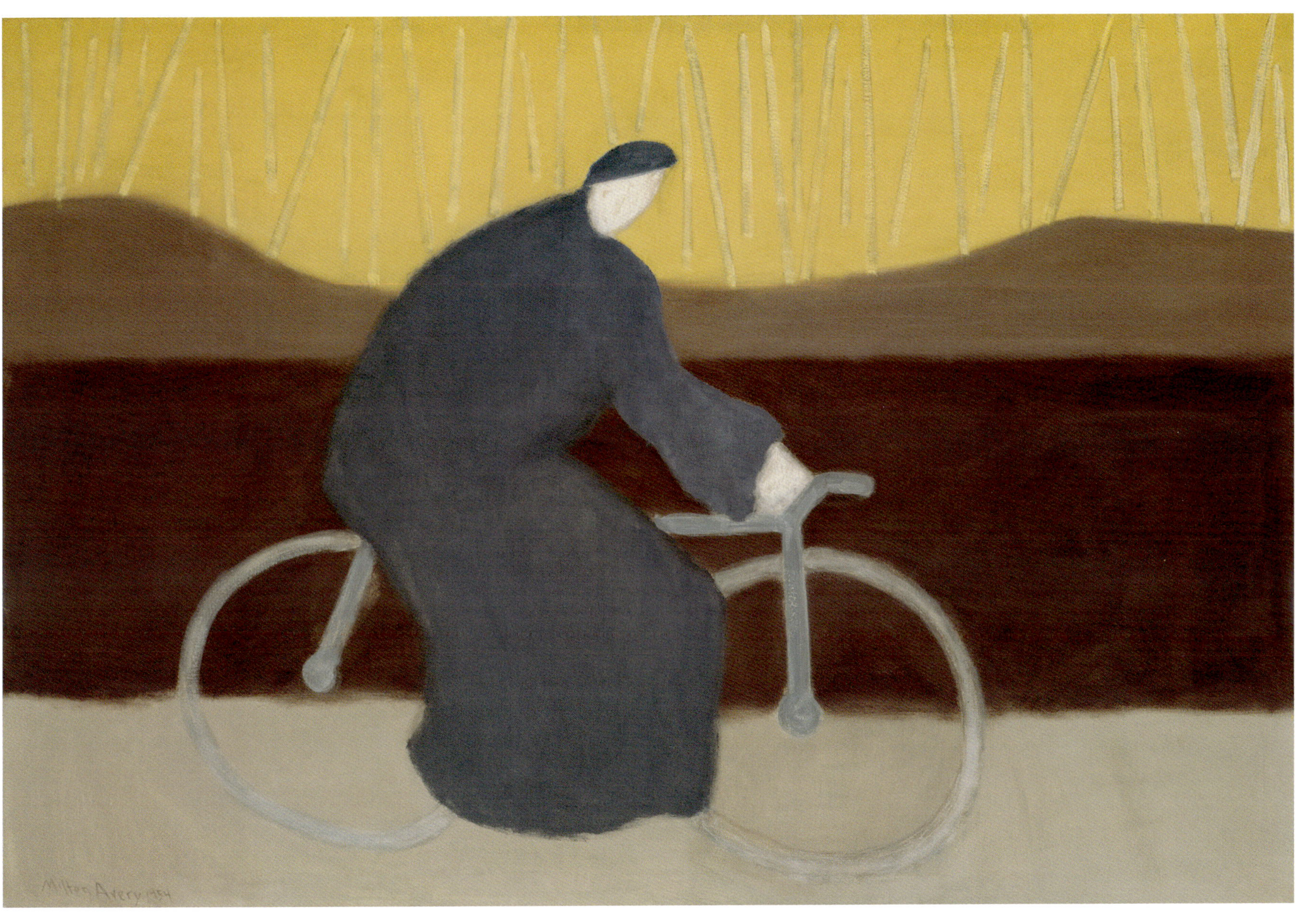
Milton Avery 1954

Hughie Lee-Smith AMERICAN 1915–1999

72 | *Transition,* 1964

Oil on canvas, 18 × 32 in.

Signed lower left: *Lee-Smith*

Gift of Mr. and Mrs. Jerome O. Eddy, by exchange, gift of Mrs. Arthur Jerome Eddy, by exchange, and partial gift of Michael Rosenfeld Gallery, New York (2002.12)

Hughie Lee-Smith, born in Eustis, Florida, studied intermittently at the Art School of the Detroit Society of Arts and Crafts and the Cleveland School of Art (now the Cleveland Institute of Arts) during the mid- to late 1930s. From 1938 to 1940 he was employed by the Works Progress Administration of Ohio and later at the Ford Motor Company's River Rouge Plant in Dearborn, Michigan. About the same time Lee-Smith began to establish close ties with other African American artists in Chicago as well as with such African American poets, writers, musicians, and actors as Paul Robeson, Margaret Burroughs, Joseph Hirsch, and Rex Gorleigh. In 1944 he joined the Navy, for which he executed mural-size paintings with patriotic themes, like *History of the Negro in the U.S. Navy.* When Lee-Smith returned to Detroit in the late 1940s, he continued his education at Wayne State University, eventually receiving his bachelor of science degree in art education in 1953. In 1958 Lee-Smith moved to New York to pursue a full-time career as an artist and teacher.[1]

The desire to convey important social and political messages was the motivating force behind much of Lee-Smith's art. While some of his paintings are meditations on the unequal power relations between blacks and whites, others are reflections on conflict between the sexes. Indeed, Lee-Smith demonstrates an acute understanding of both the African American experience as well as the human condition in general. To make his work accessible to a general audience, moreover, Lee-Smith adopted a largely realistic style, striving to create what he called a "people's art." As he wrote in the journal *New Masses,* "if art is going to be effective in [its] social task it must be understood. Form and style must, therefore, meet with the approval of the great majority of people."[2]

Yet Lee-Smith's paintings should by no means be confused with propaganda. Although they contain social and political content, they avoid overt didacticism through the incorporation of emotional and often highly personal elements.[3] Art historians, as a result, characterize Lee-Smith as a Magical Realist as much as a Social Realist, comparing him alternately with Giorgio de Chirico and Edward Hopper. Insofar as it resists definitive interpretation, the subject matter of Lee-Smith's work tends to both tantalize and teach his viewers. In almost every instance, the figures in his paintings—blacks with whites, men with women—are depicted in isolation, neither seeing nor speaking to one another. They are also often stranded in locations that fail to communicate a "clear sense of place"—deserted beaches, empty parking lots, and vacant buildings—infusing the paintings with a palpable sense of alienation and loneliness, tension and foreboding.[4]

Although *Transition* might appear at first glance to lack the human drama of Lee-Smith's other works, it is by no means bereft of the sociopolitical content of his oeuvre as a whole.[5] Two walls, an ocher rock wall and a white cement wall, dominate the middle ground. The wall is a recurring motif in Lee-Smith's work, functioning as a symbol that can be interpreted in many different ways. As a barrier, it calls to mind confinement—social as well as spiritual, physical as well as psychological. It also alludes to the history of segregation in America. Yet the wall suggests the potential for progress and liberation by pointing out "entrance ways to new lives."[6] Indeed, the walls that appear in Lee-Smith's paintings, including *Transition,* are almost always riddled with cracks, suggesting that they are not, perhaps, as durable as they might initially seem. KB

1. For more information on Lee-Smith's background, see Lowery S. Sims, "Hughie Lee-Smith: Romantic Realist or Poetic Alchemist," in *Hughie Lee-Smith: Retrospective Exhibition,* exh. cat. (Trenton, N.J.: New Jersey State Museum, 1988), and Virginia Spottswood Simon, "Qualities of Loneliness and Light," *International Review of African American Art* 16, no. 1 (1999), pp. 2–18.

2. Quoted in Sims, "Lee-Smith," p. 4. Lee-Smith played an active role in the civil rights movement, raising money by organizing events and auctioning his paintings. He also worked with students at Howard University, in Washington, D.C., where he was an artist-in-residence, on a series of murals on African American history. For more information on Lee-Smith's involvement in the movement, see Simon, "Qualities," p. 17.

3. As the artist himself once said, "I'm always trying to change things from what they are. Why should I paint a landscape the way it really is? I have to put myself into it." See Margo Mifflin, "Hughie Lee-Smith: 'It's a Topsy-Turvy World, Isn't It?'" *Artnews* 93, no. 8 (October 1994), p. 90.

4. Michael Brenson, "Visions of Uncertainty and Displacement," *New York Times,* 28 July 1989, Living Arts sec., p. 18.

5. *Transition,* as the title implies, depicts a space that exists at the threshold between two different worlds. Its subject is either an industrial landscape in the process of being reclaimed by nature or a natural landscape slowly being colonized by industry.

6. Sims, "Lee-Smith," p. 9.

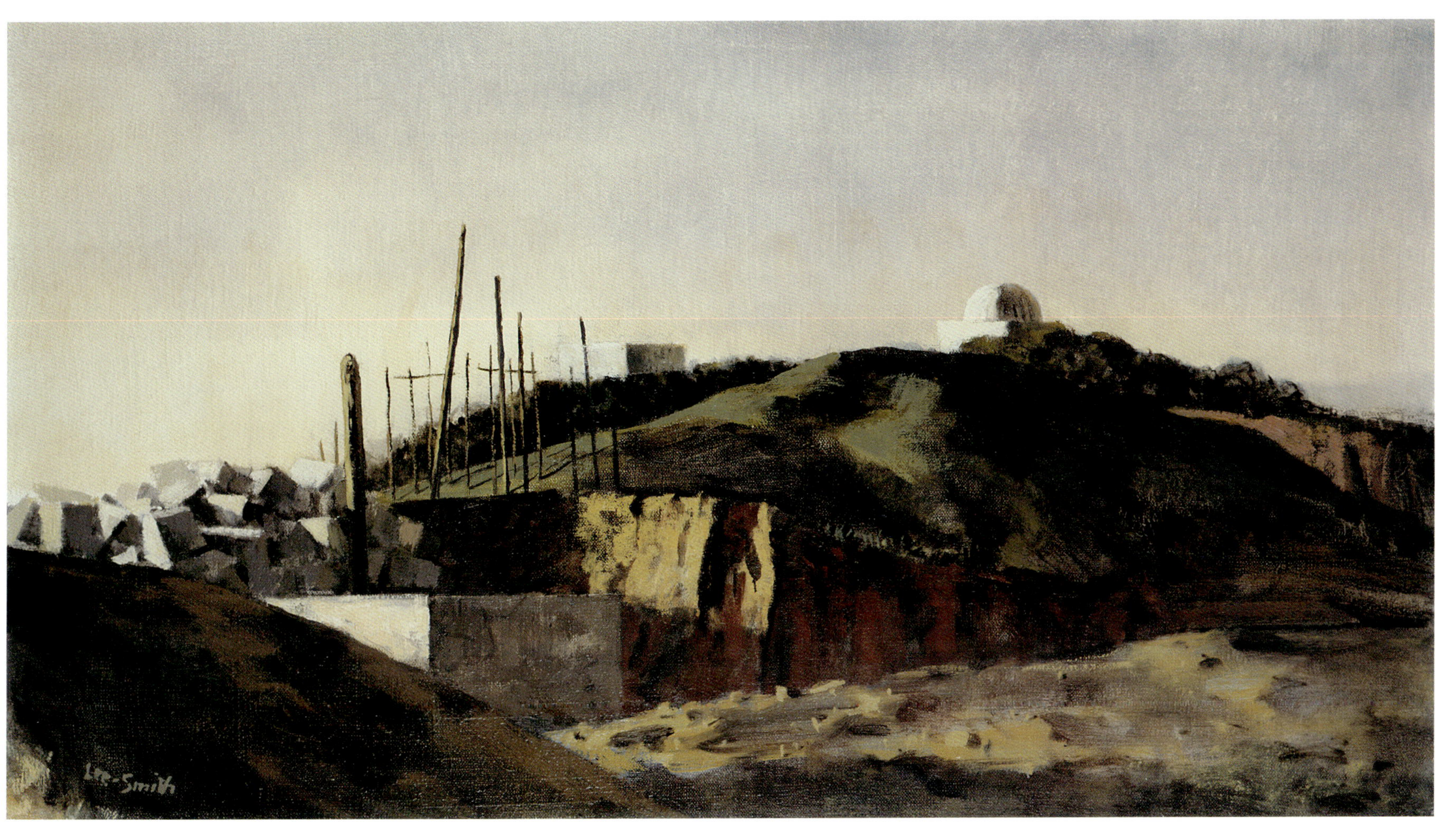
Lee-Smith

Edwin Dickinson AMERICAN 1891–1978

73 | *Landscape, Provincetown,* 1935

Oil on canvas, 11⅛ × 19¼ in.

Signed and dated upper right: *E W Dickinson 1935*; inscribed lower right side: *Provincetown*

Gift of the J. L. Hudson Gallery, Detroit (1969.1)

The work of Edwin Dickinson, a transitional figure, can be viewed as a stylistic bridge between modernism and Abstract Expressionism. Synthesizing and drawing on various artistic sources ranging from the old masters to the work of his contemporaries, he formulated an original approach that can be termed "romanticized realism." He was, however, an experimental painter and did not limit himself to any single method.

Born in Seneca Falls, New York, Dickinson attended Pratt Institute in New York City and then the Art Students League, where he studied with Charles Hawthorne, who exerted the greatest influence on his work, as well as with William Merritt Chase and Frank Vincent DuMond. He became an instructor himself, teaching at the Buffalo Academy of the Fine Arts, Cooper Union, the Brooklyn Museum Art School, and the Art Students League in a career that spanned from 1945 to 1966. He won numerous awards throughout his life and was elected an Associate of the National Academy of Design in 1948 and a full Academician in 1950. An influential artist in his day, especially recognized by his fellow artists, he was given two important solo exhibitions in the 1960s—at the Museum of Modern Art in 1963 and a retrospective at the Whitney Museum of American Art in 1965. Since his death, however, his renown has faded from its former prominence, though his work is highly regarded in artistic circles.

Dickinson led a peripatetic existence. Cape Cod is a recurring theme in his work and a region with which he is closely identified. He lived in Wellfleet for extended periods beginning in 1939 and acquired a summerhouse there; as a result, he frequently painted the surrounding areas. *Landscape, Provincetown* is typical of one aspect of Dickinson's production, the painting of numerous diminutive compositions executed rapidly and while on-site, many of them coastal views known as his *premier coup* paintings. This rapid approach was inspired by his former instructor, Charles Hawthorne. The work was originally conceived as a larger composition, but the artist appears to have cut down the canvas, as he occasionally did, probably because he was dissatisfied with some aspect of the larger image.[1]

The artist's sketchy landscapes appear artless and unstructured, conveying a sense of intimacy and immediacy. As is evident in works such as *Landscape, Provincetown,* Dickinson was fully engaged by the process of painting and revels in the medium, with broad, lavishly applied strokes of paint that create a velvety effect. The scenes are generalized, with little specific reference or detail, yet are inspired by specific locales. Though a sense of quiet pervades these compositions, they are frequently, as here, energized by a sense of movement inspired by windy conditions. Most often exhibiting a dim ethereal light and vaporous atmosphere, these subtle scenes are rendered in a subdued and limited tonal range. They eschew the dramatic for the quiet reverie of a nocturne and appear to spring from the artist's intuitive subconscious, the result of pure spontaneous creative expression. VAL

1. Helen Dickinson Baldwin to Christopher Young, 3 September 1992, curatorial files, Flint Institute of Arts.

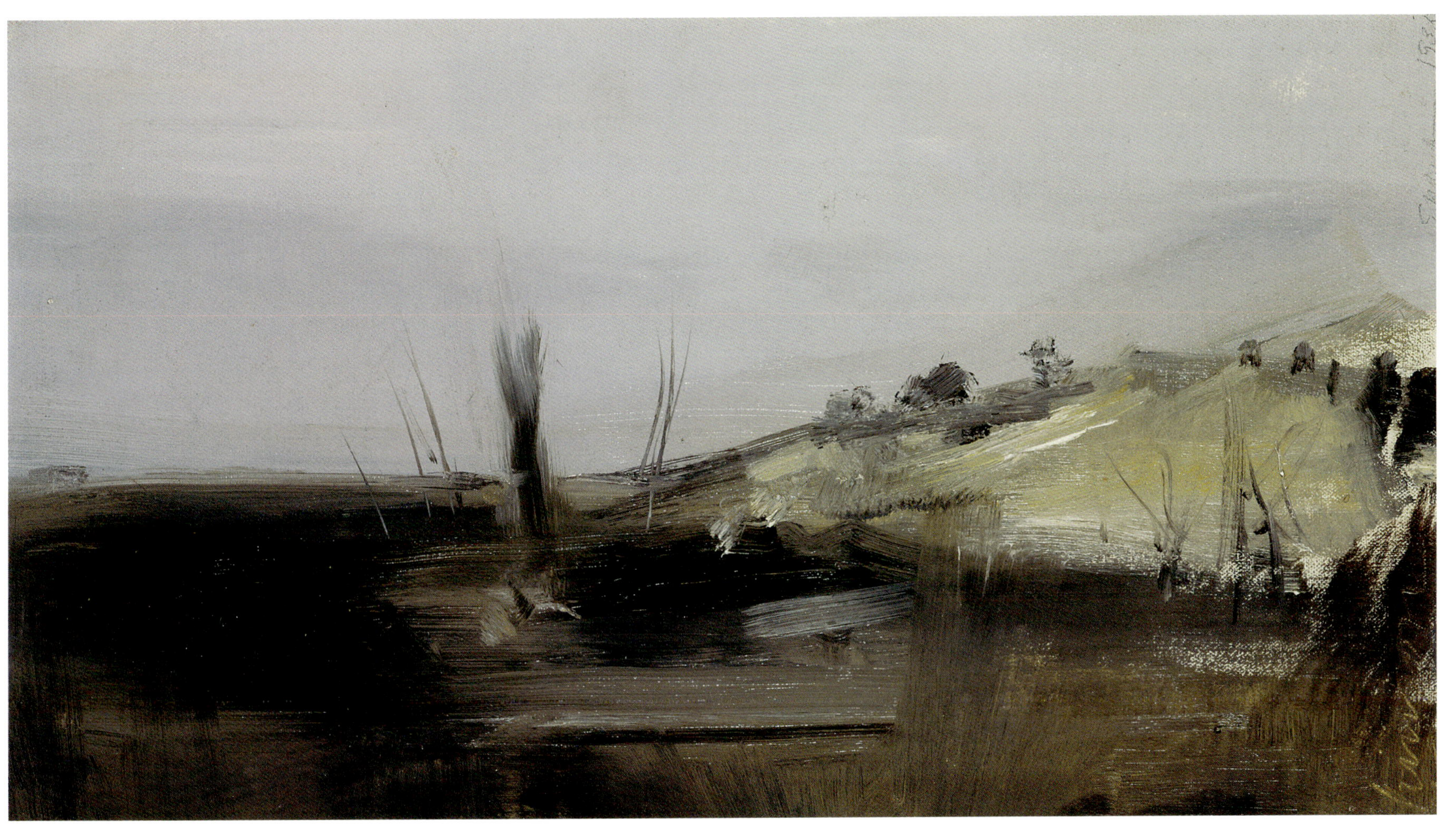

Andrew Wyeth AMERICAN BORN 1917

74 | *The Sweep*, 1967

Tempera on Masonite, 24⅛ × 35⅛ in.

Signed lower right: *Andrew Wyeth*

Gift of Mr. and Mrs. William L. Richards through the Viola E. Bray Charitable Trust (1967.29)

Andrew Wyeth, son of the well-known illustrator N. C. Wyeth, was born in Chadds Ford, Pennsylvania. Surrounded by art from an early age, he was essentially self-taught, learning by observation rather than by formal instruction. He achieved acclaim early in his career—his first solo exhibition of watercolors, in New York in 1937, completely sold out.

A large part of Wyeth's oeuvre is composed of works done in watercolor or tempera, both unforgiving media that demand great assurance and skill, and whose use requires both spontaneity and restraint. Wyeth has often noted that he was especially influenced by the work of Winslow Homer, observing, "I'm not a good enough draughtsman to be a realist. It's like the difference between Eakins and Homer: I feel I'm closer to Homer."[1] Like Thomas Eakins and Homer, Wyeth is considered, in his approach and choice of subjects, one of the quintessential American artists. Working in a straightforward style of realism that celebrates the ordinary and commonplace, he continues painting American subject matter in the tradition of the earlier American Scene painters.

Wyeth has a deeply rooted sense of place and has stated, "I feel limited if I travel. I feel freer in surroundings that I don't need to be conscious of."[2] For this reason, he divides his time between two places, Chadds Ford, in the Brandywine Valley of Pennsylvania, and Cushing, Maine, where he spends his summers. His intimate knowledge of these two environments is manifested in his art, and his work is largely devoted to subjects from these two areas. *The Sweep* pictures a view with which the artist is well acquainted, a vista from the edge of the Wyeth property in Maine, overlooking the road to the neighboring James family farm.[3] The composition references earlier depictions of nearby views, including *George's Place* (1963, watercolor; Collection of Mr. and Mrs. William E. Weiss, New York), which focuses on the stone wall, and *Distant Thunder* (1961, tempera; Collection of Mrs. Norman B. Woolworth, New York), a scene that includes the evergreen trees. Like these other works, *The Sweep* is executed with technical virtuosity, especially evident in the bristling needles of the evergreen trees, the texture of the cold, porous surface of each stone of the rock wall, and the light falling on the weathered oar leaning on the wall. The painting illustrates a key aspect of Wyeth's art: his keen ability to observe and capture fresh sights in these familiar surroundings. The image is also typical of Wyeth in its depiction of a silent, still world that is austerely cool and remote. Despite this sense of detachment, Wyeth has said, "I start every painting with an emotion—something I've just got to get out. . . . My struggle is to preserve that abstract flash—like something you caught out of the corner of your eye. . . . It's a very elusive thing."[4] VAL

1. Quoted in "Andrew Wyeth: The Artist Reflects on His Art," *The National Observer*, 9 September 1968, p. 20.

2. Quoted in "Two Worlds of Andrew Wyeth: Kuerners and Olsons," *The Metropolitan Museum of Art Bulletin* 34 (autumn 1976), p. 24.

3. *Andrew Wyeth*, exh. cat. (Boston: Museum of Fine Arts, 1970), p. 214.

4. Quoted in Wanda Corn, *The Art of Andrew Wyeth* (Greenwich, Conn.: New York Graphic Society, 1964), pp. 55–56.

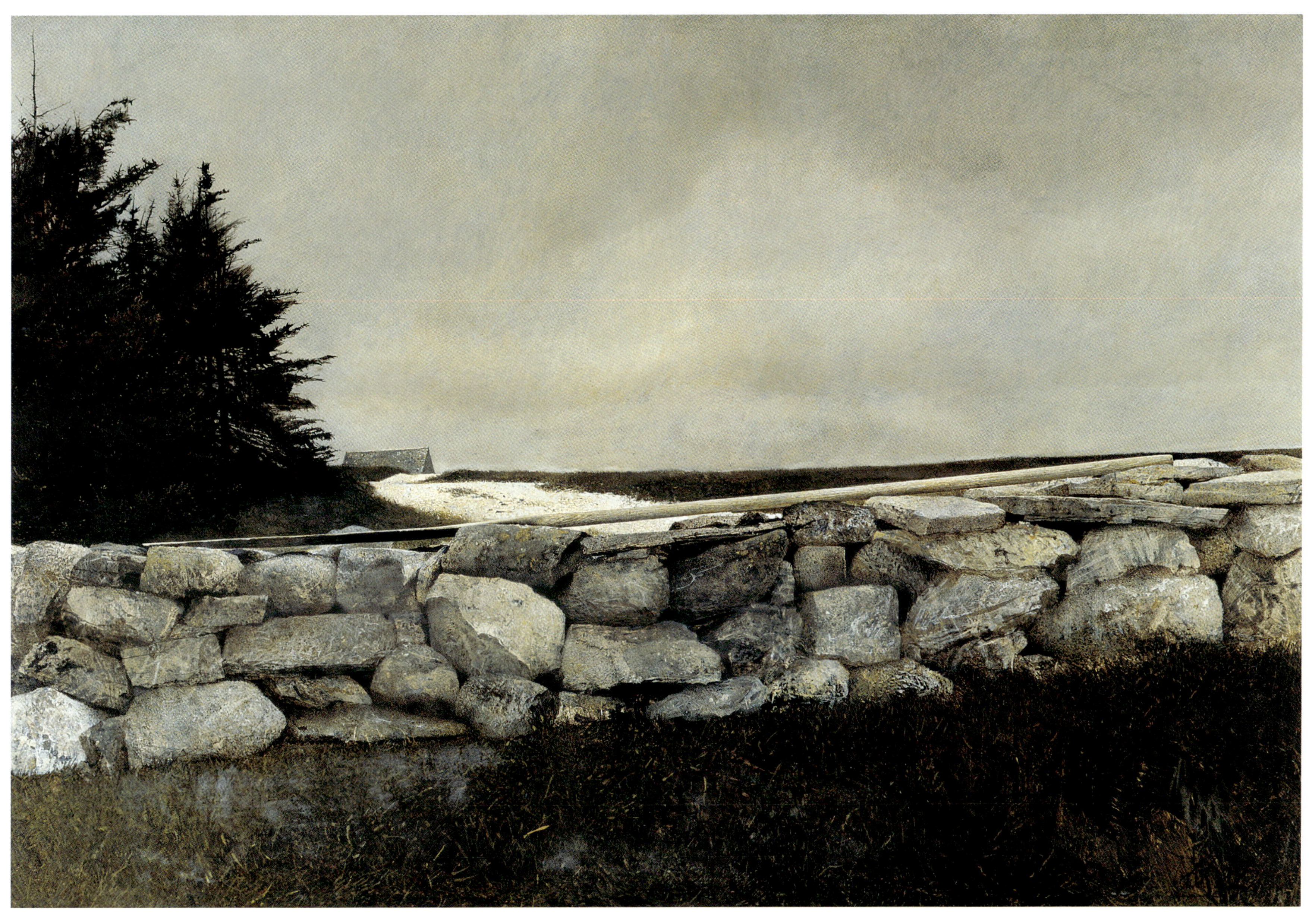

Fairfield Porter AMERICAN 1907–1975

75 | *Jimmy in Black Rocker,* 1960

Oil on canvas, 29½ × 19¼ in.

Signed and dated lower left: *Fairfield Porter 1960*

Anonymous gift (1995.13)

Born in Winnetka, Illinois, to a family of substantial means, Fairfield Porter was of the same generation as many of the Abstract Expressionists who came to prominence in the 1940s and 1950s. Although he wrote art criticism and was friendly with artists active in the movement, particularly Willem de Kooning, he did not emulate their style, choosing a different path for his own art. Against the backdrop of Abstract Expressionism, Color Field painting, Pop Art, and Minimalism—all of which had a stronghold on the art world of the time—he did not waver as he carved out his particular niche, the painting of landscapes, interiors, and portraits. Today he is recognized as one of the leading American realist painters. As Hilton Kramer noted in a 1974 review, Porter "remains one of the most accomplished representational painters we have, a master of the art of landscape and still life."[1]

Legend has it that the critic Clement Greenberg told de Kooning in the 1940s that "you can't paint figuratively today." When this story was relayed to Porter, he responded, "I think I will do just exactly what he says I can't do." Later he confessed, "I might have become an abstract painter if it were not for that."[2] The reality is probably more complex, having as much to do with the artist's tenacity, intellectual upbringing, and love of both the old masters and Post-Impressionism, as well as the personal wealth that set him apart from his contemporaries. (Unlike many of his colleagues, for instance, who matured stylistically while working on Works Progress Administration projects in the 1930s, Porter was too affluent to participate in the program.)

He enrolled at Harvard at the age of seventeen, where he studied, in addition to fine art, art history with Arthur Pope and philosophy with Alfred North Whitehead. He received his degree in 1938, listing painting as his chosen profession. Porter had traveled to Europe on a number of occasions even before college, a practice that afforded him a personal encounter with original masterpieces in foreign museums. After graduation, he studied with Thomas Hart Benton at the Art Students League in New York City and again ventured abroad. He lived in Florence for a period, where he copied from the old masters and made the acquaintance of the art dealer and Renaissance art historian Bernard Berenson, whose theories he had studied at Harvard.

Two other experiences were crucial to Porter's development. The first was a 1938 exhibition of the Post-Impressionists Pierre Bonnard and Edouard Vuillard at the Art Institute of Chicago, which was to have a profound effect on his style, particularly his interiors and figures. Of Vuillard, he could have been referring to any number of his own paintings when he noted that "what he's doing seems ordinary, but the extraordinary is everywhere."[3] The other defining influence was his own work in the field of art criticism, which he wrote for various magazines for nearly twenty years, beginning in 1951. Though he himself painted in a traditional mode, these endeavors took him out of the studio and into the wider art world, where he was exposed to myriad styles and the newest developments. He was expansive in his taste and appreciative of artists who saw the world in a different way. In a review of a de Kooning exhibition, for example, he wrote, "The paintings also remind one of nature, of autumn, say, but autumn essentially, released from the usual sentimental and adventitious load of personal and irrelevant associations."[4]

In 1949 Porter moved with his family to Southampton, New York, where he befriended Alex Katz, Jane Freilicher, James Schuyler, John Ashbery, and Frank O'Hara, all members of a large community of artists and painters living there at the time. *Jimmy in Black Rocker* is a portrait of the poet James Schuyler, who lived with the Porters off and on for close to a decade, both in Southampton and on Great Spruce Head Island, Maine, where they spent their summers. An accomplished gardener and inspirational thinker (he sometimes read to Porter as he painted), he also served as a model from time to time. There is a wonderful Cézannesque quality in the way the figure occupies space in the portrait, set against a simplified yet spatially complex interior. It is, as Porter had admired in Vuillard, "concrete in detail yet abstract as a whole."[5]
SS

1. Hilton Kramer, review of a Porter exhibition at the Hirschl & Adler Galleries, New York, quoted in, "Fairfield Porter, 68, a Realist in an Age of Abstract Art, Dies," by Grace Glueck, *New York Times,* 21 September 1975.

2. Quoted in William Agee, Malama Maron-Bersin, Michele White, and Peter Blank, *Fairfield Porter, An American Painter,* exh. cat. (Southampton, N.Y.: The Parrish Art Museum, 1993), p. 14.

3. Quoted in ibid., p. 13.

4. Fairfield Porter, "Willem de Kooning," *The Nation,* June 6, 1959, p. 520.

5. Quoted in Agee et al., p. 14.

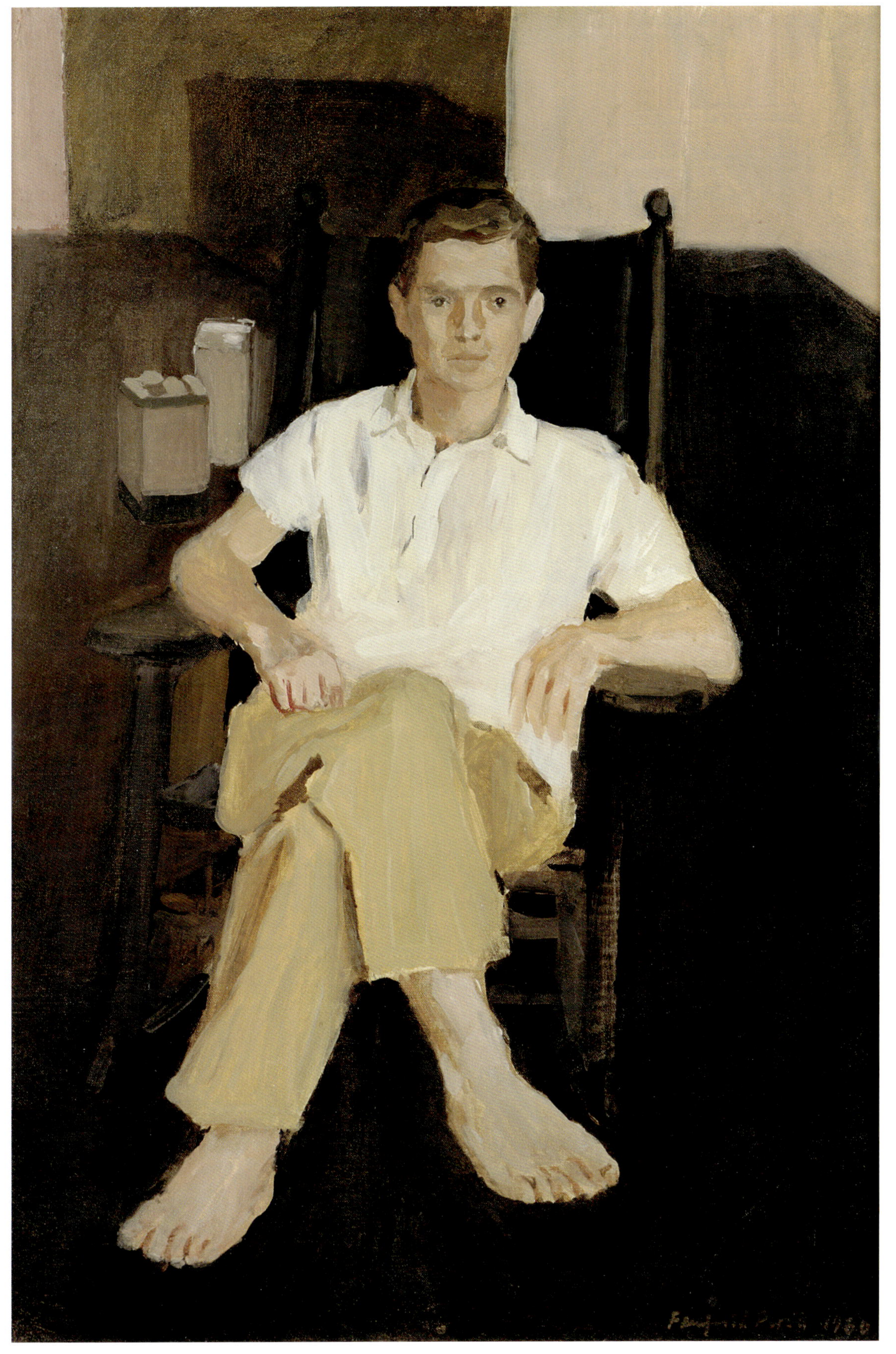

Alexander Calder AMERICAN 1898–1976

76 | *The White Sieve*, 1963

Polychromed sheet metal and wire, 13 × 21 in.; variable depth

Signed lower left corner of red part of base: AC

Bequest of Mary Mallery Davis (1990.54)

77 | *Red Fish Tail*, 1965

Polychromed sheet metal and wire, 60 × 120 in.; variable depth

Signed and dated on one of the 16 moving elements: *AC 1965*

Gift of Mrs. Aimee Mott Butler in memory of her mother, Ethel Harding Mott (1967.1)

Undoubtedly one of the most beloved sculptors of the twentieth century, Alexander Calder created magical abstract works that, whether large or small, fixed or mobile, possess a gentle grace and timeless quality. His sculptures not only display a love for modern materials but embody contemporary notions of motion, chance, and balance. They also reveal a whimsical and often humorous quality that reflects Calder's life and his interpretation of the beauty and simplicity of his surroundings. Calder stated on many occasions that he had chosen the universe as his theme and through this lens he produced work uniquely his own.

Born in Philadelphia to an artistic family—his mother, Nanette Lederer, was a painter and his father, Alexander Stirling Calder, was a sculptor, as was his grandfather—Calder was no stranger to the bohemian life. He spent his childhood frequenting artists' studios and had a workshop by the time he was ten. Despite this early interest, he decided to study science, not art, in college, attending Stevens Institute of Technology in Hoboken, New Jersey, from which he graduated in 1919 with a degree in mechanical engineering. He worked for four years in that field and then attended the Art Students League in New York City from 1923 to 1926. Although taught by such well-known artists as George Luks and Guy Pène du Bois, he was more interested in drawing and caricature than mastering the fundamentals of fine art. "I think best in wire," he once said.[1]

Calder's move to Paris in 1926 and the exposure he received to the wide array of innovative artists living in the city at the time had a tremendous effect on his artistic development. He became a close friend of Joan Miró and also made the acquaintance of Jean Arp, Piet Mondrian, and Anton Pevsner, all members, like Calder, of the Abstraction-Création group of the 1930s. In Paris Calder started his *Circus* series, for which he would later receive great acclaim. *Circus* originated in the United States, when the artist was hired by the *National Police Gazette* to make drawings of the Ringling Brothers and Barnum & Bailey circus. Using these drawings as studies, Calder fashioned miniature circus performers and tiny props from wire, fabric, and recycled materials. Acting as impresario, he brought the circus to life, guiding his characters through their performances with musical accompaniment. Over the next several decades, Calder transported the entire *Circus* in a suitcase and presented the performances in many different locations. The whimsy that inspired the making of the *Circus* and its performance is the defining element in Calder's mature work.

In 1930 Calder visited Mondrian's studio and was immediately won over to abstract art. Struck by the colorful geometric abstractions that crowded the studio, Calder stated, "Perhaps it would be fun to make these rectangles oscillate," to which Mondrian replied, "No, it is not necessary, my painting is already fast."[2] A few weeks later, with the visit still resonating in his mind, Calder began to paint his own small abstractions. These early attempts quickly led to experimentation with three-dimensional abstraction. Arp called these abstract sculptures "stabiles"; the moving sculptures were dubbed "mobiles" by Marcel Duchamp. The mobiles were at first operated by hand cranks or simple motors, which Calder abandoned in favor of the smooth and natural effects of air currents. Looking closely at a Calder mobile, it is not difficult to appreciate its close affinity with a painting by Mondrian as well as the work of Arp and Miró.

Using a relatively limited visual vocabulary and a palette of primary colors, Calder achieved an enormous variety in his work, ranging from tiny tabletop pieces to large outdoor works. By 1934 these stabiles

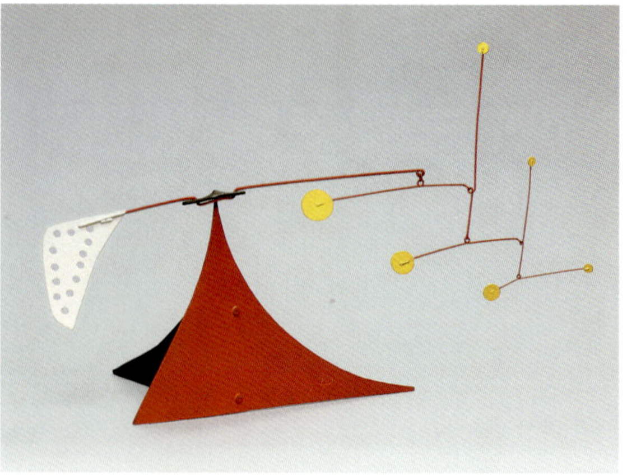

and mobiles had become Calder's primary focus, and by the mid-1940s he had advanced the concept by suspending mobiles from the ceiling. The two Calder pieces in the Flint Institute of Arts' collection perfectly exemplify his mature work. Revealing how Calder's mastery of engineering and sense of balance translates a two-dimensional work to a three-dimensional drawing in the air, *Red Fish Tail* changes before the viewer's eyes from simple metal disks to revolving fishtails whose movements are both organic and sensual. The piece also reveals his lifelong obsession with a single primary color: red. Explaining this passion, Calder said, "I almost want to paint everything red. I often wish that I'd been a Fauve in 1905."[3] *The White Sieve*, a combination of a mobile and stabile, juxtaposes the solidity of the intersecting red and black base with the delicacy of a small mobile, balanced on one side by a sievelike rudder and on the other side by spinning disks. It is indeed true that the universe has served as his artistic guide throughout his life, both physically and metaphorically. As he has remarked, "The first inspiration I ever had was the cosmos, the planetary system. . . . The simplest forms in the universe are the sphere and the circle. I represent them by discs and then I vary them."[4] SS

1. Quoted in Patterson Sims, *Whitney Museum of American Art: Selected Works* (New York: Whitney Museum of American Art), p. 97.

2. Quoted in Jean Lipman, *Calder's Universe*, exh. cat. (New York: The Viking Press in cooperation with the Whitney Museum of American Art, 1976), p. 112.

3. Ibid., p. 101.

4. Ibid., pp. 16, 18.

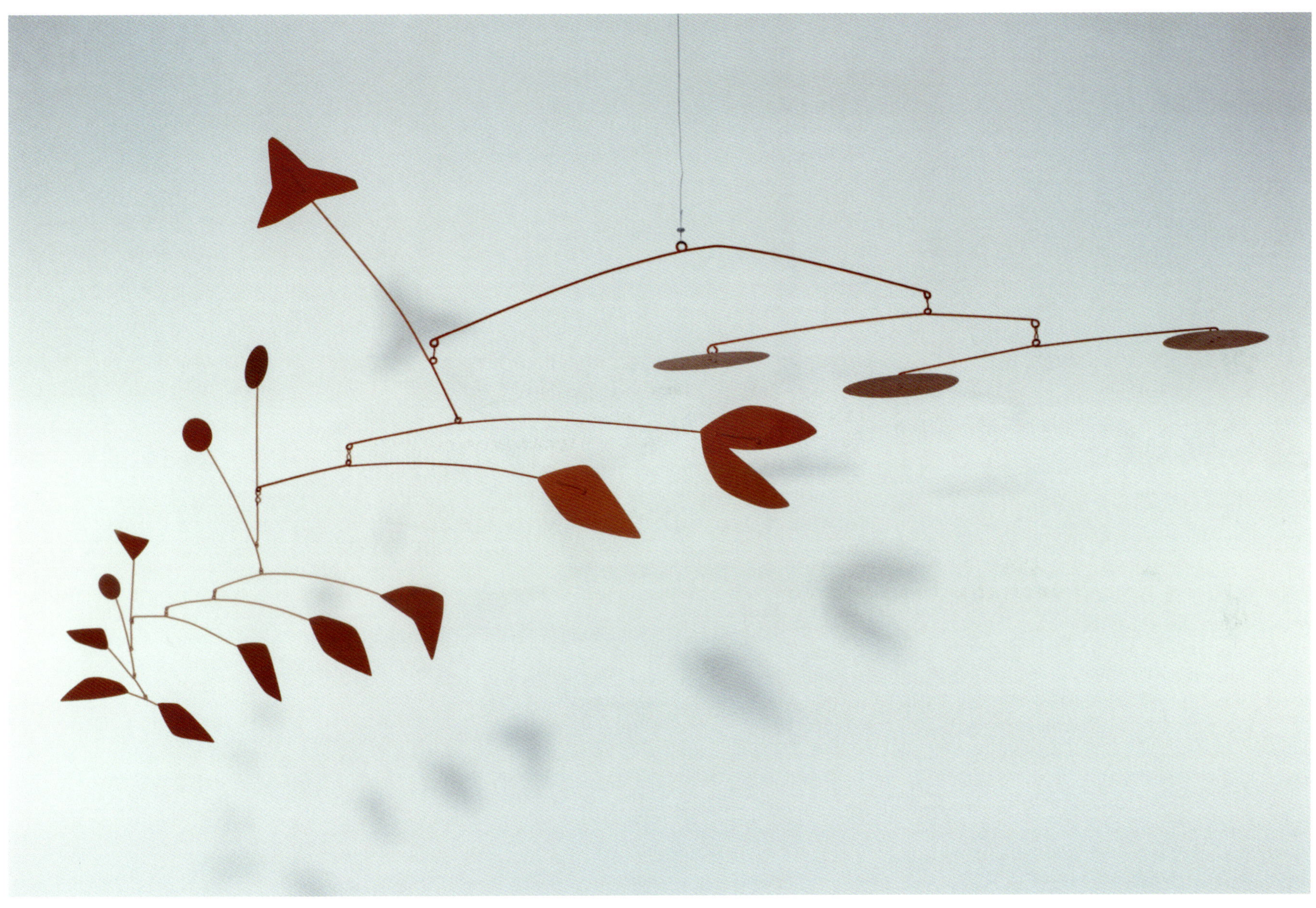

Josef Albers AMERICAN, BORN GERMANY 1888–1976

78 | *Study for Homage to the Square: With a Veil,* 1962

Oil on canvas, 30 × 30 in.

Signed and dated lower right: *A 62*

Bequest of Mary Mallery Davis (1990.13)

In 1949 Josef Albers, already an established artist and teacher, began to make works whose subject matter—the interaction of colors within a painting field—would captivate him for the rest of his life. *Study for Homage to the Square: With a Veil* is part of this series. Albers believed that the careful analysis of color relationships was sufficient as the subject of a painting, and he explored it in depth in his many *Homage to the Square* paintings. Experimenting with a broad palette, he used oil colors straight from the tube, applied in a single layer on a panel on a ground of "the whitest white."[1] Paintings from this series consist of colored squares, often of similar or related tones, nestled in sizes that ascend or descend by hue. Hard-edged against smooth background surfaces, the squares have a mechanical quality that refuses to reveal the artist's hand. While the composition of his *Homage to the Square* works appear straightforward, the process was complex, one that Albers took extreme care to document: on the back of *Homage to the Square: With a Veil,* Albers included a detailed list of the colors and paint varieties used in its production.[2] "Albers loves the non-natural," one critic observed, "he loves the square because he thinks it was created by man and is not to be found in nature."[3] In a 1964 essay Albers added to the discussion of his paintings of the square: "In consequence, they move forth and back, in and out, and grow up and down and near and far, as well as enlarged and diminished. All this, to proclaim color autonomy as a means of plastic organization."[4]

Albers's influence on decades of the twentieth-century art world is truly vast, and his role cannot be overemphasized. Such movements as Color Field painting, Minimalism, and Op Art have benefited tremendously not only from his art but also from his extensive writing and many years of teaching. Born in Germany, Albers had a rigorous education, studying at Berlin's Royal Art School, the School of Applied Art in Essen, and the Art Academy in Munich. As a student, he encountered the work of Paul Cézanne and Henri Matisse. From 1920 to 1923 Albers attended the Bauhaus in Weimar, and in 1923 he joined the faculty, teaching furniture, glass, and wallpaper design as well as color theory and drawing. Albers's experience at the Bauhaus, both as student and instructor, was crucial to the development of his mature work as an artist and theorist. Working alongside such innovators as Mies van der Rohe and Walter Gropius, he became increasingly interested in the abstract qualities of color and form and the impact they had on the viewer. Writing at the time, he noted, "The content of art is the visual formulation of our reaction to life."[5]

In 1925 the Bauhaus was moved from Weimar to Dessau, where it was closed in 1933 by the new Nazi regime. Albers immigrated to the United States, bringing with him both his own theoretical and art background and the aesthetics of his former colleagues at the Bauhaus. For the next twenty years, he held teaching positions at the most prestigious American universities. He served first as a department chairman at the Black Mountain School in North Carolina from 1933 to 1949 and then as chairman of the department of architecture and design at Yale University from 1950 to 1958. Throughout his long life, Albers wrote and published numerous theoretical texts on color. In 1971 the Metropolitan Museum of Art in New York held a retrospective of Albers's lifetime work; he was the first living artist to be accorded such an honor at the museum. SS

1. Josef Albers, "On My Homage to the Square," in *Theories and Documents of Contemporary Art: A Sourcebook of Artists' Writings,* ed. Kristine Stiles and Peter Selz (Berkeley: University of California Press, 1996), p. 109.

2. Paints used, listed from center to outside edges: Baryte Green (Lebebvre); Cobalt Green (Winsor & Newton); Mixture of Reilly's Gray 3 & 4 (Grumbacher); Gold Ochre (Rhenish).

3. Colin Naylor and Genesis P. Orridge, eds., *Contemporary Artists* (New York: St. Martin's Press, 1977), p. 21.

4. Albers, "On My Homage to the Square," p. 108.

5. Josef Albers, "The Origin of Art," in *Theories and Documents of Contemporary Art,* p. 107.

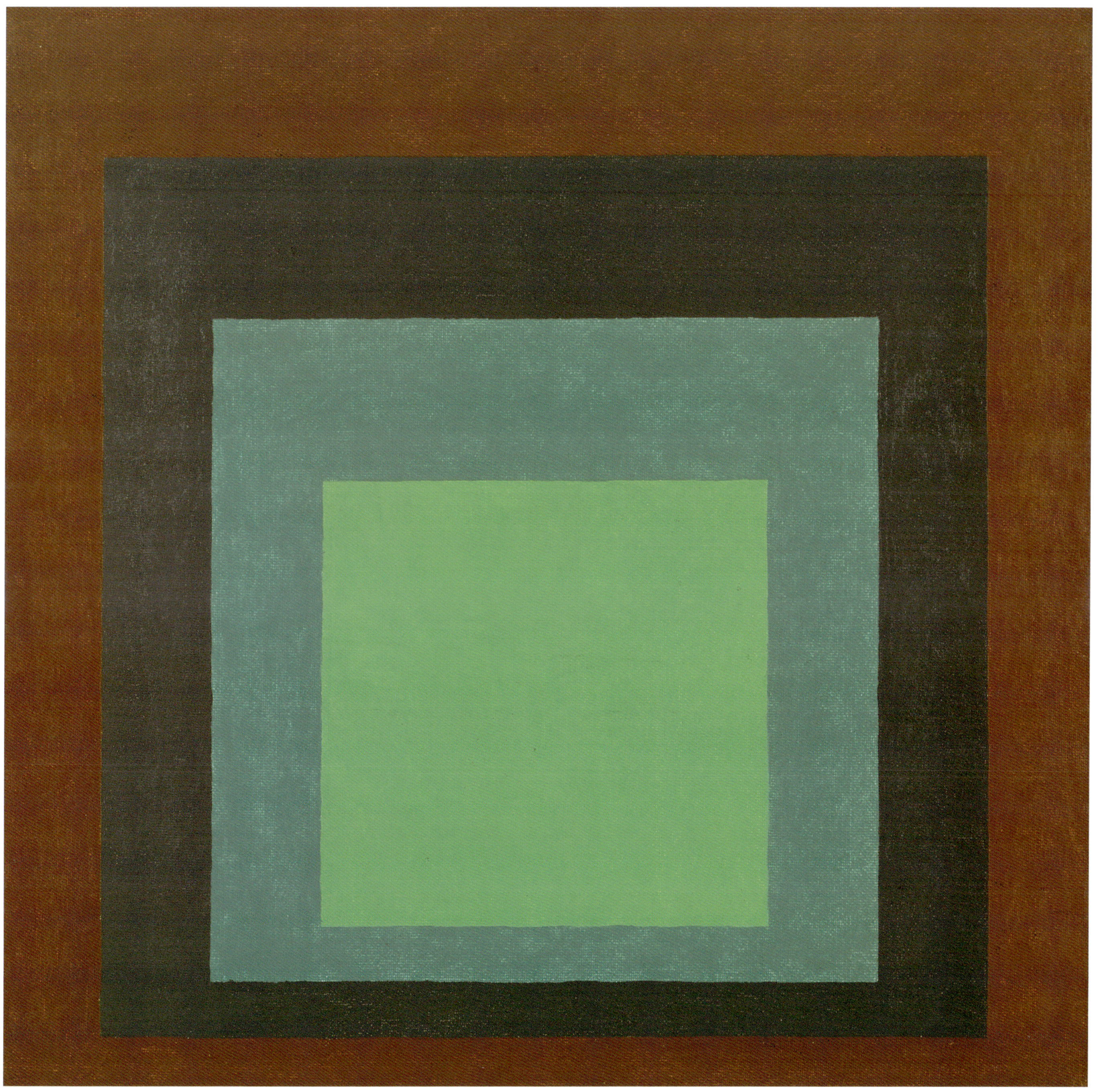

Hans Hofmann AMERICAN, BORN GERMANY 1880–1966

79 | *Untitled,* 1941

Gouache, crayon, and india ink on paper, 14 × 17 in.

Signed and dated lower right: *H.H. 41*

Flint Institute of Arts purchase with funds from the Harvey J. Mallery Charitable Trust (1992.28)

Hans Hofmann once observed that painting was "almost a physical struggle,"[1] and certainly the physicality of his work reveals an activity that is both material and mental. Hofmann is unusual in that he first made a name for himself as one of the most influential teachers of the twentieth century and only later as an accomplished artist. His life and career spanned much of the century, and he was exposed to its major art movements, from Impressionism to Abstract Expressionism. He also knew the key figures—early on, he counted among his friends Henri Matisse, Pablo Picasso, and Georges Braque, and he taught a large number of the Abstract Expressionists. One can see in the trajectory of his artistic development a struggle to move beyond the confines of Cubism, but the influence of Matisse and the Fauves—especially their love of striking, bold color—remained, defining his work throughout his career.

Hofmann was born in Weissenberg, Germany, and moved in 1886 with his family to Munich, where he attended public school and gymnasium. As a boy, he showed diverse talents in drawing, music, science, and math, combined with a love for nature and the outdoors. He left home at sixteen to work in architecture and engineering for the government. Two years later he invented an electromagnetic comptometer, a measuring device, for which he received the patent (applied for by his mother because he was too young). Contrary to the path this accomplishment might indicate, he chose to enroll in art school, although he continued to work on various inventions.

Hofmann's early art education was traditional, but his teacher, Willie Schwartz, who had been to Paris, introduced him to Impressionism. Through Schwartz, he made the acquaintance of Phillip Freudenberg, a Berlin collector and department store owner, who not only sent him to Paris but would also be his patron for the next decade. In Paris the young artist was quickly assimilated into the progressive art circles, becoming good friends with Robert Delaunay, the Cubists, and Matisse. He was soon working in a Cubist style, but with high-key color. In 1914 he returned to Munich because of illness. Soon afterward, due to the outbreak of World War I, he lost his patron. Needing to support himself, Hofmann began teaching art. The Hans Hofmann School of Fine Arts opened in 1915 in Munich and operated successfully until he closed it in 1932. He moved to New York, where he taught at the Art Students League. Two years later, he reestablished the Hans Hofmann School of Fine Arts in New York and in 1935 opened a branch in Provincetown, Massachusetts, teaching there in the summers. Hofmann's career continued to be a mixture of teaching and making his own art, which until late in his life was weighted more to the demands of the schools.

Over the years, Hofmann developed very specific theories on abstract painting. He is responsible for much of the vocabulary and ideas that define abstraction: the notion of painting as a "plastic" expression; the "push-pull" of colors and shapes working against each other spatially; and the importance of the picture plane. "Cubism was a revolution," he noted, "in that the artist broke with tradition by changing from a line to a plane concept."[2] Nature remained his source of inspiration, but color was the vehicle that transformed the experience. "Color (in nature as well as in the picture) is an agent to give the highest esthetic enjoyment," he once wrote. "The emotion-releasing faculty of the color related to the formal aspect of the work becomes a means to awaken in us feelings to which the medium of expression responds analogically."[3] This early, untitled work on paper is a beautiful example, not only of Hofmann's struggle to work through Cubism, but of his transformation of the experience of nature, here clearly a landscape, to a pictorial expression. SS

1. Quoted in William C. Seitz, with selected writings by Hans Hofmann, *Hans Hofmann,* exh. cat. (New York: The Museum of Modern Art, 1963), p. 37.

2. Ibid., p. 11.

3. Quoted in Frederick S. Wight, *Hans Hofmann* (Berkeley: University of California Press, 1957), p. 56.

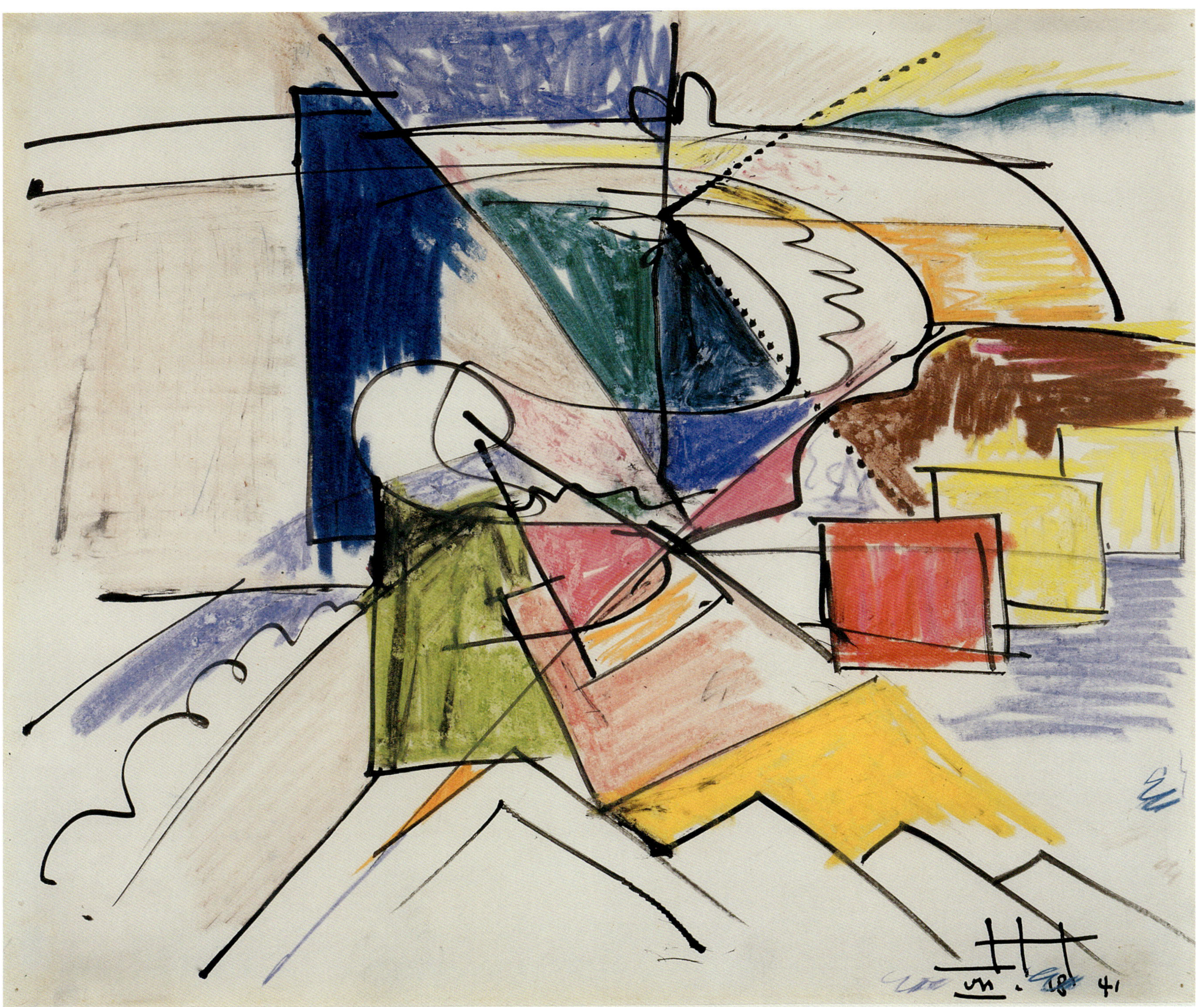

Roy Lichtenstein AMERICAN 1923–1997

80 | *Mechanism Cross Section*, 1954

Oil on canvas, 40 × 54 in.
Signed lower right: *Lichtenstein*
Gift of Messrs. Samuel N. Tomkin and Sidney Freedman (1956.2)

Roy Lichtenstein, like Andy Warhol, was a consummate Pop artist. His cool appropriation of images from myriad sources—advertising, comic strips, art history, and everyday life—and his use of a Benday dot technique that derived from commercial printing resulted in a style inimitably his own. Lichtenstein was born in New York City and studied at Ohio State University, where he earned a bachelor's degree in fine art in 1946 and a master's degree in fine art in 1949. Although he had his first exhibition in New York in 1951, it was not until his solo show at Leo Castelli Gallery in 1962 that he became aligned with the Pop Art movement.

Great artists do not materialize out of a vacuum; they are the product of their milieu and the styles and movements that preceded them. In the late 1950s, young artists generally either searched for a way to take Abstract Expressionism to its next step—for instance, the stain paintings of Helen Frankenthaler and Morris Louis—or rebelled against it, as was the case with the early "combines" of Robert Rauschenberg and the target and flag paintings of Jasper Johns. Certainly, this was true of Lichtenstein, who came to artistic maturity in the decade when Abstract Expressionism had been pushed to its limit. When asked why he quit painting his abstractions of the late 1950s, he replied, "Desperation. There were no spaces left between Milton Resnick and Mike Goldberg,"[1] two leading abstract painters of the day. Crucial to the exposure and eventual acceptance of Pop artists was the dealer Leo Castelli, who fully embraced the new aesthetic, which looked to the commercial world for both subject matter and style.

The year 1960 marked a turning point in Lichtenstein's development; he was appointed assistant professor at Douglass College, part of Rutgers University in New Jersey, where he taught until 1964. It was there he made the acquaintance of Alan Kaprow, who deeply influenced Lichtenstein's views on the integration of art and culture. He also attended a few Happenings—a "total theater," participatory art form that combined situations, theatrical events, and the visual arts—that included such artists as Claes Oldenburg and Jim Dine. Lichtenstein had been exploring aspects of abstract, gestural painting in the late 1950s, but his exposure to the irreverent and often humorous thinking of these young artists inspired him to look to contemporary culture for subject matter. In 1961 he made several paintings that included comic-strip characters such as Mickey Mouse, Donald Duck, Bugs Bunny, and Popeye. His style was formalized, employing exaggerated Benday dots and words and images taken from cartoons and advertising.

With this as his departure point, Lichtenstein explored these themes throughout his career in several series of works, executed in various media, including painting, drawing, and printmaking. He is perhaps best known for his images of women taken from romance comic books, but he also made series that parodied such art historical "classics" as Claude Monet's series of Rouen Cathedral and haystacks, art movements such as Abstract Expressionism and Art Deco, and compositions including mirrors, landscapes, and interiors.

This early painting, *Mechanism Cross Section*, is the work of a young artist grappling with the search for his own style.[2] During this time Lichtenstein was also experimenting with American themes in a Cubist grid structure. Though the picture is at first glance seemingly a pure abstraction, realistic elements can nevertheless be detected. Ernst Busch, who made a study of Lichtenstein's early work, draws a correlation between this work and diagrams of machinery with clearly delineated pipes and valves. It also resembles some sort of topographical mapping, with tunnels, a bridge, roads, and even a cul-de-sac. Lichtenstein was clearly also aware of the work of the Abstract Expressionists: the background division is reminiscent of Robert Motherwell's *Elegy to the Spanish Republic* (a series begun in the 1950s), while the loosely worked brushstrokes bring to mind the gestural qualities seen in the paintings of Willem de Kooning or even Arshile Gorky. SS

1. Quoted in John Coplans, ed., *Roy Lichtenstein* (New York: Praeger Publishers, 1972), p. 51.

2. The painting was acquired from John Heller Gallery in New York, where Lichtenstein had solo exhibitions in 1952 and 1953. Ernst Busch dates it and similar works to about 1954. See Busch, *Roy Lichtenstein: Das Frühwerk, 1942–1960* (Berlin: Gebr. Mann Verlag, 1988), unpaginated.

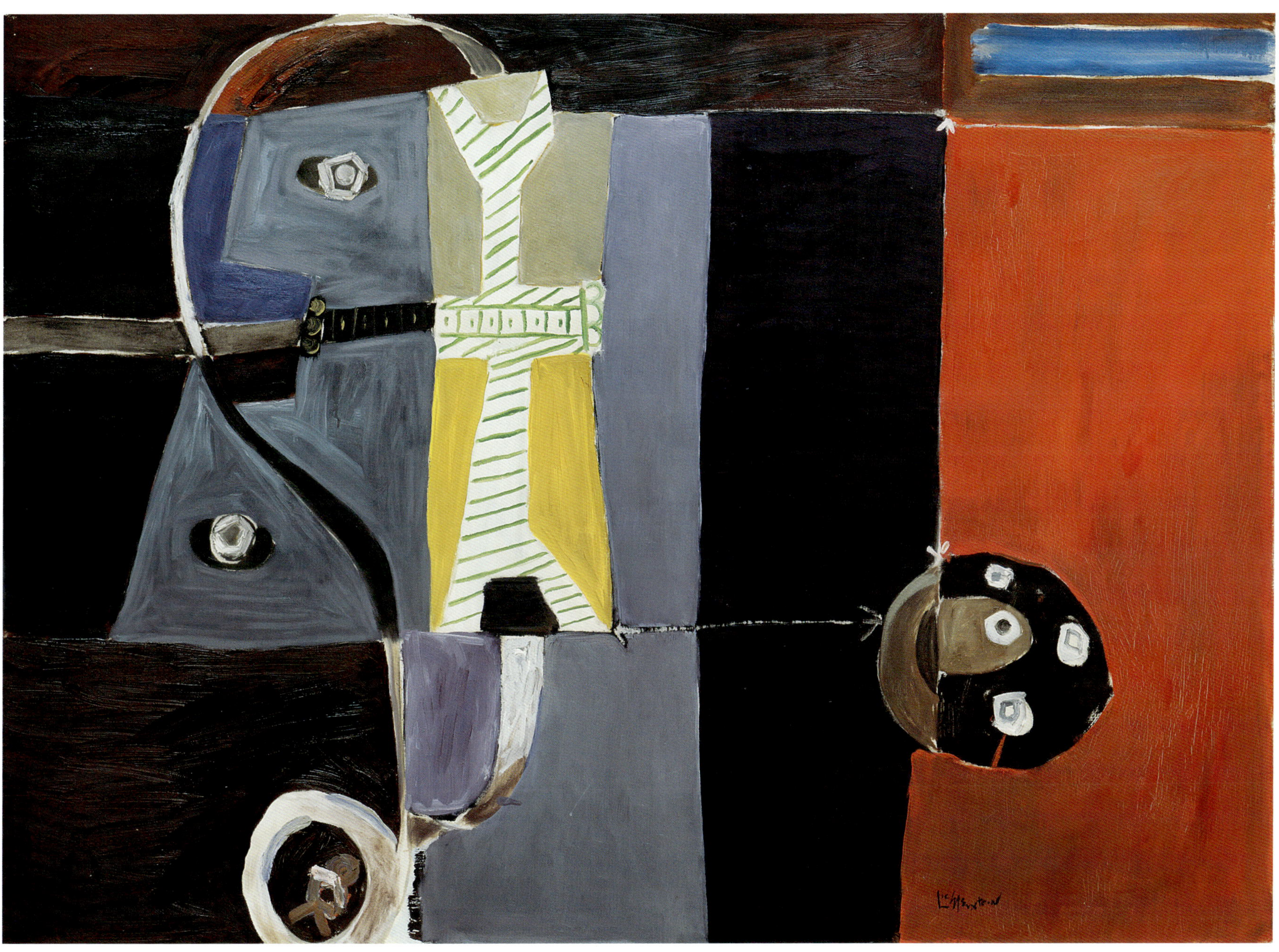

Mary Bauermeister AMERICAN, BORN GERMANY 1934

81 | *St. Peter and St. Petresse,* 1965–66

Mixed media, 20¾ × 20⅞ × 6 in.

Unsigned

Gift of the Founders Society (1966.26)

Born in Frankfurt, Germany, Mary Bauermeister, the daughter of an eminent scientist, began painting at the age of nineteen without benefit of formal art education. Increasingly interested in the ideas of Marcel Duchamp and in the qualities of chance, assemblage, wordplay, and irony that defined the work of Dada artists, she soon began making mixed-media compositions that involved a number of processes, including drawing, painting, sculpture, and assemblage. In the 1960s, a decade during which she lived mainly in New York, Bauermeister studied and collaborated with the renowned German composer Karlheinz Stockhausen, whom she later married. Her projects with Stockhausen influenced the musical qualities of primarily abstract works that seem to vibrate exuberantly.

In the 1960s Bauermeister devoted herself to a series of mixed-media works that employed such materials as glass, optical lenses, and Plexiglas, all arranged within a wood box, a strategy reminiscent of the box constructions of Joseph Cornell. In these lens boxes, Bauermeister creates spatially ambiguous compositions that manipulate light as it is filtered through glass, constantly challenging the boundaries between near and far, microscopic and telescopic. In her work, Bauermeister explains, "you discover the ambiguity of perception, you perceive the process of seeing. Certain elements combine and communicate with each other, nothing is predominant, you cannot get it."[1]

Bauermeister's interest in using glass to address seeing and perception recalls her admiration for Duchamp, whose *The Large Glass, or the Bride Stripped Bare by Her Bachelors, Even,* 1915–23 (Philadelphia Museum of Art) simultaneously employs glass as a window and an obstacle. Her use of words, both in her images and in her often equally enigmatic titles, also reminds the viewer of Duchamp's mastery of language and punning. Bauermeister will often employ language in a way that suggests her desire to assert ambiguity, a strategy that is just as much about pushing a political envelope as it is about pushing a perceptual one. In *St. Peter and St. Petresse,* for example, Bauermeister manipulates the title to create a female counterpart to Saint Peter, the founding father of the Christian church. Both visually and conceptually, Bauermeister notes that, in her art, "the theme is the equalization of certain elements, like democracy. Democracy is anti-hierarchical."[2]

Bauermeister's works, as exemplified by the lens boxes, also transcend perceptual and political interests in their almost magical quality. Full of mystery, they alternate between revealing and concealing words and images that seem somewhat familiar, yet remain perpetually elusive. Functioning as landscapes of the human mind, they also suggest the complexity that is the universe. MK

1. Interview with Pamela Wye, quoted in Wye, "Splendor in the Glass: Mary Bauermeister's Boxes and Gardens," *Arts Magazine* 64, no. 3 (November 1989), p. 76.

2. Ibid.

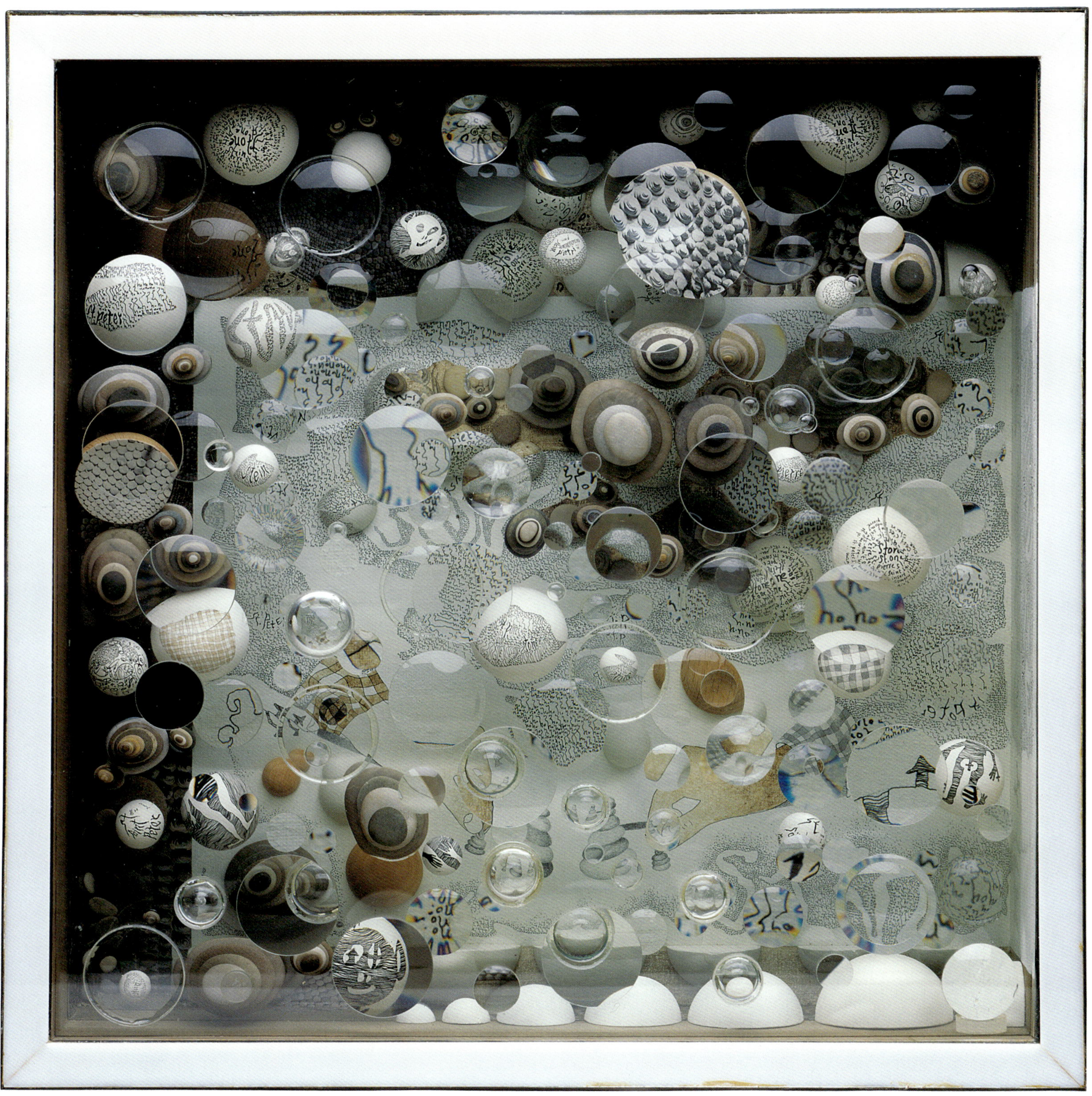

Louise Nevelson AMERICAN, BORN RUSSIA 1900–1988

82 | *Cryptic #13*, 1966

Wood, paint, and metal, 8⅛ × 8¼ × 5⅛ in.

Unsigned

Bequest of Mary Mallery Davis (1990.55)

Although smaller than her other box constructions, Louise Nevelson's *Cryptic #13* is immediately recognizable as the work of this renowned American artist. Her signature pieces are three-dimensional wood assemblages made from found objects, generally painted a uniform matte black. Like an architectural jigsaw puzzle, these asymmetric structures resemble abstract buildings or, as Nevelson has dubbed them, "cathedrals." Just as *Cryptic #13* houses a group of wood elements within its interior space, Nevelson's larger sculptural environments consist of stacked and fused boxes with myriad recesses containing her own world of objects. A path can be traced from Constructivism to Nevelson's mature work, in particular her process of assemblage, which recalls Pablo Picasso's wood constructions. "I always wanted to show the world that art was everywhere," she once said, "except it had to pass through a creative mind."[1]

Nevelson's family background, coupled with the extraordinary times in which she lived, fostered her artistic vision. Born Louise Berliawky in Kiev, Russia, Nevelson moved in 1905 with her family to Rockland, Maine, where her father operated a lumberyard. In 1920 she married Charles Nevelson and with him relocated to New York City. The move opened up entirely new worlds for Nevelson. Taking full advantage of these opportunities, she enrolled in acting and music lessons and also attended the Art Students League from 1929 to 1930. Following her time at the League, she studied in Germany with Hans Hofmann, who further encouraged her interest in Cubism. On her return to New York in 1932, she assisted Diego Rivera in the production of his large public murals. This early apprenticeship allowed Nevelson to witness the profound effect of scale in a work of art.

Much was shifting in the New York art world during these years, and Nevelson was an active member of the emerging community of artists who sought to challenge traditional approaches to subject matter, technique, and materials. Given her first one-person exhibition in 1941, she presented small Cubist-inspired sculptures made of clay, stone, wood, and metal. Two years later, as her artistic style evolved, she completed her first assemblages, made solely from furniture parts, crates, or odd pieces of wood picked up from the street. Defending her choice of material and the deep resonance it has had for her work, Nevelson observed in 1976, "I began using found objects. I had all this wood lying around and I began to move it around. I began to compose. Anywhere I found wood, I took it home and started working with it. . . . I wanted a medium that was immediate. Wood was the thing that I could communicate with almost spontaneously and get what I was looking for . . . when I am working with wood, it's very alive."[2]

Nevelson's commitment to wood as the primary material for her work is matched by her exclusive use, until the early 1960s, of matte black. Later in her career, Nevelson introduced gold and white into her palette, although black would remain, for her, the most spiritual and symbolic. "Black encompasses all colors. Black is the most aristocratic color of all. The only aristocratic color. For me this is the ultimate. You can be quiet and it contains the whole thing. There is no other color that gives you the feeling of totality. Of peace. Of greatness. Of quietness of excitement . . . the essence of it is what you call—alchemy."[3]

In 1954–55 Nevelson created her first stacked wall piece, which marked a shift in the size and scale of her work. Until that time, the boxes and columns had been configured to stand alone; now they functioned as units or "environments." The following year, this first wall piece was reconstructed at the Museum of Modern Art. In 1959 the museum once again recognized Nevelson's work by including her in the famous *Sixteen Americans* exhibition. This show was the first major forum to recognize such significant artists as Robert Rauschenberg and Jasper Johns in addition to Nevelson. Historically, the exhibition is considered a harbinger of the decades that followed, as it showcased a group of artists who began to challenge and work outside the prevailing aesthetic of Abstract Expressionism. At this point in her development as an artist, however, Nevelson was already well on her way to creating a distinctive body of work that to this day evokes a transcendent quality of beauty and greatness.
SS

1. Louise Nevelson, "Dawns and Dusks" (1976), in *Theories and Documents of Contemporary Art: A Sourcebook of Artists' Writings*, ed. Kristine Stiles and Peter Selz (Berkeley: University of California Press, 1996), p. 512.

2. Ibid., p. 511.

3. Ibid., p. 513.

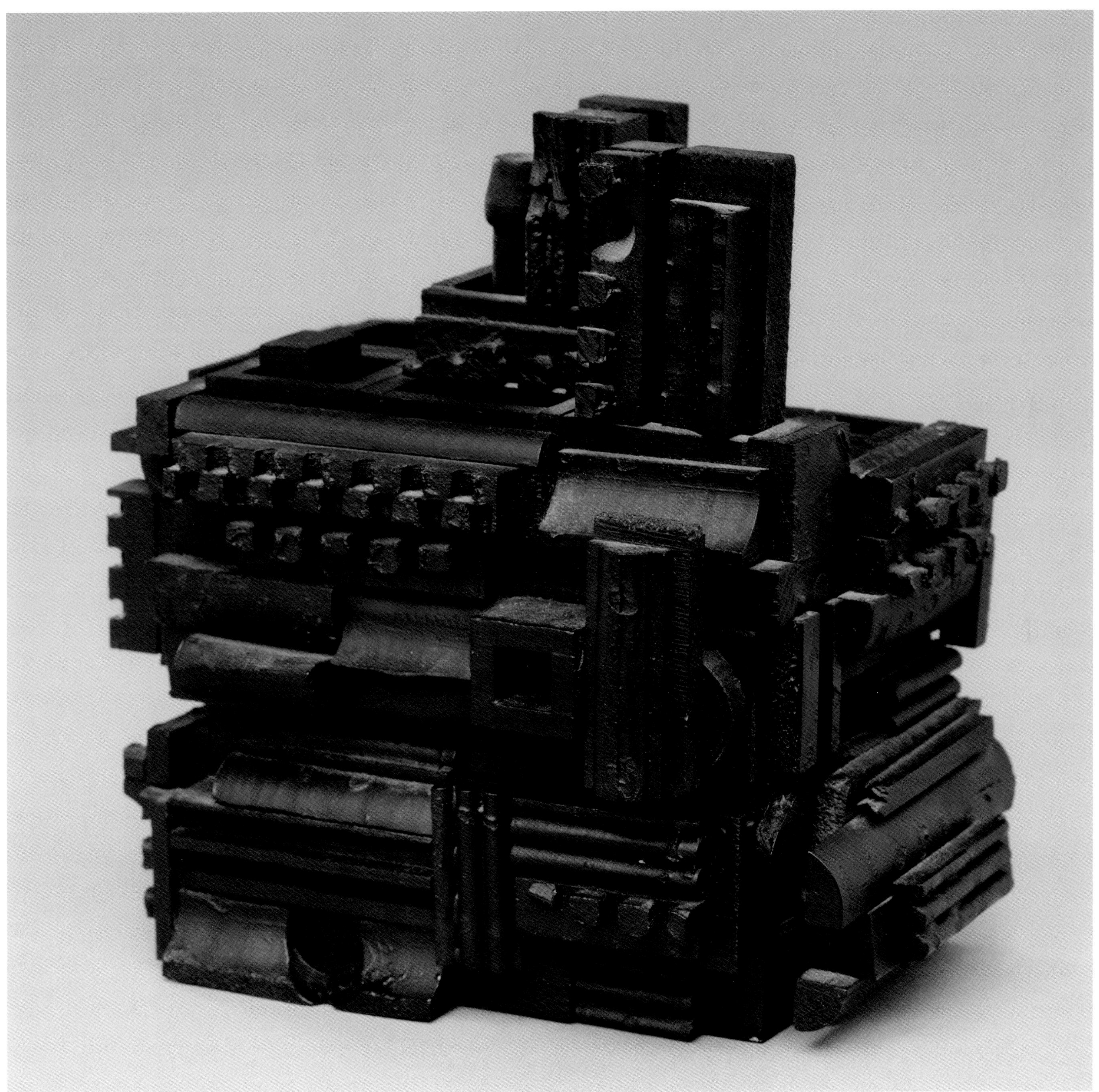

Morris Graves AMERICAN 1910–2001

83 | *Spirit Bird,* 1953

Sumi ink and tempera on paper, 28⅝ × 37⅞ in.
Signed and dated lower right: *M Graves 53*
Bequest of Mary Mallery Davis (1990.34)

Morris Graves, along with Mark Tobey, is known as a Northwest Visionary artist. Both painters lived much of their lives in the Pacific Northwest and shared an interest in the spiritual quality of the artistic process. Born in Oregon, Graves moved at the age of ten to Seattle, and he lived in the Pacific Northwest and California, outside the physical confines of the New York art scene, for most of his life. Largely self-taught as an artist, he traveled extensively, developing an aesthetic vision that combined his solitary, devout experiences with an acute awareness of New York's creative world. As a young artist, Graves was fascinated by Carl Jung's theory of the collective unconscious and the Surrealists' notion of plumbing the subconscious for subject matter. Like his contemporaries Mark Rothko and Barnett Newman, he sought to convey the spiritual in art but found he could not access this path through abstraction. Instead, he used a limited number of images—primarily vessels, birds, animals, and flowers—as metaphors for transformation and transcendence.

From 1928 to 1931 Graves worked as a seaman on a ship bound for the Far East. The journey exposed him to the fundamentals of nature painting and Eastern philosophy. He said of the experience, "In Japan, I at once had the feeling that this was the right way to do everything. It was the acceptance of nature—not the resistance to it."[1] Graves became deeply captivated by Zen Buddhism, and it soon formed the basis for his work. He studied for a brief period of time with Tobey, a fellow Seattle artist and Zen Buddhist. As if understanding how this new passion for the philosophical would affect his work, Graves addressed the subject by saying, "Zen stresses the meditative, stilling the surface of the mind and letting the inner surface bloom."[2]

Graves was an easel painter for the Works Progress Administration (1936–37) when he met and befriended the avant-garde composer John Cage in 1937. Five years later, he achieved national recognition when he was included in the exhibition *Americans 1942: 18 Artists from 9 States,* held at the Museum of Modern Art in New York. Awarded a Guggenheim Fellowship in 1946, Graves clearly stated his artistic direction in the grant's application essay: "I have learned that art and nature are the mind's Environment within which we can detect the essence of man's Being and Purpose, and from which we can draw clues to guide our journey from partial consciousness to full consciousness."[3]

An early example of Graves's work, *Spirit Bird* is a beautifully realized, delicate, and ethereal drawing. The outline of a bird, closely resembling an owl, is placed against a golden background that creates a mandala-like surrounding for the image as a whole. White marks or abstracted feathers litter the picture plane and impart the image with a spiritual aura, as if the bird is in the process of transformation. Both Graves and Tobey use this "white writing" in their work, revealing an affinity with the automatic writing of the Surrealists. In addition, it was, for Graves, a physical manifestation of his awareness of spiritual energy moving through the universe, a sense that originated when he was a young artist watching sunlight bounce off water in a rain barrel.

Graves believed that spirituality manifests itself in many forms, not only through the symbolic. The expression of the spiritual is also seen in his use of space—as he saw it, the external space of nature, the internal space of dreams and the imagination, and, last, the space of consciousness. In every aspect, both formally and conceptually, *Spirit Bird* seems to embody these three distinct spaces. Graves may have chosen the bird to symbolize nature, the gold background to represent the dream space, and, finally, the white, fleeting markings to signify the space of consciousness. SS

1. Quoted in Frederick S. Wright, *Morris Graves,* exh. cat. (Berkeley: University of California Press, 1956), p. 7.

2. Ibid., p. 19.

3. Quoted in Robert McDonald, *Morris Graves: Vessels of Transformation,* exh. cat. (New York: Schmidt-Bingham Gallery, 1990), p. 18.

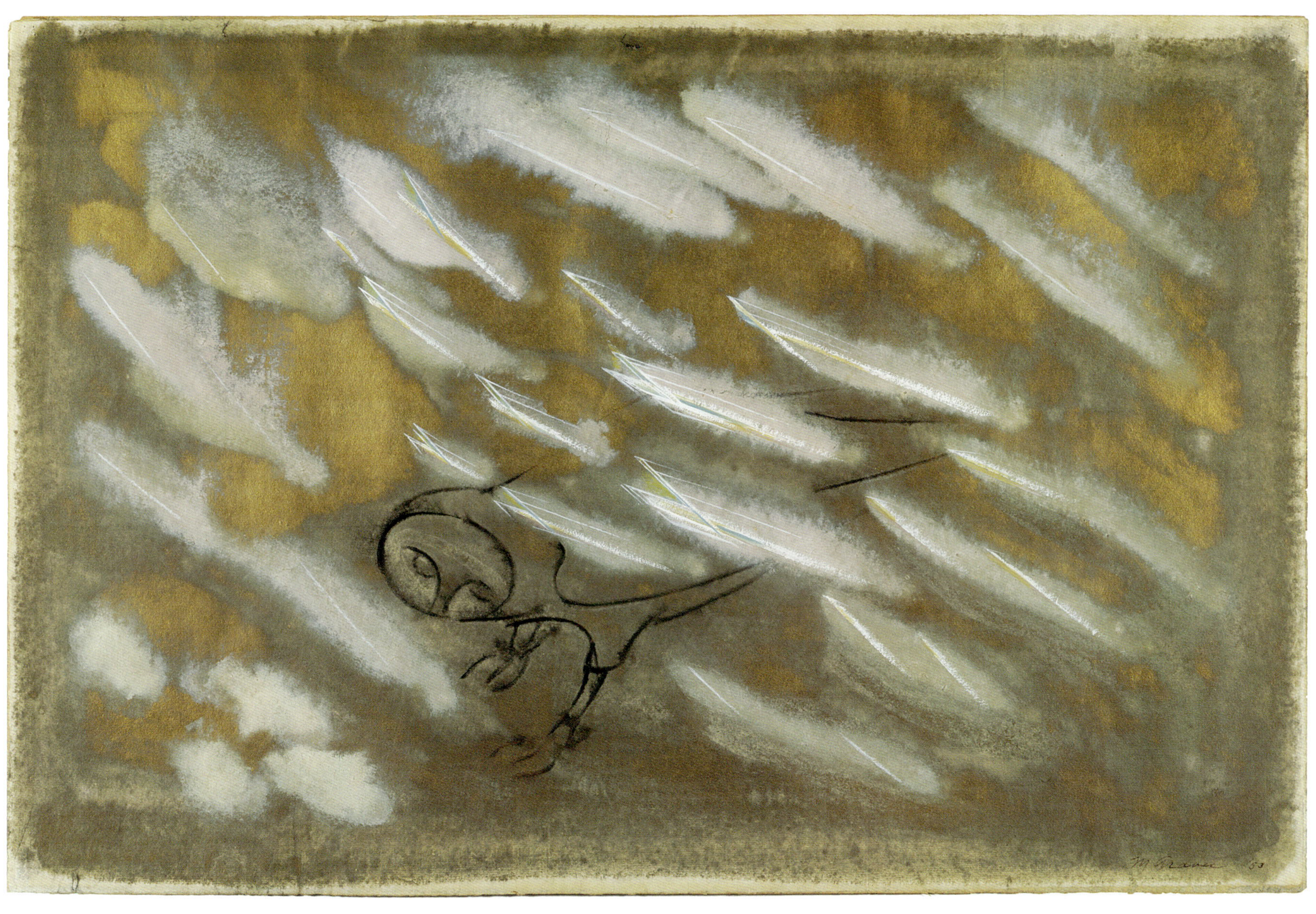

Willem de Kooning

AMERICAN, BORN THE NETHERLANDS 1904–1997

84 | *Woman,* 1964

Oil and newsprint, mounted on canvas, 20 × 27½ in.
Signed bottom, right of center: *de Kooning*
Bequest of Mary Mallery Davis (1990.23)

Willem de Kooning is considered by many to be the most significant abstract painter of the second half of the twentieth century. However, despite his renown as an artist instrumental to the development of abstraction, he always retained an element of figuration in his work. Many of his paintings, most prominently his *Woman* series from the 1950s and 1960s, incorporate the figure, and when making an abstract painting, he often simultaneously worked on meticulous, realistic figure drawings in his studio. In many ways, this duality mirrors his life, which bridged two countries and two traditions.

Born in Rotterdam, de Kooning emigrated from the Netherlands to the United States in 1926, settling in New York the following year. His early training had been a mixture of applied and fine art; an accomplished carpenter and sign painter, he was equally proficient in traditional academy techniques. Apprenticed to a commercial art firm at the age of twelve, he later enrolled in night classes at the Rotterdam Academy of Fine Arts and Techniques, where he studied for eight years. In the United States, he worked as a housepainter and carpenter and made his own art on the side. He also became part of the New York art scene, visiting museums and galleries, where he met such artists as John Graham and Arshile Gorky. In 1935 he worked for the Federal Art Project for a year, where he not only benefited from on-the-job training but also realized the importance of a full-time commitment to his art, even if it meant living in relative poverty.

The year 1938, in which he met Elaine Fried, whom he married in 1943, was also when he began painting his *Woman* series, the theme of which would occupy him periodically throughout his life. Most of his paintings are large-scale works, which he would completely rework many times before he felt they were finished. Because he worked quickly, often applying the paint thickly, he would press newspapers into the paint to help it dry, perhaps even to change the composition. It is thought that many of his works on newspaper, such as this one, were the result of this technique. If true, this oil on paper is not actually a drawing but rather a combination of a type of transfer or monotype print with drawing on top. Even in small scale, it captures the immediacy of de Kooning's gesture and the potency of his line. As he said in an interview with David Sylvester, "It is really absurd to make an image, like a human image with paint today, when you think about it. . . . But then all of a sudden it was more absurd not to do it."[1] SS

1. Quoted in Thomas B. Hess, *Willem de Kooning,* exh. cat. (New York: The Museum of Modern Art, 1968), p. 74.

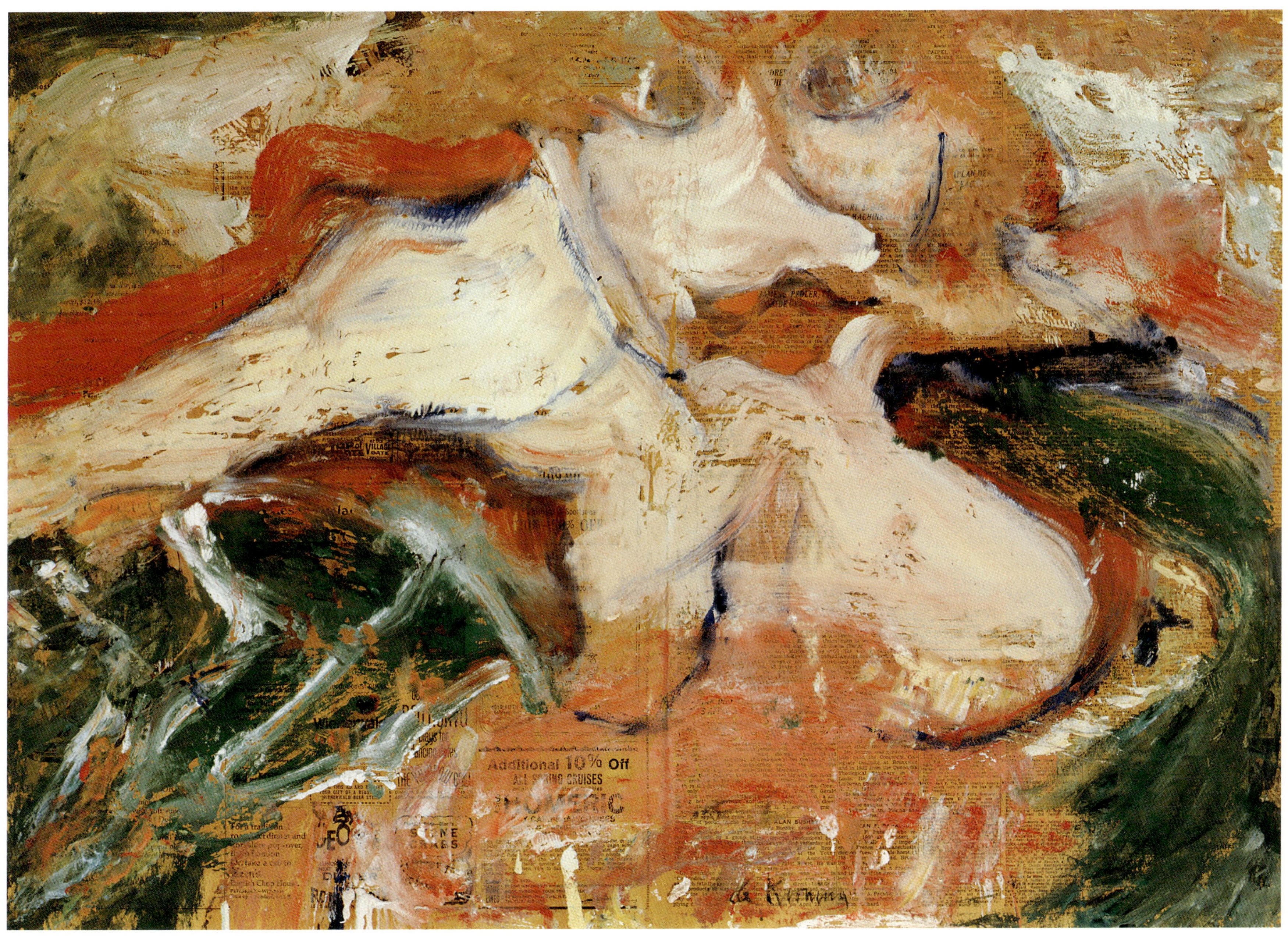
Additional 10% Off

Adolph Gottlieb AMERICAN 1903–1974

85 | *Conflict*, 1966

Oil on canvas, 72 × 90 in.

Signed, titled, and dated on verso: *Adolph Gottlieb, Conflict, 1966*

Purchase prize, first Flint Invitational (1966.23)

Adolph Gottlieb was a first-generation Abstract Expressionist and important member of what came to be known as The New York School. Along with Jackson Pollock, Willem de Kooning, Robert Motherwell, Barnett Newman, Arshile Gorky, and Mark Rothko, Gottlieb broke with the European tradition of painting and forged a new way of rendering his experience of the world. For each of these artists, the evolution was individual, taking them through several phases and into a mature style. For Gottlieb, the journey consisted of synthesizing existing avant-garde traditions such as Cubism and Surrealism with current intellectual thinking, influenced by the theories of Sigmund Freud and Carl Jung.

If Gottlieb's formal training reflected the generation before his own, much of his more radical development came later, as a result of his association with contemporary artists, writers, and philosophers. Born in New York City, he left high school before graduation. In 1919 he took evening classes at the Art Students League, studying with Robert Henri and John Sloan, artists whose urban realist works placed them in the forefront of American painting in the early part of the century. Like many American artists before him, Gottlieb sought further training abroad, departing in 1921 for Europe, where he attended the Académie de la Grande Chaumière in Paris and studied old master paintings at the Louvre.

In 1923, back in the United States, the young artist finished high school and enrolled in Parsons School of Design. By the 1930s he was exhibiting in New York as a member of The Ten, a group of avant-garde artists interested in elements of abstraction and breaking with realist traditions. However, it was in the 1940s, through his association with the Surrealists, that Gottlieb began to experiment with the ideas and methods that would ultimately lead to a breakthrough in his style. The Surrealists were fascinated by mythology and also looked to the subconscious for subject matter, often using "doodling" or automatic drawings as a means of tapping the inner workings of the mind. Gottlieb showed some of his first mythological pictures in 1943. In response to a negative review in the *New York Times*, Gottlieb, Newman, and Rothko sent the newspaper their now-famous missive stating, "There is no such thing as good painting about nothing. We assert that the subject is crucial and that subject matter is valid which is tragic and timeless."[1] The phrase "tragic and timeless" became a battle cry for an entire generation of artists determined to forge a new direction in art. By 1944 Gottlieb was sufficiently associated with Surrealism to be included in an important exhibition organized by Sidney Janis titled *Abstract and Surrealist Art in America*.

Gottlieb's earliest works of significance were his pictographs from the 1940s, paintings in which the canvas is divided into a loose grid into which totemic images—heads, eyes, hands, and various symbols and squiggles—are incised. "I did have certain symbols that were repeated and carried over from one painting to another," explained Gottlieb. "But my favorite symbols were those which I didn't understand. . . . I wanted these symbols to have, in juxtaposition, a certain kind of ambiguity and mystery."[2]

One can see in Gottlieb's evolution a move toward simplification, with a reduction of images into their purest forms. In 1952 the pictographs led to what Gottlieb referred to as his *Imaginary Landscapes*, horizontal paintings divided in the center in which solid images—circles, squares, and half moons—float above a chaotic but contained mass of scribbles. The *Imaginary Landscapes* further consolidated into the *Bursts* in 1957, Gottlieb's mature style. *Conflict* is a perfect example of this final phase, in which simple shapes in the primary colors—red, blue, and yellow—along with black float above a tangled black mass, the whole accented with black smudges and small, repeated yellow and red shapes. Placed against a clean white background, the juxtaposition of opposing marks speaks volumes. "Dualism is the pervasive theme of Gottlieb's art," noted Martin Friedman in a 1963 catalogue essay, "and his painting is the eloquent resolution of conflicting forces and emotions."[3] SS

1. Quoted in Martin Friedman, *Adolph Gottlieb*, exh. cat. (Minneapolis: The Walker Art Center, 1963), unpaginated.

2. Quoted in Jeanne Siegel, "Adolph Gottlieb: Two Views," *Arts Magazine* 42, no. 4 (February 1968), pp. 31–32.

3. Friedman, *Gottlieb*, unpaginated.

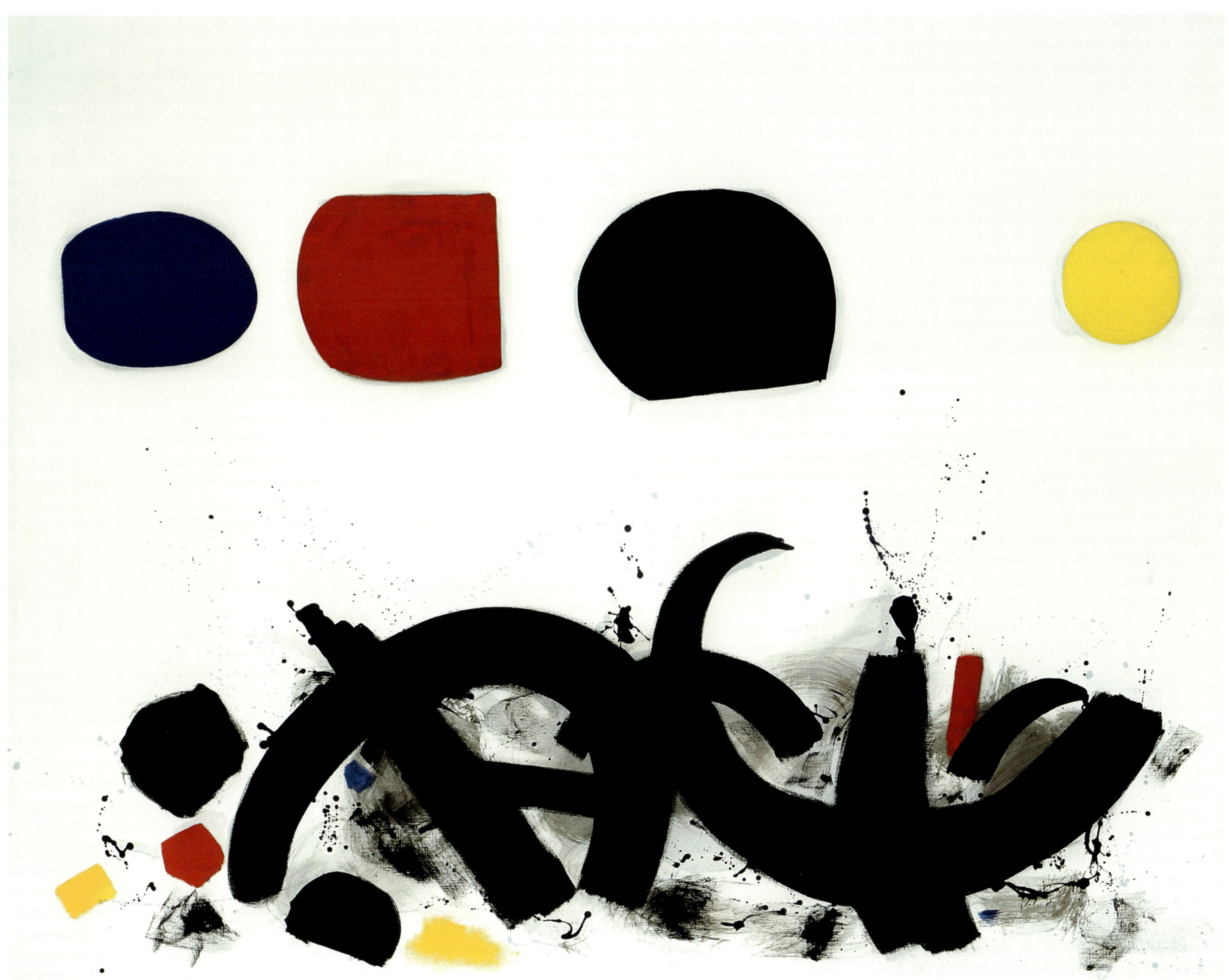

Lee Krasner AMERICAN 1911–1985

86 | *Happy Lady,* 1963

Oil on cotton duck, 58 × 75¾ in.

Signed and dated lower right: *Lee Krasner 1963*

Purchased with funds from the National Endowment for the Arts Museum Purchase Grant and the Samuel and Alma Catsman Foundation (1978.59)

Lee Krasner was one of the original members of the group of painters that came to be known as The New York School. Like most of her counterparts—her husband, Jackson Pollock, Willem de Kooning, Arshile Gorky, and Philip Guston, to name a few—Krasner came of artistic age during one of the most exciting times of the twentieth century, when nonobjective painting moved to the fore as the predominant means of expression.

American artists at the time were looking for a way to synthesize a traditional, realistic way of rendering the world with myriad European influences—Cubism, Fauvism, the abstractions of Piet Mondrian, the philosophies of the Surrealists, and Carl Jung's theories of the collective unconscious. Part of the quest was finding subject matter drawn, not from the surrounding world, but from the unconscious. In other words, they were questioning not only how to make a painting but what to paint. As Krasner developed into a mature artist, she followed a path that took her from traditional art (she was an accomplished realist painter), to controlled abstractions that retained an element of nature, then to collages made from fragmented paintings, and, finally, to the gestural, curvilinear, overall abstractions for which she is best known.

The daughter of first-generation Russian immigrants who were Orthodox Jews, Krasner (born Lena Krassner in Brooklyn) was interested in art from an early age. When she was just fourteen, she attended the Women's Art School at Cooper Union in New York, graduating in 1929. That same year, she was introduced to the work of Pablo Picasso and Henri Matisse at the Museum of Modern Art. She took some courses at the Art Students League, the National Academy of Design, and City College, but it was not until 1937, when she began studying with Hans Hofmann, that her work took a decided step toward modernism. For both artists, art was primarily about abstracting forms from nature. As she describes her development, "I think of my art training in the following way: the academy first, the break with the academy is when I hit the Hofmann School which is cubism. The next real break follows when I see Pollock's work and once more another big transition occurs. . . . It was a force, a living force, the same sort of thing I responded to in Matisse, in Picasso, in Mondrian."[1]

Happy Lady was painted after a period of intense creativity following Krasner's slow recovery from the shock of Pollock's death in 1956 and the subsequent problems in resolving his estate and, more recently, the death of her mother. She had been looking forward to an exhibition of her works, organized by Clement Greenberg, which was to be held at French and Co. When Greenberg criticized the new direction her art was taking, she angrily canceled the show. The reemergence of her productivity was heralded by the completion of *The Eye Is the First Circle* (1960), a sixteen-foot-wide loosely rendered painting executed in blacks and browns. (Due to insomnia, Krasner painted at night by artificial light; as a result, she preferred more somber colors.) Consciously or not, Krasner introduced figurative elements—eyes, faces, and other body parts—that recurred throughout the remainder of her career.

That same year, 1960, Krasner broke her right arm. Undeterred, she continued to paint, mostly by guiding the arm, still in the cast, with her left hand. *Happy Lady,* done during this time, reveals a tentative return to color in a monochromatic palette of cobalt blue. Painted on unprimed canvas, the work also shows the influence of the Color Field painters, such as Helen Frankenthaler and Kenneth Noland, who were garnering attention at the time. The name of the painting is not necessarily a reflection of her improved emotional state, however; titles, never important to Krasner, usually came after the completion of a work and were often suggested by friends. "Happy Lady" was taken from a comment by a six-year-old girl who looked at the canvas and said, "There's a lady and she's happy." When Krasner inquired why the lady was happy, the girl replied, "Don't you see she's dancing?"[2] And in fact, the verve and energy of *Happy Lady*'s execution can be seen as an abstract dancer or dance, traces of the physical body moving through space.

Although she was at the center of the Abstract Expressionist movement, still considered one of the most influential of the twentieth century, Krasner never reached the heights achieved by her counterparts. Whether the result of gender politics of the time (Hofmann once remarked, "This [study] is so good you would not know that it was done by a woman"[3]), taking care of the volatile Pollock, or simply personal limitations, one will never know. However, the past few decades or so, culminating in a traveling retrospective of her work in 2000, have shown an ongoing interest in and reevaluation of not only Krasner's art but her role in this very important development in modern art. Certainly *Happy Lady* reveals Krasner's independent spirit, talent, and particular way of rendering her simultaneous experience of both painting and the world, all of which were at the heart of Abstract Expressionism. SS

1. Quoted in Cindy Nember, "A Conversation with Lee Krasner," *Arts Magazine* 47 (April 1973), p. 43.

2. Ibid., p. 48.

3. Quoted in Robert Hobbs, *Lee Krasner* (New York: Abbeville Press, 1993), p. 25.

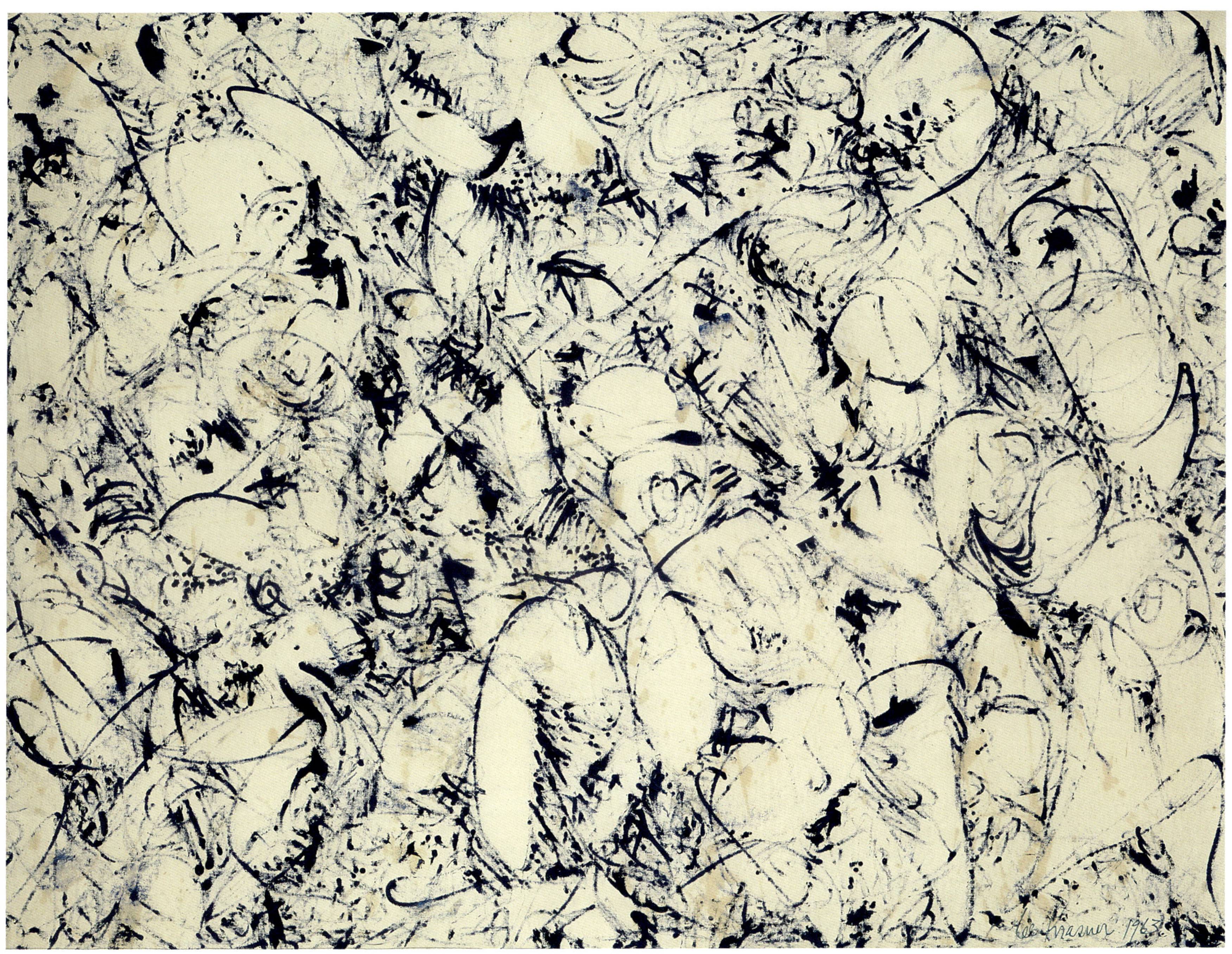

Seymour Lipton AMERICAN 1903–1986

87 | *Wind Drift*, 1982

Nickel silver on Monel metal, 33¾ × 36⅜ × 14 in.

Unsigned

Gift of the Friends of Modern Art and Michael A. and Natalie Pelavin (1985.81)

Seymour Lipton was one of the foremost sculptors of The New York School, which rose to prominence in the late 1940s and early 1950s.[1] Born in New York City, Lipton was originally trained as a dentist, but in the early 1930s, without any formal education in the arts, he began to make sculpture.

Lipton's earliest works were generally molded in plaster or carved in wood.[2] Like a great deal of art produced during and for some time after the Depression, they were expository in nature and addressed pressing social issues like racism, poverty, child labor, and class struggle. To communicate to as wide an audience as possible, Lipton utilized a figurative style enlivened by expressive distortions of form and scale. The mid-1940s, however, witnessed a shift in Lipton's technique, subject matter, and style. Thanks in part to the influence of Surrealism, which European artists such as André Breton, Max Ernst, and Yves Tanguy had imported to the United States in the late 1930s, Lipton not only began to work with metal but to adopt a more abstract idiom as well.[3] Stylistically, his sculptures from the 1940s are an amalgam of organic and mechanical forms that allude indirectly to the turmoil of World War II. At once disquieting and aggressive, they often consist of rough edges, angular contours, sharp spikes, and animated surfaces.

In the late 1940s and early 1950s Lipton developed what would become his mature style, embracing a higher degree of formal simplicity and adopting soft, sensuous shapes that alternately blossomed outward and curved inward. At the same time he pioneered a technique that he employed for the rest of his career. He began by cutting pieces from a large sheet of metal, which he then welded together to create the sculpture's form.[4] Next, he used an oxyacetylene torch to apply a layer of golden bronze or nickel silver over the exterior of the sculpture, sometimes gently hammering the surface to create variations in texture and grain. Lipton also modified his thematic program, launching a sustained investigation of the human condition in its entirety and probing such universal experiences as life and death, birth and sacrifice, struggle and redemption. He became equally concerned with giving visual form to the full range of human emotions, from anger, fear, and despair to happiness, joy, and love. According to Lipton, his primary subject was, above all, "the drama of man's life . . . with its uncertainty, mystery, pleasures and pain."[5]

Wind Drift is composed of two concave shapes—suggestive of cups or shells—perched one on top of the other. The center of the sculpture has been "pierced" and a sizable portion of its mass removed, introducing a degree of transparency not found in Lipton's earlier work. In form as well as name, *Wind Drift* evokes a great boat, its sail unfurled, floating on the buoyant waters of the sea, an effect heightened by the precarious angle at which the sculpture is perched on its base. It appears as if it might tip over at any moment, in much the same way a ship plunges down a wave. Lipton had been fascinated by sailing since a relatively young age, and he recognized in the relationship between boat and water a symbol for the relationship between man and nature.[6] Indeed, of *Wind Drift* he has said: "The lyricism of full sails on boats in fast movement . . . became a metaphor for . . . man's adventure in the limitless cosmos. . . . Man controls and is controlled by the forces of nature."[7] KB

1. Lipton, along with the sculptors David Smith, David Hare, Herbert Ferber, and others, was included in the important exhibition *The Third Dimension: Sculpture of The New York School*, held at the Whitney Museum of American Art, New York, in 1984.

2. For comprehensive information on the different phases of Lipton's career, see Albert Elsen, *Seymour Lipton* (New York: Harry N. Abrams, 1970).

3. Like many New York School artists, Lipton was also deeply impressed by African and Native American art.

4. In 1955 Lipton started using a rustproof bronze alloy called Monel metal.

5. Quoted in Judy K. Collischan Van Wagner, *Seymour Lipton: Sculpture*, exh. cat. (Greenvale, N.Y.: Hillwood Art Gallery, Long Island University, 1984), p. 4.

6. For more information on Lipton's attraction to sailing and to the sea in general, see Lori Verderame, *An American Sculptor: Seymour Lipton* (New York: Hudson Hills Press, 1999), pp. 30–31.

7. Seymour Lipton to the Flint Institute of Arts, 17 December 1985.

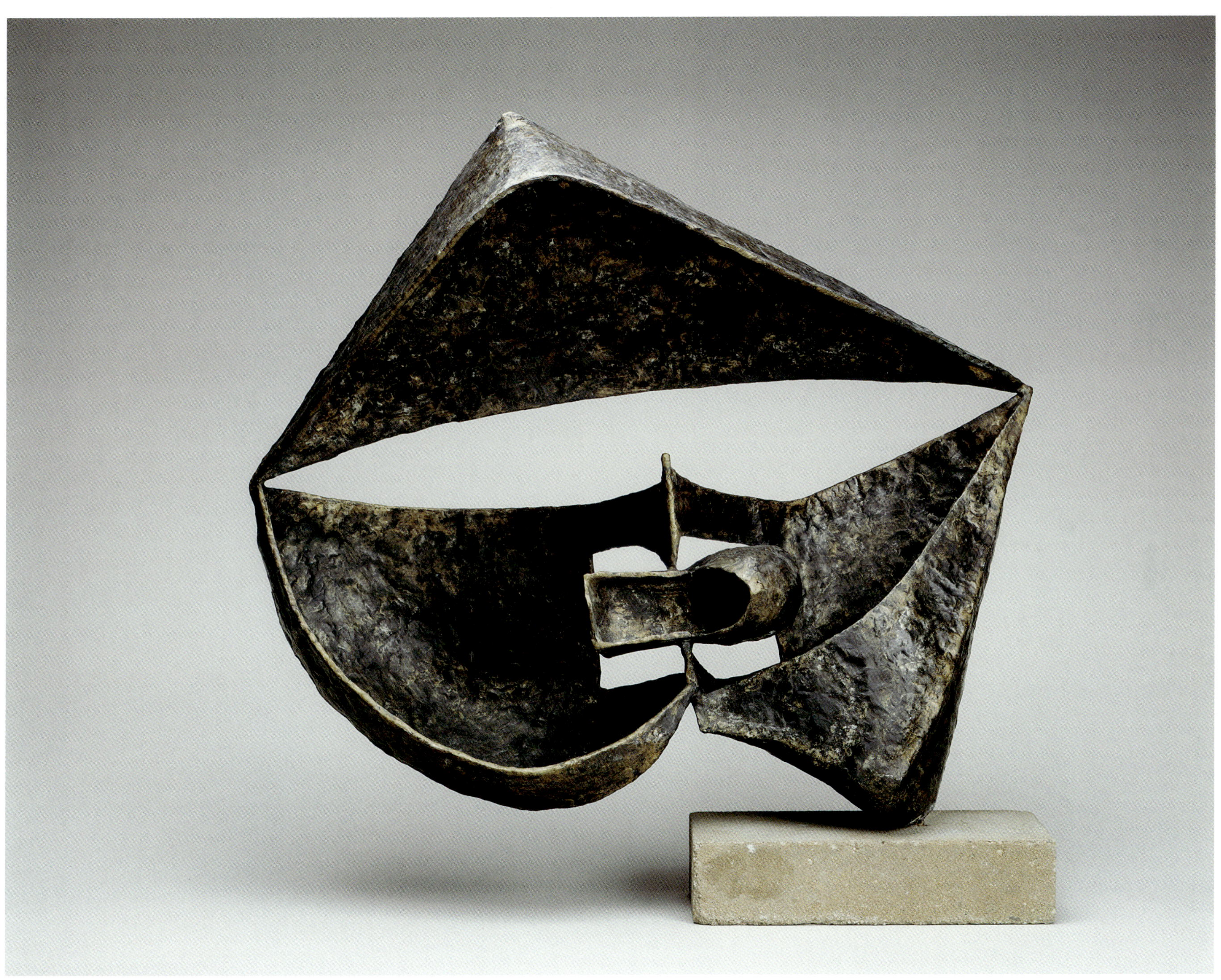

Robert Motherwell AMERICAN 1915–1991

88 | *Elegy to the Spanish Republic #173,* 1990

Acrylic on canvas, 50 × 60 in.

Signed upper right: *R.M.*

Museum purchase and gift of the Dedalus Foundation (1997.103)

Robert Motherwell began his career by studying art criticism and philosophy in Los Angeles and San Francisco before entering Harvard University in 1937. Only later, in graduate school, did he make the switch to studio art. Interspersing trips to Europe (1932 and 1938–40) with school, he combined graduate studies in philosophy at Harvard with courses in art history at Columbia University in New York. At Columbia, his professor Meyer Schapiro convinced him to switch from art history to painting, but he remained deeply committed to philosophy and art criticism throughout his life.

In New York Motherwell met a number of European Surrealists in exile and adopted their idea of automatic writing or "doodling" as a means of tapping into the subconscious. He also experimented with another Surrealist technique, collage, and became a master of the medium. He was accomplished enough to catch the eye of Peggy Guggenheim, who gave him an exhibition at her Art of This Century Gallery in New York in 1944. In 1948 he joined forces with fellow Abstract Expressionists Jackson Pollock, Mark Rothko, Clyfford Still, and Barnett Newman in opening a school called The Subject of the Artists, a name that reflected their belief that subject matter came, not from the external world, but from the unconscious mind. Motherwell felt that the role of the artist was to give visible structure to such intangibles as emotion and thought and once wrote, "The function of the artist is to make actual the spiritual, so that it is there to be possessed."[1]

In the 1950s he began his most well-known series, *Elegy to the Spanish Republic,* inspired by his reaction to the Spanish Civil War. Paintings from this series, which he would paint throughout his life, consist of simplified, stark black bars and ovoids that aggressively jut out of a white background into the viewer's space. These forms are not specific symbols of war; for Motherwell, the essence of art was not about reproducing the world as much as reordering it. Thus, his *Elegies* do not communicate specific events as much as evoke emotion through color, shape, and form. As early as 1946 he codified this approach to art, writing, "We feel through the senses, and everyone knows that the content of art is feeling; it is the creation of an object for sensing that is the artist's task."[2]
SS

1. Robert Motherwell, "Gestural Abstraction," in *Theories and Documents of Contemporary Art: A Sourcebook of Artists' Writings*, ed. Karen Stiles and Peter Selz (Berkeley: University of California Press, 1996), p. 13.

2. Ibid., p. 26.

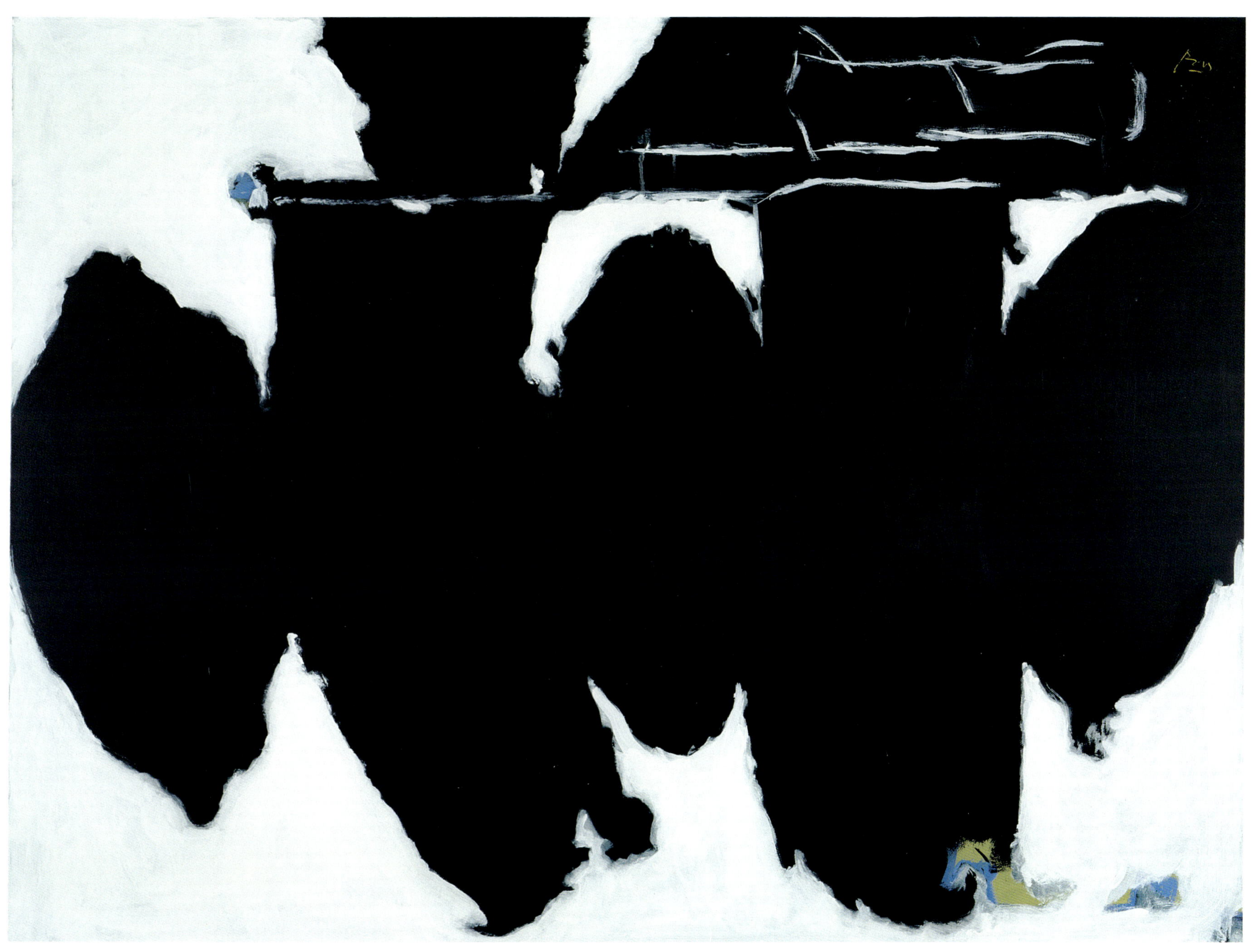

Harry Bertoia AMERICAN, BORN ITALY 1915–1978

89 | *Untitled,* 1965

Bronze, 22 × 39 × 7¾ in.

Unsigned

Gift of Mr. and Mrs. David Martin (1967.27)

The Italian-born artist Harry Bertoia is internationally recognized for both his sculpture and furniture design. A native of the town of San Lorenzo, he immigrated with his family first to Canada and then to the United States in 1930. He studied in Michigan—first at the Society of Arts and Crafts in Detroit in 1936 and then from 1937 to 1942 at the Cranbrook Academy of Arts in Bloomfield Hills. In 1943 Bertoia began working at the Evans Products Company in Venice, California, where he designed furniture, particularly chairs, with his fellow innovator Charles Eames. Of the inventive furniture Bertoia designed for Knoll Associates, the most celebrated is the Bertoia chair, introduced in 1952. In both his furniture design and his sculpture, he sought to free materials from their traditional roles. His best-known artworks are "sound sculptures," in which sound is linked to the movement of the works' metal pieces.

Bertoia came to his sound sculptures through a fascination with materials, particularly the way their properties can be made to emulate the natural world—much like trying to capture the sound, movement, and texture created by wind moving through a field of mature wheat. His static pieces carry this investigation further, exploring the relationship between materials and process. In *Untitled,* Bertoia rejected the traditional method of casting bronze, where a mold determines the shape, seeking instead to find a technique where process and chance create the form of the work. His solution was to pour the molten bronze onto sand and then, as it was cooling, "sculpt" it with a long-handled tool. "My intent was to bypass all known ways of bronze casting, particularly because the bronze was made to take forms arrived at by other material,"[1] he said. In this work, the interaction of the artist is spontaneous and the final outcome is determined by a combination of control and chance, similar to Helen Frankenthaler's manipulation of paint on unprimed canvas. The bright marine-green patina of *Untitled* is striking, bringing to mind a cluster of algae or coral waving in underwater currents. Like his sound sculptures, the allusion is to nature, but the work remains very much about the manipulation of materials.

Bertoia had come of artistic age after World War II, when the reigning aesthetic in painting was Abstract Expressionism. There was no equivalent dominant aesthetic in sculpture. It was, as the art historian Herbert Read describes, a time defined by "a diffusion of styles, the exploitation of invention, the ceaseless experiment with new materials, and not by the deployment of any coherent 'movements.'"[2] Bertoia, with his interest in modern design and his innovative use of materials and process, was the ideal artist to express this. SS

1. Harry Bertoia to Dr. Stuart Hodge, former director of the Flint Institute of Arts, 1 August 1967, curatorial files, Flint Institute of Arts.

2. Herbert Read, *A Concise History of Modern Sculpture* (London: Thames and Hudson, 1983), p. 229.

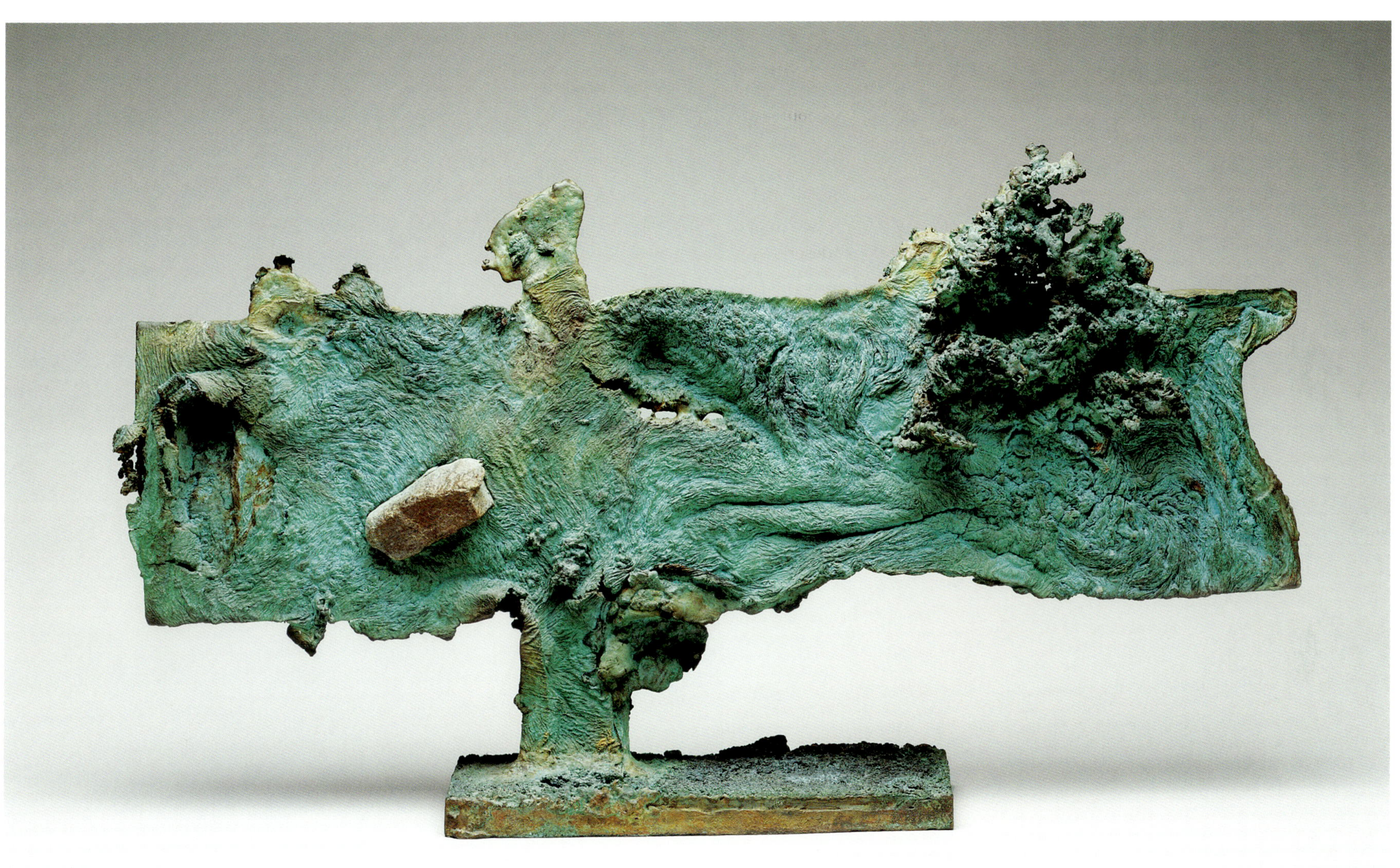

Morris Louis AMERICAN 1912–1962

90 | *I-31,* 1962

Acrylic resin on unprimed canvas, 83¼ × 15½ in.

Unsigned

Museum purchase with funds from the J. L. Hudson Company Acquisitions Challenge Grant and contributions from the Viola E. Bray Charitable Trust and other donors (1982.180)

Born Morris Louis Bernstein in Baltimore, Louis briefly studied at the Maryland Institute of Art and later lived in New York City, where in the late 1930s he worked on the Federal Art Project. He moved to Washington, D.C., in 1947 with his wife, Marcella Siegel, and resided there until his untimely death in 1962. He taught painting classes at the Washington Workshop Center for the Arts, also the venue for his first one-man exhibition in 1953.

Morris Louis gained recognition in the late 1950s and early 1960s for his large-scale, colorful abstractions made from thinned acrylic paint poured onto unsized and unprimed canvas. He came to this style later in his artistic life, experimenting with aspects of Cubism, Surrealism, collage, and Abstract Expressionism—particularly the black-and-white drip paintings of Jackson Pollock. A defining moment in his artistic evolution occurred when he met Kenneth Noland at the Washington Workshop Center for the Arts in 1953. As he said of the encounter, "Suddenly I wasn't alone."[1] Through Noland, Louis met the painter Helen Frankenthaler and the critic Clement Greenberg, both of whom proved to be extremely important in his artistic development.

Later in 1953 Louis and Noland visited Frankenthaler in her New York studio, where they saw her *Mountains and Sea* (1952; collection of the artist), a large "stain" painting that remains one of the great accomplishments of Color Field painting. For Louis, the visit was especially significant, for it provided answers to his search for the next step for abstract art. "She was," he said of the encounter, "a bridge between Pollock and what was possible."[2] He returned to Washington and began experimenting with thinned acrylic paint, bright colors, and huge canvases. Greenberg, whom Louis met that year, encouraged him along these lines. The critic not only took an interest in Louis but became highly influential in the development of the artist's mature style, visiting often and writing about him for major publications. "Back in 1953," Greenberg observed, "which was the first year of his artistic maturity, Louis discovered that the ambitious abstract painter could no longer safely take anything for granted in the making of a picture, not the shape of its support, not the nature of its surface, not the nature of its paint covering, not the implement with which he applied the paint, and not the way in which he applied it. In the thinness of paint and in an absorbent surface (whose absorbency he could control, if he chose the right dosage of size or glue) Louis found his means to a new integrity of color."[3]

Washington proved to be the perfect environment for an artist like Louis, who, though a loner, found support in the small, close-knit art community. The locale was good for him in other ways as well. As Greenberg noted in a 1960 *Art International* article on Louis and Noland, "From Washington, you can keep in steady contact with the New York art scene without being subjected constantly to its pressures to conform as you would be if you lived and worked in New York."[4] Both artists, along with Thomas Downing, Howard Mehring, and Gene Davis, became identified with what became known as the Washington Color School, a varied group whose motivating philosophy was to express content as color. Championed by Greenberg, who believed that flat, high-key abstractions were the logical direction for modern painting, the school reached its critical apogee in the early 1960s in Washington. For a time, mainly through the efforts of Greenberg, these Color Field painters rivaled in acclaim other movements that emerged simultaneously, such as Pop Art.

I-31 is part of Louis's *Stripes* series, painted in the final year of his life. It follows his larger works from the 1950s, which are usually divided into three major series: *Ambis, Veils,* and *Unfurleds.* In *Stripes,* which occupied him for close to two years, Louis worked on a smaller scale, bringing the colors together in a tight columnlike form rather than spreading them across the canvas or layering them on top of one another. He laid the colors edge-to-edge, allowing the flow of the paint to integrate organically with the weave of the canvas. However, while he indicated a flow of the paint in one direction, they were intended to hang in a way that appears upside down, as if gravity were reversed. SS

1. Quoted in *The Vincent Melzac Collection, Part One: The Washington Color Painters,* exh. cat. (Palm Beach, Fla.: Norton Gallery and School of Art, 1974), p. 34.

2. Ibid., p. 97.

3. Clement Greenberg, "Louis and Noland," in *Clement Greenberg: The Collected Essays and Criticism,* ed. John O'Brian (Chicago: University of Chicago Press, 1993), pp. 95–96.

4. Ibid.

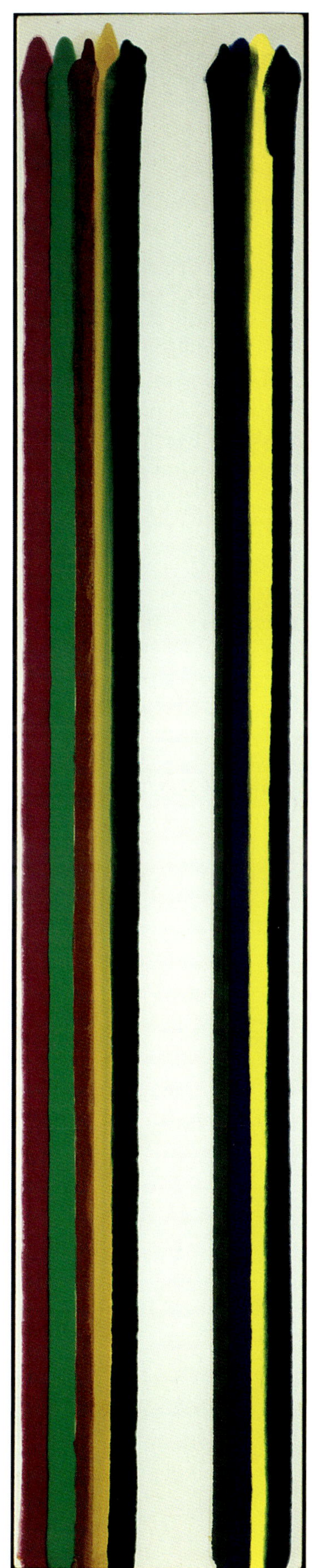

Helen Frankenthaler AMERICAN BORN 1928

91 | *Minotaur,* 1975

Acrylic on canvas, 132¾ × 81¾ in.

Unsigned

Bequest of Mary Mallery Davis, by exchange (1993.42)

In the history of art, Helen Frankenthaler stands as an important link between Abstract Expressionism and the subsequent form of abstraction that came to be known as Color Field painting, although she is primarily identified with the latter. She was interested in art from an early age, studying with Rufino Tamayo at the Dalton School in New York and Paul Feeley at Bennington College, from which she graduated in 1949. During the next few years she studied privately with Hans Hofmann, one of the great teachers of abstract painting, and came into contact with Abstract Expressionism through the work of Jackson Pollock, Willem de Kooning, and Arshile Gorky. Like the Abstract Expressionists, she was attracted to Surrealism, particularly in the emphasis given to the role of chance and the unconscious gesture of automatic drawing. As with many of the young artists committed to abstract art at the time, Frankenthaler was searching for her own style, one that would go beyond what the Abstract Expressionists, particularly Pollock, had accomplished. As she noted, "You could become a de Kooning disciple or satellite or mirror, but you could depart from Pollock."[1]

Early in her career, Frankenthaler was influenced by the critic Clement Greenberg, who believed abstraction was moving through color in the direction of flatness. Toward this end, she experimented with pouring and dripping thinned acrylic paint onto unprimed canvas, a new way of playing with both chance and gesture. Her seminal painting, *Mountains and Sea* (1952; collection of the artist), not only served as an important breakthrough for the artist; it set the tone and standards for an entire movement. When, for instance, the Washington, D.C., artists Kenneth Noland and Morris Louis visited Frankenthaler in the early 1950s and saw these large-scale, stained paintings, they realized she was the "bridge" between Pollock and the future of abstraction. Promoted by Greenberg, the new movement, Color Field painting, dominated the art scene for more than a decade and influenced many younger artists.

Minotaur is a classic example of Frankenthaler's style, with its monumental scale that commands the viewer's peripheral vision and lyrical veils of color that both saturate and hover on the surface of the work. The blue stains on the left and the pinkish red on the right, both drawn and dripped, play against the central maroon shape, made up of gradations of stains poured onto the canvas. One gets the sense of a finely tuned balance between controlled pouring, gestural drawing, and the allowance for chance. "I'd rather risk an ugly surprise than rely on things I know I can do," Frankenthaler once said, "The whole business of spotting; the small area of color in a big canvas; how edges meet; how accidents are controlled; all this fascinates me."[2] SS

1. Quoted in "An Interview with Helen Frankenthaler by Henry Geldzahler, 1965," in *Contemporary Art: A Sourcebook of Artists' Writings*, ed. Kristine Stiles and Peter Selz (Berkeley: University of California Press, 1996), p. 30.

2. Ibid., p. 31.

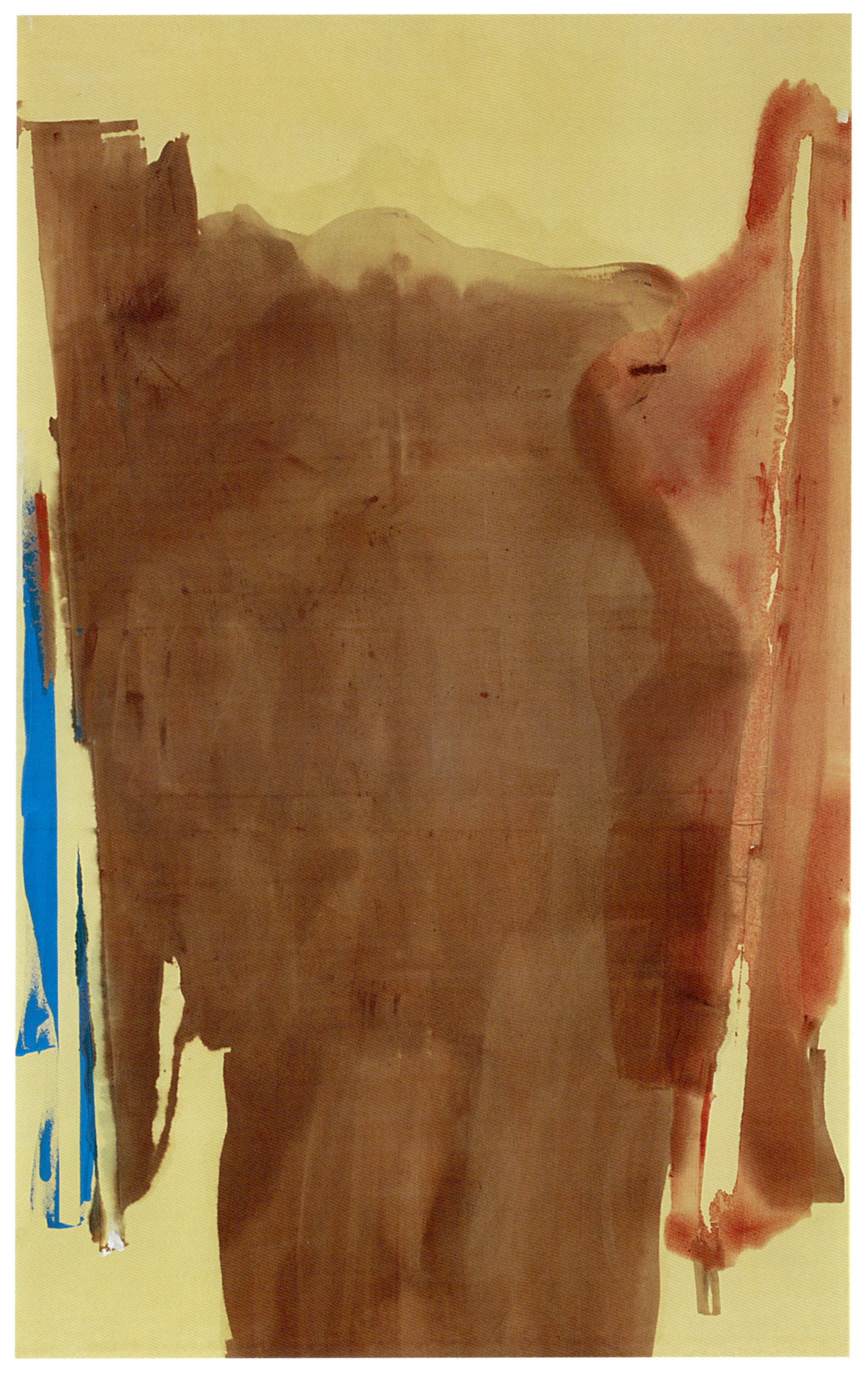

Paul Jenkins AMERICAN BORN 1923

92 | *Phenomena Forking Paths,* 1967–68

Acrylic on canvas, 113⅞ × 60 in.
Signed lower right: *Paul Jenkins*
Museum purchase (1969.45)

Paul Jenkins is best described as a Color Field painter whose work relates stylistically to that of Helen Frankenthaler and Morris Louis. Emerging in the 1950s, the Color Field painters were primarily concerned with questions of color, abstraction, and the flatness of the picture plane. Jenkins's work is distinguished among this group in that he was more involved with the fluid nature of interacting colors in the painting process than in simply creating fields of color.

Although his birthplace, Kansas City, had little to offer in the way of an artistic environment in the 1930s, Jenkins knew from a young age that his interests lay in this arena. He worked in a ceramics factory while in grade school and witnessed the transformative effect of extreme heat on various colors of glazes. Of this early aesthetic experience, Jenkins has said, "From the glazes . . . I saw strange, iridescent colors created by fire, . . . and learned that the practice of art involved this fantastic sense of timing, that it wasn't a matter of just standing in front of an easel."[1] While still a teenager, Jenkins won a scholarship to the Kansas City Art Institute's Saturday art program, afterward studying at the Art Institute in Kansas City, Missouri from 1938 to 1941. Visiting the nearby Nelson Gallery, Jenkins was especially drawn to and inspired by the collection of Far Eastern art.

In 1944 Jenkins was drafted into the Naval Air Corps. Stationed in Chincoteague, Virginia, he spent the duration of the war painting. Afterward, on the G.I. Bill, he moved to New York and studied from 1948 to 1951 with Yasuo Kuniyoshi at the Art Students League. During this time, the League was a melting pot of styles and aesthetics, and Jenkins concentrated on his figurative work. At the same time, he became aware of the work of a fellow student, Robert Rauschenberg, who was experimenting with monochromatic white paintings. Although New York's art world remained dominated by the influence of the Abstract Expressionists, this did not deter young painters such as Jenkins and Rauschenberg from searching for their own voice. Although Jenkins experimented with the flowing paint of watercolor and other media and techniques, he remained without a clear artistic path. He knew that he "couldn't continue in a figurative way, but didn't appreciate or understand the meaning of Pollock, Rothko, and Newman."[2]

The development of Jenkins's mature style came mainly from influences outside the studio classroom. A visit to Europe in 1953 provided the young painter with a fresh approach to the art world. He read Carl Jung and was introduced to the *I Ching (The Book of Changes)*. From the book *Zen and the Art of Archery,* Jenkins learned about the "kendo" stroke, described as "a movement or action whose accuracy and efficacy purportedly derive from a state of spiritual awareness so heightened that a blindfolded bowman can hit his target."[3] Philosophically and physically, the concept of the kendo stroke is central to Jenkins's artistic process, one that expanded on his early affinity to Asian art.

Since 1955 the artist has divided his time between Paris and New York. When he left for Europe in 1955, he destroyed all his existing work to make way for new modes of experimentation. Exploring how a prism diffracts light into pure color and its return back to pure light has been a main thrust in his artistic development. "It deals with origins," he has said of this fascination with the prism, "The fact light creates color is the ever-haunting presence."[4] Given his obsession with all aspects of color, it is not surprising that the nineteenth-century artists Gustave Moreau and Odilon Redon, two Symbolists who stressed the emotional content of color in their work, are among Jenkins's influences.

Since 1960 Jenkins has used thinned acrylic paint, primarily for its fluidity. Process dictates the outcome of each work and chance plays a role in the final color and composition. Beginning with an unstretched, prepared canvas, Jenkins throws paint with an urgent kendolike stroke. Carefully moving the tipped and folded canvas, he manipulates the paint's flow and direction with brushes and an ivory knife. Larger works entail the use of pulleys to reposition and move the canvas. Jenkins considers each painting a "phenomena" that masterfully combines chance with control. *Phenomena Forking Paths* illustrates how a completed painting by Jenkins resembles the unpredictable and ever-changing quality of nature. SS

1. Quoted in Jay Jacobs, "Paul Jenkins," unidentified clipping, curatorial files, p. 46, Flint Institute of Arts.

2. Ibid., p. 50.

3. Ibid., pp. 50–51. In more literal terms, kendo is a Japanese martial art involving the use of a bamboo sword; it is akin to iaido, in which a metal sword is used.

4. Quoted in Sue Scott, *Selections from the Ellen and Jerome Westheimer Collection* (Oklahoma City: Oklahoma Art Center, 1989), p. 74.

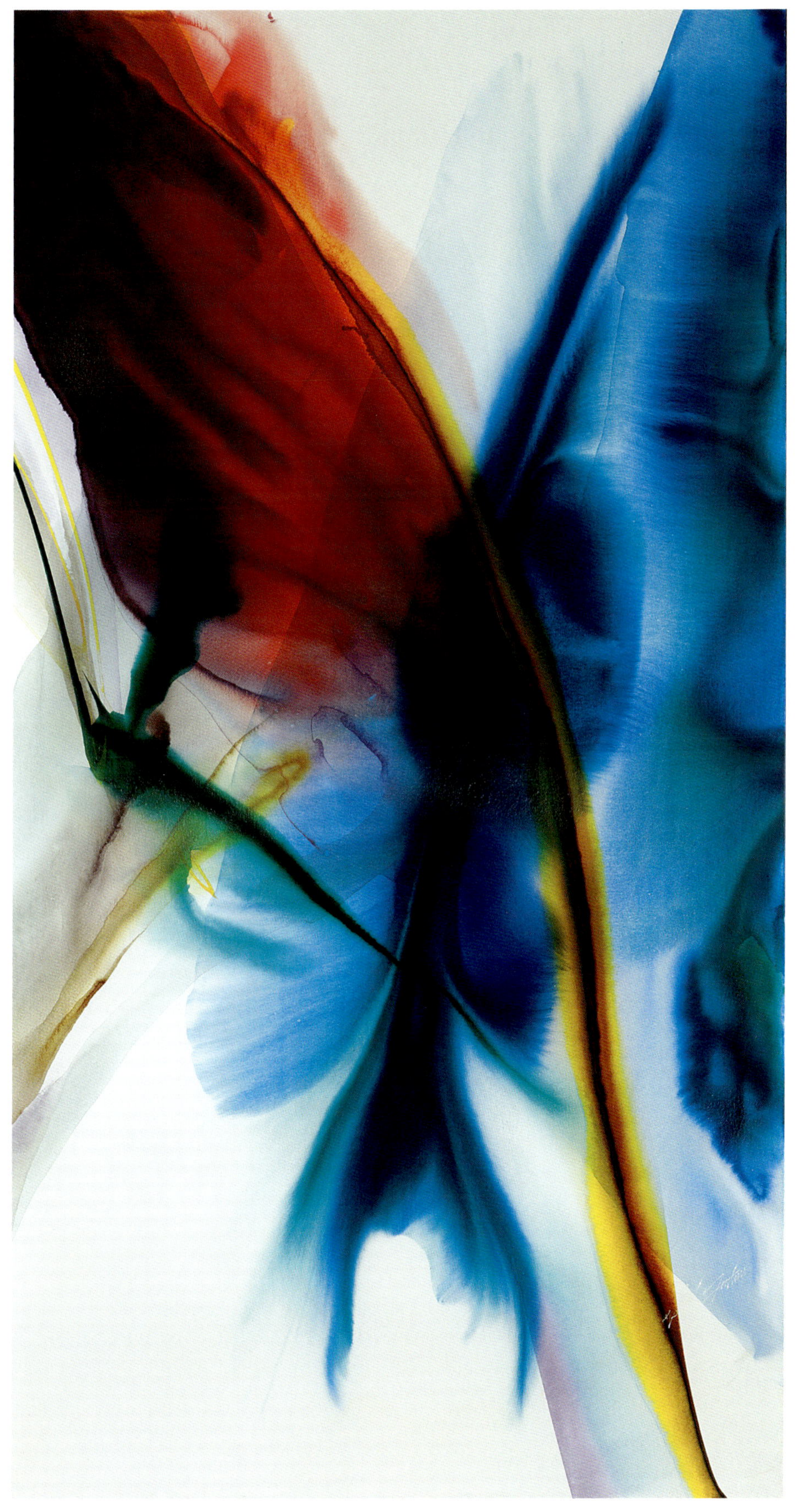

Robert Natkin AMERICAN BORN 1930

93 | *Desdemona,* 1971

Acrylic on canvas, 83¼ × 49 in.

Signed lower right: *Natkin;* signed and dated on verso, lower left: *Natkin 1971*

Gift of the Friends of Modern Art and anonymous donors (1974.2)

Robert Natkin was born in Chicago to working-class parents of Russian-Jewish descent. Although he describes the environment in which he grew up as drab, even depressing, he remembers with fondness the many trips—sometimes as many as six or seven a week—he made to the Palace Theater to see movies, musicals, and vaudeville shows. The lively colors and flickering lights featured so prominently in them would later prove to have a formative influence on the young artist.

Natkin first showed an interest in art as a teenager, which he nurtured by studying at the Art Institute of Chicago from 1948 to 1952. There he was also able to take advantage of the museum's rich collection of late-nineteenth- and early-twentieth-century art, at times skipping classes to scrutinize paintings by Paul Klee, Henri Matisse, and Pierre Bonnard. In 1957 Natkin and his wife, the painter Judith Dolnick, opened the Wells Street Gallery, where they exhibited work by artists from Chicago and New York. Before it closed two years later, the gallery showed some of the most advanced art being produced in both cities, including work by such Abstract Expressionists as Willem de Kooning, Franz Kline, and Philip Guston.

Desdemona belongs to roughly the third phase of Natkin's career, which began in the late 1960s and ended in the early 1970s.[1] The paintings he produced during this period fall into either the *Field Mouse* or the *Intimate Lighting* series and bear a superficial resemblance to works by such Color Field painters as Kenneth Noland, Jules Olitski, and Helen Frankenthaler. These works are often described as luminous, atmospheric, and ethereal because of the soft haloes of color—which range from rose and aquamarine to yellow and violet—that float across their surfaces like clouds in the sky. Anchored to neither a ground nor a horizon, the haloes melt and bleed into one another. As the critic Max Kozloff noted: "Here there are faint sprays, cottony daubs, and free-floating color smudges. In accord with this more intuitive framework, the coloring wafts itself away into tinted and pale nuances."[2] The pictures are also crowded with clusters of unidentifiable forms that call to mind a fantastic world viewed under a microscope. The forms are distributed across the entire length of the canvas in an apparently random manner, a compositional format that Natkin referred to as "scatter-balance."[3] In these works, Natkin also began to experiment in earnest with different methods of transferring pigment to canvas. The same year he executed *Desdemona,* Natkin adopted the habit of working with rags, dishcloths, and sponges instead of brushes, thereby heightening the texture and physicality of his pictures. It is no wonder, then, that so many critics have likened their surfaces to a kind of skin or, as Gerald Nordland has observed, "a breathing fabric."[4]

Although he is often categorized as a Color Field painter, Natkin denies that his pictures bear any relationship to those by Noland, Olitski, and Frankenthaler. Indeed, he has gone so far as to describe Color Field painting as "non-art,"[5] because of its emphasis on form at the expense of content. That content is as important to Natkin as form is indicated by the titles he has given his works, most of them inspired by poetry, mythology, or literature—*Desdemona,* for instance, is the name of both the tragic heroine of Shakespeare's *Othello* and a moon orbiting the planet Uranus. KB

1. For more information on the evolution of Natkin's style, see Jonathan Fineberg, "Robert Natkin: Intimate Themes," in *Robert Natkin,* exh. cat. (Philadelphia: Moore College of Art, 1976).

2. Quoted in Peter Fuller, *Robert Natkin* (New York: Harry N. Abrams, 1981), p. 101; originally published in Max Kozloff, "Robert Natkin," *Artforum* (summer 1968).

3. Quoted in Gerald Nordland, *Robert Natkin,* exh. cat. (San Francisco: San Francisco Museum of Art, 1969), unpaginated.

4. Gerald Nordland, "Robert Natkin: Color-Saturated Elastic Space," *Artnews* 72 (February 1973), p. 54.

5. Quoted in Fuller, *Natkin,* p. 22.

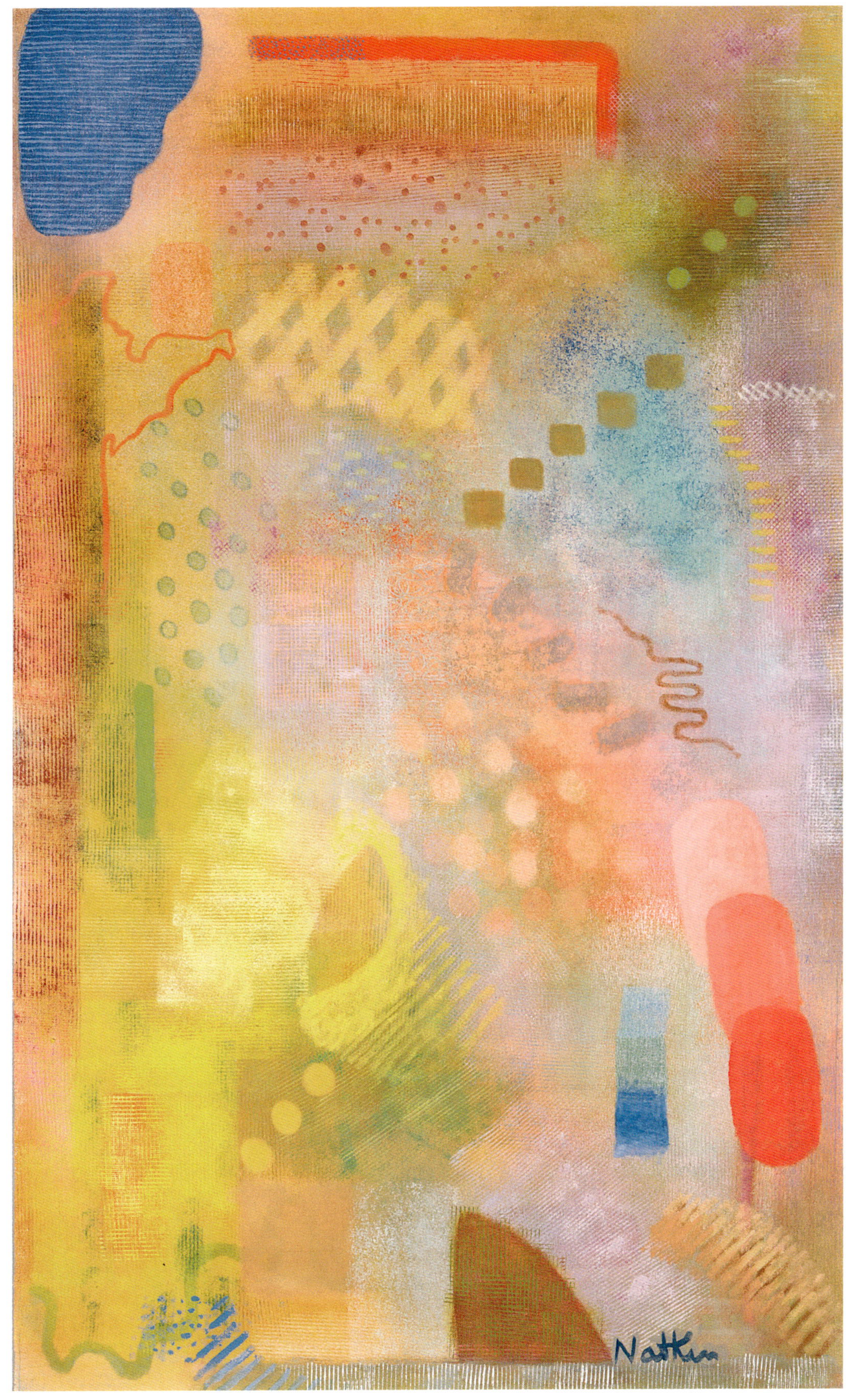

Robert Goodnough AMERICAN BORN 1923

94 | *Off White on Off White,* 1982–83

Acrylic on unprimed canvas, 48 × 64 in.

Signed and dated on verso: *Goodnough '82–83* and *Goodnough 1982–1983*

Gift of the Friends of Modern Art (1998.5)

A second-generation Abstract Expressionist, Robert Goodnough came to his mature style in the late 1960s after years of experimenting with gestural abstraction. He synthesized various aspects of abstraction—most specifically Synthetic Cubism and Hard-Edge Abstraction—to break through to a pictorial format that consists of coalesced triangular shapes set against a minimal, monochromatic field. *Off White on Off White* is a particularly subtle and beautiful example of this mature style. As with most of his work from the early 1980s, the triangular shapes are grouped to form a contiguous abstract shape, setting up a figure-ground dynamic that activates the picture plane and gives movement to the entire painting.

Goodnough was interested in art from an early age and earned a scholarship to study at Syracuse University. In 1946 he moved to New York City, where he found himself at the center of the art world from the time of his arrival. Under the G.I. Bill, he studied with Amédée Ozenfant, a founder of the French Purist School, from 1950 to 1951. He spent the summer of 1947 in Provincetown, Massachusetts, where he trained with Hans Hofmann and met such varied painters as Larry Rivers and Alfred Leslie as well as the critic Clement Greenberg. Greenberg was impressed with the young artist, whom he included in the *New Talent* exhibition he organized with Meyer Schapiro at the Kootz Gallery in 1950. The show was one of the first public forums for the second wave of Abstract Expressionists, among them Elaine de Kooning and Grace Hartigan; it was described at the time by Thomas Hess, editor of *Artnews,* as "one of the most successful and provocative exhibitions of younger artists I have ever seen."[1] Goodnough was a member of The Club, a group that met regularly to discuss the future of abstract art. He also wrote art criticism for *Artnews* from 1950 to 1957 and contributed to Robert Motherwell and Ad Reinhardt's *Modern Artists in America,* a magazine that carried the banner for modernism. He earned a master's degree in art education from New York University in 1960, supporting himself through teaching and carpentry.

The 1950s were a time of excitement and change, when many new ideas were emerging. Young artists like Goodnough were seeking ways not only to build on what the Abstract Expressionists had achieved but to add to the dialogue. From the French Purism of Ozenfant, Goodnough learned pure color and line, from Hofmann the dynamism of color. Through Hofmann and especially the writings of Greenberg, Goodnough became interested in the structure of the Synthetic Cubist grid, which is central to his work from the late 1950s.[2] These paintings are composed of loosely rendered black grids, which function as asymmetrical structures for tiny pockets of solid color. Some figurative elements are present. As Goodnough's work developed over the next two decades, the grid became less prominent, the colors and shapes more minimal, and the edges further defined. In retrospect, this evolution seems quite natural, particularly in the context of the larger art world, which was experiencing a similar change, from gestural abstraction to a more minimal aesthetic. However, one can appreciate the challenge faced by a young artist in confronting the two most dominant art movements of the twentieth century, Cubism and Abstract Expressionism, and appreciate even more his personal synthesis of the two. SS

1. Quoted in Irving Sandler, *The New York School: The Painters and Sculptors of the Fifties* (New York: Harper and Row, 1978), p. 132.

2. Greenberg believed the structure of the paintings of the first generation of Abstract Expressionists derived from Picasso's Synthetic Cubism.

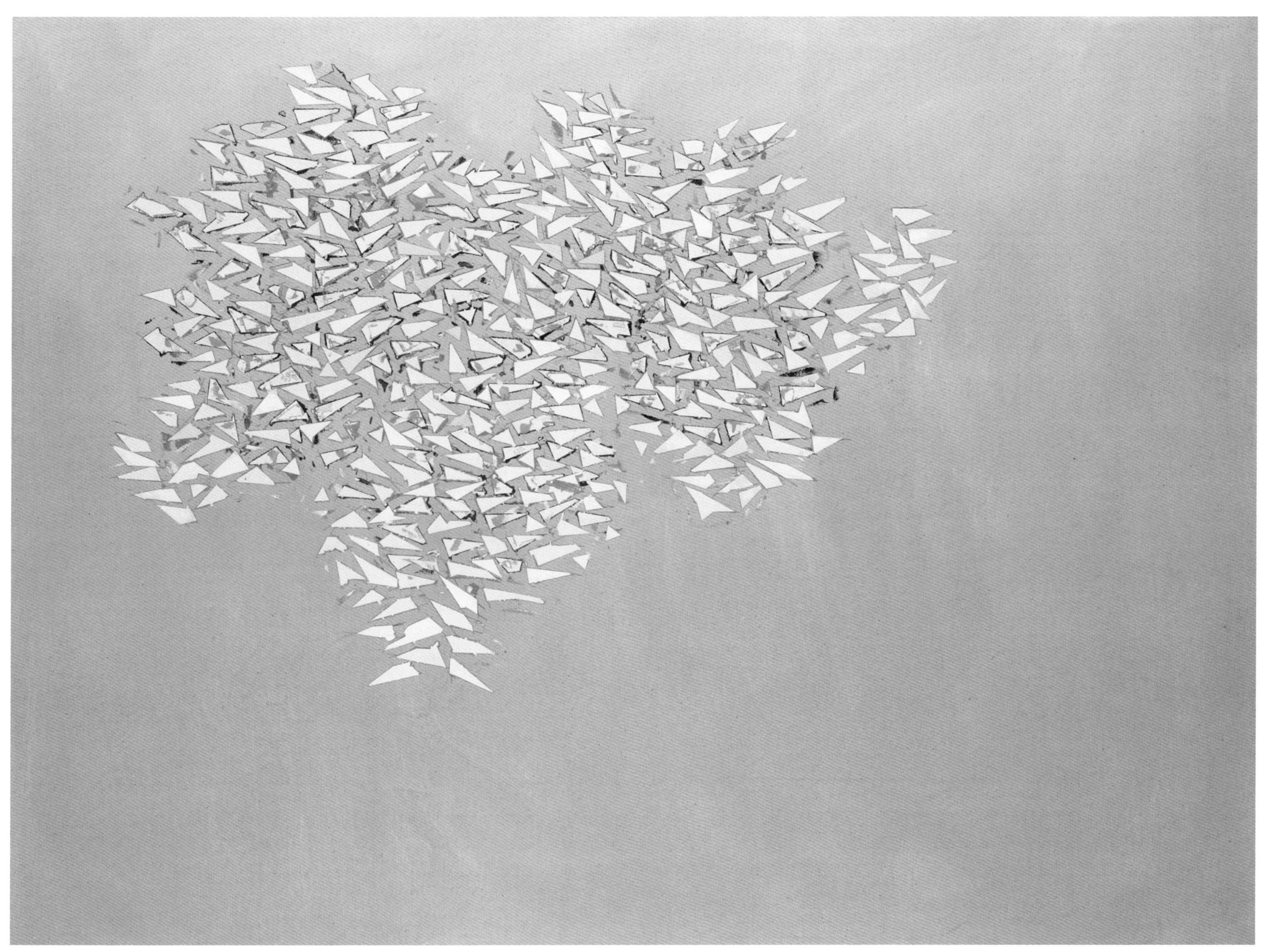

Grace Hartigan AMERICAN BORN 1922

95 | *Black Velvet,* 1972

Oil on canvas, 109⅛ × 80⅛ in.

Signed and dated lower left: *Hartigan '72*

Gift of an anonymous donor out of the Detroit area (1974.26)

In the 1950s Grace Hartigan emerged as one of the most renowned artists of the second generation of The New York School. In 1945, when she moved to New York City, her loosely figurative style was influenced primarily by Henri Matisse, but within five years she was working in an overall abstraction indebted to her contemporaries Jackson Pollock and Willem de Kooning. In 1950 she was included in the *New Talent* show organized by Clement Greenberg and Meyer Schapiro at the Kootz Gallery and in the following year had her first solo exhibition, at the prestigious Tibor de Nagy Gallery.

Pollock's exhibition of drip paintings in 1948 at Betty Parsons Gallery was particularly instrumental in Hartigan's development, although the work was shocking to her at first. "I was mesmerized and fascinated," she says of the encounter, "but I can't say that I liked the paintings initially."[1] She subsequently spent a week with Pollock and his wife, Lee Krasner, at their home on Long Island, looking at, more than talking about, his work. Hartigan was deeply affected by the experience, both stylistically and philosophically. "I knew the paintings and the person who painted them were one and the same. Painting was not an activity but a total life. And you would do anything to keep painting, even if you starved. You were the paintings and the paintings were you."[2] This infusing of self into her work led Hartigan back to figurative painting and the introduction of content into her work. As early as the mid-1950s, one begins to see a hint of biography in many of her pictures. In 1960 Hartigan married the physicist Winston Price and moved to Baltimore, Maryland. She left Tibor de Nagy and joined Gres Gallery in Washington, D.C., which closed soon after; as a result, she did not exhibit for two years. By then, Pop Art had captured much of the critical and popular imagination, and Hartigan's style, like that of Philip Guston, whom she had befriended, fell out of favor.

Black Velvet shows Hartigan's ongoing experimentation with new techniques coupled with psychological investigation. Painted in 1972, the year her father died, the work reflects her loss, symbolized by the empty chair in the center of the composition. An inkwell and a coal scuttle, gifts from her father, are at the lower left, while the upper half is filled with faces—a father and daughter—from Japanese kites she was collecting at the time. All the forms are flattened and pressed against the picture plane as if to insinuate themselves into the space of the viewer, making the overall impact somewhat claustrophobic. In technique, this painting was a departure for Hartigan, who stained the canvas with a sheepskin mitt (a tool used by housepainters) rather than employing her usual brush drawing. In addition, black was never used by those Color Field painters who practiced the staining technique, but here Hartigan uses it to represent the death of her father. She laid down the background in many layers, wiping and sanding it back, again a departure from the Color Field painters, who generally poured a single layer. Hartigan spent three months on the painting, which was a struggle both technically and symbolically. Today, however, it stands as a testament to an artist willing to push her work in new directions, even if it goes against the prevailing winds of the art world. SS

1. Quoted in Robert Saltonstall Mattison, *Grace Hartigan: A Painter's World* (New York: Hudson Hills Press, 1990), p. 11.

2. Ibid., p. 12.

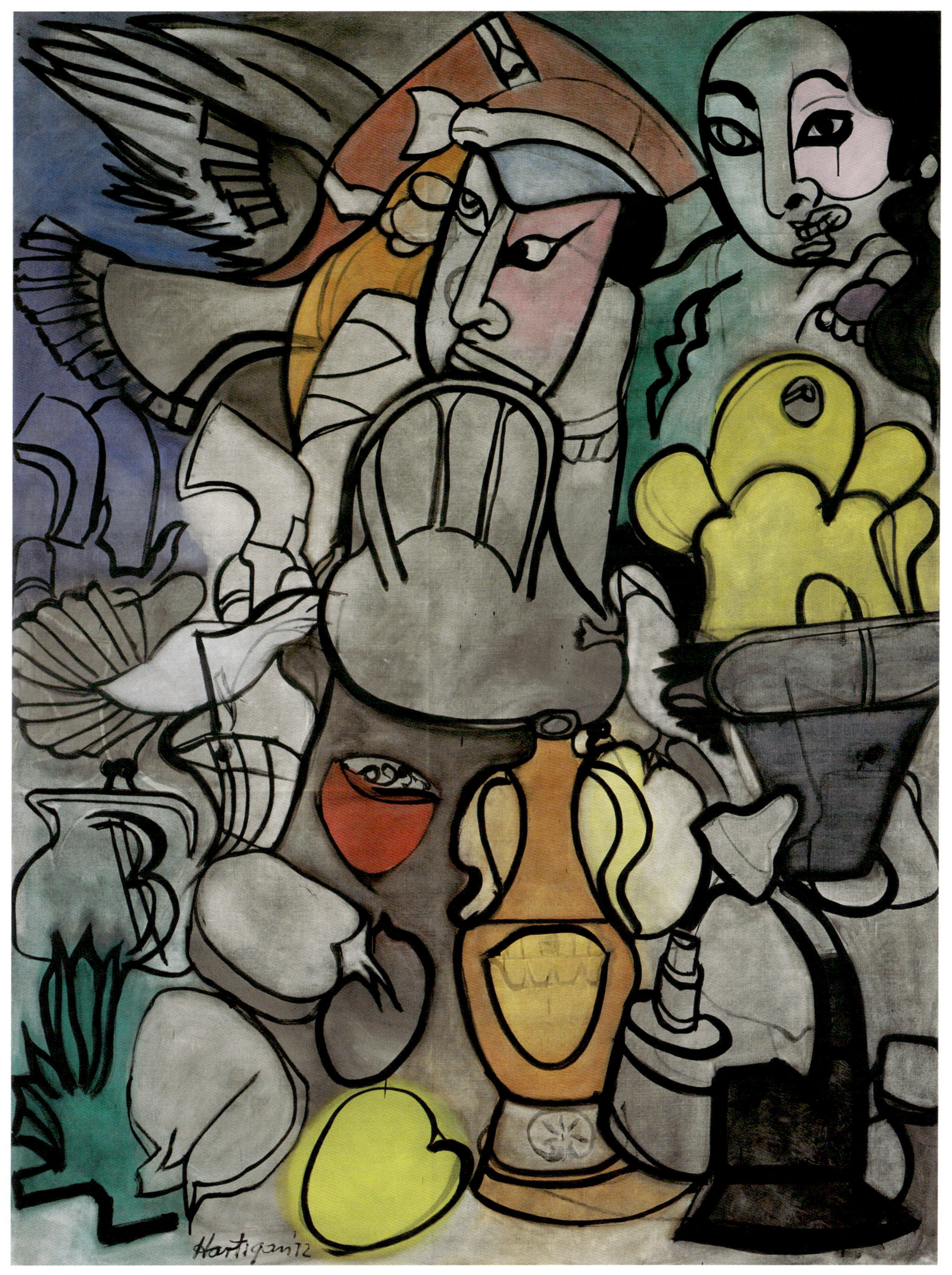
Hartigan '72

Larry Rivers AMERICAN 1923–2002

96 | *Buick Painting with P*, 1960

Oil on canvas, 47⅞ × 60⅛ in.

Titled, signed, and dated on verso: *Black Painting with P, Rivers 60*

Bequest of Mary Mallery Davis, by exchange, and partial gift of The Bishop Trust (2002.3)

Larry Rivers was a pivotal figure in the development of an innovative aesthetic that emerged from the domination of Abstract Expressionism in the 1950s. Rather than entirely rejecting the gestural painterliness of that style, Rivers fused it with old master techniques while at the same time embracing the irony, irreverence, and wittiness that came to define the emerging Pop Art movement.

Rivers believed that an accomplished technique was essential for an artist. In a 1964 mutual interview with the British painter David Hockney, he observed, "In order to project myself into this history and rivers of art, at a certain point in my work I wanted to draw and paint like an Old Master."[1] Although he is usually identified as one of the innovators of Pop Art, Rivers's reworking of historical paintings and interest in traditional rendering set him apart from such Pop artists as Andy Warhol and Roy Lichtenstein, who were more interested in commercial processes.

Born Yitzroch Loiza Grossberg in the Bronx, New York, to Russian immigrant parents, the artist changed his name to Larry Rivers when he was seventeen. Although he was trained in classical music from an early age and was given violin and piano lessons, Rivers was drawn to the liveliness of jazz, with a penchant for the saxophone. By his late teens, he was an accomplished saxophonist, playing the resort circuit with a band called Larry Rivers and the Mudcats. In 1944 he studied at the Juilliard School of Music, where he made the acquaintance of Miles Davis and Charlie Parker, and he played and performed throughout his life.

Over the next few years, a series of events conspired to turn the aspiring musician's attention to art. He met the artist Jane Freilicher through her husband, Jack, a musician Rivers encountered while playing at Old Orchard Beach, Maine. Freilicher gave Rivers his first painting lessons and introduced him to a number of other artists, among them Nell Blaine, an abstract artist who was well connected in the contemporary art world. Blaine encouraged both Rivers and Freilicher to enroll in Han Hofmann's painting school; Rivers did so in 1947, attending classes in both New York and Provincetown over the following two years. While Hofmann instructed his students in a traditional manner, working directly from the live model and from the landscape, he also stressed contemporary theories of color relationships and abstraction. Even as a nascent artist, Rivers's extraordinary ambition was not necessarily focused on contemporary thought but on mastering painting skills: "At the end of the year," he noted, "I became frantic to draw the figure. . . . If I didn't do this, I'd never be able to convince myself of my genius. . . . It was important to me to solidify my position, to be able to say, yes, don't worry, you really are an artist."[2]

Just as influential as his two years as a student at Hofmann's school was the Pierre Bonnard exhibition at the Museum of Modern Art in 1948. It was, as the art historian Barbara Rose observed, "a turning point that proved that modernism was not incompatible with figuration."[3] Rivers exhibited his Bonnard-inspired paintings in 1949 and as a result was included the following year in the now-famous *New Talent* exhibition at the Kootz Gallery, which was curated by two pivotal figures of the art world, the critic Clement Greenberg and the art historian Meyer Schapiro. That same year Rivers traveled to Europe to visit museums and see old master paintings firsthand. In addition to his time with Hofmann and the Bonnard exhibition, the gestural abstraction of Willem de Kooning was a significant influence on the evolution of Rivers's style.

Buick Painting with P is a beautiful example of Rivers's synthesis of gestural abstraction, imagery from popular culture, and aspects of realism. Three painterly horizontal strokes describe the body of the car. Another orange stroke in the center of the picture becomes the license plate, and two red circles the taillights. In 1960, the year this painting was executed, the Buick was in many ways symbolic of American life and lifestyle, and it is telling that Rivers chose to make the three horizontal bands red, white, and blue. This simple artistic choice takes the shape beyond an automobile to something both emblematic and American—a nod, perhaps, subconscious or otherwise, to Jasper Johns's famous flag paintings of the late 1950s. SS

1. Larry Rivers, in *Theories and Documents of Contemporary Art: A Sourcebook of Artists' Writings,* ed. Kristine Stiles and Peter Selz (Berkeley: University of California Press, 1996), p. 226.

2. Quoted in David Levy, Barbara Rose, and Jacquelyn Days Sewer, *Larry Rivers: Art and the Artist,* exh. cat. (Washington, D.C.: The Corcoran Gallery of Art in association with Bulfinch Press, 2002), pp. 23–24.

3. Ibid., p. 24.

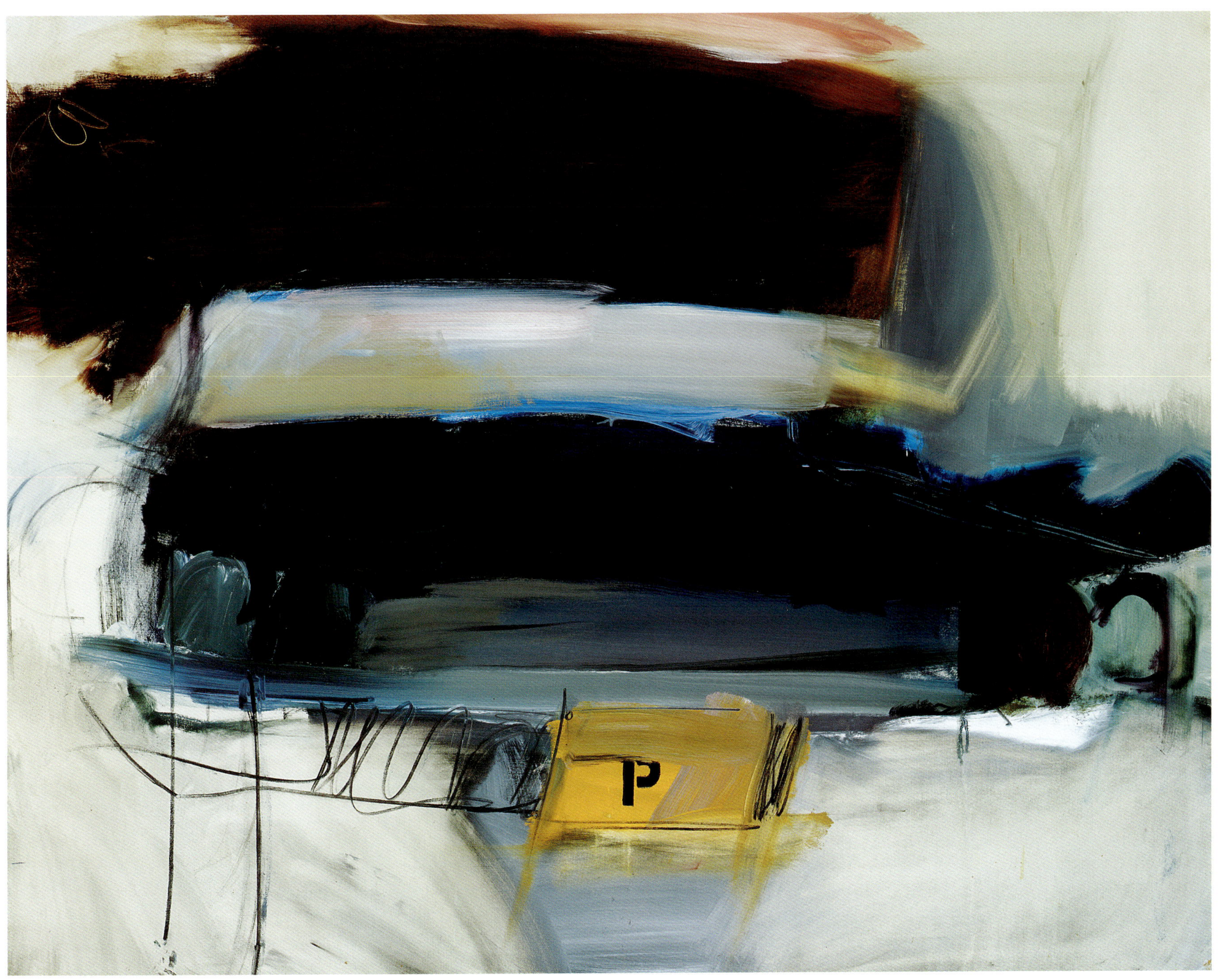
P

Wayne Thiebaud AMERICAN BORN 1920

97 | *Golden Cake,* 1962

Oil on canvas, 16 × 20 in.

Signed and dated lower left: *Thiebaud 1962*

Bequest of Mary Mallery Davis (1990.26)

Wayne Thiebaud is one of a number of artists to emerge in the 1960s after a start in commercial art; he worked for Walt Disney Studios and Universal-International Studios in Los Angeles before taking a position as layout director and cartoonist for Rexall Drug Company. It was at Rexall that his interest shifted from commercial to fine art, mostly through the influence of fellow artist Robert Mallory. When Thiebaud was twenty-nine, he returned to school at Sacramento City College and subsequently attended California State College where he earned a bachelor's and a master's degree in art. In 1956 Thiebaud moved to New York City for a year, where he learned firsthand about Abstract Expressionism, spending time with such artists as Elaine and Willem de Kooning, Franz Kline, and Barnett Newman. These two seemingly contradictory elements—a commercial art background and an intellectual interest in abstraction—became the foundation for Thiebaud's mature style.

Thiebaud is often labeled a California Pop artist. Because he sees himself more as a contemporary realist, it is a classification he resists. However, Thiebaud's first one-man exhibition in 1962, at the Allan Stone Gallery in New York, with its focus on depictions of pies, cakes, and other food items, coincided with the rise of such Pop artists as Andy Warhol, Claes Oldenburg, and Jim Dine, who were interested in similar imagery drawn from commercial or everyday sources. Critics, artists, and collectors not only responded enthusiastically to the show, but they saw him in the same light as the Pop artists. What differentiated Thiebaud from these painters who were enamored of similar techniques and imagery is his lush, even gestural, application of paint. In addition, his choice of subject matter comes from a more symbolic realm than the cool appropriation of other Pop artists. "I'm interested in foods generally," says Thiebaud, "which have been fooled with ritualistically, displays contrived and arranged in certain ways to tempt us or to seduce us or to religiously transcend us."[1]

Golden Cake is a classic example of Thiebaud's early still lifes, a single image set against a monochromatic or, at most, two-toned background. The central image is read two ways—as a realistic depiction of cake and as a combination of two geometric shapes, a circle and a triangle, that form the building blocks of painting. The lighting is dramatic, almost spotlit, elevating this object of everyday life to a higher status (a technique perhaps drawn from Thiebaud's experience in high school as a member of the theatrical department's lighting crew). The paint has been applied in a way that shapes the cake but brings to mind the actual icing, a process Thiebaud refers to as "object transference," where the paint literally takes on the appearance of the thing it is depicting. Thin, bright lines outline various parts of the cake and background, a dramatic device called "haloing" by the artist. It all combines to make the familiar extraordinary, which is in many ways the purpose of art. SS

1. Quoted in Karen Tsujimoto, *Wayne Thiebaud,* exh. cat. (Seattle: University of Washington Press in association with the San Francisco Museum of Modern Art, 1985), p. 27.

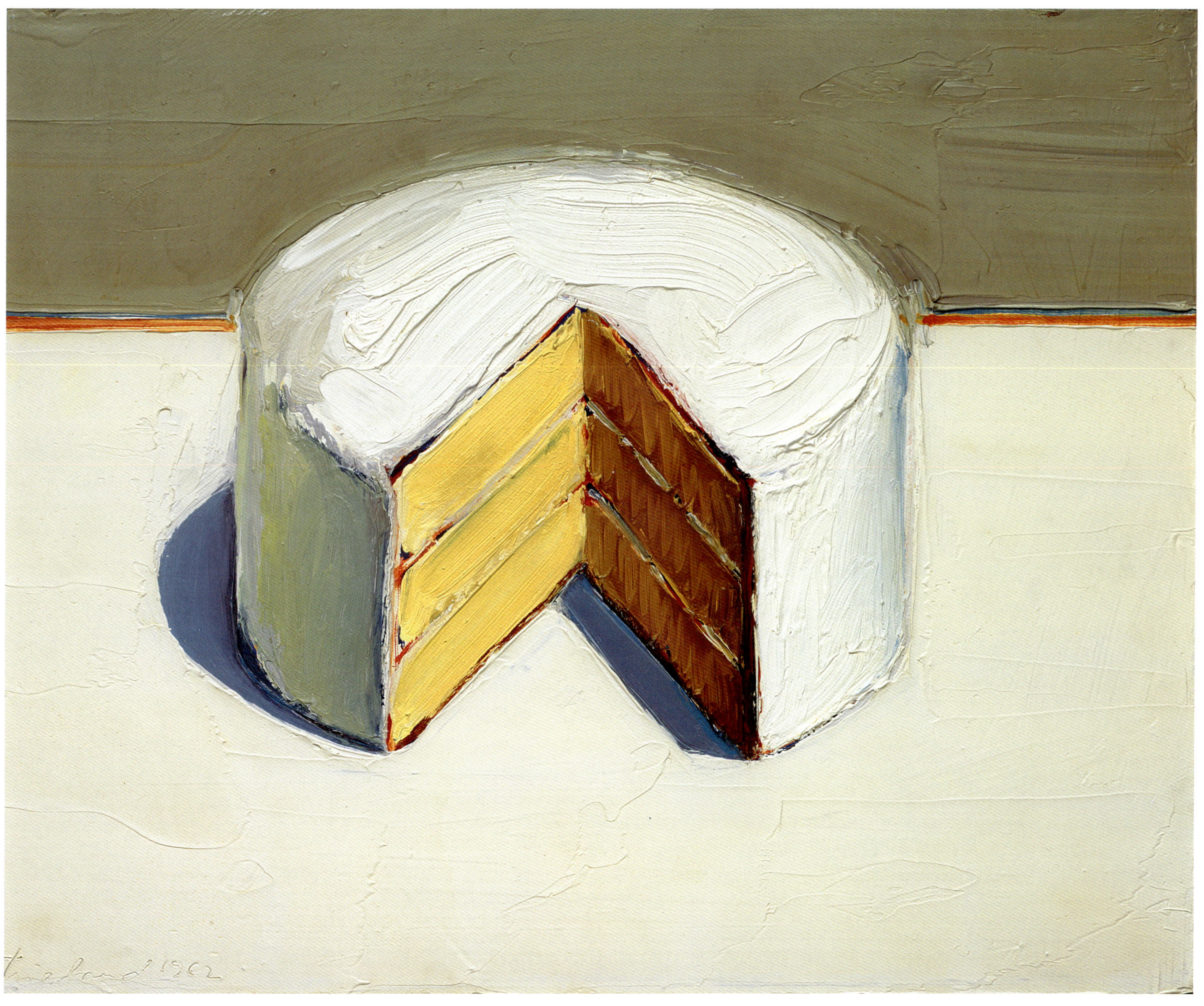

Richard Anuszkiewicz AMERICAN BORN 1930

98 | *Inflexional I,* 1966

Acrylic on canvas, 72 × 72 in.

Signed and dated on verso: *Richard Anuszkiewicz, 1966*

Purchase prize first Flint Invitational (1966.24)

Richard Anuszkiewicz, a native of Erie, Pennsylvania, began drawing and painting as a child; as a teenager he studied art at Erie Technical High. In 1948 he entered the Cleveland Institute of Art, where he was awarded a bachelor's degree in fine art five years later. His paintings from this period, inspired by those of Edward Hopper, Ben Shahn, and Charles Burchfield, are realistic in subject matter and style. In 1953, however, an event occurred that would change the course of Anuszkiewicz's career—he was awarded the Pulitzer Traveling Scholarship, which allowed him to attend the Yale University School of Art and Architecture, where he received his master's degree in 1955. While there he took classes with Josef Albers, who had taught at the Bauhaus in Germany before fleeing to America when the school was closed by the Nazis in 1933. Albers, a renowned painter, theorist, and writer, instructed Anuszkiewicz on the basics of geometric abstraction and color theory. It was not until the late 1950s, however, when he moved to New York City, that Anuszkiewicz completed the transition from realistic to abstract painting.

Anuszkiewicz is best known for the role he played in the development of Op Art (short for "Optical Art"), a movement that came to prominence in the mid-1960s. The first major exhibition of Op Art, *The Responsive Eye,* which included work by Anuszkiewicz, Bridget Riley, Victor Vasarely, and others, took place at the Museum of Modern Art in New York in 1965. According to William Seitz, the show's curator, Op Art is characterized by "sharp-edged and flatly painted shapes, colors, and lines" that "if skillfully controlled, can animate an observer's perception even against his will and bring about experiences of motion, light, deformation, [and] depth."[1]

Using purely nonrepresentational means, artists working in this style created canvases that appear to shimmer and dance, vibrate and quiver, contract and expand, advance and recede. Critics often described Op Art as hallucinatory and disorienting because of the powerful effect it had on the eye. The writer John Gruen, for example, once said that Anuszkiewicz "titillate[s] the eye with paintings whose colors and geometric patterns are so intense as to make one wince."[2] He could easily have been speaking of *Inflexional I.* Executed with an impersonal facture and almost mathematical precision, the work consists of light blue lines painted on a red ground, the majority of which are inscribed at an angle relative to the edge of the canvas. Because they intersect at the top right and bottom left corners, it appears as if they are being pulled or stretched, not unlike a rubber band. The light blue lines at the very center of the composition, by contrast, form a perfect square that echoes the shape of the canvas. When viewed more closely, however, they create the illusion of a tunnel that recedes deep into space or, alternatively, a pyramid whose very top projects toward the viewer. The confusion that *Inflexional I* creates in the visual field, an effect produced by the shifting array of complex patterns and vibrant colors, is characteristic of Op Art.

Although critics tend to identify Anuszkiewicz with Op Art, the artist has never wholeheartedly embraced the term. Indeed, he more often refers to himself as a colorist, since he pursues optical effects, not as ends in themselves, but as vehicles for the investigation of color theory.[3] As Anuszkiewicz said, "I feel that I've made a major contribution to the history of color—not in the sense of Op Art, but as a continuing esthetic idea in art history."[4] KB

1. Seitz, as quoted in Gene Baro, *Richard Anuszkiewicz: Centered Square,* exh. cat. (New York: Alex Rosenberg Gallery, 1979), unpaginated; originally published in William Seitz, "The New Perceptual Art," *Vogue* (February 1965).

2. Gruen, as quoted in Karl Lunde, *Anuszkiewicz* (New York: Harry N. Abrams, 1977), p. 29; originally published in John Gruen, "'Americans in 1963' at Modern Museum," *New York Herald Tribune,* 22 May 1963.

3. For more information on the importance of color to Anuszkiewicz, see Barry Schwabsky, "Lines of Luminosity," *Art in America* 89 (January 2001), pp. 102–3, 143.

4. Quoted in John Gruen, "Richard Anuszkiewicz: A Beautiful Discourse with Space," *Artnews* 78 (September 1979), p. 74.

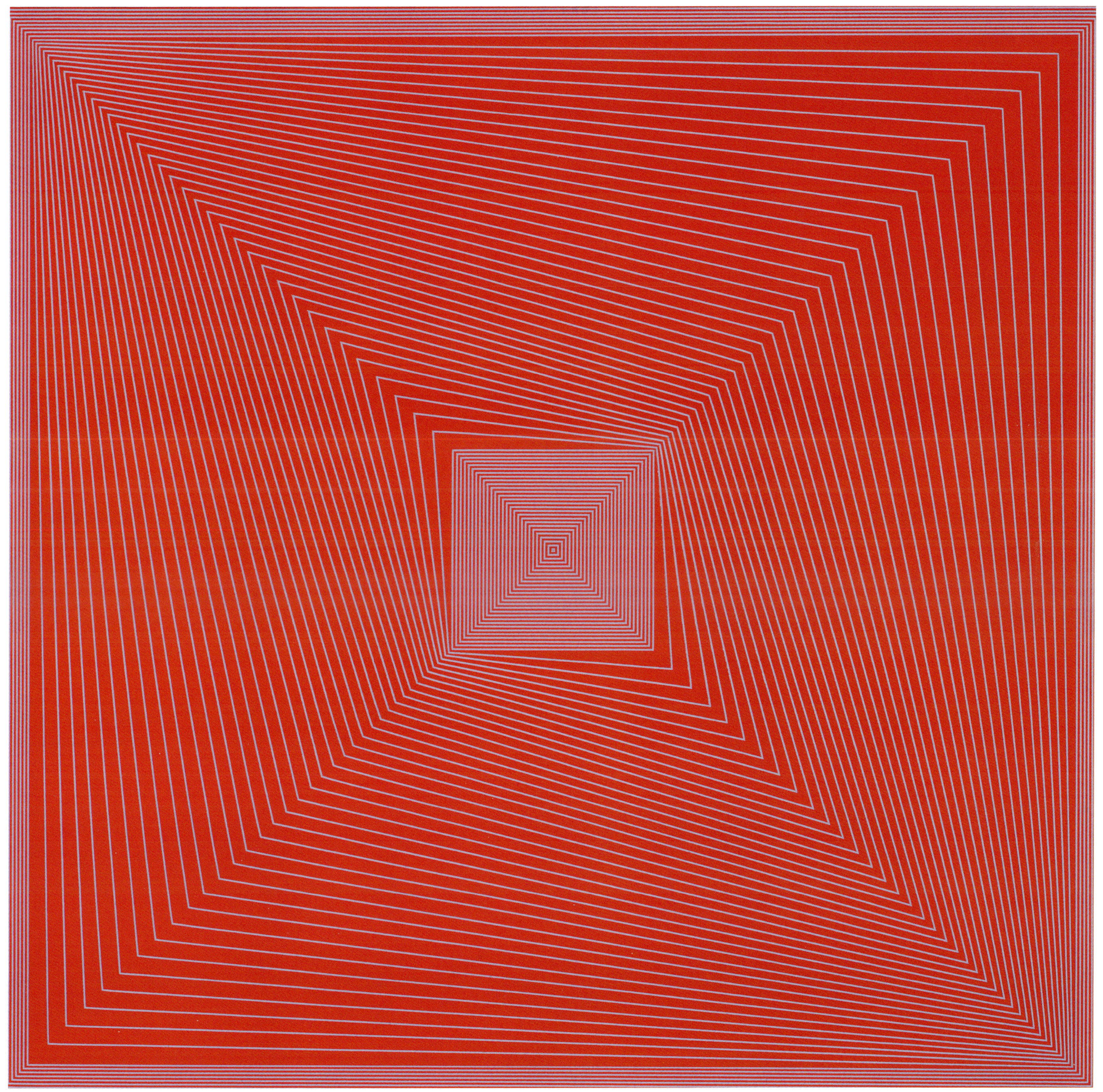

Beverly Pepper AMERICAN BORN 1924

99 | *Plus Cathedra,* 1968

Stainless steel (baked enamel), 20 × 27 × 18 in.

Unsigned

Gift of friends in memory of Joel Hodge (1969.8)

Born in Brooklyn, New York, Beverly Pepper studied painting at Pratt Institute and the Art Students League. She left New York in 1949 for Paris, where she studied with André Lhote at the Académie de la Grande Chaumière and with Fernand Léger at his studio. In the early 1950s Pepper settled in Rome, where she has spent most of her career. Her first major sculptural series, begun in 1960, consisted of wood pieces created from trees felled near her home. Pepper has since worked with many sculptural media, including bronze, stainless steel, Cor-ten steel, and forged and cast iron. Usually abstracted and often large scale, her sculpture has been associated with several movements, including Minimalism, Earthworks, and Constructivism.

Plus Cathedra is a relatively small example from a series of box sculptures Pepper created between 1967 and 1969. These pieces are essentially open-ended cubes, almost entirely sliced through. The resulting framelike shapes, fanned and opened out, appear delicately balanced. The poet and critic John Ashbery has described them as tossed "into the air where they stay, improbably cantilevered."[1]

Pepper coated the interiors of the boxes with baked enamel—white in the case of *Plus Cathedra,* although she also made red, blue, and black interiors—while the exteriors of the boxes are of highly polished, reflective stainless steel. The steel surfaces mirror the environment in which the sculpture is placed, be it a room in a museum or a landscape outdoors. As a result, when the viewer moves around the box sculptures, the exterior of the work becomes almost invisible from certain angles. These pieces create two related illusions: they both reflect their surroundings and become invisible in them. In this way, the viewer's relationship to the sculpture and, specifically, his or her movement around it are critical to the success of the piece. This engagement with the viewer is a hallmark of Minimalism, and Pepper's work of this period is often associated with the movement. Pepper questions conventional definitions of sculpture—to what degree should a sculpture be part of its environment?

Pepper has explored this question throughout her career. In most of her art, including Earthworks from the late 1960s and early 1970s, large-scale sculptures that resemble vastly oversized hand tools and later pieces that recall totem poles and funerary monuments, she considers the viewers' physical relationship with the sculpture as they approach or navigate around her art. Pepper remarked in an interview that she thinks of her work "in terms of man and the elements" and "was trying . . . to make the environment a part of the work."[2] Her commissioned work for public and private outdoor sculpture around the world, including projects in New York City, Barcelona, and the Laumeier International Sculpture Park in St. Louis, reiterate Pepper's long-standing interest in relating her art to the world it inhabits. RSR

1. J[ohn] A[shbery], "Reviews and Previews: Piero Dorazio and Beverly Pepper," *Artnews* 68, no. 1 (March 1969), p. 16.

2. Quoted in Jan Butterfield, "Beverly Pepper: 'A Space Has Many Aspects,'" *Arts Magazine* 50, no. 1 (September 1975), p. 92.

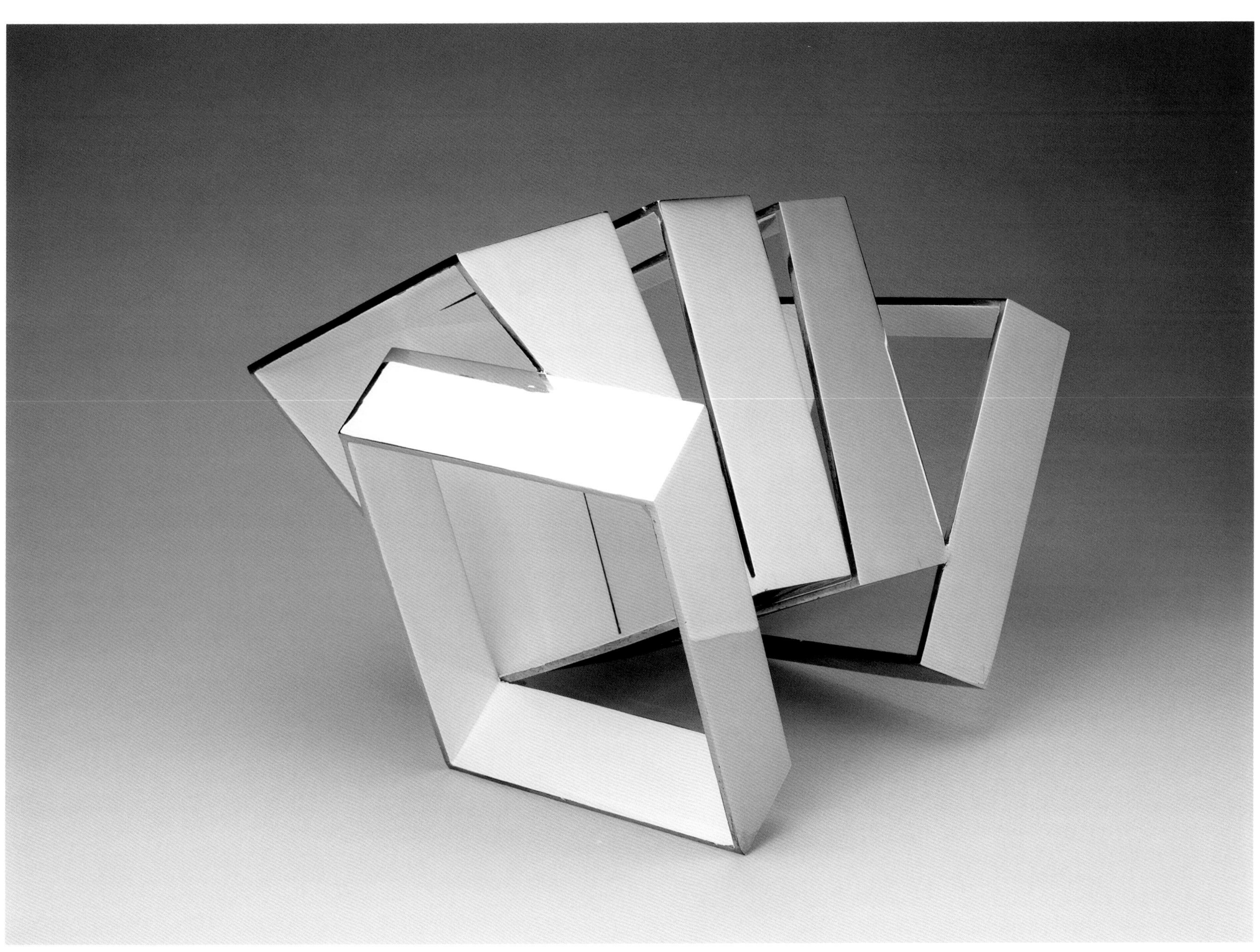

George Rickey AMERICAN 1907–2002

100 | *Two Lines Oblique—Twenty-Five Feet,* 1970

Stainless steel, 300 × 540 × 32 in.

Unsigned

Museum purchase (1969.46)

101 | *Column I,* 1962

Stainless steel, 106 × 24 in.; variable depth

Unsigned

Gift of Mr. and Mrs. Keith Davis (1972.17)

George Rickey was both an accomplished sculptor and a noted art historian. Although he began his career as a painter, he made kinetic sculptures since about 1951, and his classic book, *Constructivism: Origins and Evolutions*, originally published in 1967, is still a leading source on the topic. It is not surprising that Rickey would be drawn to Constructivism, an early-twentieth-century movement associated with the work of the Russians Naum Gabo and Vladimir Tatlin, in which nonobjective art is made from geometric forms.

One of the main goals of the Constructivists, and certainly of Rickey, is to create work that both occupies space and defines it through movement. These two works, *Two Lines Oblique—Twenty-Five Feet* and *Column I,* are classic examples of Rickey's sculpture: elegant tapered needles of forged steel, counterbalanced so that they move slowly and rhythmically in a trajectory that responds to the natural currents of the air. Clearly, to look at one sculpture is to see two works, one at rest and the other as it moves through space and time, creating what Rickey has described on numerous occasions as "drawings in space."

Rickey was born in South Bend, Indiana, but spent much of his childhood in Scotland. From the first, his course of study indicates a dual interest in art and art history. He studied at Trinity College in Glenalmond, Scotland; modern history at Balliol College, Oxford (B.A. 1929; M.A. 1931); art at the Ruskin School of Drawing, Oxford; and painting at the Académie André Lhote, Paris (1929–30). He also took classes in art history at the Institute of Fine Arts in New York and the Institute of Design in Chicago. Many of his early and middle years were spent teaching art at various schools around the country while pursuing a career as a painter. He had experimented with small whimsical mobiles while in the Army Air Corps, but it was not until 1948–49, when he attended a lecture by Naum Gabo at the Institute of Design, that he turned his attention to sculpture, first with figurative elements and soon fully embracing Constructivist beliefs. The mobiles of Alexander Calder were an early inspiration—a 1950 mobile (since destroyed) was a beautiful abstracted rendition of a flying phoenix—but as Rickey's work developed it became less anthropomorphic and more related to geometric forms and Constructivist thought.

Although Rickey's work is realized through mathematical constructs, the inspiration nevertheless originates in nature. The sculptures, whether long, thin blades or perfectly balanced squares, are transformed into movements emulating events in nature, such as blades of grass blowing in a breeze or tree branches swaying in the wind, and deriving their rhythm from the speed of the currents. Still, for Rickey, the sculpture was but a means to an end: an investigation into the phenomena of movement itself. As he once noted, "Man loves what lives and moves and renews its being and loves to makes such things if he can—whether with a green thumb or a pair of pliers. If one makes a moving thing, one is always surprised, no matter how preconceived the design, at the movement itself. It seems to have come from elsewhere—the planting or the pliers have only made the arrival possible."[1]

Rickey begins his book on Constructivism with a quotation from August Endell, the Jugendstil sculptor and architect, on his vision of "new art." Though uttered more than a century ago, it could easily describe Rickey's work today: "An art which stirs the human soul through forms which resemble nothing known, which represent nothing, and which symbolize nothing; an art which works solely through freely invented forms, like music through freely invented notes."[2]

SS

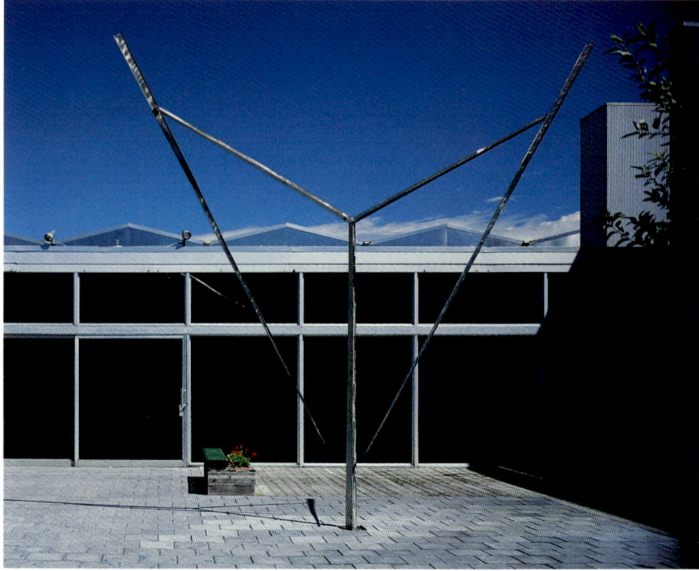

1. Quoted in Peter Selz, *George Rickey: Sixteen Years of Kinetic Sculpture,* exh. cat. (Washington, D.C.: Corcoran Gallery of Art, 1966), unpaginated.

2. Quoted in George Rickey, *Constructivism Origins and Evolution* (1967; reprint, New York: George Braziller, 1995), p. 9.

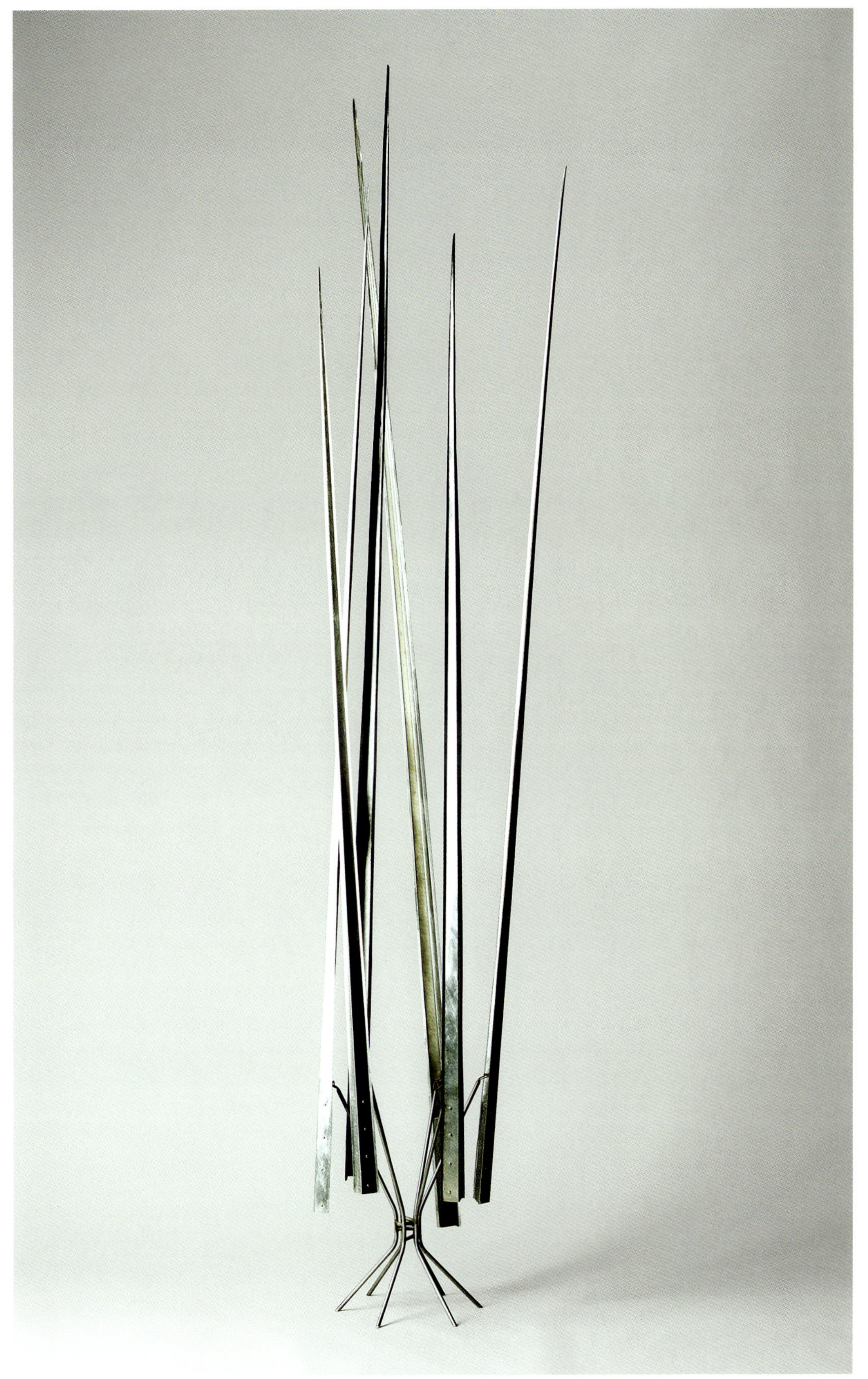

Ernest Tino Trova AMERICAN BORN 1927

102 | *Study Falling Man/Intaglio,* 1966

Bronze, 78¼ × 29½ × 29½ in.

Unsigned

Gift of Hudson's (1986.13)

Ernst Trova, a versatile artist with no formal education in the fine arts, was born in St. Louis, Missouri. He began to draw and paint in 1944 and soon expanded his repertoire to include collage, assemblage, and sculpture. In 1953 Trova traveled to New York City to see an exhibition of paintings by Willem de Kooning, whose Abstract Expressionist style exerted a strong influence on his early career. Although Trova's work from the first part of the 1960s is generally classified as Pop Art—and was included in numerous exhibitions of that movement throughout the decade—the artist prefers to describe himself as a Neo-Surrealist.[1]

In 1961 Trova introduced a new motif into his work: the Falling Man. It would not only preoccupy him for the next several years, but it would come to define his career as well. The Falling Man is not a portrait of a particular man but is instead a symbol for mankind in general. Although rendered in almost every conceivable medium, it is realized most successfully in a series of highly polished bronze (frequently chrome-plated) or stainless steel sculptures, a group that includes *Study Falling Man/Intaglio*.

The Falling Man is an altogether enigmatic figure. He has no distinguishing facial features and consequently lacks any kind of emotional expression, a state that consigns him to both the anonymous and the universal. Despite Trova's assertions to the contrary,[2] moreover, the Falling Man cannot be securely classified as adult or child, male or female, although the title implies an adult male. Age and gender are ambiguously depicted, owing largely to the absence of genitalia. While its legs are relatively strong and muscular, like those of a mature man, its small, oval head is youthful in appearance, as are its slim, graceful shoulders. Conversely, its soft contours, smooth skin, and rounded belly—with its suggestion of fertility and fecundity—are undeniably feminine, although no developed breasts are visible.

In shape and form, the Falling Man makes reference to classical sculpture as well as modern artistic forms. David Bourdon has noted a similarity between the Falling Man and statues of Egyptian pharaohs, particularly the New Kingdom Amarna rulers Akhenaton and Tutankhamun.[3] Yet its streamlined, aerodynamic contours clearly partake of the machine aesthetic that was very much in vogue in the 1960s. Given that each rendition is an almost perfect copy of the others, the Falling Man also raises the specter of the clone, the robot, the mechanomorph, and the automaton, which are associated with industrialization. As a result, it is tempting to interpret the Falling Man, as many critics have done, in a negative rather than positive light. While some have described it as a "victim of an almost uncontrollable technological apparatus,"[4] others have suggested that it represents the descent of man into barbarism and violence. Indeed, the very word "falling" has a variety of connotations and refers to many different aspects of the human condition, most of them suggestive of failure.[5] When combined with "man," moreover, "falling" also conjures numerous stories, myths, and fables about the "fall of man," both physical and moral.[6] Yet Trova insists that the Falling Man should instead be understood as a paragon of dignity and stoicism. It is "my symbol for our time," he writes. "It is the image of . . . an individual who is put into a number of predicaments," many of them perilous, but who remains nonetheless "neutral, cool and rational."[7] KB

1. Martin H. Bush, *Ernest Trova,* exh. cat. (Wichita, Kans.: Edwin A. Ulrich Museum of Art, Wichita State University, 1977), p. 23.

2. Ibid., p. 19.

3. David Bourdon, "Trova's Anatomical Provocations," in *Trova: The Seated Figure Series,* exh. cat. (New York: ACA Galleries, 1990), unpaginated. Bourdon also notes that the Falling Man, with its truncated body and missing arms, calls to mind the sculpture of Auguste Rodin.

4. These are the words Trova uses to describe the way his works are typically, and erroneously, understood. See Riva Yares, *Ernest Trova: Falling Man, Poets, Pyramids, God,* exh. cat. (Scottsdale, Ariz.: Yares Gallery, 1986), p. 6.

5. As in "to fall from grace," "to fall down," "to fall back," "to fall short of," and "to fall flat," among others. See James R. Mellow, "Trova (Notes Toward an Understanding of the Falling Man)," in *Ernest Trova: Recent Work,* exh. cat. (New York: Philip Samuels Fine Art, 1989), p. 5.

6. These include, among others, the stories of Icarus, Phaeton, and Adam and Eve. See Mellow, "Trova," p. 4.

7. Quoted in Yares, *Trova: Falling Man,* p. 5.

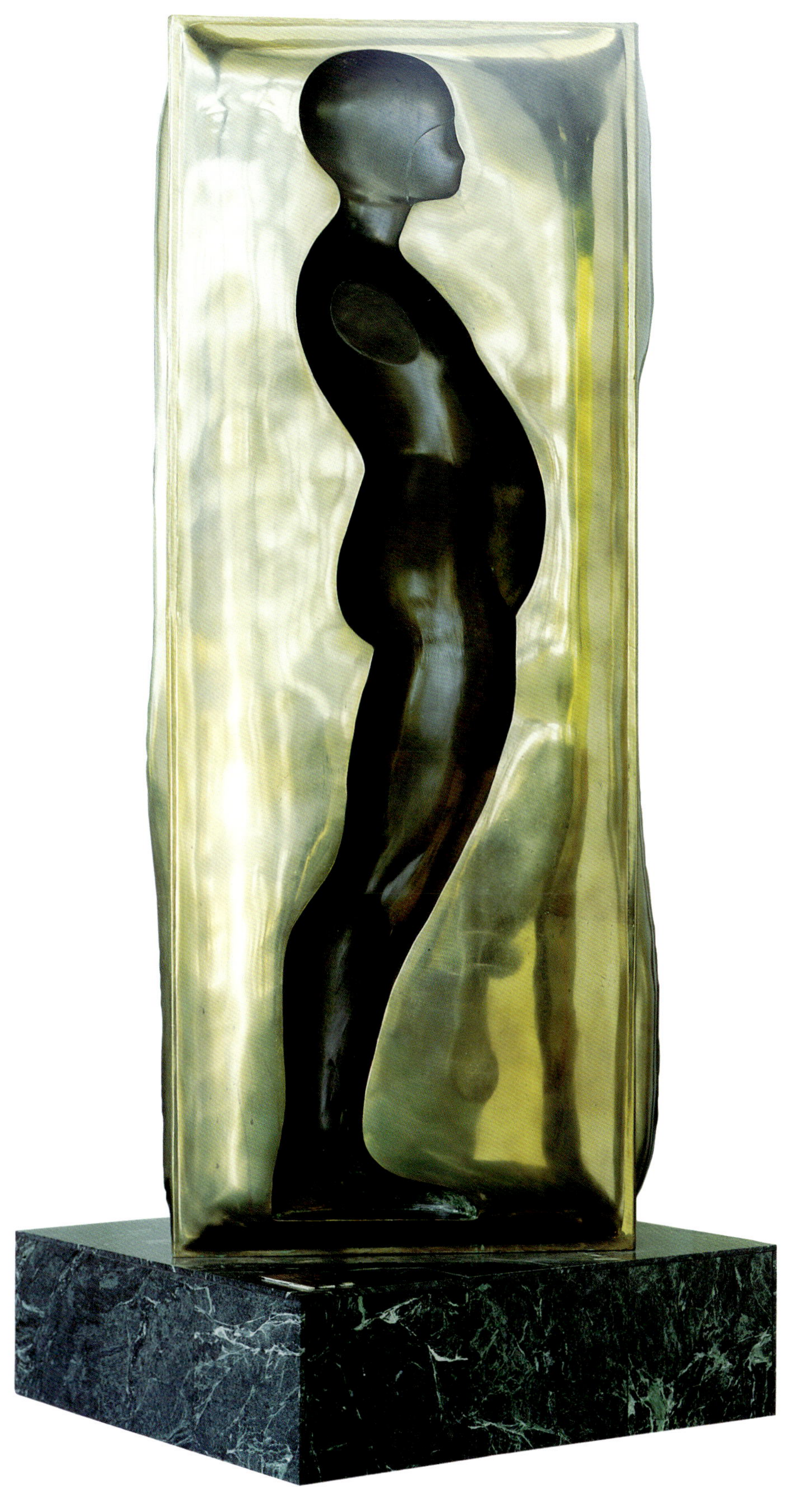

Charles White AMERICAN 1918–1979

103 | *Wanted Poster Series #17*, 1971

Oil and pencil on poster board, 60 x 30 in.
Signed and dated lower right: *Charles White '71*
Gift of Mr. and Mrs. B. Morris Pelavin (1971.43)

In the 1960s Charles White discovered a series of pre–Civil War slave-auction posters that advertised rewards for the capture of runaway slaves. They proved to be a great inspiration, and in 1969 he created his original *Wanted Poster* series, a group of paintings in oil on board that combined elements from slave-auction advertisements with portraits of contemporary African Americans. A year later, the works were issued as a series of lithographs.

Born in Chicago, White was introduced to art by his mother, who gave him his first paint set when he was seven. He was an avid reader and found Alain Locke's *The New Negro* an inspiration. He was also influenced by W. E. B. Du Bois's idea, outlined in *Criteria of Negro Art* (1926), that a black identity was dependent on a black art and literature that fostered self-respect and self-esteem, even if recognition from the majority of Americans was lacking. White's art follows Du Bois's ideas and celebrates them in his depictions of African Americans with strength and dignity. Yet it also has a broader appeal, enabling people of all races to see the American ideal of freedom realized with hope and respect despite oppression and the severest treatment.

In 1934, at sixteen, White received scholarships to two art schools, both later revoked when the schools discovered his race. In 1937 he received a third scholarship, to the Art Institute of Chicago, where he completed the two-year program in only one year. He was employed by the Works Progress Administration in the 1930s and moved in the following decade to New York City, where he studied printmaking at the Art Students League and further developed his realistic style.

In *Wanted Poster Series #17* the central figures, a woman and a child, are visually anchored to the picture surface by a rectilinear grid, the Stars and Stripes of the American flag, and stenciled letters advertising slaves for sale. The figures' downcast glances, sad expressions, and oppressed demeanor evoke feelings of pity, shame, and indignation in the viewer. They are placed beneath a dove, a symbol of peace, and stenciled letters spelling the word "sold." The sharp contrast of dark and light used to model the figures increases the dramatic impact as well as the sense of isolation.

White's interest in the subject of runaway slaves was also strongly influenced by the lynching of three of his uncles and two of his cousins in the South over a fifteen-year period. As he explained, "Paint is the only weapon [that] I have with which to fight what I resent. If I could write I would write about it. If I could talk I would talk about it. Since I paint, I must paint about it."[1]

White was given a retrospective at the Whitney Museum of American Art in 1951 and, after a lifetime of exhibitions and honors, was elected to the National Academy of Design in 1971, the same year this painting was completed. MMD

1. Quoted in Sharon F. Patton, *African-American Art* (New York: Oxford University Press, 1998), pp. 148–49.

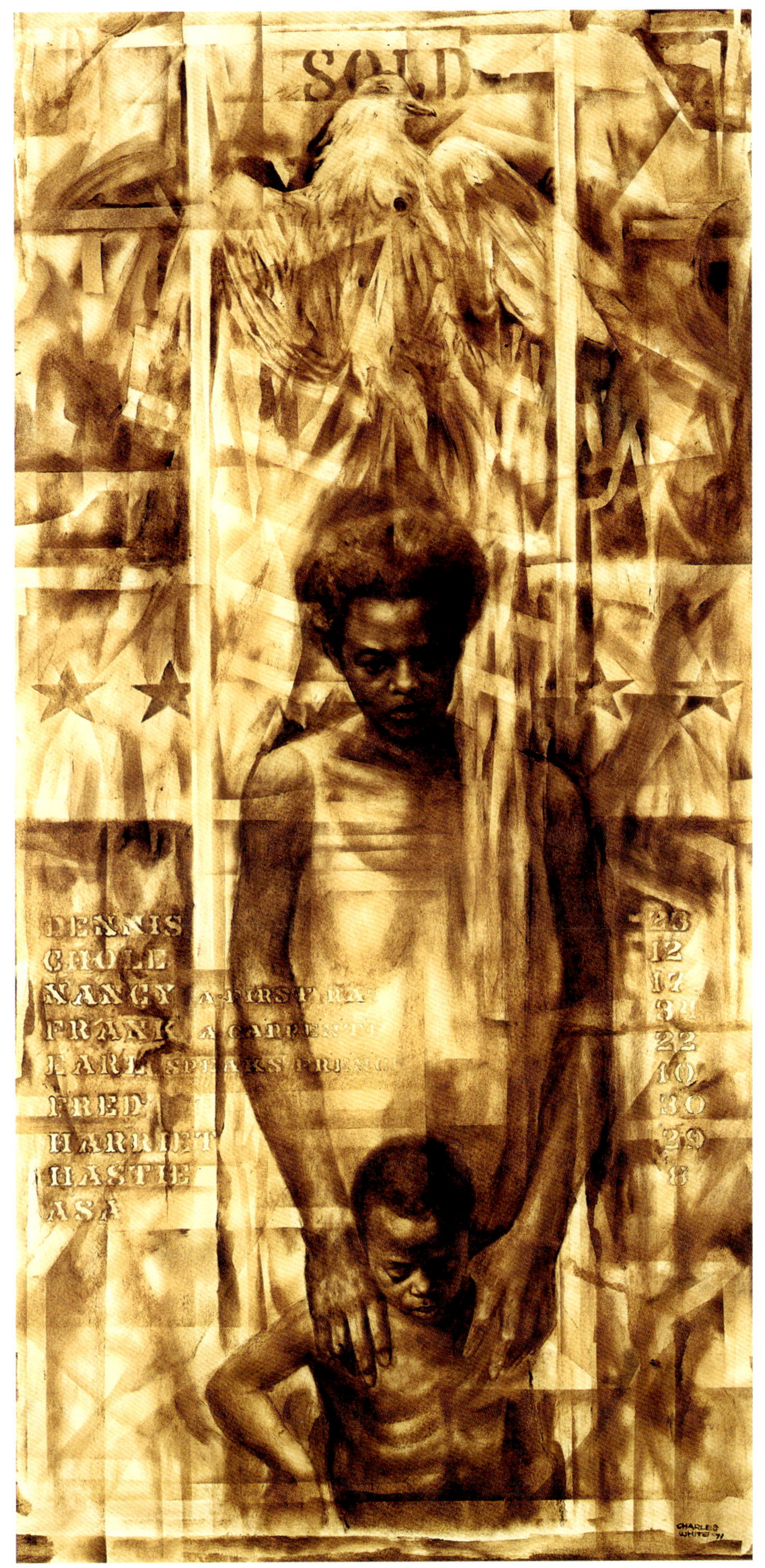
SOLD
DENNIS 23
CHOLE 12
NANCY 17
FRANK 34
EARL SPEAKS 22
FRED 10
HARRIET 30
HASTIE 29
ASA 8
CHARLES WHITE

Frank Owen AMERICAN BORN 1939

104 | *Untitled,* 1971

Acrylic on canvas, 58⅛ × 68⅛ in.

Signed and inscribed on verso: *Franklin Owen 450 Broadway, New York, NY*

Anonymous gift (2000.35)

Frank Owen, born in Kalispell, Montana, studied art at the California State University at Sacramento and then at the University of California at Davis, from which he received his bachelor's and master's degrees, in 1966 and 1968 respectively. He has received two grants from the National Endowment for the Arts and has been featured in numerous exhibitions across the United States. A dedicated educator, he has been teaching steadily since the late 1960s and in 1992 was appointed assistant professor of art at the University of Vermont, Burlington, a position he still holds today.

Owen came to artistic maturity in the 1970s and 1980s while living in New York City, where he showed at such galleries as Leo Castelli and Nancy Hoffman. In the early 1970s Owen devised a unique method of transferring pigment to canvas, inspired in part by Jackson Pollock and Helen Frankenthaler. Rather than applying paint with a brush, Owen pours it with great care and precision directly onto the canvas. He then pushes and pulls the paint across the surface until he achieves the desired effect, variegated strata of color resembling an aerial photograph or topographical map. Indeed, *Untitled* calls to mind craggy mountain peaks and serpentine rivers glimpsed out of an airplane window. This method of painting, however, requires a nearly Herculean effort. Owen typically plans up to a month in advance before beginning a new work. Because the picture has to be completed all at one time, mainly to control the drying time of the various pigments, his painting sessions often last thirty-six continuous hours.

Although not formally associated with the movement, Owen was influenced to a great extent by Abstract Expressionism.[1] Indeed, his paintings share something of Pollock's "terribilita"[2] in their large format and heroic scale. They are, as one critic aptly put it, "tumultuous, electrifying" and filled with "explosive patterns."[3] The latter is very much a function of the decentered, nonhierarchical compositions that both Owen and Pollock employed. In works such as *Untitled,* the composition is spread from edge to edge, animating the entire surface of the canvas.

What distinguishes Owen's work from that of such artists as Pollock and Frankenthaler is his penchant for bright, intense, even psychedelic, colors. Streams of almost every imaginable hue—from lavender and tangerine to mustard yellow and pink—meander across the surface of *Untitled,* not unlike veins in the human body. From a distance, they appear to fuse and mix, creating the illusion of a shimmering mirage. On closer viewing, however, they regain their specificity: each remains distinct from the other, its borders crisp and intact, a testament to Owen's adroit handling of paint. The artist himself best described the overall effect that his works, in their color, style, and technique, have on the viewer. "I prefer," he said, "to isolate out sets of rather persistent themes and weave them into fragile nets of sometime [*sic*] puzzling and contradictory meaning. I [wanted to] do this in a way that is beautiful, but a terrifying kind of beauty: sharp, controlled and ultimately, elusive."[4] KB

1. According to Lyle Rexler, critics in the 1970s often described Owen, along with the painters Jeff Way and David Diao, as a "lyrical abstractionist." See Lyle Rexler, "Frank Owen," *Review*, 15 September 1998, pp. 6–7.

2. John Fitz Gibbon, "Frank Owen: The Machine in the Ghost," in *Frank Owen: Selected Paintings from 1970–90*, exh. cat. (Plattsburgh, N.Y.: Plattsburgh State Art Museum, 1991), unpaginated. It should come as no surprise that Owen also admires, according to Fitz Gibbon, the paintings of the French Romantic artist Théodore Gericault.

3. Atirnomis, "French and Co. Gallery," *Arts Magazine* 45 (March 1971), p. 60.

4. Quoted in Fitz Gibbon, "Frank Owen."

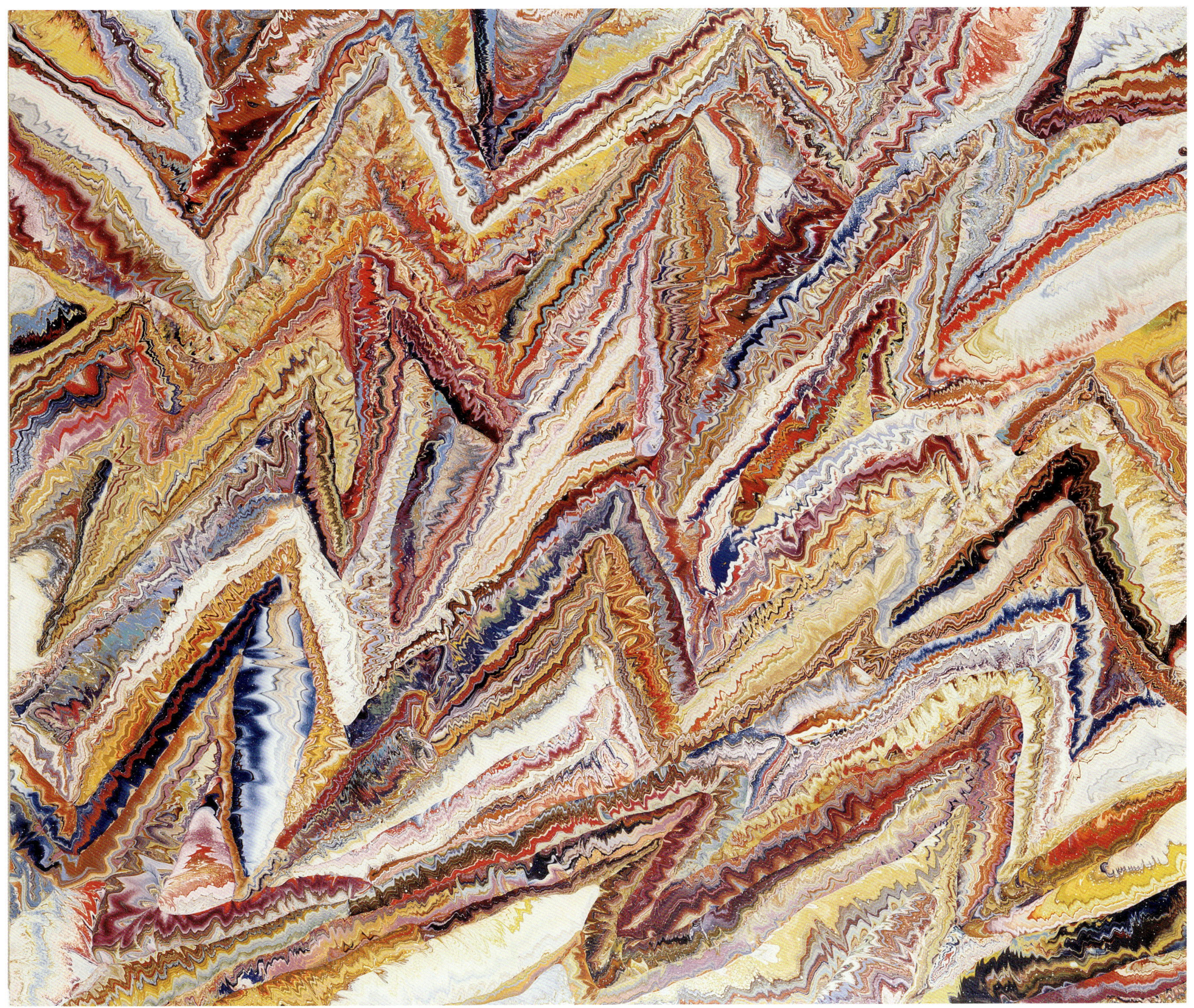

Claes Oldenburg AMERICAN, BORN SWEDEN 1929

105 | *Geometric Mouse, Scale C,* 1971, edition of 120

Anodized aluminum, 19 × 20 × 13 in., dimensions variable

Signed and inscribed on one eye disk: *CO 40/120*

Gift of Dr. Bernard J. and Arlene D. Harris (1991.30)

Everyday objects undergo a surprising metamorphosis in the work of the immensely talented and internationally renowned artist Claes Oldenburg. An apple core, a pair of scissors, and a constellation of numbers become, respectively, a torso, the Washington Monument, and a map of Chicago. Oldenburg's undeniable cleverness and relentless humor clearly inform how he handles the mundane in his work. Presenting one object while suggesting another, he challenges one's perception while engaging the notion of visual play. This perceptual game is conveyed most deliberately in Oldenburg's soft sculptures, the works for which he is best known. A drum set, a saxophone, and a teapot are reconstituted in soft material, often presented in a supine position, as if hinting at entirely different objects. "It's not about anthropomorphizing," Oldenburg has said, "it's about releasing the many identities of forms. In animated film that happens in real time. In a sculpture, the fluctuations have to be superimposed. The sculpture should look different each time you see it, and that should keep it alive."[1] This process is evident in Oldenburg's *Geometric Mouse, Scale C,* in which two circles and a square are transformed into the head of a mouse.

Born in Stockholm, Sweden, Oldenburg moved with his family to the United States in 1936. He majored in art and English literature at Yale University, from which he graduated in 1950. He then attended the School of the Art Institute of Chicago for two years, where he studied painting with Paul Weighardt while working as a part-time reporter for the Chicago city news bureau. In 1956 Oldenburg moved to New York City, where he met and befriended fellow artists Jim Dine, Allan Kaprow, and George Segal, all of whom would have a lasting effect on his work. Together, the artists staged what has become known as Happenings, which combined drama, events, and various visual media to make a new form of art. Opening his studio in 1961 as The Store, Oldenburg "sold" painted plaster replicas of fruit, vegetables, canned foods, and other goods. These everyday objects, copied from advertisements, were a clever twist on the idea of art and commodity.

In 1977 Oldenburg began to collaborate with his second wife, Coosje van Bruggen. Their work focused on the making of large-scale public works, many of which had originated as small, whimsical drawings. The titles of these sculptures, like the items in The Store, directly suggest their source in popular culture—*Pool Ball, Giant Switches, Flashlight,* and *Fishing Pole*, among others.

By the early 1980s Oldenburg and van Bruggen's combined artistic efforts took their work in two directions, one toward outdoor public commissions and the other toward more intimate, indoor sculpture. *Geometric Mouse, Scale C* is a study for an outdoor sculpture subsequently realized in multiple variations of size, scale, and color. Examples can be found at the Walker Art Center in Minneapolis and the Hirshhorn Museum and Sculpture Garden in Washington, D.C. The largest, *Geometric Mouse, Scale X, Red* (1971; Public Library, Houston, Texas), measures eighteen feet high.

Oldenburg was a leading figure in the Pop Art movement in the late 1950s and early 1960s and his unique perception of objects has sustained his art in the subsequent decades. His quirky yet magical way of viewing the world has remained his inspiration. An artist's statement issued at the beginning of his career conveys Oldenburg's devotion to experiencing the fantastic in the everyday: "I am for the art of things lost or thrown away, coming home from school," he commented, "I am for the art of the cock-and-ball trees and flying cows and the noise of rectangles and squares."[2]
SS

1. Quoted in Arne Glimcher, *Claus Oldenburg,* exh. cat. (New York: The Pace Gallery, 1992), p. 12.

2. Claes Oldenburg, "I Am for an Art," in *Theories and Documents of Contemporary Art: A Sourcebook of Artists' Writings,* ed. Kristine Stiles and Peter Selz (Berkeley: University of California Press, 1996), p. 337; originally published in a briefer version in *Environment, Situations, Spaces,* exh. cat. (New York: Martha Jackson Gallery, 1961); reprinted in an expanded version in Claes Oldenburg and Emmett Williams, eds., *Store Days: Documents from The Store (1960) and Ray Gun Theater (1962)* (New York: Something Else Press, 1967), pp. 39–42.

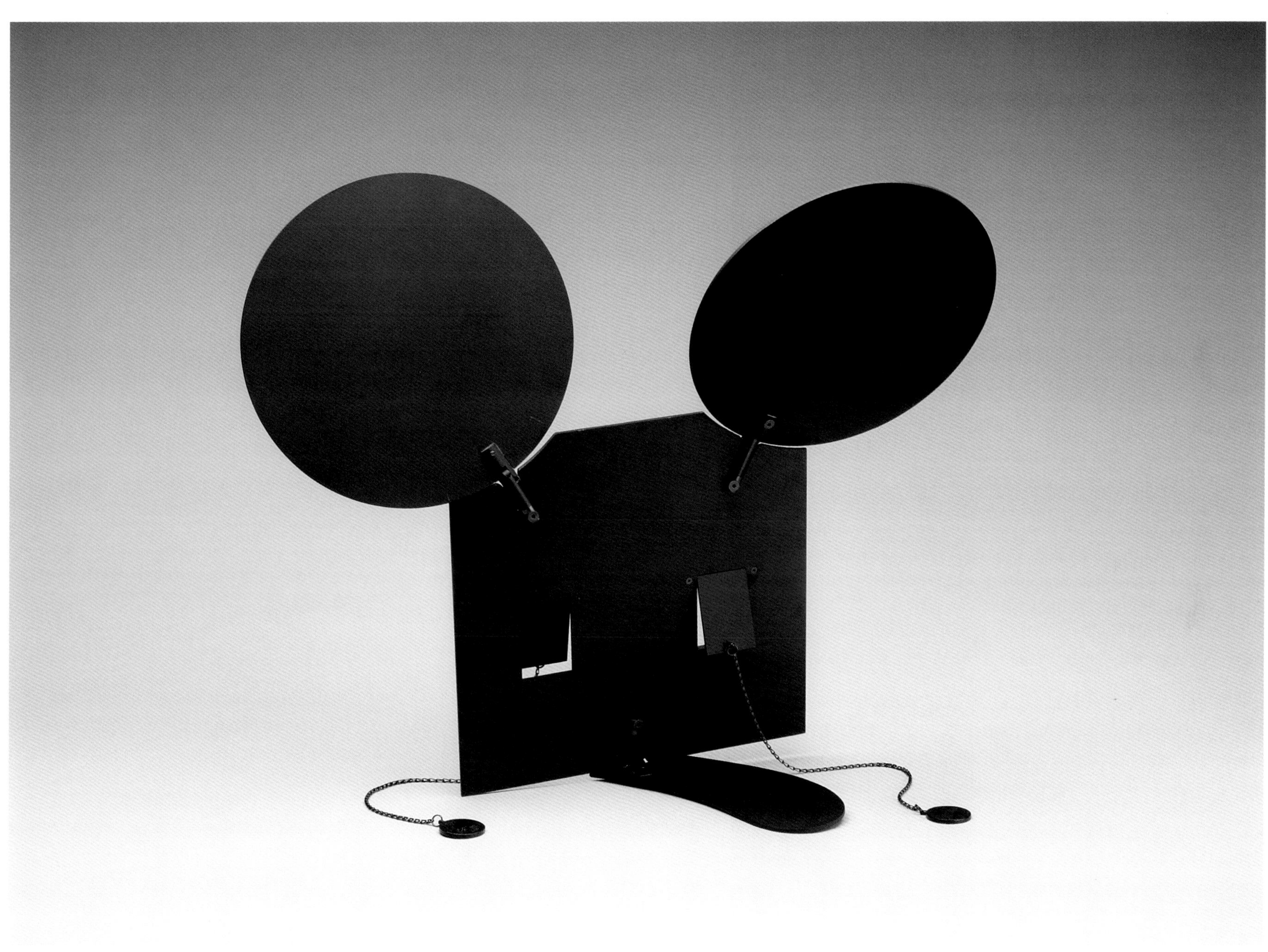

Romare Bearden AMERICAN 1914–1988

106 | *Prevalence of Ritual: Reverend John's Sermon No. 1,* 1973

Collage and acrylic on board, 56 × 46 in.

Signed lower right: *Ro / mare / Bear / den*

Flint Institute of Arts purchase (1973.69)

Reverend John's Sermon No. 1 is one of a series of collages by Romare Bearden called the *Prevalence of Ritual.* The title of the group is the result of a collaboration between Bearden and his friend Albert Murray, who used the phrase to suggest the universal dimension of Bearden's work. The works explore situations and emotions common to all people by combining images from Bearden's African American heritage with those from his traditional art training. As the artist explained, "In my work, if anything, I seek connections so that my paintings can't be only what they appear to represent. People in a baptism in a Virginia stream are linked to John the Baptist, to ancient purification, and to their African heritage. I feel this continuation of ritual gives a dimension to the works so that the works are something other than mere designs."[1]

Bearden was born in Charlotte, North Carolina, and raised in New York City's Harlem. He attended high school in Pittsburgh, where he became interested in drawing and cartooning. In 1935 he received a bachelor's degree in mathematics from New York University but decided to train to be a professional artist. The following year, he enrolled at the Art Students League, where he studied under the German Expressionist George Grosz. During this time, he supported himself as a caseworker for the New York City Department of Social Services. It was not until 1966, at the age of fifty-two, that he was able to leave his job as a social worker to concentrate on art.

Throughout the 1940s Bearden was more interested in using his work as an instrument of social change than with questions of style. As he explained, "As far as I was concerned at the time . . . aesthetic technique was simply the means that enabled the artist to communicate his message—which as I saw it then was always essentially social if not political."[2] He turned to Abstract Expressionism in the late 1940s and continued to work in that style through the 1950s, but abandoned it because he felt it lacked a meaningful philosophy. In the 1960s he synthesized all that he had learned and created the photomontage style for which he is best known. The shallow space, flat areas of color, art historical references, and African design that characterize his mature work grew out of Bearden's heritage and these earlier artistic influences and were the result of his efforts to find universal symbols common to all cultures.

When Bearden was a child, he was taken to hear a sermon delivered by a follower of the famous Baptist preacher John Jasper (1812–1901). For more than sixty years, Jasper's dramatic orations, focusing on stories from the Old Testament, were heard in Virginia, Maryland, and New Jersey. Thousands flocked to hear the Reverend John, and many ministers imitated his oratory style and adapted the content of his sermons. In *Reverend John's Sermon No. 1,* Bearden recalls his childhood experience. Using a photomontage technique, he combines images from the Middle Ages, including a city and knights in armor, to create the image of a battle scene. Although composed of many fragments, the composition is unified through the use of color and the juxtaposition of detailed and textured images with flat shapes. The resulting collage is a celebration of the victory of the human spirit over oppression. MMD

1. Quoted in Alexandra Anderson-Spivy, *Romare Bearden: The Human Condition,* exh. cat. (New York: ACA Galleries, 1991), unpaginated.

2. Quoted in the Papers of African American Artists, Archives of American Art, Smithsonian Institution website, www.aaa.si.edu/guides/afriamer/bearden.htm, accessed 11 May 2001.

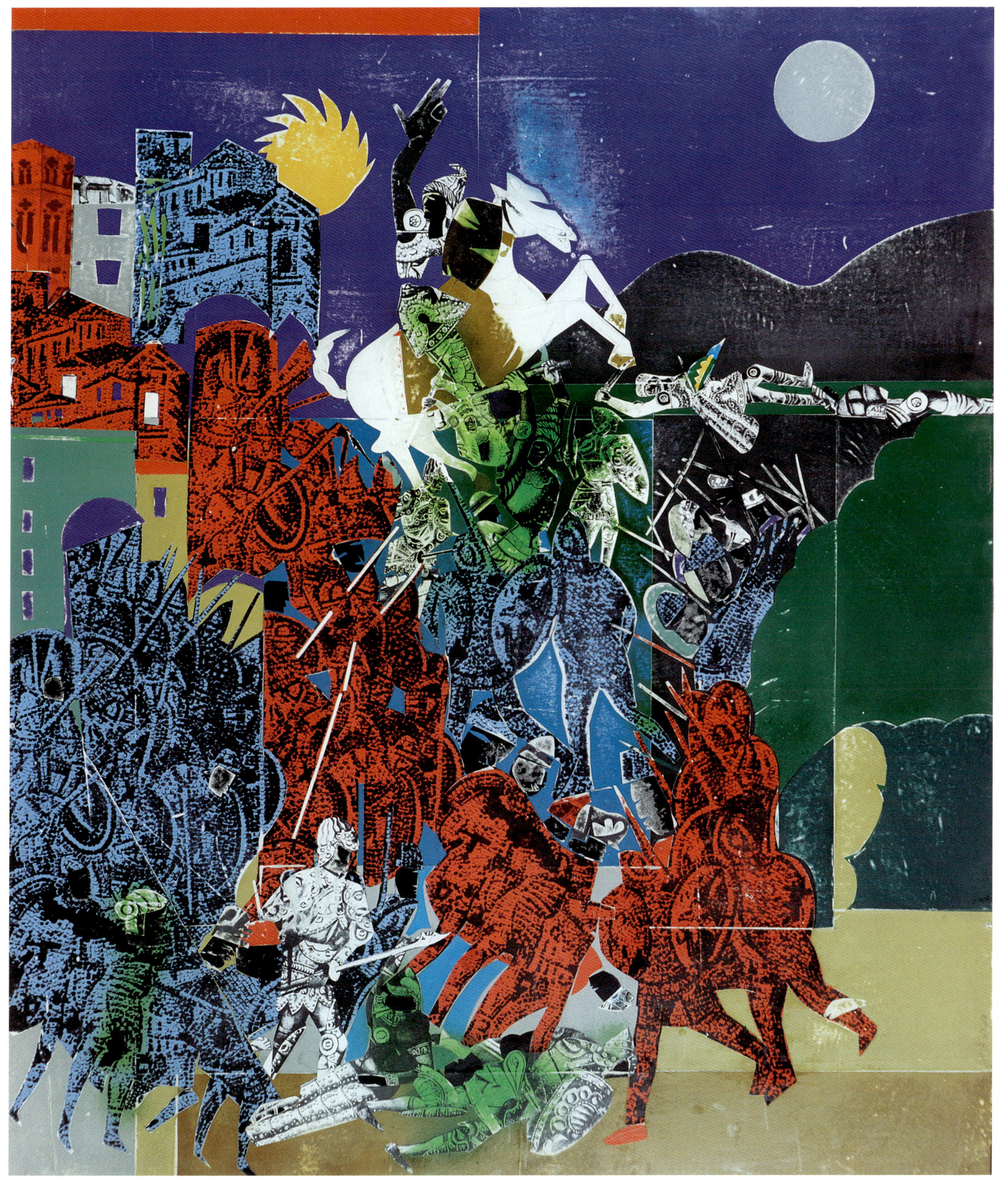

David Buchanan Parrish AMERICAN BORN 1939

107 | *Parkway,* 1979

Oil on canvas, 86⅞ × 71¼ in.

Signed and dated lower right: *David Parrish '79*

Purchased with funds from the National Endowment for the Arts Grant and the Samuel and Alma Catsman Foundation (1978.79)

David Parrish, born in Birmingham, Alabama, attended Washington and Lee University in Lexington, Virginia, from 1957 to 1958. Following a trip to New York City, he returned to his home state, transferring to the University of Alabama, from which he graduated in 1961. Unable to establish a career as a magazine illustrator, his original goal, Parrish found employment making technical drawings for the aerospace industry. In 1964 he executed his first painting based on a photograph, which depicted a group of poor men and women standing in front of a country store. Although he would soon abandon such highly charged subject matter, the work was prophetic, for it made use of a style and technique that would come to define his oeuvre.

Along with such artists as Richard Estes, Chuck Close, Audrey Flack, and Ralph Goings, Parrish is closely associated with the Photorealist movement, which came to prominence in the late 1960s and early 1970s.[1] Photorealism, as its name suggests, aims to reproduce the visible world as accurately as possible, largely by relying on photographs as source material.[2] Characterized by a high degree of verisimilitude, these paintings are typically rendered in a careful, meticulous hand with smooth, even strokes, which imbues them with an air of neutrality, impartiality, and factuality, although they are, in fact, wholly contrived. Like the Pop artists who emerged slightly earlier, the Photorealists were fascinated by commercial culture and the urban environment. For both, the primary subject matter is the everyday contemporary world of automobiles and storefront windows, canned food and skyscrapers, strip malls and neon signs.

Parrish's work after 1970 is dominated by a single motif—the motorcycle. The artist claims that his interest in the motorcycle lies not in its connotations of virility and rebellion, but in its association with consumerism. Indeed, he recognizes in bikes "something akin to commercially manufactured sculpture."[3] Like most Photorealists, Parrish begins a painting, not by making a sketch, but by taking a photograph; at times he uses as many as 150 different exposures before arriving at the desired image. Parrish tends to photograph motorcycles on view in showrooms as well, which suggests that it is indeed the bike as a commodity that appeals to him. The photograph is then printed as a slide, projected onto the canvas, and traced by the artist.[4]

Parrish's paintings of motorcycles make repeated use of the close-up, a photographic technique that tends to decontextualize and thus distort familiar objects, rendering them strange and incongruous. Only a small portion of the motorcycle in *Parkway*—the handlebars, instrument panel, ignition, and gas tank—for instance, is visible. The disorientation produced by the close-up, moreover, is exacerbated by the oblique angle from which the bike is represented. The viewer, standing somewhere near the front tire, seems to peer down at the motorcycle. The bike's vivid colors, shiny surfaces, and, most important, glass windshield—in which a vast cityscape is reflected—also contribute to the almost hallucinogenic effect. As Mitchell Kahan has pointed out, paintings such as *Parkway* seek a "jarring, off-balance effect," creating an "eerie feeling of visual dislocation and lack of control."[5] KB

1. Louis Meisel provides a thorough history of the term "Photorealism" in *Photo-Realism* (New York: Harry N. Abrams, 1980), pp. 12–13. For more information on Photorealism, see John Arthur, *Realism/Photo-Realism* (Tulsa, Okla.: Philbrook Art Center, 1980), and Linda Chase, "Photo Realism: Post-Modernist Illusionism," *Art International* 20 (March–April 1976), pp. 14–29.

2. The making of photographs has always been subject to the same processes of selection and alteration as the making of paintings and sculptures. While the medium has been employed as an aid to the artist since its invention, its use was no longer a hidden part of the process in Photorealism. It was, instead, presented as an integral part of the technique.

3. Mitchell Douglas Kahan offers other reasons for Parrish's attraction to the motorcycle; see Kahan, *David Parrish,* exh. cat. (Montgomery, Ala.: Montgomery Museum of Fine Arts, 1981), p. 7. Parrish was not the only Photorealist to use the motorcycle as a subject. See Edward Lucie-Smith, *Super Realism* (Oxford: Phaidon Press, 1979), p. 46. On the aesthetic merits of the motorcycle itself, see Matthew Drutt, ed., *The Art of the Motorcycle,* exh. cat. (New York: Solomon R. Guggenheim Museum, 1998).

4. For more on Parrish's working method, see Kahan, *Parrish,* pp. 8–10. Parrish discusses his technique in an interview with Nancy Foote (*Art in America* 60 [November–December 1972], pp. 83–84).

5. Kahan, *Parrish,* p. 17.

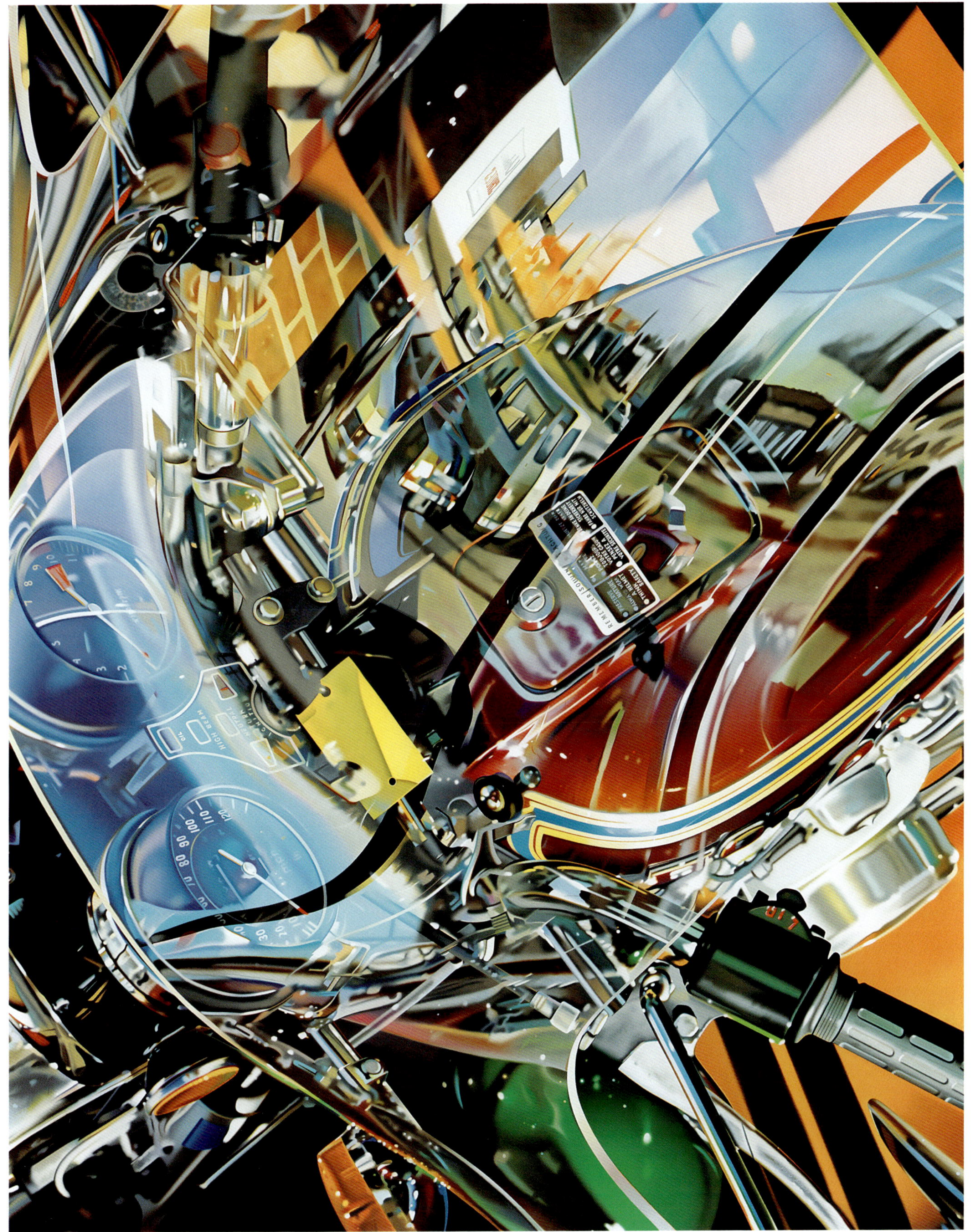

Jim Peters AMERICAN BORN 1945

108 | *The Spiritual and Physical/The Pull (for Joseph Bueys)*, 1986

Oil, wood, sticks, wax, glass, and tin on canvas, 91 × 77¼ in.

Signed and dated on verso: *JS Peters 86*; signed on other parts of panels: *JSP*

Gift of Ellen and Richard U. Levine (1999.23)

Graduation from the United States Naval Academy and a master's degree in nuclear engineering from the Massachusetts Institute of Technology are unusual beginnings for an artist, especially one whose work is as filled with tension and ambiguity as Jim Peters's is. Born in Syracuse, New York, Peters first became interested in painting in high school. He excelled in mathematics and "liked to build things,"[1] and after graduation accepted an appointment to the Naval Academy to study atomic engineering. His talent in science led to a fellowship at MIT in Cambridge, Massachusetts, and a master's degree in nuclear physics. While in Cambridge, he visited the Museum of Fine Arts in Boston often, where he rediscovered his interest in painting. After receiving his degree from MIT, he returned to the Navy to complete his tour of duty. Assigned to the aircraft carrier *John F. Kennedy*, he set up a studio in the mechanical room and began to paint in earnest. His next naval posting was in Connecticut, where he became involved with a group of artists known as the Mystic Art Association.[2] Within a year, he decided painting would be his vocation, and he left the Navy to enroll in the graduate program of the Maryland Institute for the Arts.

Personal and provocative, Peters's paintings are collections of memories—psychological imprints from childhood to the present collaged to form a visual interpretation of the people, places, and events in his life. Autobiographical, the works reveal his passion for academics, architecture, and film. These introspective constructions nevertheless depict moments in the universal human condition and common experiences to which viewers can relate.

The Spiritual and Physical/The Pull (for Joseph Bueys) is typical of Peters's constructed tableaus. The surface combines the traditional painting materials of canvas and paint with such unconventional materials as wood sticks, glass, wax, and tin. A strong sense of architectural space prevails, both through the illusionistic rendering of buildings, fences, and platforms and by the addition of three-dimensional structural elements. Peters likes to compare the process of making his paintings to filmmaking—like a film, they are composed of many different frames, often layered over each other. The placement of the figures frequently changes until the "final frame" freezes them in situ, where they must remain. The process of making these paintings is revealed in the pentimenti and uncorrected surface changes, devices Peters uses to heighten the drama between the artist, the artwork, and the viewer.

Beyond the formal qualities of the painting's surface lie Peters's enigmatic subjects. There one finds a disturbing balance between opposites: familiar and unknown, dreamlike and real, male and female. His women are often portrayed as heroic but seem to exist in a play where the values are uncertain. In *The Spiritual and Physical/The Pull (for Joseph Bueys)*, the protagonist is his wife. A young mother, she rarely has time to herself after dealing with the demands of baby, husband, and home. Standing in a tub, preparing to bathe, she is momentarily alone, facing an open sky beyond the ocean's horizon where her thoughts drift far and free, if only briefly. Still, there is a sense more of tension than of relaxation—the tub is placed in the confines of a fenced-in compound outside the house where her husband and child sit at the window—needing her—and pulling her back with their needs.

At the time this painting was done, Peters, his wife, and child were spending the summer in a twelve-by-sixteen-foot cabin on the coast of Massachusetts. Artistically, Peters likes the tension created by the close proximity of figures situated in small places. Water, an important element in Peters's work, is symbolic of his father's Navy career and, later, his own. Signifying safe harbors, sanctuary, and repose, water and tubs appear in many of his pictures.

The title of this work is enigmatic and ambiguous, offering only veiled clues as to its meaning. *The Pull* alludes both to psychological and emotional ties and to their visual manifestation in the sketched elliptical lasso that binds the woman to her two family members in the house. The dedication to Joseph Bueys, by contrast, is more coincidental—the older artist, whose work influenced Peters, died while the painting was in progress. JBH

1. Jim Peters, telephone conversation with author, April 2002.

2. The Mystic Art Association is a group of amateur painters working in the Mystic Seaport area in Connecticut. They paint landscapes and figural works in a predominantly realistic style.

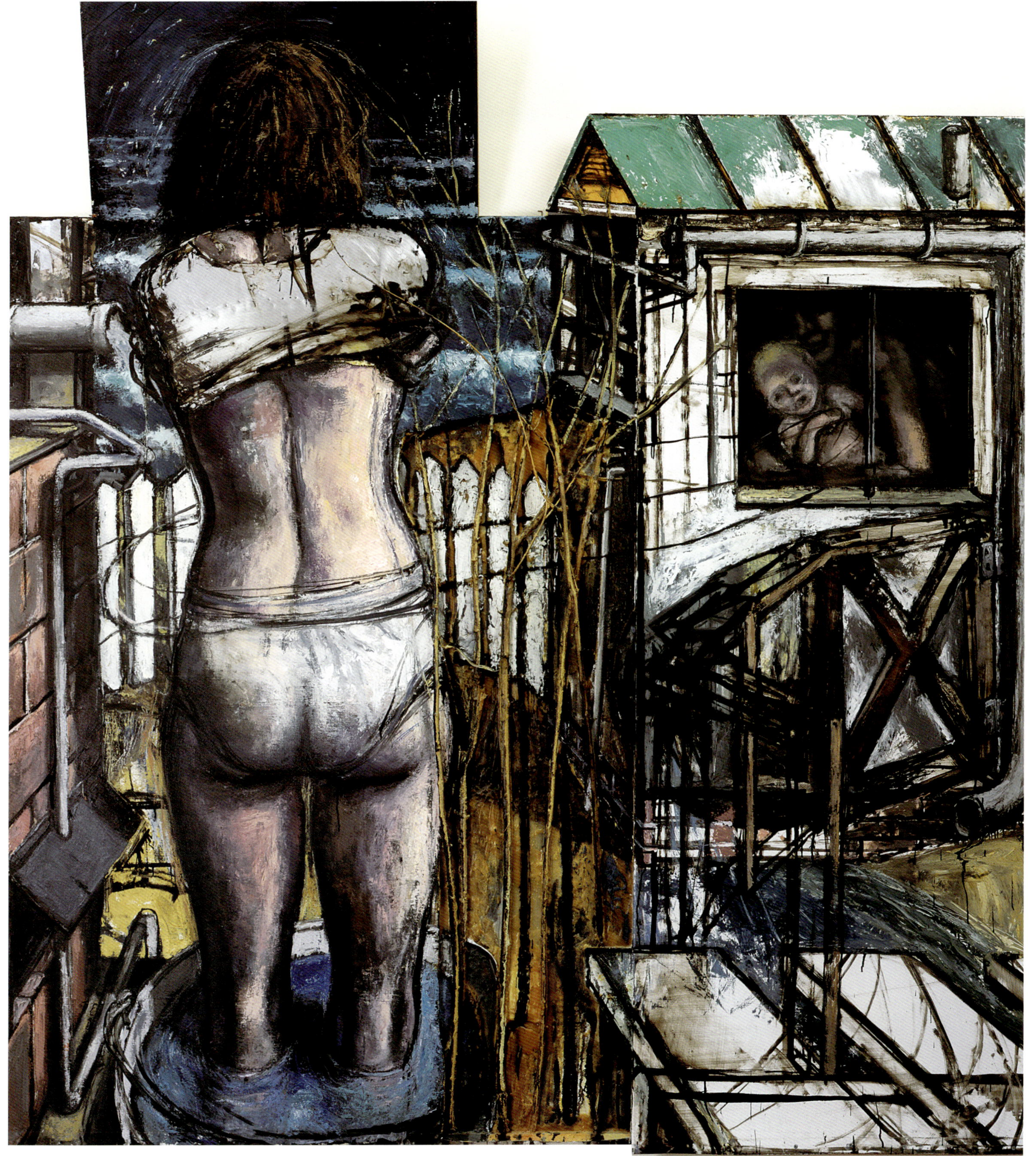

Duane Hanson AMERICAN 1925–1996

109 | *College Student,* 1990

Polychromed bronze, cloth, fiber, leather, paper, and rubber, 70 × 24 × 18 in.

Unsigned

Bequest of Mary Mallery Davis, by exchange (1994.1)

Duane Hanson's place in the history of art is one of contrasts and contradictions. His hyperreal sculptures—cast from life and dressed in actual clothing—not only document a certain stratum of society in the United States in the late twentieth century, but they also connect to a tradition of realist sculpture that can be traced back to ancient Greece. These predecessors have as their contemporary counterparts such Super-realist painters as Richard Estes and Ralph Goings, who, in their quest for verisimilitude, rebelled against abstraction as a style and as a vehicle for the expression of emotion.

From a young age, Hanson knew he wanted to be a sculptor. As an undergraduate, he attended three schools before graduating from Macalester College in St. Paul, Minnesota, in 1946 with a degree in art. In 1951 he earned a master's degree in fine art from the Cranbrook Academy of Art in Bloomfield Hills, Michigan. Although abstraction was in vogue at the time, Hanson always retained a connection to realism, even during his experimental student days. "I would try to do abstract work," he said of this early experience, "but I always put a bit of an arm or nose in it. I never could do just nonfigurative work."[1]

The decade following graduation was challenging for Hanson as he searched for his own style. After a brief stint teaching in Connecticut, he moved to West Germany, where he lived for seven years. The most remarkable aspect of his tenure there, in terms of his artistic development, was making the acquaintance of Georg Grygo, a sculptor who was working at the time with polyester resin and fiberglass. In 1960 Hanson returned to the United States, where he took a position teaching at Oglethorpe College in Atlanta, Georgia, and began his own experimentation with the contemporary materials used by Grygo. If his time in Germany was instrumental in his move toward using new materials, the five years spent in Atlanta, an epicenter for the civil rights movement, awakened in him a desire to make art with a social conscience.

The year 1965 was a critical juncture in Hanson's career. He moved to Miami, Florida, to join the faculty at Miami Dade Community College. It was also the year he made a controversial sculpture that was to take him in a new direction, as well as result in the college administrators banning him from his studio. The sculpture *Abortion* deals with the horrors of illegal, backstreet operations. Made of wood and cloth coated with plaster, the piece brings to mind the sculptures of George Segal. Thematically, this and subsequent works such as *Gangland Victim* (1967) and *Bowery Derelicts* (1969) are reminiscent of works by Edward Kienholz. Both Segal and Kienholz were artists Hanson admired.

As he worked to develop his style, Hanson moved from overt social commentary to documenting and commenting on the everyday world around him, much as Pop Art took its inspiration from the commercial world and the banal. By the early 1970s, Hanson was making the sculptures for which he is best known today—working- and middle-class Americans going about their everyday lives. The technique of casting from life, which he first attempted in 1967, enabled Hanson to achieve a sense of realism that surprises in a different way—not through horrific subject matter, but by creating a moment when the viewer realizes that what he sees is not a live figure but art. Hanson's work is thus most effective when installed in a less traditional venue or in an everyday environment—leaning against the wall in a museum, like *College Student,* "walking" in an airport terminal, or situated in an office building—rather than placed on a pedestal or behind glass. His characters rarely, if ever, engage the viewer through direct eye contact. They have been made to inhabit a private world, their gaze directed down, remaining alone with their thoughts, fatigue, dreams, or disappointments.

For close to three decades, Hanson's work has enjoyed mass appeal, yet it was not until recently that he has received a level of critical attention to match his popularity. Perhaps one of the reasons for the resurgence of interest in Hanson is the current use of mannequins as a metaphor to comment on society by artists such as Kiki Smith, Robert Gober, and Charles Ray. Though perhaps in a less obvious way, Hanson, too, saw his sculptures as surrogates that mirror the world: "They have a life of their own, they had a life when I made them and now they have to go on, to face the world."[2] SS

1. Quoted in Christine Giles, Elizabeth Hayt, and Katherine Plake Hough, *Duane Hanson: Virtual Reality,* exh. cat. (Palm Springs, Calif.: Palm Springs Desert Museum, 2000), p. 45.

2. Quoted in Kirk Varnedoe, *Duane Hanson* (New York: Harry N. Abrams, 1985), p. 32.

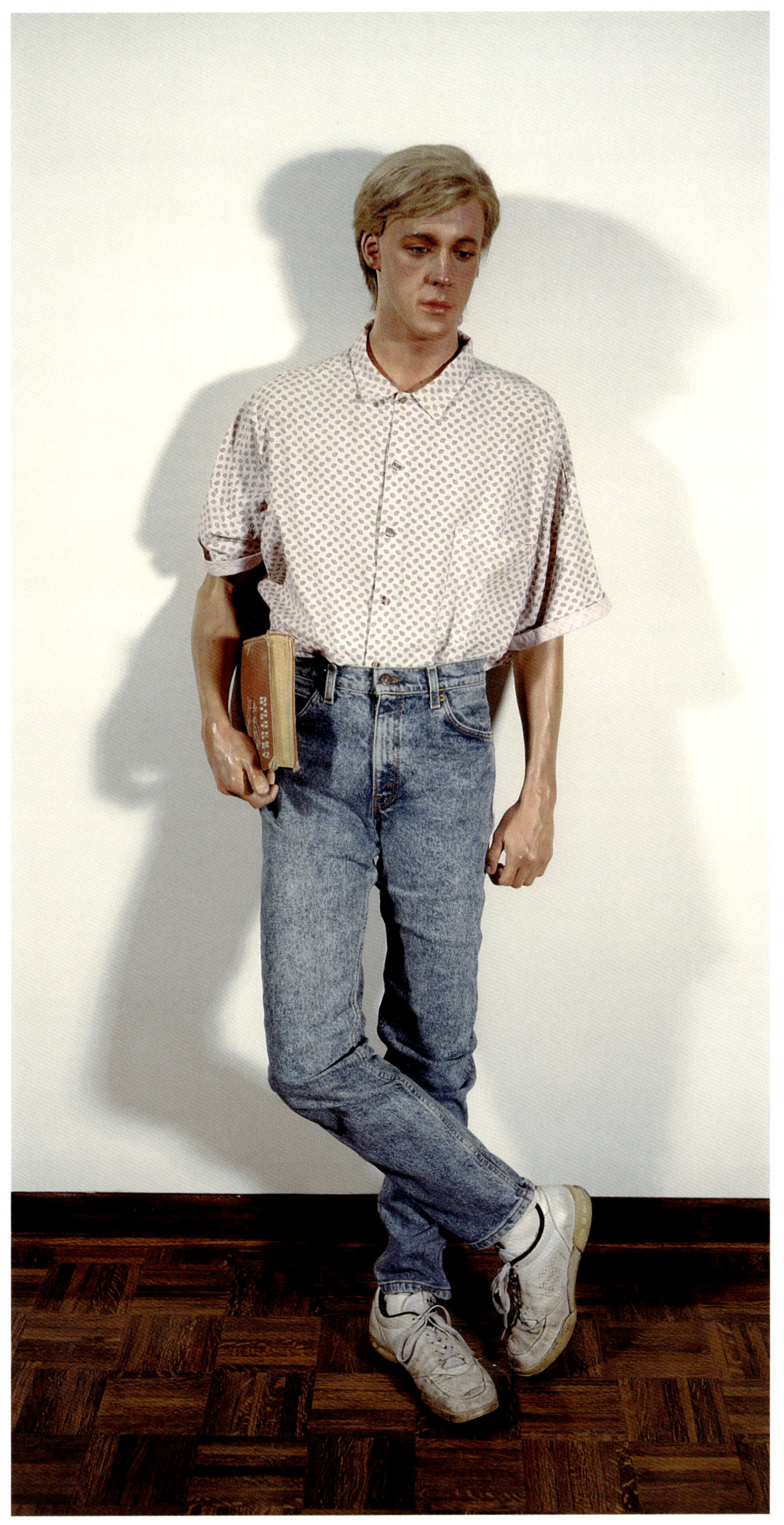

Joseph Raffael AMERICAN BORN 1933

110 | *Le Printemps I,* 1988

Watercolor on paper, 61 × 44¾ in.

Signed lower right: *Raffael*

Flint Institute of Arts purchase (1989.71)

Early in his career, Joseph Raffael made a name for himself with his beautiful, realistic paintings of water, fish, flora, and fauna. As he did then and still does today, Raffael seeks to bring the world of nature alive on the canvas or paper. Nature is his primary source, usually filtered through the lens of the camera that serves as his initial study or sketch. He is known as one of the great watercolorists of our time, not only for his mastery of the medium but also because of his contemporary approach in terms of size, scale, and process. For Raffael, painting is not just about the final result but also about the transformation of the artist and medium that takes place as the painting is completed. "When I begin I don't even know how to paint the image I want. The act of painting coming through pushes me to a creative edge which is unimaginable at the outset. With each painting I grow as a painter and as a person. My paintings teach me."[1]

Raffael attended Cooper Union in New York from 1953 to 1954 and earned his bachelor's degree from Yale University, where he studied with Josef Albers, the abstract painter and renowned color theorist. Although Raffael did not pursue abstraction as a style, the considered use of color nevertheless has remained an essential part of his work. In 1966 Wayne Thiebaud invited the young artist to teach for a semester at the University of California at Davis. Inspired by the landscape, proximity to the outdoors, and the intense, unfiltered light, Raffael relocated to California two years later. "I've always felt most myself and most alive when I've been in nature," observed Raffael. "Moving to California and to the country provided me with a daily immersion in nature. As a result, it empowered my energy and creative impulse."[2] During this time, Raffael became known for his realistic paintings of flowers, water, and carp, beautifully rendered in an allover abstract composition that is as much indebted to his predecessors the Abstract Expressionists as to any type of realistic nature painting.

In 1987 Raffael moved again, this time to the south of France, to fulfill a lifelong dream of living and working in a place that not only boasts a beautiful, sun-drenched landscape but also is equally rich in the history of art. Painted one year after his move, *Le Printemps I* is from a series of watercolors and oils that had as its muse Raffael's new wife, Lannis, pictured with one of their white cats. Moving his attention indoors and focusing on the human figure is, in a sense, a departure for the artist. He might argue, however, that it is simply a continuum. As he once noted, "painting is the subject of my work, and nature the inspiration. . . . The process of painting the work. What happens from moment to moment. What occurs. The events that take place before my eyes."[3] Nevertheless, one can see that the source of his creativity has expanded. "Before," noted Irene McManus, "vast nature was Raffael's acknowledged inspiration. Now he finds his light, color, energy, and emotion in one woman, one mystic source. You might say that for Raffael today, all nature is this one woman, this strange Primavera."[4]
SS

1. Quoted in Henry T. Hopkins, *A Dream Remembered,* exh. cat. (New York: Nancy Hoffman Gallery, 1986), p. 9.

2. Ibid.

3. Quoted in Irene McManus, "Joseph Raffael's 'Lannis Series, Part One,'" *Arts Magazine* 62 (March 1988), p. 28.

4. Ibid.

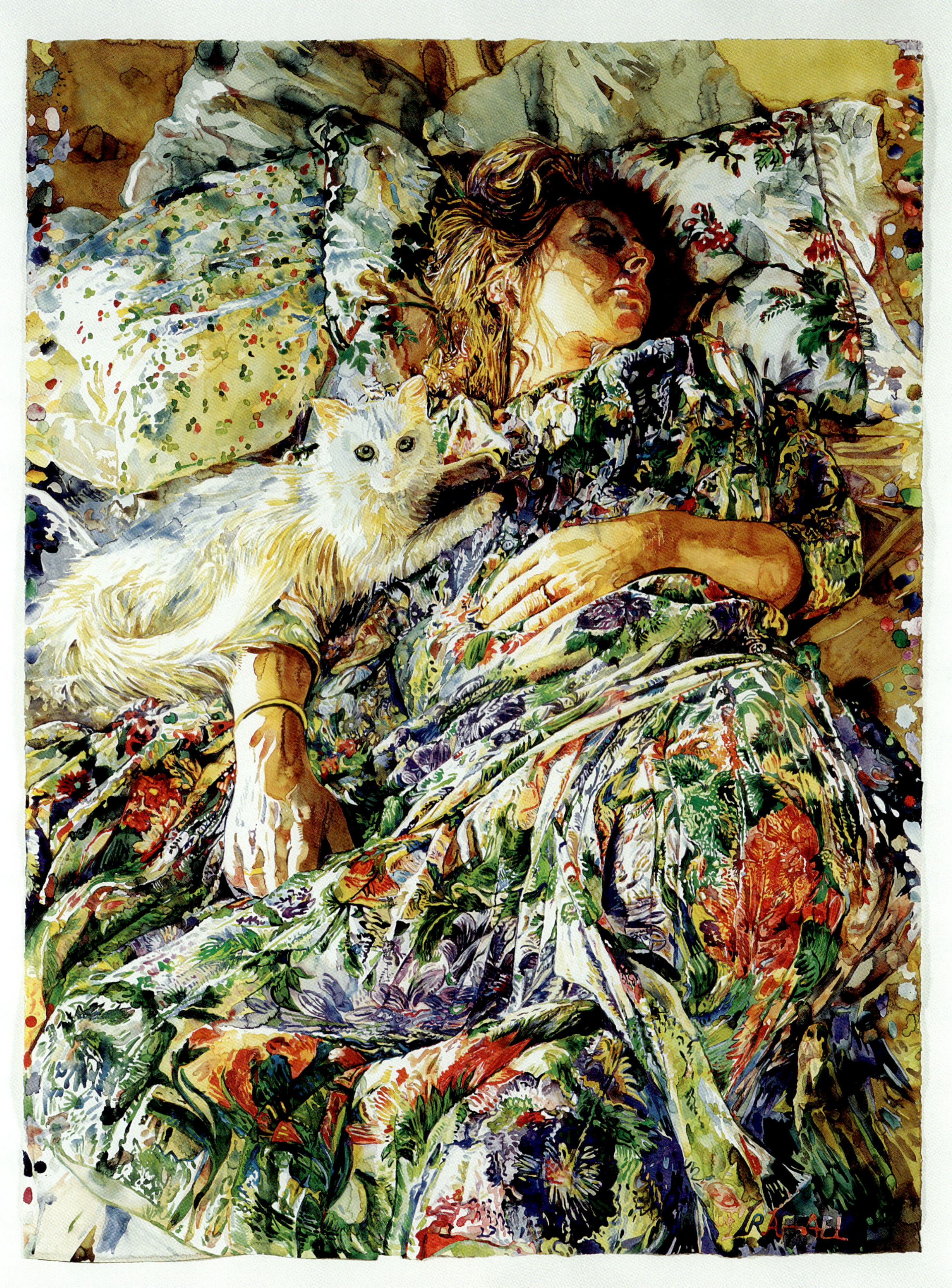
RAFFAEL

Neil Welliver AMERICAN BORN 1929

111 | *Cedar Water Brook,* 1988

Oil on canvas, 72 × 72 in.

Signed lower right: *Welliver*

Flint Institute of Arts purchase in memory of Mr. and Mrs. Donald E. Johnson (1989.72)

Neil Welliver is one of the leading American landscape painters working today. His distinctly contemporary way of rendering these views borrows from a vast array of art historical precedents. Although his imagery brings to mind the landscapes of such early modernists as Marsden Hartley and John Marin, the scale and loose mark-making are indebted to the Abstract Expressionists. His method of painting out-of-doors is aligned with that of the Impressionists, and yet the final product is as studied as any academic painting. Like the Impressionists, Welliver begins each composition as a study, working *en plein air* for many hours to capture the changes in light and temperature. The finished painted sketch is used in the studio to make a charcoal sketch on paper, which is transferred to a large canvas. The sketch is the cartoon, or full-scale guide, for the final painting, which is completed methodically, from the top of the canvas to the bottom. This way of working may in part account for the overall composition of most of his paintings, in which space is compressed and the imagery cropped.

Welliver earned a bachelor's degree in fine art from the Philadelphia Museum of Art's College of Art in 1953, but it was his studies with Josef Albers at Yale University, where he received a master's degree in fine art in 1955, that were to have the strongest influence on his development. From Albers, whose theories on color could be applied to abstraction and realistic imagery alike, Welliver learned about color relationships. He restricts his palette to eight colors—lemon yellow, cadmium yellow, white, ivory black, light green, ultramarine blue, cadmium red scarlet, and manganese blue (although to achieve the full brilliance of a Maine autumn, he adds cadmium red)—and yet achieves a full array of values, shadows, and contrasts through color placement.

Since 1962, when Welliver was invited to Maine by the painter Alex Katz, the unadulterated forests of this Northern state have served as his source of inspiration. That same year, he bought a small cabin in Lincolnville, moving there permanently in 1970. Initially, Welliver peopled his scenes, painting nudes or some animals in the woods, but by the mid-1970s his work had given way to exploring the purity of the landscape alone. *Cedar Water Brook* is a classic example of this investigation, one that speaks of the solitary experience of nature.

Welliver's particular approach to nature is not the grand vistas of such Hudson River School artists as Asher B. Durand and Frederic E. Church but a personal, one-on-one experience of the natural world. He presents this experience, not as a static window on his world, but as a re-creation of the dynamic moment. Scale, immediacy of the mark, and a compressed sense of space create the dynamic of, as Welliver sees it, "the spectator being able to, in fact, not see the picture as an object, but really actively entering into it."[1]
SS

1. Quoted in Laurie S. Hurwitz, "Neil Welliver," *American Artist* 55, no. 586 (May 1991), p. 29.

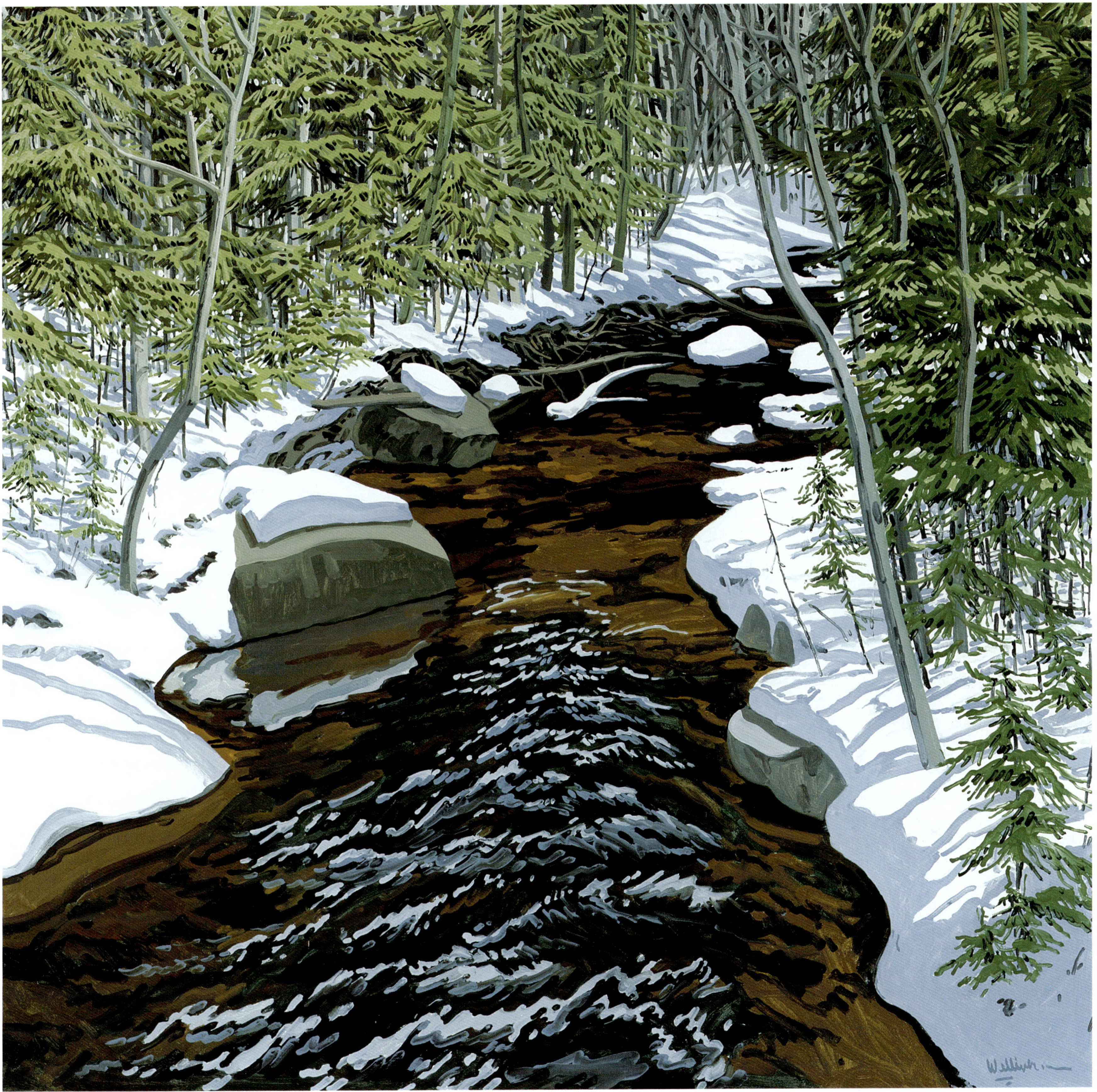

Don Eddy AMERICAN BORN 1944

112 | *Altarboy Day Dreamer II,* 1987

Acrylic on canvas, 56 × 40 in.

Signed, with measurements, on verso: *Don Eddy, 56 x 40*

Flint Institute of Arts purchase in memory of Mary Mallery Davis (1989.70)

In 1968 the New York art dealer Louis Meisel coined the term "Photorealist" to refer to artists who rely on the use of a camera to make highly realistic paintings. Many artists associated with the movement were also interested in removing all evidence of the artist's hand, an aim they often accomplished by using an airbrush, which rendered brushstrokes indiscernible. Don Eddy is considered one of the primary artists in the movement. As with many of the artists identified with Photorealism in its nascent stages—Chuck Close, Malcolm Morley, and Audrey Flack, to name a few—Eddy has pushed beyond an early, surface-oriented style, one that was primarily about technical virtuosity and the beauty of reflections, to making paintings that are equally concerned with subject matter. Though he still uses photography and works with an airbrush, these Photorealist trademarks are now a means to the end of integrating formal concerns with content.

In looking back over the course of Eddy's early life, one can see that his development as an artist was informed as much by life experience as by formal study. Born in Long Beach, California, in 1944, Eddy, like many of his generation in California, developed a passion for surfing. As a teenager, he worked in his father's auto-body and custom shop, where he became proficient in mixing colors and in the use of the airbrush (he still uses the same airbrush he acquired when he was thirteen). He also used his talents customizing surfboards for himself and friends. After high school he attended Fullerton Junior College for one year and the following year went to the University of Hawaii, where he received a bachelor's degree in fine art in 1967 and a master's degree in fine art in 1969. In Hawaii Eddy was able to indulge his zeal for surfing and to pursue intellectual interests that from the beginning were a fusion of psychology and art. He also worked as a photographer for one of the many agencies in Hawaii taking "aloha" pictures of arriving tourists. Thus he has easily and almost naturally incorporated the camera as a tool in his picture making since 1968.

Eddy first made a name for himself by painting highly realistic, often closely cropped cars set in junkyards or behind chain-link fences. He pushed his incredible skill with the airbrush to the next level with subsequent series that involved depicting glassware and silver tableware on reflective surfaces. However, by the early 1980s Eddy was not entirely satisfied with these mainly technical exercises and looked to incorporate history, personal history, memory, and psychology with the formal challenges—space, abstraction, representation, and shifts in perception—that can all be simultaneously present in a painting. Today, Eddy is still interested in technical precision. He begins each work with a meticulous underpainting in three colors—first green, then burnt sienna, and finally purple—applied in tiny circles across the surface. Sometimes as many as thirty additional layers of color are thinly applied to give the final, rich surface in the final work.

Altarboy Day Dreamer II is a perfect example of the formal and conceptual integration Eddy was seeking. It is an extension of an earlier work, *Altarboy Day Dreamer* (1985; private collection), in which objects float against the interior of a Baroque church dome. In *Altarboy Day Dreamer II,* the backdrop is more specific and brought in closer, and similar objects—toys, candy, fruit, and postcards—float against a painting by Nicolas Poussin depicting the Assumption of the Virgin Mary surrounded and supported by putti (c. 1626, National Gallery of Art, Washington, D.C.). In both works, one is bombarded with the collision of the deep space of the historical work and the flatness of the objects floating on the surface. It is as if Eddy has concocted an invisible screen, one side of which is the historical work (a trip back in time) and the other side is the contemporary work (the present). The hovering objects are also a meditation on his earlier work. Many critics have seen *Altarboy Day Dreamer* as a rendition of the daydreams of an altarboy as he sits in church. Certainly, *Altarboy Day Dreamer II* is equally a painting that investigates both literal space and the space of the mind.

Eddy could well have been describing *Altarboy Day Dreamer II* when discussing spatial concerns in art: "In its specific problems, the paintings are about the development and maintenance of spatial tensions: the tension that results from the creation of a space that is both logical and illogical, a space that simultaneously strains toward the illusionary depth and flatness."[1] SS

1. Quoted in Colin Naylor and Genesis P. Orridge, eds., *Contemporary Artists* (New York: St. Martin's Press, 1977), p. 274.

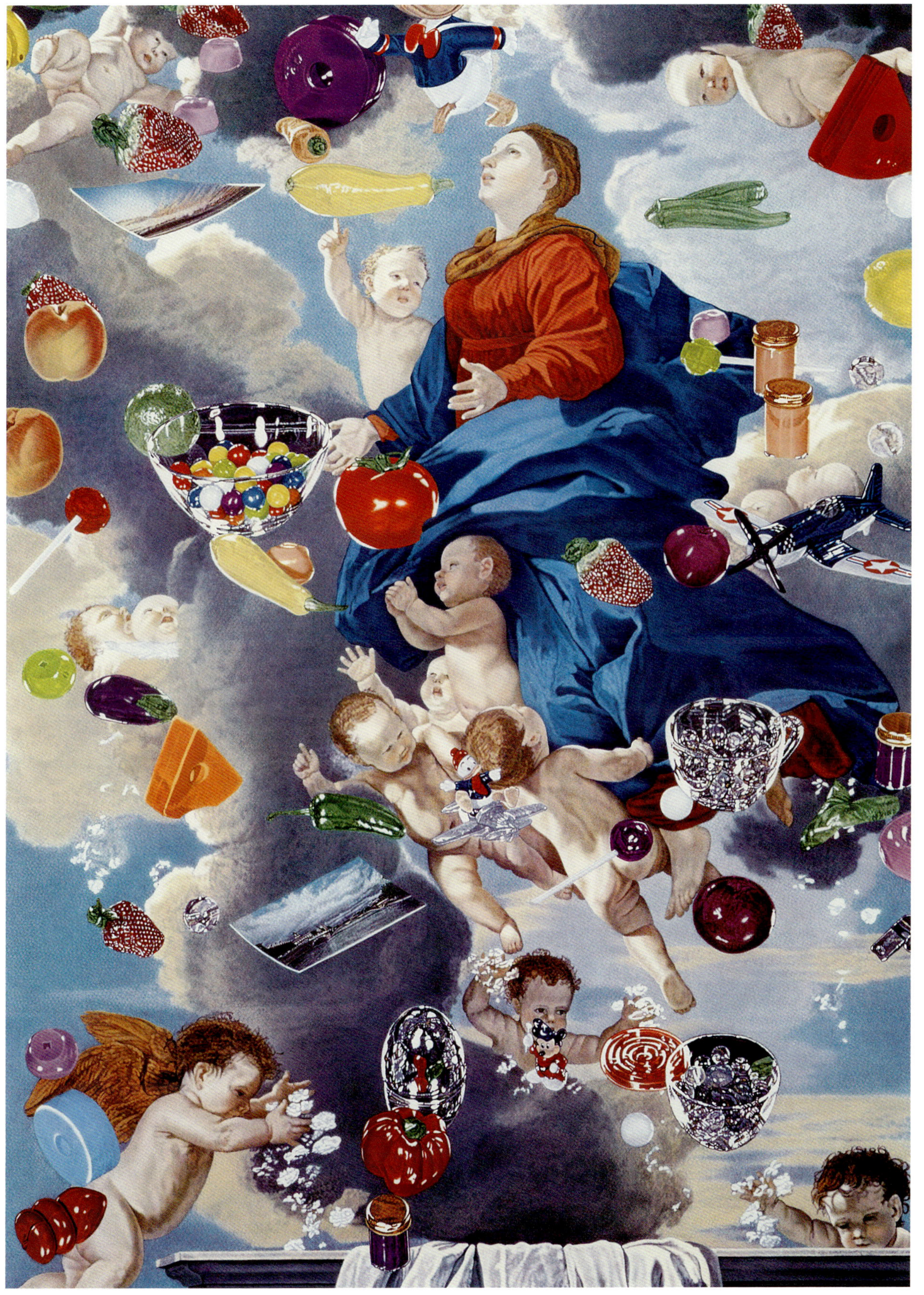

Philip Pearlstein AMERICAN BORN 1924

113 | *Entrance to Lincoln Tunnel, Daytime,* 1992

Oil on canvas, 72 × 72 in.

Signed and dated lower right: *Pearlstein 92*

Gift of Mrs. Cecil Boksenbom, by exchange (1993.40)

Philip Pearlstein emerged in the 1960s as a leader of the New Realism movement. Developing simultaneously with Pop Art and Hard-Edge Abstraction, New Realism embodied the "cool" aesthetic of the time while tapping into the long history of figure painting. The noted art critic Irving Sandler wrote of this shift in aesthetics, "The appearance of art changed from one decade to the next. Instead of the hot, dirty, direct-from-the-self look of fifties art, sixties art looked cool, clean, distanced-from-the-self."[1]

After graduating from the Carnegie Institute of Technology in 1949, Pearlstein shared an apartment in New York City with fellow Pittsburgh native Andy Warhol. The roommates could not have followed more divergent paths in their work. Their early decisions are significant, however, as their choices encompassed two of the dominant artistic directions of the sixties: Pop Art and Hard-Edge Abstraction. As a young artist in New York, Pearlstein confronted pure abstraction's stronghold over the 1950s art world and sought another avenue for his work. His paintings were loosely brushed abstracted landscapes, hardly a style or subject matter that addressed the current trends. "I use nature in a calculated way as a source of ideas," he said of his choice of subject matter, "they allow me to remain uninvolved. I can look at them abstractly and just concentrate on painting."[2]

Pearlstein's artistic approach wavered between two very different styles of painting. The first was a rigorous allegiance to fluid figure painting from the model; the second was a concerted effort to tighten his canvases or rid them entirely of expressive brushstrokes. Like many of his generation, Pearlstein was stimulated by the intellectual dialogue surrounding modernism, regardless of the stylistic choices he made in his own art. He earned a master's degree in art history at the Institute of Fine Art in New York, where he wrote his thesis on the French artist Francis Picabia. He also contributed occasionally to art magazines, primarily to defend his vision of realism. By the mid-1960s he was producing the work for which he is best known: male or female nudes posed in an artificially lit studio. Pearlstein employed artificial lighting to increase the depth of shadows and render the figures' skin more porcelain-like. In addition, the models were posed with patterned blankets and rugs or set against mirrors and chairs. The total effect enhanced the nonconfrontational, removed, and self-absorbed quality he sought in his paintings. He achieved his uniquely cropped compositions by first painting a specific feature, such as a knee or an elbow, within the picture plane. He followed this choice by working in a circular fashion until the whole canvas was complete, making the space of the painting and the viewer's angle slightly skewed.

Pearlstein was criticized both for his subject matter and his depiction of an uncalculated, illusionistic space. Sanctioned by the writings of Clement Greenberg, space in contemporary painting was organized as abstract and flat. From early in his career, Pearlstein has maintained that his primary interest lay neither in the psychological nor the emotional but was propelled by the formal constraints of space, composition, form, and color. His subject matter, he claims, whether nudes, landscapes, or cityscapes, was merely an unconscious decision that best served his formal concerns. "Since the early 1960s, when I discovered that realistic painting can be aggressive, I have usually dismissed subject matter as such, and have relied on stylistic motivation instead. That is, I have paid little attention to content of the psychological aspects of content, letting the chips of interpretation fall where they will. I have concentrated instead on the formal problems of realist paintings as I became aware of them in succession."[3]

Entrance to Lincoln Tunnel, Daytime beautifully shows the view of New York City from Pearlstein's studio. The windowsill frames the painting's subject, which is reminiscent of the patterned textiles that often occupy part of his interior scenes. The small sculpture of a horse is integral to the work's shallow space. It is juxtaposed with the windowsill, leaving a viewer to see what is inside in contrast to the grid and patterning of the city behind it. Though best known for his interior scenes with figures, the artist has, since the 1970s, represented land- and cityscapes as well, ever experimenting and playing with space, form, and composition. SS

1. Irving Sandler, "Philip Pearlstein and the New Realism," in Russell Bowman, Irving Sandler, and Philip Pearlstein, *Philip Pearlstein: A Retrospective,* exh. cat. (New York: Alpine Fine Arts Collection, 1983), p. 16.

2. Quoted in Irving Sandler, *The New York School: The Painters and Sculptors of the Fifties* (New York: Harper and Row, 1978), p. 132.

3. Quoted in Russell Bowman, "A Realist Artist in an Abstract World," in *Philip Pearlstein: A Retrospective,* p. 13.

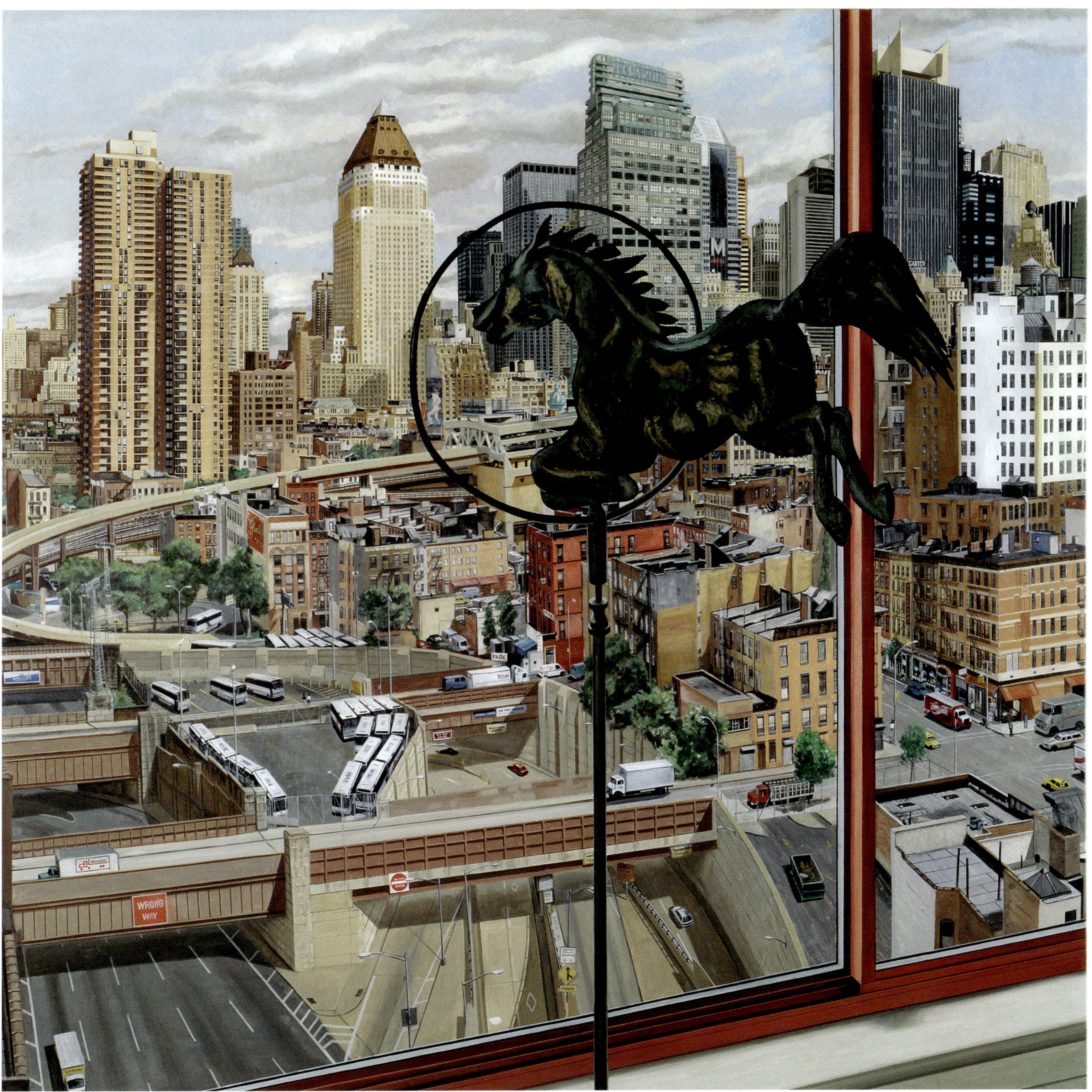
PARK
WRONG WAY

Carolyn Brady AMERICAN BORN 1937

114 | *Tree Roses/Giverny,* 1989

Watercolor on paper, 51¼ × 76½ in.

Signed and dated lower right: *Carolyn Brady 1989*

Flint Institute of Arts purchase in memory of Kathryn Chambers (1989.69)

Carolyn Brady is considered one of the leading watercolorists working today. Like other masters of this lush but unforgiving medium whom she admires, Charles Demuth and Charles Burchfield among them, Brady finds inspiration both in nature and in her immediate surroundings. Brady studied art in the late 1950s, graduating from the University of Oklahoma with a bachelor's degree in 1959 and a master's degree in 1961—both in fine art—and, like most of the artists of her generation, was taught to paint abstractly. Though she developed a distinct representational style, she nevertheless still sees painting through an abstract lens. "I'm always making a synthesis of realism and abstraction," she once noted, "coming to abstraction by illusionistic means."[1]

Early in her career, Brady was identified with the Photorealists because she used photography as part of her process. Today, the association seems too limiting when one views the surface richness of her paintings—for instance, she uses a sable brush to achieve the passages of pure abstraction, rather than the airbrush preferred by many Photorealists. Though essential to her working method, the photograph functions for Brady merely as the drawings for the paintings and not something to be slavishly reproduced. It is one step in a process—first, a slide is projected and the image is "mapped" onto the paper with pencil. When she begins applying the watercolor, Brady may crop the picture, flatten space, heighten color, or alter perspective in creating the final painting.

Perhaps inspired by the domestic material being used by some female counterparts at the time (one thinks of Miriam Shapiro), Brady's works from the early 1970s were appliqués sewn on linen. In search of a more immediate connection to her environment, this process gave way to small watercolors of objects found around the house. It was during this time that she began working in New York as a textile designer, something she did for seven years until she was able to quit and devote herself full-time to painting. As Brady's competence in watercolor increased, so did the intricacy of the work. By the mid-1970s she was painting the large-scale, compositionally complex still lifes of flowers and objects for which she first earned recognition. From the beginning, watercolor was the perfect medium to translate Brady's particular vision of the world. "There is a kind of pulse to the watercolor, a fluttering quality that is not as easy to get with oils," she once noted.[2] Though Brady thinks of her work in abstract terms, noting that "the flowers are really just vehicles for color in my work,"[3] her choice of objects, food, flowers, and gardens are autobiographical, a part of her everyday life.

In the late 1980s Brady turned her attention to the out-of-doors, inspired both by her garden in Maine and a visit to Giverny, France, the site of the extraordinary home and gardens of Claude Monet, another artist Brady clearly admires. She also heightened the spatial play in her paintings, often juxtaposing close-ups of flowers or objects with a background landscape. Certainly, a direct result of her visit to Monet's beautiful gardens was this painting. It is interesting that Brady chose to focus, not on the water lilies for which Monet is best known, but on roses. Yet the formal layout, in which the roses float against the background, is compositionally very much like Monet's lily ponds. Although the viewer may approach Brady's work as a window onto the world, it also has a connection to the various art styles that preceded it, from Impressionism to Abstract Expressionism. As the critic Gerrit Henry observed, this "highly formalist painter is not without a Realist vision of the simple, yet complex glories of this present day and world."[4] SS

1. Quoted in Susan Stiles Dowell, "Art Imitates Life," *Baltimore Magazine* 88 (March 1995), p. 86.

2. Quoted in Nancy G. Heller, "The Southern Artist," *Southern Accents* 12 (September–October 1989), p. 178.

3. Quoted in Alan Singer, "Carolyn Brady," *American Artist* 49 (May 1985), p. 95.

4. Gerrit Henry, *Carolyn Brady Watercolors*, exh. cat. (Tulsa, Okla.: Philbrook Museum of Art, 1989), p. 17.

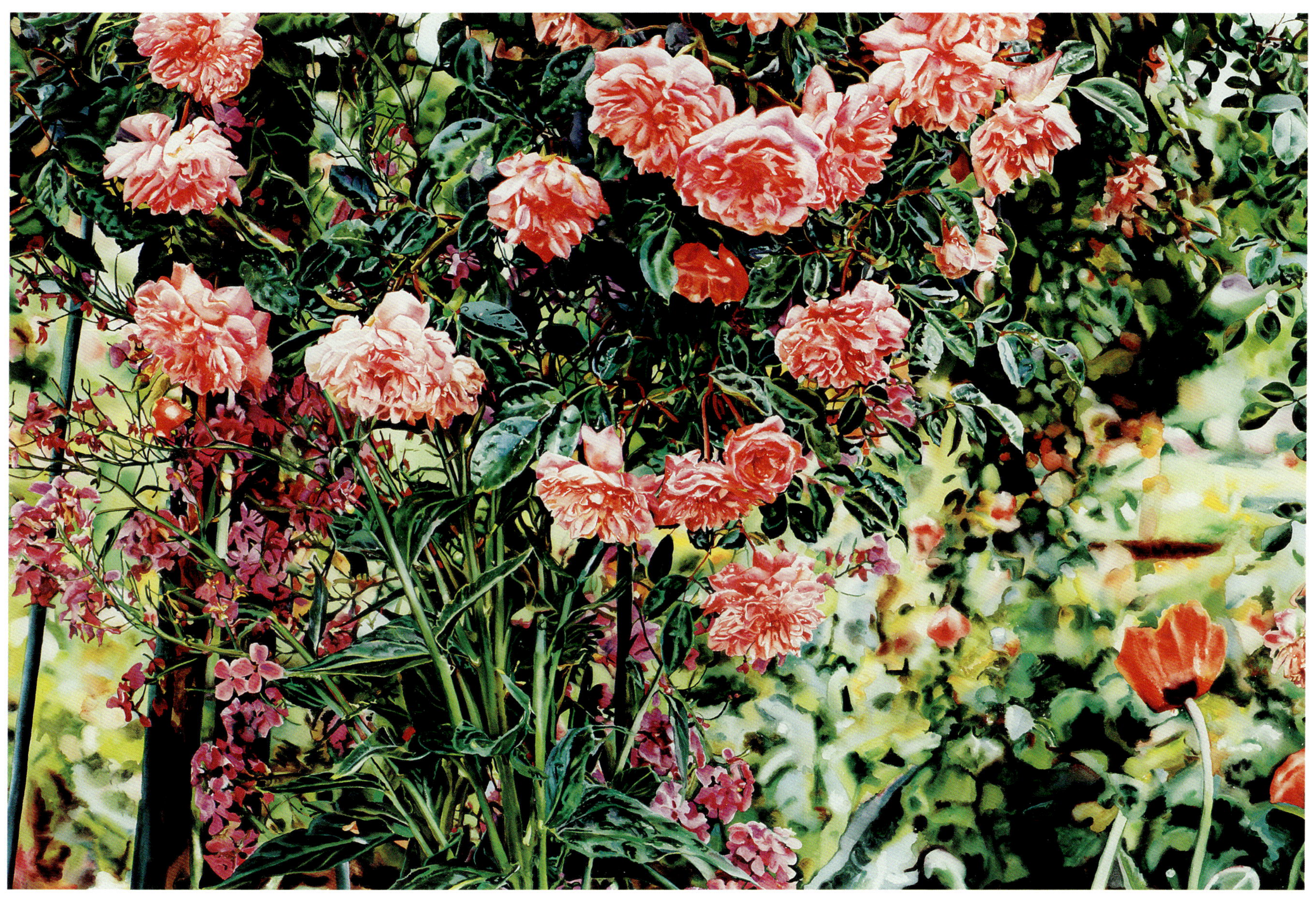

Marilyn Levine AMERICAN, BORN CANADA 1935

115 | *Johann's Jacket,* 1990

Ceramic and mixed media, 35 × 19 × 7 in.

Signed, dated, and numbered on tag inside jacket: *Levine 90-1A*

Gift of The Harding Foundation (2002.18)

Marilyn Levine, born in Alberta, Canada, was originally trained as a chemist. She began to study art, including ceramics, at the age of twenty-six. In 1969 she enrolled at the University of California at Berkeley, receiving her master's degree in 1970 and a master's in fine art, with a specialty in sculpture, in 1971. Levine is one of a number of artists active in the Bay Area, including Barbara Brown and Jerry Rothman, who work primarily in clay, the aesthetic and technical possibilities of which they have greatly expanded. Indeed, Levine, Brown, and Rothman, among others, helped to dissolve the rigid boundaries that often separate ceramics and sculpture and, in a larger sense, the fine and applied arts.

Initially, Levine created colorful, geometric boxes embellished with amorphous protrusions, but between 1969 and 1970 she began to fabricate realistic facsimiles of everyday objects.[1] Her work since that time can aptly be described, in the words of the critic John Perreault, as "trompe l'oeil sculpture"[2] in that it is characterized by such a high degree of verisimilitude that it tricks the eye into believing the object it represents is real. *Johann's Jacket,* for example, is an uncanny and altogether convincing simulation of a man's leather jacket. With a careful, meticulous hand, the artist faithfully reproduces the size and color of the original, including every seam, wrinkle, and fold and going so far as to incorporate an actual zipper and real buttons. She is even able to capture, in the rigid, unforgiving medium of fired clay, the exact texture of soft, supple leather.[3] Finally, she has enhanced the illusion of veracity by making a coat rack on which she "hangs" the "jacket." In this respect, *Johann's Jacket* is as much a philosophical conundrum as it is a perceptual puzzle. It presents the viewer, in Levine's own words, "with a dilemma or confrontation. The conflict between visual and tactile clues disturbs one's sense of reality, with the result that one's relationship to the object can no longer be the same."[4]

Johann's Jacket is typical of the kind of subject matter depicted by Levine. Generally, she selects banal, ordinary objects such as suitcases, clothing, purses, shoes, socks, and gloves, which have about them an air of the cast-off and forgotten.[5] The jacket in *Johann's Jacket,* like all of the objects used by Levine, appears to have been worn or used, its very history registered in the scuffs and discolorations that the artist so carefully reproduces. As much as it implies the passage of time, the jacket also suggests the presence of a unique individual. What attracted Levine to such source material was the opportunity it afforded to represent human subject matter, albeit indirectly. According to Levine, her work is concerned above all with recording the "traces" people leave behind in and on the world. "Trace," she claims, "is the accumulation of the marks left by the realization of man's intent, such as trampled grass, grease spots and dirt. In trace . . . we find richness, a humanity often omitted in intent. Trace always tells a story. My work is involved with the story told by trace."[6] If the jacket recreated in *Johann's Jacket* is the trace of a specific human being, the sculpture as a whole recounts the story of the person who once wore it. In other words, *Johann's Jacket* is as much a portrait of the object's owner as it is a representation of the object itself. KB

1. For more information on the development of Levine's sculpture, see Stephen Prokopoff, *Marilyn Levine: A Decade of Ceramic Sculpture,* exh. cat. (Boston: Institute of Contemporary Art, 1981), and Susan Peterson, "The Ceramics of Marilyn Levine," *Craft Horizons* 37, no. 1 (February 1977), pp. 40–43.

2. John Perreault, "False Objects: Duplicates, Replicas and Types," *Artforum* 16, no. 6 (February 1978), p. 26.

3. For information on Levine's technique, see Elaine Levin, "Portfolio: Marilyn Levine," *Ceramics Monthly* 33, no. 3 (March 1985), pp. 40–46, and Edward Lucie-Smith, "Virtual Reality," *Ceramic Review,* no. 179 (September–October 1999), pp. 16–19.

4. Nancy Foote, interview with Marilyn Levine in "The Photo-Realists: 12 Interviews," *Art in America* 60, no. 6 (November–December 1972), p. 84. Levine's sculptures share many of the same qualities seen in the 1970s Superrealist or Hyperrealist movement, exemplified by the paintings of David Parrish and the sculpture of Duane Hanson. Nineteeth-century American trompe-l'oeil paintings also exerted a profound influence on her work.

5. Levine has also been known to heighten the seeming insignificance of her objects by scattering them unceremoniously around the floor of the gallery instead of placing them on a pedestal. See Alan Meisel's review in *Craft Horizons* 31, no. 5 (October 1971), p. 53. Levine's preference for the commonplace links her to the artists Fumio Yoshimura, Scott Burden, and Marjorie Strider, who also re-create everyday items. There is also some similarity to Pop Art, although Levine's sculpture lack the coolness and neutrality and the ironic perspective seen in that movement. See Foote, "The Photo-Realists," p. 85.

6. Quoted in ibid.

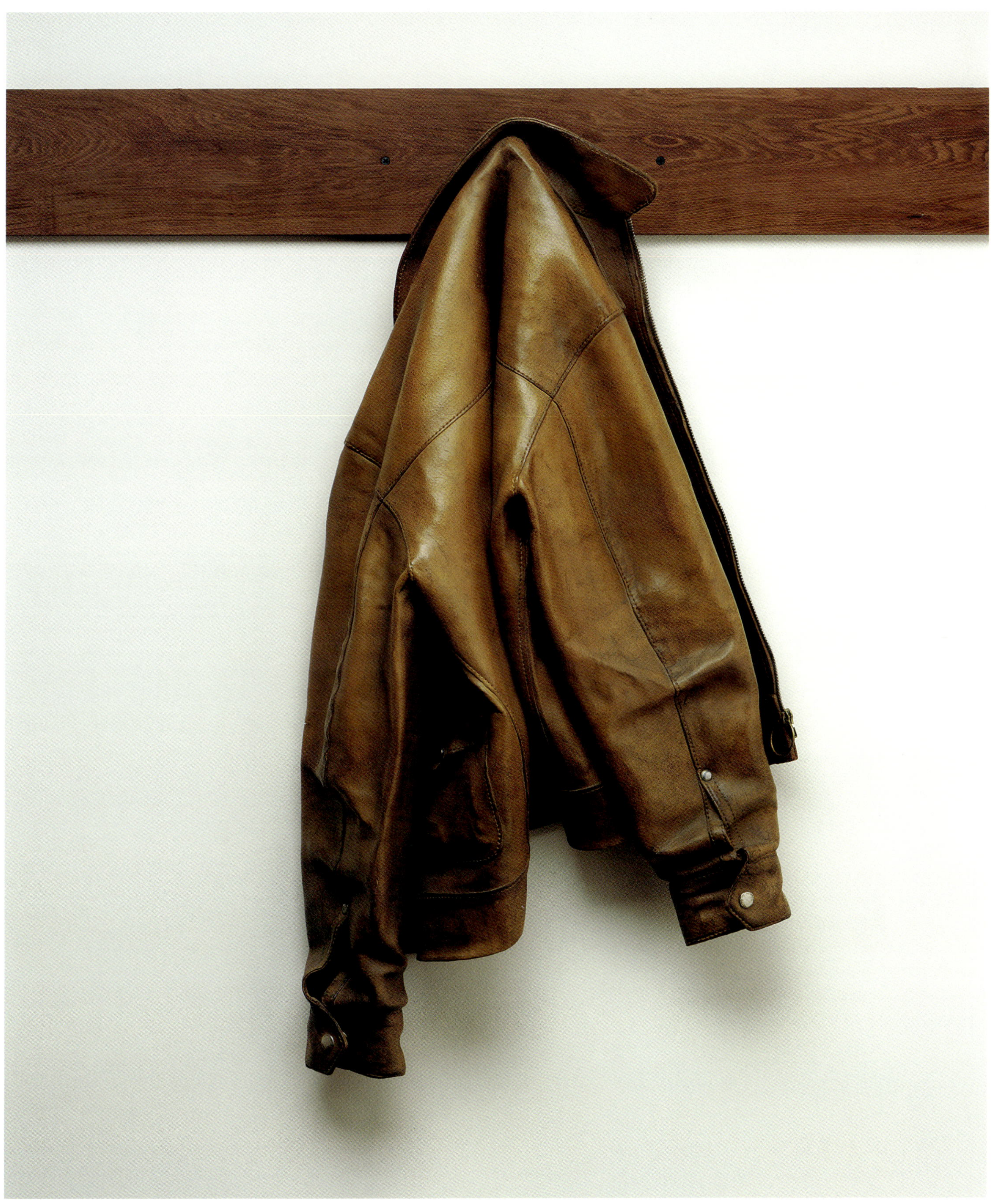

Jack Beal AMERICAN BORN 1931

116 | *Sondra with Gladioli,* 1992–93

Oil on canvas, 35¾ × 115½ in.

Unsigned

Gift of Mrs. Cecil Boksenbom, by exchange (1993.41)

Jack Beal is one of the preeminent realist painters to emerge from the long shadow cast by the dominant style of The New York School. As with most young painters in the late 1950s, he began his career as an abstract painter but by the early 1960s was searching for an individual style. On the strength of his large abstract canvases, Martha Jackson offered him an exhibition in 1962 but he declined, choosing instead to work odd jobs as a way of distancing himself from the art process. He spent that summer with his wife, Sondra Freckleton, also an artist, on the Oswegatchie River in upstate New York, finding in nature the direction he needed. As he says, "I wanted to give Art one more try: I had this vague notion that I wanted to get more natural form and color back into my painting, although at that time I had no notion at all of becoming a representational painter."[1] Works from this time are gestural, with thickly applied paint, but the forms are recognizable.

It was not until 1964, during a summer spent at Cabin John's Creek in Maryland, that Beal merged the philosophical implications of abstraction with the actuality of his life in a painting titled *The Saw* (Mellon Bank Corporation, Pittsburgh, Pennsylvania). This large-scale, dynamic work is packed with specific imagery of country living—a round saw blade, fences, grasses, fields, and a cabin—transformed into diagonals and patterns that lead the viewer into and through the painting. The works that immediately followed were equally dense and full of imagery, a matrix that functions both representationally and formally and that has become a Beal trademark.

Painting the figure was a logical progression for Beal, and by the mid-1960s he was making work that focused on the figure or at least implied a human presence. His favorite model is his wife, usually nude, whom he frequently rendered allegorically. Controversy compelled Beal to abandon painting nudes of his wife, although he continued to depict her clothed, surrounded by flowers, exotic fabrics, and other props. *Sondra with Gladioli* is a classic Beal work, a still life in which Sondra, seated behind a small table, reads contemplatively. The floral-patterned wallpaper behind her and the floral silk robe she is wearing are juxtaposed against the brightness of the real flowers in a vase and, more subtly, a basket of fruit. The throw rug at the lower left and the curved, delicate legs of the table form an angle that draws the viewer deep into the picture. The resulting play of patterns, angles, and real and painted flowers lends the work a visual wittiness and imbues the picture with the richness and mood of a Victorian painting. SS

1. Quoted in Eric Shanes, *Jack Beal* (New York: Hudson Hills Press, 1993), p. 14.

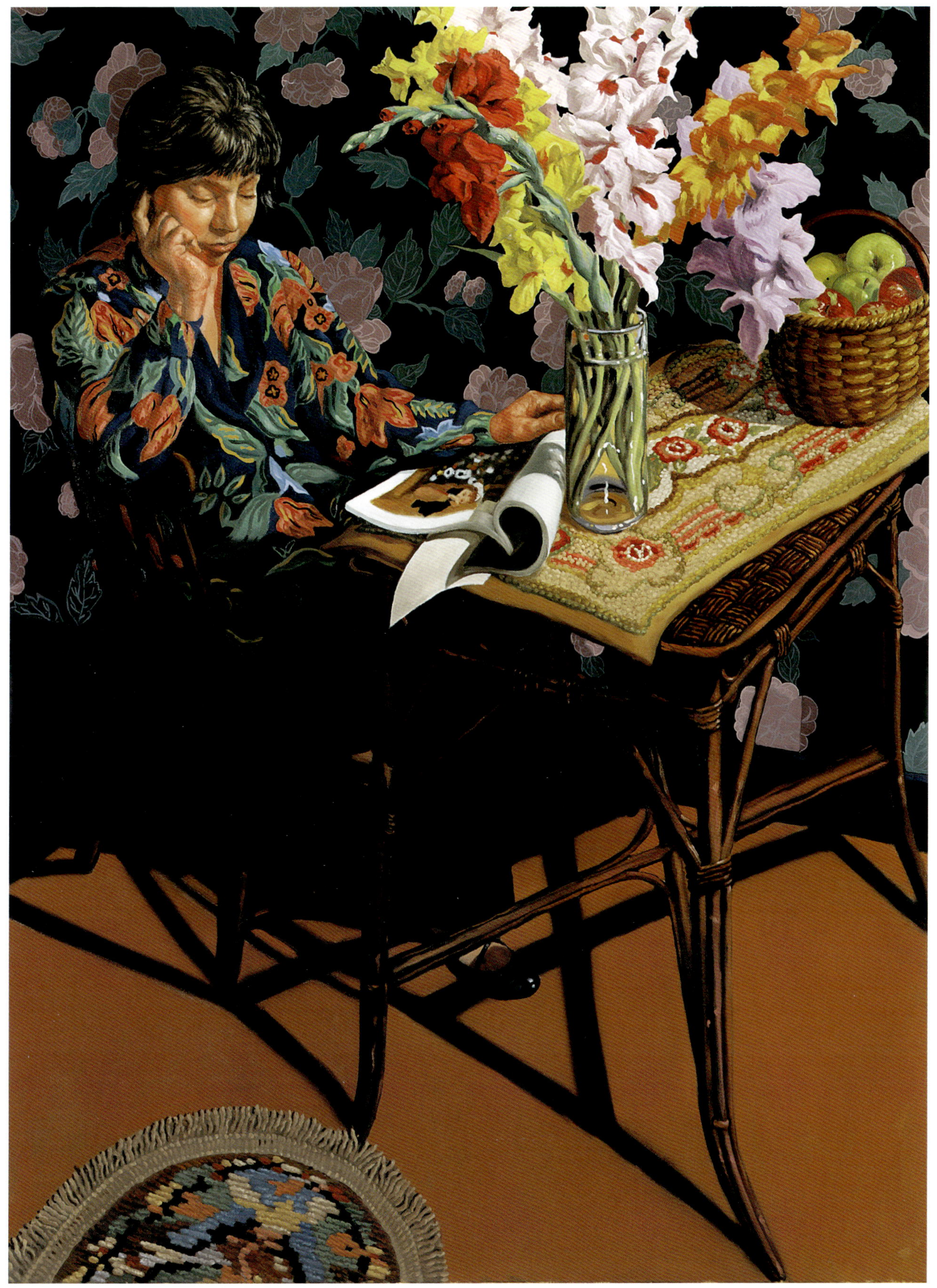

Stone Roberts AMERICAN BORN 1951

117 | *Portrait of a Marriage,* 1988

Oil on canvas, 47 × 35 in.

Signed and dated lower right: *J. Stone Roberts 1988*

Purchased with Traditional Art Fund (1995.11)

From an early age, Stone Roberts has been captivated by visual images. When he was five, he came across reproductions of old master paintings in the book *Fifty Centuries of Art,* published by the Metropolitan Museum of Art. As he later explained:

> I never confused them with photographs. And I immediately knew they were not like the illustrations I saw in children's books. These were images that lived in a world of their own. I had little interest in whether they were telling a story or not. I was consumed by their sheer visual presence. And I knew somehow that they were very old. I felt it miraculous that they spoke so directly to me through time. Most of all, I was amazed that a person could put so much together out of his imagination and make it all *fit.*[1]

Stone Roberts was born in Asheville, North Carolina. He enrolled at Yale University in 1969 to pursue what he thought would be a career in law or business. In his junior year, however, he took a drawing class taught by the well-known realist painter William Bailey. It was there, copying from old masters and from life, that he discovered the power of drawing. In 1972 he attended Yale's summer school for art, where his realist drawings and paintings remained outside the mainstream. He continued his studies with graduate work at the Tyler School of Art in Philadelphia, and he also attended the school's branch in Rome. After completing his fine arts degree, he worked in corporate finance at a Wall Street bank. Although successful in the business world, in 1981 he followed the urging of his wife and quit his job to become a full-time artist. In April of the following year he began work on his first large-sale realistic painting, *Janet,* which was later acquired by the Metropolitan Museum of Art. By the fall of 1982 Roberts began showing his work at the Schoelkopf Gallery in New York.

Roberts's paintings are often developed over a considerable period of time, sometimes as long as twelve years. He approaches them as if writing a novel, in which the original concept is further developed as a result of repeated viewing, like a plot that unfolds over time. *Portrait of a Marriage* is more than a portrait of two people. In its precise realism the viewer encounters a vast array of details that, when considered together, speak as much about the realities of contemporary life as they do about the two individuals depicted. Complex and subtle, the narrative quality of the work suggests, but does not fully reveal, the story of these people.

Commissioned by Thomas and Louise McNamee, the painting is a scene from life. As with many of his paintings, Roberts developed the composition in a series of drawings. The wife, a successful businesswoman, is dressed in a red suit. Pen in hand, she sits on the floor surrounded by a briefcase and carefully arranged papers, contemplating the work before her. The husband, a writer, is equally focused as he busies himself at his computer. Leaning across his keyboard to adjust the monitor, his body forms an arch that suggests his traditional role as protector. Yet in his self-absorption, he is as disconnected from his wife as she is from him.

By shifting perspective within the painting, Roberts creates changing points of view that draw the observer into the painting. He places the husband and wife parallel to the picture plane. The husband occupies the upper half of the painting. He is in the background while the wife, placed in the middle ground, dominates the center of the composition. The lower third of the painting is flattened so that objects of the wife's attention—cassette recorder, bulging briefcase, datebook, and papers—are seen in great detail, while the couple's black cat is shown on the left. Captivated by the precise details and carefully arranged composition, the viewer is challenged to make sense of the union of this disconnected couple. The Flint Institute of Arts acquired the painting after the couple's divorce. Originally named after them, the title was changed to *Portrait of a Marriage* at their request. MMD

1. Quoted in Charles Michener, *Stone Roberts: Paintings and Drawings* (New York: Harry N. Abrams, 1993), p. 7.

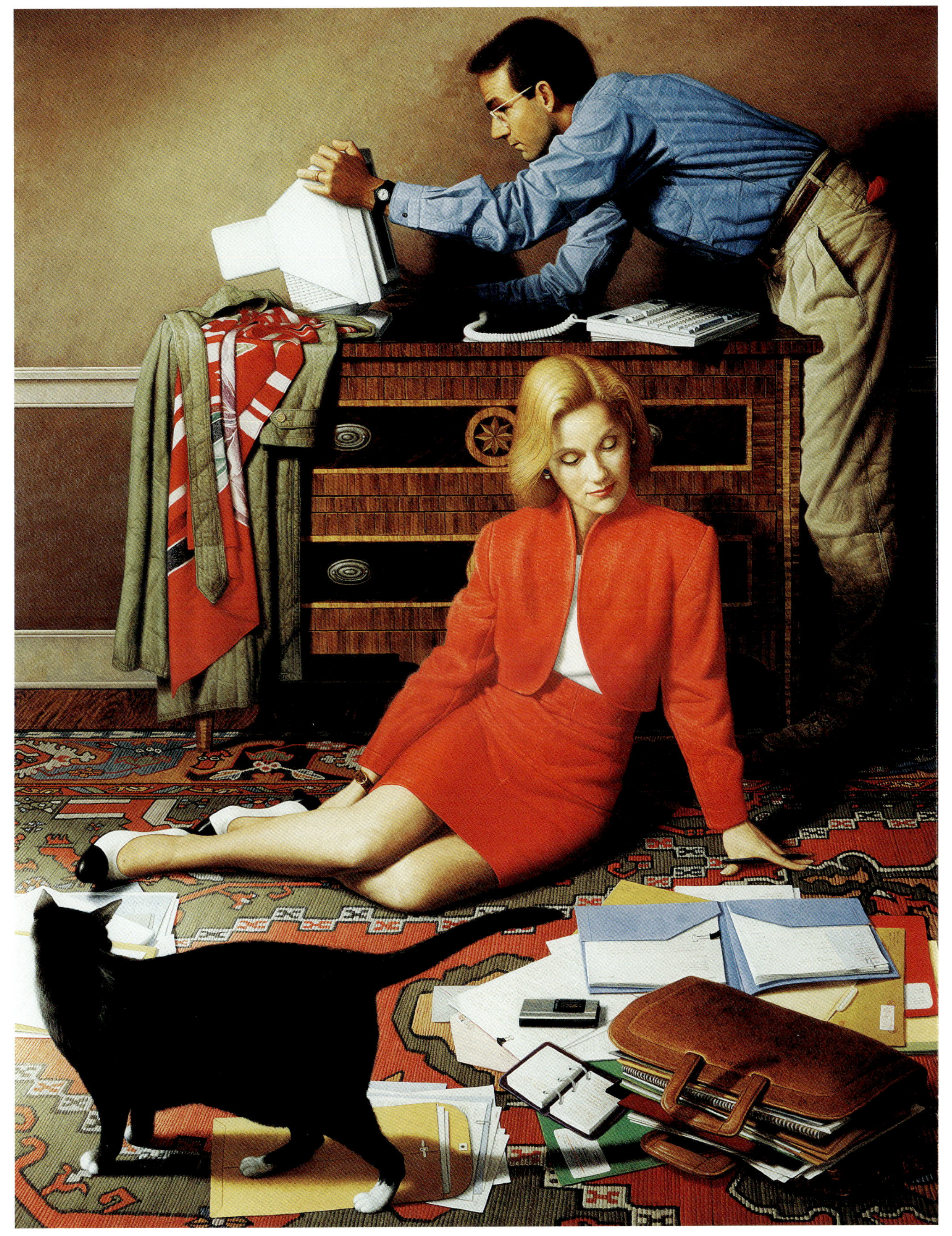

Scott Fraser AMERICAN BORN 1957

118 | *Metronome,* 1990

Oil on panel, 13¼ × 21¼ in.

Signed lower right: *Scott Fraser*; inscribed on vertical bar of metronome: *Scott Fraser*

Flint Institute of Arts purchase (1991.2)

Scott Fraser is a contemporary realist who paints carefully orchestrated, exquisitely detailed still lifes that are layered with symbolic and often personal significance. His influences are as varied as seventeenth-century Dutch still lifes and works by the contemporary realist-expressionist painter Gerhard Richter. Fraser, who attended the Kansas City Art Institute and the Atelierhaus in Worpswede, Germany, began his career painting landscapes. In the 1980s, frustrated by the genre and inspired by the humor and mystery in Joseph Cornell's work, Fraser began making still lifes exclusively. Fascinated by Cornell's assemblages of seemingly unrelated objects, Fraser recalls his epiphany: "It didn't matter to me what if anything Cornell was trying to say. I only remember thinking, 'This is what I want to do in paint.'"[1]

Fraser's meticulously painted, highly illusionistic canvases also recall the American trompe-l'oeil realist tradition, established in the early nineteenth century by Raphaelle Peale, that thrived in the 1880s and 1890s in the hands of William Michael Harnett and John Frederick Peto. However, unlike Harnett and others who used the trompe-l'oeil still life to express a certain nostalgia, Fraser emphatically seeks to reflect his own time and his personal realities in very self-conscious ways. "I can't exist in the present and have my works look like they are from the past, even though I love to study and admire historical works. It's good to borrow from them, but they must be changed and revamped to suit this time in which I live."[2] Over time, of course, such a strategy of using objects from his present reality—bubble wrap, sneakers, and Band-Aids—will have the ironic effect of dating his paintings. This irony, which is surely not lost on Fraser, speaks volumes about "reality" and "realism" as constantly shifting, personally and historically contingent concepts.

As Fraser suggests in *Metronome,* however, personal realities may have universal applications. The work represents a contemporary *vanitas* (vanity) with a metronome, a device used by musicians and dancers to measure time, here stopped by a taut string attached to a table by a pushpin. On one, personal level, the metronome is a reference to his wife, who gives piano lessons at their home. According to Fraser, the painting's arrested metronome reflects his desire to stop time for his wife, who had experienced a difficult illness.[3] But beyond the autobiographical significance, Fraser explores larger questions about time and the fragility of human life, both references to *vanitas* painting. He depicts an egg precariously (and miraculously) perched atop the metronome, which is surrounded on either side by eggs and eggshells. The intact, cracked, and uncertainly suspended eggs symbolize the delicate cycle of life and death and serve as reminders of mortality. Easily disturbed by even the slightest movement, the eggs and the tightly pulled string ridicule the notion of human control over life. MK

1. Quoted in Bonnie Gangelhoff, "Mystery and Resonance," *Southwest Art* 29, no. 10 (March 2000), p. 113.

2. Scott Fraser, "Scott Fraser on Contemporary Realism," *Southwest Art* 29, no. 10 (March 2000), p. 114.

3. Marilynne S. Mason, "Realism with a Hint of Mystery," *Christian Science Monitor,* 30 August 1993, p. 16.

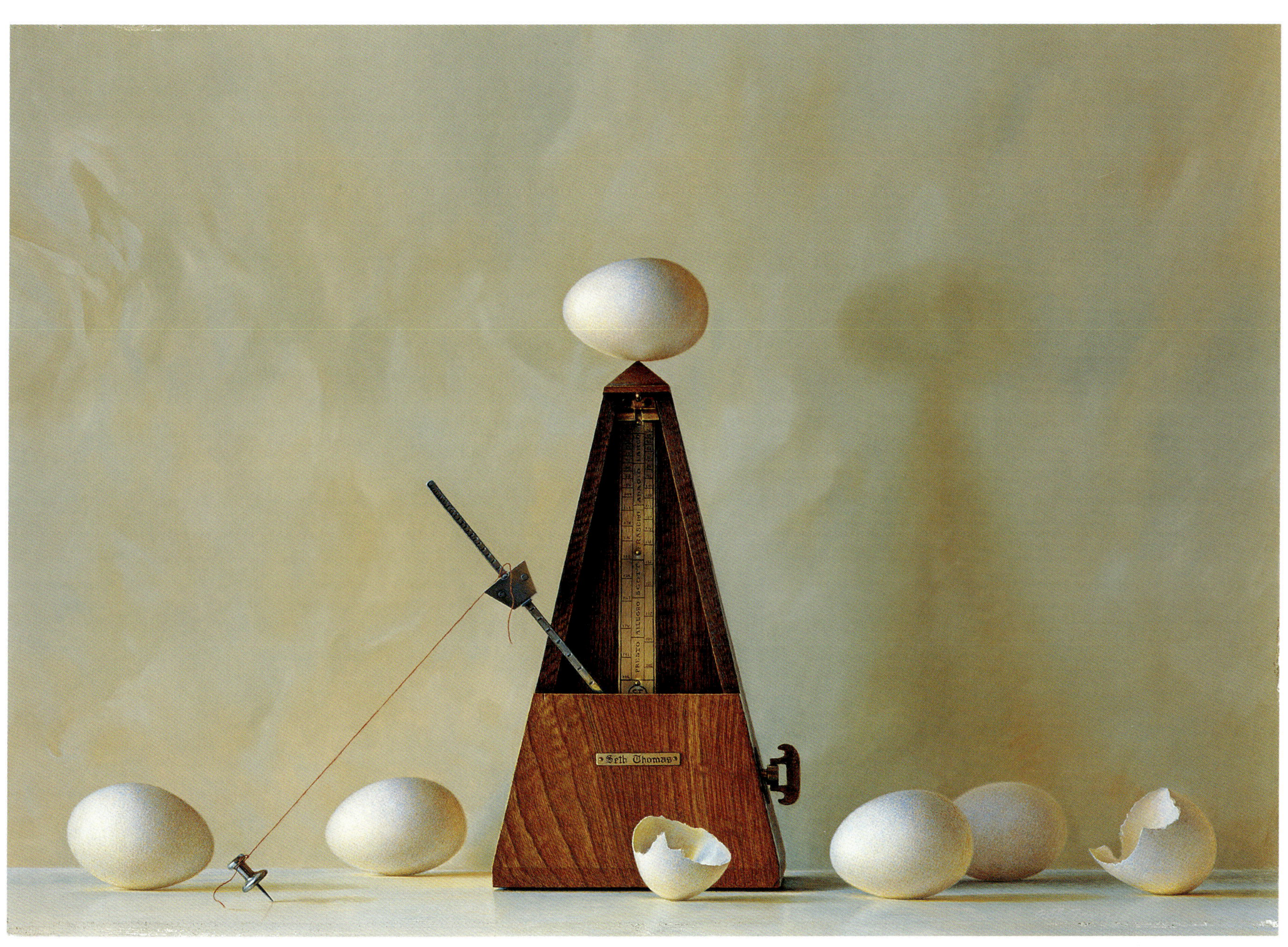
Seth Thomas

Dennis Oppenheim AMERICAN BORN 1938

119 | *Upper Cut,* 1999

Wood, pressed board, hard foam, art books, and metal, 58 × 55 × 43½ in.

Unsigned

Purchased in memory of Dr. Stuart Hodge, Director of the Flint Institute of Arts (1959–1980), with funds from the Dr. Stuart Hodge memorial and partial gift from The Dennis Oppenheim Foundation (1999.34)

Dennis Oppenheim burst onto the contemporary art scene in the mid-1960s, when he became known primarily as an Earth Artist. He created works that as much investigated a conceptual vein as they were dedicated to traditional object-making. At the same time, he experimented with Body Art—in which the body of the artist is used as both the form and the medium—and Performance Art, where he explored a wide range of universal and personal themes—world history, art history, popular culture, comedy, and his own psyche. The only extant evidence of these performances and events is informal photographs taken at the time to record the experience. Later, in the early 1970s, Oppenheim began to experiment with video and technology, making what he has referred to as his "machine pieces." The works generated during this period negotiated different systems of thought and ways of making art, finding their final form as installations. As a whole, Oppenheim's practice during these two decades can be seen as a far-reaching exploration of ideas, techniques, and materials newly surfacing in the discourse on and making of contemporary art.

Oppenheim first became interested in art while attending high school in the mid-1950s, when he developed an affinity with the powerful aesthetics of the Abstract Expressionists. He was particularly drawn to the work of Willem de Kooning, largely because he saw an antipainting stance in de Kooning's backward strokes. In 1958, after graduating from high school, Oppenheim attended the California School of Arts and Crafts, Oakland, for two years. Thereafter, his career, like his work, followed a circuitous path. After art school in California he married and moved to Hawaii, where, taking a brief hiatus from art, he took a job as a construction worker. He returned to the California School of Arts and Crafts, where he earned a bachelor's degree in 1964. The following year, his enrollment in the art department at Stanford University set him on a more serious course. About his time at Stanford Oppenheim has stated, "That's where the interest in art theory, philosophy and tremendous attention to the East Coast and a real competitiveness began."[1] Along with many of his contemporaries in the Bay Area, Oppenheim was interested in Neo-Dada, which, like its counterpart in the music world, Funk, explored the off-key and dissonant. The influence of Neo-Dada can be traced through most of his mature work.

Following a retrospective exhibition held at various European venues in the early 1990s, Oppenheim commented on the disjointed, almost fractured, quality of the relationship among the various stages of his career: "When I see all of this work together, it looks like it was done by ten different artists. It's rather horrifying. There are these big machine pieces next to a picture of me eating a gingerbread cookie. It's clear that my career has not been a linear thing at all."[2] However, what is evident in reviewing Oppenheim's oeuvre is that his relentless experimentation, persistence, and humor have greatly influenced generations of young Conceptual artists. Oppenheim has left his mark on Earth Art, Body Art, Performance Art, Conceptual Art, and on the history of art from the 1960s on. As he noted in a 1993 interview, "Dematerialization was the watchword, and you could do a qualified art work that would have the integrity of a sculpture, but would consist simply of a photograph, a work, or a postcard. Things were done quickly and no one was inclined to fine-tune the final work too much. The tendency was to claim an arena and leave it quickly so that you left a lot of material for other people."[3]

The connection between Oppenheim's earlier and later pieces is found in his references to the body. In many of the sculptures, this imagery can be understood as an autobiographical thread that joins his work. In the Flint Institute of Arts' *Upper Cut,* a wide-open mouth reveals specifically chosen books, mainly on art and philosophy, in lieu of teeth.[4] It has some missing "teeth," perhaps a metaphor for educational gaps or stray thoughts. In this work, and in the various styles and media that preceded it, Oppenheim successfully transforms simple materials into a multi-dimensional artistic statement, at once humorous and meaningful. SS

1. Quoted in Germano Celant, *Dennis Oppenheim,* exh. cat. (Milan: Editions Charta, 1997), p. 28.

2. Quoted in Eleanor Heartney, "Dennis Oppenheim, a Process of Discontinuity," *Art Press* 176 (January 1993), p. E1.

3. Ibid., p. E2.

4. The titles include *Zero Communication* by Walter de Maria; *Below Indigo: Depression in Art* by Mark Rothko; *Not Understanding Art* by Arthur Danto; and *Spending Your Husband's Money* by Sylvia Fleury.

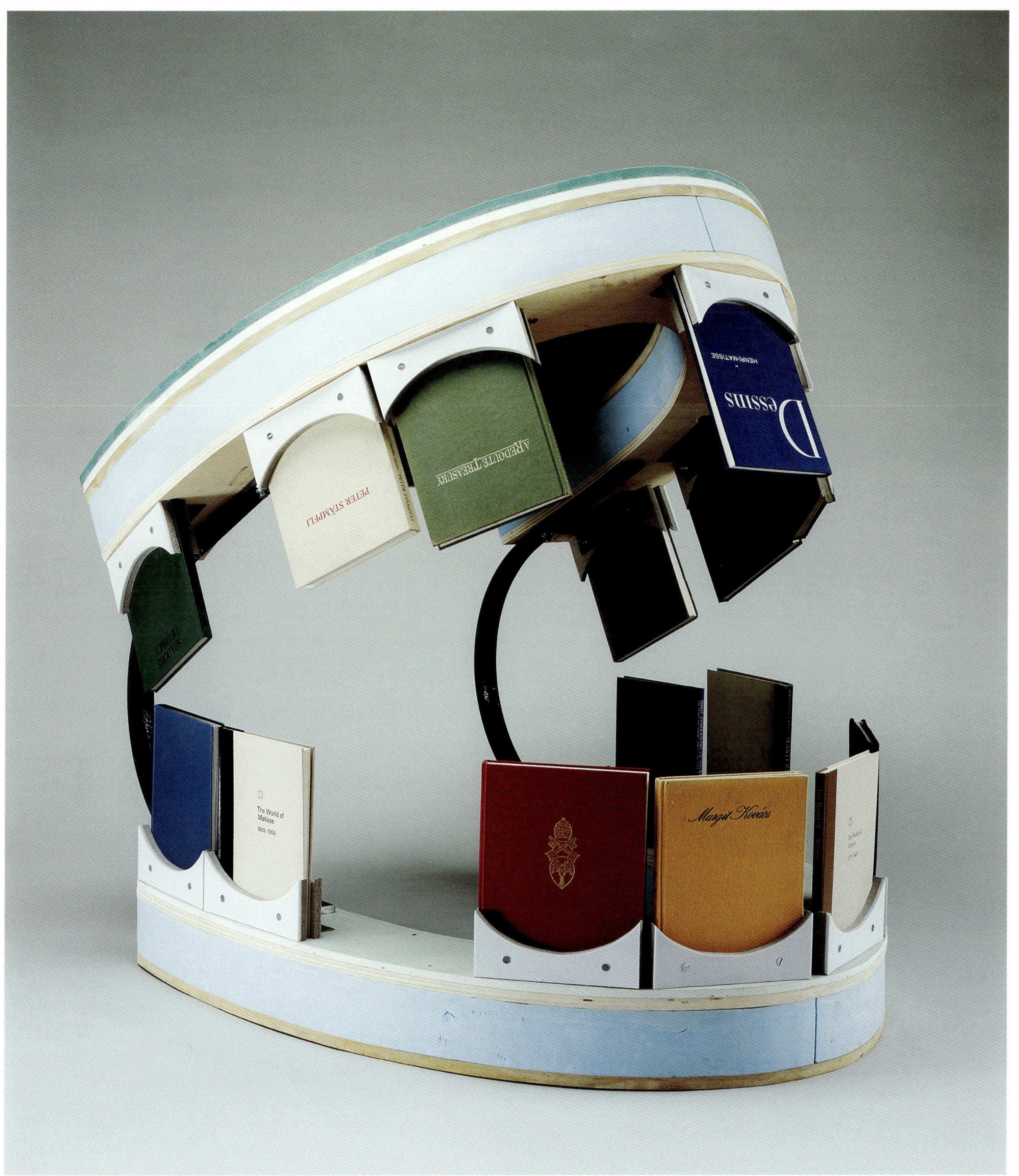
PETER STÄMPFLI
A REDOUTÉ TREASURY
HENRI MATISSE
Dessins
The World of
Matisse
1869–1954
Margit Kovács

Richard Maury AMERICAN BORN 1935

120 | *Interior with Stefania,* 1992

Oil on canvas mounted on panel, $55\frac{1}{8} \times 43\frac{3}{8}$ in.

Unsigned

Gift of Mary Mallery Davis, by exchange (1994.6)

The work of Richard Maury, a leading contemporary realist painter, is aligned more with that of the old masters than with the development of twentieth-century abstract and Conceptual Art. Born in Washington, D.C., Maury remained in the city of his birth to study at the Corcoran Gallery of Art from 1955 to 1956. He then moved to New York City, where he studied at the Art Students League until 1959. Although Maury matured artistically while Abstract Expressionism was still the prevailing style of painting, he found it difficult to embrace its philosophical framework. "I was feeling even more guilty about my continuing to be mainly interested in realistic drawing and painting," he said of the experience. "We all know that Realism was a thing of the past while Abstraction was the only true path for the creative spirit. The trouble was that I had absolutely no ability in anything abstract."[1]

In 1960 Maury moved permanently to Florence, Italy, where the historic city's pace, sensibility, and museums, filled with the masterpieces of Fra Angelico and Titian, reinforced the direction of his art. The natural light of Florence fills Maury's studio and is transposed into the interior spaces of his paintings. Working in a classical manner, Maury begins a composition with a preliminary pencil drawing and then transfers this study to a gesso-covered canvas mounted on a wood panel. Many thin layers of glaze are then painstakingly applied to the composition to achieve the exquisitely articulated final work.

Best described as a genre painter, most of Maury's work consists of interiors, still lifes, and portraits. The influence of seventeenth-century Dutch painters, particularly Jan Vermeer, is evident not only in his rigorous attention to detail but also in his subjects' tranquil activities—writing, knitting, and reading. Maury looks to his immediate surroundings for inspiration, and the objects that fill the painting field are chosen, not for their metaphoric or symbolic meaning, but for their contribution to a harmonious visual arrangement. Maury has stated in reference to his choice of subject matter, "I think that 'Realist' is the most apt single word to describe my work. . . . I have many colleagues who paint imagined scenes, but I am interested artistically only in the here and now. The fact that I live in this out-of-the-ordinary house, in this out-of-the-ordinary town, I am sure obscures the present day reality which is the aim in my work. I would like to feel that this quotidian and thus, I hope, eternal quality can easily be perceived."[2]

Interior with Stefania is a beautiful example of Maury's seamless blending of the old with the new. The subject, seated in a chair reading, is placed between the curved arch of the doorway and the rectilinear edges of a cabinet filled with glass and china. Several devices and visual ploys are used to play with the viewer's perception. Although the woman's clothes are modern, the specific era to which they belong is unclear—her Capri pants and matching shirt could be from any decade in the last half of the twentieth century. In contrast to this open-ended reading of the woman's outfit, the blue blades of the electric fan, whose hue matches that in the china pattern, indicate that the painting is set in contemporary times. Formally, the large green bottle of wine, jutting into the observer's space, serves as a visual counterpart to the fan. Both objects are visual cues that command attention. In the space of the composition, they are extraordinary objects in an otherwise ordinary setting. "I am doing no intentional selection in regard to the making of a painting," Maury says. "It is only, I am certain, to make something beautiful."[3] SS

1. Quoted in Philip Eliasoph, "Letter from Florence: The Art of Richard Maury," *American Arts Quarterly* 14 (winter 1997), p. 16.

2. Ibid.

3. Ibid., p. 18.

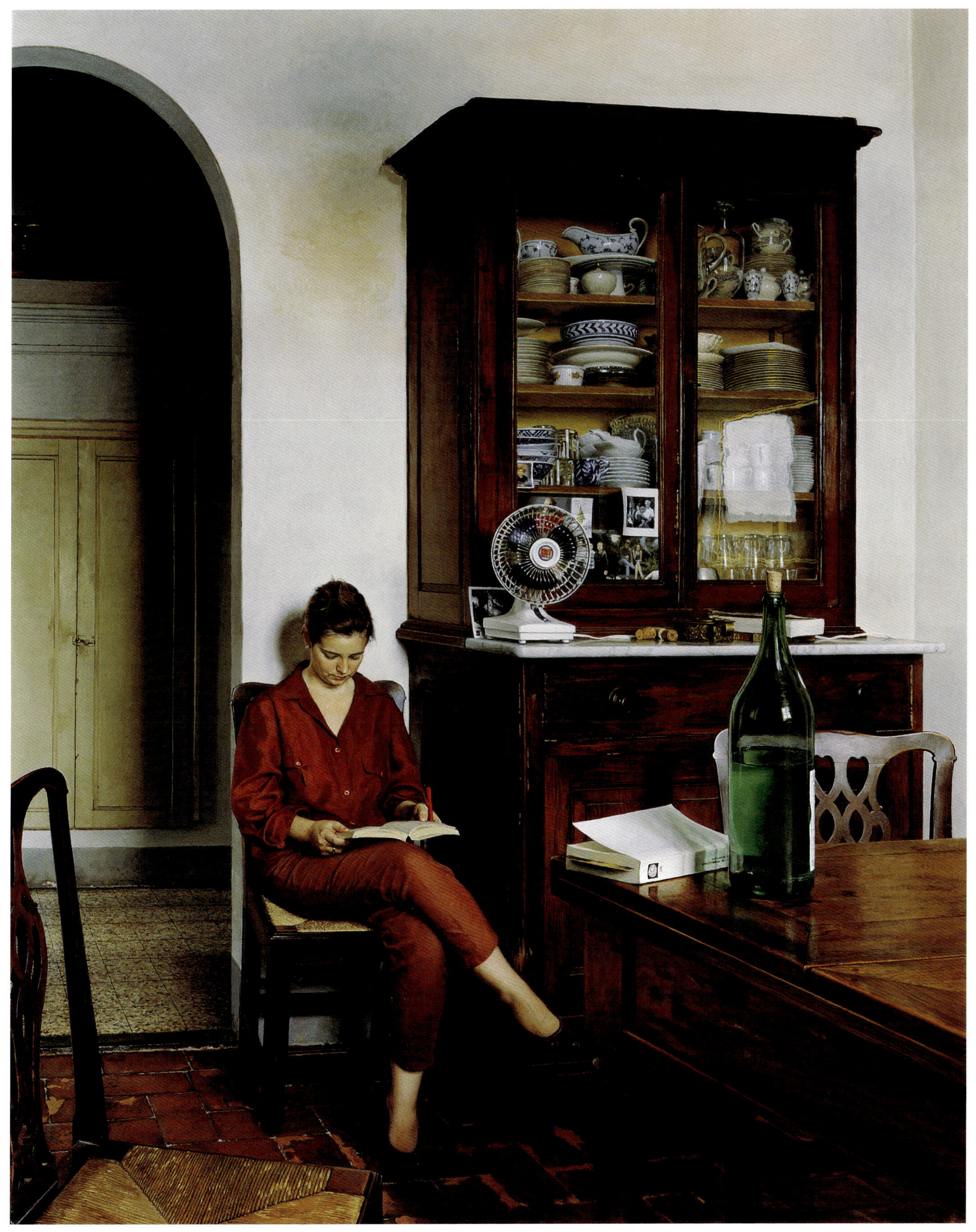

Deborah Deichler AMERICAN BORN 1948

121 | *The Chocolate Thief,* 1995

Oil on canvas mounted on aluminum panel, 19¾ × 29¾ in.

Signed lower right: *Deichler*

Gift of the Founders Society (1995.12)

Born in Bryn Mawr, Pennsylvania, Deichler's interest in art was first piqued in high school, where she took classes in printmaking, oil painting, and photography. She continued her studies at the Philadelphia College of Art, earning a bachelor's degree with a certificate in art education in 1970. After graduation, Deichler accepted a job as a teacher at a junior high school in New England. In 1976, however, she returned to her first passion—painting. She attended classes at the Pennsylvania Academy of the Fine Arts from 1976 to 1980, including those taught by the realist painters Ben Kamihira, Louis Sloan, and Arthur DeCosta.[1] It was only then, with the encouragement of her family, that she committed herself to a full-time career as an artist.

Deichler's choice of both subject matter and style has been profoundly influenced by the work of Northern European and Italian painters from the Renaissance and Baroque periods. A realist in the tradition of such artists as Jan van Eyck and Caravaggio, Deichler has demonstrated over the years a marked preference for figure studies and still lifes, which she renders in meticulous, painstaking detail. Her figure studies often depict women who exude a powerful, mysterious sexuality, one that is accentuated by the cornucopia of accessories—bracelets, medals, hats, and necklaces—that cover them. Her still lifes likewise radiate a palpable eroticism. Filled with succulent fruits and shiny objects, they tempt the eye as well as the appetite.

Although painted in a realistic style, Deichler's pictures are not as straightforward as they might seem at first glance. They combine a naturalistic technique with what can only be described as a Surrealist sensibility. Critics have often compared them to fairy tales, because of their inclusion of bizarre, fantastic, and strange elements. Deichler is not content to merely reproduce or copy reality, despite the formal qualities of her works. Indeed, the artist herself has said that she strives to construct a reality that is "ironic, ridiculous, and absurd, yet one that is also playful."[2]

The reality that Deichler creates in her paintings is often infused with symbolism, as can be seen in *The Chocolate Thief.* The painting depicts an old wood table, whose white surface is illuminated by a dramatic shaft of light. On the table are the remains of what appears to have been a delicious afternoon tea, complete with raisin bread, butter, peaches, and chocolate. At the back of the table toward the right is a glass vase containing a bouquet of brown, wilted flowers. The only activity in the painting takes place at the left edge of the canvas, where a mouse—the thief after whom the painting is named—eagerly nibbles away at a hunk of chocolate, its tiny paws wrapped around the candy as if in an amorous embrace. While the half-consumed food suggests the presence of a human being, no one is visible. Indeed, the person who originally partook of the meal probably left some time ago, judging from the state of the flowers and the presence of the mouse. *The Chocolate Thief* is thus a modern *vanitas,* a type of still life especially popular with seventeenth-century Dutch painters that symbolizes the brevity of human life, the inevitability of death, and the transience of earthly pleasures and achievements. In this painting, a seemingly straightforward and unambiguous still life, Deichler has embedded a hidden message that speaks to the human condition throughout the ages. KB

1. William P. Scott, "Deborah Deichler," *American Artist* 52 (May 1988), p. 36.

2. Ibid.

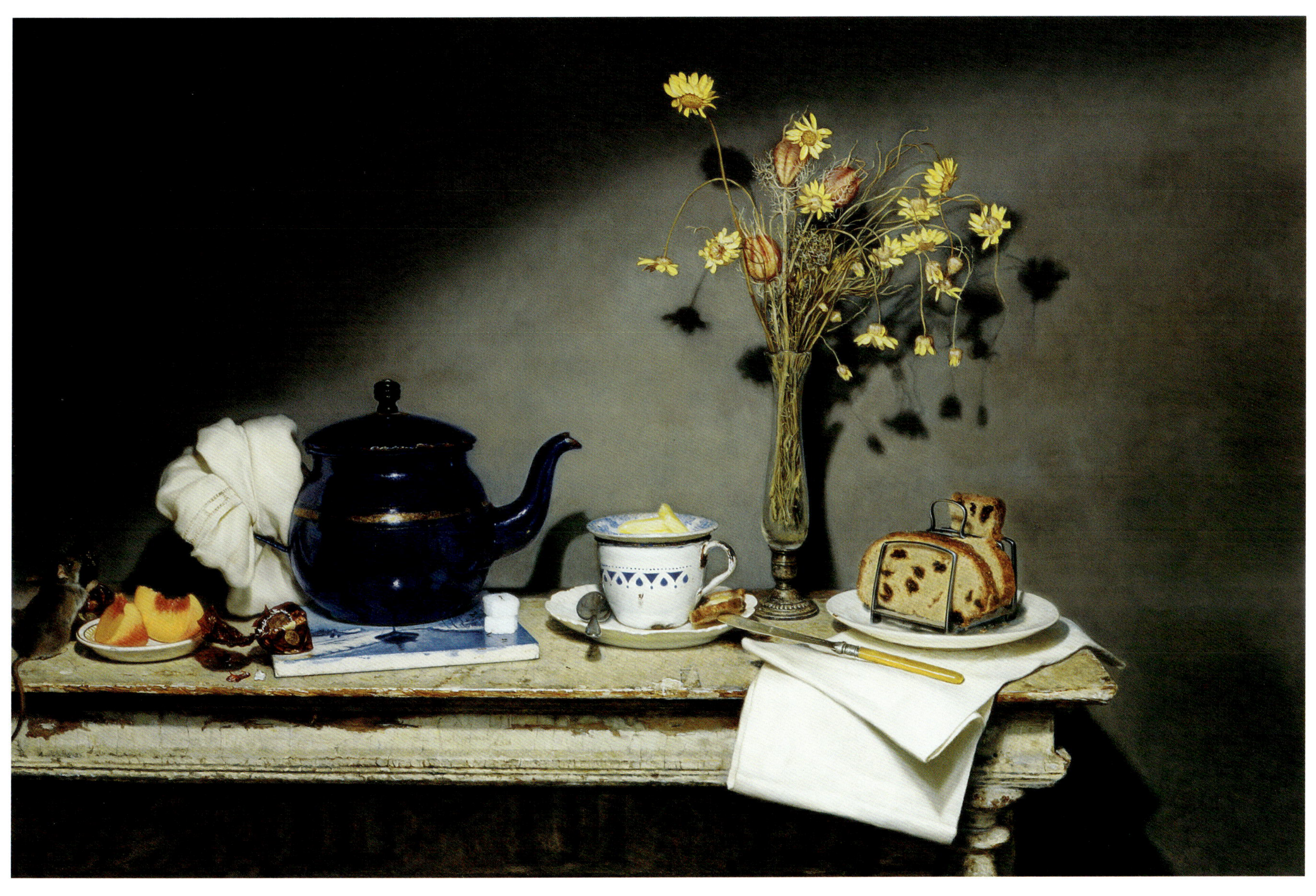

Melvin Edwards AMERICAN BORN 1937

122 | *Ida's Voice,* 1992

Welded steel, 10⅛ × 11 × 11 in.

Unsigned

Museum purchase with assistance from the Richard Florsheim Art Fund, the Loeb Charitable Trust, and Mark and Charlotte Lippincott (1998.27)

Melvin Edwards, born in Houston, Texas, learned to draw and paint in high school. He proved to be naturally gifted and, when a junior, was chosen to attend art classes at Houston's Museum of Fine Arts. Also a talented football player, he went to the University of Southern California at Los Angeles on an athletic scholarship, although he continued to have a strong interest in art. He enrolled at Los Angeles City College and, later, the Los Angeles County Art Institute, with the intention of becoming a painter. This objective changed, however, after he took a welding class in 1960—from that time he has worked primarily as a sculptor.

An avid reader, Edwards developed an interest in art and culture at an early age. He became acquainted with art history—African art, Renaissance painting, and the art of many other countries and periods. He was interested in the work of his contemporaries, especially the painters Charles White, Romare Bearden, David Siqueiros, and Diego Rivera and the sculptors Julio González, David Smith, and Alexander Calder. Edwards also traveled extensively through Europe, South America, the Caribbean, and Africa, and his journeys exposed him to a wide range of cultural influences, which he incorporates into his works. In addition to providing aesthetic ideas, his studies and travels have made him privy to the many manifestations of the human condition. The disparities he observed firsthand both at home and abroad made a deep impression on both his life and work.

In 1963, compelled by the civil rights movement to explore themes of racism and social injustice, Edwards began a series of sculptures called *Lynch Fragments.* The title of the series is based on stories he heard from childhood about the lynching of African Americans, still prevalent at the time of his youth, but it also applies to all forms of racism and injustice. Edwards has said that the sculptures represent "a continuance of the resistance against oppression" and that they are a "private conversation—most of them relate to my personal experience or specific incidents within the history of racism throughout the world."[1]

The objects in Edwards's work are often common, identifiable metal tools—gears, saw blades, bolts, and chains. His virtuosity in welding enables him to blend these disparate objects together as if they were made of soft clay. Generally the size of a human head, these high-relief sculptures are intended to hang on the wall six feet off the floor. A mixture of black and gray steel, they are strangely familiar, not only because they are made of recognizable parts but because the overall form often resembles a face or mask. Yet the combination of these parts takes on new meaning because of the association Edwards has created between them and the fact that the masklike shape remains abstract—it is left to the viewer to associate a washer with an eye or a bolt with a nose.

The likeness of Edwards's sculptures to African masks is no accident—he has been deeply interested in African culture since he was young and has traveled to Africa many times to visit and teach, at the same time seeking out carvers and bronze casters. His works incorporate many characteristics of the ritual objects, especially their abstract and enigmatic character. While his titles sometimes use African words or names as a reference to this influence, he feels that the works must ultimately stand on their own merits, apart from their titles.

Meaning in Edwards's sculptures is elusive: tools can be symbolic of work and progress or oppression and slavery. They may, in addition, simply serve as shapes defining the overall form. Like the African mask-maker, Edwards does not intend for his work to be taken literally. His forms are evocative and allude to many things, including his personal experiences, formal training in the arts, and interest in social and cultural issues.

Today Edwards is a professor of drawing, sculpture, and art history at Rutgers University in New Jersey. He has received a number of commissions for large-scale, freestanding, outdoor sculptures but continues to make the *Lynch Fragments,* which now number more than two hundred. JBH

1. Quoted in Valerie J. Mercer, "Sculptor's Horizons Have No Limits," *New York Times,* 3 June 1990, p. 12.

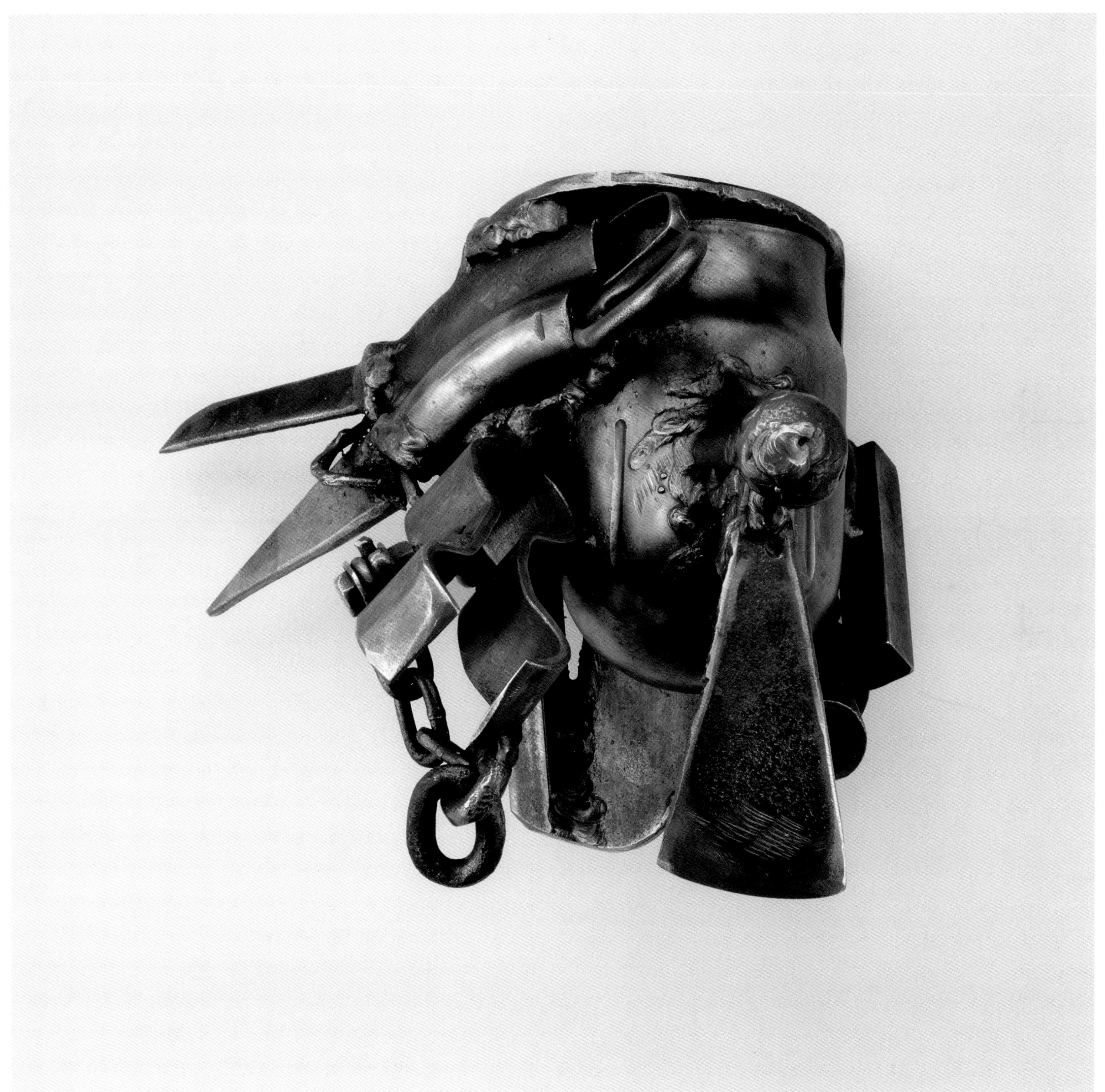

John Gittins AMERICAN BORN 1940

123 | *Gray's Mirror,* 1985

Acrylic on canvas, $65\frac{1}{2} \times 36\frac{1}{2}$ in.

Signed, titled, and dated on stretcher: *John Gittins, "Gray's Mirror", 1/85*

Gift of the artist (2002.8)

John Gittins worked for years as a psychologist before devoting himself to painting and photography. His interest in art, lying in the borderland between psychology and analytic philosophy, centers on the relationship of language and thought, much affected by the idea that each area of mental life, including art, has its own way of structuring experience.

Today, Gittins's rigorous training in psychology forms the intellectual foundation for his approach to painting, a seemingly curious departure point for an artist who works in an abstract style. "I'm interested in a sense of human presence behind the work," he once said. This element attracts him to a wide variety of work, regardless of style, from the biomorphism of Joan Miró to the geometry of Piet Mondrian.[1] Of his contemporaries, he finds the paintings of the German Gerhard Richter—both his abstract and his realistic pictures—particularly intriguing. Gittins's insight into Richter is equally telling for his own work. "What I get in Richter is representation in all ways," he has said. "There's a tremendous exuberance in his pictures, he's a masterful handler of paint. But there's a mental, mindful side of him too, a tragedy in his work in which he makes something come back. He re-represents it but it is never like the original so one comes away with a sense of loss. It seems analogous to Proust and memory."

There is a physical aspect to Gittins's work that belies his intellectual underpinnings. His working method—extruding paint through a tube with a nozzled head, pouring, splashing, rolling with a roller, and even at times molding paints and gels with his hands—invites chance and opens up the picture to undeliberated decision making. "When I work," Gittins has said, "I go on faith that an unconscious structuring is at work." This awareness of the dichotomy of human actions—at times consciously thought out and other times guided by the subconscious—is something Gittins observed in his own life many years ago. As a young man he played football, both offensive and defensive positions. He has spoken more than once about the contrast between playing the two sides, the one more systematic and the other responsive, and the analogy to his painting, a fusion of conscious thought and subconscious reaction.

For more than ten years, Gittins has been exhibiting with a group of artists known as the New New Painters, with whom he shares an interest in abstraction, new materials, unorthodox processes, and high-key color. *Gray's Mirror,* an example of an early point in Gittins's evolution, was made when he began associating with the group. It is more subdued in its palette than the bright, contrasting colors of much of his later work. There is clear figure-ground delineation, the background of pale gray craquelure and the black foreground conjuring images as diverse as Chinese calligraphy or the skeleton of an arthropod. The central figure exhibits an anthropomorphic quality and a sense of movement as well, as if it is in the process of either dissolving or coming together or even emerging out of a gray mist. SS

1. This and subsequent quotations, John Gittins, telephone conversation with author, 17 January 1999. This entry is excerpted from an essay that originally appeared in Sue Scott, *The New New Painters,* exh. cat. (Flint, Mich.: Flint Institute of Arts, 1999).

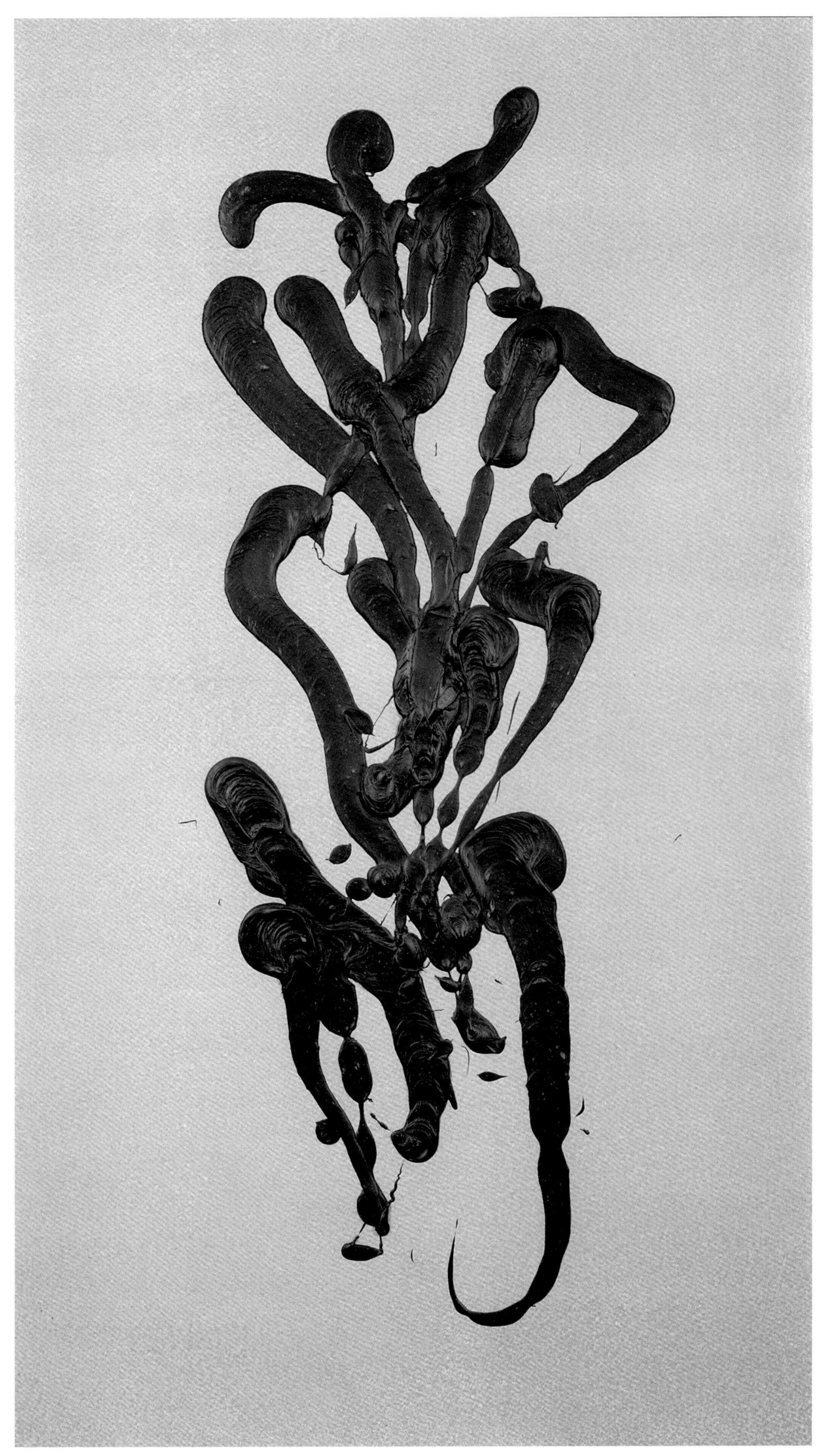

Jerald Webster AMERICAN BORN 1953

124 | *Rites of Spring,* 1992

Acrylic on canvas, 42¼ × 78⅜ in.

Titled, dated, and signed on verso: *Rites of Spring 1992, Jerald Webster*

Gift of the artist (2001.2)

Jerald Webster grew up on a farm in upstate New York, and in his paintings one can see the landscapes he knew as a child—a purity of light and color and an allusion to earth and sky are evident in even the most abstract of his works. Visiting the Albright-Knox Art Gallery in Buffalo as a teenager, he was drawn to the paintings of Henri Matisse and Hans Hofmann as well as to those by Clyfford Still and many of the other Abstract Expressionists. He saw in their work an extraordinary beauty made possible through the language of abstraction. He knew if he were to pursue a career in art, that was the language he wanted to speak.

While attending Syracuse University in the early 1970s, he became interested in the work of Morris Louis, Friedel Dzubas, Kenneth Noland, Jules Olitski, and Jack Bush. Their ability to express the sublime through pure color in simple compositions struck a chord with Webster, and their work continues to inspire him today. He also began reading the writings of Clement Greenberg, who gave him a critical and philosophical framework for understanding art. "Greenberg's writing," he says, "matched intuitively what my eyes had been telling me all along."[1] It was also at Syracuse that he met fellow student Steve Brent and the visiting artist Joseph Drapell, both of whom had aesthetic interests similar to Webster's and who would eventually exhibit with him as members of the New New Painters. Later, working on his own outside the artistic milieu of New York City, his only confidant and critic was Drapell.

Webster begins a work without a preconceived notion of what he wants to paint. "I make all my decisions on the spot," he said. "I want to make the painting as spontaneous as I can." Within this spontaneity, however, is a certain amount of conscious decision-making or, as he sees it, "focused improvisation." The first layer is like a drawing in which he configures angles, hard edges, and points with tape, changing and responding to each shape until the final composition is satisfactory. Next he stains these shapes different colors, intuitively choosing the hues as he moves through the composition. The top layers are again like drawing, this time textured marks of color against the stained hard-edged background. Webster first used acrylic gels when he was attending a Triangle Artists Workshop class in 1986, in Pine Plains, New York, turning to the medium as a way of getting color that was more concrete and physical. Metallic and reflective additives were later used to get an even more varied and tactile surface. In the end, it is drawing, whether stained areas of color or surface marks, that provides the composition's overall structure and space.

After painting in an abstract mode for more than twenty years, Webster has grown proficient in its language even as he reinvents it. Yet one realizes it is not so much a new language as it is a particularly American dialect, in which one can discern the influence of not only the Abstract Expressionists and Color Field painters but the clean lines of Charles Sheeler and the bold, pure colors and drawing of Marsden Hartley. "As much as I love the elegance of Color Field painting, there is a certain amount of inherent awkwardness to my paintings," says Webster. "I'm a farm boy at heart." SS

1. This and subsequent quotations, Jerald Webster, telephone conversation with author, 13 December 1998. This entry is excerpted from an essay that originally appeared in Sue Scott, *The New New Painters,* exh. cat. (Flint, Mich.: Flint Institute of Arts, 1999).

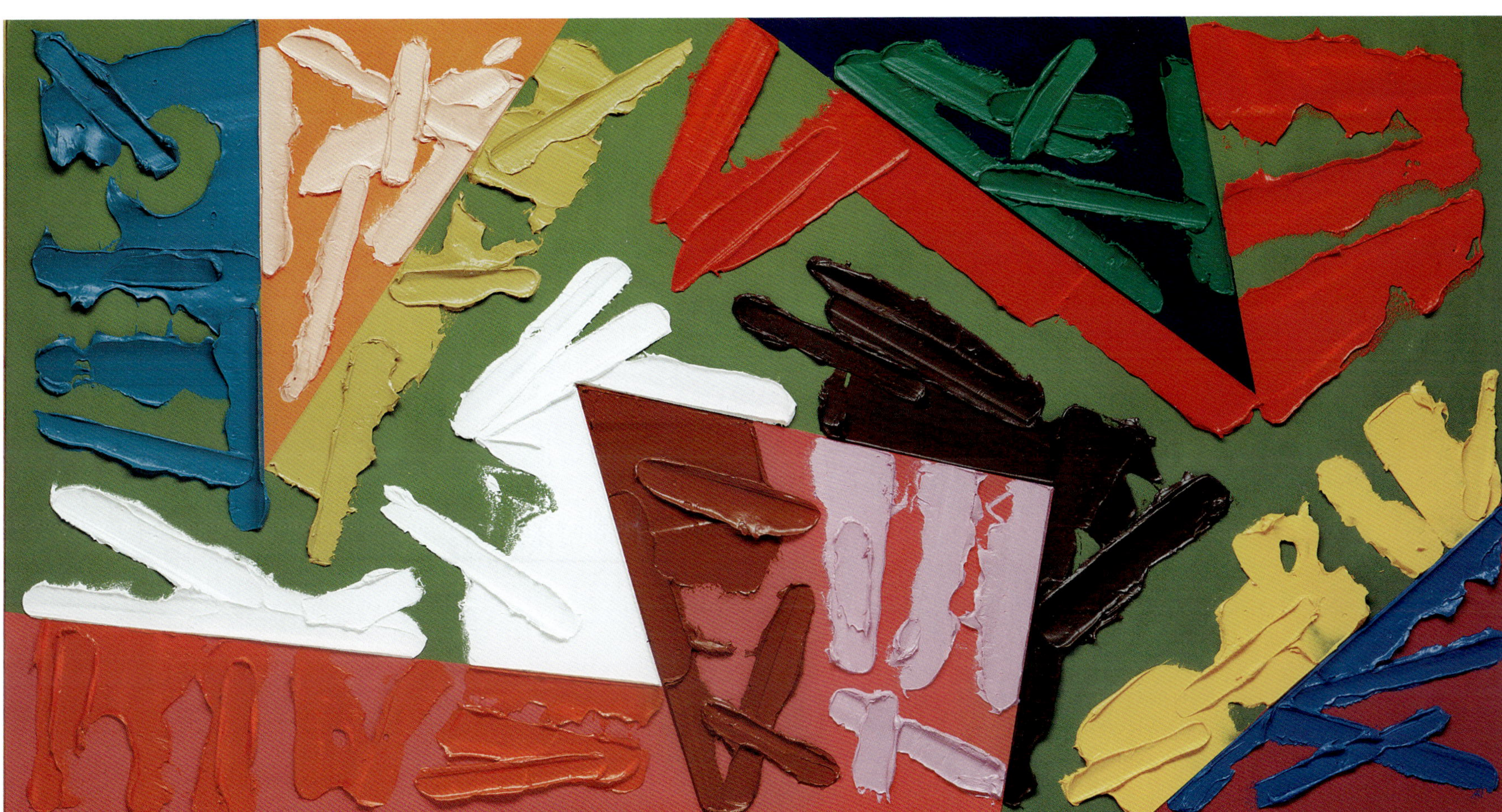

Marjorie Minkin AMERICAN BORN 1941

125 | *Anu*, 1997

Acrylic on Lexan, 96 × 60 × 12 in.

Signed, dated, and titled on verso: © *Marjorie Minkin, 1997, Anu*

Anonymous gift (2000.25)

As a Boston native, Marjorie Minkin had frequented the Museum of Fine Arts since childhood. But it was a visit in the early 1970s—when she saw an exhibition of *Unfurleds*, Morris Louis's series of paintings—that changed both the way she looked at and made art. She knew Louis had been deeply influenced by the critic Clement Greenberg, with whose writing she was also familiar, but the exposure to Louis's work caused her to delve more deeply into Greenberg's writings.

Although Minkin was already working abstractly on unprimed canvas with thinned acrylic paint, as did Louis and other Color Field painters, she was cognizant that her work did not fit neatly into that category—it had discrete shapes, value differentiation, and clear delineation between figure and ground, all of which fell outside the standard formalist practice of the movement. Interestingly, one can see in these early works, which have the diaphanous, flowing quality of Louis's *Veil* and *Ambi* series of the late 1950s, the interest in light and sculptural form that would come to define her mature work.

Minkin eventually became acquainted with Greenberg through Kenworth Moffett, former curator of twentieth-century art at the Museum of Fine Arts, when she was invited by Moffett to accompany him on two days of studio visits in Toronto in 1981. It was also through Moffett that Minkin met two other members of the New New Painters, Jerald Webster and John Gittins, who share with Minkin an interest in abstraction, high-keyed colors, textured surfaces, and new materials. The three artists have exhibited together internationally since 1992. The following summer she met Greenberg again at the inaugural session of the Triangle Artists Workshop, held in Pine Plains, New York. Both meetings offered a lesson in how to look at painting. Although the artist and the writer often disagreed on aesthetics, the two events marked the beginning of a relationship with Greenberg, one of the most powerful critics of the twentieth century, which lasted until his death, in 1994.

At the time, Minkin was working with a custom tool, layering colors in a diagonal shape against an elongated rectangular canvas, continuing her interest placing a "figure" against a ground. Greenberg questioned her use of space and encouraged her to work directly with the shape on a diamond-shaped canvas. She subsequently returned to a traditional rectangular format, but it is clear that the exercise was crucial for her later work with a polycarbonate plastic, a background material that provided both shape and surface relief. Initially, she layered partially painted plastic sheets over painted canvas but by 1987 had begun constructing pieces of free-form, molded Lexan. Lexan, an industrial plastic used in ships, skyscrapers, and airplanes, provided Minkin the opportunity to experiment with both space and light.

Although she has been influenced by contemporary theory and relies on modern materials, Minkin's aesthetic is also grounded in a classical sensibility. In her fifth year at the Museum School in Boston, she was awarded a travel fellowship, which she used to visit Northern Italy and the south of France, later traveling to Greece. Her exposure to the surface and texture of frescoes, the drapery of classical Greek sculpture, and the light-filled environment of the churches, chapels, and temples was to have a lasting effect.

Minkin's references are at once figurative, architectonic, and even geologic. *Anu* can be read as both figure and landscape, shaped like a torso but with an energetic surface treatment that emphasizes its topography. "It is about nature, the forest and the feminine element in nature," noted Minkin. "The name refers to an ancestor goddess of Ireland known as a force of prosperity and abundance. Anu may also be the same goddess as Aine or Danu."[1]

Like other members of the New New Painters, Minkin has found her métier through the use of contemporary materials. At the same time, it is clear her work is not just about new materials but the use of the material as a means to an end. As a result, Minkin has created a body of work that alludes to space while capturing an impression of transitory light and color. SS

1. Marjorie Minkin, e-mail to author, 29 July 2002. This entry is excerpted from an essay that originally appeared in Sue Scott, *The New New Painters*, exh. cat. (Flint, Mich.: Flint Institute of Arts, 1999).

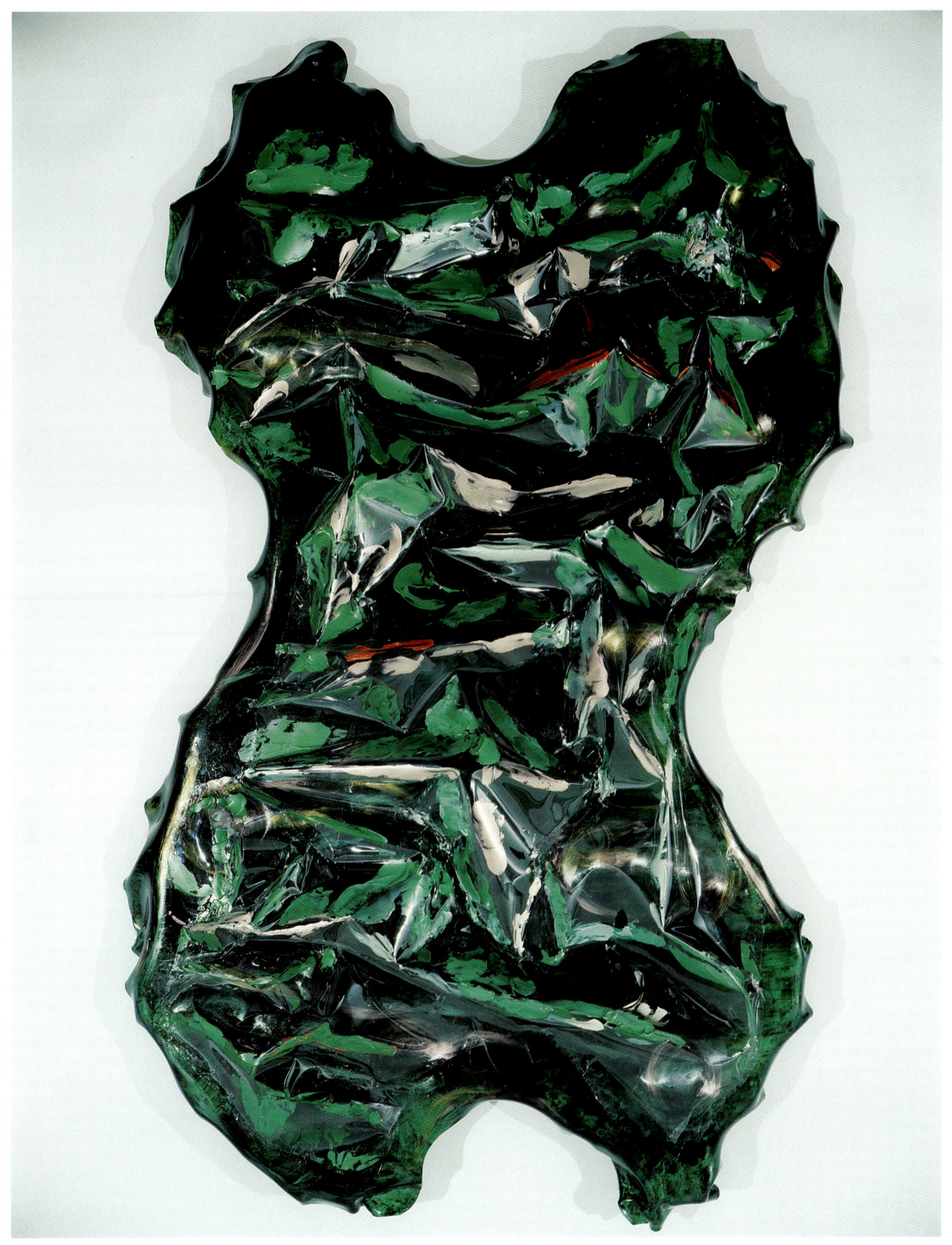

Robert Rohm AMERICAN BORN 1934

126 | *Untitled (Caged Core),* 2001–2

Steel, mesh, and encaustic, 85½ × 11 × 11 in.

Unsigned

Gift of Marilynn and Ivan C. Karp (2002.15)

For forty years, Robert Rohm has been making sculptures that, as he once noted, examine the "fundamental aspects of sculpture."[1] Rohm studied art at Pratt Institute in Brooklyn, New York, and earned his master's degree from the Cranbrook Academy of Art in Bloomfield Hills, Michigan, in 1960, and he came to artistic maturity during the following decade, when Minimalism, Process Art, and Earth Art were the defining movements. Rohm's early sculpture reflects these influences, particularly in the way the artist has experimented with a wide range of industrial materials and in his use of simple forms. In the evolution of his mature work, however, Rohm has gone beyond his contemporaries to examine the history of sculpture, particularly artists and movements of the twentieth century. He has drawn freely from such diverse movements as Surrealism, abstraction, figuration, and Minimalism as well as from numerous international cultures.

Rohm, who has been a professor at the University of Rhode Island since 1965, was awarded grants by the National Endowment for the Arts in 1974 and 1987. The latter grant, combined with a sabbatical from teaching, provided an opportunity for him to travel to such exotic places as India, Burma, Thailand, Japan, Hawaii, and eastern Africa. The expedition not only awakened an interest in the figure, but it resulted in Rohm's examination of social issues and the human condition, an intellectual component that had been excised from Minimalist aesthetics. If his early work brought to mind assemblage art with a Surrealist element—a slanted tabletop or a ladder balanced on a chair—the work executed after his time abroad became more figuratively based, often with oblique references to social or emotional commentary. "I tend to think of the human figure as a container," Rohm observed of this change in artistic direction, "and this is one of the links between my new work and what I've done in the past. Yes, there's a darker side to these sculptures, but I'd like to think they're open enough to elicit other meanings."[2]

The new sculpture was exhibited at the O. K. Harris Gallery in New York in the spring of 2002 as part of a series of large-scale works made from steel, mesh, and encaustic. Consisting of vertical armatures of steel and mesh that encase abstract shapes, the sculpture addresses both formal and conceptual issues. Formally, Rohm investigates interior and exterior spaces, bringing to mind work as diverse as Barbara Hepworth's and Henry Moore's, while his notions of containment and figuration function on a psychological plane within a Surrealist context. Indeed, on a formal level, Rohm plays with traditional sculpture by placing the armature on the exterior, thus making the viewer privy to interior spaces. At the same time, the armature exists as a cage that confines the "figure," adding a psychological component to the work. In this way, Rohm integrates formal elements of several diverse influences, merging traditional figurative sculpture with the psychology of the Surrealists while using the industrial materials of the Minimalists. In an artist's statement accompanying the O. K. Harris exhibition, Rohm observed:

> I am interested in the "figure" as a relationship of parts, as a vessel or container. Can the figure be "present" through the manipulation of the forms of its shell or covering and can the core of the self be exposed as being present, in the process of departing, or absent? Can that form or combination of forms have compelling resonance while being familiar and unknown at the same time? The sculptures come from a distillation and synthesis of complex and overlapping feelings about the self and are meant to elicit reflective and contemplative responses in the viewer.[3]

SS

1. Quoted in Kenneth Baker, "Art: Rohm's Rhapsody in Rope," *Boston Phoenix,* 12 December 1972, p. 14.

2. Quoted in Bill Van Siclen, "Travel Gave Shape to Rohm's Work," *Providence Sunday Journal,* 6 March 1988, p. I-3.

3. Artist's statement, O. K. Harris Gallery, March 2002.

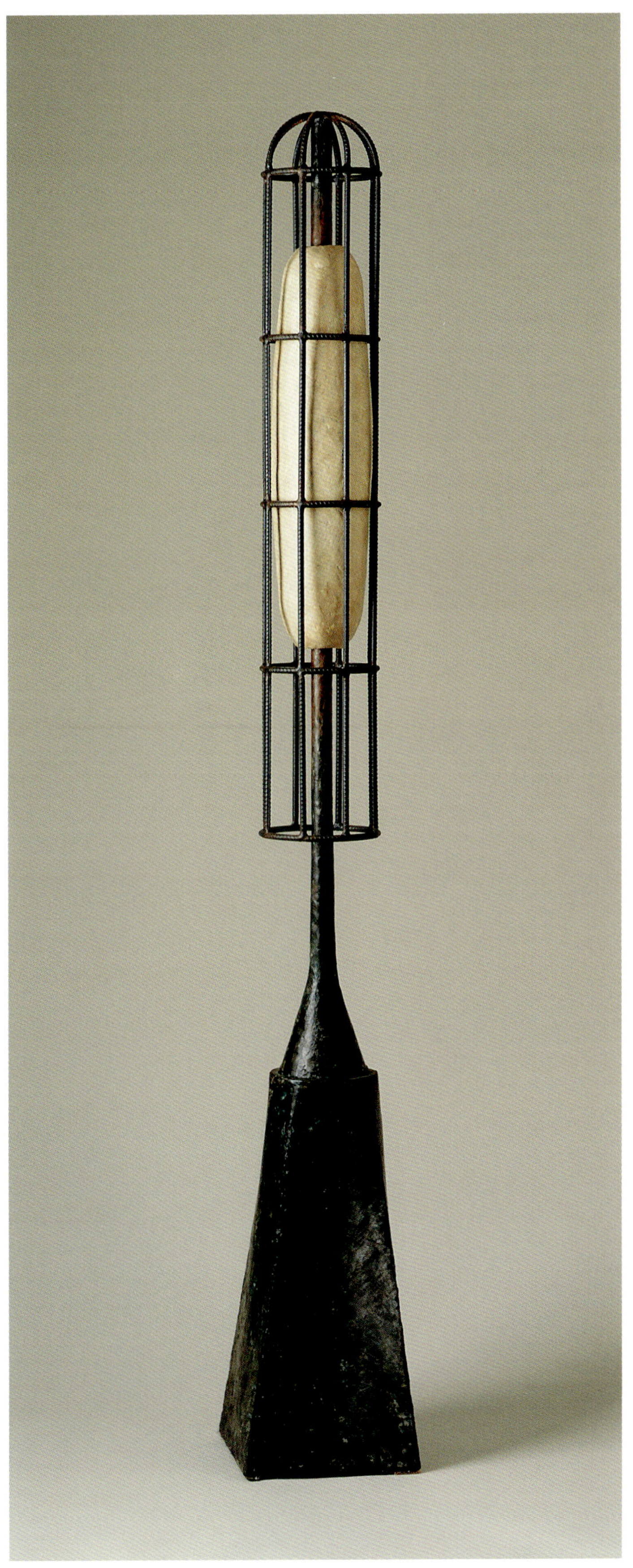

Chakaia Booker AMERICAN BORN 1953

127 | *India Blue,* 2001

Rubber, tires, and wood, 73 × 43 × 38 in.

Unsigned

Bequest of Russell J. Cameron, by exchange, and partial gift from the Friends of Modern Art (2002.11)

Chakaia Booker creates monumental and personal sculptures using old tires from automobiles, trucks, motorcycles, and bicycles. Arising from the tradition of assemblage, Booker's work is infused with a personal vision that takes it beyond mere abstraction or the use of unconventional materials. An African American, Booker finds inspiration in her cultural background; in her hands, the mundane material rubber, mounted on armatures of wood or metal, is cut, shredded, curled, nailed, and otherwise manipulated into visual metaphors that speak of identity, ritual, sexuality, and masking.

Even the color of the rubber is seen by Booker as symbolic. As Charlotta Kotik has noted, "Booker also relates the 'blackness' of her pieces to the issues of black identity—it is a symbolic color of her own heritage. And just as Booker challenges our preconceived notions that tires are uniformly black, she encourages us to reexamine our other assumptions around the complex meaning of the word 'black.'"[1] The extension of this idea is particularly apparent when comparing shades of black within a single sculpture or shades in different works. Under the rubric "black" can be seen hues ranging from deep blues and browns to grays. Dark ebony may be threaded with red or green or naturally "decorated" with pieces of glass and tiny rocks. "Rubber is not new, of course," Booker notes, "but I think I process and construct it in a new way. I see it more monumentally, more sculpturally, more archeologically. The different textures are important to me, the colors, the smells."[2]

Born in Newark, New Jersey, Booker grew up in a family that encouraged all forms of artistic expression. Her grandmother, aunt, and sister designed and sewed unique outfits, and when Booker first explored her creativity it was in the form of wearable art and jewelry. She makes herself an extension of her art, expressing her identification with it by wearing elaborate headdresses and colorful robes, incorporating African patterns in her own custom-designed materials. Booker studied sociology at Rutgers University, where she earned a bachelor's degree in the subject in 1976. In 1993 she received a master's degree in fine art from City College in New York. Today, sociological investigation still forms the foundation of much of her work.

Initially, Booker made baskets, and her ceramics were on a sculptural scale. Feeling a need to be more experimental while increasing the size of her work, she looked to castoffs from junkyards and construction sites—old chairs, wood, cabinets. But discarded tires had a particular resonance. "I liked how they could be adapted, how I could make different shapes out of them, how they could be indoors and how I could bring them back outdoors. Rubber is primary for me. It's necessary to my vision, but in the end, the materials I use depend on the work I'm doing."[3] Although she had been dubbed "the Queen of Rubber Soul,"[4] Booker explores other materials, for example bones and fruits, as well as other genres such as landscape painting. Nevertheless, it is for her monumental rubber sculptures that she first received acclaim, particularly at the 2000 Whitney Biennial and the groundbreaking *Greater New York* exhibition the same year at P.S. 1 in Queens, New York.

In accordance with the tradition of assemblage and found objects, one of Booker's objectives is for the material to transcend itself. *India Blue* is a beautiful example of Booker's ability to transform her medium into a work that speaks of growth and movement, an organic form that can at once be a mass of entwined flowers and vines, a knot of seaweed flowing through the water, or a headdress spilling out layers of entwined dreadlocks. SS

1. Charlotta Kotik, *Chakaia Booker: New Sculptures*, exh. cat. (New York: Marlborough Galleries, 2001), p. 4.

2. Quoted in Lilly Wei, "Queen of Rubber Soul," *Artnews* 101 (January 2002), p. 88.

3. Ibid., p. 90.

4. Ibid., p. 88.

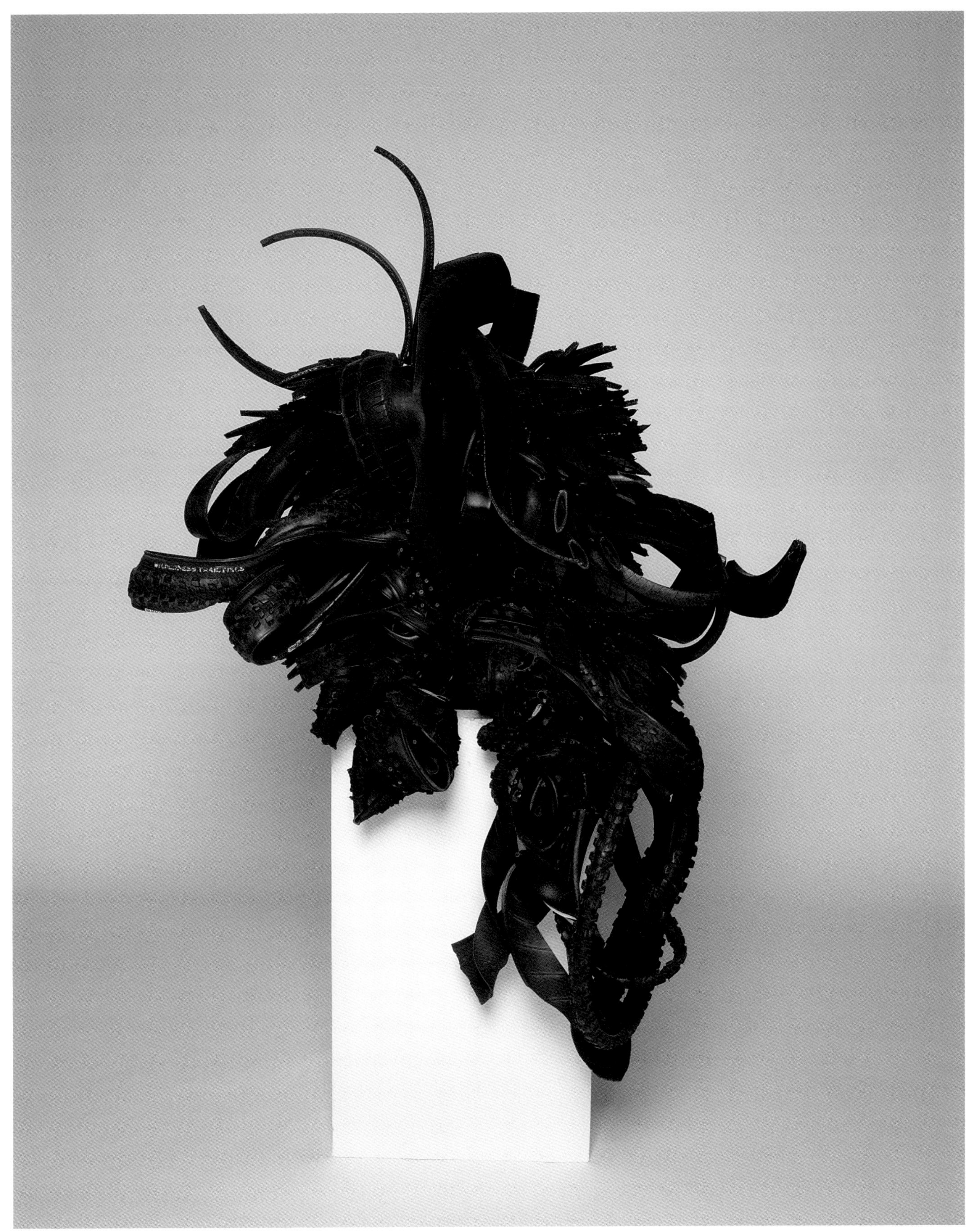

Nabil Nahas AMERICAN, BORN LEBANON 1949

128 | *A Carnation for Rimbaud,* 1998

Acrylic on canvas, 36 × 36 in.

Signed on verso: *N. R. Nahas*

Gift of the American Academy of Arts and Letters, New York; Hassam, Speicher, Betts and Symons Funds (2002.17)

In his art, Nabil Nahas draws from a rich Islamic heritage, an understanding of French art and literature, and a fascination with the progression of abstract painting in the history of contemporary art. Born in Beirut, Lebanon, Nahas lived there and in Cairo until he was twenty, at which time he moved to the United States to go to college. He graduated from Louisiana State University in 1971 with a bachelor's degree in fine art and in 1973 earned his master's degree in fine art from Yale University. While at Yale, Nahas studied with the abstract painter Al Held, so it is not surprising that much of his early work explored variations in geometric abstraction. His time in Beirut, where the connections to France and Europe are strong, instilled in Nahas a cultural awareness that informs his art to this day.

In the late 1990s Nahas began making paintings that presented an overall textured field made by combining acrylic paint with powdered pumice, a volcanic rock. The abstract forms, which were less hard-edged and more organic than earlier in his career, were inspired by a walk along the beach in Southampton, New York, where he saw hundreds of starfish that had been washed up by a storm. He perceived in nature's pattern a naturally occurring geometry and began using the shapes in his painting, first imprinting casts of starfish into a thick layer of white paint, which he used as a foundation over which to build up a sculptural texture of color and form.

Nahas applies the paint in small dabs or clusters, creating color and form simultaneously. Space is not only implied, it is real—the sculptural depth of the painting varies from two to three inches. An active gardener, Nahas finds inspiration in nature. His choice of palette in his paintings is often high keyed and contrasting, but it is always taken from the natural world. The resulting colorful, organic abstractions, which bring to mind rich images ranging from encrusted reefs and underwater sponges to elaborate Islamic decoration, were a breakthrough for the artist and were hailed by the critic Roberta Smith as "the best of his career."[1]

Nahas mixes up ideas of abstraction, science, and nature. One thinks of Jackson Pollock's overall skeins, where the paint splatters across the canvas, edge to edge. Yet although they cover every inch of the canvas, Nahas's abstractions speak less of an eruption of paint than they do of slow growth, like the evolution of a coral reef. There is a considered repetition of form in the painting *A Carnation for Rimbaud,* in which the same flowerlike shape recurs across the picture plane. These fractals, or irregular geometric shapes, differ just slightly from one to the next, just as the same kind of flower varies slightly in nature. Nahas often uses titles from literature or science. This work, which refers to the French Symbolist poet Arthur Rimbaud, has an elegiac, almost Victorian, quality that calls to mind dried petals—it is at once an abstract field of repeated images and a blueprint from nature. SS

1. Roberta Smith, "Art in Review: Nabil Nahas," *New York Times,* 17 January 1997, p. C27.

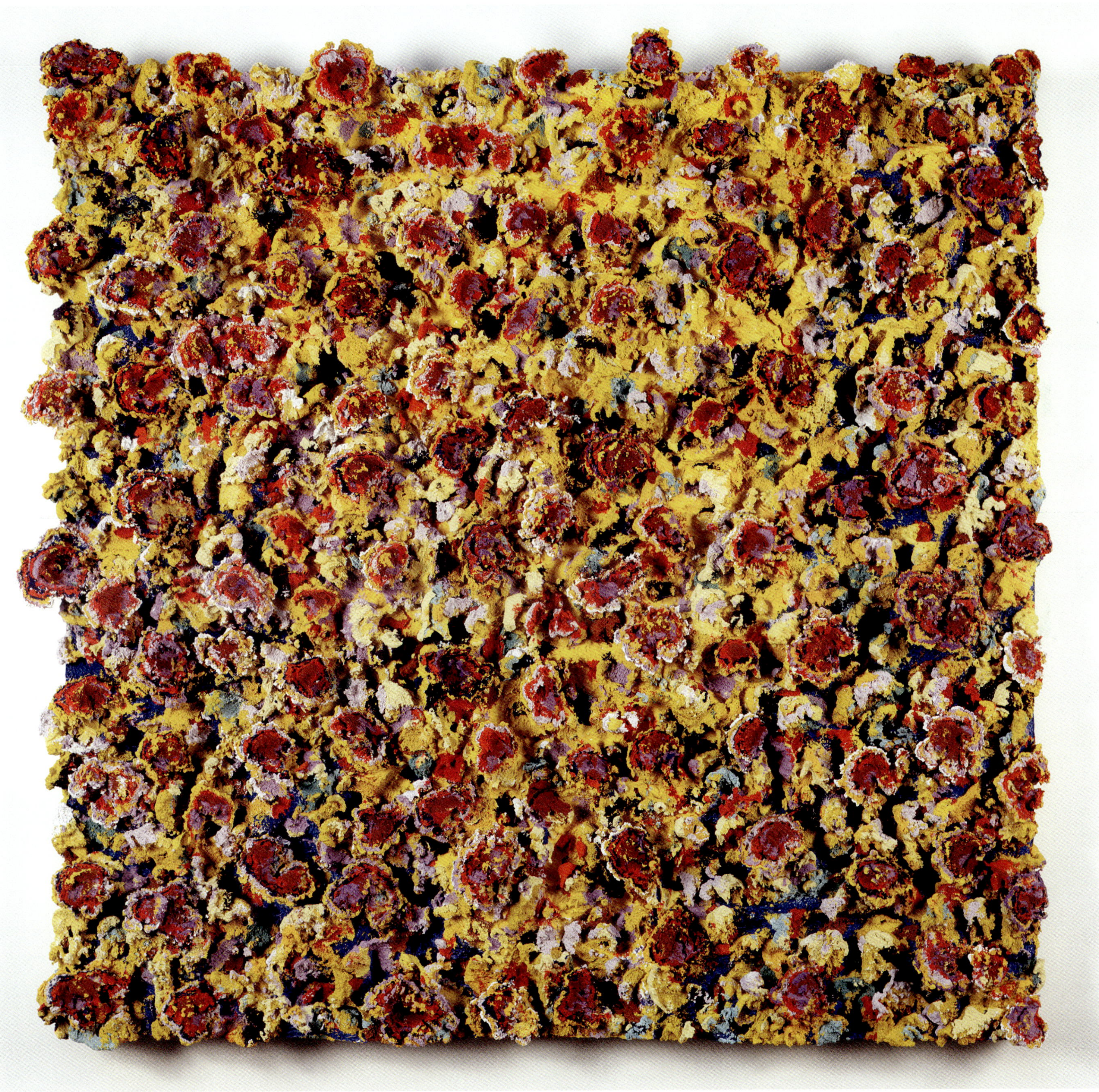

Whitfield Lovell AMERICAN BORN 1959

129 | *Epoch*, 2001

Charcoal on wood with found objects, 77½ × 55 × 17½ in.

Signed, titled, and dated on verso: *Whitfield Lovell, Epoch, 2001*

Gift of Mr. and Mrs. William L. Richards, by exchange (2002.13)

Whitfield Lovell fuses his African American heritage with training in contemporary art to create works that speak of collective memory and personal experience. The result is "tableaux," or assemblages, that combine beautiful charcoal drawings rendered on wallboard with related sculptural objects—old bottles, vases, glass lanterns, or shabby furniture—found at flea markets and rummage sales. The drawings have their source in late-nineteenth- and early-twentieth-century photographs. An accomplished draftsman, Lovell captures the emotion and immediacy of the photographs while infusing the images with an aura of nostalgia. Initially some photos were of family members (his father was an avid amateur photographer), but the recent past has seen him use unknown faces taken from anonymous portraits unearthed in archives or found at flea markets or in junk shops.

Born in the Bronx, New York, Lovell has spent most of his life in and around New York City. His mother hailed from South Carolina, and from an early age Lovell visited the South, where he was not only fascinated by the rural culture but also struck by the separation between blacks and whites.[1] This heritage, and his growing sociological awareness, inspired an ongoing investigation that today forms the conceptual foundation of Lovell's work.

Lovell's attraction to art, which began when he was in junior high school, deepened in 1972, when he enrolled at the Fiorella LaGuardia High School of Music and Art in Manhattan. There his focus turned to creative writing and poetry. His interest in painting was revitalized during a visit in 1977 to the Museo del Prado in Madrid. Lovell briefly attended the Maryland Institute College of Art but, seeking a more urban environment, left to enroll at the Cooper Union School of Art in New York City, from which he graduated with a bachelor's degree in 1981. In 1995, while participating in an artist's residency program at Rice University in Houston, he began making drawings on board and combining them with found objects. The first of these works, the site-specific installation *Echo*, was created in an abandoned shotgun house. Drawn directly on the walls, these images take on a mystical presence, as if conjuring ghosts from a distant past.

The narrative quality in Lovell's work reflects his interest in history, literature, and poetry. Of the present work, he notes:

> The image in *Epoch* is taken from an old tattered photograph of a World War I soldier. For some time now I have been interested in the contradictions surrounding the role of African Americans in the military and particularly in the Civil War and WW I. Enlisting in the military gave many young Black men an opportunity to see the world and also provided employment during times when opportunities were rarely available to them in the United States. They were however, fighting for a democracy, which they were themselves denied. Many soldiers experienced scorn upon their return, because it was not considered appropriate to honor an African American along with the white war heroes.[2]

Epoch is executed on wallboards taken from the interiors of old houses in Texas. The muslin strips attached to the planks are what remains of the insulating layer of fabric that was stretched and nailed across the walls. Nail holes and paint stains add to the texture of the surfaces. Lovell prefers to leave such remnants intact and works them into the composition. The flowers, handmade in silk and other fabrics, have a faded quality that refers to the passage of time, adding an elegiac quality to the work. "I was attracted to this image because of the very chiseled features of the young man and the elegance of his pose. The way his ankles are crossed imply a sort of gentility and decorum while the stubby cigar in his left hand, the crumpled uniform, and worn boots suggest ruggedness." On a shelf are nine volumes of *Great Epochs in American History* from a set found in a junk shop, which Lovell felt added a poignant reference for "the incongruity of this slice of history." "Actually," he notes, "the text inside of these books which related to African Americans was so disturbing that I could have done a piece with the books opened, which would have broadened the irony in the piece, but I felt it was more eloquent to follow my original plan." SS

1. Lilly Wei, "The Tableaux of Whitfield Lovell," in *Whitfield Lovell Portrayals*, exh. cat. (Purchase, N.Y.: Neuberger Museum of Art, Purchase College, State University of New York, 1998), p. 10.

2. This and subsequent quotations, Whitfield Lovell, e-mail to author, 9 April 2002.

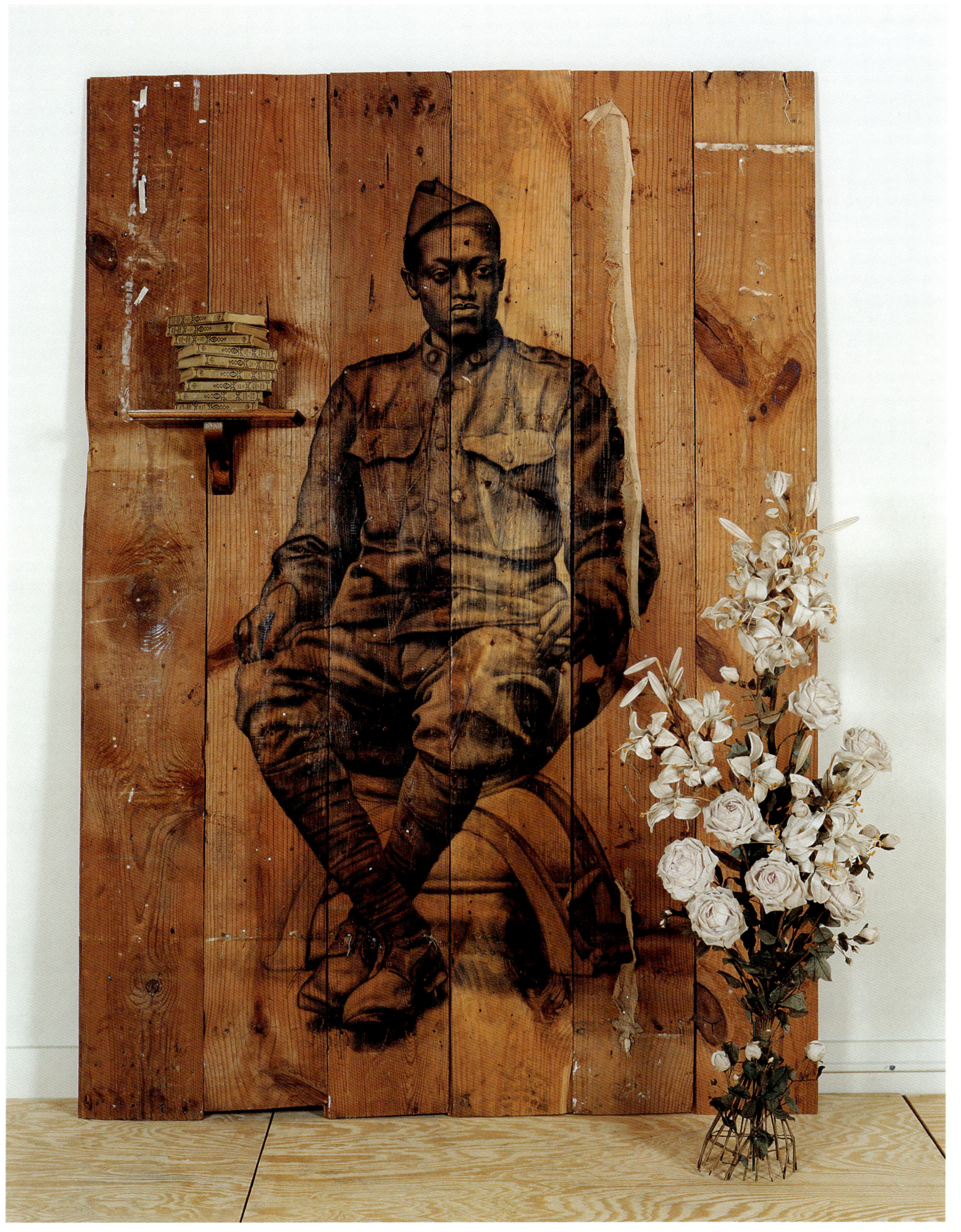

Robert Gniewek AMERICAN BORN 1951

130 | *The Stone Burlesk,* 1998

Oil on linen, 14 × 22 in.

Signed lower right: *Gniewek*

Museum purchase (2000.69)

The second-generation Photorealist Robert Gniewek has lived in Michigan his entire life. He earned his bachelor's degree in fine art from Wayne State University in 1973, but it was not until he began working on his master's degree, also at Wayne State University (he graduated in 1979), that he became interested in Photorealism, particularly the work of Richard Estes. Today, Gniewek, who lives in Dearborn, exhibits internationally. Most significantly, he has shown with Louis Meisel, the progenitor of Photorealism, since the early 1990s and was included in Meisel's important survey book, *Photorealism since 1980*.[1]

Like all Photorealists, Gniewek's work begins with the camera. He may take as many as a thousand photographs for a single series, selecting various sites that interest him and shooting them from different angles and vantage points. Because Gniewek is interested in nightscapes, most of his photography takes place in the dark; he uses a tripod and changes the exposures to ensure a range of lights and darks.

The first day of work in the studio begins with projecting the image from a slide and penciling in the composition. Once that process is complete, Gniewek makes several prints from the slides, selecting different exposures and varied viewpoints of the same image, which he uses for reference. The result is what Gniewek calls a "composite" taken from many sources. He may additionally augment or heighten the color. As he notes, the goal is not slavishly to reproduce the photograph but to "make an interesting painting" both formally and conceptually.[2]

The Stone Burlesk is part of the *Detroit Theatre* series Gniewek executed in 1997–98, a group of paintings that have as their subject old theaters in and around Detroit. He initially photographed the source images for *The Stone Burlesk* in the early 1980s, when he painted an earlier version. The theater was torn down sometime in the mid-1990s, so Gniewek had to rely on the slides from his previous series for the later painting.

"This work is typical of the subject matter I've been dealing with for twenty years," says Gniewek, "consisting of city landscapes and old buildings, with all of their character, color, and light." He is particularly drawn to buildings with neon lights within the nightscapes, noting that "Neon signs were an integral part of American cities from the '30s, '40s, '50s, and '60s, but now they are literally fading from the landscape."[3] This painting is a poignant reminder of that disappearance. In its contrasting neon lights and dark shadows, the work brings to mind the stark realism and underlying loneliness of a painting by Edward Hopper. The scene is deserted, with only a fragment of a truck in the shadows to indicate a human presence. Nevertheless, the bright lights and oversized neon sign beckon the viewer. SS

1. Louis Meisel, *Photorealism Since 1980* (New York: Harry N. Abrams, 1993).

2. Robert Gniewek, telephone conversation with author, 21 August 2002.

3. Ibid.

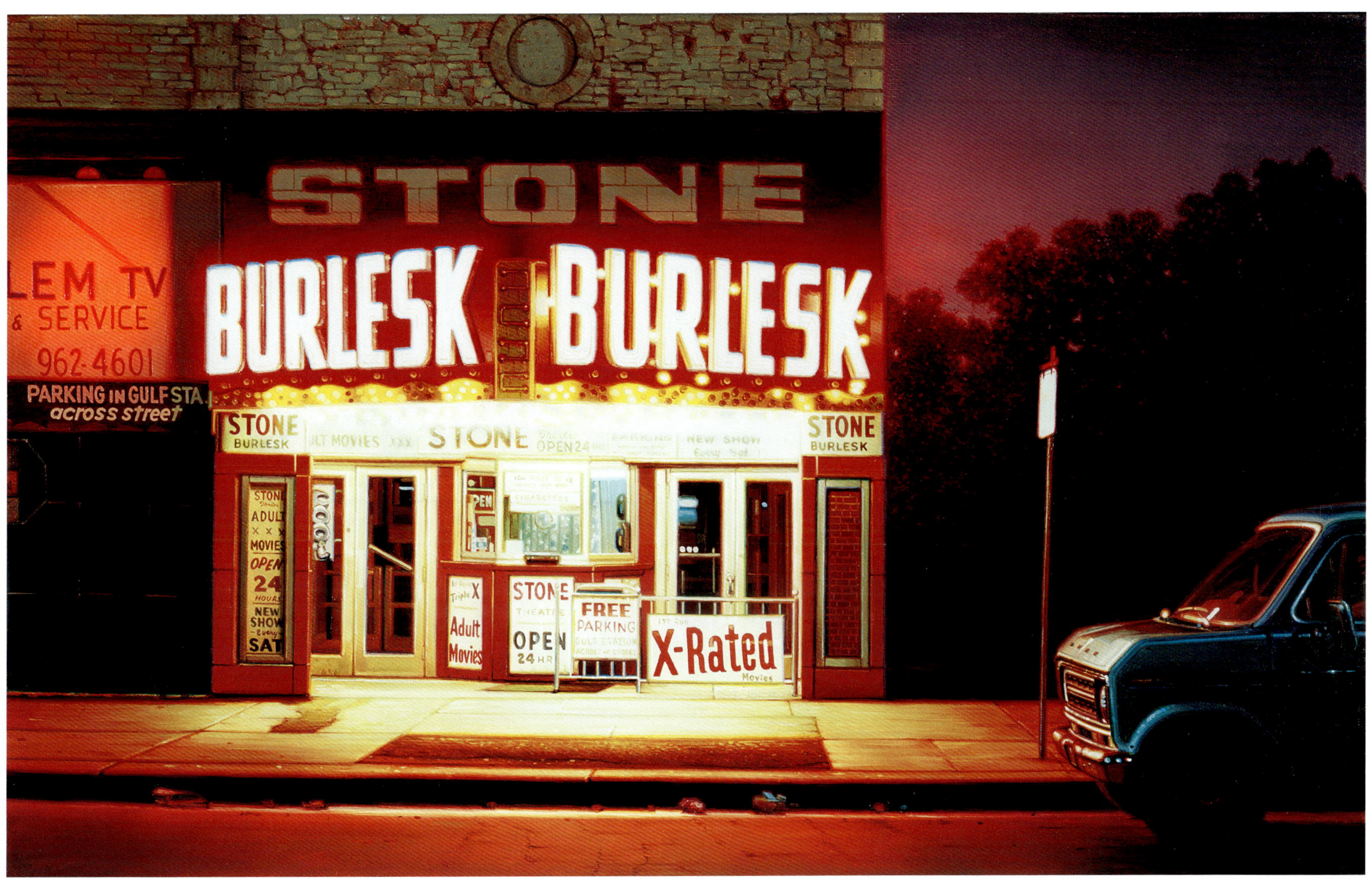
STONE
BURLESK
BURLESK
LEM TV
& SERVICE
962-4601
PARKING IN GULF STA.
across street
STONE
BURLESK
STONE
NEW SHOW
STONE
BURLESK
ADULT
MOVIES
OPEN
24
NEW
SHOW
SAT
Adult
Movies
STONE
OPEN
24 HRS
FREE
PARKING
X-Rated

Ralph Goings AMERICAN BORN 1928

131 | *Half and Half Creamer,* 2000

Oil on canvas, 15¾ × 15¾

Signed and dated lower right: *Goings 2000*

Gift of the Friends of Modern Art (2002.9)

One of the most well known of the original group of Photorealists, Ralph Goings has been making his highly detailed, photo-based paintings for more than three decades. Like his Photorealist counterparts who surfaced in the late 1960s and early 1970s, Goings first studied art in the 1950s, when abstraction was at its height of influence. Receiving his bachelor's degree in fine art from the California College of Arts and Crafts in Oakland in 1953, he taught art in high school and college, and in 1966 earned his master's degree in fine art from the California State University at Sacramento. Even when he painted abstractly as a young artist, it is telling that Goings used photographs from magazines to inspire the composition.

In the mid-1960s Goings began photographing and then painting the pickup trucks that abounded in Northern California. These trucks were not the beat-up vehicles of John Steinbeck's Depression-era California but the shiny new symbols of suburban status and identity. Perhaps the influence of such Pop artists as Andy Warhol and Roy Lichtenstein, who emerged in the early 1960s and took inspiration from commercial advertising, helped Goings to break from abstraction and into this new territory of rendering the world around him. He found himself not only attracted to the variety of shapes, colors, and models of trucks but even more to the concept of painting from a photograph. "I wanted to paint from a flat, two-dimensional surface. There was something there that interested me in the way images looked that were derived from a photograph as opposed to reality."[1]

The highly detailed, beautifully executed paintings of vehicles were introduced to the New York audience at an exhibition at the O.K. Harris gallery in 1970. In 1975, looking for a change of pace and scenery, Goings moved with his family to a farm community in upstate New York, where he lives today. With these new surroundings came different subject matter, which seemed to follow a logical trajectory from trucks to the exteriors of supermarkets and diners where they were parked and, finally, to an investigation of the interiors of such structures. Today, Goings is as known for his still-life paintings of catsup bottles, sugar dispensers, creamers, and salt and pepper shakers as he is for the classic trucks of the 1970s.

As with his fellow Photorealists, photography is the departure point for each of Goings's paintings. He may take hundreds of photographs of a subject before selecting the final image, which is then developed as a slide that is projected onto a canvas. Although in the beginning, he used only "found" compositions, he has recently taken to arranging, lighting, and photographing his own created setups. After meticulously drawing the projected image in pencil, the artist begins the laborious process of transferring the composition, often unedited, to the canvas. A large print made from the slide is hung next to the paintings for reference.

It is interesting to consider Goings vis-à-vis the proliferation of fine art photographers in the late 1990s, many of whom also turned their lens to aspects of banality in Middle America. Photography is in some form a presentation of reality, either real or constructed. Goings's paintings are twice removed from the reality presented by these photographers, having gone through the process of transcription by the artist's brush. It takes longer to read one of his paintings than it does a photograph because the viewer is not only engaged with the image but also with Goings's virtuosity in rendering it.

Half and Half Creamer is a simple yet beautiful example of Goings's gift for verisimilitude. The background consists of two horizontal bands of color, one gray, the other black. The references are to both landscape painting and Minimalism, yet the gray Formica tabletop is rendered with subtle shadows and reflections that distance it from the flatness preferred by the Minimalists. A simple stainless-steel creamer sits solidly in the center of the composition, occupying three-dimensional space, while light shining on it reflects an abstract pattern of luminosity and color. Many Photorealists eschew particular readings of their paintings, but this simple object brings to mind a very specific, yet universal place: the American diner. Singled out, it becomes almost iconic. As Goings once observed: "My paintings are all about me and the world I live in."[2] SS

1. Quoted in Jane Cottingham, "Techniques of Three Photo-Realists," *American Artist* 44 (February 1980), p. 64.

2. Ibid.

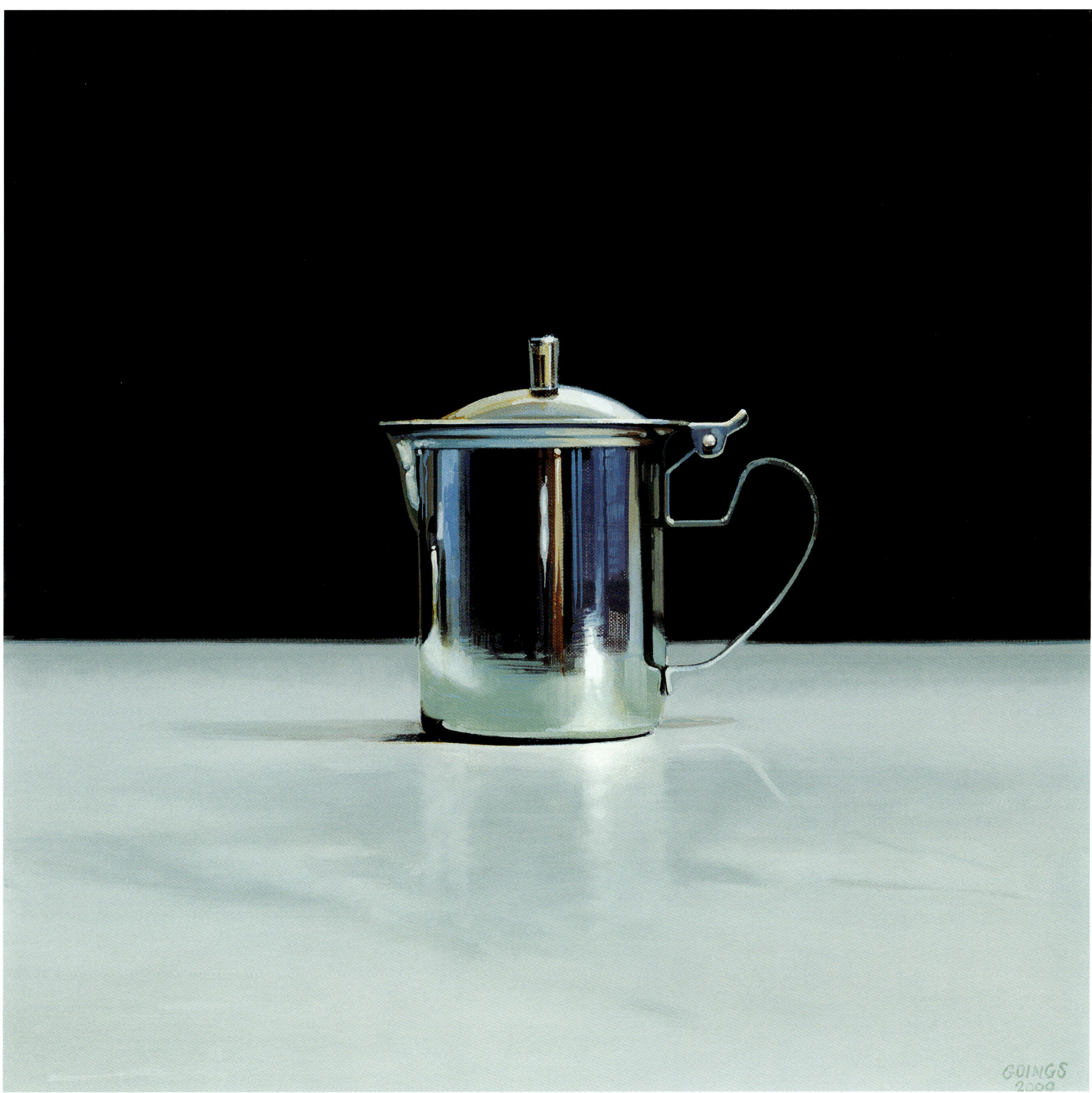
GOINGS
2009

Index

Illustrations (*italic* page numbers) follow page numbers. For those artists and works represented in the catalogue, the page and catalogue numbers of the entry (**cat. no.**) are in **bold**.

N

O

P

R